Biophysics of Water

Biophysics of Water

Proceedings of a Working Conference
held at
Girton College, Cambridge
June 29–July 3, 1981

Editor: **Felix Franks**
Associate Editor: **Sheila F. Mathias**
*Department of Botany,
University of Cambridge*

A Wiley–Interscience Publication

JOHN WILEY & SONS LIMITED
Chichester · New York · Brisbane · Toronto · Singapore

Copyright © 1982, by John Wiley & Sons, Ltd.

All rights reserved.

No part of this book may be reproduced by any means nor transmitted, nor translated into a machine language without the written permission of the publisher.

Library of Congress Cataloging in Publication Data:

Main entry under title:

Biophysics of water.

'A Wiley–Interscience publication.'
Includes index.
1. Water of hydration. 2. Biophysics. I. Franks, Felix. II. Mathias, Sheila F.
QP535.H1B56   574.19'212   82-2839
                                      AACR2

ISBN 0 471 10229 6

British Library Cataloguing in Publication Data:

Biophysics of water.
1. Waters—Congresses   2. Biophysics—Congresses
I. Franks, Felix   II. Mathias, Sheila F.
574.19'1   QH505

ISBN 0 471 10229 6

Typeset by Preface Ltd, Salisbury, Wilts.
Printed at Page Bros. (Norwich) Ltd.

This work relates to Department of the Navy Research Grant N00014-81-G-0014 issued by the Office of Naval Research. The United States Government has a royalty-free licence throughout the world in all copyrightable material contained herein.

Contents

Foreword xiii

Preface xvii

List of participants xix

Section 1 Macromolecular hydration and biological function

Plenary Lecture
Molecular hydration and biological function 3
  R. H. Pain

Poster Contributions
Dynamical and structural aspects of protein hydration studied by high-resolution neutron scattering 15
  J. Randall and H. D. Middendorf
Comparative studies of some different models of the solvent effect on the conformations of biological molecules 21
  B. Robson, G. Douglas, A. Metcalfe, K. Woolley and J. S. Thompson
Correlation between aqueous solubility and partitioning in an hydrated dextran gel (Sephadex® G-15) 23
  Å. Ch. Haglund and N. V. B. Marsden
Characterization of the state of water within synthetic membranes by water sorption isotherms and heat capacity measurements 27
  W. Lukas and W. Pusch
Computer simulation of water around biomolecules 32
  H. F. J. Savage, J. M. Goodfellow, J. L. Finney and P. Barnes
An investigation of the hydration of lysozyme using a direct difference infra-red technique 36
  P. L. Poole and J. L. Finney
Water bridges in myoglobin 39
  J. R. Grigera and I. G. Mogilner
Low temperature oxyhaemoglobin hydration in dependence on protein concentration 42
  J. Brnjas-Kraljević and S. Maričić

An NMR study of isotope distribution and the state of water in the
hydration layer of DNA 45
   R. Mathur-De Vré, R. Grimèe-Declerck and P. Lejeune
The role of solvation in protein structure stabilization and unfolding . 48
   S. N. Timasheff, T. Arakawa, H. Inoue, K. Gekko, M. J. Gorbunoff,
   J. C. Lee, G. C. Na, E. P. Pittz and V. Prakash
Statistical state solvation sites: $[(CHO)_2]_{aq}$ 51
   F. T. Marchese, P. K. Mehrotra and D. L. Beveridge

Discussion Panel
Solvent effects in biomolecular processes 55
   J. L. Finney
Molecular hydration and its possible role in enzymes 58
   G. Careri
Some views of solvation effects in the light of a Monte Carlo 62
simulation
   B. Robson
The soluble Frankenstein: polyoxyethylene action in protein solutions
and cell suspensions 66
   S. Vuk-Pavlović
Preferential interactions in protein–water–cosolvent systems . . . 70
   S. N. Timasheff

Plenary Lecture
Towards a molecular picture of liquid water 73
   J. L. Finney

Discussion summary: Macromolecular hydration 97
   Reporter: J. M. Goodfellow

Section 2 Macroscopic surfaces and hydration interactions

Plenary Lecture
Surface forces in biological systems 105
   B. W. Ninham

Poster Contributions
The osmotic properties of haemoglobin under physiological
conditions—implications for the osmotic behaviour of red cells . . 121
   B. Wittmann and G. Gros
NMR relaxation and water dynamics at the protein surface 125
   R. G. Bryant
Structural water of phospholipid bilayers. A realistic calorimetry study 127
   L. Ter-Minassian-Saraga and G. Madelmont

Small angle scattering study of water bound to a protein 134
  M. S. Lehmann and G. Zaccaï
On the role of interfacial water in protonmotive systems 137
  D. B. Kell and J. G. Morris
Phospholipid bilayer hydration—interbilayer repulsion and intrabilayer
structural changes 140
  R. P. Rand and V. A. Parsegian
Model for a cooperative structure wave 144
  J. G. Watterson
The ordered water ion channel 148
  D. T. Edmonds
Free energies at the biosurface–water interface: relationships between
surface thermodynamics and interfacial structure 151
  D. J. McIver and S. Schürch
Water/ice: electrical conductivity—a conjectural relationship . . . 154
  D. C. Pressey
Kinetics of vacuum dehydration in the study of tissue water 160
  A. I. Popescu, E. Katona, C. Ganea and V. Vasilescu

Discussion Panel
The occurrence and extent of vicinal water 163
  W. Drost-Hansen
The non-exchangeable water fraction inside microsomes 170
  G. Pifat
Some electrical properties of small isolated water molecule arrays . . 173
  D. T. Edmonds
Molecular mechanism of the hydration force 176
  S. Marčelja
Water at the protein surface 178
  R. G. Bryant

Plenary Lecture
Double-layer, van der Waals and hydration forces between surfaces in
electrolyte solutions 183
  J. N. Israelachvili and R. M. Pashley

Discussion summary: Effects of macroscopic surfaces on interactions
involving water 195
  Reporter: P. T. Beall

Section 3 Dynamics of water in cellular systems

Plenary Lecture
Osmosis: the push and pull of life 205
  H. G. Hempling

Poster Contributions

Protonic beta-aluminas: model systems for proton transfer in biological processes 215
   J. O. Thomas and G. C. Farrington

Evidence for an increase in viscosity of water associated with ion pumping 218
   P. M. Wiggins and G. A. Bowmaker

NMR of water nuclei in heterogeneous systems. Relaxation theory and oxygen-17 data from aqueous solutions of proteins, polyelectrolytes and micelles 221
   B. Halle, L. Piculell, G. Carlström, T. Andersson, H. Wennerström and B. Lindman

Facilitated proton transfer in protein solutions by rotational and translational protein diffusion 225
   G. Gros, H. Gros and D. Lavalette

Proton NMR relaxation and diffusion study of water sorbed in oriented DNA and hyaluronic acid samples. 231
   G. Lahajnar, I. Zupančič and A. Rupprecht

Dynamics of water in the peripheral nerve 235
   E. Katona, C. Ganea, A. I. Popescu and V. Vasilescu

The influence of the dynamic properties of water on protein fluctuations 238
   R. B. Gregory and A. Rosenberg

Tritiated water distribution in the glycerol-extracted muscle during contraction, relaxation and rigor. Relevance for ionic changes in muscle activity 242
   C. T. Dragomir, M. Perianu, A. Petre, S. Botea, D. Calin, A. Barbier and R. Chirvasie

O-17 and proton spin–lattice relaxation time studies in supercooled H_2O and D_2O enriched with O-17 246
   E. W. Lang and H.-D. Lüdemann

Discussion Panel

Dynamics of water in cellular systems 249
   W. Derbyshire

Hydrogen exchange kinetics as a tool in the study of macromolecule water interactions 253
   A. Rosenberg

Determination of water relation parameters of individual higher plant cells 256
   A. Deri Tomos and U. Zimmermann

The contribution of dielectric relaxation and nuclear magnetic relaxation measurements to our understanding of the dynamics of

hydration in solutions of biomolecules and in cellular systems . . . 261
   K. Hallenga
A mechanism of ATP-driven cation pumps 266
   P. M. Wiggins
Water permeation through lipid bilayer membranes 269
   D. A. Haydon

Discussion summary: The dynamics of water in cellular systems . . . 271
   Reporter: W. Drost-Hansen

Section 4 Physiological water stress

Plenary Lecture
Physiological water stress 279
   F. Franks

Poster Contributions
Hydration dependent phase changes in a biological membrane . . . 295
   J. H. Crowe, L. M. Crowe and D. W. Deamer
Membrane water and its role in a thermodynamic model of membrane
damage 300
   J. J. McGrath
Physical and temporal factors involved in the death of embryos that
contain ice 303
   W. F. Rall, C. Polge and D. S. Reid
Fish glycopeptide and peptide antifreezes: their interaction with ice and
water 306
   A. L. DeVries
Evidence for a protein stabilizing mechanism in plant cells under water
stress 309
   B. Schobert
Biological systems with low water content: NMR approach to the
state of water in plant seed 312
   S. Ratković, M. Denić, G. Lahajnar and I. Zupančič
The effects of growth under water stress on the structure, metabolism
and cryopreservation of cultured sycamore cells 315
   H. W. Pritchard, B. W. W. Grout, K. C. Short and D. S. Reid
Freeze-induced dehydration: effects on the plasma membrane of
isolated plant protoplasts 319
   P. L. Steponkus, M. F. Dowgert, R. Y. Evans and W. J. Gordon-Kamm
NMR relaxation times of water protons in cultured cells under freezing
and osmotic stress conditions 323
   P. T. Beall

Water relations in the epidermal cells of the halophyte *Suaeda maritima*   327
  A. Deri Tomos and R. G. Wyn Jones

Discussion Panel
Water relations and resistance mechanisms in bacteria 333
  G. W. Gould
Towards a physical chemical characterization of compatible solutes . 335
  R. G. Wyn Jones and A. Pollard
The relation between ionic selectivity and enhanced interactions of water molecules in *Halobacterium marismortui* 340
  B.-Z. Ginzburg and M. Ginzburg
Freezing injury and cold acclimation in plants 343
  J. V. Carter
Membrane damage following freeze-induced dehydration 347
  G. J. Morris
Physiological water stress: cellular components under extremes of physical conditions 352
  R. Jaenicke

Discussion summary: Physiological water stress 356
  Reporter: H. leB. Skaer

Section 5   Matters arising

Plenary Lecture
Alternative views on the role of water in cell function 365
  J. S. Clegg

Discussion following Clegg's lecture 385
  Reporter: H. leB. Skaer

Summarizing Discussion   386
  Reporters: H. leB. Skaer and F. Franks
NMR relaxation of water in heterogeneous systems—consensus views?   389
  R. G. Bryant and B. Halle

Subject index 395

Compound index 399

Foreword

M. F. Perutz

The first person to determine the solvation of a protein was the Cambridge physiologist Gilbert Adair (1896–1979).[1] He developed the measurement of osmotic pressure to a fine art; he was also an excellent physical chemist and mathematician which allowed him to calculate the effects that membrane potentials would have on the osmotic pressure. By this means he worked out the molecular weight of haemoglobin as 67 000 and published it in 1924, a year before Svedberg did.[2] Later he became interested in the effect of hydration on osmotic pressure, especially at high protein concentration, since this would remove a portion of the solvent and thus raise the effective protein concentration. In 1928 he suggested that 0.21 g H_2O/g protein would fit his results.[3] In 1936, Gilbert and his wife Muriel Adair reexamined the problem by measuring the densities of protein crystals in various media. They found the density of a salt solution in which a wet haemoglobin crystal just floated to be higher (1.34) than that of the dried protein (1.28). They attributed the higher density of the wet haemoglobin crystals to their permeability to water and to electrostriction of the interstitial water by the polar groups of the protein. The density of haemoglobin in the wet crystals was equal to $1/V_{sp}$, the apparent specific volume of the protein in solution.[4]

I began working with Adair in 1937 when he made me the first crystals of horse haemoglobin for my X-ray work. Their unit cell dimensions showed that the dry protein occupied only 48.6% of the crystal volume, the rest being taken up by water of hydration and ammonium sulphate solution. Variations of the density of the wet crystals (floating in benzene–bromobenzene mixtures) as a function of the ammonium sulphate concentration of their original suspension medium showed as much as 0.3 g H_2O/g protein to be unavailable as a solvent to the diffusible electrolytes.[5] Where was that water? Inside or outside the protein? A few years later comparisons of Patterson projections at various stages of swelling and shrinkage of the crystals taught me that the protein molecules must be largely impermeable to water, which meant that the water of hydration must be located at their surface. If haemoglobin was assumed to be spherical, then 0.3 g H_2O/g protein just about sufficed to cover it with a monomolecular layer of water all round. This was in 1947.[6] For the next 30 years I wondered what this bound water looked like.

Gradually the resolution of our X-ray analysis improved to the point where bound water molecules appeared as distinct peaks on our electron density maps. Only very few electron density peaks that are not protein are seen inside the chains of oxymyoglobin or haemoglobin, but such peaks, spaced at hydrogen bonding positions from the polar groups of the protein, are prominent at the contacts between the four subunits of haemoglobin and take part in the allosteric transition between its two forms. Many water molecules are also bound to polar groups at the protein surface. However, the total number of water molecules which show up clearly in the electron density maps of haemoglobin is less than 100, or less than 1/10 of those not available as solvent to diffusible electrolytes. Those not accounted for must be attached too loosely to stay in one place during the long time it takes to collect X-ray diffraction pictures.[7,8] So far no one has seen 'ice-bergs' of immobilized water molecules covering non-polar side chains at the protein surface. Incidentally, crystallographers never proposed that proteins had a structure with hydrophilic side chains out and hydrophobic side chains in, as one speaker at this meeting writes. The rule which we advanced was the exclusion of strongly polar side chains from the interior, and this has stood the test of time. Interior charged residues appear only at the active sites of enzymes where they take part in the catalytic mechanism.

In agreement with Timasheff's prediction we find no sulphate ions inside the protein (ammonium ions would be indistinguishable from water), while X-ray analysis of crystals of lysozyme soaked in urea solutions does show urea molecules attached to polar groups inside the protein. I note that Maričić and his colleagues, in a paper in this volume, find by NMR that the quantity of water restricted in its rotational and/or translational mobility by haemoglobin in dilute solution is only 0.04 g H_2O/g protein and that it rises tenfold at a haemoglobin concentration of ~18 mM haem. It is interesting that this corresponds to the concentration in the red cell where the freely rotating haemoglobin molecules are close-packed like the atoms of a liquid metal, so that the hydration shells of neighbouring molecules can interact.[9] Yet there is a paradox here: while interaction between neighbouring haemoglobin molecules increases the number of water molecules restricted in their mobility, it has no influence on another indicator of hydration, namely the partial specific volume which is independent of protein concentration and remains the same in wet crystals and in dilute solutions.[4]

What does X-ray analysis tell us about solvation of nucleic acids? In transfer RNA water molecules and octahedrally hydrated magnesium ions form an essential part of the three-dimensional structure.[10] This structure is therefore destroyed by chelating agents such as EDTA. DNA is known to exist in two forms: the extended B structure at high and the contracted A structure at low humidity. Dickerson and his colleagues have now discovered by X-ray analysis of crystalline oligonucleotides that both forms are stabilized by water molecules bridging the turns of the helical grooves. In the wide groove of B-DNA the water molecules form a lacework bridging the phosphates of neighbouring turns. These results are consistent with those obtained by NMR by Mathur-de Vré et al. and reported in these pages, namely that ^1H_2O is concentrated near the strongly ionizing phosphates. In the narrow groove of B-DNA water molecules are bound to NH and CO groups of the bases. These hydrogen bonds appear to be weaker than those linking the phosphates. On reduction of the humidity, the water molecules in the narrow groove therefore dissociate from the DNA, the groove closes up and the double helix contracts to the A-form where only the lacework of water molecules between the phosphates is maintained.[11] Here at last X-ray analysis has provided a picture of the effect of water stress—drying—on an important biological macromolecule. I hope that it will provide equally satisfying explanations for many other of the natural phenomena described in F. Franks' interesting lecture and discussed at this conference.

References

1. P. Johnson and M. F. Perutz, Gilbert Smithson Adair, *Biographical Memoirs of Fellows of the Royal Society*, **27**, 1 (1981).
2. G. S. Adair, A comparison of the molecular weights of the proteins, *Proc. Camb. Phil. Soc. Biol. Sci.*, **1**, 75 (1924).
3. G. S. Adair, A theory of partial osmotic pressures and membrane equilibria, *Proc. Roy. Soc. Lond.*, A**120**, 573 (1928).
4. G. S. Adair and M. E. Adair, The densities of protein crystals and the hydration of proteins, *Proc. Roy. Soc. Lond.*, B**120**, 422 (1936).
5. M. F. Perutz, The composition and swelling properties of protein crystals, *Trans. Faraday Soc.*, **47B**, 187 (1946).
6. J. Boyes-Watson, E. Davidson and M. F. Perutz, An X-ray study of horse methaemoglobin I, *Proc. Roy. Soc. Lond.*, A**191**, 83 (1947).
7. M. F. Perutz, The role of bound water in haemoglobin and myoglobin, *Biosystems*, **8**, 261 (1977).
8. S. E. V. Phillips, Structure of oxymyoglobin at 1.6 Å resolution, *J. Mol. Biol.*, **142**, 53 (1980).
9. M. F. Perutz, Submicroscopic structure of the red cell, *Nature*, **161**, 204 (1948).
10. A. Jack, J. E. Ladner, D. Rhodes, R. S. Brown and A. Klug, A crystallographic study of metal-binding to yeast phenylalanine transfer RNA, *J. Mol. Biol.*, **111**, 315 (1977).
11. B. N. Conner, T. Takano, S. Tanaka, K. Itakura and R. E. Dickerson, The molecular structure of d(^{I}CpCpGpG), a fragment of right-handed double helical DNA, *Nature*, **295**, 294 (1982); also references quoted therein.

Preface

The initiative for a conference on the biophysics of water came from the US Office of Naval Research which sponsors research programmes on several of its aspects. At a preliminary meeting held in January 1980 at Bethesda, Maryland, the objectives, format and venue of such a conference were discussed and Carlton F. Hazlewood of Baylor College, Houston, Texas, and I agreed to act as joint organizers. At that time we decided to depart from the conventional conference format and to adopt instead a novel approach, combining a very limited number of lectures with selected poster displays and panel discussions, led by invited contributors. The emphasis of the conference was to be on *discussion*, a much neglected commodity at most meetings where lecture follows lecture, follows lecture. As the date of the conference drew nearer we became apprehensive whether our approach had been too bold and that it might result in long silences. In the event, our fears were shown to be unfounded.

In order clearly to define the subject matter of the conference, we chose four scientific topics as being in need of detailed treatment; one day to be devoted to each topic. A plenary lecture was to introduce each topic, after which a limited number of posters would be introduced by their authors, viewed for a period and then discussed in plenary session. The afternoons were to be devoted to discussions, introduced by invited panel members, drawn from different disciplines. All discussions were to be summarized by reporters for subsequent publication. The programme was completed by a number of evening lectures which, while not specifically relating to the topic of the day, were of more general relevance to the subject of the conference.

Very few changes were made subsequently and the conference took place as originally planned. Girton College, Cambridge, was chosen as venue because of its attractive situation and facilities. The conference attracted some 120 participants from 17 countries, encompassing a wide range of disciplines: applied mathematics, physics, chemistry, biochemistry, cytology, physiology, biophysics, microbiology, marine biology, botany and zoology. Unfortunately, during the period prior to the conference, Carlton Hazlewood decided to resign as co-organizer; his place was taken by John Finney of Birkbeck College, London.

The conference duly took place on June 29–July 3, 1981, and if the subsequent mailbag is a reliable guide, then the choice of the novel format was completely vindicated. It was particularly gratifying to observe that not only were national barriers broken down almost immediately, but that a productive dialogue quickly developed between members of different disciplinary 'religions'.

The list of acknowledgements is of necessity a long one, because a successful conference only materializes through the close co-operation between the organizers, the secretariat, the College staff, the financial benefactors and the participants. Adopting the above order, I should like to thank John Finney for his constant support, especially during the conference. The *real* organization was in the capable hands of my wife Hedy and Sheila Mathias, ably supported by Alison Yarwood and Anna-Marie Edwards, both students at Girton. A special thank you goes to Bill Harker, Girton College catering manager, and his staff who came in for lavish praise from the international gathering for the standard of the cuisine. The Office of Naval Research supported the conference with a generous grant, and further support was provided by the Gesellschaft für Biologische Chemie, through the good offices of Rainer Jaenicke. Finally, it is a pleasure to acknowledge the support from the participants who entered into the spirit of the meeting with great gusto. A very unusual feature was the promptness with which the manuscripts for this volume reached me. Special thanks go to the plenary lecturers and the four reporters: Julia Goodfellow, Walter Drost-Hansen, Paula Beall and Helen Skaer, who turned the Babel of lively discussion into a coherent story.

To all those who have asked when the next conference is to be staged, the reply is that the experience was encouraging, but also involved much hard work, and that the venture is not one that is likely to be repeated, at least not in a hurry.

Cambridge   FELIX FRANKS

List of participants

N. D. Atherton	Department of Chemistry (Postgraduate), University of Aston in Birmingham, Gosta Green, Birmingham B4 7ET, UK.
P. Barnes	Department of Crystallography, Birkbeck College, Malet Street, London WC1 7HX, UK.
G. Barone	Istituto Chimico, Via Mezzocannone 4, Napoli 80134, Italy.
H. Bank	Department of Pathology, Medical University of South Carolina, Charleston, South Carolina 29425, USA.
J. B. Bateman	6, Colney Hatch Lane, Muswell Hill, London N10 1DU, UK.
P. T. Beall	Department of Physiology, Baylor College of Medicine, 1200 Moursund, Houston, Texas 77030, USA.
M. J. Beilby	Botany School, Downing Street, University of Cambridge, Cambridge CB2 3EA, UK.
D. L. Beveridge	Chemistry Department, Hunter College, City University of New York, 695 Park Avenue, New York, N.Y. 10021, USA.
M. Bonilla	Queen Elizabeth College, Physics Department, Campden Hill Road, London W8 7AH, UK.
J. Brnjas-Kraljević	Department of Physics-Biophysics, School of Medicine, University of Zagreb, Salata 3, 41000 Zagreb, Yugoslavia.
E. Brosio	Istituto di Chimica Fisica, Università degli Studi di Roma, Piazzale A. Moro 5, 00185 Rome, Italy.
R. G. Bryant	Chemistry Department, University of

	Minnesota, 207 Pleasant Street, S.E. Minneapolis, MN.55455, USA.
G. CARERI	Istituto Fisico Marconi, Università di Roma, 00185 Rome, Italy.
J. V. CARTER	Department of Horticultural Science, University of Minnesota, St. Paul, MN.55108, USA.
A. CLARKE	British Antarctic Survey, Madingley Road, Cambridge CB3 0ET, UK.
J. S. CLEGG	Department of Biology, University of Miami, Coral Gables, Florida 33124, USA.
G. E. COULSON	Culture Centre of Algae and Protozoa, 36 Storey's Way, Cambridge CB3 0DT, UK.
J. H. CROWE and L. M. CROWE	Department of Zoology, University of California, Davis, California 95616, USA.
W. DERBYSHIRE	Department of Physics, University of Nottingham, Nottingham NG7 2RD, UK.
A. L. DEVRIES	524 Burrill Hall, University of Illinois, Urbana, Illinois 61801, USA.
A. DINOLA	Istituto di Chimica Fisica, Piazzale A. Moro 5, 00185 Rome, Italy.
J. DORE	Physics Laboratory, University of Kent at Canterbury, Canterbury, Kent, CT2 7NR UK.
C. T. DRAGOMIR	Victor Babes Institute, Spl. Independentei 99–101, Bucharest 76201, Romania.
W. DROST-HANSEN	Laboratory for Water Research, Department of Chemistry, University of Miami, Coral Gables, Florida 33124, USA.
J. EDEN	6, Sunnyhill, Rhostrehwfa, Llangefni, Anglesey LL77 7YU, UK.
D. T. EDMONDS	Clarendon Laboratory, Parks Road, Oxford OX1 3PU, UK.
H. ELMGREN	Institute of Physical Chemistry, Uppsala University, P.O. Box 532, 751 21 Uppsala, Sweden.
J. L. FINNEY	Crystallography Department, Birkbeck College, Malet Street, London WC1E 7HX, UK.
F. FRANKS	Department of Botany, Downing Street, University of Cambridge, Cambridge CB2 3EA, UK.
B. J. FULLER	Academic Department of Surgery, Royal Free

List of participants

	Hospital, Pond Street, London NW3 2QG, UK.
C. GABRIEL	Physics Department, Queen Elizabeth College, Kensington, London W8 7AH, UK.
A. GIANSANTI	Istituto di Fisica 'G. Marconi', P.le A.Moro 5 (Citta Univ.), 00185 Roma, Italy.
B. Z. GINZBURG	Department of Botany, The Hebrew University, Jerusalem, Israel.
J. M. GOODFELLOW	Department of Crystallography, Birkbeck College, Malet Street, London WC1E 7HX, UK.
M. J. GORBUNOFF	Graduate Department of Biochemistry, Brandeis University, Waltham, MA 02254, USA.
G. W. GOULD	Unilever Research Laboratory, Colworth House, Sharnbrook, Bedford MK44 1LQ, UK.
K. GOUNARIS	Department of Biochemistry, Chelsea College, University of London, Manresa Road, London SW3 6LX, UK.
J. R. GRIGERA	Instituto de Fisica de Liquidos y Sistemas Biologicos, IFLYSIB, 59-789, c.c. 565, 1900 La Plata, Argentina.
G. GROS and H. GROS	Institut für Physiologie, Universitätsklinikum Essen, Hufelandstrasse 55, 4300 Essen, West Germany.
B. W. W. GROUT	Department of Biology, North East London Polytechnic, Romford Road, London E15 4LZ, UK.
E. HAGELBERG	Biochemistry Department, University of Cambridge, Tennis Court Road, Cambridge CB2 1QW, UK.
Å. HAGLUND	Department of Physiology and Biophysics, Box 572, S-751 23 Uppsala, Sweden.
B. HALLE	Physical Chemistry 1, Chemical Centre, P.O. Box 740, S-22007 Lund 7, Sweden.
K. HALLENGA	Vrye Universiteit Brussel, Department of Organic Chemistry, Pleinlaan 2, B-1050 Brussels, Belgium.
D. A. HAYDON	Physiological Laboratory, Downing Street, Cambridge, UK.
R. J. W. HEFFORD	Port Sunlight Laboratory, Quarry Road East, Bebington Wirral, Merseyside L63 3JW, UK.

H. G. Hempling	Department of Physiology, Medical University of South Carolina, 173 Ashley Avenue, Charleston, S.C. 29403, USA.
C. A. Hoeve	Chemistry Department, Texas A & M University, College Station, Texas 77843, USA.
J. F. Holzwarth	Fritz-Haber-Institut der Max-Planck-Gesellschaft, Faradayweg 4-6, 1000 Berlin 33, West Germany.
J. N. Israelachvili	Department of Applied Mathematics, I.A.S., Research School of Physical Sciences, Australian National University, Canberra, A.C.T. 2600, Australia.
R. Jaenicke	Biochemie II, Nat. Fak., Universitätstrasse 31. D-84 Regensburg, West Germany.
E. R. James	Winches Farm, 395 Hatfield Road, St. Albans, Herts., UK.
C. F. Jenner	Waite Agricultural Research Institute, Glen Osmond, South Australia 5064.
N. B. Jones	Upjohn Limited, Fleming Way, Crawley, West Sussex, RH10 2NJ, UK.
R. L. Jones	Research Unit, Royal London Homoeopathic Hospital, Great Ormond Street, London WC1, UK.
E. A. Katona	Department of Biophysics, Faculty of Medicine, Dr. P. Groza Blvd., 8, 76241 Bucharest, Romania.
R. L. Kay	Carnegie-Mellon University, 4400 Fifth Avenue, Pittsburgh PA 15213, USA.
D. B. Kell	Department of Botany and Microbiology, U.C.W., Penglais, Aberystwyth, Dyfed SY23 3DA, UK.
V. A. Knight	King Faisal University, Colleges of Medicine and Medical Sciences, P.O. Box 2114, Dammam, Saudi Arabia.
G. Lahajnar	Institut 'Jozef Stefan', E. Kardelj University of Ljubljana, 61000 Ljubljana, Jamova 39, Yugoslavia.
M. S. Lehmann	Institut Laue-Langevin, Avenue des Martyrs, F38042 Grenoble, France.
H. Levine	General Foods Corp., Tech Ctr T22-1, Tarrytown, NY 10591, USA.
H. D. Lüdemann	Universität Regensburg, Institut für Biophysik und Phys. Biochemie, Postfach 397, D-8400 Regensburg, West Germany.

List of participants

W. Lukas	Max-Planck-Institut für Biophysik, Kennedy-Allee 70, D-6000 Frankfurt am Main 70, West Germany.
G. Maass	Medizinische Hochschule Hannover Zentrum Biochemie OE.–4350–Abt. Biophysikalische Chemie, Postfach 610180, Karl-Wiechert-Allee 9, 3000 Hannover, West Germany.
J. J. McGrath	201 Engr. Bldg., Michigan State University, E. Lansing, Mi. 48824, USA.
D. J. L. McIver	Department of Pharmacology, University of Western Ontario, London, Ontario N6A 5C1, Canada.
E. MacRobbie	Department of Botany, Downing Street, University of Cambridge, Cambridge CB2 3EA, UK.
G. I. Malinin	Physics Department, Georgetown University, Washington D.C. 20057, USA.
S. Marčelja	Department of Applied Mathematics, RS Phys S, Australian National University, Canberra, A.C.T. 2601, Australia.
N. V. B. Marsden	Department of Physiology and Biophysics, Box 572, S751 23 Uppsala, Sweden.
D. Marvin	E.M.B.L., Postfach 10.2209, Heidelberg, West Germany.
S. F. Mathias	Department of Botany, Downing Street, University of Cambridge, Cambridge CB2 3EA, UK.
R. Mathur-DeVré	Institut d'Hygiène et d'Epidémiologie, 14 Rue J. Wytsman, Brussels 1050, Belgium.
G. Mela	Istituto per i Circuiti Elettronici, C.N.R., Via Opera Pia 11, 16145 Genova, Italy.
H. D. Middendorf	Department of Biophysics, University of London King's College, 26–29 Drury Lane, London WC2B 5RL, UK.
G. J. Morris	Culture Centre of Algae and Protozoa, 36 Storey's Way, Cambridge CB3 0DT, UK.
B. W. Ninham	Department of Applied Mathematics, I.A.S., Research School of Physical Sciences, Australian National University, Canberra, A.C.T. 2600, Australia.
R. H. Pain	Department of Biochemistry, University of Newcastle upon Tyne, NE1 7RU, UK.
M. F. Perutz	MRC Unit of Molecular Biology, Cambridge, UK.

L. Piculell	Physical Chemistry 1, Chemical Center, P.O. Box 740, S-22007 Lund 7, Sweden.
G. Pifat	Institute Rudjer Bošković, Bijenička c. 54, 41000 Zagreb, Yugoslavia.
P. L. Poole	Crystallography Department, Birkbeck College, Malet Street, London WC1E 7HX, UK.
D. C. Pressey	Clinical Research Centre, Watford Road, Harrow HA1 3UJ, UK.
H. W. Pritchard	Department of Biology, North East London Polytechnic, Romford Road, London E15 4LZ, UK.
W. Pusch	Max-Planck-Institut für Biophysik, Kennedy-Allee 70, D-6000 Frankfurt am Main 70, West Germany.
W. F. Rall	ARC Institute of Animal Physiology, Animal Research Station, 307 Huntingdon Road, Cambridge CB3 0JQ, UK.
R. P. Rand	Zoology Department, University of Nottingham, Nottingham NG7 2RD, UK.
S. Ratković	Maize Research Institute, P.O. Box 89, 11080 Zemun-Beograd, Yugoslavia.
G. Rialdi	Centro Studi Chimico Fisici, Macromolecole-CNR, Corso Europa 30, 16132 Genova, Italy.
S. Ridella	Istituto per i Circuiti Elettronici, C.N.R., Via Opera Pia 11, 16145 Genova, Italy.
I. Roberts	Department of Botany, Plant Science Labs., University of Reading, Whiteknights, Reading RG6 2AS, UK.
B. Robson	Department of Biochemistry, University of Manchester, Oxford Road, Manchester M13 9PL, UK.
A. Rosenberg	Box 198, Mayo Dep of Laboratory Medicine, University of Minnesota, Minn 55455, USA.
H. F. J. Savage	Department of Crystallography, Birkbeck College, Malet Street, London WC1E 7HX, UK.
B. Schobert	Lehrstuhl für Botanik, Technische Universität, Arcisstr. 16, D-8000 München 2, West Germany.
H. leB. Skaer	Department of Zoology, University of Cambridge, Downing Street, Cambridge CB2 3EJ, UK.
L. Slade	General Foods Technical Center T23-1, 555 South Broadway, Tarrytown NY 10591, USA.

List of participants

P. L. STEPONKUS	Department of Agronomy, 609 Bradfield Hall, Cornell University, Ithaca, New York 14853, USA.
S. SVETINA	Inštitut za biofizico, Medicinska fakulteta, Lipičeva 2, 61105 Ljubljana, Yugoslavia.
L. TER-MINASSIAN-SARAGA	Physico-Chimie des Surfaces et des Membranes, CNRS, UER Biomédicale, 45 rue des Saints-Pères, 75270 Paris cedex 06, France.
J. O. THOMAS	Institute of Chemistry, Uppsala University, Box 531, 751 21 Uppsala, Sweden.
S. N. TIMASHEFF	Graduate Department of Biochemistry, Brandeis University, Waltham, MA 02254, USA.
A. D. TOMOS	Department of Biochemistry and Soil Science, U.C.N.W., Bangor, Gwynedd, Wales.
C. TOPRAKCIOGLU	Physics Laboratory, University of Kent, Canterbury, Kent CT2 7NR, UK.
S. VUK-PAVLOVIĆ	Institute of Immunology, Rockefellerova 2, 41000 Zagreb, Yugoslavia.
I. WADSÖ	Thermochemistry, Chemical Center, University of Lund, P.O. Box 740, S-22007, Lund, Sweden.
J. G. WATTERSON	Department of Pharmacology, University of Zurich, Gloriastrasse 32, CH-8006 Zurich, Switzerland.
P. M. WIGGINS	Department of Medicine, University of Auckland School of Medicine, 85 Park Road, Auckland, New Zealand.
B. WITTMANN	Institut für Physiologie, Universitätsklinikum, Hufelandstr. 55, 43 Essen 1, West Germany.
R. G. WYN JONES	Department of Biochemistry and Soil Science, U.C.N.W., Bangor, Gwynedd, Wales.
U. ZIMMERMANN	Arbeitsgruppe Membranforschung am Institut für Medizin, Kernforschungsanlage Jülich, GmbH, Postfach 1913, D-5170 Jülich, West Germany.

Section 1 Macromolecular hydration and biological function

Molecular hydration and biological function

Roger H. Pain
University of Newcastle upon Tyne, UK

Summary

The interaction of water with biological macromolecules is of prime significance in determining their structure and function. Water may act as a 'good' solvent or as a 'poor' solvent, and the importance of each of these modes of interaction is illustrated by particular examples.

Evolution has taken place in an environment of which water is one of the major components. It is not surprising, therefore, that the interrelationships between this superficially simple molecular species and biological systems are very delicate and sophisticated. While biochemistry seeks to understand organisms at the molecular level, such explanations frequently raise further questions for the biophysicist, questions which concern the involvement of water.

Water is a unique liquid, many of whose properties are critical for the continued support of life, and Henderson's early monograph still makes interesting and stimulating reading on this point.[1] As a 'biochemical' it plays a central role in many enzyme catalysed processes in biosynthesis, metabolism and catabolism and, in a quite unique way, in photosynthesis. It is its property as a solvent, however, that I wish to discuss in this introductory lecture. The ability to dissolve a large number of metabolites, nutrients and waste products, energy storing molecules, hormones and the like, forms the basis for the transport of energy and information through the simple cell and round the 'plumbing' of more complex organisms. Having enabled access to appropriate parts of the body for these various materials, water then governs their distribution between itself and appropriate sites. Substrates distribute between cytoplasm and enzymes, hormones between blood and receptors, sugars between extra-cellular water and membrane pores. Simple solvation can affect the specificity of transport and ions, as suggested for the preferred passage of potassium over sodium through valinomycin. The preferential solubility of phosphate ions in water, as opposed to lipid, prevents the passive diffusion across membranes of phosphorylated sugar metabolites.

Many of these examples describe the function of water as a *good* solvent but the cell would not exist were not certain molecular species and assemblies rather poorly soluble in water. There is a basic need for selective barriers to enable the cell to exist and operate as a partially closed system. Structures for rigid levers, filters and mechanical energy transducers must be insoluble, while enzymes and receptors depend on structures to express their specificity. Either in the assembly of these structural components or in their continued stabilization there is frequently the active involvement of water as a poor solvent.

Many biological structures, such as the double-helical form of DNA, globular proteins and certain gels depend for their existence on a delicate balance between the 'good' and 'poor' solvent characteristics of water. The resulting marginal stability can be seen as having been rather precisely selected according to the requirements of biological function. I want to examine these phenomena in the light of two examples, in which water functions mainly as a poor and as a good solvent respectively. Both systems are well understood at one or more levels but at the same time illustrate the need for a greater contribution from the biophysics of water.

Water as a poor solvent: the hydrophobic effect

Non-polar molecules and groups are poorly soluble in water and the unfavourable free energy of solubilization arises in the entropy and not the enthalpy term.[2] In Figure 1 the thermodynamics of transfer of methane between inert solvent, gas phase and water are summarized. The small $+\Delta H$ for transfer from liquid to gas reflects the small van der Waals between methane molecules. The favourable enthalpy change on transfer to water may therefore include a negative ΔH for the water as well as a presumed van der Waals interaction with neighbouring water molecules. The remarkable parameter is the entropy change which is large and negative for transfer into water and

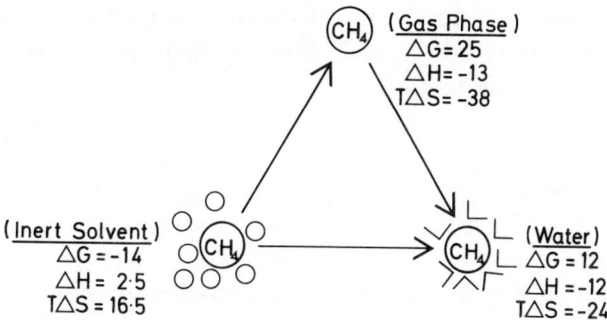

Figure 1 Thermodynamic parameters for the transfer of a molecule of methane from an apolar solvent to water directly or via the gas phase (after W. P. Jencks[2]; reproduced by permission of McGraw-Hill)

which must be associated with ordering of the poor solvent. The volume change is also negative, suggesting that the cavity created to receive the non-polar group is compensated to some extent by a reduction in the unoccupied space in the solvent. Characteristic of this transfer process is the large increase in the specific heat ΔC_p of the system characteristic of a decrease in the degrees of freedom, presumably largely of the solvent since the apolar group does not interact appreciably with water.

The hydrophobic interaction occurs when two such apolar groups are brought together in water and is accompanied by a favourable increase in entropy. The free energy change for the interaction is proportional to the surface area of the groups involved. The largest component of the overall decrease in free energy is associated with the entropy change, far outweighing any favourable inter-solute attractions. The situation becomes complicated at temperatures outside the normal biological range because of the large ΔC_p term. I shall take the situation only where there is a favourable interaction accompanied by a large increase in entropy and outline some of the ways in which this problem has been approached in terms of 'water structure'.

Water may be best represented, at biologically significant temperatures, by a continuously bonded lattice, each oxygen being at the centre of four hydrogen bonds.[3] There is a temperature dependent equilibrium between a more open, regular structure with tetrahedral bonding on the one hand, and a more compact, less well ordered arrangement with hydrogen bonds which are strained in both angles and length and occasionally broken. Looked at another way, water consists of a series of polyhedra of various sizes which hydrogen bond into the surrounding lattice with different degrees of ease. The whole structure is highly mobile.

On this simplified model, the main effect of inserting a non-polar group is to induce reorientation of water molecules at the interface in such a way as to maximize the number of hydrogen bonds which can be made with neighbouring water. This restraint leads to a hydrogen-bonded 'net' of water molecules over the apolar surface, and the degree to which the net matches the stereochemistry of the surrounding water will govern the overall volume of water disturbed by the presence of the apolar group. Later contributions in this conference will emphasize that such preferential orientations of water molecules are still very mobile and do not constitute a 'structure' in the common usage of the word.

Hydrophobic association may now be pictured as arising in two alternative ways. A non-polar solute dimer will expose a reduced surface area to water compared with the separated monomers, with fewer water molecules being restrained, both in the close 'net' and beyond. Alternatively, the stereochemistry of a surface net round a non-polar group may be such as to allow the component water molecules to hydrogen-bond to the net over a neighbouring group, with fewer additional constraints than are involved in each net separately maximizing its hydrogen-bonding to bulk water. The latter model, described by Stillinger and based on structures for super-coiled water, presumes that the surface net forms part of an unstrained, ideal polyhedron. Both models account for the observed entropy change and for the linear relationship shown to exist between hydrophobicity and solute surface area. Recent Monte Carlo and molecular dynamics simulations support the formation of clathrate lattices round isolated, small apolar molecules and reduction in the solvent shell on association of an alkyl pair. More detailed calculations of the interaction as a function of distance in the case of two methane molecules, led to oscillatory functions which suggest the possible existence of hydrophobic association with differing amounts of water separating the apolar surfaces as well as contact association.[4] This possibility had previously been suggested on the basis of thermodynamic studies and offers interesting possibilities which will be referred to later on.[5]

Hydrophobic association is very important in biological systems. The association of insulin monomers and of tobacco mosaic virus subunits, and the binding of chymotrypsin to substrate are examples of interactions which show the characteristic thermodynamic parameters. There are many other examples where the equilibria cannot readily be measured and where thermodynamic measurements are less easily available, unless it be in the presence of a third component. The stability of globular proteins, for example, is generally accepted as depending substantially upon hydrophobic interactions but it is not possible to assess the contribution in quantitative terms. The configurational entropy tending to destabilize the protein is estimated to be of the order of several hundred kJ/mol whereas the experimentally measured resultant stability is close to 10 kJ/mol. The stabilizing interactions, which include hydrogen bonds, van der Waals interactions, coulombic interactions as well as hydrophobic interactions, are therefore very large compared with the marginal stability and the component contributions cannot be estimated experimentally. Present estimates of the contribution of hydrophobic interactions depend upon the use of small molecule solubility data. The known structures of globular proteins show that the old 'hydrophilic out, hydrophobic in' concept is far from the truth, with up to 50% of the surface area of known examples being non-polar in nature.

To understand more about the stability of proteins and of the way in which they fold, it is essential to understand better and to be able to calculate quantitatively the contribution of the aqueous solvent.

In order to underline the curious and complex nature of some of the problems associated with the hydrophobic interaction in the context of protein stability, I want to describe some experiments on the enzyme penicillinase.[6] Penicillinase is unusual in being denatured by urea, guanidinium chloride or acid to a stable state of intermediate conformation, viz:

$$\text{Native} \rightleftharpoons \text{Intermediate} \rightleftharpoons \text{Unfolded}$$
$$(N) \qquad\qquad (H) \qquad\qquad (U)$$

ΔG 10 kJ/mol   10 kJ/mol

The apparent free energy difference between the states is as shown. State N is globular and folded, state U has no regular structure and state H has nearly as much secondary structure as the native enzyme but is considerably expanded. It has been shown that the native state consists of three closely interacting domains which separate but remain folded in low concentrations of denaturant to give state H. The stabilizing interactions for H relative to U are thus *intra*domain interactions while those which stabilize state N relative to state H are *inter*domain. It is possible to study the two sets of equilibria independently and in this way to assess the relative contribution of hydrophobic association to the two transitions. Three types of information exemplify this approach.

(i) The transitions can be examined as a function of denaturant concentration and the respective apparent free energies extrapolated to zero. In this way values of $\Delta G_0'$ can be obtained as a function of temperature and these show a marked temperature dependence (Table 1). The native state exhibits a pronounced minimum in values of $-\Delta G_0'$ at 15 °C, characteristic of hydrophobic interactions. For state H, $\Delta G_0'$ levels off below 15 °C but shows no clear minimum. These results are complex to interpret but are compatible with hydrophobic interactions being more important in the N–H than in the H–U transition.

(ii) The denaturation experiments described above can be carried out using either urea or guanidinium chloride (GuCl) as denaturants. Extrapolated values of $\Delta G_0'$ are the same for both denaturants, confirming that the conformational states of the protein are the same in each case. It has been established from model compound studies that GuCl is a more effective denaturant than urea on a molar basis and that its greater effectiveness is more marked in solubilizing the peptide bond than it is in solubilizing apolar groups. The relative effectiveness in driving the two transitions of penicillinase has been measured and expressed in terms of the ratios of $E = (d \ln K_D/d \, [\text{denaturant}])$ for GuCl and urea. The values of $E_{\text{GuCl}}/E_{\text{urea}}$ for the N–H and H–U transitions respectively are 2.06 and 2.60. This difference again suggests a higher proportion of apolar groups relative to peptide backbone groups being exposed in the former transition than in the latter.

(iii) Sulphate is well known for its ability to stabilise globular proteins against denaturation. This effect has been quantitated in the case

Table 1 The variation of free energy of stabilization of *staphylococcal* penicillinase with temperature

Temperature °C	ΔG_0 (kJ.mol^{-1})	
	N–H	H–U
8	6.8	23.4
15	20.5	24.6
30	7.8	9.8

of penicillinase for the two transitions by performing unfolding experiments with urea at different concentrations of sulphate. The results, given in Figure 2, show that sulphate has a far greater effect in stabilizing state N relative to state H than state H relative to state U. The model compound solubility studies of Nandi and Robinson[7] show that sulphate will salt out apolar amino-acid sidechains much more strongly than it does peptide bonds. The conclusion is again that hydrophobic interactions play a greater part in stabilizing interdomain association than intradomain interaction.

Chothia[8] has analysed the structures of several globular proteins of

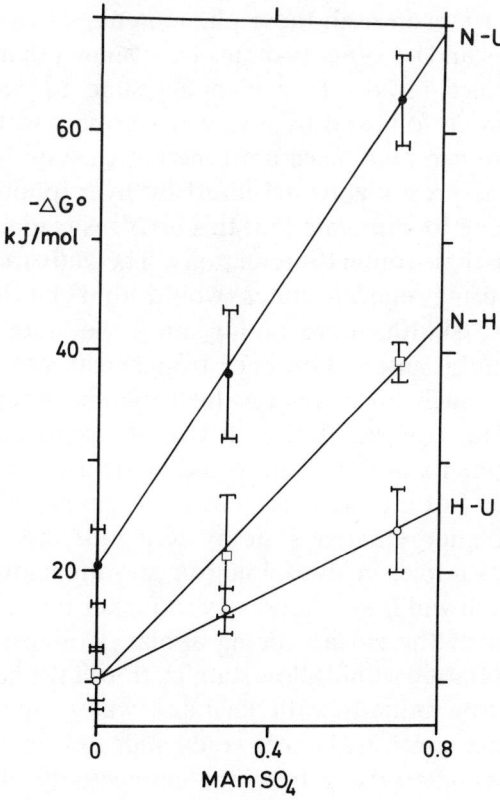

Figure 2 The stabilization of state N relative to states H and U (N–H and N–U, respectively) and of state H relative to state U (H–U). Apparent free energies of stabilization of states N and H are plotted as a function of concentration (mol/l) of ammonium sulphate. (C. Mitchinson, Ph.D Thesis, University of Newcastle upon Tyne)

known conformation and shown that unfolding a domain results in the exposure of a higher proportion of peptide groups than when two subunits or domains are separated. This is therefore in keeping with the above conclusions and these experiments serve to confirm the model proposed on the basis of other evidence for the stepwise reversible unfolding of penicillinase.

This example shows that an empirical interpretation of denaturation can provide useful qualitative information about the involvement of hydrophobic association in globular protein stabilization. It raises, however, many questions as to the mechanisms of denaturation by urea and GuCl, of stabilization by sulphate and of the nature of the involvement of water in both these phenomena.

Studies on this and on other proteins have shown that the process of folding takes place rapidly to a compact state in which secondary structure is formed, followed by a slower step in which 'shuffling' of units of structure can take place until the native state is attained. The collapsed state is presumably stabilized by hydrophobic association, but it is interesting to speculate that this involves trapped water which leads to weaker-than-contact interactions. The activation barriers between neighbouring energy states would thus be lower and the molecule able to shuffle more rapidly until the state with stronger, contact hydrophobic interaction and stronger van der Waals interaction is reached. Such lower energy hydrophobic interactions would have the advantage of stabilizing an overall conformation in which appropriate segments of the chain would be near to one another, and yet allow a variety of interactions to be explored rapidly in the search for the low free energy native state by acting effectively as a kind of lubricant. For example, in the folding of apo myoglobin certain segments of the chain will have a tendency to flicker into helical cylinders with one aspect of the surface being apolar. Collapse to a compact spherical conformation would allow stabilization of the helices by hydrophobic association, initially with included water. In the search for native helix–helix contacts, helices could slide across each other with ease, with constraints arising from the connectivity of the cylinders, until a series of contact associations are arrived at cooperatively, with most or all of the water being expressed from the globular structure.

It must be pointed out that such favourable interactions will be restricted to contacts between small apolar areas. They are not likely to occur when two large areas of apolar surface approach with intervening layers of water approaching one molecule thick. In this case, an appreciable proportion of hydrogen bonds would remain unsatisfied with considerable energy cost.

Water as a good solvent: the formation of mucous gel

Mucus is a widespread and vital component in the continued existence and function of slugs, fish and humans. Physiological processes such as breathing, locomotion, digestion and reproduction are dependent on the viscoelastic properties of mucus which provide protection, lubrication and selective permeability. Although differing in detail, most mucous secretions are composed of highly glycosylated glycoprotein molecules which interact in such a way as to produce the physical properties particular to the given physiological function.[9,10] The glycoprotein whose properties I shall discuss comes from pig gastric mucus which lines the surface of the stomach forming a phase boundary between the cells in the wall and the heterogeneous contents of the stomach. It has an average molecular weight of 2×10^6 and contains 87% carbohydrate arranged in chains on four polypeptide chains in what is described as the bottle brush structure (Figure 3).

This glycoprotein, as might be expected from the large content of hydroxyl bearing sugar moieties, interacts strongly with water. Water acts towards it as a 'good' solvent as indicated by the relatively low degree of intermolecular interaction at low to moderate concentrations and by the high degree of expansion of the molecule in aqueous solution. The effective volume has a value of $V_e = 50$ ml.g^{-1}; that is, more than 98% of the volume within the sphere of influence of the molecule is composed of water. Water thus competes very effectively for hydrogen bond donors and acceptors on the glycoprotein molecule and there is very little intermolecular hydrogen bonding. The extent of strong interaction with water is, however, small: non-frozen water (determined at 250 °K by ^{1}H N.M.R.) amounts to approximately 0.5 g per gram of glycoprotein or about 1% of the water within the effective volume. 'Masking' of reactive groups with relatively small amounts of water leaves the flexible molecule free to expand in such a way as to maximize its conformational entropy. Flexibility has been demonstrated by the ability of the molecule to contract in solution, containing guanidinium chloride or caesium chloride, and to expand in solutions of low ionic strength.

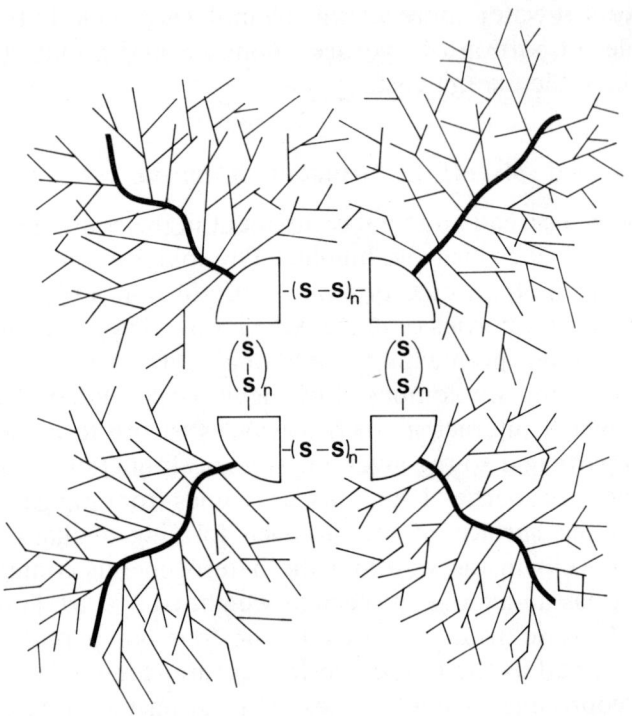

Figure 3 Diagrammatic representation of the glycoprotein from porcine gastric mucus. Each of the four disulphide bridged units has a molecular weight of 5×10^5 daltons. The non-glycosylated, cysteine containing parts of the polypeptide may or may not be folded. The actual composition is 87% carbohydrate and 13% protein. Approximately one amino-acid residue in three in the glycosylated part of the polypeptide chain (heavy line) is glycosylated

A distinct transition in properties occurs on lowering the water content in a solution of glycoprotein. Flow properties reflect a sharp rise in intermolecular interaction and, as the water content is reduced further, a gel forms corresponding to the physiological gel from which the glycoprotein was originally extracted. The concentration of glycoprotein at which strong interaction becomes appreciable is that at which the molecular domains occupy the solution. In other words, the molecules are now touching one another and all the solvent is intramolecular. As the concentration is raised further, the gel changes from a sloppy, viscoelastic gel to one which is much more firm and less readily dispersed on dilution. At these concentrations, either the effective volume is decreased with the decreased activity of water or there is mutual interpenetration of the molecular domains, in either case increasing the probability of cooperative intermolecular hydrogen bonding. In either case, gel formation occurs when molecules are forced together by reducing the water content. The phenomenon of a transition can be repeated in another way by taking a solution of glycoprotein at 10 g.l^{-1} and steadily lowering the ionic strength. The molecules expand and the solution becomes more viscous until a gel is formed. The addition of salts reverses this process. Here, intermolecular interaction and gel formation occurs as the molecules expand and again invade the domains of their neighbours, allowing glycoprotein to compete effectively with water for hydrogen bonding groups on neighbouring glycoprotein molecules.

Under given conditions, therefore, the water content of the glycoprotein solution determines the physical properties of the system. This balance is quite delicate. Although the phenomenon of interaction of the glycoprotein is conceptually simple and involves only a small fraction of the total water in the system, the volume fraction of the total water is the major factor in determining the rheology of the mucous gel. This balance can be seen to be operating in the following physiological examples.

Respiratory mucus gel coats the 'ciliary escalator' in which a layer of gel, on to which foreign particles lodge, is moved away from the lung by the concerted movement of underlying cilia. The rheological properties of the gel are critical to this operation. Increase in water content allows the gel to be sheared more readily and decreases the purchase of the cilia on the gel. Decreased water content increases the shear resistance so that the gel follows the cilia in both directions of their beat with loss of net translation of the gel. In chronic obstruction lung disease the water content becomes lower still and characteristic bronchial 'plugs' are produced which can be dispersed only with difficulty.

Cervical mucus varies in its rheological properties as a function of time in the menstrual cycle. Most of the time, it exists as a homogeneous gel with relatively low water content and high viscosity, and acts as a barrier to sperm. At menstruation, more glycoprotein is produced together with an overall higher proportion of water so that the viscosity is lower, allowing the movement of sperm. It has been suggested that at this time the glycoprotein is extruded rapidly from crypts at a relatively high concentration in such a way that layers or cylinders of viscous and slowly dispersing gel are aligned along the cervix, providing directional guidance for sperm to swim up the low viscosity channels in between. Whether this model is correct in detail or not, the rheology and hence the water content of the gel is critical in this physiological function.

The 'goodness' of the solvent properties of water towards these glycoprotein molecules is seen to vary in a sensitive manner depending, for a given set of conditions, on the water content. Only a small percentage of the water is involved in solvent interactions with the glycoprotein and the properties of the bulk of the water remain apparently unchanged while the properties of the total system change dramatically. Physiological systems of this sort will provide some fascinating contexts for the study of the biophysics of water.

References

1. L. J. Henderson, *The Fitness of the Environment*, Macmillan, New York (1913).
2. C. Tanford. *The Hydrophobic Effect*, 2nd edn., Wiley, New York.
   F. Franks, in *Water—A Comprehensive Treatise* (ed. F. Franks) Vol. 4, Ch. 1, pp. 1–94, Plenum Press, New York (1975).
   W. P. Jencks, *Catalysis in Chemistry and Enzymology*, Ch. 8, McGraw-Hill, New York.
3. R. H. Stillinger, *Science*, **209**, 451 (1980).
   W. B. Dandliker and V. A. de Saussure, in *Chemistry of Biosurfaces* (ed. M. L. Hair), Vol. 1, Ch. 1, pp. 1–43, Dekker, New York (1971).
4. S. Swaminathan and D. L. Beveridge, *J. Amer. Chem. Soc.*, **101**, 5832 (1979).
5. F. Franks, *Phil. Trans. R. Soc. Lond.*, B**278**, 33 (1977).
6. B. Adams, R. J. Burgess, E. A. Carrey, I. R. Mackintosh, C. Mitchinson, R. M. Thomas and R. H. Pain, in *Protein Folding* (ed. R. Jaenicke), pp. 447–467, Elsevier, Amsterdam (1980).
7. P. K. Nandi and D. R. Robinson, *J. Amer. Chem. Soc.*, **94**, 1299–1308 and 1308 (1972).
8. C. Chothia, *J. Mol. Biol.*, **105**, 1 (1978).
9. R. H. Pain, in *The Mechanical Properties of Biological Materials* (ed. J. F. V. Vincent and J. D. Currey), pp. 359–376, Society for Experimental Biology, London (1980).
10. M. W. Denny and J. W. Gosline, *J. exp. Biol.*, **88**, 375 (1980).

Dynamical and structural aspects of protein hydration studied by high-resolution neutron scattering

Sir John Randall
University of Edinburgh, UK

and

H. D. Middendorf
University of London, King's College, UK

Summary

The scattering of cold neutrons (λ_0 = 2.5 to 10 Å) from protein powders and films has been used to study the surface dynamics of sorbed water molecules, the hydrogen-weighted spectrum of low-frequency modes, and the hydration-induced order in the arrangement of subunits. Partially and fully *in vivo* deuterated samples of the phycobili-protein C-phycocyanin were investigated. Wet-minus-dry difference broadenings $\Delta E(k)$ measured in quasi-elastic scattering experiments (k = 0.15 to 1.7 Å^{-1}) show a hydration-dependent oscillatory structure. At sub-monolayer hydration levels this has allowed average distances between primary hydration sites to be determined, together with the residence time of water molecules at such sites. Time-of-flight difference spectra (10 to 800 cm^{-1}) have been obtained as a function of water uptake and those show the gradual development of spectral features characterizing the rotational and vibrational water–protein interaction. The contribution of intramolecular modes can be assessed by varying the deuteration level of the protein and the H_2O/D_2O contrast in the water of hydration. Low-angle diffraction patterns demonstrate a reversible order to disorder transition in the spatial arrangement of subunits.

X-ray and neutron diffraction studies have in the past provided much useful information on the hydration of polypeptides, proteins and nucleic acids.[1] Only more recently has it become possible to complement these studies dynamically by also performing energy analyses of the scattered radiation. Advanced neutron spectrometers[2] using cold neutrons with incident wavelengths $\lambda_0 = 2$–12 Å can now resolve energy transfers $\hbar\omega$ in the range 10^{-4} to 10^3 cm^{-1} corresponding to nuclear motions with frequencies from 3×10^6 to 3×10^{13} Hz. For scattering angles 2θ between $\approx 1°$ and $140°$, the range of momentum transfers $\hbar k$ covered simultaneously is $k = (4\pi/\lambda_0)\sin\theta \approx 0.01$–$3$ Å^{-1} so that dynamical processes are sampled over scale lengths $2\pi/k$ extending from bond lengths to macromolecular dimensions.

Spectral analysis of the neutrons scattered into a solid angle element centred on any fixed angle 2θ (compare Figure 1) reveals an elastic peak ($\hbar\omega \approx 0$) which may be broadened symmetrically by diffusive motions with energies $\hbar\omega \leqslant 1$–10 cm^{-1} (quasi-elastic scattering), together with an energy-gain spectrum extending up to roughly $5k_BT \approx 1000$ cm^{-1} which represents the inelastic spectrum proper. In each of these regimes, the scattering from biomolecules consists of an incoherent and a coherent component. Because of the very large incoherent scattering cross-section of protons (80 barn*) relative to all other nuclei (<0.4 b) present in natural biological

* 1 barn = 10^{-24} cm^2.

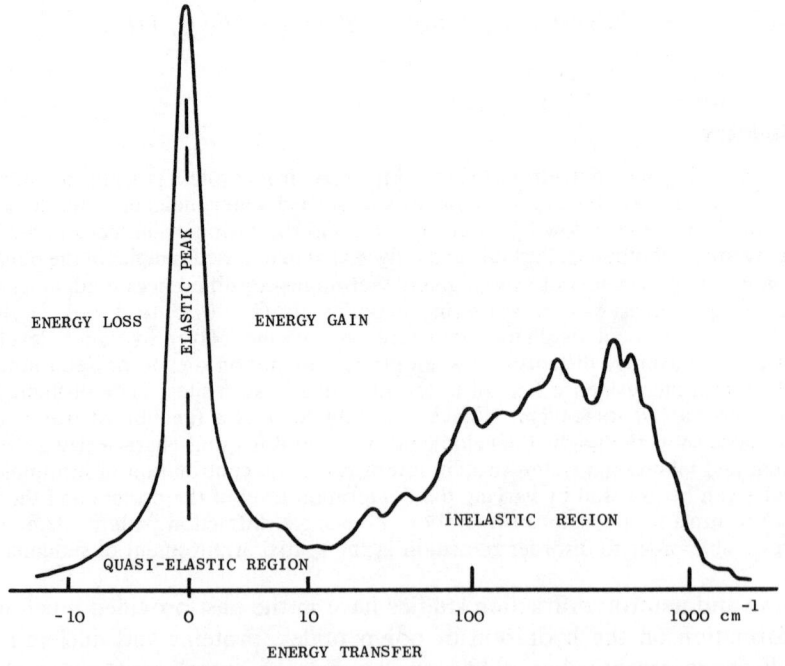

Figure 1 Typical appearance of neutron spectrum from hydrated biopolymers at $2\theta = $ const. (intensities in inelastic region exaggerated relative to elastic peak)

samples, the incoherent scattering is almost entirely due to hydrogenous groups and water molecules. By replacing some or all of the carbon-bound hydrogens with deuterium (2 b), or changing the H/D ratio in the water of hydration, it is possible to 'fade out' the proton signal selectively and to accentuate either the scattering from the bulk protein or that from the water of hydration.

Partially and fully *in vivo* deuterated samples[3] of the phycobiliprotein C-phycocyanin were investigated. These were isolated from blue-green algae by H. L. Crespi at Argonne National Laboratory, USA. C-phycocyanin is a multimeric chromoprotein located between the thylakoid membranes, and its function is that of a light-harvesting protein involved in photosystem II. The crystallographic structure of C-phycocyanin has been determined[4] to a resolution of 5 Å. It is often found in hexameric form (MW ≈ 200 000) and is composed of $(\alpha\beta)$ subunits each carrying three phycocyanobilin chromophores. The $(\alpha\beta)_6$ molecule is shaped like an oblate ellipsoid (diameter 110 Å, thickness 40 Å) with a central solvent channel of 10 Å radius.

Neutron diffraction patterns from H_2O-hydrated powder samples of fully *in vivo* deuterated phycocyanin (d-PC) show five subsidiary peaks or bands centred on $k \approx 0.085, 0.20-0.25, 0.7, 1.4$ and 2.0 Å^{-1}. Dry d-PC gives a very steep fall in intensity at small k, indicative of large scattering units (radius of gyration $R_g \gtrsim 150$ Å). As the sample takes up H_2O, a conspicuous subsidiary maximum appears first at $k \approx 0.25$, increases in intensity and gradually shifts to $k = 0.21$ Å^{-1} at 0.25 g H_2O/g protein. At any fixed hydration level, this maximum disappears almost completely on changing the H/D contrast from 100% H_2O stepwise to 100% D_2O. Using the neutron spin-echo spectrometer IN 11 at the Institut Laue-Langevin (I.L.L.), Grenoble, it was possible experimentally to separate the coherent from the incoherent scattering. These measurements[5] demonstrate a hydration-induced, fully reversible transition to medium-range order in the three-dimensional arrangement of the subunits of an oligomeric protein.

The IN 10 backscattering spectrometer[6] was used to record quasi-elastic neutron spectra at several scattering angles corresponding to $k = 0.15$ and 1.68 Å^{-1}. The dependence of the quasi-elastic difference broadening ΔE on k and hydration level is of principal interest here and has been reported in detail.[7,8] If the water dynamics is described by a space–time correlation function $G_s(r, t)$, the scattering law $S_{incoh}(k, \omega)$ follows from this by double Fourier transformation and $\Delta E(k)$ is the associated width function. Hydration difference broadenings measured for a powder sample of d-PC at four hydration levels (expressed as hydration numbers per $(\alpha\beta)$ subunit) are given in Figure 2. These results show that $\Delta E(k)$ possesses an oscillatory structure with a first maximum between $k_{max} = 0.4$ and 0.8 Å^{-1}. The position of this maximum shifts to higher k with increasing hydration, while its intensity increases and the following minimum at $k_{min} = 0.7$ to

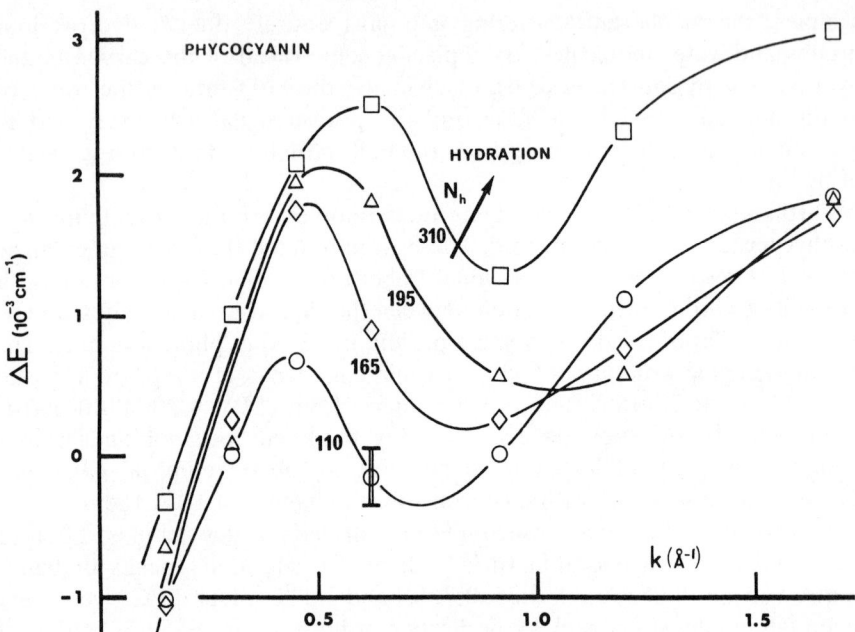

Figure 2 Quasi-elastic broadening $\Delta E(k)$ for H_2O-hydrated d-PC (reproduced from ref. 8 by permission of The Royal Society)

1.3 Å^{-1} becomes progressively more shallow. A Chudley–Elliott jump diffusion model was adopted as a working hypothesis to extract a characteristic length (water migration distance a) and a characteristic time (residence time τ_0 at a hydration site) from the $\Delta E(k)$ data. Values of a = 6 to 9 Å and τ_0 = 5 to 30 ns were obtained for the powder sample and agree well with average jump distances derived from topographical considerations in conjunction with hydration number estimates.

High-resolution inelastic spectra were obtained using the IN 5 multichopper spectrometer[9] at I.L.L. and three examples are shown in Figure 3. It is seen, first of all, that a distinct hydration difference spectrum between the dry and the H_2O-hydrated sample is observed already at a relatively low hydration level (equivalent to about 80 H_2O molecules per $(\alpha\beta)$ subunit). The prominent peak at 495 cm^{-1} is due to torsional oscillations of the H-bonded water of hydration; on partial desorption (not shown here) this peak shifts to higher cm^{-1} values, indicative of tighter 'binding' and loss of mobility. The inelastic spectrum for a D_2O-hydrated sample, on the other hand, does not differ appreciably in its overall intensity from that of the dry sample, and its most conspicuous feature is the considerably depressed peak at 575 cm^{-1}. The sets of spectra obtained to date are rather limited and a full analysis of the complex pattern of spectral changes is not yet possible. The appropriate

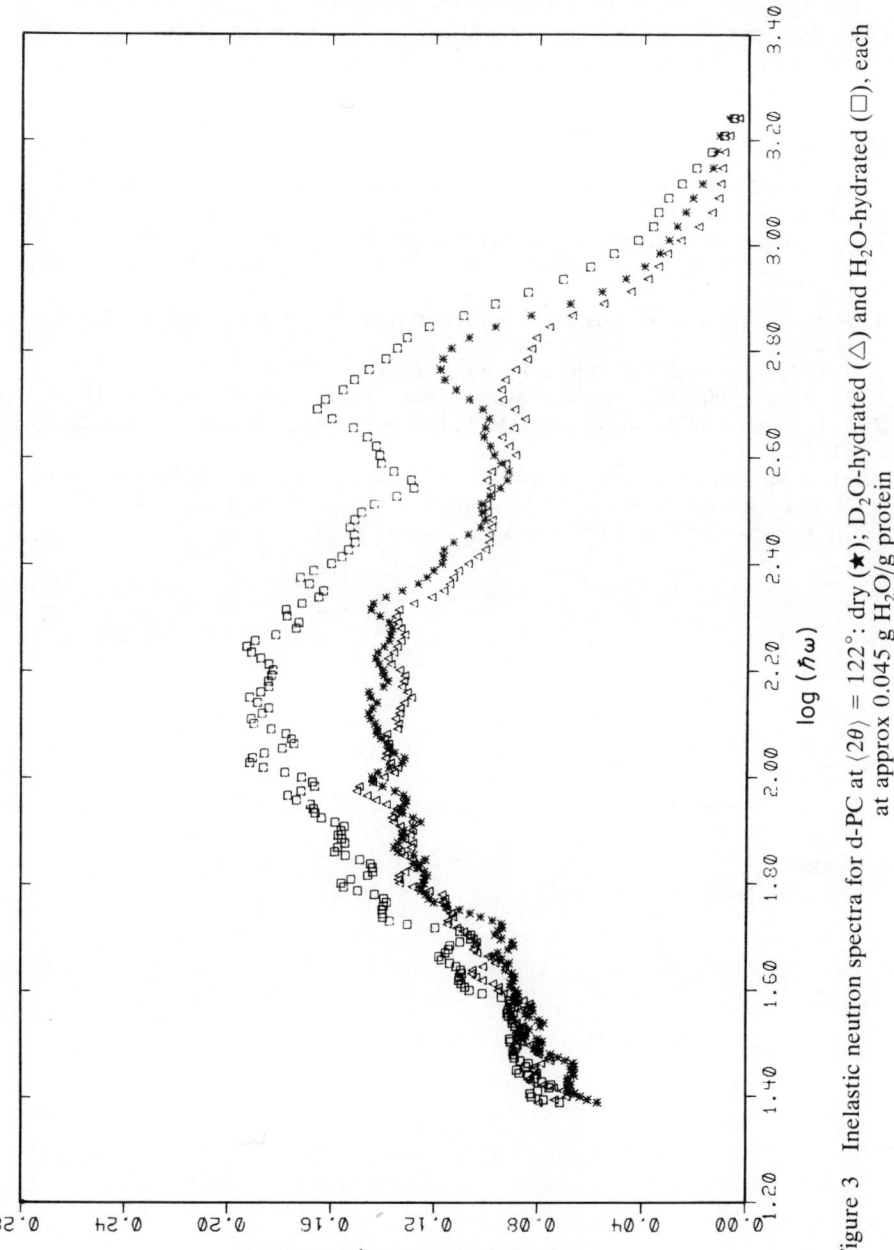

Figure 3 Inelastic neutron spectra for d-PC at $\langle 2\theta \rangle = 122°$: dry (★); D_2O-hydrated (△) and H_2O-hydrated (□), each at approx 0.045 g H_2O/g protein

hydration and contrast difference spectra reflect the way in which the various degrees of freedom of the protein–water system are repartitioned, and it is clear that spectra of this kind are a potentially rich source of information on details of the dynamic properties of hydrated proteins.

References

1. H. J. C. Berendsen, in *Water—A Comprehensive Treatise* (ed. F. Franks), Vol. 5, Ch. 6, Plenum (1975).
2. T. Springer, *Phil. Trans. R. Soc. Lond.*, **B290**, 673 (1980).
3. H. L. Crespi, in *Stable Isotopes in the Life Sciences*, p. 111, I.A.E.A., Vienna (1977).
4. R. G. Fisher, N. E. Woods, H. E. Fuchs and R. M. Sweet, *J. Biol. Chem.*, **255**, 5082 (1980).
5. J. T. Randall, *et al.* (submitted for publication).
6. M. Birr, A. Heidemann and B. Alefeld, *Nucl. Instr. Meth.*, **95**, 435 (1971).
7. J. T. Randall, H. D. Middendorf, H. L. Crespi and A. D. Taylor, *Nature*, **276**, 636 (1978).
8. H. D. Middendorf and J. T. Randall, *Phil. Trans. R. Soc. Lond.*, **B290**, 639 (1980).
9. R. E. Lechner, F. Volino, A. J. Dianoux, F. Douchin, H. Hervet and G. C. Stirling, I.L.L. Rep. No. 73L85 (I.L.L., Grenoble, 1973).

Comparative studies of some different models of the solvent effect on the conformations of biological molecules

B. Robson, G. Douglas, A. Metcalfe, K. Woolley and J. S. Thompson
University of Manchester, UK

Summary

Simple models of the solvent effect reveal trends in stability when applied to the conformational analysis of biological oligopeptides, and further ways by which sequence determines conformation.

To tackle in reasonable time some problems concerning short heteropolypeptides, we have been obliged to use simplified models of the solvent effect. Solvation shell perturbation models, emphasizing the hydrophobic interaction, have been used by us,[1] but are highly empirical and not well justified theoretically. For small peptides it is fortunate that Monte Carlo calculations reveal gross electrostatic phenomena such as the effect of a continuum reaction field to be dominant.[2] Fairly well founded analytical representations of the reaction field contribution[3] imply that conformations with large dipole moments and small molecular dimensions tend to be stabilized, steric factors permitting. The effect of electrostatic interactions within the solute molecule may change the conformation to increase or decrease the dipole moment and increase or decrease the molecular dimensions. Counterions decrease the intramolecular electrostatic interactions. Thus we have a complex interplay of frequently competing effects. The precise sequence of residues, especially charged residues, determines the outcome, and this is currently being explored. It is an important factor in the sequence-conformation relationship.

In the case of enkephalins, combined second derivative and SIMPLEX minimization[1] from a variety of starting points locates a small number of minima for most extended and compact (turn) forms. The compact forms always have considerable stability with or without the reaction field, with or without explicit inclusion of counterions. Similar calculations on a biologically highly active cyclic peptide suggest that such compacted forms are strongly determined to be the biological ones, as do comparison with morphine and its derivatives. In the case of the unionizable thyroid hormone releasing factor (TRF) and its analogues, counterions have no effect, but now the reaction field is required to produce consistency between the theoretical and the experimental biological activities. For example, TRF produces three classes of conformer on minimization, which according to the spatial arrangement of the three rings are called Propeller (P), Cup (C) and Y-shaped or ring-stacked (Y). With respect to the P conformer, the Y and C energies are 2.8 and 6.8 kcal mol^{-1} respectively. When the histidine residue is N'-methylated, we obtain 6.1 and 21.6 kcal mol^{-1}. Since this analogue is eight times more active, a role for the P form is further indicated. When pyroglutamic acid is replaced by the similar proline residue, the Y and C conformers are now more stable by -2.3 and -13.6 kcal mol^{-1}, consistent with the inactivity of this analogue, and so on.

The peptide cross-link of the peptidoglycan cell walls of streptococci is an interesting example. The N-acetyl N' methylamide end-blocked analogue contains eight D and L residues with three carboxyl groups and one charged lysyl group, giving a structure as $(-) \cdot (+) \cdot (-) \cdot (-)$. *In vacuo*, the lysyl group attracts the three carboxyls, closing the structure in the manner of a cup. The reaction field produces a U-band conformer with the lysine at the elbow and the carboxyls at the ends of the U arms. When the positions of sodium and chloride ions are included in the minimization, the structure becomes more extended and floppy. The situation in the cell wall is clearly dictated by global charge repulsions, since the wall lattice *contracts* as the ionic strength is increased: nonetheless, an electrostatic tension between two carboxyl groups, relaxed in the presence of the counterions, appears to be an important trigger, releasing a class of more stable, fairly open conformers.

References

1. B. Robson and D. J. Osguthorpe, *J. Mol. Biol.*, **132**, 19 (1979).
2. A. T. Hagler, D. J. Osguthorpe and B. Robson, *Science*, **208**, 599 (1980).
3. V. Madison and K. D. Kopple, *J. Amer. Chem. Soc.*, **102**, 4855 (1980).

Correlation between aqueous solubility and partitioning in an hydrated Dextran gel (Sephadex® G-15)

Åsa Ch. Haglund and N. V. B. Marsden
Uppsala University, Sweden

Summary

Distribution coefficients of 1-alcohols and cycloalkanes are highly correlated with their aqueous solubilities as are those of aromatic hydrocarbons, the aromatic regression line being the higher. This is consistent with affinity for non-polar solutes being due to an hydrophobic interaction whereas aromatics have another additional interaction. The latter is not due to aromaticity but simply an additive effect of three double bonds.

This highly cross-linked gel acts as a molecular sieve towards polar aliphatic solutes. However, less polar, or π-electron containing compounds are not excluded on a size basis; their distribution coefficients (K_d) exceed unity and increase with mol. weight indicating affinity for the gel.[1] These relationships are shown in Figure 1.

The hydrophobic nature of this interaction has been discussed previously;[1] it was proposed that the affinity reducing effect of hydroxyl substitution (Figure 1) simply results from weakened hydrophobicity. In this context it should be noted that saturated and unsaturated compounds behave differently. Whereas there are only small irregular differences between the ΔG^0 values of cyclohexane, cyclohexene, the cyclohexadienes and benzene a decrease in ΔH^0 of about 2 kJ for each double bond indicates an energetic interaction. Neither conjugation nor aromaticity have any special influence; benzene thus behaves as 'cyclohexatriene'.

If hydrophobic interactions are involved in the affinity, the latter should be correlated with the aqueous solubility of the solute, as shown in Figure 2 for

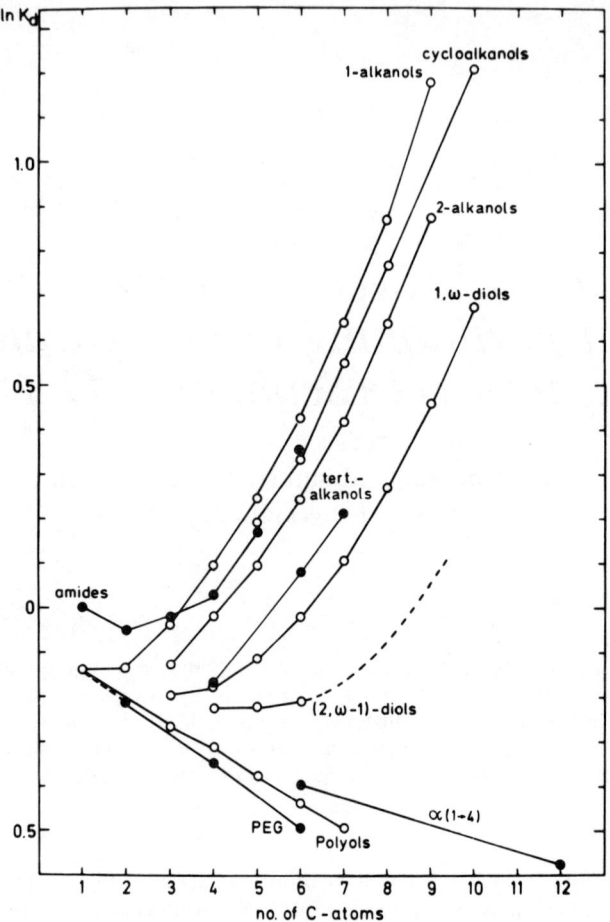

Figure 1 ln K_d values for different homologous series. PEG = polyethyleneoxides, $\alpha(1 \to 4)$ = slope of maltodextrins

six 1-alkanols, cyclopentane, cyclohexane and 1-chlorobutane with the following regression equation:

$$\ln K_d = 0.150 \ln(1/m_{sat}) + 0.053 \qquad (1)$$

with $n = 9$, $r = 0.992$, $SD_{slope} = 0.007$, where m_{sat} is the molal concentration at saturation.

This result also supports the hypothesis that the hydroxyl (or chlorine) has only a short-range influence and that the groups do not interact attractively with the gel but merely act to reduce the number of carbon atoms effective in the hydrophobic interaction.

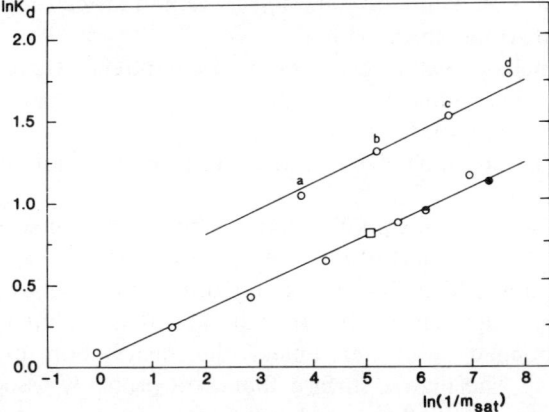

Figure 2 Relation between ln k_d and solubilities (ln $1/m_{sat}$) for 1-alkanols, cyclopentane, cyclohexane and 1-chlorobutane (lower line) and alkylbenzenes (upper line). ○ = 1-alkanols, C_4-C_9; ◐ = cyclopentane, ● = cyclohexane; □ = 1-chlorobutane, a = benzene, b = toluene, c = ethylbenzene and d = n-propylbenzene

As expected aromatic compounds do not fit the saturated line (Figure 2). The aromatic equation has a slope nearly the same as that for saturated solutes but displaced to a lower free energy value.

Figure 3 shows that cyclic hydrocarbons with one or two double bonds lie

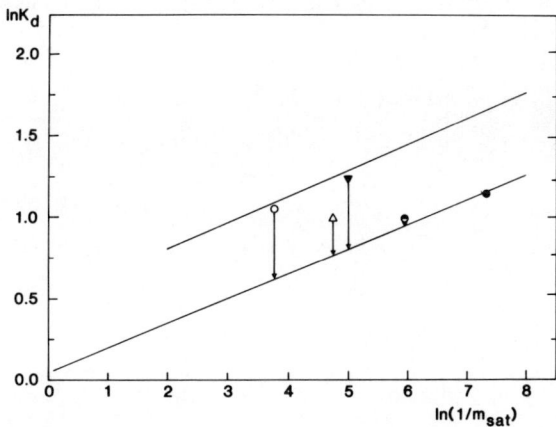

Figure 3 Relation between ln k_d of unsaturated compounds and their solubilities. ● = cyclohexane, ◐ = cyclopentane, △ = 1,4-cyclohexadiene, ○ = benzene and ▼ = cycloheptatriene. The two lines are as in Figure 2

between the saturated and aromatic lines; the non-aromatic cycloheptatriene lying very near to the aromatic line.

We also conclude that with unsaturated compounds there is some interaction due to the double bond, superimposed on a residual hydrophobic interaction. Enthalpy data[2] further suggest that the double bond effect is additive but that aromatic electron delocalization does not play a significant role.

The hydrophobic affinity implies that it is favourable for such solutes either to associate with some part of the matrix surface or to be accommodated in the internal water, which almost certainly differs from bulk water due to the closeness of the matrix chains. It is thus unlikely that a solute in the gel can be entirely surrounded by water unless the distribution of the latter is heterogeneous.[3] The matrix surface therefore probably associates with the hydrocarbon moieties and thus reduces their contact area with water. Hydrophobic reactions in sugar residues are known[4] but the disproportionately high affinity of this gel suggests there may be a cooperative effect due to a stable array of non-polar faces of the anhydroglucose residues.

References

1. Åsa Ch. Haglund and N. V. B. Marsden, *J. Polymer Science*, Polymer Letters Edition, **18**, 271 (1980).
2. Åsa Ch. Haglund and N. V. B. Marsden, *Proc. Second Romanian Nat. Conference of Biophysics*, Bucharest, 57 (1976).
3. P. Flodin, *Dextran Gels and Their Applications in Gel Filtration*, Meijel, Halmstad (1962).
4. A. Suggett, in *Water—A Comprehensive Treatise*, ed. F. Franks, Plenum, New York, Vol. 4 (1975).

Characterization of the state of water within synthetic membranes by water sorption isotherms and heat capacity measurements

W. Lukas and W. Pusch
Max-Planck-Institut für Biophysik, Germany

Summary

The state of water within synthetic membranes, particularly asymmetric and homogeneous cellulose acetate membranes, is characterized by the thermodynamic functions of water sorption, $\Delta \bar{H}_w$, $\Delta \bar{S}_w$ and $\Delta \bar{G}_w = \Delta \mu_w^m$ as well as by the partial specific heat of water within the membranes. Using the thermodynamic functions of water sorption and the partial specific heat of water within the membranes, the absolute thermodynamic functions of sorbed water, $\bar{H}_w$, $\bar{S}_w$ and $\bar{G}_w = \mu_w^m$ can be calculated.

Introduction

Reid and Breton[1] proved homogeneous cellulose acetate (CA) membranes to be relatively permeable to water and to be effective barriers to certain solutes. Concurrently, Loeb and Sourirajan[2] unintentionally discovered the so-called modified or asymmetric CA membranes composed of a very thin active layer and a porous support (matrix) making up nearly the entire film. The active layer of about 0.1 μm up to 0.5 μm thickness, viewed as an extremely thin homogeneous CA membrane, governs the solute and solvent transport across such modified membranes. Poor solute permeability results from both low diffusion and low partition coefficients. When the solutes are electrolytes, a small partition coefficient might originate from Donnan exclusion, on the one hand, and from a specific water structure within the membrane, on the other hand. The water structure within synthetic membranes may be characterized by water sorption isotherms,[3,4,5] calorimetric measurements[6,7] and IR spectroscopic investigations.[8,9]

Results and discussion

The purpose of this study was to characterize the state of water within synthetic membranes by both water sorption isotherms and calorimetric measurements. Using homogeneous CA membranes of three different degrees of acetylation (32, 39, 44 wt.-%), a Du Pont polyamide (B-10) and a sulphonated PTFE (Nafion) membrane, water sorption isotherms within 20% up to 100% relative humidity were measured at 25 °C, 35 °C and 45 °C. In addition, the heat capacities of membrane samples with different but constant water contents were measured at temperatures ranging from −40 °C up to +30 °C. The following expression relates the measured heat capacity, c_m, to the partial specific heats of the water within the membrane and the membrane material, c_w and c_p:

$$(1 + v^*) \cdot c_m = c_p + c_w \cdot v^*$$

where $v^* = m_w/m_p$ is the relative water content of the membrane, m_w is the weight of water within the membrane and m_p its dry weight. When $(1 + v^*) \cdot c_m$ is plotted against v^* for homogeneous CA membranes of different acetyl content, straight lines are obtained demonstrating that c_w and c_p are independent of the water content of the membrane. The resultant partial specific heats are plotted as functions of the temperature in Figure 1. As is obvious from this figure, the partial specific heat of water within these membranes is always larger than that of bulk water and ice at the respective temperatures. These experimental findings coincide with results obtained from DSC measurements where the partial specific heat of water sorbed by different polymers[10] and phospholipids[11] was measured as a function of the temperature. Water present in homogeneous CA membranes with a specific heat larger than that of bulk water might be considered as 'bound' water interacting with the membrane matrix.

Figure 2 exhibits the water sorption isotherms of two homogeneous CA membranes, prepared from BAYER Cellit K-700 and T-900, measured at 35 °C and 45 °C. As can be seen from this figure, the water content of the K-700 membrane decreases with increasing temperature, whereas that of the T-900 increases. The corresponding enthalpies and entropies of sorption are thus negative or positive, respectively. From a statistical mechanics point of view, a negative entropy of sorption, found with the K-700 and E-320 membrane, might be correlated with a more ordered state of water within the membrane or, in general, with fewer statistical degrees of freedom of the bound water.

Using the partial specific heat of water, the corresponding thermodynamic functions of sorption, and the values of the thermodynamic functions of bulk water at a certain temperature, the absolute thermodynamic functions, $\bar{H}_w, \bar{S}_w$ and μ_w^m, of the water within the membrane can be calculated as functions of

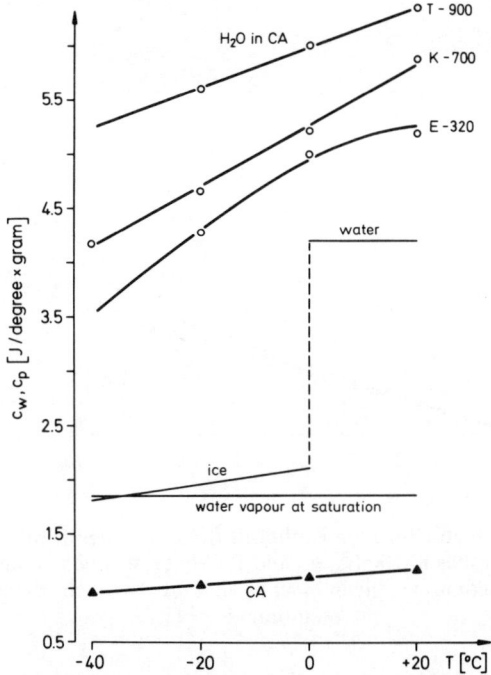

Figure 1 Partial specific heat of water, c_w, within homogeneous cellulose acetate membranes of different acetyl content, cast from either BAYER Cellit K-700 and T-900 or Eastman Kodak Cellulose Acetate E-320, as a function of the temperature, T. The specific heats of ice, water and water vapour at saturation are presented for comparison. The partial specific heat of BAYER Cellit K-700, c_p, is also shown as a function of the temperature[6,7,12,13]

the water content, v, and the temperature[12,13] ($v = 100 \cdot v^*$ is given in wt.-%). Using the calculated chemical potentials of water within a K-700 membrane at different water contents, $\mu_w^m(v, T)$, a state diagram of sorbed water can be drawn as demonstrated in Figure 3.

The asymmetric polyamide and CA membranes, as well as the Nafion membranes exhibited a diffuse melting region in the curves of heat capacity versus temperature at different but constant water contents. Such membranes are therefore surmised to contain free water in addition to bound water. With increasing water contents of the Nafion and asymmetric CA membranes, the peak of the diffuse melting region shifts to higher temperatures indicating the melting of ice within pores of increasing diameters. On the other hand, the peak of the heat capacity versus temperature curves of the B-10 (polyamide)

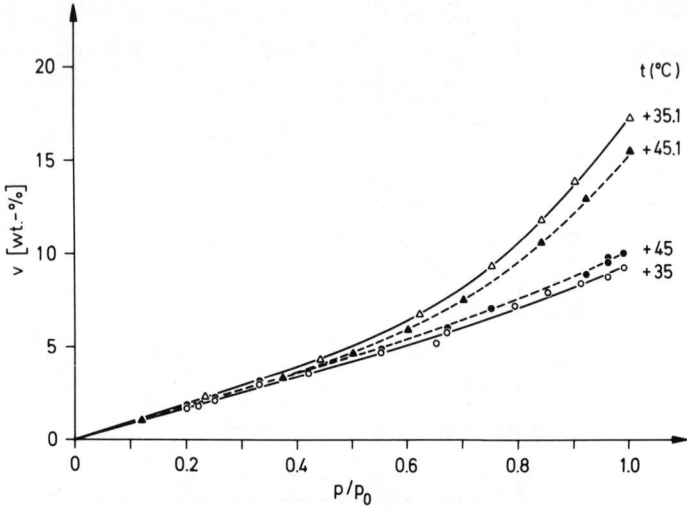

Figure 2 Water sorption isotherms of homogeneous cellulose acetate membranes K-700 (△, ▲) and T-900 (○, ●) at 35 °C and 45 °C. The water content v, given in wt. −%, refers to the dry weight of the membrane[6,7,12,13]

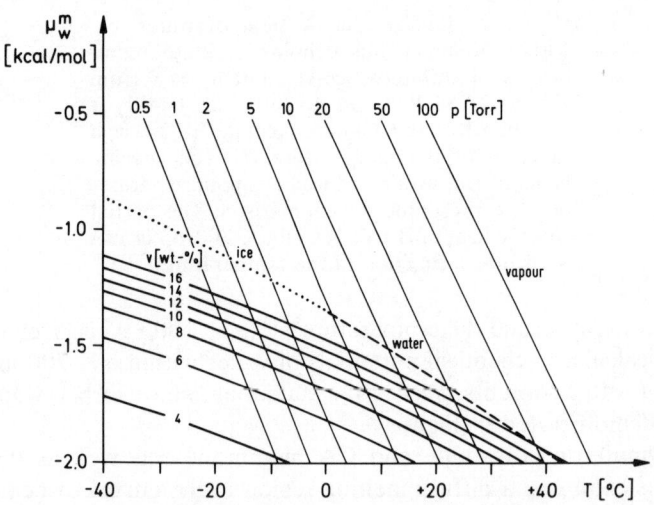

Figure 3 Calculated chemical potential of water, $\mu_w^m(v,T)$, within a homogeneous CA membrane K-700 as a function of temperature, T, at different water contents of the membrane (v = constant). The chemical potentials of ice and bulk water as well as of water vapour at different but each time constant vapour pressure (isobars) are also shown

membranes remains, independent of the water content, at the same temperature and is comparatively narrow. This indicates a very narrow pore size distribution of the pores present in the matrix of the B-10 membranes.

References

1. C. E. Reid and E. J. Breton, *J. Appl. Polymer Sci.*, **1**, 133 (1959).
2. S. Loeb and S. Sourirajan, *Advan. Chem. Ser.*, **38**, 117 (1962).
3. W. Vieth and A. S. Douglas, *J. Macromol. Sci. Phys.*, **B3**, 737 (1969).
4. J. L. Williams, H. B. Hopfenberg and V. Stannett, *J. Macromol. Sci. Phys.*, **B3**, 711 (1969).
5. H.-G. Burghoff and W. Pusch, *J. Appl. Polymer Sci.*, **20**, 789 (1976) and **24**, 1479 (1979).
6. H.-G. Burghoff and W. Pusch, *J. Appl. Polymer Sci.*, **23**, 473 (1979).
7. W. Lukas, *Thermodynamische Charakterisierung des in homogenen Celluloseacetat-Membranen gebundenen Wassers*, Diplomarbeit, Johann-Wolfgang-Goethe-Universität Frankfurt am Main, September 1980.
8. W. A. P. Luck, D. Schiöberg and U. Siemann, *J. Chem. Soc., Faraday Transactions II*, **76**, 136 (1980).
9. C. Toprak, J. N. Agar and M. Falk, *J. Chem. Soc., Faraday Transactions I*, **4**, 803 (1979).
10. C. A. J. Hoeve, Private Communication, unpublished results.
11. L. Ter-Minassian-Saraga and G. Madelmont, This volume pp. 127–133.
12. H.-G. Burghoff and W. Pusch, *Polymer Engin. Sci.*, **20**, 305 (1980).
13. W. Pusch, Final Res. Rept. to the 'Bundesministerium für Forschung und Technologie', Bonn-Bad Godesberg, März 1981.

Computer simulation of water around biomolecules

H. F. J. Savage, J. M. Goodfellow, J. L. Finney and P. Barnes
Birkbeck College, UK

Summary

Monte Carlo computer simulation techniques have been used to investigate water–biomolecule interactions at the molecular level. By extending the polarizable electropole model for water we have developed a set of interatomic potentials describing water–protein interactions. This model specifically accounts for non-pair-additive (cooperative) effects which are known to be important in hydrogen bonded systems. Using as test systems amino acid hydrate crystals in which the solvent molecules are well defined, we have found that the final predicted water structure is very sensitive to the input parameters for the potential. Using an optimized set of potential parameters, we are extending our work to examine in detail the solvent organization of vitamin B12 coenzyme.

Although interactions with solvent are thought to play a major role in many aspects of protein behaviour, e.g. stability, dynamics, folding and enzyme activity, the thermodynamics of these processes has yet to be related to changes in structure at the molecular level. An initial part of such a study is to be able to predict solvent organization around a biomolecule in one particular state, using Monte Carlo simulation techniques. In addition to having a high resolution X-ray/neutron structure of the protein, this requires that we can efficiently parameterize the individual atomic interactions between water and protein molecules as well as between water molecules themselves.

A variety of interatomic potentials have been developed in attempts to model pure water. They are almost always 'effective' pair potentials (e.g. ST2, CI). However, there is evidence that non-pair-additive (cooperative) effects are important in the formation of hydrogen bonds in aqueous systems. This has led us to develop a water model which attempts to describe cooperative effects explicitly via the use of a polarizable dipole. This polarizable electro-

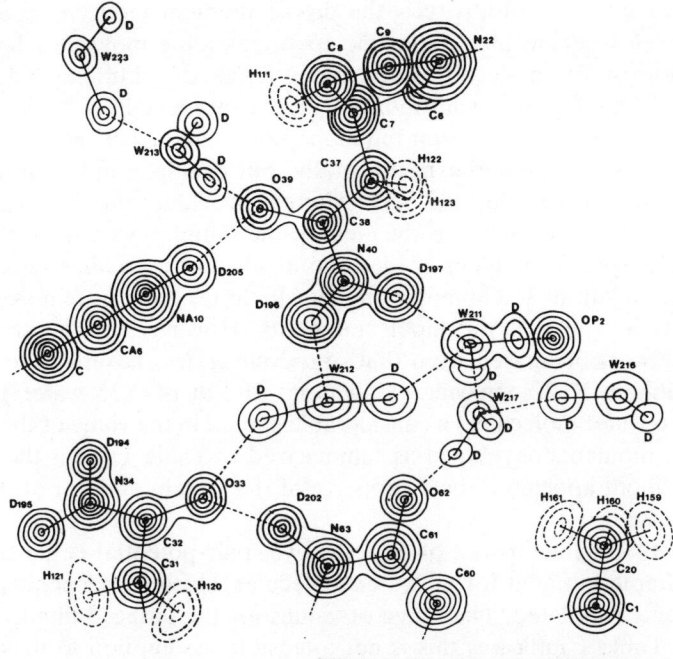

Figure 1 Neutron scattering density from vitamin B12 coenzyme

pole (PE) model[1] has been shown to reproduce a variety of known properties of the gas phase, ice and liquid water.

To extend this PE model to describe water–amino acid interactions which occur in systems of biological interest, we need to know the fractional atomic charges and the non-bonded coefficients of each atom type in the biomolecule. All these quantities are difficult to obtain with any certainty. For this reason we have investigated the sensitivity of the predicted solvent organization to the values of these parameters which are input to the potential energy functions.[2] This study involved the simulation of several amino acid hydrate crystals in which the water molecules were experimentally very well-defined. Careful comparison of the predicted with the experimental structures lead to the choice of an optimum set of potentials.

These optimized potential energy functions are being used to investigate properties of the solvent network in medium sized biomolecule hydrate crystals. One property of interest is the extent of non-pair-additive (cooperative) effects in such systems, as these effects may limit the use of 'effective' pair potentials. Non-pair-additivity is a consequence of the effect of environment (i.e. the surrounding molecules) on the properties of each molecule. One measure of non-pair-additivity is the dipole moment induced on a solvent molecule because the local field due to surrounding molecules has led to polarization of the molecule's electronic charge distribution. We found a range of values for the mean induced dipole moment in different systems (Table 1) which varied between the monomer value of 1.855 D to the value for ice Ih 2.6–3.0 D found experimentally. For example, in serine the mean dipole moment has a value of 2.77 D whereas in azidopurine it was predicted to be only 2.1 D. Not only was the mean value found to vary with the system but also the spread in values around the mean. In the smaller systems (e.g. L-arginine dihydrate and homoproline tetrahydrate) there were no significant differences in value of the dipole moments. However, as the size of the solvent network increased from that of α-cyclodextrin hexahydrate through that of vitamin B12 coenzyme (17 waters) and dCpG (25 waters) to bulk water (216 water molecules) a considerable spread in the value of the individual dipole moments developed as summarized in Table 1. Thus the induced dipole moment appears to be a property of the system and not of the water molecule itself.

One of the characteristics of an 'effective' pair potential is the use of an average dipole moment for all water molecules which is independent of the system being simulated. The range of values for the induced dipole moment shown in Table 1 indicates this is not a feasible assumption to make in our model. The use of an average dipole moment for all solvent molecules within one system and which is different for each system is a possible approximation

Table 1 Dipole moments for water molecules in several biomolecule hydrate crystals

System	Dipole moments in Debyes
Water–bulk	2.5 (range 1.9–3.1)
Serine monohydrate	2.77 ± 0.13
Azidopurine monohydrate	2.11 ± 0.04
L-arginine dihydrate	2.43 ± 0.09
	2.49 ± 0.09
Homoproline tetrahydrate	2.58 ± 0.03
	2.45 ± 0.23
	2.48 ± 0.23
	2.46 ± 0.20
α-cyclodextrin hexahydrate	2.32 ± 0.11
	2.15 ± 0.04
	2.07 ± 0.11
	2.18 ± 0.08
	2.15 ± 0.09
	2.09 ± 0.10
dCpG-proflavin complex-17 hydrate	2.41 (range 1.9–2.8)

to make but, first, it requires *a priori* knowledge of the value to use and, secondly, neglects any significance in the spread in individual dipole moments within each system. We have found that using the fixed average value for the induced dipole moment in each system leads to an underestimate of the final energy compared with that obtained with the original 'unfixed' simulation for systems bigger than L-arginine dihydrate. This discrepancy was a maximum of 1 kcal mol^{-1} (i.e. 13% of the original energy) for bulk water with 216 water molecules.

A second method for simplifying the energy calculations involves a procedure of periodically updating the dipole moments of each individual water molecule. It has been found that an updating frequency of once every fifty configurations leads to no significant differences in the final predicted solvent organization compared with the original 'unfixed' simulations in which the dipoles were updated every configuration. Moreover, a considerable reduction in required computer time is found by using this method which makes it feasible to carry out full Monte Carlo simulation on large water–protein systems of direct biological interest while using a potential which attempts to account for cooperative effects.

One system we have studied in some detail is that of vitamin B12 coenzyme. This molecule was chosen for the study because its structure is much better defined than any protein so far with both X-ray and neutron data having been collected by us to about 0.9 Å resolution. This data has been refined by several independent methods in order to compare possible bias in any one refinement method. The refined model (R—13%) contains about thirty partially occupied water positions which can be divided into two regions: (a) an ordered monolayer and (b) a partially ordered region. The initial stages of the full Monte Carlo simulations show that the solvent molecules in region (a) are moving consistently with the crystallographic data but the movements in the partially ordered region are significantly greater. The analysis of the dipole moments has shown a wide range of values (1.9–2.8 D) with the mean at 2.4 D.

References

1. P. Barnes, J. L. Finney, J. D. Nicholas and J. E. Quinn, *Nature Lond.*, **282**, 459 (1979).
2. J. M. Goodfellow, J. L. Finney and P. Barnes, *Proc. Roy. Soc. B*, in press.

An investigation of the hydration of lysozyme using a direct difference infra-red technique

P. L. Poole and J. L. Finney

Birkbeck College, UK

Summary

A direct difference infra-red technique has been developed and used to investigate the hydration events of lysozyme. Four main atom groups are studied: amide I, amide II, non-ionized carboxyl acid and a peak at 1330 cm^{-1}. It was found that the atom group hydration results agreed with expectations from model compound work. Similar measurements on the sequence-homology protein α-lactalbumin indicate significant differences in the uptake of water.

A method of obtaining difference IR spectra of protein glasses by direct means has been developed and used to investigate the hydration of specific atom groups of lysozyme. Although a direct method has been used for the study of serum albumin hydration,[1] this procedure was unsatisfactory because of the arbitrary nature of the normalization procedure, due to lack of control of the film thickness. In other work difference spectra have been produced by computer processing of spectra. Recently reported was a study of lysozyme,[2] where these computed difference spectra were used to follow hydration of the amide I and the ionized carboxyl group. An attempt to correlate this with other techniques; that of heat capacity, diamagnetic susceptibility and enzymatic measurements was carried out on lysozyme powders.[3]

The problems with computer difference techniques include those of 'baseline' assignment and the need to carry out separate scannings of samples. In order to avoid these problems, we have developed a method which uses wedge-shaped samples that can be moved perpendicular to each beam so as to normalize correctly the amount of protein in the spectrometer. The wedge-shaped glasses are formed in cells that are specially made to contain a groove

Hydration of lysozyme

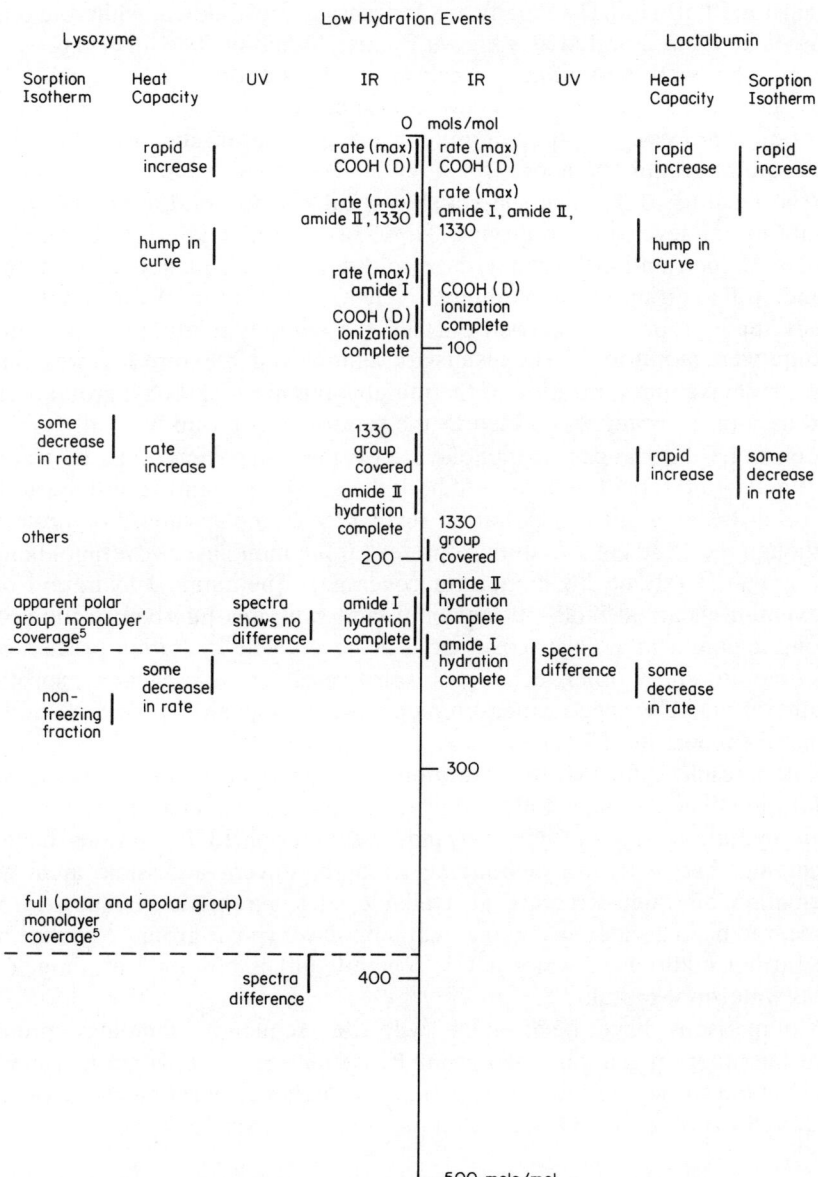

Figure 1 Low hydration events for lysozyme and α-lactalbumin as determined by IR and some other techniques. Apparent 'monolayer' coverage is that given by Golton[5], and is used here purely as a reference point

so as to form the shape of the protein glass. The glasses are equilibrated against a 50:50 H_2O/D_2O mixture. One glass is dryed down, while the other glass is kept equilibrated at a known relative humidity. The 'dry' glass is run against the 'wet' glass after normalization at 2850 cm^{-1} (CH stretch). The 'dry' glass is rehydrated in a stepwise fashion so as to be able to follow the hydration process. The spectra are converted to absorbance with the aid of a computer graphics system.

The resulting difference spectra show peaks corresponding to changes in hydration of several atom groups. Those of particular interest are amide I, amide II, non-ionized carboxyl acid and a group frequency at 1330 cm^{-1} (unidentified group(s) assigned tentatively to a side group(s) vibration(s)). A study for lysozyme was carried out and the features relating to these atom groups were monitored.[4] The results are summarized in Figure 1. It was found that the maximum ionization of the initially unionized carboxyl group occurred as soon as water was added to the sample; this group was fully ionized around one-third apparent monolayer coverage of polar groups by water.[5] The maximum rate of hydration of both the 1330 cm^{-1} feature and the amide II occurred at a higher hydration level (25–40 mols water/mol protein), although the 1330 cm^{-1} feature saturates (at 0.6 monolayer coverage) before the amide II (about 2/3 monolayer coverage). The amide I hydration rate maximum occurs at ~60–70 mols/mol, and saturates just before full polar group apparent monolayer coverage is achieved. The hydration process was also monitored by other techniques: some results of heat capacity, sorption isotherm and UV spectra measurements are also given in Figure 1, and in general support the IR results.

These results show that the hydration of dry lysozyme results initially in the ionization of acid groups, followed by the hydration of available polar groups. This hydration of polar groups might be determined by various factors, including that of hydrogen bonding strength, solvent accessible area, and formation of water structure at available sites. Aromatic residues do not appear to be in a water environment at monolayer (polar group) coverage but on further addition of water a UV spectral shift is observed at about 400 mols water/mol protein.

Comparisons have been made with the sequence homology protein α-lactalbumin. In general, polar group hydration seemed to occur in a similar fashion but the saturation values seem to be higher, suggesting more water is required for coverage. Other techniques indicate a similar result.

References

1. R. Brodersen et al., *Acta Chemica Scandinavica*, **27**, 573 (1973).
2. G. Careri et al., *Biopolymers*, **18**, 1187 (1979).
3. G. Careri et al., *Nature*, **284**, 572 (1980).
4. P. L. Poole and J. L. Finney, unpublished results.
5. I. Golton, Ph.D. thesis, University of London (1980).

Water bridges in myoglobin

J. Raul Grigera and **Ines G. Mogilner**
La Plata, Argentina

Summary

Water sorption isotherm on to myoglobin and single crystal NMR spectra have been interpreted using an exchange water model. Water sorbed on to primary binding sites is considered to be responsible for the NMR doublet. Good agreement exists between results from these studies and diffraction data. Denaturation by drying is clearly shown.

Water vapour sorption studies were done on sperm whale myoglobin (ex Sigma) using the resonant quartz crystal method.[1] Experiments were done at 30 °C and experimental data fitted with Guggenheim isotherm.[2] Figure 1 shows the isotherm of 'native' material (desorption) and the complete loop sorption–desorption for the material after complete drying. It is clear from the figure that once the protein is completely dehydrated it behaves as a different material from the point of view of the sorption isotherm. The dehydrated substance has a normal behaviour, exhibiting the regular characteristic of sorption in the presence of hysteresis. From sorption parameters it is seen that the number of primary sites increases by drying, suggesting dramatic conformational changes. As for the native protein one can observe that the number of primary sites corresponds to 78 water molecules per myoglobin molecule. This is in excellent agreement with the results of X-ray[3] and neutron diffraction.[4] The sorption isotherm allows us to compute the fraction of the total water fixed to primary binding sites at a given relative humidity.[5]

Wide line NMR spectra of water in myoglobin single crystal were done for two crystal orientations with a home-made spectrometer operating at 21 MHz using signal averaging to improve the signal noise ratio. Quality of spectra is far from ideal and can certainly be improved. Figure 2 shows the spectra for two orientations of the crystal when lying in the AB plane.

From these spectra it is possible to get a rough estimation of the splitting at

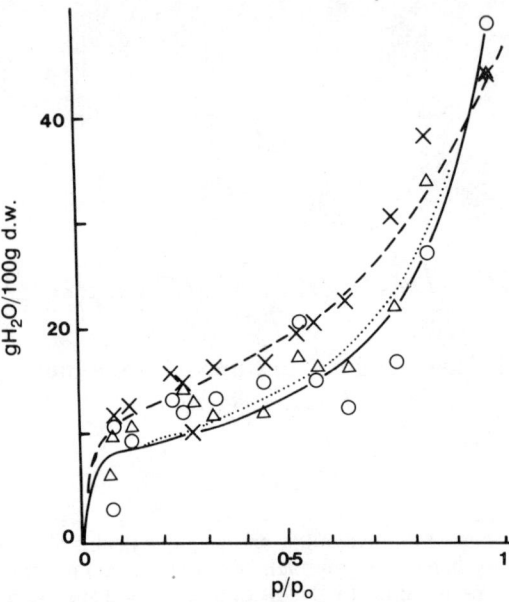

Figure 1 —○ = desorption native; ···Δ = adsorption after drying; —— × = desorption after drying and rehydration

each orientation giving $\Delta H/2\alpha\,(90°) = 0.0105$ and $\Delta H/2\alpha\,(0°) = 0.0051$, and from these we can obtain[6] one of the Saupe parameters as $S_{22} = 0.010$.

Results can be analysed by an exchange model[5,7] in which we have:

$$1/T_2^{ob} = f/T_2^b + (1-f)/T_2^c \qquad (1)$$
$$S_{22}^{ob} = fS_{22} + (1-f)S_{22}^c$$

where 'b' and 'c' stand for the different types of water molecules that exchange in between. In another version of the model[8] a third type of water

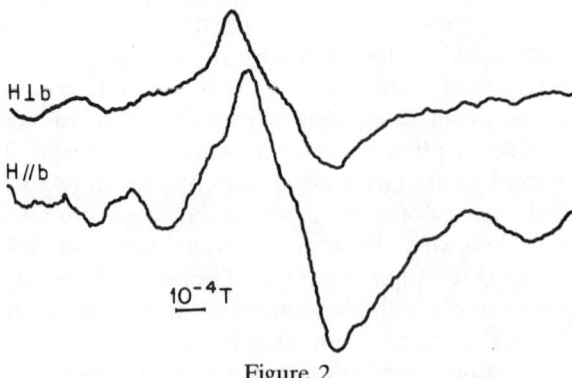

Figure 2

'a' is considered as a possible type which does not exchange with the other fractions. The value of f can be obtained, as was mentioned, from the sorption isotherm. Applying this model to our data we get: $S_{22}^b = 0.038$ (assuming that the fraction 'c' rotates isotropically, i.e. $S_{22}^c = 0$) and $T_2^b = 6.9 \times 10^{-3}$ s (generalizing the results of dielectric relaxation for other proteins that give an estimation of $T_2^c \simeq 600$ ms).

From the results shown it seems that the water detected by the sorption isotherm as fixed in primary binding sites can be identified with the water of hydration that can be observed by diffraction techniques. It seems that the 'a' water does not exist in myoglobin. The anisotropy of 'b' water would be responsible for the NMR doublet although we do not know if the 'c' water is isotropically oriented. A conclusive test (not yet done) would be to compute the NMR splitting using this model and diffraction data. The contribution of water to the stabilization of protein structure is not a new fact, but the identification of the water in primary sorption sites (which cause stabilization) with the water detected by diffraction allows us to consider the stabilizing water not only as the water that links amino acids belonging to the same protein but also to the ones that produce intermolecular linking in the protein crystals. NMR spectra of oriented fibres of collagen and DNA have similar characteristics with myoglobin single crystals. In collagen the exchange model has been applied with success.[7] DNA results may be interpreted in a similar way.

Acknowledgements

The work was partly supported by the Organization of American States.

References

1. M. G. Kennerley, *Polymer*, **15**, 216 (1962).
2. E. A. Guggenheim, *Application of Statistical Mechanics*. Clarendon Press, Oxford, 1966.
3. T. Takano, *J. Mol. Biol.*, **110**, 569 (1977).
4. B. P. Shoenborn, Cold Spring Harbor Symposium, *Quant. Biol.*, **36**, 569 (1971).
5. J. R. Grigera, *J. Phys. Chem.*, **83**, 2145 (1979).
6. A. D. Buckingham and K. A. McLauchlan, in *Progress in Nuclear Magnetic Resonance Spectroscopy*, Vol. 2, Emsley, Feeney and Sutcliffe editors. Pergamon Press.
7. J. R. Grigera and H. J. C. Berendsen, *Biopolymers*, **18**, 47 (1979).
8. J. R. Grigera and S. Mascarenhas, *Studia Biophysica*, **73**, 19 (1978).

Low temperature oxyhaemoglobin hydration in dependence on protein concentration[1]

J. Brnjas-Kraljević and S. Maričić

University of Zagreb, Yugoslavia

Summary

The specific hydration of oxyhaemoglobin measured at subzero temperatures has a threshold around 18 mmol haem/1000 ml, with a maximum hydration of 0.42 g H_2O/g Hb in the higher concentration region. The threshold Hb-concentration depends neither on the absolute amount of hydration nor on the type of ion.

It is widely believed that there is a fraction of water molecules which interact with macromolecules in such a way that they 'sense' some aspects of the macromolecular structure and motions.

A biphasic proton magnetic relaxation behaviour which was observed in the isotopically diluted haemoglobin solutions at concentrations above 15 mmol/1000 ml was ascribed to the association of haemoglobin tetramers and the fast relaxing phase of protons to the additional haemoglobin hydration at higher concentrations[2] due to the associated molecules.[3]

In order to determine the hydration of haemoglobin more directly up to the highest protein concentration and in ordinary water solutions, the Kuntz method was used.[4] We measured the dependence of solvent proton magnetization, M_0, on temperature from +25 °C to −20 °C.

In our measurements the ratio of M_{0F} (proton magnetization of the unfrozen water in the frozen haemoglobin solution) to M_{0L} (proton magnetization of liquid solutions corrected for the M_0 due to the protein protons) is proportional to the amount of water molecules in the hydration shell, it being defined as all the water molecules which become restricted in their rotational and/or translational mobility because of their interaction with the protein.

The concentration dependence of the calculated haemoglobin hydration is

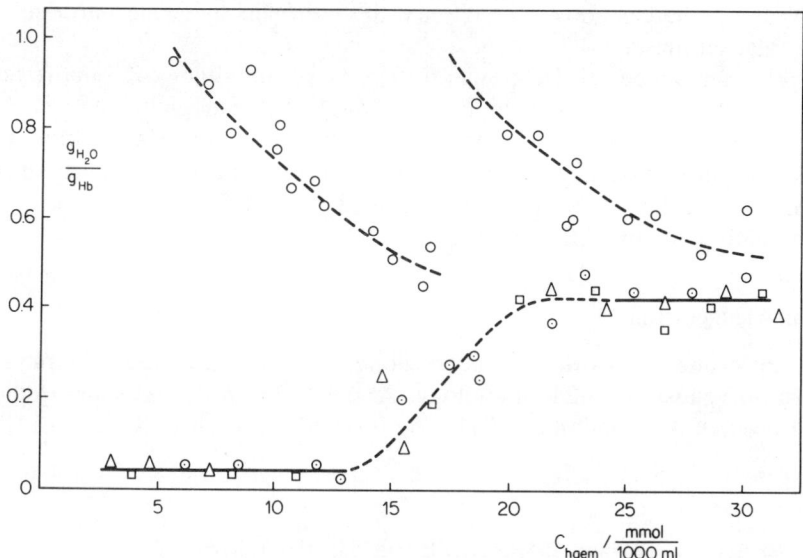

Figure 1 The specific hydration in g H$_2$O per g protein from solutions of oxyhaemoglobin in 0.1 M phosphate buffer, pH 7 (○); 0.1 M LiCl, pH 7 (△); 0.1 M KCl, pH 6.9 (□); deionized H$_2$O, pH ? (⊙)

presented in Figure 1. The hydration is similar in the presence of 0.1 M monovalent cations (Li$^+$ and K$^+$) with their common chloride anion, and in deionized solution, but a completely different behaviour is observed in potassium phosphate buffer solutions. In the monovalent ion solutions two haemoglobin hydration plateaus are well defined; 0.04 g H$_2$O/g Hb for the low concentration region and 0.42 g H$_2$O/g Hb for the higher one. The hydration of haemoglobin molecule in phosphate buffered solutions decreases from 0.9 g H$_2$O/g Hb to 0.5 g H$_2$O/g Hb in the same manner for both concentration regions. However, common to both sets of ionic solutions is the transition in the hydration around 18 mmol haem/1000 ml.

Two conclusions may be drawn:

(a) the hydration of haemoglobin is neither a function of the extremes in the ion double layer structure, nor of the type of monovalent ions;

(b) the threshold haemoglobin concentration does not depend on the absolute amount of hydration and the type of ion, although the concentration dependence is unique for the phosphate ion.

There are two concentration regions of the protein within which the specific hydration is constant (only for the monovalent ions solutions). This can be interpreted as that below $c_1 = 10$ mM the $(\alpha\beta)_2$-haemoglobin tetramers exist in solution, whereas above $c_2 = 16$ mM the tetramers associate into defined molecular entities.

The latter range of Hb-concentration is of physiological importance. Hence, the association behaviour of normal oxyhaemoglobin and its hydration should be considered in various structure–function relationships. The self-association of oxyhaemoglobin appears to be an intrinsic property of the normal molecule, whereas the amino acid substitution in the sickle cell haemoglobin enhances the effect.

Acknowledgements

The experimental work has been done in Macromolecular Biophysics Laboratory, Institute of Immunology, Zagreb. The work was supported by the Research Association of SRH, The Biomedical Science, No C–1–14.

References

1. J. Brnjas-Kraljević and S. Maričić, BBRC, **83**, 1048 (1978).
2. J. Brnjas-Kraljević, S. Maričić and V. Bračika, *Biophys. Chem.*, **6**, 191 (1977).
3. D. Desnica, *Biopolymers*, **18**, 1685 (1979).
4. I. D. Kuntz, T. S. Brassfield, G. D. Law and G. V. Purcell, *Science*, **163**, 1329 (1969).

An NMR study of isotope distribution and the state of water in the hydration layer of DNA

R. Mathur-de Vré, R. Grimèe-Declerck and P. Lejeune
Institut d'Hygiène et d'Epidémiologie, Brussels, Belgium

Summary

We have applied ³H NMR spectroscopy to study the hydration of DNA by tritiated water, and investigated by ¹H and ²H NMR the relative distribution of water protons and deuterons in the hydration layer. The results indicate that the distribution of isotopes occurs preferentially, this is defined as the 'hydration isotope' effect. Radiobiological and biophysical implications of the results are pointed out.

Water molecules in the hydration layer of biological macromolecules exhibit markedly different characteristics from those of free water, and they exercise an important influence on the molecular functions of water in various biophysical and radiobiological processes. We have investigated the localization of tritiated water and the nature of isotope distribution in the hydration layer of DNA with a view to provide an insight into: (i) the microscopic heterogeneous character of the hydration layer and (ii) microdistribution of the radionuclide ³H from tritiated water in the vicinity of DNA (the radiosensitive biopolymer).

In frozen biological samples, the unfrozen water is generally recognized as the hydration water[1,2] and is responsible for the NMR signal of water nuclei observed at sub-zero temperatures. We measured quantitatively the percentage of solvent ³HHO present in the hydration layer of DNA by ³H NMR spectroscopy. The percentage of deuterated water in the hydration layer of DNA and in the corresponding free solvent was compared for a series of mixed $H_2O/^2H_2O$ solvents by means of ²H NMR. The T_1 values of water tritons, protons and deuterons were measured in liquid solutions at +5 °C. Finally, we applied ¹H and ²H NMR to investigate the relative distribution of isotopes in the hydration layer of DNA by studying the combined effects of temperature (−5 to −45 °C) and partial deuteration of the solvent on the spin–lattice relaxation time (T_1) of water protons and deuterons, quadrupolar splitting (Δ_q) for deuterons and, spin–spin relaxation times (T_2) and ($T_{1\rho}$) of water protons.

The quantitative measurements revealed[3] that 3–4% of solvent ^{3}HHO is localized in the hydration layer of DNA (0.75% solution in tritiated water). The amount of ^{2}H$_2$O present in the hydration layer was found to be higher than in the corresponding free solvent. Furthermore, we observed[3] marked changes in the temperature-dependent behaviour of proton T_1 and, T_1 and (Δ_q) of deuterons by changing the H$_2$O/^{2}H$_2$O composition of the solvent. The proton T_1-temperature curves showed a well-defined minimum at −18 °C for 100% H$_2$O; by lowering the fraction of H$_2$O in the solvent we obtained narrower curves with a concurrent shift of the minimum to higher temperatures. At the position of the minimum $\omega_0 \tau_c \cong 1$, where ω_0 is the Larmor frequency and τ_c the correlation time of bound water molecules. The results were interpreted in terms of the dynamic behaviour of water molecules in partially deuterated hydration layer. By lowering the ^{2}H$_2$O fraction, the T_1 values of hydration water deuterons increased and exhibited enhanced temperature-sensitivity, whereas the temperature-dependence of T_2 (or linewidth) of water protons in the range −6 to −25 °C decreased considerably at lower proportions of H$_2$O. Contrary to the behaviour of T_1 and T_2, the temperature-dependence of $T_{1\rho}$ for water protons was found to be much less sensitive to changes in the proportion of H$_2$O in the solvent.

The above mentioned results imply that the distribution of water protons and deuterons in the hydration layer is not random but occurs selectively, in such a manner that the protonated water bonds tend to localize in the regions of strong interactions, i.e., in the vicinity of negatively charged phosphate groups.[4] The combined effects of differential interaction potentials experienced by H$_2$O near DNA[4] and important differences in the hydrogen bonding abilities of O—H, O—^{2}H and O—^{3}H bonds in water due to a large isotopic mass ratio favour selective distribution of water protons and deuterons in the hydration layer. The selective distribution of isotopes together with increased amount of hydration ^{2}H is defined as the 'hydration isotope' effect.

The observation of the 'hydration isotope' effect is consistent with the microscopically heterogeneous state of water molecules in the hydration layer. The combined effects of specific interactions, selectivity and heterogeneity in the hydration layer contribute to the inherent micromolecular functional basis of water in macroscopic evolution of biophysical and radiobiological processes in an aqueous medium.

The results showing the presence of ^{3}HHO in the hydration layer of DNA, and the 'hydration isotope' effect applied to ^{3}H bear far-reaching radiobiological implications. It is well-known that in biological systems the damage induced by ionizing radiations is localized in the DNA molecule. The very short range (0.69 μm in water), low energy and high specific activity of tritium β-rays result in almost complete self-absorption of ^{3}H energy, and make tritiated water an important internal source of radiation; whereby the initial molecular damage induced by β-radiation localizes in the close vicinity of the radionuclide. Therefore, a concrete knowledge of the molecular basis of the behaviour of tritiated water in the hydration layer of DNA is essential for describing the microdistribution of initial energy deposition from ^{3}HHO and for a comprehension of certain molecular aspects of the radiobiological effects of tritiated water.

Acknowledgements

We gratefully acknowledge the help and collaboration of Mr. Parmentier in this work. Thanks are also due to Dr A. J. Bertinchamps (Commission of the European Community) for several useful discussions regarding the radiobiological aspects of tritiated water.

References

1. R. Cooke and I. D. Kuntz, *Ann. Rev. Biophys. and Bioeng.* (L. J. Mullins, Ed.), Vol. 3, 95 (1974).
2. R. Mathur-De Vré, *Prog. Biophys. Molec. Biol.*, **35**, 103 (1979).
3. R. Mathur-De Vré, R. Grimèe-Declerck and P. Lejeune, *Radiat. Res.* (In Press.)
4. A. Pullman, B. Pullman and H. Berthod, *Theoret. Chim. Acta*, **47**, 175 (1978).

The role of solvation in protein structure stabilization and unfolding

Serge N. Timasheff, Tsutomu Arakawa, Hideo Inoue,
Kunihiko Gekko, Marina J. Gorbunoff, James C. Lee, George C. Na,
Eugene P. Pittz and V. Prakash

Brandeis University, USA

Summary

A systematic study of the relation between protein solvation (and hydration) and structural stability has been carried out with the aim of elucidating the mechanism of protein structure stabilization by polyhydric compound containing solvents. Direct measurements of the preferential interaction between protein and solvent components made by dialysis equilibrium showed a uniform pattern for structure stabilizing solvent additives.

It has been the practice for many years among biochemists and biologists to stabilize the biological activity of isolated enzymes, organelles, etc. by keeping them in polyhydric compound containing solvents, such as aqueous glycerol, sucrose and hexylene glycol (2-methyl-2,4-pentanediol, MPD). With the aim of elucidating the mechanism of protein structure stabilization by such substances, a systematic study has been carried out of the relation between protein solvation (and hydration) and structural stability. The approach has been that of the direct measurement of the preferential interaction between proteins and solvent components by dialysis equilibrium, monitored by precision densimetry or differential refractometry, with analysis of the results in terms of multicomponent thermodynamic theory, coupled with the Wyman linkage relations. As a result of these studies a uniform pattern emerged. All structure stabilizing, self-association promoting and crystallizing solvent additives studied are preferentially excluded from the domain of the protein molecules, namely the preferential interaction parameter $(\partial m_3/\partial m_2)_{\mu_3}$, is negative (Table 1). This is true for sucrose, glucose, glycerol, MPD, concentrated crystallizing salts and structure-stabilizing amino acids, in combination with a

Solvation in protein structure stabilization

Table 1 Preferential interaction of proteins with structure-stabilizing solvents

Cosolvent	Protein	$(\partial m_3/\partial m_2)_{\mu_3}$ mol/mol	$(\partial \mu_3/\partial m_2)_{m_3}$ (kcal/mol)^2/1000 g H$_2$O
Sucrose, 1 M	α-chymotrypsin	−7.6	4.2
	Ribonuclease	−7.6	4.3
	Tubulin	−34.2	18.9
Glycerol, 30%	α-chymotrypsin	−27.5	2.8
	Ribonuclease	−12.9	1.3
	Tubulin	−151.8	16.4
MPD, 40%	Ribonuclease	−55.0	6.5
20%	Ribonuclease	−5.2	1.6
	Lysozyme	−12.0	3.7
Glycine, 2 M	Lysozyme	−14.9	3.9
	BSA	−62.2	16.5
Na$_2$SO$_4$	BSA	−32.0	33.6

variety of proteins, covering a broad spectrum of surface polarity, structural hydrophobicity and molecular size. Thus, structural stabilization is linked directly to preferential hydration of the proteins due to totally non-specific interactions related to the perturbation of solvent structure by contact with the protein surface. Assuming the preferential exclusion to be statistically distributed over the surface of the protein, the N → D reaction, which involves an expansion of the protein molecule, should increase this effect. Since $(\partial m_3/\partial m_2)_{\mu_3} = -(\partial \mu_3/\partial m_2)_{m_3}/(\partial \mu_3/\partial m_3)_{m_2}$, an increase in the negative value of preferential interaction leads to an increase in the chemical potential of the co-solvent. This situation being thermodynamically unfavourable, the

Table 2 Preferential interactions of proteins with structure-destabilizing solvents

Protein	$(\partial m_3/\partial m_2)_{\mu_3}$ mol/mol	Protein	$(\partial m_3/\partial m_2)_{\mu_3}$ mol/mol
6 M GuHCl		8 M Urea	
Ribonuclease	0	Ribonuclease	2
α-chymotrypsin	44	α-chymotrypsin	38
Lysozyme	14	α-lactalbumin	12
β-lactoglobulin	16	β-lactoglobulin	44
Tubulin	55		
2-Chloroethanol, 40%		Methoxyethanol, 40%	
β-lactoglobulin	166	β-lactoglobulin	24
Lysozyme	80		
BSA	482		
Insulin	103		

system reacts by maintaining a minimal total protein–solvent interface, i.e. the extent of denaturation is minimized and the protein structure stabilized.

The converse situation is true for denaturants. In this case, all substances examined (urea, guanidine hydrochloride, 2-chloroethanol, methoxyethanol) were found to interact preferentially with proteins (Table 2) inducing their unfolding, this being the thermodynamically favoured reaction. Detailed analysis showed that urea and guanidinium ion interact with peptide groups, while the alcohols interact with the non-polar residues, relieving the hydrophobic pressure of water and permitting the structure to loosen.

Acknowledgement

This work was supported by grants from the National Institutes of Health, GM 14603 and CA 16707.

Further reading

J. C. Lee, K. Gekko and S. N. Timasheff, *Methods in Enzymology*, **27**, 82 (1971).
S. N. Timasheff, J. C. Lee, E. P. Pittz and N. Tweedy, *J. Coll. and Inter. Sci.*, **55**, 658 (1976).
S. N. Timasheff, *Acc. Chem. Res.*, **3(2)**, 62 (1970).
J. C. Lee and S. N. Timasheff, *Biochemistry*, **13**, 257 (1974).

Statistical state solvation sites: $[(CHO)_2]_{aq}$

Francis T. Marchese, P. K. Mehrotra and **David L. Beveridge**
Hunter College of the City University of New York, USA

Summary

A general procedure for the determination of solvation sites from molecular distribution functions obtained by means of liquid state computer simulations is described. The procedure is illustrated by results obtained from a Monte Carlo simulation on $[(CHO)_2]_{aq}$.

In order to understand the nature of biomolecular hydration processes it is necessary to obtain a description of the local aqueous solution environment around solute atoms or functional groups having ionic, hydrophilic, hydrophobic or mixed characteristics. A multiplicity of these interactions are involved in a typical aqueous solution. The resultant solvation is a complex competition between energetic and geometrical factors characteristic of both solute and solvent species.

Recent theoretical treatments of biomolecular solvation have focused on the determination of solvation sites, i.e. regions where water molecules are most likely to be found in the vicinity of the solute molecule.[1] In the definition most widely used to date, solvation sites are equivalenced with the local minima of the solute–solvent potential energy surface. This approach, however, does not include a consideration of water–water interactions, temperature effects and the statistical nature of the solute–water system.

A more general procedure for the analysis of the local solution environment of a dissolved solute based on molecular distribution functions has been proposed from this laboratory.[2] Here the structural and energetic characteristics of the aqueous solution such as coordination number, binding energy and pair interaction energy can be obtained in the general framework of generic molecular distribution functions for the system. For large solutes or solutes with multifunctional groups the solute–water distribution can be partitioned into atomic, functional group or fragment distributions. This is accomplished by invoking the 'proximity criterion'.

The proximity criterion assigns each water molecule in the various N-molecule configurations of the solute–water ensemble to the closest or most proximal solute atom. Using this technique the primary (1°) and higher order hydration for each solute atom can be determined. The proximity criterion also can be used to further resolve the total probability density into atomic and functional group components. A computer graphic analysis of these results leads to solvation sites. Since these sites include temperature factors, N-molecule interactions, and statistical weights they have been appropriately termed 'Statistical State Solvation Sites.'

As an example of the statistical state solvation site concept, we present results for a liquid state (T, V, N) ensemble Monte Carlo computer simulation on a dilute aqueous solution of trans-glyoxal.[3] General aspects of the calculations and related recent results are reviewed in references 4 and 5 and literature cited therein. The 90% probability density distribution of these molecules was determined and displayed using computer graphics (Figure 1).[6]

The envelope containing the probability of finding 1° coordinated water molecules around trans-glyoxal in aqueous solution is shown in Figure 1(a). The water density is seen to be space-filling, but not otherwise readily interpretable. The probability density of 1° coordinated water was then decomposed into contributions identified with the various solute atoms using the proximity criterion with the following results.

For the carbonyl oxygen, the average coordination number was found to be 2.30. The probability density distribution for solvation of the carbonyl oxygen is shown in Figure 1(b). The statistical state solvation sites here are well localized into two specific regions, corresponding to the pair of solute–water hydrogen bonds involving the carbonyl oxygen unshared electron pairs.

The average 1° coordination number of the glyoxal carbon atom was calculated to be 0.73. This relatively low value is a consequence of the reduced water accessibility of the carbon atom. The statistical state solvation sites, Figure 1(c), are localized above and below the molecular plane and correspond to the interaction of water molecules with the pi electrons of the carbonyl group.[7]

The glyoxal hydrogen atom was found to have a 1° coordination number of 5.78. The water probability density associated with the solute hydrogen by the proximity criterion is shown in Figure 1(d). The density envelope for the hydrogen solvation was found to encompass a large spatial region around the atom, and here the statistical state solvation of the hydrogen is a single site, broad and diffuse in character.

The localized nature of the solvation of the carbonyl oxygen and the more diffuse character of the CH group solvation emerge clearly and quantitatively from this analysis. The former illustrates how the statistical state solvation site

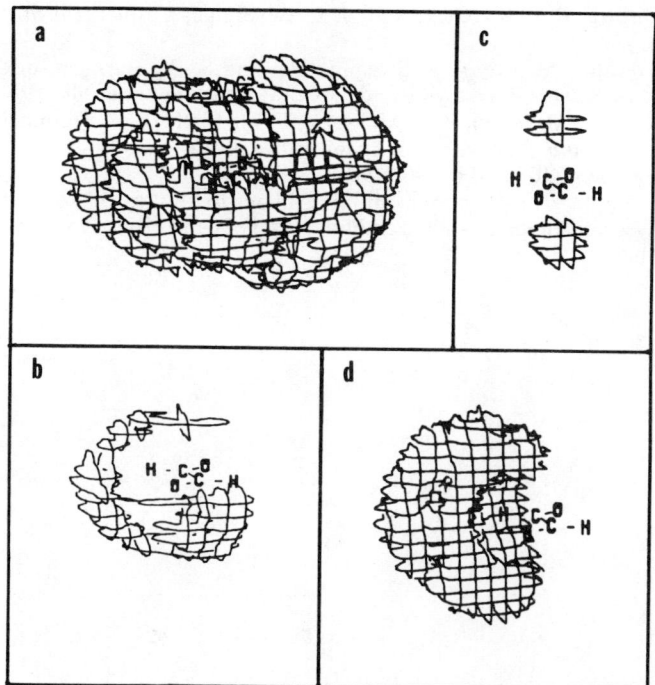

Figure 1 Calculated 90% probability densities for solvent molecules in the first solvation shell of trans-glyoxal in the system $[(HCO)_2]_{aq}$ at 25 °C. (a) total molecule, (b) oxygen atom, (c) carbon atom, (d) hydrogen atom

concept accommodates directional hydrogen bonding. The latter indicates that incipient evidence of hydrophobic hydration is present for even the smallest hydrocarbon fragment in a molecule. The essential features of the aqueous hydration of glyoxal are thus well represented in terms of statistical state solvation sites. We feel that statistical state solvation sites are a highly promising basis for the development of a comprehensive descriptive structural chemistry of aqueous solutions.

Acknowledgement

This research was supported by NIH Grant #GM-24149 and a CUNY Faculty Research Award.

References

1. A. Pullman and B. Pullman, *Q. Rev. Biophys.*, **7**, 505 (1975).
2. P. K. Mehrotra and D. L. Beveridge, *J. Am. Chem. Soc.*, **102**, 4287 (1980).

3. P. K. Mehrotra, F. T. Marchese and D. L. Beveridge, *J. Amer. Chem. Soc.*, **103**, 672 (1981).
4. D. L. Beveridge, M. Mezei, S. Swaminathan and S. W. Harrison, in *Computer Modelling of Matter*, P. G. Lykos, ed., ACS Symposium Series, **86**, 191 (1978).
5. D. L. Beveridge, M. Mezei, P. K. Mehrotra, F. T. Marchese, V. Thirumalai and G. Ravi-Shanker, *Ann. N.Y. Acad. Sci.*, **367**, 108 (1981).
6. W. L. Jorgensen, *QCPE*, **11**, 340 (1979).
7. This and all other density plots should be symmetric with respect to the molecular plane; this is not completely realized in the level of convergence for the simulation reported here.

Solvent effects in biomolecular processes

J. L. Finney
Birkbeck College, UK

Solvent effects are widely implicated in biomolecular processes, such as protein folding, substrate binding and association. Conventionally, these effects are discussed in terms of charge effects, hydrogen bonding and hydrophobic interactions, the latter often being considered dominant. In order to try to understand the detailed molecular level changes involved in such processes, attempts have often been made to connect known molecular level changes indicated from crystallography with the measured thermodynamics of a particular process. It is instructive to see how far such an approach can be taken at the present time in order to assess the limitations and the potentialities of energy calculations, for e.g., folding proteins or binding substrates in the computer in particular, and for connecting molecular level changes with thermodynamic quantities in general.

Consider for example the folding of a protein the size of lysozyme or ribonuclease. Experimentally, the free energy change of folding $\Delta G_{E \to F}$ is about 10–20 kcal mol^{-1}. This is a very small value, emphasizing the (functionally important) marginal stability of the molecule. Looked at slightly differently, this free energy change is equivalent to the energy loss on breaking only 2–5 hydrogen bonds; this is around only 1% of the total number of hydrogen bonds in the crystallographic folded structure.

Although the conformation of the 'denatured' protein is unknown, for the sake of this discussion we take it as the fully extended chain. Referring to the crystallographic folded structures, we can make the following observations:[1]

1. Forty to fifty per cent of the exposed surface is generally classified as 'apolar'. Using Chothia's figure of 22 cal Å^{-2} for the free energy change on burial[2] (but see caveat in note to Table 1), this means about 70 kcal mol^{-1} of potential 'hydrophobic free energy' is unrealized (perhaps because to do so would cause greater unfavourable free energy changes from, e.g., unsatisfied hydrogen bonds?). On the same assumptions, the *realized* 'hydrophobic free energy' from apolar group burial is ~130–150 kcal mol^{-1}. Clearly hydrophobic effects are not maximized independently of other factors: only about 65% of the theoretically available hydrophobic contribution is realized.

2. The extended chain structure has about 600 polar sites available for hydrogen bonding, presumably to solvent water. In the folded structure, half of these make internal hydrogen bonds, leaving about 250–300 exposed polar sites available for solvent hydrogen bonding[2] (a number of which corresponds to the fraction of water that fails to freeze at low temperatures).[3,4] Consequently, assuming all exposed polar

Table 1 Tentative balance sheet of contribution to the free energy change on folding of lysozyme and ribonuclease

	Term	Comments	Estimated magnitude/ kcal mol^{-1}
$\Delta G_{E \to F}$	Free energy change on folding	SMALL: ~3–5 hydrogen bonds	10–20
= ΔG_{titr}	pKa changes on folding		−5?
+ ΔG_{charge}	Changes in surface charge–charge interactions	Estimate at neutral pH	~0?
+ ΔG_ϕ	Hydrophobic free energy change	Surface exposure model^2 Possible range*	−130 −40 → −600!
+ ΔH_ψ	Several hydrogen bonding effects: (a) Difference in strength of water–polar group and polar–polar group (b) Hydrogen-bond distortion (c) Unsaturated polar groups	Average of several quantum mechanical values^1 Using water–water energy surface^7	−75 +100 → +200 +70
− $\eta_c T \Delta s_{config}$	Configurational entropy change per residue	Value of between 2–5 cal K^{-1} (residue mol)$^{-1}$ used^1	+70 − +200
− $\eta_w T \Delta s_{release}$	Release of water from polar interactions to bulk solvent	Assumes 25% of value for ice melting (underestimate?)	−120
+ other terms, e.g. ΔH_{VDW}	Changes in van der Waals interactions	Protein denser than water, implying some stabilization? Possibly included in ΔG_ϕ above	?
+ $\Delta H_{\psi-\phi}$	Polar–apolar interactions within protein	See reference 1	?
+ $T \Delta S_{vibr}$	Vibrational entropy changes	Potentially large and solvent-related	?

* Evidence is growing that the simple proportionality between buried accessible area and free energy change is probably not valid.^{10} The range quoted is based on trial calculations by Karplus and Pratt quoted in reference 10.

sites do hydrogen-bond to water (but see reference 5), the following contributions to $\Delta G_{E \to F}$ need be considered.

(a) Any difference in hydrogen bond strength between water–water and water–polar group hydrogen bonds will be magnified by a factor of about 300. Thus even a small energy difference of 0.5 kcal mol^{-1} (~10%) will scale up to a total energy change of 150 kcal mol^{-1}, an order of magnitude larger than the total $\Delta G_{E \to F}$.
(b) Up to 300 waters will be released from polar sites to solvent. The entropic consequences could be large.

3. Only very few (10–20) polar sites are *either* unsatisfied internally *or* geometrically incapable of solvent interaction. Considering the complexity of the protein structure, this is a high degree of saturation suggesting at least that *lack* of internal hydrogen bond saturation is strongly destabilizing: at 5 kcal mol^{-1} for each hydrogen bond, this deficit scales up to 5–10 times the total $\Delta G_{E \to F}$. The need to hydrogen bond internally is underlined by the behaviour of water as an internal 'hydrogen-bond filler' in larger proteins, where otherwise-separated polar groups are hydrogen-bonded through water.[6]

4. Internal hydrogen bonds are distorted by 0.2 Å and 25° (RMS values). Using our knowledge of the water–water hydrogen bond,[7] this distortion is equivalent to 0.5 to 1 kcal mol^{-1}, or ~1–2 kT. Any energetic significance of this is difficult to separate from dynamic effects, and made even more uncertain by the unknown state of water–polar group hydrogen bonds in the extended chain. It would seem that internal hydrogen bond distortion could act to either stabilize or destabilize the folded structure.

The table is an attempt to draw up a balance sheet of these and other effects. In considering the values presented, the difficulties of making realistic estimates should be borne in mind, especially for the hydrophobic free energy change and entropic changes from both chain folding and from release of waters from polar groups to bulk solvent.

One major point stands out: all but two of the contributions are potentially very large compared with the overall $\Delta G_{E \to F}$. Taken at face value, the figures suggest that, as far as our attempt to connect molecular level structure with thermodynamics is concerned, no one effect dominates: protein folding appears to be a complex maximization of several competing effects. Secondly, small differences in strengths of individual hydrogen bonds will be magnified by a factor of about 300 for the whole protein. Thus, if one wishes to realistically fold a protein *ab initio* using energy criteria, we need to know the forms of the many different potential functions in very considerable detail. This is beyond our current knowledge.[8,9] We might discuss whether or not such detailed information is even in principle obtainable to give useful information on energy *differences* between the starting and finishing structures in a biomolecular process. Similar magnification factors hold for other terms involving a large number of water molecules such as the entropy change on release of water from hydrogen bonding with polar groups to the bulk solvent.

References

1. J. L. Finney, B. J. Gellatly, I. C. Golton and J. M. Goodfellow, *Biophys. J.*, **32**, 17 (1980).
2. C. Chothia, *Nature*, **248**, 338 (1974).
3. I. C. Golton, Ph.D. thesis, University of London (1980).
4. J. L. Finney, J. M. Goodfellow and P. L. Poole, Procs. NATO ASI/FEBS school on 'Current Methods in Structural Molecular Biology', 1980 (in press).

5. R. L. Biltonen, in *Colloques Int. CNRS No 246*: 'L'eau et les systèmes biologiques', CNRS, Paris, p 13 (1976).
6. J. L. Finney, in: *Water: A Comprehensive Treatise*, ed. F. Franks, Plenum, New York, **6**, 47 (1979).
7. J. L. Finney, paper presented at this meeting.
8. H. F. J. Savage, J. M. Goodfellow, J. L. Finney and P. Barnes, this meeting.
9. J. M. Goodfellow, J. L. Finney and P. Barnes, *Proc. Roy. Soc.*, **B 214**, 213 (1982).
10. F. M. Richards and M. Karplus, *Biophys. J.*, **32**, 45 (1980).

Molecular hydration and its possible role in enzymes

G. Careri
Università degli Studi di Roma, Italy

Summary

Enzymes are flexible proteins that change conformation during the performance of their function. This can be accomplished by the presence of substructures, called domains, which behave as Brownian particles driven by inter-domain hydration bridges. This picture is substantiated by hydration studies of lysozyme powder.

For a long while one tenet of biochemistry was that specific functions of biological macromolecules were determined by the precise three-dimensional geometries, of conformations of the molecules. The description was dominated by two limiting structures, highly structured ones seen by crystallographic techniques and unstructured, random coils attributed to 'denatured' proteins. Experimental and theoretical evidence against these oversimplified views has accrued in the last years. Today the notion of globular proteins as flexible entities that change conformation during the performance of specific biological functions is widely accepted.[1] My aim here is to call attention to the close relationship that must exist between flexibility and hydration in globular proteins. I shall limit myself to one wide class of globular proteins, the enzymes, and make specific references to lysozyme because this enzyme has been studied by a variety of techniques. I shall first consider the pertinent features of enzyme action and of molecular hydration of lysozyme, and then mention some more general problems.

As is well known, the mechanism of enzyme catalysis can be pictured as the binding of substrate to a sterically specific site on the enzyme, which triggers a series of conformational changes which optimize the active site environment. This optimization involves proper orientation of functional groups and restriction of possible substrate structures, thus reaching a great entropic advantage over the reaction in solution. Cooperative transitions of a flexible macromolecule can assist not only in this optimization, but also by dynamically participating in the elementary kinetic steps which are characterized by rate constants typically in the range 10^8 sec^{-1}. Large proteins and enzymes usually consist of several massive and nearly rigid domains,[2] to which active groups are attached, and which change their relative position in the course of the catalytic pathway. The recent finding of the global incompressibility[3] of the mac-

Molecular hydration and its possible role in enzymes

romolecule on one hand, and the evidence for local fluctuations of its structure on the other,[1] allows one to conclude that the enzyme can work because of interdomain and of substrate mobility. Stated in different words, each domain moves as a kind of Brownian damped oscillator in the mean field of interdomain weak forces, finding by thermal fluctuations the best orientation of the attached functional groups. The same holds for the substrate. In this way catalysis can be fast, because domain rigidity reduces the number of the fluctuating degrees of freedom of the polypeptide chain, and the search time for optimization of the active site environment can become much shorter. In this picture domain coordinates are seen as statistical macrovariables, driven by the interdomain fluctuating forces.

Within this framework we understand that hydration must be of great importance for enzyme dynamics because, according to the fluctuation-dissipation theorem, the viscosity of the solvent is the kinetic property which governs the Brownian motion. As a matter of fact, recent studies on ligand binding[4] and enzyme catalysis[5] show that local viscosity-dependent structural fluctuations control the transition over the reaction barrier. And we must expect that the smaller the region where the water molecules are confined, the higher to be the r.m.s. amplitude of their displacements and therefore the dynamical influence towards the surrounding domains.

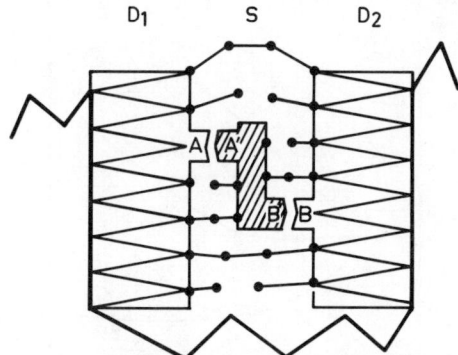

Figure 1 Schematic representation of the role of interdomain water molecules (black dots), to assist by fluctuating bridges the correct position of active groups A and B, located on protein domains D_1 and D_2, towards the complementary groups A' and B' located on substrate S. The heavy line represents the protein polypeptide chain, which is rigid inside each domain and floating elsewhere. The larger number of water molecules bound on the protein surface is not shown, because their fluctuations are less relevant to the effect considered here

The above picture of enzyme hydration can be better visualized in the case of lysozyme, where the substrate binding cleft is the interdomain region which must continuously fluctuate, because formation and breaking of interdomain water bridges give rise to forces acting between substrate and domains. And we must expect that in lysozyme powder, when the region near the binding cleft becomes progressively hydrated, the enzymatic activity will depend on the number of such interdomain water bridges that have been created. As we shall see below, this seems indeed to be the case.

Here I shall limit myself to studies on protein films or powders, because these solid samples allow controlled variations of water activity over a wide range. Studies of this kind have been carried out for lysozyme, where the so-called 'water of hydration' is 0.38 h (g of water/g of protein) equivalent to 300 molecules of water/molecule of lysozyme, about one-half of the amount needed for monolayer coverage.[6] Various measurements indicate that the conformation of the protein in the powder is the same as in solution, pointing out the absence of large conformational changes with hydration.[7] On the other side, the onset of enzymatic activity is at 0.2 h.[6] At this same hydration the development of the dynamic properties is revealed by an ESR probe,[7] and the water electronic structure reaches its normal value as is demonstrated by diamagnetic susceptibility studies.[6] This critical hydration value is located where the coverage of binding sites weaker than the backbone peptides starts.[8] Only above this

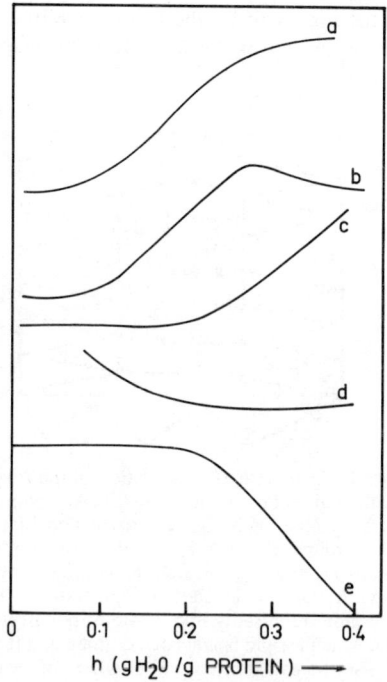

Figure 2 Effect of hydration on lysozyme powder. From top to bottom the curves are: (a) amide I shift of peptide backbone; (b) apparent specific heat capacity; (c) enzymatic activity; (d) diamagnetic susceptibility; (e) rotational relaxation time of an ESR probe. Curves (a) to (d) adapted from reference 6 and curve (e) from reference 7. The observed changes, near 0.2 hydration, are discussed in the text

critical coverage, the partial molar thermodynamic quantities become close to bulk water values.[6]

Let us discuss these findings within the framework of catalysis assisted by interdomain fluctuations. It seems quite likely that in lysozyme, only above 0.2 h hydration, a number of interdomain water bridges can be formed and broken at random, because of weak binding energies of these bridges in comparison with thermal energy. These random events can give rise to Langevin forces acting in the region between the domain and the substrate, providing the dynamical state of the cleft needed for catalysis.

This picture is substantiated by the fact that in lysozyme the pattern of atomic displacements reveals[9] that the lips of the active site cleft are located in a region of high displacement, while the intramolecular 'hinge mode' of the two lobes of this cleft do not account for much of the observed displacement. This means that the two lobes are not the substructures relevant for dynamics, but that domains must be some smaller units. As a matter of fact, very recently the spatial spread of atomic motions in the backbone of lysozyme has been found to be well correlated with the reciprocal density of various interactions along the polypeptide chain, mainly hydrogen bonds.[10] Of course, more definitive conclusions will be reached only when the anisotropy of the atomic displacements will be conveniently mapped.

I believe that the conclusions reached above in the specific case of lysozyme can be extended to other globular proteins. Protein substructures must always behave as Brownian particles, and *water is the medium which provides the random forces to control these substructures to their functions*. Then the entire design of globular proteins may have evolved just to make the best use of such water induced fluctuations. Of course to the quite general 'physical' effects discussed above, one must add the more specific 'chemical' effects induced by hydration on the protein sidechains.

Acknowledgement

The author thanks Dr E. Gratton for several stimulating discussions on this matter.

References

1. G. Careri, P. Fásella and E. Gratton, *Ann. Rev. Biophys. and Bioeng.*, **8**, 69 (1979).
2. O. B. Ptitsyn, *FEBS Lett.*, **93**, 1 (1978).
3. C. Hardy, B. Gavish and E. Gratton, *Biophys. Journ.*, Abstracts of the American Biophys. Soc., Denver, in press (1981).
4. D. Beece, L. Eisenstein, H. Frauenfelder, D. Good, M. C. Marden, L. Reinisch, A. H. Reynolds, L. B. Sorensen and K. T. Yue, *Biochemistry*, **19**, 5147 (1980).
5. B. Gavish and M. M. Werber, *Biochemistry*, **18**, 1269 (1979).
6. G. Careri, E. Gratton, P. H. Yang and J. A. Rupley, *Nature*, **284**, 572 (1980).
7. J. A. Rupley, P. H. Yang and G. Tollin, in 'Water in Polymers' (ed. Rowland, S. P.), *ACS Symposium Series*, **127**, 111 (1980).
8. G. Careri, A. Giansanti and E. Gratton, *Biopolymers*, **18**, 1187 (1979).
9. P. J. Artymiuk, C. C. F. Blake, D. E. P. Grace, S. J. Oatley, D. C. Phillips and M. J. Sternberg, *Nature*, **280**, 563 (1979).
10. B. Gavish, Preprint Dept. Phys. U. of Illinois, Urbana, April 1981.

Some views of solvation effects in the light of a Monte Carlo simulation

B. Robson
University of Manchester, UK

Summary

While it may be dangerous to draw too many conclusions from a single series of Monte Carlo simulations of solution behaviour, such simulations do provide a wealth of detail in reasonable accord with current understanding based on experimental data, and may yet resolve outstanding paradoxes.

Introduction

The Monte Carlo approach to the study of solution behaviour is computationally fairly expensive but can provide a wealth of detail. Recently, we collaborated with Dr. Hagler's laboratory to apply this technique to a simple peptide, N-acetyl alanyl N'-methylamide, in water.[1] Briefly, about 350 water molecules were placed around the peptide solute so as to reproduce the experimental density, and periodic boundary conditions were imposed in such a way as to avoid a water–vacuum interface while emulating infinite dilution.

The present discussion is not a review of that study but rather a personal account of the effect the results have had on the relatively naïve way we must normally introduce solvent effects into conformational and other types of calculations.

The reaction field

One clear lesson from the Monte Carlo study was that the reaction field can have a dominant effect and cannot, in general, be neglected. The reaction field implies the cumulative, if individually very weak, electrostatic effects of water molecules at some distance from the solute. For the N-acetyl alanyl N'-methylamide used in the Monte Carlo calculation, the reaction field contributed a stabilizing energy of 5.6 kcal mol^{-1} to the conformer with parallel peptide group dipoles compared with the conformer in which the two peptide groups were engaged in an intramolecular (C_7) hydrogen bonded ring arrangement. In this case, the reaction field contribution was still not quite strong enough to overcome the preference for the C_7 conformer on steric and hydrogen bonding grounds.

The pleasing aspect of this result is that the reaction field can always be approximated by a simple analytical function. Assuming the solute occupies a spherical cavity, workers have used[2]

$$E_{rf} = -14.4 \frac{\mu^2}{R^3}\left[\frac{\varepsilon - 1}{2\varepsilon + 1}\right] \tag{1}$$

The cavity radius R is, however, problematic: we prefer the root mean square distance between all non-covalently bonded atoms of each solute conformer which lies between the maximum enveloping radius of the conformer and the Lagrange radius of gyration; this is consistent with cavities estimated by eye for space filling molecular drawings of the molecule in each conformation.

Solvation effects and Monte Carlo simulation

The supermolecule

The supermolecule approximation[2] treats the solvent effect in terms of water molecules strongly bonded to the solvent, and thus capable of being regarded as chemical extensions of it. The Monte Carlo results confirm that the solvent forms strong hydrogen bonds to the solute amide and carbonyl groups with a high degree of occupancy by the water molecule. The results also suggest, however, that if the water molecule is to be linked to the solute in an energy calculation using the supermolecule approximation, the $O \cdots H-N$ or $H \cdots O=C$ valence angles must be allowed to vary. Further, bifurcate arrangements are also possible, such as

$$\begin{array}{c} O\!\!-\!\!H \\ | \\ H \\ H \diagup \\ \diagdown \\ A O O\!\!=\!\!C \\ \diagup \\ H \\ H \\ | \\ O\!\!-\!\!H \end{array}$$

where water molecule A occupies a solute hydrogen bond site as far as its oxygen to carbonyl oxygen distance is concerned, though its hydrogen atoms point in the opposite direction. Such an orientation would not be energetically feasible in a supermolecule representation if only *one* water is sited at the carbonyl group.

The solvation shell

While on the one hand the much used *solvation shell* model implies that the effect of the solute on the solvent is confined to its vicinity, one may equally well imagine, *a priori*, a propagation of the structuralizing effect of the solute well out into the solution. Certainly, the application by Hagler and Moult[3] of the same Monte Carlo technique to the lysozyme crystal shows structuralized water bridges between adjacent protein molecules, but this was not found for the calculation of N-acetyl alanyl N'-methyl-amide intended to emulate infinite dilution. Rather, more than two water molecule diameters distant from the solute surface the water already behaved in a manner analogous to that of bulk pure water, according to several criteria.

In bulk pure water, or any liquid capable of exerting a strong solvophobic effect, there are a wide range of orientations in which a single constituent molecule will be able to hydrogen bond to neighbours. A three-dimensional lattice in this sense provides greater orientational freedom for each constituent molecule (in ethanol, in contrast, each molecule has few orientations in which it can encounter a low enthalpy, hydrogen bonding situation). The presence of the solute, however, locally reduces this orientational freedom of water. In particular, the non-polar groups reduce the possible hydrogen bonded orientations of first shell water by some 20%. That this is not a larger reduction appears to be due to the possibility of distorted and bifurcate $(O \cdots H \cdots O)$ hydrogen bonds. Also, this seems to explain why the solute effect here does not

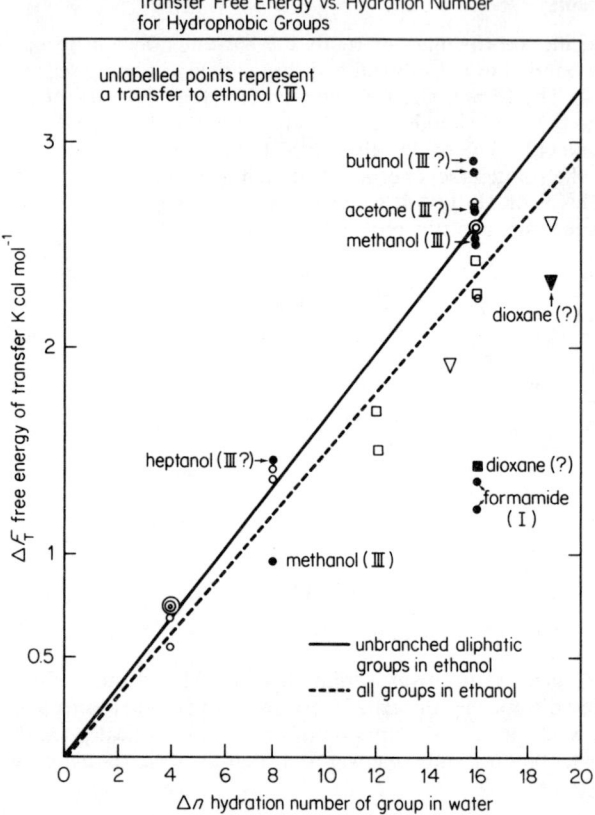

Figure 1 Experimental free energies of transfer of various hydrophobic amino acid sidechains from water to ethanol and other solvents, plotted against 'hydration number' of the sidechain (strictly, the estimated number of neighbouring waters with significantly restricted orientational freedom). The receptor solvent class according to Ray[4] is indicated. Class III solvents are believed to be incapable of forming extensive hydrogen bonded networks, and then the transfer free energy approximates in value to the change in orientational free energy of a water molecule on entering the sidechain solvation shell of a non-polar group

propagate outwards: the bifurcate hydrogen bonds introduce a reserve of structural laxity, at low enthalpy cost, which damps out long range propagation of entropically unfavourable orientating effects.

Is such a small reduction to 80% of the pure water orientational freedom sufficient to explain the hydrophobic effect? Even neglecting enthalpic and translational entropy contributions, $-RT \ln 0.8$ kcal (mol water)$^{-1}$ is consistent with the 0.15 kcal (mol water)$^{-1}$ suggested by transfer experiments (see Figure 1). Here data has been collected for polar recipient solvents (to minimize enthalpic contributions to the transfer free energy), but which are, in the notation of Ray,[4] predominantly class III solvents (to minimize a solvophobic effect).

Denaturation phenomena

The Monte Carlo results for a peptide also suggest, albeit indirectly, the manner and extent to which urea may affect water structure in protein denaturation studies. Briefly, looking at the number of water molecules which have orientations significantly restricted near peptide NH and CO groups, the molarity of strongly bound solvation shell water in a urea solution will be about 10 molar per molar urea, already of the order of the molarity of pure water. Clearly the statements (a) that these denaturants affect the structure of the water as a whole, and (b) that like peptide groups they should only affect near neighbour waters, are not inconsistent. There are, however, far more challenging paradoxes more worthy of Monte Carlo. For example, why is a *mixture* of urea and guanidinium chloride a much worse protein denaturant than one would predict for a simple mixture? This general result from our laboratory is exemplified in Figure 2, where the first order rate constant of hen egg white lysozyme denaturation is charted as a function of the denaturant mix. From our preliminary amino acid transfer experiments, we tentatively suggest that the anomaly arises most obviously *only* in connection with charged groups, which *prefer* to be in the mix far more than one would expect from the ionic and neutral denaturants alone. This is consistent with the fact that charged groups on a protein are *less* (*c.* 20%) exposed in a denatured random coil than on the native protein surface, but provides a thermodynamic, rather than detailed mechanistic explanation. Consideration of solvent ordering *per se* suggests nothing about this paradoxical effect of the urea–guanidinium chloride mix on the transfer of charged groups. Monte Carlo simulation of a water, urea, guanidinium, chloride system is, however, close to becoming a practical proposition, and would exemplify a specific, practical application.

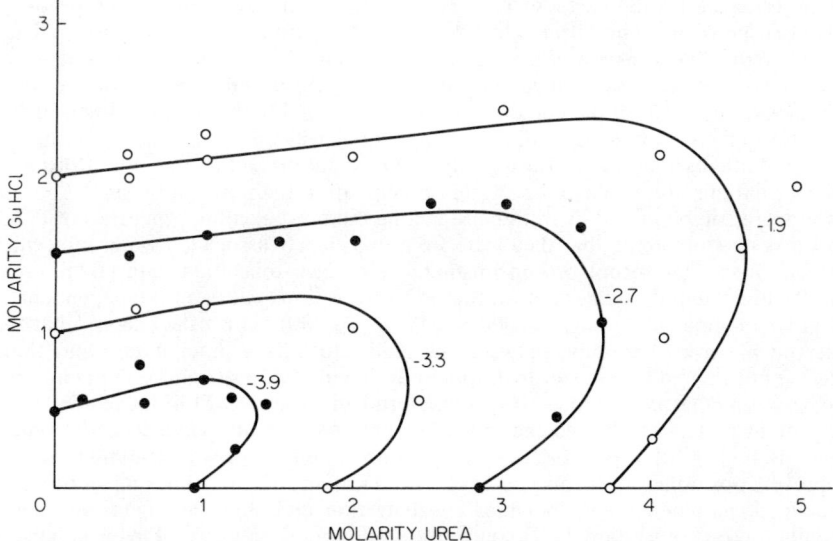

Figure 2   Concentrations of urea and guanidine hydrochloride plotted at a constant k_{app} of lysozyme unfolding. The lines represent the average contour of constant $\log_{10} k_{app}$. Urea and guanidinium chloride mixes have unexpectedly poor denaturing effects on lysozyme. This paradox may be fundamental to denaturation phenomena and Monte Carlo simulations are a possible approach to resolving it

References

1. A. T. Hagler, D. J. Osgurthorpe and B. Robson, *Science*, **208**, 599 (1980).
2. V. Madison and K. D. Kopple, *J. Amer. Chem. Soc.*, **102**, 4855 (1980).
3. A. T. Hagler and J. Moult, *Nature*, **272**, 222 (1978).
4. A. Ray, *Nature*, **231**, 313 (1971).

The soluble Frankenstein: polyoxyethylene action in protein solutions and cell suspensions

S. Vuk-Pavlović

Institute of Immunology, Zagreb, Yugoslavia

Summary

Polyoxyethylene (POE) induces protein precipitation and cell fusion, presumably with the same physicochemical mechanism. I speculate that it induces aggregation of membrane proteins and intercellular association of these aggregates. Divalent cations, excluded from the POE domain, are accumulated in the intercellular space and mediate the actual fusion of lipid bilayers.

Polyoxyethylene (POE) excludes proteins from solutions[1] and induces the fusion of cells in suspension.[2] The latter effect results in the formation of chimaeric cellular monsters (the Frankenstein effect). Both phenomena are technologically important (fractionation of proteins from composite solutions, cell fusion in monoclonal protein technology, etc.). These phenomena can be important for the understanding of the deposition of circulating molecules on the arterial walls and of various membrane associated microscopic events during cell–cell recognition and interaction. More data and speculations are available on protein precipitation than on cell fusion.

The mere solubility and hydration are among the most exciting properties of POE. Most investigators agree that they arise from two closely associated water molecules per each mer. Our recent proton magnetic resonance relaxation data (Benko and Vuk-Pavlović, unpublished) confirm that POE hydration (per mer) is independent of the polymer molecular weight ($1000 \leq MW \leq 20\,000$). This effect shows that the observed positive correlation between the ability to induce precipitation and chain length is not related to polymer hydration only. Therefore, a search for direct interaction between POE and proteins was also undertaken. However, POE is excluded from the protein precipitates[3,4] and the molar concentration of the polymer in the supernatant is higher after precipitation than before (Benko, private communication). Moreover, positions of ^{13}C nuclear magnetic resonance (NMR) lines in solutions of albumin do not depend on polymer concentration and show no significant POE-albumin interactions at any POE concentration (Samulski and Vuk-Pavlović, unpublished). On the basis of these and other data, especially the extensive work of Ingham,[5-8] it appears that the POE's precipitating action (and presumably of other uncharged hydrophilic polymers) is due to the exclusion of organic cosolvent from the domain of the protein, an effect mediated largely by the charge induced phase separation.[4,9]

Pittz and Timasheff[9] described the crystallization of ribonuclease A from aqueous 2-methyl-2,4-pentanediol (MPD). Similar to POE, MPD does not interact directly with the protein. Small concentrations of salts induce phase separation in the MPD–water system, and analogous to it, Pittz and Timasheff postulate the occurrence of microscopic multipoint phase separation at the fixed surface charges of the protein.[9] Since these charges cannot detach and migrate into the aqueous phase, water migrates towards them excluding MPD from the protein neighbourhood. As formation of this excessive hydration is entropically unfavourable and as it increases the chemical potential of MPD, protein aggregation takes place in order to remove a part of its hydrated surface from solution and to reduce the chemical potential of the cosolvent. It is noteworthy that both MPD-water and POE-water phase separation, as well as albumin precipitation and microtubule formation from tubulin monomers are similarly enhanced by neutral salts, apparently according to the Hofmeister series[6,10] showing that salt induced surface tension changes may contribute to these effects.[11] However, these simple thermodynamic considerations may not be sufficient to account for all the systems, as the NMR studies of the water–sodium dodecyl sulphate micelles–POE system did reveal electrostatic interactions of POE ether oxygens and sulphate groups via the sodium counterions and entropy-mediated interactions of POE and detergent hydrocarbon groups.[12]

Thus what is the molecular mechanism of cell fusion—the Frankenstein effect? I speculate that cell fusion is mediated essentially by the same mechanism as protein precipitation (whatever its molecular details really are). The available literature data I quote provides some circumstantial and qualitative support for this hypothesis.

The cell membrane is a continuous bilayer of amphiphilic phospholipids and glycolipids into which proteins, occupying most of the cellular surface, are inserted. Some of them undergo rapid translational and/or rotational diffusion, some of them occupy fixed and defined mutual sterical relations. Fusion of cells is, in the first instance, fusion of two membrane continua into one. This process consists of at least three 'elementary' steps (Figure 1): (1) Aggregation of membrane proteins. This step removes proteins from certain parts of the membrane resulting in formation of larger areas of membrane which consist mostly of bare phospholipids and glycolipids. (2) The encounter step. Cells overcome mutual repulsion. (3) Fusion. More membranes merge into one.

Aggregation of membrane proteins is normally induced by a number of physiological agents (hormones, antibodies, etc.).[13] If POE induces the same effect in the exposed part of the membrane proteins as in the soluble globular molecules, then aggregation of these membrane components is the only way to reduce the excessively hydrated surface area and the chemical potential of POE. Therefore, protein aggregation in membranes can be formally considered as two-dimensional precipitation. I am not aware of any data showing that POE induces protein aggregation in membranes. There are, however, data available on some altered properties of these molecules. For instance, low concentrations (2 to 5%) of POE 4000 or 6000 enhance the antigenicity of tumor cells as detected by the reactions in mixed lymphocyte cultures.[14] Antigenicity arises from non-lipid parts of membranes and, therefore, any instant change of antigenicity must be related to alterations of membrane protein structure. Aggregation of antigenic sites might provide the basis for such a phenomenon, since POE probably does not interact with membrane proteins directly, and because, for the same reason, it probably does not induce conformational changes of these proteins.

The two-dimensional protein aggregates can further reduce their surface through contacts with similar aggregates on surfaces of adjacent cells. Thus, these patches of aggregated proteins can become points of multiple intercellular attachment. At this point the role of mobile divalent cations, particularly Ca^{2+} which is always present in

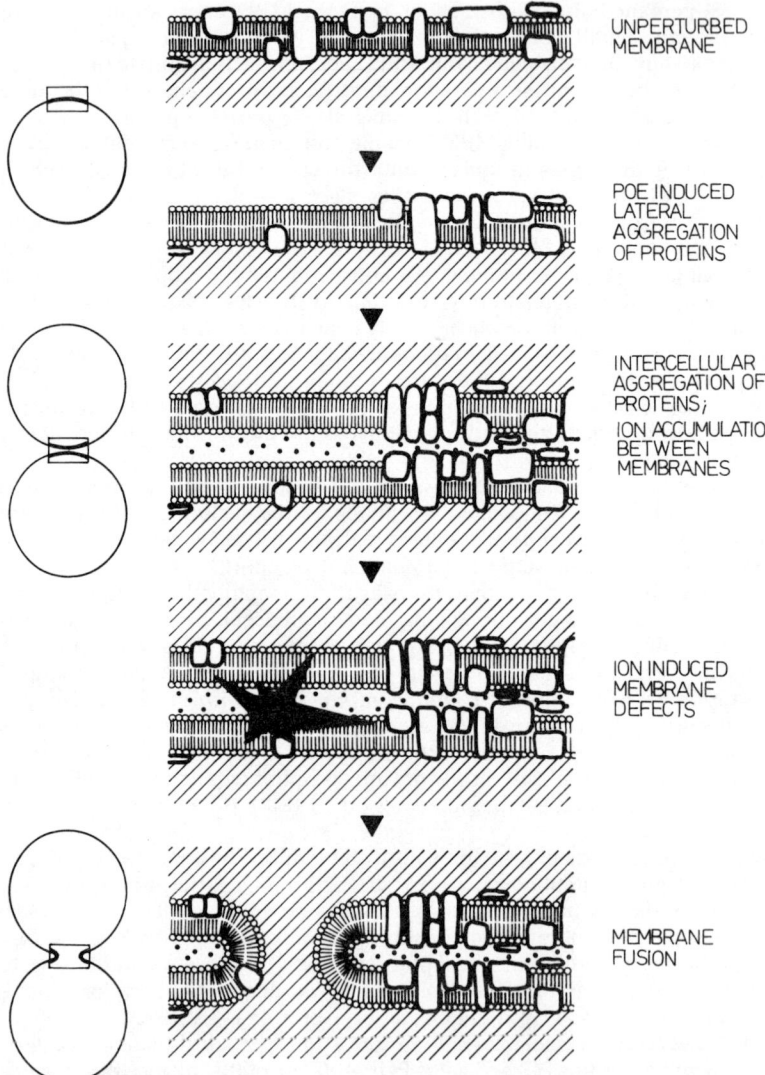

Figure 1 The hypothetical steps of the polyoxyethylene (POE) induced cell fusion. The addition of POE induces lateral aggregation of membrane proteins by a mechanism analogous to the induced protein precipitation from solutions. Further intercellular protein aggregation and ion accumulation between the membranes are analogous to the respective events during protein precipitation. The subsequent membrane fusion is probably due to the ion induced membrane defects[15] and it does not depend on the presence of POE directly. The circles on the left represent membranes to aid the proper orientation within the more detailed scheme

cell culture media, becomes important. As already mentioned, these ions are excluded from the vicinity of POE and they will migrate into the space between membranes, neutralize surface charges and reduce their repulsion.[15]

Mixing and transfer of lipids between adjacent bilayers would be energetically very unfavourable and, therefore, the actual fusion must include transition states of low activation energy. These transition states probably evolve through calcium binding and membrane surface charge neutralization paralleled by an increase of the membrane phase transition temperature.[15] In other words, calcium induces local acyl chain crystallization of the outer layer of the membrane. This induced in-plane and transmembrane heterogeneity leads to transient destabilization of the membrane enabling the actual fusion step to take place.[15] However, the most recent freeze fracture electron microscopic data show that POE promotes defect formation in phosphatidylcholine and phosphatidylethanolamine unilamellar vesicle dispersions. Phosphorus-31 NMR of the same system revealed the 'existence of a non-bilayer (isotropic) phase' which 'may be associated with an intermediate stage of membrane fusion'.[16] If the actual fusion step takes place according to the mechanism proposed in Reference 15, it does not depend on the presence of POE directly.

The present speculation leaves many questions open. The answers to two of them can be instrumental to the understanding of the Frankenstein effect: What is the molecular mechanism of the charge induced phase separation? Are we able to explain two-dimensional aggregation of proteins substantially embedded in the amphiphilic semi-solid matrix solely by knowledge obtained with protein precipitation by POE in three-dimensional aqueous solutions?

References

1. A. Polson, G. M. Potgieter, J. F. Larfier, G. E. F. Mears and F. J. Joubert, *Biochim. Biophys. Acta*, **82**, 463 (1964).
2. Q. F. Ahkong, J. I. Howell, J. A. Lucy, F. Safwat, M. R. Davey and E. C. Cocking, *Nature*, **255**, 66 (1975).
3. C. R. Middaugh, W. A. Tisel, R. N. Haire and A. Rosenberg, *J. Biol. Chem.*, **254**, 367 (1979).
4. J. C. Lee and L. L. Y. Lee, *Biochemistry*, **18**, 5518 (1979).
5. K. C. Ingham, *Arch. Biochem. Biophys.*, **184**, 59 (1977).
6. K. C. Ingham, *ibid.*, **186**, 106 (1978).
7. S. I. Miekka and K. C. Ingham, *ibid.*, **191**, 525 (1978).
8. S. I. Miekka and K. C. Ingham, *ibid.*, **203**, 630 (1980).
9. E. P. Pittz and S. N. Timasheff, *Biochemistry*, **17**, 615 (1978).
10. T. F. Busby and K. C. Ingham, *Vox Sang.*, **39**, 93 (1980).
11. W. Melander and Cs. Horvath, *Arch. Biochem. Biophys.*, **183**, 200 (1977).
12. B. Cabane, *J. Phys. Chem.*, **81**, 1639 (1977).
13. J. Schlessinger, *Trends Biochem. Sci.*, **5**, 210 (1980).
14. S. A. Ben-Sasson and P. A. Henkart, *J. Immunol.*, **119**, 227 (1979).
15. D. Papahadjopoulos, W. J. Vail, C. Newton, S. Nir, K. Jacobson, G. Poste and R. Lazo, *Biochim. Biophys. Acta*, **465**, 579 (1977).
16. L. T. Boni, T. P. Stewart, J. L. Alderfer and S. W. Hui, *Biophys. J.*, **33**, 118a (1981).

Preferential interactions in protein–water–cosolvent systems

Serge N. Timasheff
Brandeis University, USA

It has been known for many years that the native structure of globular proteins can be stabilized in aqueous solution by addition of high levels (~1 M) of polyhydroxy compounds, such as sucrose, glycerol or hexylene glycol (2-methyl-2,4-pentanediol, MPD), or of concentrated salts, such as sodium or ammonium sulphate or sodium phosphate. In an effort to understand the manner in which these solvent additives exercise their protein structure-stabilizing action, we undertook a number of years ago a study of the interactions which may impart the stabilizing activity on these compounds. The results of these studies which were essentially dialysis equilibrium measurements and which are summarized in our poster, have revealed a uniform pattern, namely, all the protein structure-stabilizing compounds are preferentially excluded from contact with the protein surface, i.e. the preferential interaction parameter, ξ_3, is negative. $\xi_3 = (\partial g_3/\partial g_2)_{\mu_3}$ is in fact the 'binding' measured by dialysis equilibrium, or gel permeation. Using the notation Component 1 = H_2O, Component 2 = protein, Component 3 = cosolvent, ξ_3 has the meaning of grams/cosolvent in excess over bulk solvent found per gram of protein inside the dialysis bag at dialysis equilibrium (μ is chemical potential, and g_i is concentration in grams of i per gram of water).

A negative value of ξ_3, i.e. negative binding of cosolvent to protein, necessarily has two consequences. The first one is that addition of Component 3 to an aqueous solution of the protein is thermodynamically unfavourable, since it signifies an increase in the chemical potential of both protein and cosolvent when these are mixed, as

$$\left(\frac{\partial g_3}{\partial g_2}\right)_{\mu_3} = - \left(\frac{\partial \mu_3}{\partial g_2}\right)_{g_3} \bigg/ \left(\frac{\partial \mu_3}{\partial g_3}\right)_{g_2}$$

This result gives the thermodynamic explanation for protein structural stabilization by the cosolvent, since denaturation, or expansion of the protein molecule would even augment this unfavourable effect by increasing the total contact surface area between protein and solvent. The second conclusion is that, in such a three-component system, there is an excess of water in the immediate domain of the protein over the bulk solvent, since preferential hydration, ξ_1, is related to preferential solvation by the cosolvent by

$$\xi_1 = - \frac{g_1}{g_3} \xi_3$$

Decomposition of the preferential interactions into total interactions, namely, total hydration A_1 (grams of water per gram of protein), and total solvation, A_3 (grams of cosolvent per gram of protein) present within the immediate domain of the protein, makes evident that preferential hydration measured by dialysis equilibrium is actually a measure of the difference between solvent compositions within the immediate domain of the protein and in the bulk solvent, since

$$\left(\frac{\partial g_1}{\partial g_2}\right)_{\mu_3} = A_3\left(\frac{A_1}{A_3} - \frac{g_1}{g_3}\right)$$

From this equation, it is evident that preferential hydration is simply a measure of the excess of water and deficiency of cosolvent in the domain of the protein surface. The question to ask is: what is the origin of this solvent composition perturbation? Is it the result of attraction of water molecules by the protein or repulsion of cosolvent molecules? Four possible situations present themselves.

1. There is a hydration layer which cannot be penetrated by the cosolvent molecules due to the strong forces of attraction between water and the protein surface;

2. The protein is indifferent to both water and cosolvent molecules, but the cosolvent molecules, being bulkier than water molecules, cannot approach the protein as closely, with the result that there is a steric exclusion which manifests itself as an apparent hydration. This is the model already proposed by Kauzmann a number of years ago.

3. The third possibility is based on the concept of protein structure stabilization by the hydrophobic and solvophobic effects, according to which unfavourable interactions between water or cosolvent molecules and the non-polar residues force these residues to coalesce as much as possible in the interior of the globular structure. If now, in a mixed solvent, the cosolvent were to interact less favourably with protein non-polar residues than water, the cosolvent molecules would be preferentially repelled from the protein surface leaving behind an excess of water which would manifest itself as an apparent hydration. The same result would prevail if the cosolvent were to enhance solvent ordering in water cosolvent mixtures, strengthening the hydrophobic effect.

4. Finally, the micro-phase separation at the protein surface could be due to an increase by the cosolvent of the water surface free energy, or surface tension. A consequence of this, made necessary by the Gibbs adsorption isotherm, would be a depletion of cosolvent molecules at interfaces, again giving rise to an excess of water, or an apparent hydration.

A detailed examination of the results of our preferential interaction studies may help to sort out these possibilities. We shall concentrate on four cosolvent systems, namely, glycerol, sucrose, MPD and concentrated salts. The key observation is that ξ_3 varies both with the nature of the cosolvents and of the proteins. The preferential hydration was decomposed in self-consistent manner into A_1, i.e. total hydration and A_3, i.e. total solvation, and results were correlated with physical and chemical properties of the proteins, namely surface area per gram of protein, hydrophobicity and polarity, as defined by Bigelow. The first, and most striking result is that in none of the systems is there any correlation between ξ, A_1 or A_3 and protein hydrophobicity. This was to be expected, since hydrophobicity is an internal rather than surface property. Second, there is no simple correlation of these parameters with molecular volume of the cosolvents and size of the proteins. This argues against the Kauzmann exclusion principle if one treats it in terms of hard spheres impenetrable to each other, although the excluded volume effect must certainly play a role.

Similarly, there is no evidence for an impenetrable shell of water, as no correlation was found between ξ_1 or A_1 and the surface properties of proteins. Two effects, both of which are related to the properties of the solvent and not the protein, were found to play a significant role. First, in the case of sucrose and concentrated Na_2SO_4 and NaCl,

ξ_3 was found to correlate well with the values predicted from the effect of these cosolvents on the surface tension of water, namely on the faces of cohesion between water molecules and the degree of solvent order. In the case of the glycerol system, A_3 was found to correlate with protein polarity, which is consistent with the concept of glycerol repulsion from surface hydrophobic areas on the proteins. Finally, in the case of MPD, the hydration values reach 1 gram water per gram of protein. This can be explained best by a repulsion of MPD molecules from ionized groups on the surface of the protein.

In conclusion, a detailed analysis of the preferential interactions between proteins and solvent components in water-structure stabilizing cosolvent systems indicates that the structural stabilization is due to a microphase separation of the solvent at the protein surface, with water molecules accumulating at that surface. This excess of water need not be interpreted, however, in terms of a hydration layer consisting of water molecules ordered on the protein surface. In fact, the observed solvent interactions are related to the structure of the solvent and the unfavourable interactions between protein surface and cosolvent molecules. The water molecules, on the other hand, appear to be innocent bystanders which are left in the vicinity of the protein molecules, since the latter find their environment less unfavourable than that of the cosolvent molecules. In this manner, any hydration measured in such systems could be an accidental consequence of complex interactions between water and cosolvent molecules and cosolvent molecules and protein, but as such the apparent hydration layer seems not to play any major role in protein structure stabilization.

Biophysics of Water
Edited by F. Franks
© 1982 John Wiley & Sons Ltd

Towards a molecular picture of liquid water

J. L. Finney
Birkbeck College, University of London, UK

Summary

The currently available models of liquid water are reviewed in the light of different model pair potentials. It is shown that most potential functions are only able to account for the measured properties over a limited range of physical conditions. The variables which determine the water dimer potential energy surface are discussed and it is concluded that the non-pair-additivity contributions must play a significant role in water–water hydrogen bonding. Various ways of incorporating such effects in the calculations are suggested.

1 Introduction

Water is a liquid. Therefore, structure models inconsistent with liquid properties must be rejected—for example, disordered crystal models that have no fluidity. Water is water, not an assembly of icebergs.

A valid description of any liquid has two main aspects: molecular *mobility* and instantaneous *structure*. It is perturbations close to biomolecule surfaces of both *mobility* and *structure* of the water from its bulk nature that we must quantify if we are to understand at the molecular level the solvent contribution to the thermodynamics of a biomolecular process such as enzyme-substrate binding.

Molecular mobility is in principle straightforward. Correlation times of the order of 10^{-11}–10^{-12} sec for rotational (τ_R) and translational (τ_D) motions can be measured by dielectric relaxation and NMR. Changes in these correlation times close to a macromolecule surface will contribute to the thermodynamics of our substrate binding process. Measurement of these dynamic perturbations is possible in principle, although difficult in practice.*

It is much more difficult to describe perturbations in liquid *structure* usefully. We are required to specify a reference structure, with respect to which perturbations can be quantified. For crystals, a perfect lattice reference state can be used, and structural deviations due to thermal motions, vacancies and dislocations characterized in a thermodynamically useful way. For liquids, specifying a meaningful reference structure when that structure is essentially non-crystalline and disordered is a problem. Devising a thermodynamically useful order parameter to quantify deviations from that structure is more problematical, especially for heterogeneous systems.

In what follows, we shall set up an overall conceptual framework within which to consider liquid water structure. However, the subtleties of the solvent-related effects that occur in our model enzyme-substrate binding process make our overall framework insufficient.[1] We require a much more detailed, quantitative picture of the hydrogen bond interaction than is currently available, and problems related to this are discussed.

2   Liquid and crystal structure

Over twenty years ago, Bernal argued that a liquid was a 'homogeneous, coherent, and essentially irregular assemblage of molecules containing no crystalline regions.'[2] For an idealized liquid of equal hard-sphere molecules, such a model could be built in the laboratory. Figure 1 illustrates the essential contrast between the molecular arrangements in the liquid and the crystal. The upper part of the mass in the figure shows the regular long-range ordered arrangement of atoms that is characteristic of the ideal liquid. It contains no crystalline regions; any attempt to describe this structure as a disordered crystal will lead to inconsistencies. However, it should not be considered to be totally random; the fact that no atom centre can be closer than one diameter to another imposes considerable restrictions on the assembly, which should therefore be considered as a structure with *restricted disorder*.

This idealized model can be described as an *adequately dense, disordered arrangement of molecules which contains no crystalline regions, yet which is consistent with the intermolecular interaction*. The inter-

---

* See the statement in this volume by R. P. Bryant *et al.* concerning the problems of relaxation time measurements by NMR.

Towards a molecular picture of liquid water

Figure 1 An idealized model of a simple liquid (upper) contrasted with the regular crystalline structure (below)

molecular interaction here is that of hard spheres, but the concept can be extended to other liquids provided we can build into the model the geometrical consequences of the intermolecular interaction. For example, for Lennard-Jones atoms, the essential structure is the same, although the soft repulsive core together with the weak van der Waals attractions result in small structural changes. For water, we can take a related path, and ask: *What adequately-dense non-crystalline structure can I build which is consistent with the intermolecular interaction?* Before we can begin to answer this question, we must consider the nature of the intermolecular interaction: the water–water hydrogen bond.

3 An idealized structural model for water

The simplest picture of the molecule assigns partial charges to the two hydrogens and the two lone pairs which are considered to be disposed in an approximately tetrahedral manner (Figure 2(a)). Each molecule is capable of forming four hydrogen bonds to neighbouring molecules in each of which a proton is directed approximately at a lone pair of a neighbour (Figure 2(b)). In these four interactions, one molecule acts as a proton donor in two of them, and as a proton acceptor in the other two. This geometry is idealized in the low-pressure ices, in which the angular disposition of first neighbours is very close to tetrahedral.

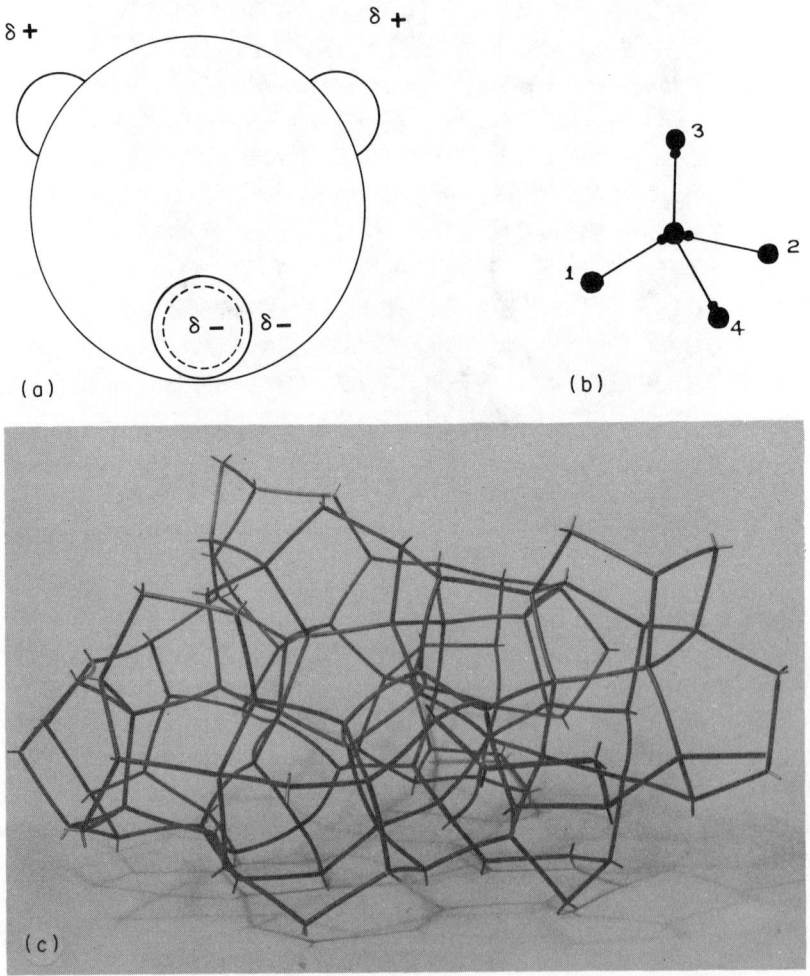

Towards a molecular picture of liquid water

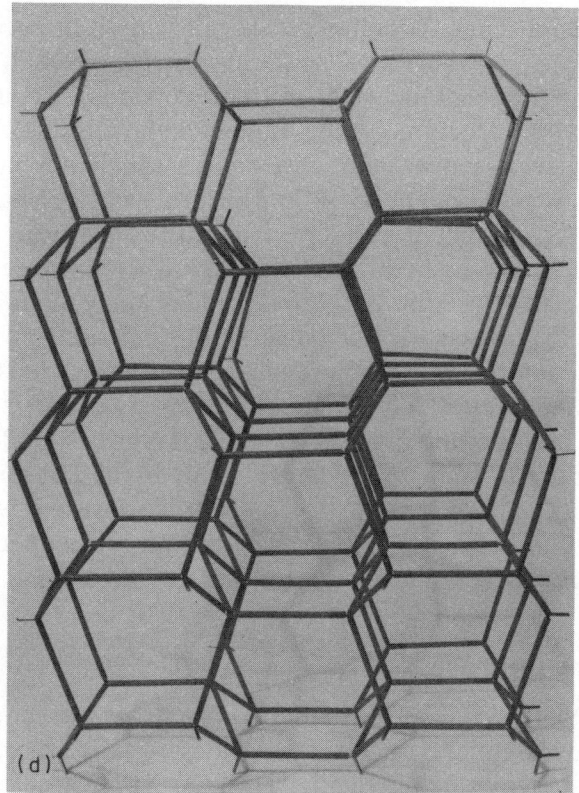

Figure 2 (a) The 'classical' picture of the water molecule showing schematically the tetrahedrally disposed protons (δ^+) and electron lone pairs (δ^-). (b) Nearest neighbour tetrahedral coordination of water molecules in ice Ih. (c) An idealized random tetrahedral network (cf. liquid water). (d) An idealized regular tetrahedral network (cf. ice Ih)

Leaving aside for the present the validity of this simple model, we can use this basic tetrahedral building block to construct a model of a non-crystalline structure which is adequately dense and yet is consistent with approximately tetrahedral geometry. Such a model is shown in Figure 2(c): the non-crystalline 'random' aspect of the network model is seen when contrasted with the crystalline tetrahedral network of Ice Ih (Figure 2(d)).

This conceptual first order model serves well as a starting point from which to consider the molecular nature of liquid water. It represents an approximation to the instantaneous structure (but which changes to a statistically equivalent though geometrically different network every 10^{-11} to 10^{-12} sec) which is consistent with the geometrical consequences of our model of the water–water interaction. In contrast to the *random packing* structure of the simple liquid discussed above, in which the intermolecular interactions were spherically symmetrical, the structure is a *random network* in which the intermolecular interactions are strongly angle-dependent. The distortions from tetrahedral geometry necessary to build such a random network are small (say $\sim \pm 10°$), and the structure naturally contains many pentagonal rings. This is to be expected when the constraint of long-range periodicity is removed: the internal angle of a regular planar pentagon is 108°, very close to the ideal tetrahedral angle of 109.5°.

The foundations of the random tetrahedral network model were laid by Bernal and Fowler in 1933,[3] yet it is only in the last ten years that the general ideas have become accepted. It is consistent with the distorted hydrogen-bond model of Pople,[4] and was developed further by Bernal and co-workers,[2] and more recently by Sceats and Rice.[5]

4 Improving the model

Unfortunately this conceptual model is inadequate for our purposes. It contains the essential structure, but does not incorporate enough quantitative detail to help us understand the significance of the subtle changes in water structure and mobility that occur at or near biomolecule interfaces. Improvement of the model requires progress on two fronts. First, we need to improve our simple model of the hydrogen bond. Secondly, although useful in the early stages, laboratory model-building is no longer adequate. We require much more subtle techniques if we are to understand the structural consequences of the potential function we choose to model the water–water interaction.

4.1 Computer simulation techniques

An adequate theory of the liquid state in general would allow us to calculate structural, thermodynamic and time-dependent properties from a knowledge of the potential function. Although a variety of approximate methods exist for simple liquids, the problems of applying them to water, where the potential function is strongly angle dependent, are severe. Fortunately, we can avoid this problem through computer simulation techniques, which enable us to evaluate *numerically* liquid properties from an assumed knowledge of the intermolecular potential. The literature on these Monte Carlo and molecular dynamics techniques is extensive, and their application to water has been reviewed recently by Wood.[6] For our purposes, we merely note that, given an assumed form for the intermolecular potential function, we can obtain structural, thermodynamic and dynamic properties which can be compared with experiment.

The application of computer simulation to water can be regarded as the exploration of the properties of model liquids whose molecules interact in a prescribed way. The properties of simulated water will depend ultimately on the detailed assumptions made about the hydrogen bond. The problem of a molecular picture of liquid water thus is reduced to the problem of an adequate picture of the hydrogen bond interaction. It is upon this, and upon some of the structural and thermodynamic consequences of a variety of hydrogen bond models, that we now concentrate.

4.2 *The nature of the water–water hydrogen bond*

The simple model of four tetrahedrally-disposed charges that we used to develop our random network model is inadequate. It relies too much upon the local coordination found in ice structures, where it can be argued that the requirement to form a regular lattice forces a near-perfect tetrahedral local organization. In the liquid, the lattice constraint is absent, therefore we should examine the details of the water–water interaction in the absence of such constraints.

Very large basis set *ab initio* quantum mechanical calculations can give a good approximation to the energy surface of two molecules. The predicted minimum energy configuration of two water molecules,[7] is in essential agreement with the results of microwave beam experiments.[8] Moreover, the computed wave functions give an indication of the electron distribution in both the isolated molecule and in the dimer.

Two major points can be drawn from these theoretical studies. First, the lone pair region *does not* consist of two distinct, separated lobes of electron density in well-defined tetrahedral positions. Rather, the charge density seems to form a single region, whose centre is approximately trigonally disposed with respect to the two protons. An expected consequence of this is that the tetrahedrality of the water–water interaction is considerably less than we are led to believe

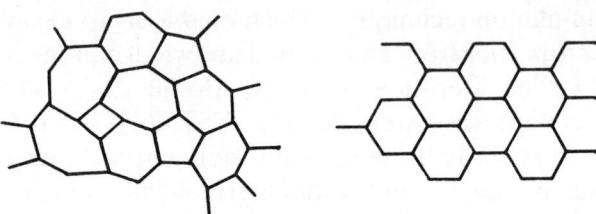

Figure 3 Idealized two-dimensional 3-coordinated 'crystal' and 'liquid'

from the ice structure. In liquid water, therefore, where lattice constraints are absent, we might expect a less-perfect tetrahedrality than in the ices. Because each water molecule can donate two protons to a region of negative charge, we would still expect overall a coordination of four in liquid water, although with significant deviations from the ideal tetrahedral angle. Once this proton donor–acceptor balance is upset, however, as would occur at polar group interfaces, the deviations from four-coordination would be expected to be greater. Crystallographic studies on small molecule crystal hydrates bear out this prediction,[9,10] as do high resolution studies on protein and other macromolecule crystals where a significant fraction of water molecules are clearly three-coordinated.[11,12]

The second point concerns the *pair-additivity* of the water–water hydrogen bond. In simple liquids, the assumption is normally made that the total energy of an assembly of N molecules can be calculated by adding together the energy of interaction of each *pair* of molecules in turn. The total energy is the sum of individual *pair* energies, and the potential function is *pair-additive*. Put differently, if molecule 3 is brought close to molecules 1 and 2, then the energy of interaction E_{12} of molecules 1 and 2 is unaltered. For simple liquids, this is a good approximation. For water, both experimental evidence[13,14] and theoretical calculations[15,16] suggest the approximation is relatively poor, as was proposed earlier by Henry Frank[17] on the basis of chemical arguments.

The consequences of non-pair-additivity—or cooperativity—for water structure are presently unclear. Most work on water argues that these effects can be included in an 'average' manner, and so 'effective' pair potential functions have been developed which attempt to do this. At interfaces such as protein molecule surfaces, however, these arguments break down. What limited work that has been done with non-pair-additive potentials suggest that cooperative effects must be considered specifically if sensible results are to be obtained in heterogeneous systems.[14,30,31]

4.3 Models of the water molecule

Bearing the above two points in mind, we now consider the use of the following three models of the water–water hydrogen bond in studying the molecular nature of liquid water.

(a) *ST2*[18] This model incorporates four point charges arranged tetrahedrally, being designed to reproduce hydrogen-bond tetrahedrality. It was designed from the previous four point charge BNS[19] model, which was itself fitted to the second virial coefficient.

(b) *CI*[20] This analytical potential was designed to be consistent with high level quantum mechanical calculations (including electron correlation) of the interaction energy of two water molecules. Energy values calculated for 66 configurations were used to fix the parameters of an analytical form, which is effectively a three point charge model. As the 'charge' locations are not tetrahedrally disposed, we would expect this model to be less 'tetrahedral' than ST2.

(c) *PE*[14,21,22] This model represents the water molecule electron distribution in terms of an electrical multipole expansion. The experimental dipole moment and quantum mechanical quadrupole (in agreement with recent experiments) are used, *together with a dipole polarizability to try to handle the cooperative effects discussed above*. Non-bonded parameters are fitted to the known equilibrium dimer.[8] Work so far using this model has truncated the expansion after the quadrupole, though a detailed examination of the consequences of this is under way.[23]

Before proceeding to examine a few predictions of these models, we should note the following points.

(i) Both ST2 and CI are pair-additive models, while PE attempts to incorporate cooperativity. ST2 is an 'effective' pair potential, while CI attempts to reproduce the interaction of two water molecules accurately; hence, we might reasonably expect ST2 to perform well in the liquid (for which it has been optimized) and poorly in the gas phase, while for CI the reverse should be the case. PE is designed to handle both gas and condensed phases.

(ii) ST2 is expected to be tetrahedral, CI and PE not necessarily so.

4.4 Sample model predictions

Although all three model potentials have predicted successfully a wide range of properties of liquid water,[14,18,20] none is totally satisfactory. As an illustration of some of the features of these models, we examine two properties: the second virial coefficient and the radial distribution function of the liquid.

(a) *Second virial coefficient*. This gas phase property is a Boltzmann-weighted integration over the two-molecule energy surface. Remembering the sources of our three sample models, we would thus expect ST2 to do poorly (it is an 'effective' pair potential optimized for the liquid) while CI (*fitted to* the dimer surface) and PE should fare better. The various predictions are shown in Figure 4. The only surprise is that CI does very poorly, a particularly odd result for a potential designed to fit the very surface that defines the second virial. The reason, as we shall see below, is that the analytical form fails to reproduce the dimer energy surface adequately, presumably because

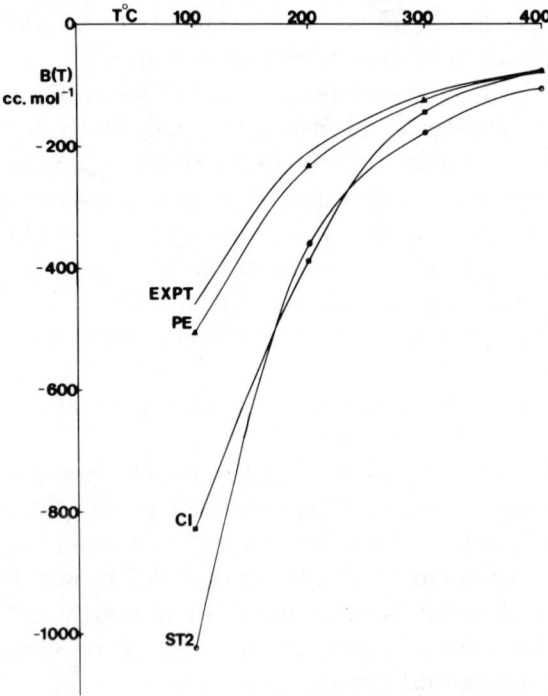

Figure 4 The second virial according to three models of water

of the distribution and small number (66) of points used to fit a six-dimensional surface. That ST2 and CI both perform poorly in the gas phase suggest it is dangerous to use them for calculations in heterogeneous assemblies where local differences in water molecule number density will invalidate the assumptions upon which 'effective' pair potentials are based.[14]

(b) *Radial Distribution Function* (RDF). This function describes the probability of finding a molecule (or atom) at a given distance from any other atom. Its form for simple liquids is a first peak showing the spread in first neighbour distances, the area under this peak corresponding to the number of first neighbours (Figure 5). At larger distances, two or three further oscillations occur, after which little structure is evident.

The RDF is in principle obtainable experimentally from X-ray and neutron scattering measurements. However, as the scattering cross-sections for X-rays and neutrons of the various atoms in water (or D_2O) are different, the RDFs from the two sources are rather different. The X-ray experiment sees mainly the oxygen atoms, and the resulting RDF ($g_x(r)$) shows largely the oxygen atom distribution. Water molecule orientation effects are therefore absent. For neutrons, the cross-sections of deuterium and oxygen are of the same order of magnitude, and the neutron RDF ($g_N(r)$) weights the two atoms more equally. Thus this latter function contains information on local molecular orientations.

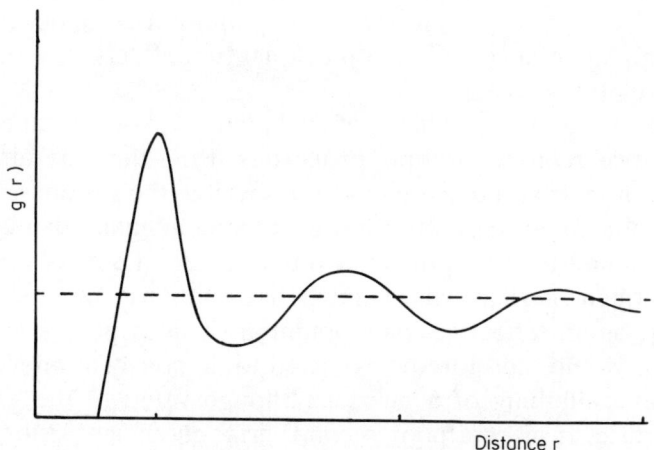

Figure 5 The form of the (normalized) radial distribution function for an inert gas

As ST2 is optimized for the liquid, we expect a good $g_x(r)$. At first sight this is indeed the case,[18] with the positions of the first three maxima well reproduced. The first maximum is, however, too high, with the following first minimum correspondingly reduced. A possible implication is that the first neighbour coordination shell is too ordered, which might be a consequence of the tetrahedrality of the model. This suggestion is reinforced by the predicted $g_N(r)$, which shows two sharp peaks at low r, corresponding to first neighbour (intermolecular) —O⋯H and H⋯H separations,[16,18] in contrast to the experimentally-observed broad shoulder.[24] ALthough quantum effects may act to reduce the sharpness of these peaks, the hypothesis that the inherent tetrahedrality of ST2 may result in over-strong first neighbour orientation correlations seems reasonable. PE follows the form of $g_N(r)$ fairly well,[14] although there are problems of scaling which call for a reassessment of the non-bonded interaction parameters. These scaling problems are apparent also in $g_x(r)$, which also suggests the PE angular correlations may be too *weak*.

As CI was fitted to points on the dimer surface, it necessarily ignores cooperative effects in condensed phases. Hence we would not expect good predictions of liquid state properties. The predicted $g_x(r)$ is, however, relatively good;[20] there are also indications that agreement is improved if simulations are run at temperatures (~50 degrees) higher than those of the experimental RDF being compared.[32] Although detailed comparisons with the neutron $g_N(r)$ have not been made, there are indications that the O⋯H correlations may be too strong in this model also,[20] suggesting local orientational correlations may be too strong. Again, a consideration of quantum effects may smear out these correlations.

An interesting, if somewhat confused picture, results from considering these two relatively simple properties. PE—the only attempt to consider non-pair-additive effects—does well in the gas phase, but has scaling problems in the liquid; moreover, the angular correlations of first neighbours may be predicted too weakly. ST2 does well in the liquid, though perhaps its angular correlations are too strong; moreover, as an 'effective' pair potential, it does poorly in the gas phase, and would therefore be expected to do poorly at interfaces. CI appears as something of a puzzle: although fitted to the gas phase dimer surface, it gives a poor second virial coefficient. Moreover, it does relatively well in the liquid, where we would expect it to perform poorly. The following more detailed discussion of these potentials leads us to suggest tentative explanations of these points.

5 The dimer energy surface

The minimum energy water dimer configuration is shown in Figure 6. Keeping the O_1O_2 distance constant at 3.0 Å, we can plot the energy as we rotate independently either the donor angle θ_D or acceptor angle θ_A. These two sections of the total dimer surface are particularly relevant to the angular correlations of the first neighbour coordination discussed above (Section 4.4). These sections for our three sample models can be compared with available quantum mechanical calculations at SCF level, together with a very limited number of points which include electron correlation effects. Although these *ab initio* calculations cannot be taken as a fully reliable reference point, the main features of the energy variations should be indicated correctly. Thus this data gives us some guidance in assessing the validity of the corresponding energy surface sections of the three models.

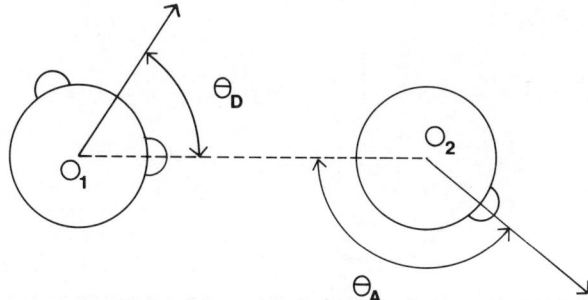

Figure 6 The equilibrium water dimer showing the definition of acceptor (θ_A) and donor (θ_D) angles

5.1 Acceptor angle section

Figure 7 shows the model acceptor angle sections, together with the available SCF and configuration interaction points. There are clear differences both between the models themselves, and between the models and the *ab initio* points. Close to the minimum, the following points are of interest (see Figure 7):

(i) Both ST2 and PE predict the minimum θ_A angle in essential agreement with experiment and the quantum mechanical calculations. Although derived by fitting an analytical form to dimer quantum mechanical calculations, the CI minimum is displaced by some 20°.

(ii) ST2 exhibits a double minimum separated by a barrier of about 1 kcal mol^{-1}. The weaker minimum corresponds to the *cis* dimer con-

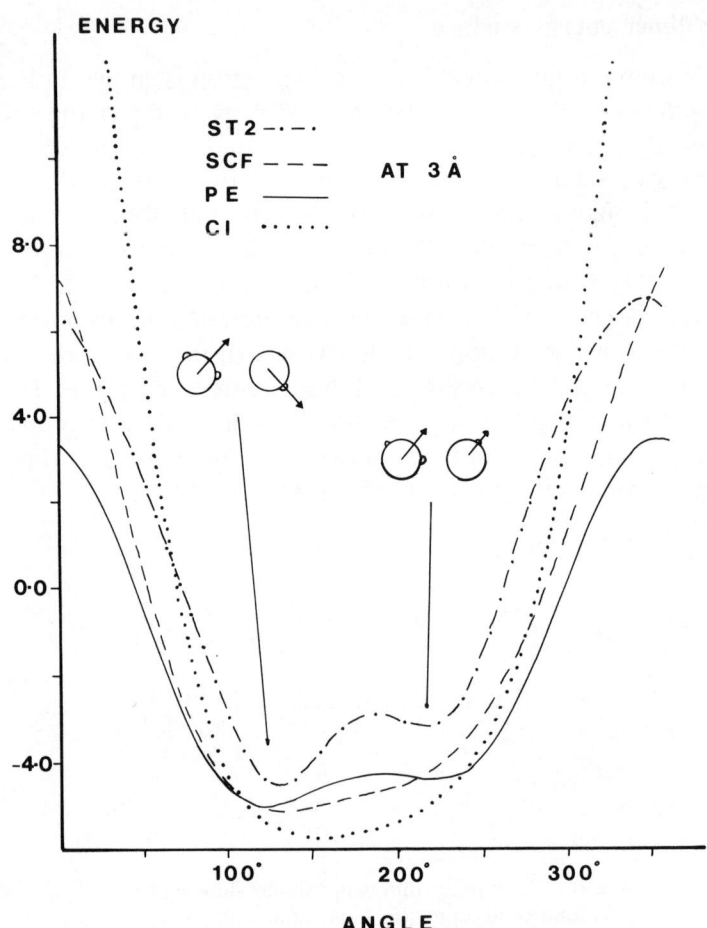

Figure 7 The acceptor angle section of the water dimer for $O_1O_2 = 3.0$ Å, $\theta_D = 52°$ according to three water models. The motifs indicate the relative orientations for the two ST2 minima. The ST2 curve should be displaced *down* by 2 kcal mol^{-1}

figuration. PE shows here only a *very* shallow minimum, with a much lower barrier of 0.5 kcal mol^{-1}. Neither CI nor the quantum mechanical results show any sign of a double minimum, the force constant for the *trans* ↔ *cis* rotation being very soft.

This latter point underlines the poor directional control on the hydrogen bond of the lone pair region, and also reflects the lack of two distinct lone pair regions on the water molecule as discussed in Section 4.2. That ST2 shows two distinct minima corresponding to the 'classical' tetrahedral lone pair positions suggests that it is likely to overemphasize the angular correlations in local coordination. This seems to be consistent with the tentative conclusions drawn from the RDF discussion above. The remnant (albeit minimal) double minimum (or minimum plus shoulder) found for PE may also be a defect, although with an intervening barrier of the order of kT, the structural consequences of this feature at room temperature may be relatively small.

In the repulsive region (corresponding to hydrogen–hydrogen repulsion along the O_1O_2 vector (Figure 6)), both ST2 and PE are inadequately repulsive by about 3 and 4 kcal mol^{-1} respectively if the SCF curve is taken as a yardstick (no quantum mechanical CI points are available in this region). *Clementi's CI fitted potential is dramatically too repulsive by about 11 kcal mol^{-1}*. Further investigation[23] suggests that this large discrepancy from the quantum mechanical values to which this analytical potential was fitted arises from a poor distribution of the fitting points over the whole energy surface. As the fitting procedure could use only 66 points to sample a six-dimensional surface, the occurrence of such problems is not surprising.

It might be argued that this large discrepancy will have little effect on liquid properties at room temperature—or indeed on the second virial coefficient—as the wings of the curve will not be sampled significantly (kT ~ 0.5 kcal mol^{-1}). However, this strong repulsion has the secondary effect of reducing the *width* of that part of the θ_A well which *is* sampled. As reference to Figure 7 shows, for energies higher than -3 kcal mol^{-1}, the CI potential well becomes progressively narrower than the calculated SCF well. Taken together with possible complex geometrical effects of the shifted minimum of the CI potential, the effects on predicted liquid structure are likely to be significant. As shown by Figure 4, the effects on the second virial coefficient (presumably augmented by other 'fitting' discrepancies elsewhere on the total energy surface) are large. In the light of this narrowing of the θ_A well-depth, it is not surprising that the temperature rescaling mentioned in Section 4.4 gives improved experimental agreement.

PE shows (smaller) deviations from SCF in the opposite sense—the PE well is broader by about 20° up to an energy level of about 0 kcal mol^{-1}, above which the difference increases rapidly. This is consistent with the inadequate angular correlations this model is suspected to give (Section 4.4(b)). The ST2 well is if anything narrower than SCF except within 50° of the maximum repulsion, suggesting an opposite conclusion for this model consistent with the liquid RDF discussion above (Section 4.4(b)).

5.2 Donor angle energy variation

The variation of energy with the donor angle θ_D is shown in Figure 8. Apart from one point, no SCF data are yet available to serve as a benchmark in discussing the three model curves.

In the central repulsive region (corresponding to lone pair–lone pair opposition along O_1O_2) ST2 and CI are essentially indistinguishable; PE is of the same general shape, but with a maximum about 1 kcal mol^{-1} lower. The PE barrier is significantly narrower than either ST2 or CI, again suggesting somewhat weaker angular correlations.

In the attractive region, ST2 and CI show two distinct but asymmetrical minima with a small barrier between them; these minima correspond to the two classical hydrogen bonding configurations with molecule 1 as the proton donor. The relative differences in the well

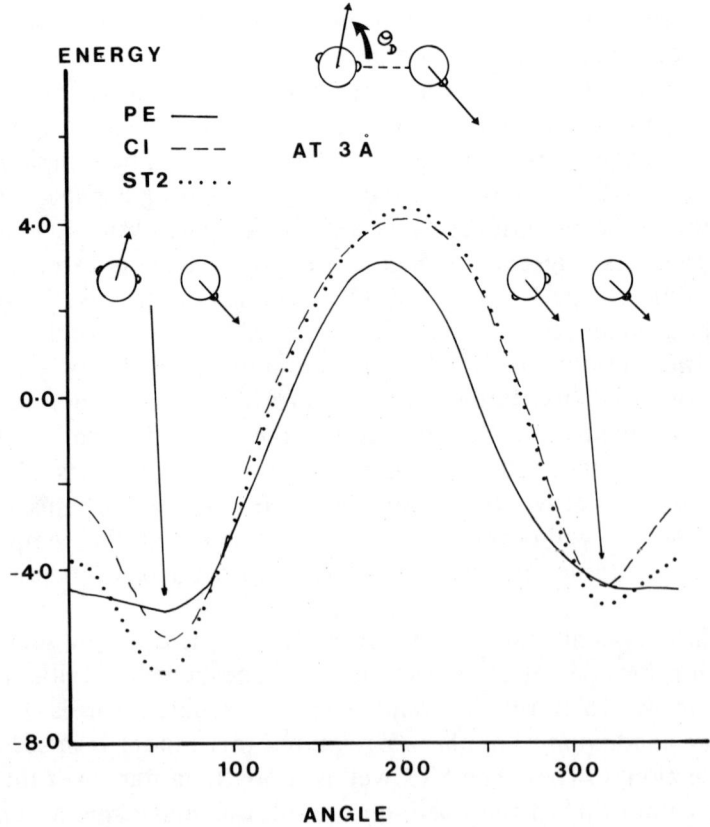

Figure 8 The donor angle section of the water dimer

depths and the intervening barrier would be expected to lead to differences in detail in local angular structure, but in both cases the population of states intermediate between the two well configurations (a 'bifurcation') will be significantly lower than the populations of the two minima themselves. In contrast, PE shows no maximum separating these two classical hydrogen-bonding configurations, and hence this potential will show weaker angular control by the proton donor. Although quantum mechanical calculations are not available for this donor angle section of the energy surface, the strong directional control of hydrogen bonding by the proton donor suggested from crystal data (Section 4.2) argue for the PE model being defective in this region.

5.3 Discussion

To draw conclusions concerning the structure of dense many-body assemblies from the dimer surface is dangerous. We have also ignored all but two sections of the (θ_A, θ_D) surface, and all energy variations with O_1O_2 distance and out-of-plane rotations, where additional differences between the three models are seen.[23] Nevertheless, the differences in the angular dependencies of the dimer energies of the different models are highly suggestive of apparently reasonable rationalizations of the RDF features discussed in Section 4.2. In terms of the relative strengths of local angular correlations, we would argue that all three models are imperfect. Improving them with respect to real water is not an easy problem, not least because of an imperfect knowledge of the details of the energy surface for real water. Experiment can yield useful information on force constants close to a minimum energy configuration. *State-of-the-art* quantum mechanical calculations *including electron correlation* can be reliably performed on the dimer, but even with the increasing availability of vector processor computers, it is feasible to explore only a limited selection of points on a six-dimensional surface. Even if we had a good numerical representation of the energy surface from quantum mechanics, there are then significant problems in fitting an analytical form. Some of these are seen in comparing the analytical form fitted by Clementi with the numerical representation of the energy surface: choice and distribution of sample points for the fitting procedure is difficult, and can lead to unphysical features such as the exaggerated repulsive barrier seen in Figure 7. Nevertheless, work along these lines is the most promising way forward and such a programme is under way at Birkbeck.

6 Cooperative effects

The previous section ignored the problem of *non-pair-additivity* of the water–water hydrogen bond raised in Section 4.2. We conclude with a discussion of the limited attempts that have been made to quantify this, and to model the consequences of cooperativity in liquid water. Of the three water models discussed above, only PE attempts to model non-pair-additivity specifically: this it does through allowing the dipole moment to change under the influence of the polarizing field from the surrounding molecules (Section 4.3).[14]

6.1 3- and 4-body effects

Non-pair-additivity can be considered in terms of the effect on the energy E_{12} of an isolated pair of molecules of bringing up a third molecule. In principle it is a many-body effect in that bringing up a fourth molecule may similarly affect the energy E_{123} of the triplet, and so on; however, it has been argued from quantum mechanical perturbation theory that only the 3-body contribution is likely to be significant.[27] Although PE is designed to consider n-body effects, our calculations confirm that only the 3-body contribution is significant in the model. Defining a non-pair-additivity energy as the difference between the energy of the triplet and the three constituents pairs $[\Delta E^{(3)} \equiv E_{123} - (E_{12} + E_{13} + E_{23})]$, the 3-body term can contribute up to 20%. In contrast, the 4-body correction term $\Delta E^{(4)}$ rarely amounts to more than 1%, and can be argued to be negligible. This result suggests that the computational complexities of PE might be simplified if an analytical 3-body potential were constructed. However, remembering the difficulties of analytical fitting to the six-dimensional dimer surface (Section 5.1), the problems of fitting an analytical form to the twelve-dimensional trimer surface look formidable.

6.2 Quantum mechanical calculations of 3-body energies

The problems of calculating 3-body corrections from quantum mechanics are enormous. The *dimer* energy calculations discussed in Section 5, yield a *small difference* between *two large numbers*. With

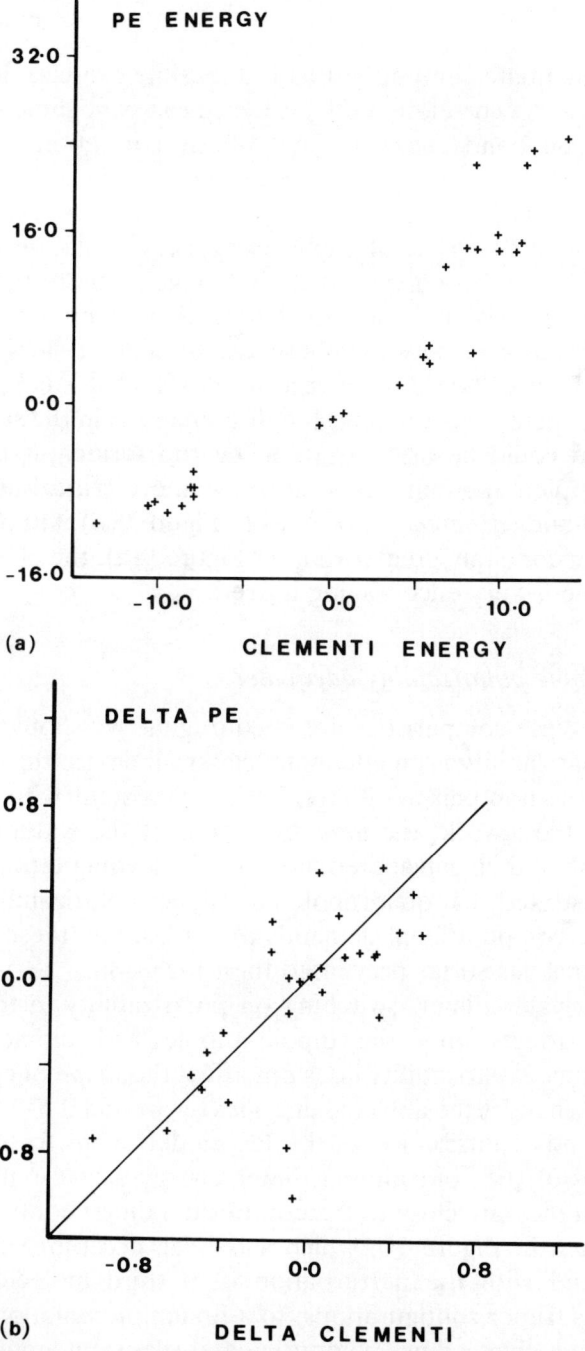

Figure 9 (a) Water trimer energies predicted by PE and estimated from quantum mechanics by Clementi *et al.*[16] (b) 3-body contributions to water trimer energies according to PE and Clementi

care and adequate computing this is a feasible exercise, including significant electron correlation effects which can contribute up to 20% of the hydrogen bond energy.[26] The 3-body correction is much more difficult; not only must we consider many more electrons, but the result we seek is a *second* order difference between two large numbers.

The most extensive set of published trimer calculations to date have been performed by Clementi at SCF level; the results should be regarded as provisional until further work is done with larger basis sets. A comparison between these results and PE for 28 trimers is shown in Figure 9(a). For energies below about +6 kcal mol^{-1} the agreement seems encouraging; the discrepancies in the strongly repulsive region could be argued not to be too serious as this region is poorly-sampled at room temperature. A more critical test is to compare the 3-body *differences* $\Delta E^{(3)}$, as in Figure 9(b); although the scatter is understandably greater than in Figure 9(a), the clustering about the 45° line is very encouraging indeed.

6.3 Is dipole polarizability adequate?

Although these comparisons are encouraging, we should ask whether dipole polarizability is an adequate 'classical' device through which to try to mimic non-pair-additivity. To be consistent with this electron distortion framework, the *total* distortion of the water electron distribution should be considered, not just the leading term, unless it can be demonstrated that quadrupole and higher polarizability effects are small. The computational demands of considering these higher order polarizations has so far prevented their inclusion.

For the water dimer, switching on polarizability in the PE model therefore affects only the dipole–dipole and dipole–quadrupole energy terms. Polarizability does not affect the *shape* of either surface, but rather changes the absolute energies by around 0.5–1.0 kcal mol^{-1}.

The 3-body contribution in the PE model seems to similarly leave the shapes of the contributing dimer energy surfaces unchanged, at least when they are close to the equilibrium dimer configuration. This is illustrated in Figure 10, which shows an acceptor surface section without and with the perturbation of a third molecule in one of Clementi's trimer configurations: to a first approximation, the level of the surface is changed by an approximately constant amount, but there is no significant perturbation of the shape of the curve. Plots of the total perturbed $E(\theta_A, \theta_D)$ surface show similar behaviour: whether or

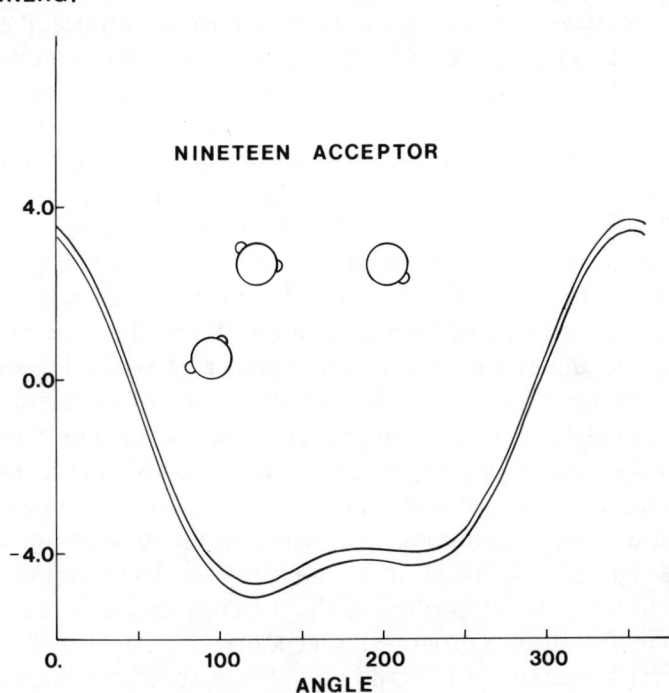

Figure 10 Perturbing effect of a neighbouring third molecule on the effective energy surface of a water dimer

not this is a realistic representation of what happens in reality is presently not clear. If it can be shown to be so, there may be computationally simpler ways of handling the 3-body correction. Further progress on this point must await planned computationally expensive state of the art quantum mechanical calculations on selected points on the trimer energy surface.

7 Summary

At one level, it can be argued that the instantaneous structure of water is solved in principle: it is a random network of molecules of adequate density that is consistent with the intermolecular potential. However, this conceptual picture is inadequate to help us understand the often subtle solvent-related effects observed in biological processes. Useful progress in this direction requires a much better quantitative understanding of the details of the water–water hydrogen bond.

Selected consequences of three models for the water molecule suggest we as yet have no adequate model to serve our purpose. Particular problems surround the angular dependencies of all three models, and consequently none gives a fully satisfactory account of even such a crude property as the radial distribution function. Cooperativity is significant; PE seems to make a promising attempt at handling it, though further work is necessary to test whether or not the use of dipole polarizability is sufficient. All the models discussed are rigid body models, which ignore quantum effects; these are likely to be significant, yet little attempt has so far been made to allow for them.

In the absence of experimental data on all but the near-minimum region of the dimer energy surface, further progress in designing potentials for *real* water must depend upon state-of-the-art quantum chemical calculations at beyond Hartree–Fock level. For the dimer, this is feasible, although computational limitations restrict us to only a limited sampling of a five-dimensional surface. To test models of the significant 3-body contribution, the problems are at least an order of magnitude greater. Work is under way[29] to see how far the 3-body energy surface can be probed with currently-available computing power. Whether further progress with cooperative effects will be more efficient via an extended PE-type model or a specific 3-body correction is still an open question. Success with molecular-level calculations on aqueous biomolecule systems depends upon its being answered.[30,31]

Acknowledgements

My colleagues Barry Gellatly and John Quinn who initiated and executed the energy surface calculations are responsible for many of the ideas presented. They are not responsible for erroneous interpretations. Paul Barnes developed the early work on the PE potential, including the original computer programs used in the energy calculations.

References

1. J. L. Finney, J. M. Goodfellow and P. L. Poole, in *Current Methods in Structural Molecular Biology: Techniques and Applications*, ed. D. B. Davies, Plenum, New York (in press).
2. J. D. Bernal, *Proc. Roy. Soc.*, **A280**, 299 (1964).
3. J. D. Bernal and R. H. Fowler, *J. Chem. Phys.*, **1**, 515 (1933).
4. J. A. Pople, *Proc. Roy. Soc.*, **A205**, 163 (1951).

5. M. G. Sceats and S. A. Rice, *J. Chem. Phys.*, **72**, 3260 (1980).
6. D. W. Wood in *Water: A Comprehensive Treatise*, ed. F. Franks, Plenum, New York, Vol. 6, p. 279 (1979).
7. G. H. F. Diercksen, *Theor. Chim. Acta*, **21**, 335 (1971).
8. T. R. Dyke, K. M. Mack and J. S. Muenter, *J. Chem. Phys.*, **66**, 498 (1977).
9. I. Olovsson and P.-G. Jönsson, in *The Hydrogen Bond*, eds P. Schuster, G. Zundel and C. Sandorfy, North-Holland, Amsterdam, Vol. 2, p. 393 (1976).
10. J. L. Finney, *J. Mol. Biol.*, **119**, 415 (1978).
11. J. L. Finney, in *Water: A Comprehensive Treatise*, ed. F. Franks, Plenum, New York, Vol. 6, p. 47 (1979).
12. H. F. J. Savage, Unpublished work.
13. J. L. Finney, *Farad. Disc. Chem. Soc.*, **66**, 80, 86 (1978).
14. P. Barnes, J. L. Finney, J. D. Nicholas and J. E. Quinn, *Nature*, **282**, 459 (1979).
15. D. Hankins, J. W. Moskowitz and F. H. Stillinger, *J. Chem. Phys.*, **53**, 4544 (1970).
16. E. Clementi, W. Kołos, G. C. Lie and G. Ranghino, *Inter. J. Quant. Chem.*, XVII, 377 (1980).
17. H. S. Frank and W. Y. Wen, *Disc. Farad. Sci.*, **24**, 133 (1957).
18. F. H. Stillinger and A. Rahman, *J. Chem. Phys.*, **60**, 1545 (1974).
19. A. Ben-Naim and F. H. Stillinger, in *Water and Aqueous Solutions*, ed. R. A. Horne, Wiley–Interscience, New York, p. 295 (1972).
20. G. C. Lie, E. Clementi and M. Yoshimine, *J. Chem. Phys.*, **64**, 2314 (1976).
21. P. Barnes, in 'Report of CECAM Workshop on Molecular Dynamics and Monte Carlo Calculations on Water', ed. H. J. C. Berendsen, CECAM, Orsay, France, p. 77 (1972).
22. P. Barnes, in *Progress in Liquid Physics*, ed. C. A. Croxton, Wiley, Chichester, p. 391 (1978).
23. B. J. Gellatly and J. E. Quinn, unpublished work.
24. I. P. Gibson, thesis, University of Kent (1978).
    I. P. Gibson and J. C. Dore, in preparation.
25. B. J. Gellatly, unpublished work.
26. G. H. F. Diercksen, W. P. Kramer and B. O. Roos, *Theor. Chim. Acta*, **36**, 249 (1975).
27. J. N. Murrell, personal communication.
28. J. E. Quinn and J. L. Finney, unpublished work.
29. J. O. Baum, J. L. Finney and V. Saunders, unpublished work.
30. J. M. Goodfellow, J. L. Finney and P. Barnes, *Proc. Roy. Soc.*, **B214**, 213 (1982).
31. J. M. Goodfellow, *Proc. Nat. Acad. Sci. (USA)*, in press.
32. I. McDonald, personal communication.

Macromolecular hydration

Reporter: **Julia M. Goodfellow**

Discussion of posters

Initially the discussion centred on the interpretation of excluded volume effects around proteins in mixed solvents. In reply to a question by Clegg, Timasheff said that there is no universal molecular mechanism to explain the general pattern of preferential exclusion of solvents which stabilize protein structure. The preferential interaction parameter appears to correlate with the polarity of the protein for glycerol as cosolvent, but with the increase in water surface tension induced by the sugar for sucrose as cosolvent. All structure stabilizing cosolvents enhance the polymerization of tubulin, a result which is consistent with the reduction of the unfavourable thermodynamic effect of solvent exclusion from the vicinity of the protein by a decrease in the total surface area of the protein exposed to the solvent. The interpretation of the excluded volume data becomes more complex when one studies enzymically active proteins, for then one must consider the interactions of both the active site with solvent and also the substrate with the mixed solvent; a cosolvent induced change in conformation of the substrate may lead to an observed change in enzyme activity. One system described in the literature which is consistent with cosolvent exclusion is that of ribonuclease in concentrated ammonium sulphate solution. However, Pain noted that the effect of sulphate on enzyme kinetics must be enzyme-substrate specific because the rates of hydrolysis of penicillin by penicillinase are independent of sulphate concentration up to 2 M, although sulphate is known to stabilize the enzyme and to inhibit a conformational change to a substrate-deactivated form.

A discussion followed on the possible explanations of the results of Robson who found that mixtures of urea and guanidinium chloride showed no denaturing effect, whereas these compounds individually are used universally as denaturants. One possible reason for these unexpected results was that the urea and guanidinium chloride dimerized but there was no evidence for this. Robson described further experiments with the mixed solvent, involving transfer of individual amino acids from water to the urea/guanidinium chloride mixture. These experiments show that polar amino acids behave as expected, when transferred to denaturing conditions, but charged residues show anomalous behaviour. This is consistent with the premise that the mixed solvent does not denature the native structure because of stabilization of the charged groups which are preferentially on the surface in the folded state.

Derbyshire requested a model for the effects of ionic concentration and specific ionic species on the hydration levels in haemoglobin. Brnjas-Kraljevič found no molecular mechanisms able to explain all her results. In general, the hydration shell of haemoglobin changed as expected from the known structure inducing behaviour of the ions. However, the effect of phosphate ions could only be explained in terms of three effects; that of solvation of the phosphate ions, binding of the ions to the protein and the hydration of the protein. Rosenberg said that his results on oxygen uptake isotherms for 10 mM haemoglobin solutions showed no such differences in behaviour in the presence of phosphate. This discrepancy was rationalized by Kell who thought that the differences in results occurred because the experiment of Rosenberg was looking at the active site alone while those of Brnjas-Kraljevič involved the whole protein molecule.

The experiments of Mathur-De Vré on the differential binding of H_2O and D_2O to DNA were discussed, but here again there was no molecular mechanism which could explain the large differences in binding. In reply to more detailed questions from Bryant, the author stated that most of the observed NMR results showed a single exponential decay and that no experiments on differential binding had been undertaken on small model compounds in solution.

Franks initiated a heated discussion of the problems associated with defining 'bound' or 'hydration' water. Does such water exist? How far does it extend? How do its properties differ from those of bulk water? Careri thought that a satisfactory definition might be achieved by consideration of the magnitude of the binding energy of a water molecule relative to the thermal energy kT. 'Bound' water molecules would have binding energies greater than kT. However, Careri realized that his definition depends on the notion of a 'mean field' acting on one representative molecule, and for this reason may not be generally useful where there are too few water molecules or a non-uniform field. Israelachvili emphasized that when considering interactions around macromolecules, free energy differences of 0.1 or 0.01 kT could be important when summed over large numbers of atoms in a macromolecular assembly. For this reason he supported a distance criterion for defining 'bound' water.

In answer to Finney, Bryant thought that a 'dynamic' measurement from NMR signal intensity was useful but was also somewhat arbitrary, as it depended on 'bound' water measurements relative to those on a frozen sample. Moreover, specific heat measurements would be likely to give a slightly different value, as now the reference system was changed to an equally arbitrary standard—the gas phase properties of water. A proposal that the timescale relevant to a biological process, e.g. enzyme catalysis, should be used was put forward by Kell. A further definition came from Middendorf as that of a density of states function, intermediate between that of the solid protein and the bulk water continuum.

The obvious lack of a coherent definition was apparent in the view of Ter-Minassian-Saraga that 'bound' water was effectively an artefact, whether measured experimentally or defined from calculations. Finney observed that 'bound' water had never been a useful concept and would not be useful even if we succeeded in agreeing on a definition. The discussion was perhaps best summarized by Beveridge who felt that 'bound' water could be best described at the present time as 'non-bulk' water.

Panel discussion (format: questions were asked after each speaker)

(1) Finney—Estimates of free energy of protein folding

It was suggested by Wiggins that the large sizes of some enzymes (up to 1000 amino acid residues) gave these molecules a greater flexibility and capacity for storing free energy. A slight change in energy of one type of interaction became considerably magnified when summed over all possible interactions in such a large molecule. In response to a question by Bryant, Finney emphasized that the free energy difference between the native and the unfolded states was relatively small, of a magnitude equivalent to the energy of a few hydrogen bonds, i.e. a few kT. However, this small net difference arose from the balance of several large opposing free energy changes. Moreover, each of these large free energy components derived from small differences in free energy for one interaction, added over all the possible interaction sites of this type in the macromolecule.

The calculations of such free energy differences depend critically on accurate estimates of many small quantities, and Robson suggested that it may not be either necessary or feasible to calculate them because: (a) we are interested only in the native state which, by definition, has the lowest free energy and, (b) the reference state—that of the unfolded protein—known as a random coil, is not well-defined. Wadsö also thought that such calculations were premature and that we could learn more from a simpler system, such as a ligand-binding reaction, especially as we could then correlate predictions with thermodynamic measurements. Israelachvili suggested the development of an equation of state so that it was not necessary to define each individual molecular interaction. However, an attempt at this type of an approach already existed in the literature and had not been found to be particularly useful.

(2) Careri

The relationship of the model proposed by Careri for the enzymic behaviour of lysozyme to the molecular dynamics results of Karplus *et al.* was discussed in reply to a question by Middendorf. It appeared that Careri's model was consistent with the motion of the lips of the cleft, calculated from the crystallographic refinement of anisotropic temperature factors (Blake *et al.*) but not with the large 'hinge' motions found in the molecular dynamics calculations. An upper limit to the fluctuation energy of the domains in phycocyanin had been found to be 4×10^{-7} kT by Middendorf.

The experiments described by Careri were based on dry lysozyme films, and although catalytic activity could be measured from hydration levels greater than 0.29 g/g, it was not clear how this related in magnitude to the activity of the enzyme in dilute solution. Lüdemann further asked whether any experiments had been performed to assess the 'activity' of the unfolded protein, as it was known that one could get spurious activity of the proteins in a random coil conformation. Pain asked whether the substrate could diffuse to the active site at such low hydration levels. This was not known, as in the experiments described the substrate was already frozen in the active site before measurements began. Although a statistical mechanics approach was proposed by Careri in order to correlate thermodynamic behaviour with molecular interactions, Kell questioned the use of such an approach for proteins, because any one protein molecule would behave in an identical way as, say, other such protein molecules. He concluded that a *macroscopic* statistical mechanics approach was no good to describe such behaviour. Careri, however, was using a statistical mechanics approach to study all the molecular interactions in one protein molecule and not the statistical behaviour of different protein molecules.

(3) Robson

Finney suggested that the degree of directionality of the hydrogen bonding implicit in the water model used in this computer simulation of solvent around a dipeptide would directly influence the number of 'bifurcated' hydrogen bonds. Franks asked about the relative strengths of the hydrogen bonds in the 'second' hydration shell relative to those in the 'first' shell and to bulk water. Robson replied that they were not necessarily weaker bonds but that the orientational freedom was restricted in the first and second hydration layers. These results were discussed in relation to the hydration of

Ni^{++} ions, where there is known to be a well-defined first hydration layer from the neutron scattering results of Enderby and Neilson.

The question of what constitutes a bifurcated hydrogen bond was considered by Lehmann. The usual notation refers to one hydrogen accepting electrons from two oxygen atoms. The other kind where the oxygen donates to two hydrogens is quite normal, considering that oxygen has several sets of electrons to donate to the bonds. Robson agreed that his definition of 'bifurcated' could refer to this latter type. The relationship between these results of loss in orientational freedom for a maximum of three shells only and the phenomenon of heterogeneous nucleation of an aqueous fluid supercooled to about -12 °C was mentioned by Bank. However, it would be necessary to carry out simulations at these low temperatures before a meaningful comparison could be made. Two limitations of these simulations were mentioned. Pressey commented on the treatment of all particles in a classical sense, so that there was no mechanism to allow for quantum effects, such as proton tunnelling. The second, more serious limitation, raised by Edmonds, was that the interpretation of the results in terms of large entropic cost and a small enthalpic cost to the water being close to the protein would have to be changed if the cooperative effect of hydrogen bonding was taken into account. The increase in dipole moment of the water molecule in such a cooperative system may give an appreciable enthalpic cost.

(4) Timasheff and Vuk-Pavlović

The contributions by Timasheff and Vuk-Pavlović on interactions in mixed solvents were discussed together.

Timasheff showed that his results with MPD (methyl pentane diol) as cosolvent were consistent with repulsion from charged groups on the protein surface. Israelachvili asked how it was possible to measure these charges. In fact, the values for these charges can be calculated if the pH of the solvent is known. Hefford thought that the negative adsorption of sulphate ions at a polymer/solvent interface is the cause of phase separation of a PEG (polyethylene glycol)-rich phase from a PEG/sulphate mixture. This is equivalent to the lowering of the lower critical solution temperature to room temperature. However, the interesting question was why sulphate ions should do this. The lowering of the binodal (limit of phase separation) to lower concentrations as the molecular weight increases is due to the reduction of the combinational entropy of mixing, since the enthalpic term is due to the number of segment/segment interactions and is not very dependent on molecular weight. Hefford concluded his remarks with the comment that polymer/polymer incompatibility is a general phenomenon, whereas polymer/polymer mixing is less common.

Pressey remarked that from a knowledge of other organic semi-conducting materials (see R. Pethig—*Dielectric and Electronic Properties of Biological Materials*, John Wiley, 1979) it is probable that polyethylene glycol will function as an electron transfer agent, i.e. it will serve to discharge the potentials between points on a membrane. This session ended with a solution to the 'hair wash' problem, first raised by Vuk-Pavlović which seemed to perplex some visitors who were not used to English plumbing.

Discussion after Finney's lecture

Dore commented on the neutron diffraction results for structural studies of liquid water (D$_2$O). The pair correlation function (or radial distribution function) $g^N(r)$ shown by Finney was for intermolecular contributions only (i.e. the intramolecular r_{OD} and r_{DD} distances do not feature in the distribution) and comprises a mixture of

Macromolecular hydration

functions which are termed the partial distribution functions. These arise from the time-averaged distribution of the different atom types about each other and for a two-component system like D_2O, there are three partial functions which can be expressed as $g_{OO}(r)$, $g_{OD}(r)$ and $g_{DD}(r)$. The X-ray measurements are primarily dependent on the oxygen positions and give the $g_{OO}(r)$ function, whereas the neutron function is a composite function

$$g^N(r) = 0.091 g_{OO}(r) + 0.421 g_{OD}(r) + 0.489 g_{DD}(r);$$

this function is sensitive to the relative orientation of the molecules. In principle, it is possible to determine the separate partial functions if three independent diffraction measurements can be made but, although much progress has recently been made, there is not yet an established set of partial functions.

Dore further agreed with Finney that most computer models seem to overestimate the degree of local tetrahedral order, but it also appears that they fail to give sufficient structure at larger distances, typically in the 3–5 Å region. Recent neutron studies of water show that temperature and pressure have a very significant effect on the structure. A detailed geometric interpretation of the changes has not yet been developed but it is likely that these are due to rather subtle changes of orientational correlation between the molecules. Water is a liquid which exhibits a much greater change in its structural characteristics as a function of temperature than any other liquid studied so far. The ability to reproduce these effects in the simulations imposes considerable difficulties on the formulation of a satisfactory intermolecular potential. At present it is probably true to say that there are two forms of water—'computer' water and 'real' water. It is to be hoped that the two descriptions will eventually converge on a single form but this situation has existed for some time. Current developments in theory and experiment are very encouraging but it would be premature to suggest that a 'solution' is near at hand.

Beveridge pointed out that there are now extensive comparisons between the various pairwise potentials and their abilities to describe liquid water. He believed that results for the structure, via $g(r)$, as well as a number of other important properties, are remarkably well modelled by pairwise potentials. It would therefore be helpful to discuss how successful these approaches have been, rather than to create the impression that an entire understanding awaits a consideration of three-body, and higher polarizability effects in the potential.

Section 2 Macroscopic surfaces and hydration interactions

Biophysics of Water
Edited by F. Franks
© 1982 John Wiley & Sons Ltd

Surface forces in biological systems

B. W. Ninham
The Australian National University, Canberra, Australia

Summary

The key problem was posed by Poisson exactly 150 years ago. He maintained that there should be a density profile at an interface which must be taken into account in a theory of capillary action—contrary to the assumption of Laplace and Young. The general question of solute or surface-induced liquid structure and its influence on interactions has been with us since. Except for Clerk Maxwell who in 1876 derived a decay length for structural forces in thin water films of 3 Å, the matter was dropped. Primitive models, involving continuum approximations to the solvent outside some 'effective' hard core, 'hydration', Stern, . . . layer, have dominated ideas concerning forces between solute molecules and between surfaces. Van der Waals and electrostatic forces based on continuum theories for biological systems do show peculiarly delicate and subtle forms, presaging the onset of a rich hierarchy of behaviour in the last 50 Å. Theoretical and experimental work on the forces in even the simplest liquids now show that continuum theories break down at distances of 10–20 molecular diameters (depending on surface and liquid). Similar work on electrolytes throws new light on the meaning and definition of terms like hydration, Stern layers, Born energy, dielectric constant profiles, and on the extraordinary complexity of structural forces in water. These new developments will be reviewed.

Introduction

Of the two words, surface forces, the second at least admits of definition. Two objects can be moved towards each other, an operation which occasions a *measurable* force. But in biophysical problems especially that dubious abstraction which assumes that a surface exists, and further, that it can be defined, is very much more tenuous. This question is central: There is a problem in deciding where a surface begins and where bulk water ends. With biological entities those molecules like lipids which make up the structure are in a constant state of interchange with monomers, micelles, vesicles, . . . , whose existence

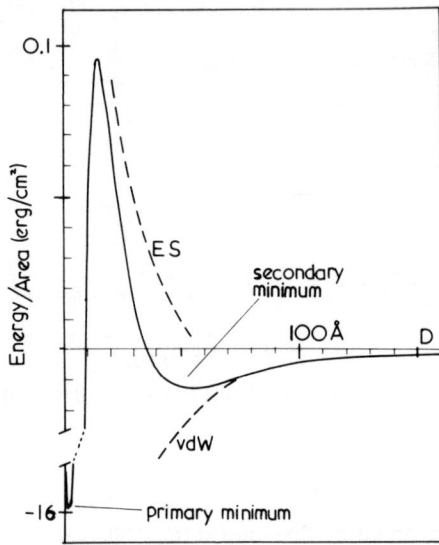

Figure 1 Conventional picture[1,4] of interaction potential between two planar lyphobic colloidal particles: − − − attractive van der Waals and repulsive electrostatic double-layer interactions and ——— total potential

and form will be altered by changes in chemical potential induced by a neighbouring 'surface'. With this very real complication in mind, let us agree to accept the concept of a surface and see how far we can proceed with it.

The classical problem of surface forces in colloid science on which most of our intuition is based begins with the idea of a bulk electrolyte solution separating two *solid* surfaces. We then consider that there are two distinctly different opposing forces.[1] There are (i) van der Waals forces (usually attractive); and (ii) electrostatic or double-layer forces (usually repulsive). A plot of the combined potential of interaction against distance (Figure 1) yields the conventional picture with a barrier to flocculation, primary and secondary minima. The calculation of these forces involves two diametrically opposed notions.

Van der Waals forces

The central assumption here is that a liquid adjoining a solid surface (or a solute molecule in solution chemistry) is uniform with bulk liquid

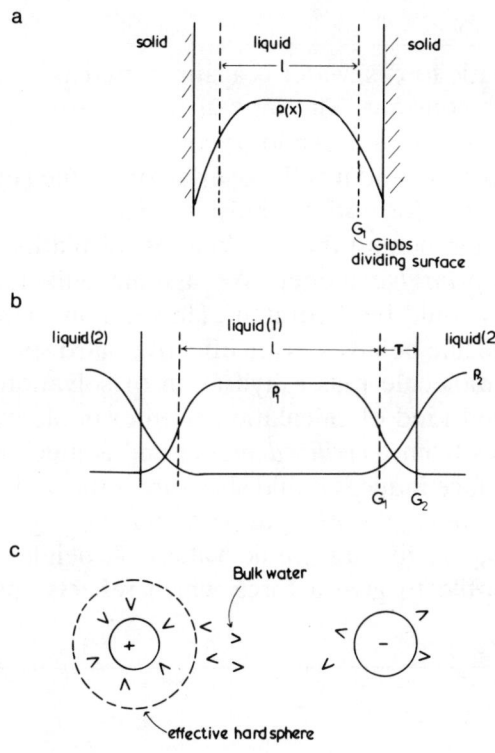

Figure 2 Basis of 'primitive' model in particle interactions or solution theory. The profile of liquid density, polarization, etc. is subsumed in an 'effective' hard sphere radius or Gibbs dividing surface, beyond which liquid is treated as a continuum. (a) Density profile of liquid between two large solid particles; (b) a thin film of liquid (1) separating an immiscible liquid (2) – the Gibb's dividing surfaces are now separated and (c) ionic solution

properties up to the 'interface' (Figure 2). For a single surface or for two simple immiscible liquids in contact, this idea was well established by Gibbs, who gave a precise formal definition of an interface in terms of adsorption excesses. In turn these can be defined formally in terms of distribution functions of statistical mechanics. Then in estimating van der Waals forces by Lifshitz theory,[2,3] the free energy change with distance as two surfaces are brought together is treated as a perturbation, i.e. the adsorption excesses (surface-induced liquid structure, surface-free energies) are unperturbed to lowest order.

Double-layer forces

For the electrostatic forces, water is again treated as a continuum with a given dielectric constant. The ions of the electrolyte now play the role of an intervening liquid. An ionic concentration gradient is set up by the charged surface, and it is the overlap of profile (Figure 3) which is responsible for the (osmotic) repulsive force.

The simplification behind the first kind of calculation leads to what will be called a *primitive* model: We assume bulk liquid up to an 'interface', which could be 'hydrated'. (In solution theory we assume that a solute molecule behaves as an 'effective' hard sphere comprising the bare solute molecule plus a hydration or solvation shell (Figure 2(c)).) The second kind of calculation is an example of a 'structural' force which arises from a *civilized* model and is much more sophisticated. Here a surface induces liquid structure, reflected in the decay of profile in density, polarization, hydrogen bond arrangements, concentration gradients, ... to bulk liquid values. A neighbouring surface perturbs that profile to give a force which reflects change in liquid

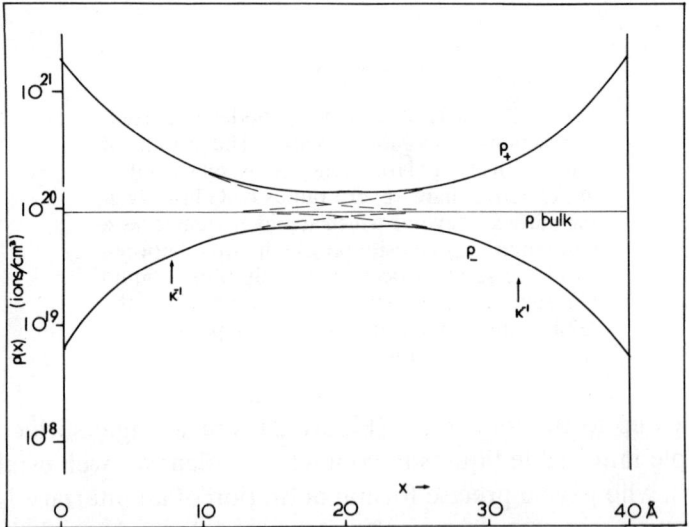

Figure 3 The first civilized model: Gouy-Chapman picture of ionic charge profile induced by charged surface. Water is treated as continuum of dielectric constant $\varepsilon = 80$. Overlap[5] (———) of individual (- - -) ionic profiles, which decay gradually to bulk electrically neutral concentrations, gives rise to double-layer force

structure. In both cases the force measures the change in chemical potential with distance, but the nature, and mechanism of transmission, of the force is very different.

A further idea is contained in the extension of classical double-layer theory to include charge regulation. In a situation where a surface has dissociable groups, cation binding and therefore surface charge changes self-consistently due to the proximity of another surface.[5] There is now not only a force due to surface-induced liquid structure, but the force depends too on liquid-induced surface structure. (The liquid is here the primitive electrolyte, with the water treated as if passive.)

Experiments over the past few years have confirmed the classical theories of van der Waals and electrostatic forces at 'large' distances.[4] This is to be expected. Liquid structure reflects the granularity of matter, unimportant far from a surface or a solute molecule, and water can be treated as a continuum at low enough salt concentration. The answer to the question of how large is large turns out for water to be somewhere about and less than 50 Å, depending on the surface. Much more interesting is that new experiments[6] have revealed a rich diversity of behaviour and dramatically new phenomena of obvious importance to biophysical problems. Many of these new results are described qualitatively by new theoretical developments which embrace the 'civilized' model[7,8] or extension of older ideas about 'hydration'. Hydration forces dominate interactions below 30 Å, depending on the surface, can be attractive or repulsive, depending critically on pH and cation concentration.[4] Like the double-layer forces with which they are inextricably entangled, they are par excellence forces due to surface-induced liquid structure, accessible and comprehensible only within the civilized model which admits that matter is made up of molecules, and that thin liquid films can change the nature of surfaces.

Van der Waals forces

To see how older theories and experiments have been modified it is useful to maintain the fiction that in water a decomposition into several kinds of force is permissible. Lifshitz theory[2] which appeared 26 years ago represented a truly major advance which did more than finally put numbers to the Hamaker[9] constant. Subject to the validity of the primitive model (a point repeatedly stressed by Hamaker and

Lifshitz, and ignored) the theory showed that the interaction energy between surfaces was very much more complicated and subtle than the simpler familiar form $E = -A/12\pi l^2$ based on two-body summation of dispersion forces. Included in the theory which relied on macroscopic dielectric data were extremely delicate effects:[3] Many-body forces not accessible through earlier theories; effects of temperature, which dominate forces in biophysical systems; retardation, which gradually damps out ultraviolet contributions beyond 40–50 Å, infrared contributions reflecting dipole-induced dipole correlations due to intramolecular vibrations, spatial dispersion, which can give rise to very long-range forces between long molecules, non-additive effects of different geometries. The highly cooperative strong temperature dependent forces which dominated interactions in biological systems (low Hamaker constant), exhibited qualitatively those features expected of the hydrophobic interaction.[10] These new temperature-dependent forces were screened by addition of salt, an observation only recently confirmed which bears on salting-in and salting-out phenomena. (This effect shows immediately that van der Waals and double-layer forces are intimately coupled.) The Hamaker constant is not constant but, especially in water–oil systems, a very complicated function of surface separation. All these things are known and understood. Germane to the thesis of this paper, however, are several matters which were overlooked:

(a) Below distances of 30–50 Å interaction forces cannot generally be computed to an accuracy of more than a factor of 2, because dielectric data at the far ultraviolet frequencies required is simply not available.[3,8] Claims that continuum theories describe interactions to contact deserve some scepticism.

(b) Extrapolation of Hamaker or Lifshitz theory down to atomic separations to compute surface-free energies of simple hydrocarbon liquids, as had been done by several authors,[11] is not permissible, and highly misleading. Such phenomenological descriptions of hydrocarbon interfacial energies are useful, but depend on the 8th power of an unknown molecular cut-off distance.[8] The density profile is important, as can be seen by applying the same methods to liquid argon.[8]

(c) Surface forces are intrinsically *many-body* forces, and cannot be computed accurately via methods of liquid state statistical mechanics using two-body molecular potentials, e.g. one can deduce quite rigorously from Lifshitz theory that for two solute molecules (2) immersed in a simple liquid (2) of density ρ_1, whose molecules interact via dispersion forces only, the potential of mean force is[7]

$$W_{22}(r) = \frac{3\hbar}{\pi r^6} \int \frac{d\xi}{\varepsilon_1^2} [\alpha_2 + \rho_1\alpha_1 \int h_{21}(r) \, d^3r]^2, \tag{1}$$

where $\alpha_j = \alpha_j(i\xi)$ are molecular polarizabilities, h_{21} measures the adsorption excess of solvent (1) about a solute molecule (2) and $\varepsilon_1 \simeq 1 + 4\pi\rho_1\alpha_1$ is the dielectric constant of the solvent. If we use a two-body force description and derive the corresponding result from statistical mechanics, the factor ε_1^2 reflecting many-body forces is missing. For the special case of small solutes at large distances Lifshitz theory does reflect liquid structure implicitly—through $h_{21}(r)$. The theory breaks down at small distances, because the weak overlap approximation implicit in perturbation theory fails. With temperature-dependent van der Waals forces in water it is clear that even the qualitative form of interactions is not remotely accessible through two-body force summation.

(d) An indication of when the primitive model breaks down can be found as follows: Imagine (Figure 2(b)) two half-spaces of a liquid (2) separated by another liquid (1), e.g. an oil–water system. These two liquids are immiscible and there will be a density profile at each surface. Choose the 2–1 interface to be the Gibbs dividing surface of species 2 (G_2) whose separation is $X = l + 2\tau$. The actual density profile for each species can be replaced by a step function uniform up to the Gibbs dividing surface of each species. Denote their separation by τ. Then the system can be regarded as a triple film in which the region τ is a vacuum. The energy of interaction is then (approximately)

$$\begin{aligned}E(X) &= -\frac{1}{12\pi}\left(\frac{A_{22}}{X^2} - \frac{2A_{21}}{(X-\tau)^2} + \frac{A_{11}}{(X-2\tau)^2}\right) \\ &\simeq -\frac{1}{12\pi}\left(\frac{[A_{22} - 2A_{21} + A_{11}]}{X^2} - \frac{4\tau(A_{21} - A_{11}) + \cdots}{X^3}\right).\end{aligned} \tag{2}$$

If the spaces (2) were hard walls so that l is well-defined, an identical expression can be derived rigorously from statistical mechanics, and τ is related to adsorption excesses. The formula is only qualitatively correct—because of restriction to two-body forces, but τ can be estimated from techniques of liquid state physics to be of the order of a molecular diameter at least. The first term represents the continuum result, and the second tells us how rapidly that result breaks down and goes over to a different force law at small distances. If we substitute

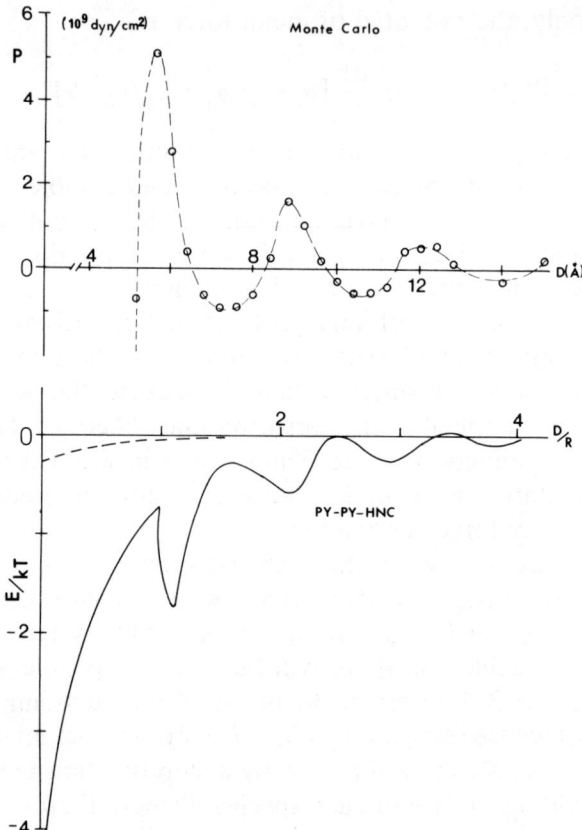

Figure 4 Monte Carlo calculations of the force and theoretical estimates of the energy per unit area between hard walls separated by a Lennard-Jones liquid.[7] Beyond about 6–10 molecular diameters (~50 Å) the continuum results take over

typical Hamaker constants, we see that the second term is as large as the first (and the continuum result totally invalid) at distances around 10 to 20 molecular diameters. The actual force law which takes over at these distances can be roughly deduced from techniques of liquid state physics. For Lennard-Jones or hard sphere fluids between hard walls, the results are as indicated (Figure 4). Such theoretical computations are severely limited, apart from their restriction to two-body forces, but they do indicate that continuum theories can be grossly erroneous at distances less than 30–50 Å. Subsequently this was confirmed by the remarkable experiments of Horn and Israelachvili who measured

Surface forces in biological systems

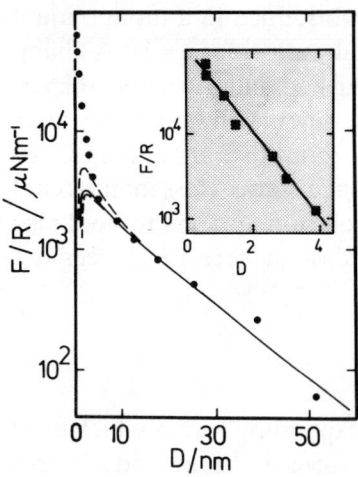

Figure 5 Experimental measurements[6] of force and energy per unit area between molecularly smooth mica plates separated by the liquid octamethylcyclotetrasiloxane, which is essentially a hard sphere of diameter 9–10 Å. Measured oscillations extend to and merge into usual continuum van der Waals force (dotted curve) only after about eleven diameters. (b) The nett force plotted on a reduced scale

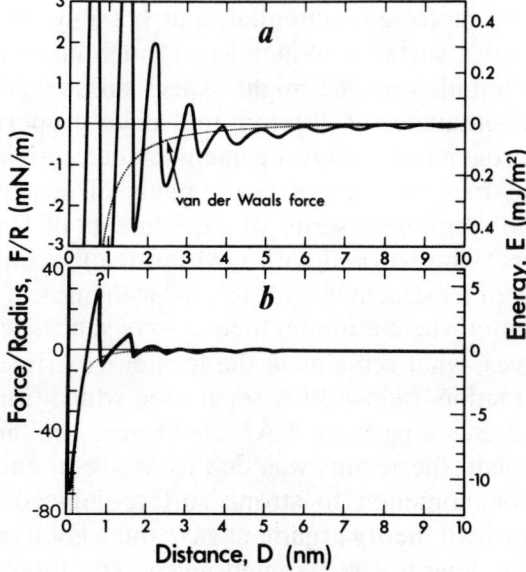

Figure 6 Forces measured[4] between mica surfaces in 5×10^{-4} M NaCl solution at pH 8.9 (●). The exact DLVO theory including surface charge regulation is shown at the full line and the upper and lower dashed lines are for constant charge and potential, respectively. The nett exponential hydration force (decay length ~ 9 Å) is shown in the inset. Earlier results with lipid membranes[6] are discussed by Rand, pp. 140–143

oscillatory forces between molecularly smooth mica in a model liquid (Figure 5). The liquid has nearly spherical molecules (≈ 10 Å diameter) which interact only via hard core repulsion and attractive dispersion forces. Together with their earlier experiments on liquid crystals,[12] and on cyclohexane, they do show that primitive model approximations to van der Waals forces break down at distances less than around 10 or more molecular diameters. That conclusion appears to hold also for fluid (biological) surfaces in water, although here the forces are monotonic[6] (Figure 6).

Hydration forces

Next in a logical development are the corresponding forces which exist in water—free from the complications of surface charge and electrolyte. The oscillations in surface forces discussed above reflect the organization imposed on the liquid by a surface due to the hard core repulsion of the molecular potential, and possibly by the hard wall nature of the mica surfaces. Water has a much more open structure than a simple liquid, and one might expect surface-induced order to reflect the predominance of different molecular properties like polarization, or hydrogen bond rearrangements in determining distribution functions. The first accurate measurements of structural forces in water were the continuing series of experiments of Rand, Parsegian and co-workers[6] who worked with (zwitterionic) lecithin multilayers, and later those of Israelachvili and Adams[4] with mica. If van der Waals forces—calculated via continuum theory—are subtracted out from the measured curves, what remains in the former experiments is a strong repulsive interaction, below 30 Å separation which fitted to an exponential, had decay length of 2 Å. The forces are monotonic! An attempt to explain the results was due to Marčelja and Radić,[13] who ascribed the phenomenon to strong surface-induced dipolar orientation. A mean-field theory argument gave out a good description provided the decay length was assumed given. The theory had obvious and admitted deficiencies, but represented an important advance, capturing for the first time the idea of surface-induced structural forces. The same theoretical ideas later saw good service in elucidating similar problems which abound in hydrophobic and hydrophilic solutions.[10,14] The important observation is that solute–solute interactions cannot be described in terms of primitive models. There are difficulties with interpretation of the multilayer experiments because it is hard to disentangle the supposed surface force (due to water removal on compression) from a consequent induced lateral compression of the multilayer head-group and hydrocarbon moieties. The forces operating between multilayer surfaces are nonetheless real, repulsive, and several orders of magnitude larger than any continuum electrostatic forces. A complementary set of experiments due to Pashley and

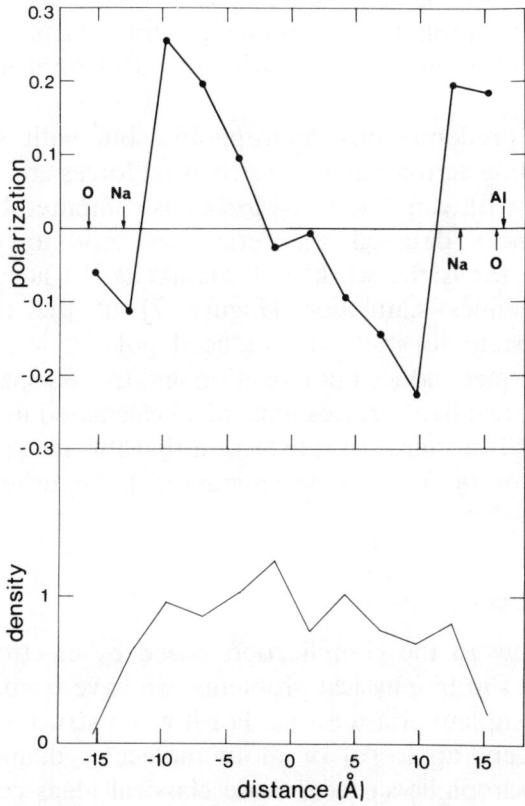

Figure 7 Molecular dynamics calculation[13] of polarization and density profiles ST 2 water between mica surfaces. The polarization is displayed as a fraction of the polarization value for fully oriented water dipoles at bulk water density, while density is measured relative to bulk density. The bin size, i.e. the distance between successive layers, is 2.76 Å which approximately corresponds to the distance between successive molecular layers. Since the system is small and not yet fully equilibriated there is substantial scatter in the data

Israelachvili[6] with surfactant bilayers adsorbed on mica again shows strong hydration forces, roughly exponential, with decay length around 3–8 Å, depending on surfactant concentration. The strength of the force, however, is somewhat less than those observed by Rand and Parsegian, an observation which presumably reflects the different head-groups in the mica and bilayer surfaces. The origin of the forces here is presumably different. If the bilayers are replaced by monolayers, thereby altering the nature of the interacting surfaces from hydrophilic to hydrophobic, the repulsive structural force disappears and is apparently replaced by an attractive structural force of quite different form.

With mica, predominantly hydrophobic, but with some surface dipoles interacting across water any structural forces are either absent, or comparable with van der Waals forces as computed by continuum theory. The sole detailed theoretical attempt to model these phenomena so far is the work of Gruen *et al*.[13] who carried out a molecular dynamics simulation (Figure 7) of the charge mica–water–mica system to study the induced polarization profile. The decay of the surface-induced polarization and the associated repulsive forces between two like surfaces have been calculated in detail for the ice structure. It is a source of satisfaction that this result confirms the mean field theoretic ideas, which augurs well for future theoretical understanding.

Electrostatic forces

If we come now to the complication posed by electrolyte, and by charged surfaces in biophysical problems, we have from a theoretical viewpoint, a complete disaster area. For if water structure can extend, as we have seen, up to 10 or more molecular diameters from a charged, or hydrophilic surface, those classical ideas concerning the double-layer embodied in Figure 8 must be inadmissible. Words like Stern layers, zeta potential, outer and inner Helmholtz planes, capacitance of the inner layer, dielectric constant profile, discreteness of charge effects, ionic hydration must be viewed with extreme suspicion. Fortunately there have been some important recent theoretical and experimental developments which do throw a deal of light on the problem. The situation has been reviewed elsewhere, but in summary form:

(1) In DLVO theory a balance between van der Waals and electro-

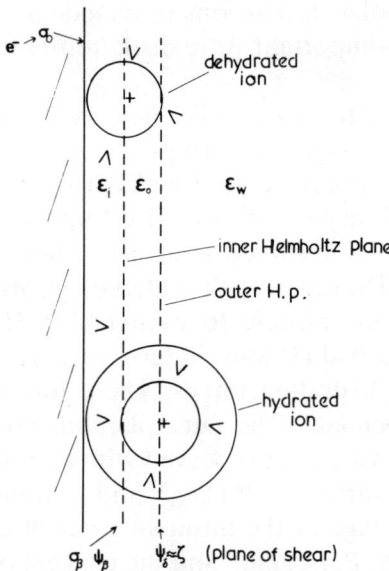

Figure 8 Conventional picture of the double-layer as developed for the mercury–water interface

static forces occurs at secondary minimum distances typically of the order of the Debye screening length, for 1:1 electrolytes, $\kappa^{-1} \simeq 8$ Å (0.1 M), 30 Å (10^{-2} M), 100 Å (10^{-3} M), with many interesting concentrations in colloid science centred around 10^{-2}–10^{-3} M. This corresponds to distances 30 Å $\lesssim \kappa^{-1} \lesssim$ 100 Å, and here the classical theories are expected to be almost correct. This is borne out by experiment. For biological systems the continuum theories are certainly incorrect.

(2) A careful analysis[15] of bulk electrolyte activities confirms that the primitive model description of ions is a reasonable approximation for simple 1:1 and 2:1 electrolytes like LiCl, NaBr, $CaCl_2$. It breaks down for CsCl, and is totally erroneous for ions like NO_3^-, SO_4^-, Al^{+++}.

(3) Extensive theoretical work by Chan and others[16] on both bulk electrolytes and of the double-layer within the extended confines of a civilized model, have revealed much new information on the concepts of ionic hydration, breakdown of continuum solvent approximation, meaning of the Stern layer, Born energy and polarization profiles at interfaces. The models studied are ion–dipole mixtures with the ions represented as hard charged spheres and the solvent as hard spheres

with embedded dipoles. Extensions to include quadrupole interaction and polarizability—important to realistic representation of water are in progress.

(4) The experimental work of Pashley and Israelachvili[4,6] discussed by the latter in this Symposium brings to order a wealth of confusion, and is of much importance to biophysical problems. Briefly, for mica–water–mica systems, with added H^+ up to pH 4, no short-range hydration repulsion is observed and the surfaces come into primary minimum contact. However, with added electrolyte, at a predictable critical concentration, specific to each cation (Figure 6), hydrated cations replace adsorbed H^+ ions, induce water structure, and give rise to strong repulsive hydration forces. These forces have a magnitude which is cation dependent. The same phenomenon is now recognized to be ubiquitous, having been observed with air bubbles,[17] latex coagulation,[18] mercury,[19] surfactant,[20] clay,[21] and lecithin surfaces.[6] There is here a fruitful marriage of the intuitive ideas of charge regulation of the author and V. A. Parsegian,[5] and the concept of ion-induced water structure. The work on multilayer surfaces of Rand and Parsegian is obviously of the highest importance and is discussed separately by Rand.

Future developments

Future theoretical progress can be expected on several lines: (a) formal statistical mechanics of model systems; (b) approximate statistical mechanics of model systems; (b) approximate statistical mechanics of real electrolytes. In summary, we have probably gone about as far as it is reasonably possible theoretically given the present limited understanding of water. In biophysics, what is needed now is theoretical work on head-group interactions, which ultimately takes us back to solutions.

References

1. E. J. Verwey and J. Th. G. Overbeek, *Theory of the Stability of Lyophobic Colloids*, Elsevier, New York (1948). B. V. Derjaguin and L. D. Landau, *Acta Phys. Chem.*, **14**, 633 (1941); *J. Exp. Theor. Phys. (USSR)*, **11**, 802 (1941), reprinted **15**, 662 (1945).
2. E. M. Lifshitz, *J. Exp. Theor. Phys. (USSR)*, **29**, 94 (1955); *Sov. Phys. JETP*, **2**, 73 (1956). I. E. Dzyaloshinskii, E. M. Lifshitz and L. P. Pitaevskii, *Adv. Phys.*, **10**, 165 (1961).

3. J. Mahanty and B. W. Ninham, *Dispersion Forces*, Academic Press, London–New York (1976).
4. J. N. Israelachvili and G. E. Adams, *Nature*, **262**, 774 (1976); *J.C.S. Far. Trans. II*, **74**, 975 (1978). R. M. Pashley, *J. Coll. Interface Sci.* (2 papers, in press, 1981).
5. B. W. Ninham and V. A. Parsegian, *J. Theor. Biol.*, **31**, 405 (1971). T. W. Healy and L. R. White, *Adv. Coll. Interface Sci.*, **9**, 303 (1978).
6. V. A. Parsegian, N. Fuller and R. P. Rand, *Proc. Natl. Acad. Sci. (U.S.A.)*, **76**, 2750 (1979). R. G. Horn and J. N. Israelachvili, *Chem. Phys. Letts.*, **71**, 192 (1980); *J. Chem. Phys.* (in press, 1981). R. M. Pashley and J. N. Israelachvili, *Colloids & Surfaces*, **2**, 169 (1981).
7. D. J. Mitchell, B. W. Ninham and B. A. Pailthorpe, *J.C.S. Far. Trans. II*, **74**, 1098 (1978); *J. Coll. Interface Sci.*, **64**, 194 (1978). D. Y. C. Chan, D. J. Mitchell, B. W. Ninham and B. A. Pailthorpe, *J.C.S. Far. Trans. II*, **76**, 776 (1980). J. E. Lane and T. W. Spurling, *Chem. Phys. Letts.*, **67**, 107 (1979). I. Snook and W. van Megan, *J.C.S. Far. Trans. II*, **75**, 1095 (1979); *J. Chem. Phys.*, **72**, 2907 (1980).
8. See also B. W. Ninham, *J. Phys. Chem.*, **84**, 1423 (1980), for recent review, and *Adv. Colloid Interface Sci.*, Proceedings IUTAM-IUPAC Symposium on Interaction of Particles in Colloidal Dispersions, Canberra (1981).
9. H. C. Hamaker, *Physica*, **4**, 1058 (1937).
10. D. Y. C. Chan, D. J. Mitchell, B. W. Ninham and B. A. Pailthorpe, in *Water, A Comprehensive Treatise* (ed. F. Franks), Plenum Press, New York (1979), vol. 6.
11. See e.g. F. M. Fowkes, *J. Phys. Chem.*, **66**, 832 (1962); **72**, 3700 (1968). R. J. Good and E. Elbing, *Ind. Eng. Chem.*, **62**, 54 (1978). J. N. Israelachvili, *J.C.S. Far. Trans. II*, **69**, 1729 (1973).
12. R. G. Horn and J. N. Israelachvili, *J. Physique*, **42**, 39 (1981).
13. S. Marčelja and N. Radić, *Chem. Phys. Letts.*, **42**, 129 (1976). S. Marčelja, *Croatica Chem. Acta*, **49**, 347 (1977). D. W. R. Gruen, S. Marčelja and B. A. Pailthorpe, *Chem. Phys. Letts.* (submitted).
14. S. Marčelja, D. J. Mitchell, B. W. Ninham and M. J. Sculley, *J.C.S. Far. Trans. II*, **73**, 630 (1977).
15. B. A. Pailthorpe, D. J. Mitchell and B. W. Ninham, *J. Phys. Chem.* (to appear).
16. S. A. Adelman and J. M. Deutch, *J. Chem. Phys.*, **60**, 3935 (1974). G. N. Patey and J. P. Valleau, *J. Chem. Phys.*, **63**, 2334 (1975). J. S. Høye and G. Stell, *J. Chem. Phys.*, **68**, 4145 (1978). D. Y. C. Chan, D. J. Mitchell and B. W. Ninham, *J. Chem. Phys.*, **70**, 2946 (1979). D. Y. C. Chan, D. J. Mitchell, B. W. Ninham and B. A. Pailthorpe, *J. Chem. Phys.*, **69**, 691 (1980). S. L. Carnie, D. Y. C. Chan, D. J. Mitchell and B. W. Ninham, *J. Chem. Phys.*, **73**, 2949 (1980). D. Y. C. Chan, D. J. Mitchell and B. W. Ninham, *J. Chem. Phys.*, **72**, 5159 (1980). S. L. Carnie, D. Y. C. Chan, D. J. Mitchell and B. W. Ninham, *J. Chem. Phys.*, **74**, 1472 (1981).
17. R. R. Lessard and S. I. Ziemanski, *Ind. Eng. Chem. Fundam.*, **10**, 260 (1971).
18. T. W. Healy, A. Homola, R. O. James and R. J. Hunter, *Farad. Disc.*, **65**, 156 (1978).
19. S. Usui and T. Yamasaki, *J. Phys. Chem.*, **71**, 3195 (1967); *J. Coll. Interface Sci.*, **29**, 629 (1969).
20. J. S. Clunie, J. F. Goodman and C. P. Odgen, *Nature*, **216**, 1204 (1967).
21. H. van Olphen, *Clays & Clay Minerals*, **2**, 419 (1954); *An Introduction to Clay Colloid Chemistry*, Wiley–Interscience (1963).

The osmotic properties of haemoglobin under physiological conditions—implications for the osmotic behaviour of red cells

Bernhard Wittmann and **Gerolf Gros**
Universitätsklinikum Essen, Germany

Summary

We have investigated the osmotic coefficients, ϕ, of human haemoglobin at concentrations up to 10 millimolal under physiological conditions. Our values of ϕ are higher than previously published data at all concentrations of haemoglobin studied. A significant increase in ϕ with increasing ionic strength was observed. The volume response of red cells, as predicted by these values of ϕ, was calculated and compared with experimental data.

Volume changes of red blood cells exposed to media of varying tonicities are less than expected from van't Hoff's law.[1] Several attempts have been made to attribute this non-ideal osmotic behaviour to the osmotic coefficient of haemoglobin, ϕ_{Hb} (i.e. the ratio of real haemoglobin osmolality to haemoglobin molality), which increases progressively with increasing haemoglobin concentration.[2] However, the values of ϕ_{Hb} necessary to describe the observed volume changes[3] are significantly higher than the values of ϕ_{Hb} measured by Adair.[4] But, as Adair performed his experiments far from the physiological situation, the measurements of red cell volume alterations and ϕ_{Hb} are not strictly comparable. We have therefore reinvestigated the osmotic properties of haemoglobin under physiological conditions.

We determined the osmotic pressure of human haemoglobin at concentrations up to 10 millimolal in an electronic membrane osmometer with a short time constant (Fa. Knauer, Berlin). From these measurements we calculated the osmotic coefficients of haemoglobin, ϕ_{Hb}, and evaluated their role for the osmotic behaviour of red cells.

Results

Figure 1 shows the osmotic coefficients of haemoglobin, derived from osmotic pressure measurements of human HbCO at $T = 37\,°C$, ionic strength $\mu = 0.15$ and pH = 7.0 (isoelectric). It is obvious that our values of ϕ_{Hb} are significantly higher than the values of Adair (1929), which were obtained from sheep blood at $0\,°C$, $\mu = 0.2$ and pH = 7.8.

To test whether these differences in ϕ_{Hb} are due to differences in the experimental conditions we determined ϕ_{Hb} at $T = 27\,°C$ (unfortunately our osmometer does not allow measurements at lower temperatures) and found only slightly lower values than those measured at $37\,°C$. Variation of pH between pH 6.5 and 7.5 at $\mu = 0.15$ and low protein concentrations (and therefore negligible Donnan effect) did not result in alterations of ϕ_{Hb}, nor did the variation of pH between 6.0 and 8.0 at high protein concentrations and $\mu = 2.5$ (where also no Donnan effect exists). 2,3-DPG, which might have been present in the haemoglobin preparation used by Adair, when added in concentrations of 4 and 8 mM respectively to our haemoglobin solutions, did not change the observed values of ϕ_{Hb}. The only parameter which was of significant influence on ϕ_{Hb} was variation in the ionic strength.

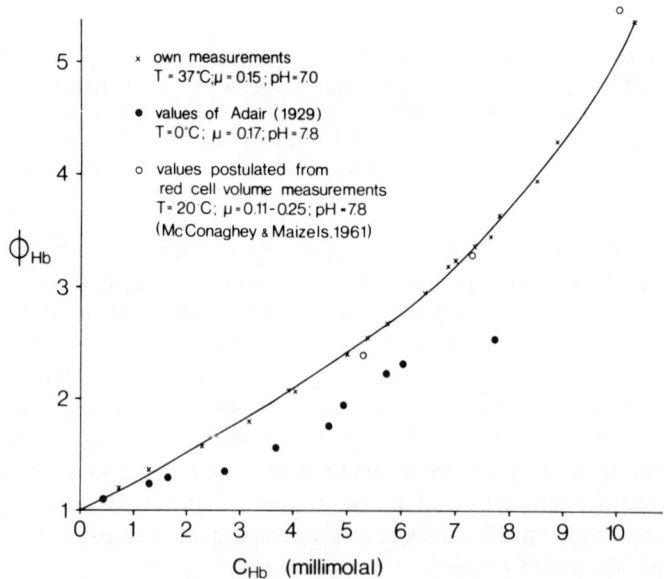

Figure 1 The osmotic coefficient of haemoglobin, Φ_{Hb}, at various molal concentrations of haemoglobin. Our values of Φ_{Hb} (x) are significantly higher than the values estimated by Adair (●). The open circles show the values of Φ_{Hb} postulated by McConaghey and Maizels (1961) from red cell volume measurements

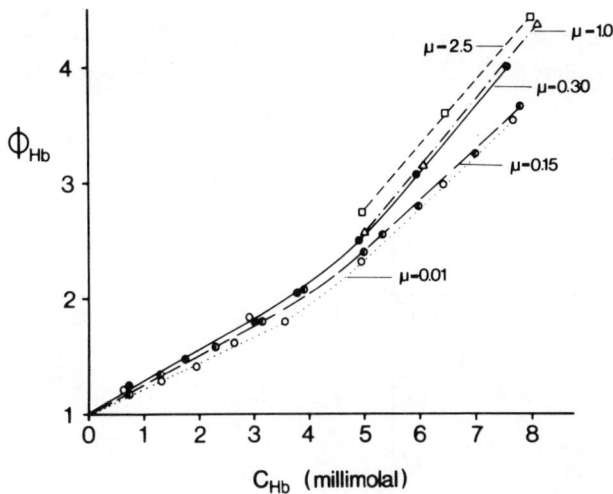

Figure 2 Variation of Φ_{Hb} with ionic strength, μ, at various molal concentrations of haemoglobin. Note that there is only small increase in Φ_{Hb} at ionic strengths higher than $\mu = 0.30$

As shown in Figure 2, ϕ_{Hb} increases with ionic strength when the latter increases from $\mu = 0.01$ to $\mu = 2.5$. At physiological concentrations of haemoglobin the most pronounced increase in ϕ_{Hb} occurs between $\mu = 0.15$ and $\mu = 0.30$, a range of ionic strength which may well occur in the red cell under osmotic stress. It appears from our measurements that the osmotic properties of haemoglobin are mainly influenced by variations in ionic strength and to a smaller extent by alterations in temperature. If the temperature dependence of ϕ_{Hb} is the same between 0 °C and 27 °C as it is between 27 °C and 37 °C, both effects fail to explain the observed differences to the results of Adair.

Conclusions

What are the volume responses of red cells predicted by the osmotic behaviour of haemoglobin? The results of our calculations are shown in Figure 3. It is evident from the figure that at hypotonic situations ($\pi/\pi_0 < 1$) the observed volume changes of red cells can be well described by our predictions. In the hypertonic range ($\pi/\pi_0 > 1$) however, the degree of deviation from ideal osmotic behaviour appears to be significantly smaller than what has been measured directly by several authors.

It should be noted that our calculations are based upon values of ϕ_{Hb} which hold for $\mu = 0.15$. In the course of cell shrinkage, however, ionic strength

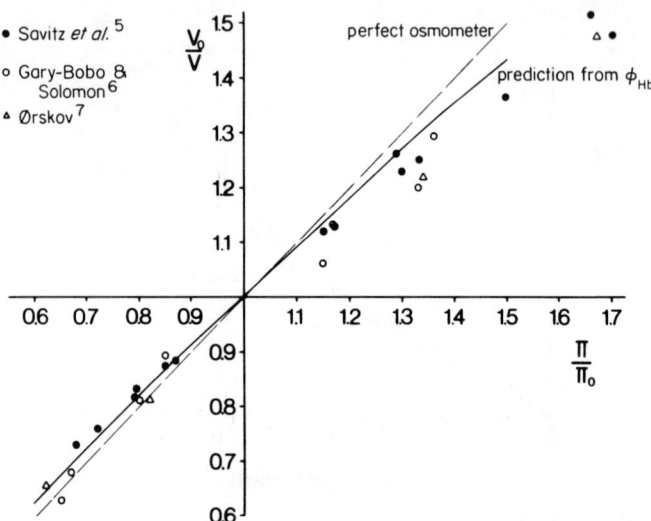

Figure 3 Osmotic behaviour of red cells at various medium osmolalities. V/V_o is the water volume ratio of red cells (V_o = red water volume at isotonicity). π/π_o, is the osmolal ratio (π_o = 290 m OsM). The broken line indicates perfect osmotic behaviour. The curve represents the osmotic behaviour as predicted by the values of Φ_{Hb} from Figure 1. The different symbols refer to red cell volume measurements of various authors (see insert)

within the red cell will increase (e.g. at $\pi/\pi_0 = 1.5$ to $\mu = 0.21$) which will lead to an increase in ϕ_{Hb} as can be seen in Figure 2. The rise in ϕ_{Hb} then results in a greater deviation from osmotic ideality. But some more data on ϕ_{Hb} at high ionic strength and high haemoglobin concentrations are necessary to quantitatively describe this effect.

We conclude that the osmotic behaviour of red cells at hypotonic medium osmolalities can be explained in terms of the osmotic properties of haemoglobin. Whether the effect of ionic strength on the osmotic behaviour of haemoglobin can explain the osmotic response of red cells placed in hypertonic media deserves further investigation.

References

1. E. Ponder, *Hemolysis and Related Phenomena*, New York (1948).
2. D. A. T. Dick and L. M. Lowenstein, *Proc. Roy. Soc.*, **B148**, 241 (1958).
3. P. D. McConaghey and M. Maizels, *J. Physiol.*, **155**, 28 (1961).
4. G. S. Adair, *Proc. Roy. Soc.*, **A126**, 16 (1929).
5. D. Savitz, V. W. Sidel and A. K. Solomon, *J. Gen. Physiol.*, **48** (1), 79 (1964).
6. C. M. Gary-Bobo and A. K. Solomon, *J. Gen. Physiol.*, **52**, 825 (1968).
7. S. L. Ørskov, *Acta Physiol. Scand.*, **12**, 202 (1947).

NMR relaxation and water dynamics at the protein surface

Robert G. Bryant
University of Minnesota, USA

Summary

Nuclear magnetic resonance techniques have been used for the study of water dynamics at macromolecular surfaces. The interpretation of data collected is discussed in the context of appropriate existing relaxation theory.

Nuclear magnetic resonance (NMR) relaxation rates are related directly to the correlation times that characterize motion of the observed molecule and thus provide a powerful means for studying water dynamics at protein and other macromolecular surfaces.[1] The dynamical problem may be simplified if bulk rotation of the protein is eliminated as in the powder or crystal, but the nuclear spin relaxation remains complicated by efficient magnetic coupling between the macromolecule spins and the usually more mobile water spins.[2] Study of both the water and protein relaxation over a wide temperature range has demonstrated the importance of this efficient cross relaxation at all temperatures, though the direction of transfer depends on temperature and composition. At low temperatures where water motion is slower than methyl rotation, the water spins add to the relaxation load of the protein methyl groups thus lengthening the apparent protein proton T_1. At temperatures above approximately 200 K water motion is sufficiently rapid to provide an efficient relaxation path for both water and protein protons. The addition of the protein proton relaxation load to the water protons effectively lengthens the water relaxation time: however, careful measurements using selective pulses provide a straightforward though cumbersome means for extracting the more fundamental relaxation parameters from the coupled spin systems. These procedures yield a transfer rate, and two other rates that approximate better the relaxation rates of the water and the protein spins, though this identification cannot be strictly valid.[3] Interpretation of the relaxation parameters has focused on deducing correlation times that bring observations into agreement with a relaxation theory such as that by Bloembergen, Purcell and Pound appropriate to isotropic diffusional motion.[4] To get any sort of agreement with the isotropic theory it has been customary to postulate a distribution of correlation times for the water motion. In the present case such a strategy leads to broad distributions and activation parameters that correspond to values in excess of the desorption enthalpies, an important difficulty.

Relaxation of the assumption that motion of water is isotropic at the surface represents a different type of distribution of the parameters in the relaxation equation. Anisotropic motion implies that rotation about one axis is faster than about others; hence, there are at least two correlation times in the problem. The orientation of the rotation axes in the system may not all be identical, hence, a distribution of the effective strength of the interaction is also implied. In the present case a model in which water rotates rapidly about a primary hydrogen bond at the surface (either O- or H-bonded), and rotates more slowly about the other two directions also fails to agree quantitatively with the data, but it does solve the difficulty of very short T_2 values usually found for such systems and brings the activation energy required well below the desorption enthalpy. To account for the NMR data, effects of both anisotropic motion and a *small* distribution of at least two primary correlation times which may differ by an order of magnitude or more, are suggested. The picture of the adsorbed water suggested by the NMR data is therefore one where water rotates rapidly about a unique, presumably a hydrogen bond axis and more slowly about the other axes which would also permit translation on the surface. Complete orientational averaging implied by lack of ^{2}H quadrupole splittings must occur on a time scale of the order of a microsecond.[5]

References

1. R. G. Bryant, *Ann. Rev. Phys. Chem.*, **29**, 167 (1978).
2. H. T. Edzes and E. T. Samulski, *Nature (Lond.)*, **265**, 521 (1977).
3. W. M. Shirley and R. G. Bryant, *J. Amer. Chem. Soc.*, submitted (1981).
4. H. A. Resing, *Adv. Mol. Relox. Pruc.*, **1**, 109 (1967).
5. B. Borah and R. G. Bryant, unpublished results.

Structural water of phospholipid bilayers. A realistic calorimetry study

Lisbeth Ter-Minassian-Saraga and Georgette Madelmont
Université Paris V, France

Summary

This poster presents an original interpretation[1] of thermograms obtained with the differential scanning calorimeter DSC Du Pont de Nemours 990-910. The samples consisted of planar multibilayers of either PI, the natural (wheat) acidic phosphatidylinositolmonophosphate, or DPPC, the synthetic amphoteric 1,2-dipalmitoyl-3sn-phosphatidylcholine, at various degrees of hydration. The results obtained using the present interpretation[1] and a previous one[2] are compared.

Our technique is presented in Figure 1. It is based on the use of equal amounts of water in both the sample and the reference cups. In Figure 2 the thermogram obtained by this technique is compared with the previous one.[2] The thermograms obtained for PI at various degrees of hydration are shown in Figure 3. Figure 4 shows the model used for the structural water: the water which constitutes the aqueous spacings between bilayers.

The bilayers are supposed to be quasi-planar. They interact through net forces (electrostatic, van der Waals, etc. . . . .) represented by the springs and determine the behaviour of the structural water.

Above 0 °C (Figure 4(a)) or below 0 °C (Figure 4(b)) the free energy of the interbilayer structural water is modified by the action of phospholipid molecules. This action is equivalent to a bilayer surface field of force. Its effect on the water free energy decreases with the distance y from the bilayer 'surface' following the power law (Equation (a1)) in the appendix, as suggested in (1, 3). In Figure 4(a), (b) and (c), the variation of the water free energy shift $\delta\bar{\mu}^w$ (from the bulk value) with y is shown at various temperatures. This variation involves that of the equilibrium position of the frozen melted structural water front, named $y = l$, with a temperature shift $\hat{T} = (T - 273.15)°$: see Equation (a2) and l_1, l_2, l_3 in Figure 4(c).

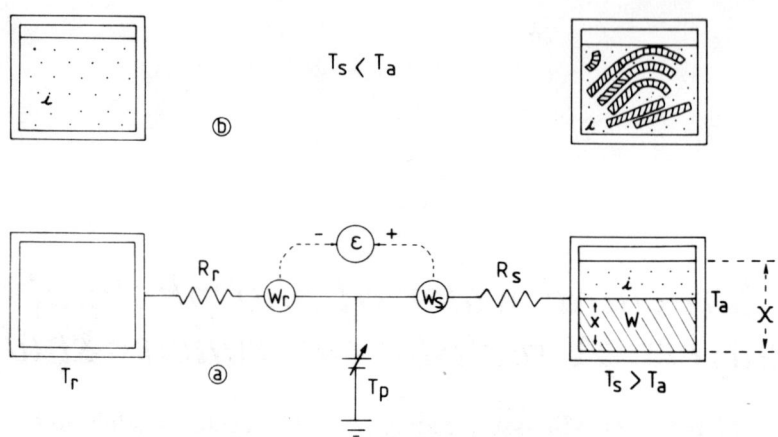

Figure 1 Ice melting by conventional DSC and by the present differential isothermal calorimetry. (a) Conventional DSC. Pure ice and water. $r \equiv$ reference (left); $s \equiv$ sample (right); T = holder temperature; T_p = temperature source; W, R power supply, thermal resistance; ε recorded differential power signal; $T_a = 0\,°C$; x = thickness of melted ice; $w \equiv$ water; $i \equiv$ ice. (b) Ice melting in a lamellar phase by the present differential isothermal calorimetry. The reference cup (left) contains ice or water. The sample cup (right) contains water and a lamellar phase. The temperature is below $T_a = 0\,°C$

The shape of the thermograms is obtained by noting that the net heat effect inside the sample δQ^s is the sum of various contributions (Equation (b1) and Equation (b2)) due to phase transitions, thermal expansion and increase in sample temperature. The area of the peak corresponding to melting of the frozen structural water (Equation (b3)) depends on the amount of structural water m_s, on the 'non-freezing' and 'non-melting' $(2l_0/L)$ percentage of this water and on its melting molar enthalpy L. In our technique (Figure 1 and Figure 2) m_s is obtained directly from the 'exothermic' peak located at 0 °C (Figure 1(c)). It is smaller than the calibration peak (Figure 1(a)) obtained with an empty cup upon the sample holder. The percentage $(2l_0/L)$ of non-freezing structural water is obtained from the value of L and the difference between the 'exothermic' peak at 0 °C and the broad endothermic one (located in the range of temperature shifts $\hat{T}_{max}$ and $\hat{T}_{min}$) in Figure 1(c). This value is very much dependent on the accuracy and performance of the DSC apparatus.

The value of L is obtained from the plots of thermograms (Figure 5) according to Equation (b2) where (dQ^s/dt) is the thermogram ordinate, $\hat{T}$ is the shift deduced from the corresponding temperature, read on the abscissa, and $\alpha = 2$. The plots in Figure 5 constitute controls of our interpretation which is verified only by planar lamellar systems. It is not verified by the hydrated

Structural water of phospholipid bilayers

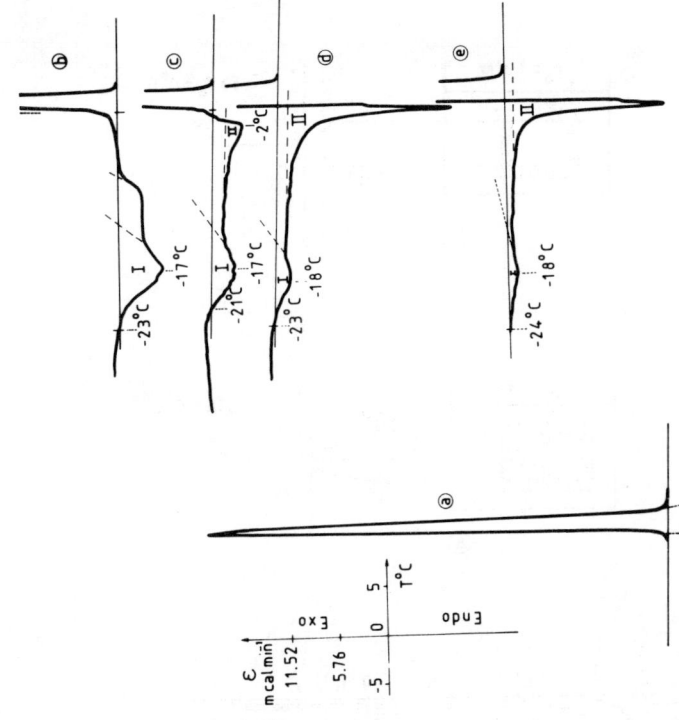

Figure 2 Thermograms for fully hydrated DPPC. Heating rate $2°$ min^{-1}. 50% (w/w) water. (a) 0.520 mg water in reference cup. Sample cup empty. (b) Conventional DSC thermogram: reference = empty cup; sample = 0.5 mg DPPC + 0.52 mg H$_2$O. (c) Our technique: (a) and (b) opposed. (d) DPPC chain melting transition and pretransition. $\hat{T}_{min}$ is the temperature shift at which all frozen structural water is melted. $\hat{T}_{max}$ is the temperature shift at which the frozen structural water at $y = l_0$ starts melting (see model in Figure 4)

Figure 3 Thermograms for PI. Heating rate = $2°$ min^{-1}. (a) Ice melting in reference cup; 0.44 mg water; sample cup empty. (b) Water 15% (w/w) in sample cup (2.5 mg PI + 0.44 mg H$_2$O) reference cup as in (a); (c) Water 20% (w/w) in sample cup (1.94 mg PI + 0.480 mg H$_2$O); reference cup 0.5 mg H$_2$O

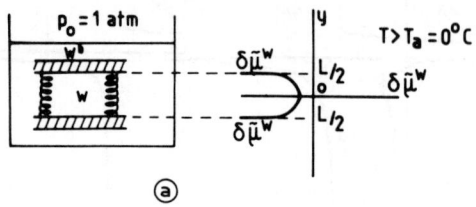

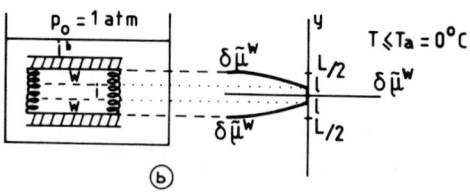

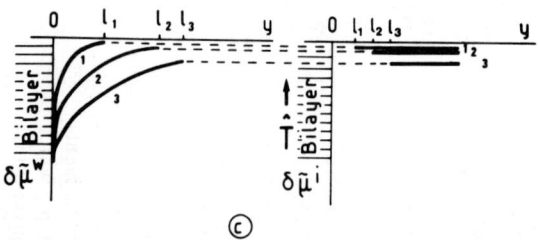

Figure 4 Model for hydrated lamellar systems and shift of free energy of water inside the aqueous separation at various temperatures. (a) w^b, w = bulk water, structural water (inside the aqueous spacings); L = width of aqueous spacing; y = distance from bilayer water interface. Springs: model for interbilayer force. $\delta\tilde{\mu}^w$ = shift of water molar free energy for structural water. (b) i^b, i = bulk ice, frozen structural water; frozen/melted structural water interface position at $y = 1$. (c) qualitative plots of $\delta\tilde{\mu}^w$ and $\delta\tilde{\mu}^i$ versus y at three temperatures, $T < 273.15$K. l_1, l_2, l_3 are corresponding equilibrium positions for the ice water front. When $\hat{T} \to \hat{T}_{max}$, $l \to l_0$ corresponding to the amount of non-freezing structural water (non-freezing in Table 1)

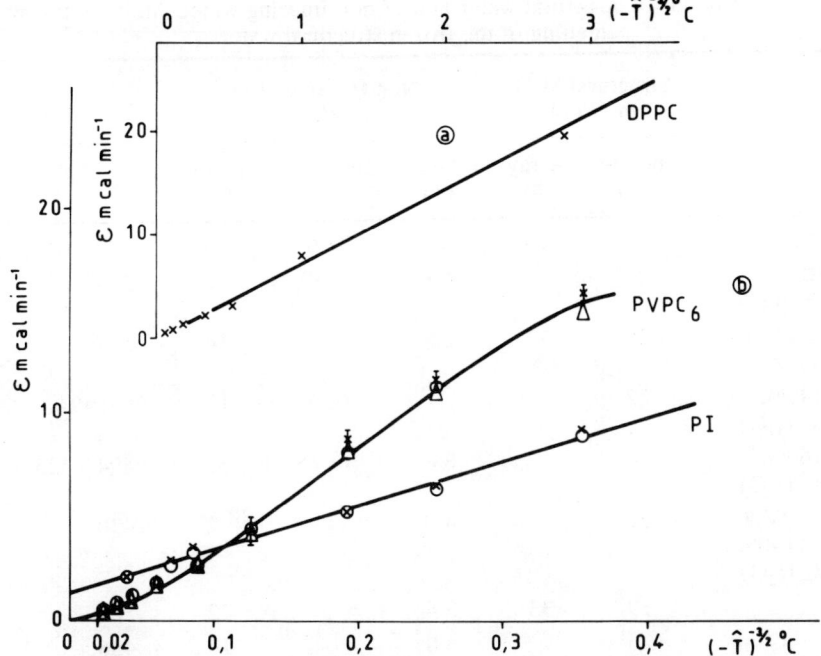

Figure 5 Plot of thermograms according to equation (b2). $dQ/dt = \varepsilon$ = differential power input; $-\hat{T}$ = ice fusion temperature depression (shift). (a) Fully hydrated DPPC (see Figure 2 and Table 1). (b) Polysoap PVPC6 + H_2O (60% water w/w) and fully hydrated PI + H_2O (60% water w/w) (see Table 1 and Figure 3)

polysoap PVPC 6 (2-methyl-5-vinyl-1-hexylpyridinium bromide), Figure 5(b).

In Table 1 the results obtained using the present interpretation and one in the line of reference (1) are compared. The amount of structural water m_s is compared to that obtained from X-ray studies.[4]

The conclusion is presented in Table 2.

Appendix

(a) *Structural Water*

$$\delta\tilde{\mu}_{T,p0} = -ay^{-\alpha}\left\{1 + \left(\frac{y}{L-y}\right)^{\alpha}\right\} = -ay^{-\alpha}\phi(L,l) \tag{a1}$$

Table 1 Amount of structural water and of non-freezing water. Molar enthalpy of melting of the frozen structural water

Fully hydrated systems	Structural H$_2$O mol/mol		Non-freezing H$_2$O mol/mol			L cal mol^{-1}	
	Thermo-gram	X-ray (4)	1st route (1)	2nd route (1)	previous (2)	1st	2nd
DPPC	21	19	3.4	1; 6	13	743	648; 626
DPPC + PVPC6 (1/1)	29		6.8		16	324	
DPPC + Ch (1/1)	20	23	2.8		14	517	
PI (40%, w/w, H$_2$O)	22			6; 6	15	564; 494	
PI (60%, w/w, H$_2$O)	40		8.8	6; 15	32	394	323; 338
PI + PVPC6 (1/1) (40%, w/w, H$_2$O)	21		4.0		2	1430	
EL	39	33	3.4		22	587	
EL + Ch (1/1)	26		4.0		16	486	
PVPC6 (40%, w/w, H$_2$O)	16				6		
Ch	9				5		

Hydration of DPPC samples (pure or mixed) and Ch: 50% (w/w) H$_2$O. Column 'previous': assuming $L = 1440$ cal mol^{-1}. PVPC 6 = poly(2-methyl-5-vinyl-1-hexylpyridinium bromide); EL = egg lecithin; Ch = cholesterol; PI = phosphatidylinositolmonophosphate (wheat).

The first route and the second route correspond to the two ways by which the amount of non-freezing water was deduced from the data: 1st route from the values of $\hat{T}_{min}$ and $\hat{T}_{max}$, and the expression $(2l_0/L) \simeq \sqrt{(\hat{T}_{min}/2\hat{T}_{max})}$ of (1); 2nd route is explained in the text.

solid/liquid transition at $T < 0$ °C; position of the interface at $T < 0$ °C: $y = 1$.

$$\frac{L}{T_a}\hat{T} + \frac{a}{l^\alpha}\phi(L, 1) = 0, \qquad T = T_a + \hat{T} \qquad (a2)$$

definition: $l = L/2$; $\hat{T} = \hat{T}_{min}$; $\hat{T}$ = 'cryoscopic' effect of surface forces.

(b) *Calorimetric (DSC) Measurements*

$$\delta Q^s = T\delta S_p = \underset{\text{transition}}{\delta Q} + \underset{\text{bil. expansion}}{\delta Q} + \underset{\text{(small)}}{C_{p,A,L,l}\, dT} \qquad (b1)$$

$$\left(\frac{dQ^s}{dt}\right)_{obs} = \dot{T}\left\{C_{p_0,A,L,l} - 2T\left(\frac{\partial\sigma}{\partial T}\right)_{p_0,A,L,l}\frac{dA}{dT} + AT\left(\frac{\partial\Pi}{\partial T}\right)_{p_0,A,L,l}\left(\frac{dL}{dT}\right)\right.$$

$$\left. + \underbrace{\frac{m_s L}{18\alpha}\left[\frac{\phi(L,1)}{\phi(L,2)}(-\hat{T}_{min})\right]^{1/\sigma}}_{\text{slope}} \underbrace{(-\hat{T})^{-\alpha+1/\alpha}}_{\text{variable}}\right\} \quad (b2)$$

$$\underbrace{Q^{s,w}}_{obs} = \underbrace{\frac{m_s L}{18}\left(1 - \sqrt{\frac{\hat{T}_{min}}{2\hat{T}_{max}}}\right)}_{\text{first route}} = \underbrace{\frac{m_s L}{18}\left(1 - \frac{2l_0}{L}\right)}_{\text{second route}} \quad (b3)$$

Percent (of freezing and melting water) $2l_0/L$.

Conclusions

Table 2

Past		Present
observed	← Q^s →	observed
assumed high, non-specific	← L →	determined small, specific to charge and fluidity
?	← m_s → (structured water)	observed amount
determined high, specific	← non-freezing water →	determined small, not very specific
?	← power law mechanism →	assumed and controlled
?	← power law parameter α →	determined

References

1. L. Ter-Minassian-Saraga and G. Madelmont, *J. Colloid Interface Sci.*, **81**, 369 (1981).
2. B. D. Ladbrooke, R. M. Williams and D. Chapman, *Biochim. Biophys. Acta*, **180**, 333 (1968).
3. R. P. Gilpin, *J. Colloid Interface Sci.*, **68**, 235 (1979).
4. R. P. Rand, *Ann. Rev. Biophys. Bioeng.*, **10**, 277 (1981).

Small angle scattering study of water bound to a protein

M. S. Lehmann and G. Zaccaï
Institut Laue-Langevin, Grenoble, France

Summary

Small angle neutron scattering measurements of papain in water (D_2O and H_2O), water–dimethylsulphoxide (D_2O–$(CH_3)_2SO$) and water–ethanol (D_2O–CH_3CH_2OD) have been used to estimate the extent of the region next to the protein which is inaccessible to the probe molecules. It is found that around 3/4 of the surface is directly accessible to ethanol and dimethylsulphoxide.

The method used resembles the standard method of contrast variation,[1] whereby two parameters are obtained as a function of solvent composition, the forward scattered intensity $I(O)$ and the radius of gyration, R_G.[2] From $I(O)$ the excess scattering length of the molecule can be extracted as $\sqrt{I(O)} = \Sigma b_i - \rho_s V$, where V is the 'molecular' volume and Σb_i is the sum of the scattering lengths inside this volume. The solvent density, ρ_s was varied by varying the content of ethanol or dimethylsulphoxide; we could thus obtain Σb_i and V.

The basis of the analysis lies in the interpretation of V. This volume is defined by a boundary around the molecule beyond which the solvent is homogeneous in composition. A simple picture of this is given in Figure 1. If the scattering density of the solvent (e.g. D_2O–dimethylsulphoxide) is much different from D_2O, then any group of water molecules irreplaceably bound to the molecules will, by this interpretation, be included in V. Assuming the partial volume of the molecule to be the same in H_2O and H_2O:ethanol mixtures, the volume of bound water can be derived. A similar calculation can be done for Σb_i.

Measurements were done on solutions holding up to 33% of ethanol or dimethylsulphoxide. Wavelengths were in the range of 4.5 Å to 10 Å. A measurement in H_2O was used to normalize the observations as the molecular

Small angle scattering study of water bound to a protein

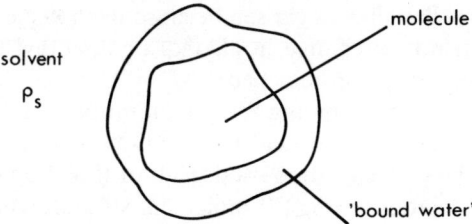

Figure 1 Example of molecule in a solvent ρ_s. The scattering density of the solvent is obtained from the mixture. Σb_i and V are summed for all points up to the boundary beyond which the solvent is homogeneous of density ρ_s This includes the bound water region

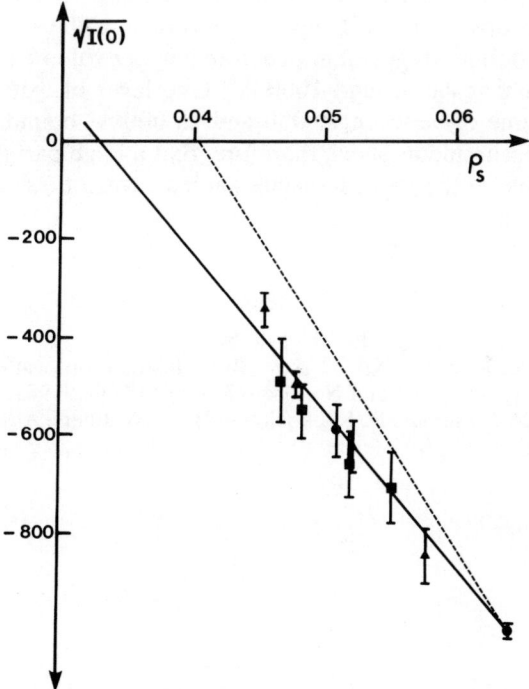

Figure 2 The observed relationship $\sqrt{I(O)} = \Sigma b_i - \rho_s V$. ρ_s is in 10^{-12} cm/Å^3, $\sqrt{I(O)}$ in 10^{-12} cm. The full line is a least squares fit. The broken line is for the case of 0.3 g/g of water bound to the surface (i.e. a volume of approximately 12 000 Å^3)

weight is known. Papain was chosen because its molecular structure is known and it is known not to change in alcohol or dimethylsulphoxide solutions.[3] Parameters for this protein are $M_r = 23\,400$, Σb_i (in D_2O buffer) = 880×10^{-12} cm assuming 80% deuteration of labile hydrogen.

The radius of gyration is around 16 Å in D_2O and drops to around 14 Å for the highest probe concentration used. Half of this drop can be accounted for from model calculations using the molecular structure and the rest is undoubtedly caused by the bound water found on the surface. The results are shown in Figure 2. The least squares line is 1050–32 000 ρ_s. From the least squares line we get $\Sigma b_i = 1050$, i.e. the scattering of bound water is 170×10^{-12} cm, corresponding to approximately 90 water molecules or a volume of 3500 Å^3. The volume of the molecule can be estimated using standard density for proteins and is around 28 500 Å. In this estimate, there is an implicit assumption that, on average, the density of bound water around the protein is the same as bulk. We find this reasonable since the protein surface is heterogeneous and contains charged groups which will electrostrict water as well as hydrophobic groups which will repel it. Subtracting the molecular volume from the total volume we get an impenetrable water volume of 3500 Å^3. The error is estimated to be around 1000 Å^3. One layer of water would correspond to a volume of between 10 000 and 15 000 Å^3 bound to the surface. The present measurements show, therefore, that a large part of the surface is directly accessible to the probe molecules at least when these are in relatively low concentrations.

References

1. B. Jacrot, *Rep. Prog. Phys.*, **39**, 911 (1976).
2. G. Zaccaï, in Proc. of the NATO Adv. Study Institute on Scattering Techniques Applied to Supramagnetic and Non-Equilibrium Systems, 1981.
3. J. Drenth, J. N. Jansonius, R. Koekoek and B. G. Wolthers, *Adv. Protein Chem.*, **25**, 78 (1971).

On the role of interfacial water in protonmotive systems

Douglas B. Kell and J. Gareth Morris
University College of Wales

Summary

The nature and role of protonmotive systems in bioelectrochemical information transfer is briefly reviewed. It is likely that 'energized' coupling protons are relayed from their sources to their sinks along the surfaces of the coupling membrane. The possible role of interfacial water molecules and other factors in effecting this transfer is outlined. Attention is drawn to those areas to which water biophysicists can contribute an improvement in our understanding of protonmotive systems.

Introduction

It is now widely accepted that an important means of bioelectrochemical energy transduction and information transfer is effected by a current of 'energized' protons, which are pumped across 'coupling' membranes that themselves serve to separate two aqueous compartments. Such systems are known as protonmotive systems. Current controversy is focused upon the extent to which such energized coupling protons are osmotically active. In the chemiosmotic formulation[1,2] the coupling protons are described energetically as forming a protonmotive force between the two bulk aqueous phases that the membrane serves to separate, given as a sum of electrical and chemical terms:

$$\Delta p = \Delta \psi - 2.3RT\Delta pH/F \qquad (1)$$

where Δp is the protonmotive force, $\Delta \psi$ is the electrical potential across the membrane, ΔpH is the pH differential across the membrane, and R, T and F have their usual thermodynamic meanings. In this view the protonmotive force between one membrane surface and the other is equal to that between the two bulk phases in the steady state. In an alternative view, generalized by

Williams[3] and developed in more specific terms by others,[4,5] the coupling protons do not become osmotically active and are retained on the membrane surfaces. It is at present unknown whether such a retention of energized coupling protons is engendered by additional proteins, by biophysical forces including hydrogen-bonded chains of interfacial water molecules, or by both. It is, however, important to realize that this type of protonmotive system behaves as a molecular machine, as defined by McClare,[6,7] and care must be exercised in its thermodynamic description.

Space does not permit an extensive analysis of the evidence favouring the view that the 'energized' coupling protons of processes such as electron transport phosphorylation, active solute transport and flagellar rotation are indeed membrane-bound, and such evidence has been reviewed at some length elsewhere;[4,5] we confine our present enquiries to the relative importance of interfacial water molecules and 'proton-transferring proteins' in effecting such directed vectorial proton transfer.

Proton transfer along membrane surfaces; what is the mechanism?

The existence of a layer of 'structured' water within the inner Helmholtz plane adjacent to biological membrane surfaces could, in principle, give rise to a vectorial proton transfer pathway parallel to a membrane surface.[3] There is at present little evidence available to indicate whether or not this actually occurs *in vivo*. However, it is obvious that for those working in the field of 'vicinal water'[8,9,10] the possibility that such water molecules may be involved in bioelectrochemical proton transfer seems well worth exploring. In this regard it is worth noting Freund's proposal[11] that proton transfer in bioenergetic systems occurs not via the mechanism believed to occur in ice[12] but via a dual 'proton band' mechanism, as found for certain inorganic hydroxides.[13]

The alternative to an involvement of 'structured' water in effecting preferential H^+ transfer parallel (as opposed to perpendicular) to a coupling membrane surface is that there exists in such coupling membranes proteins whose normal function is specifically to channel 'energized' protons between their membrane-located sources and sinks.[4,5] Such proteins are taken to interact cooperatively, and we have referred to the proton-transferring network that they constitute as a 'protoneural' network.[5] In this type of model the energy of the 'energized' protons is conserved in the form of field-induced strained protein conformational states, which relax as they pass energized protons to the next element of the network, finally delivering them to a proton sink, such as an ATP synthase enzyme, which will perform useful biological work.

Thus, at our present state of knowledge, it is of the greatest importance to find or to develop methods which will allow us to distinguish between proton transfer along chains of adsorbed water molecules and proton transfer along chains of H-bonding amino acid residues, both along the surfaces of coupling membranes[4,5] and through channels within the proton pumps themselves.[14-16]

The existence, likely nature and properties of strongly-adsorbed water molecules at the surfaces of membranes and proteins have been excellently summarized by the other contributors to this volume. Our task is to draw the attention of water biophysicists to the possible involvement of such water molecules in vectorial proton transfer as a means of bioelectrochemical information transfer. Schwartz[17,18] has outlined the thermodynamics of membrane-located proteins containing large (hundreds of Debye units) permanent dipoles, and the significant conformational changes that even single bond charges can exert upon them as a transmembrane field is set up. We therefore hope that the extremely barren outline of protonmotive systems that we have given here may stimulate workers in the field of water biophysics to join the interdisciplinary effort that will be needed to further our understanding of protonmotive bioenergetic systems.

References

1. P. Mitchell, *FEBS Lett.*, **78**, 1 (1977).
2. P. Mitchell, *Science*, **206**, 1148 (1979).
3. R. J. P. Williams, *FEBS Lett.*, **85**, 9 (1978).
4. D. B. Kell, *Biochim. Biophys. Acta*, **549**, 55 (1979).
5. D. B. Kell, D. J. Clarke and J. G. Morris, *FEMS Microbiol. Lett.*, **11**, 1 (1981).
6. C. W. F. McClare, *J. Theoret. Biol.*, **30**, 1 (1971).
7. C. W. F. McClare, *Ann. N.Y. Acad. Sci.*, **224**, 74 (1974).
8. W. Drost-Hansen, in *The Chemistry of the Cell Interface*, Part B (ed. H. D. Brown), pp. 1–184, Academic Press, New York (1974).
9. H. H. G. Jellinek (ed.), *Water structure at the water-polymer interface*, Plenum Press, New York (1972).
10. R. Cooke and I. D. Kuntz, *Ann. Rev. Biophys. Bioeng.*, **2**, 95 (1974).
11. F. Freund, *Trends Biochem. Sci.*, **6**, 142 (1981).
12. N. Riehl, B. Bullmer and H. Engelhardt (eds), *Physics of Ice*, Plenum Press, New York (1969).
13. F. Freund and H. Wengeler, *Ber. Bunsenges. Phys. Chem.*, **84**, 866 (1980).
14. M. K. F. Wikström and K. Krab, *Biochim. Biophys. Acta*, **549**, 177 (1979).
15. S. R. Caplan and M. Ginzburg (eds), *Energetics and Structure of Halophilic Microorganisms*, Elsevier/North Holland, Amsterdam (1978).
16. A. K. Dunker and D. A. Marvin, *J. Theoret. Biol.*, **72**, 9 (1978).
17. G. Schwartz, *J. Membr. Biol.*, **43**, 127 (1978).
18. G. Schwartz, *J. Membr. Biol.*, **43**, 149 (1978).

Phospholipid bilayer hydration—interbilayer repulsion and intrabilayer structural changes

R. P. Rand
Brock University, Canada

and

V. A. Parsegian
National Institutes of Health, Bethesda, USA

Summary

Measurements of interbilayer repulsive forces as a function of bilayer separation, and intrabilayer lateral pressure as a function of molecular area have been made by X-ray diffraction techniques for a variety of lipid systems. The chemical potential of water in the interbilayer space, relative to bulk water, varies smoothly with bilayer separation. Large variations in lateral pressure, bilayer compressibility and structural transitions exist among these lipids on water removal.

In aqueous systems most diacyl phospholipids form lamellar phases made up of alternating layers of water and bimolecular lipid leaflets. We have measured by X-ray diffraction bilayer thickness, molecular area and bilayer separation. With increasing amounts of water, the bilayers both deform, becoming thinner, and increase separation either to a fixed distance of 20–30 Å in the case of electrically neutral bilayers, or to an indefinitively large distance (100's of Å) in the case of charged bilayers. By controlling the chemical potential of the water in three ways, osmotically, by hydrostatic pressure and by vapour pressure, we have measured the work of water removal and divided it into that of overcoming bilayer repulsion and that of deforming the bilayers. Thus, we have measured interbilayer repulsive forces, F_R, as a function of bilayer separation (see Figure 1 for examples) and intrabilayer lateral pressure, F_{LP}, as a function of molecular area[1] for the following lipid systems:

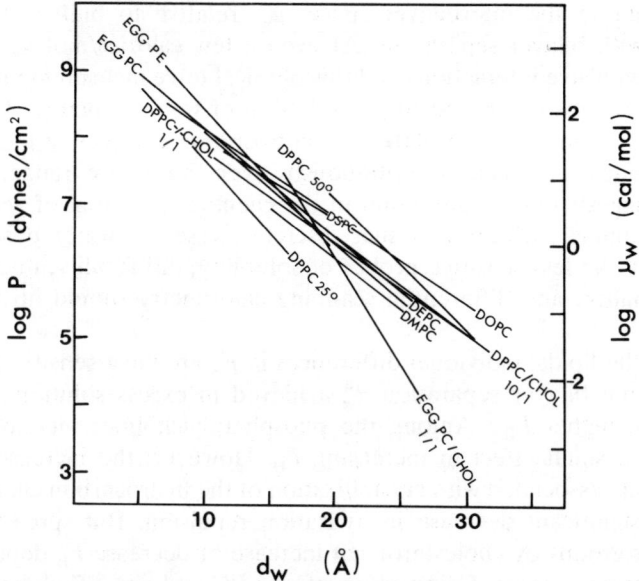

Figure 1 P is the interbilayer hydration repulsion, μ_w is the chemical potential of interbilayer water relative to bulk water, and d_w is the interbilayer separation. The lines are best-fit exponentials to data points[9] for the lipids listed in the text and, with the possible exception of egg PC/cholesterol 1/1, are not detectably different. Thus, whether the hydrocarbon chains of the bilayers are melted or frozen, shorter or longer, homogeneous or heterogeneous or contain cholesterol or have different polar head groups, the decay constant of the hydration force is about 2.5–3.0 Å. This suggests that the force is independent of the molecular structure of the hydrophilic surface

dilauryl-, dimyristyl-, dipalmitoyl-, dioleyl-, distearyl- and egg phosphatidylcholines, some of these with cholesterol, melted or frozen chains, egg phosphatidylethanolamine, and some charged lipid bilayers containing phosphatidylserine, phosphatidylglycerol, or phosphatidylinositol.

Although individual differences exist beyond about 25 Å, out to this separation interbilayer repulsion for this entire set of lipids[3] shows an exponentially decreasing 'hydration force', F_H, similar to that we first reported,[2] with a decay distance of 2–3 Å. This force dominates electrostatic repulsion and, with the important exception of divalent cations[4] and charged lipids, is negligibly dependent on bilayer electric charge and medium ionic strength. It is likely to exist for all hydrophilic surfaces and is likely to be a characteristic of water and not of the molecular structure of that surface.[6] The chemical potential of water in the interbilayer space, μ_w, relative to bulk water, varies smoothly with bilayer separation. At even a few calories/mol μ_w translates into large repulsive interactions and this physical force measurement provides an extremely sensitive probe of perturbation of water structure. Near complete dehydration, μ_w extrapolates to the hydration energies of ions and cell surface groups. μ_w changes continuously over this entire range, and this strongly suggests that a continuum in the chemical potential of water exists near hydrophilic surfaces and that discrete classes of water described by studies with the less sensitive probes of solubility, diffusibility, nuclear magnetic resonance, and differential scanning calorimetry should no longer be assumed.

Among the lipids, individual differences in F_H are most sensitively seen in the maximum bilayer separation d_w^0 achieved in excess solution, larger d_w^0 reflecting a higher F_H.[7] Among the phosphatidylcholines increasing chain length has a small effect in increasing F_H. However, the increase in polar group density associated with crystallization of the hydrocarbon chains results in a very significant decrease in hydration repulsion. But spreading apart these polar groups by cholesterol can increase or decrease F_H depending on the cholesterol content. Comparison of egg PC and egg PE shows that the smaller polar group results in a significant decrease in d_w^0 and F_H, to the extent that we would predict that contact between two vesicles of PC/PE mixture would result in lipid segregation where PE accumulates in the areas of closest approach.[7] Contact between vesicles of other lipid mixtures would also result in structural changes in the contact region.[7,8]

Bilayers containing even small amounts of the anionic phospholipids separate to indefinitively large values in water and to ≈ 25 Å in high ionic strength monovalent solutions, i.e. hydration repulsion dominates electrostatic.[5] But divalent cations dramatically vitiate hydration repulsion allowing these charged bilayers to reach molecular contact.[5]

Large variations in lateral pressure, bilayer compressibility and structural transitions exist among these lipids on water removal.[7,9] Double bonds and cholesterol increase bilayer deformability; freezing the hydrocarbon chains does not dramatically increase deformability; lateral compression can induce crystallization of the hydrocarbon chains and cause lipid segregation in mixed lipid systems.

References

1. V. A. Parsegian, N. Fuller and R. P. Rand, *Proc. Natl. Acad. Sci.*, **76**, 2750 (1979).
2. D. M. LeNeveu, R. P. Rand and V. A. Parsegian, *Nature*, **259**, 601 (1976).
3. L.-J. Lis, M. McAlister, N. Fuller, R. P. Rand and V. A. Parsegian, *Biophys. J.* (In Press).
4. A. C. Cowley, N. Fuller, R. P. Rand and V. A. Parsegian, *Biochemistry*, **17**, 3163 (1978).

5. M. Loosley-Millman, Ph.D. Thesis, Guelph University (1980).
6. S. Marcelja, N. Radic, *Chem. Phys. Lett.*, **42**, 129 (1976).
7. R. P. Rand, *Ann. Rev. Biophys. Bioeng.*, **10**, 277 (1981).
8. R. P. Rand, V. A. Parsegian, J. A. C. Henry, L.-J. Lis, M. McAlister, *Can. J. Biochem.*, **58**, 959 (1980).
9. L.-J. Lis, M. McAlister, N. Fuller, R. P. Rand, V. A. Parsegian, *Biophys. J.* (In Press).

Model for a cooperative structure wave

J. G. Watterson
University of Zurich, Switzerland

Summary

Cooperativity in water interactions is used to construct a model predicting that both structure and energy are propagated through the liquid in the form of sinusoidal waves.

Cooperativity in water links the concepts of structure and energy. The non-additivity of the hydrogen bond means that ordered regions induce energetically favourable bonding with neighbouring molecules facilitating the structure building process. Thus, we do not consider local changes as resulting from random fluctuations, but as taking definite quantifiable values. We introduce $s(x, t)$ to represent the density of structure at position x and time t. Assuming structure building is proceeding at x as depicted in Figure 1, we have the incremental increase

$$\Delta s = -(ds/dx) \cdot \Delta x \quad (1)$$

and s becomes the dashed curve. The reaction thus appears like a polymerization travelling at that moment from left to right with velocity $c(s) = \Delta x/\Delta t$, allowing us to write s in terms of t

$$\Delta s = -(\partial s/\partial x) \cdot c \cdot \Delta t \quad (2)$$

Defining now another density function $\varepsilon(x, t)$ associated with the energy liberated by structure formation, whereby for small changes $\Delta \varepsilon = \sigma \cdot \Delta s$, we can use Equation (2) to link s and ε

$$(\partial \varepsilon/\partial t) = -\sigma \cdot c \cdot (\partial s/\partial x) \quad (3)$$

We can also regard s as the degree of a chemical reaction since its change measures a redistribution of bonds. This reaction is viewed as happening at or close to equilibrium and hence, in the language of irreversible thermo-

Model for a cooperative structure wave

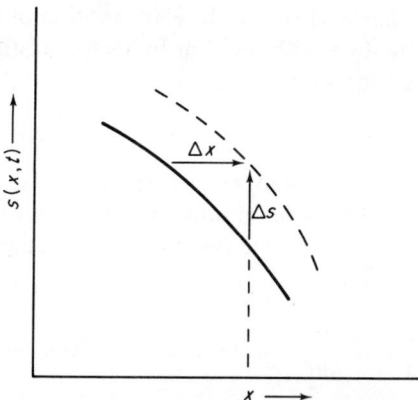

Figure 1 Schematic representation of how the structure function $s(x,t)$ appears to move with velocity $c = \Delta x/\Delta t$. Assuming there is local build-up occurring, then molecules to the left which already have a high degree of order promote structuring on the right via the cooperative interactions and so the process travels in the positive x-direction

dynamics, its rate can be equated to an affinity or potential difference between products and reactants. The values of s at x and $x - \Delta x$ represent the reactants and products, provided the reaction is proceeding as depicted in Figure 1, and over the same distance the potential drop is $(d\varepsilon/dx)\,\Delta x$, and the reaction rate in the small volume Δx is

$$(\partial s/\partial t) = -\gamma \cdot (\partial \varepsilon/\partial x) \qquad (4)$$

This equation has the form of a phenomenological equation where the 'flux' ds/dt is set proportional to the driving 'force' $-(d\varepsilon/dx)$.

Combining Equations (3) and (4) leads directly to the classical wave equations

$$\frac{\partial^2 \varepsilon}{\partial t^2} = c^2 \cdot \frac{\partial^2 \varepsilon}{\partial x^2} \qquad \frac{\partial^2 s}{\partial t^2} = c^2 \cdot \frac{\partial^2 s}{\partial x^2} \qquad (5)$$

provided the velocity can be expressed as $c = \sigma \cdot \gamma$. This result implies that both structure and energy are transmitted as waves in a medium where the mechanism of intermolecular interactions is cooperative.

The exact form that a structure wave would take is an open question, so for discussion we take the simplest stationary sinusoidal form

$$\varepsilon = 2\cos(kx)\cos(\omega t) \qquad s = 2\sin(kx)\sin(\omega t) \qquad (6)$$

where $k = 2\pi/\lambda$, $\omega = 2\pi\nu$ and $\lambda\nu = c$. In wave motion of this type the energy is not given directly by the oscillation but by its quadratic form, so we introduce two new density functions

$$E = 4a\,\cos^2(kx)\cos^2(\omega t) \qquad I = 4b\,\sin^2(kx)\sin^2(\omega t) \qquad (7)$$

As the wave passes it causes changes in $E\,dx$ and $I\,dx$, i.e. the local energy and structure content in the small volume dx. After introducing a factor T to equalize the amplitudes, $a = bT$, we can add these changes together to obtain another oscillating function

$$\frac{\partial E}{\partial t} + T\frac{\partial I}{\partial t} = -4\omega bT\,\cos(2kx)\sin(2\omega t) \qquad (8)$$

This represents another local change and, if taken as a displacement wave describing the to and fro motions of the water molecules accompanying the fluctuations in E and I, it is simply the local volume change. This new wave has the form

$$y = -2Y\,\sin(2kx)\cos(2\omega t) \qquad (9)$$

whereby small volumes change with the rate $d(dy/dx)/dt$. This argument allows us to identify Equation (8) with the thermodynamic statement, $dE = T\,dS - P\,dV$, connecting changes in internal energy, entropy and volume. This condition for the wave motion prescribes that the wavelength is proportional to the ratio P/T since it follows

$$\lambda = \frac{4\pi Y}{b} \cdot \frac{P}{T} \qquad (10)$$

From Equation (7) b is an amplitude giving the maximum density of order or structure building centres. Considering the ratio P/T as a measure of the density of degrees of freedom, then Equation (10) tells us that the wave has longer wavelengths in systems where there are more degrees of freedom per ordering centre. This picture seems reasonable, since it predicts that local order extends over a larger region, i.e. we have bigger clusters or networks, when there are more modes of interaction available to each building centre.

Another consequence of Equation (8) is that the changes in the function I represent negative changes in entropy. The work of Brillouin has established this form of function, the so-called negentropy, in theoretical physics. It is built around the idea that at the molecular level negative entropy can be identified with information. We are thus led to the conclusion that information can be transmitted through an aqueous medium without requiring a permanent covalently linked structure. It also provides us with a thermodynamic definition of the variable $s(x,t)$ which was introduced in quite a different way in Figure 1. On the other hand, $\varepsilon(x,t)$ being the square root of

Model for a cooperative structure wave

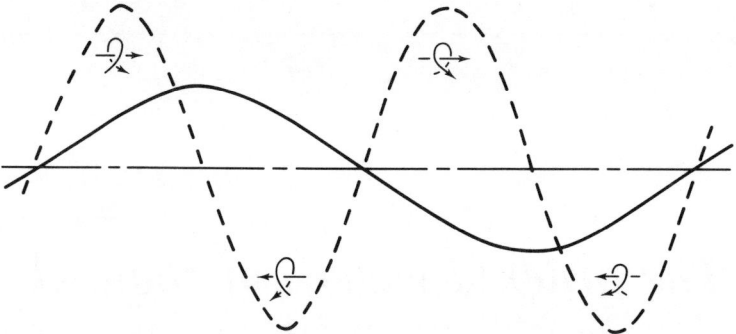

Figure 2 Regions of defined molecular rotations and translations according to $\varepsilon(x,t)$ (solid curve) and $y(x,t)$ (dashed curve). In each of the four half-wavelengths of y is a different combination. $s(x,t)$ shown by the broken curve is taken to be zero at this moment, $\sin(\omega t) = 0$

energy, is a more familiar quantity. It probably represents the momentum associated with rotations, as the molecules reorientate to fit into or break away from ordered clusters. Their translations are given by Equation (9), which in combination with these proposed rotations $\varepsilon(x,t)$, are depicted in Figure 2.

Within the bulk of liquid water we cannot expect any preferred direction of propagation. The build-up and break-down of structured regions should then appear as random clustering and molecular cross-linking as randomly percolated hydrogen bonding. But a solute–solvent interface might force direction and order into these fluctuations. The living cell abounds in regions of layered membrane systems and the aligned protein filaments of the cytoskeleton in registered arrays. These macroscopic structures present networks of parallel interfaces to the solvent medium, so that, assuming they impose direction on the structure wave, the entire region is filled with the solvent medium fluctuating in a concerted way.

The wave model depicts how cooperativity could have far-reaching influence which operates without the existence of an interposed covalently bonded structure. It does not predict the molecular details of any structure, as do computer simulations, but it does predict that they repeat themselves periodically over larger distances and that structural changes can be transmitted beyond the local region of their occurrence. Such a mechanism may underlie the observations of long-range effects seen even in the absence of detectable ordering in the intervening solvent medium.

The ordered water ion channel

D. T. Edmonds
The Clarendon Laboratory, Oxford, UK

Summary

A protein defined pore, lined with an electrically ordered water molecule array is capable of modelling many of the known properties of ion channels in excitable membranes.

The model

A. The channel consists of a clathrate-like cage or net structure of water molecules composed largely of planar pentagon or puckered hexagon rings.[1,2] These configurations allow each water molecule four tetrahedrally oriented hydrogen bonds, two donors and two acceptors. One particularly stable channel may be formed by stacking dodecahedra[3] formed only of planar pentagon rings.

B. The channel is supported by five (pentagon channels) or six (hexagon channels) parallel rod-shaped protein structures that span the membrane perpendicularly and enclose the channel.[1,2] The whole structure is stabilized by matched water channel–protein rod hydrogen bonds.

C. Calculations[3] show that the water ring centres are low energy ionic binding sites which are selective for unhydrated ion size, valence and charge sign. Particularly low energies are found for Na^+ in the planar pentagon and K^+ in the puckered hexagon. Adjacent sites are separated by as little as 0.3 nm and ion mobility may be high.

D. Because of its position, shielded from high dielectric fluid, and its elongated shape the water electric dipole array is ordered[1,3] with a net dipole moment parallel or antiparallel to the channel axis in the two ground states. This leads to large electric fields within the channel so that ion transfer may be controlled by electric fields alone without the need of gating particles.

E. The channel can switch[1,2,3] between the two lowest energy electrically ordered configurations solely by water molecule rotation. It can be triggered by the membrane field (electrical gating) or by the proximity of a suitable charged group (chemical gating).

Evidence for the model

A. In order to provide low energy binding sites for ions within a membrane, electrically charged groups or mobile dipoles are required. Only dipole arrays are capable of combining closely spaced sites and low electrostatic energy in the absence of the ions.[2,3,4]

B. The five or six protein rod structure required to match the pentagon or hexagon water rings are both found experimentally for the post-synaptic acetylcholine activated ion channel in real tissue.[5] The repetition length of the individual rods has been found[6] to be 0.52 nm and 0.63 nm which matches that required to support typical water channels (0.6 nm for the dodecahedral channel).

C. Large scale structures consisting of five consecutive edge connected water pentagons have been measured recently[7] for a deoxydinucleoside-drug complex.

D. The calculated charge transfer[1,2] on channel switching of between $1.6|e|$ and $1.2|e|$ depending on the structure is in good agreement with the 'gating charge' transfer found[8,9] for the sodium channel in the squid axon of $1.3|e|$.

E. Using a voltage-controlled channel model based upon the calculated electric field gradients expected for ordered water channels, approximate agreement is obtained[4,10] with the measured current-voltage characteristic[11] for both K^+ and Na^+ transfer in the squid axon using physiological ion concentrations.

Predictions of the model

A. Ion channels in membranes have two configurations and the channel switch corresponds to the transfer between them.[10] *Both* configurations may conduct in an appropriate membrane voltage range. This is in contrast to mechanical gating particle models in which a channel switches between open and shut.

B. The dipole moment of the channel undergoes a large change or switching. For an eight section dodecahedral channel it is about 150 Debye.

C. The water channel ends are charged and the sign of the charge changes on switching. In a resting membrane ($V(\text{in}) < V(\text{out})$) the outer end of the channel is negative and so should selectively bind positively charged poisons and other channel blockers such as Zn^{++}. In a depolarized membrane the inner end of the switched channel becomes the negatively charged end. Selective binding studies in resting and depolarized membranes should reveal this.

D. The model treats sodium and potassium channels identically. The very different characteristics obtained are due to the different ion concentrations and thus the different Nernst potentials (membrane voltage for no transfer) for these two ions in a physiological context. For a K^+ concentration of 400 mM both internally and externally (Nernst potential is zero) the model predicts[4] a sodium type switching characteristic and a K^+ action potential. Such a characteristic has in fact been measured[12] in the squid axon with these K^+ concentrations.

E. The model predicts[10] channel activation by hyperpolarizing pulses at large negative membrane voltages ($V(\text{in}) \ll V(\text{out})$). Such activation has recently been detected.[13,14]

References

1. D. T. Edmonds, *Chem. Phys. Lett.*, **65**, 429 (1979).
2. D. T. Edmonds, *Biochem. Soc. Symp.*, No. 46, London (1980).
3. D. T. Edmonds, *Proc. R. Soc.*, **B211**, 51 (1980).
4. D. T. Edmonds, *Trends in Biochemical Sciences*, April, 92 (1981).
5. D. M. Fambrough, *Physiol. Rev.*, **59**, 165 (1979).
6. M. J. Ross, M. W. Klymkowsky, D. A. Agard and R. M. Stroud, *J. Mol. Biol.*, **116**, 635 (1977).
7. S. Neidle, H. M. Berman and H. S. Shieh, *Nature*, **288**, 129 (1980).
8. C. M. Armstrong and F. Benzanilla, *J. Gen. Physiol.*, **63**, 533 (1974).
9. R. D. Keynes and E. Rojas, *J. Physiol.*, **239**, 393 (1974).
10. D. T. Edmonds, *Proc. R. Soc.* (In press) (1981).
11. A. L. Hodgkin and A. F. Huxley, *J. Physiol.*, **117**, 500 (1952).
12. J. W. Moore, *Nature*, **183**, 265 (1959).
13. H. Brown, D. Difrancesco and S. Noble, *J. Exptl. Biol.*, **81**, 175 (1979).
14. D. Atwell and M. Wilson, *J. Physiol.*, **309**, 287 (1980).

Free energies at the biosurface–water interface: relationships between surface thermodynamics and interfacial structure

Donald J. McIver and **Samuel Schürch**
University of Western Ontario, Canada

Summary

The driving force for spontaneous interactions at cell surfaces is a decrease in the surface free energy. Non-covalent bonds between biological molecules and their surrounding aqueous solvent probably play an important role in determining the free energies of interaction between biological surfaces. For example, the free energies of such processes as cellular adhesion, membrane fusion and the binding of drugs and hormones to cellular receptors probably receive major contributions from water–surface interactions.[1]

We have approached the quantitative investigation of these and similar processes from the viewpoint of macroscopic surface thermodynamics, adapted for the extremely low interfacial free energies found at the biosurface–water interface.

In a three-phase system, when a non-deformable solid is wetted by two immiscible liquids, the equilibrium contact angle between the liquids and the solid is a unique function of the interfacial free energies, γ, given by Young's equation.

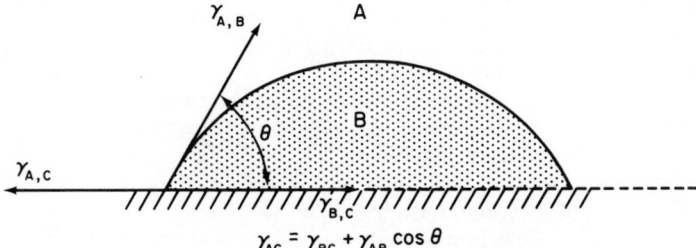

Figure 1   Equilibrium relation between interfacial free energies γ, at a three-phase boundary

γ_{AC} is a function of the intermolecular forces across the surface AC, and in aqueous systems is largely determined by the surface–water interaction. Only γ_{AB} and the contact angle θ are experimentally accessible.

Initially we studied the wetting of biological surfaces by polar hydrophobic fluids such as isopropyl salicylate:[2] estimation of γ_{AC} from measurements of γ_{BC} and an empirical equation of state[3,4] indicated that γ_{AC} on cell surfaces is less than 6×10^{-5} J.m^{-2}. The sensitivity of these wetting studies may be considerably improved by reducing γ_{BC} to the $10^{-5} \sim 10^{-6}$ J.m^{-2} level.

In phase-separated solutions of aqueous polymers such as dextran and poly(ethylene glycol), γ_{AB} may be set at any value by varying the polymer concentration. We have used these systems to measure contact angles on living cells, and then examine the response of the cell surfaces to various stimuli.[5] Measurements of θ and γ_{BC} are related to γ_{AC} either by the critical spreading approach of Zisman[6] or the interaction parameter Φ of Good and Elbing.[7] Both approaches yield comparable results.

Studies on model systems reconstituted from phospholipids and purified cell surface glycoprotein (glycophorin) have allowed us to reproduce the thermodynamic properties of intact cells and have shown that the pronounced hydrophilicity of the cell surface reflects the presence of high molecular weight polymers, whose interfacial properties resemble those of other polymer solutions. The results of these experiments are summarized in Table 1.

These studies allow us to interpret the wetting of biological surfaces by polymer solutions as illustrated schematically in Figure 2; when $\theta \to 0$, γ_{BC} approaches a minimum, which may equal zero if the forces of adhesion and

Table 1

Test System:	Interface	γ_{AC} (J.m^{-2})
	1. Dextran 500K/PEG 20K	
	Erythrocytes	0.65×10^{-6}
	Neutrophils	0.85×10^{-6}
	Pulmonary macrophages	0.93×10^{-6}
	Platelets	0.75×10^{-6}
	2. Isopropyl salicylate/0.9% NaCl	
	Fluorocarbon oil	4.5×10^{-2}
	Fluorocarbon oil + dipalmitoyl lecithin	5×10^{-3}
	Fluorocarbon oil + dipalmitoyl lecithin + glycophorin	$<10^{-5}$
	3. Dextran 500K/PEG 20	
	Fluorocarbon oil	$\sim 3.0 \times 10^{-2}$
	Fluorocarbon oil + dipalmitoyl lecithin	1×10^{-3}
	Fluorocarbon oil + dipalmitoyl lecithin + glycophorin	1×10^{-6}

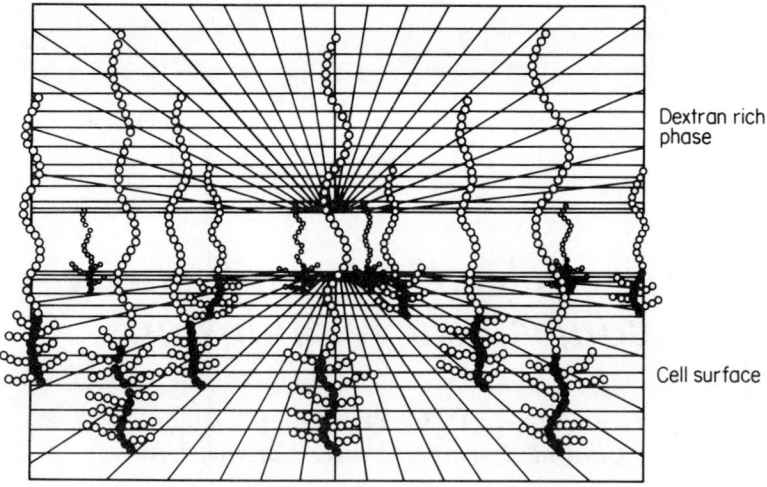

Figure 2 Schematic diagram of dextran–cell interactions when $\gamma_{BC} \to 0$

cohesion are of the same type ($\Phi = 1$). The dextran contact angle thus titrates the surface activity of cell surface polymers, particularly glycosylated proteins and lipids.

Calcium ions play a central role in controlling cell surface interactions. The influence of calcium on cell surface energy was investigated by using agents which have been shown histochemically to displace cell surface calcium, including the ionophore A-23187, zymosan particles, complement and antigen–antibody complexes. Surface energy measurements showed that calcium displacement rendered the cells more hydrophilic. These findings are in general agreement with predictions of calcium–biosurface interactions based on a combination of ion exchange theory and surface thermodynamics.[1]

Acknowledgement

Supported by Canadian MRC and University Hospital, London, Ontario.

References

1. D. J. L. McIver, *Physiol. Chem. Phys.*, **11**, 289 (1980).
2. J. F. Boyce, S. Schürch and D. J. L. McIver, *Atherosclerosis*, **37**, 361 (1980).
3. A. W. Neumann, R. J. Good, C. J. Hope and M. Sejpal, *J. Colloid Interf. Sci.*, **49**, 291 (1974).
4. S. Schürch and D. J. L. McIver, *J. Colloid. Interf. Sci.*, **83**, 301 (1981).
5. S. Schürch, D. F. Gerson and D. J. L. McIver, *Biochim. Biophys. Acta*, **640**, 557 (1981).
6. W. A. Zisman, in *Contact Angles*, Advances in Chemistry Series 43, ed. R. F. Gould, pp. 1–51, American Chemical Soc., Washington, D.C. (1964).
7. R. J. Good and E. Elbing, *Ind. Eng. Chem.*, **62**, No. 3, 54 (1970).

Water/ice: electrical conductivity—a conjectural relationship

D. C. Pressey
Clinical Research Centre, Harrow, UK

Summary

Criticisms of the ionic theory of electrical conductivity are briefly summarized and a conjectural model for water as a semiconductor, based on solid state concepts of a band model, is proposed.

1 Known properties of ice/water

Hexagonal ice (Ih) has a wurtzite structure resembling ZnS. Liquid water has, at least residually, the tetrahedral structure of diamond or germanium. The latter has been used as a basis for a random lattice bond model structure of water.[1] An amorphous ice also exists (Tg ~ −142 °C). All three types of structure mentioned above are typical of semiconductor materials. Properties of a few of these, together with ice and water, are tabulated opposite.

A singular property of semiconductors is that the conductivity/temperature relationship is of the form

$$\sigma = \sigma_0 \exp(E_A/kT)$$

This applies to both water and ice.

The presently accepted theory of electrical conductivity in aqueous solutions is subject to criticism on the grounds that it is: (a) inexact,[4] (b) 'based on a picture of ions as impenetrable charged spheres in a solvent treated as a continuous and structureless dielectric,'[5] (c) in contravention of electrostatic principles,[6] and that (d) ions are hydrated and move in activated jumps.[7,8] Relevant properties are plotted in Figure 1.

Table 1 Properties of selected semiconductor materials

	SiC	ZnS	Ice	Ge	Si	InSb	Water	Am.Si
Electron mobility ($cm^2 v^{-1} s^{-1}$)	100	100	$20^{(2)}$	3800	1900	78,000	?	~0.5
Hole mobility ($cm^2 v^{-1} s^{-1}$)	20	20	$6.4 \times 10^{-3\,(3)}$	1820	500	750	?	—
Conductivity σ ($ohm^{-1} cm^{-1}$)	—	—	$\sim 4 \times 10^{-9}$	2	4.3×10^{-4}	—	5.6×10^{-8}	10^{-9}
Nearest neighbour distance Å	1.88	2.34	1.75	2.44	2.35	2.81	1.85	~2.3
Ban gap (eV)	2.8	3.6	$\sim 1.2^{(2)}$	0.67	1.107	0.165	(1.229)	0.62

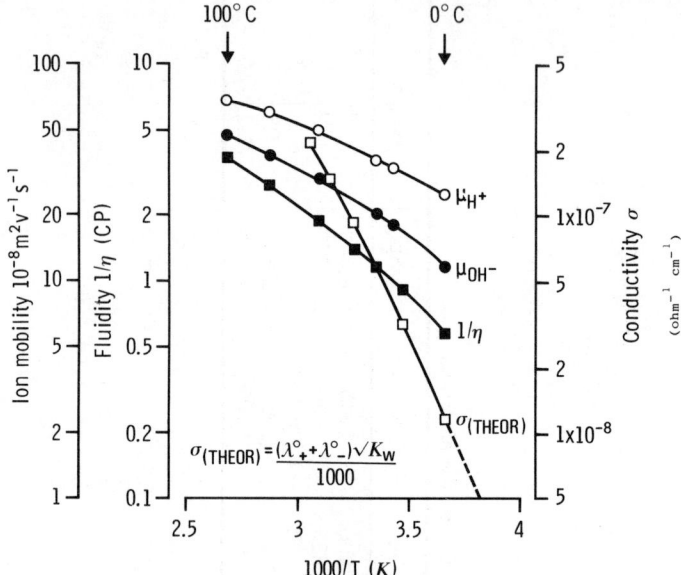

Figure 1   Showing that ionic mobility (μ) is not a simple inverse relationship to viscosity (η). Conductivity is theoretically related to the sum of the limiting ionic equivalent conductances $\lambda°$ (ohm^{-1} cm^2 equiv^{-1}) and the ionic constant K_w as shown. (The mobility

$$\mu = \lambda/F)$$

2 Conjectural model for ice/water conductivity

It is proposed that the observed conductivity of water/ice can be better accounted for by regarding water/ice as a semiconductor. Whilst different models for amorphous and crystalline forms would be more appropriate, a single simple model is indicated in Figure 2.

The essential feature of conduction in semiconductors is that it is effected by means of positive and negative charge carriers, normally electrons and holes, where the holes are defects in the lattice which migrate in the opposite direction to the electrons.

In its simplest form, the energies of the carriers lie within conduction and valence bands respectively, though discrete levels are possible.

The model assumes a band structure with a conduction band edge E_C and valence band edge E_V. The band gap $E_g = E_V - E_C = 1.229$ eV (at 25 °C), this being the potential at which carriers are discharged. The Fermi level is by definition the chemical potential. This is conventionally taken as zero, but this is not the absolute thermodynamic potential. A value of 4.73 eV has been determined,[9] though a value nearer 7 eV can be obtained.

It is obvious that change of pH and/or the presence of ionized impurities,

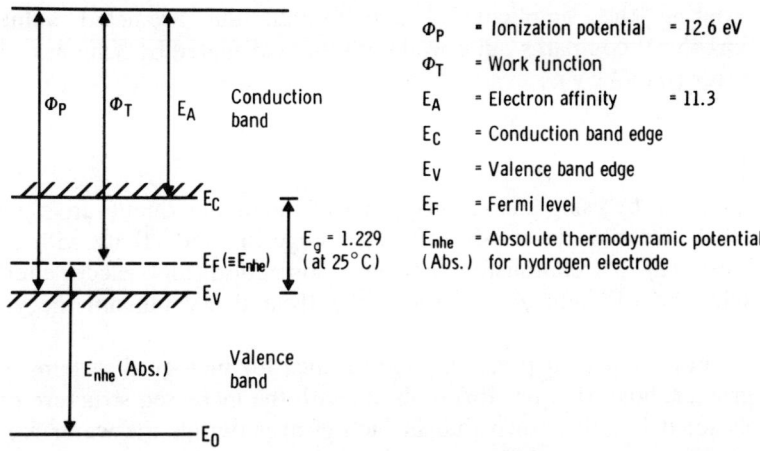

Figure 2 Postulated band structure with energy levels for water as a semiconductor. The Fermi level ≡ the potential of a normal hydrogen electrode at pH = 7

e.g. $Ce^{++++/+++}$—for purely historical reasons chemists denote these as oxidized/reduced states—will determine the Fermi level and hence $(E_C - E_F)$ and $(E_F - E_V)$. This fact clearly accounts for the observed phenomenon of Fermi level pinning.[10]

Similarly, introduction of a solid semiconductor into an aqueous solution will create a Schottky barrier—this has also been observed.[11]

The ionization potential is known to be $E_I = -12.56$[12] so that the electrical affinity

$$E_A = E_I - E_g = -11.231 \text{ eV}$$

This agrees closely with the value of -11.30 eV (-270.6 ± 2.5 kcal mol^{-1}) obtained by extrapolation from single ion hydration enthalpy values.[13]

The activation energy $E_A = E_g/2 = 0.6145$ eV for conduction does not agree well with the value quoted from Pethig[14] but attributable to Duecker and Haller,[15] as given in the preprint.

Better agreement is obtained with a recent figure obtained by laser irradiation of water[16] of 57 kJ/mol (= 0.594 eV).

An essential feature of the model is the recognition of the identity

$$\text{hole} \equiv \text{proton}$$

It is further assumed that conduction takes place exclusively by means of protons and electrons, i.e. is non-ionic, which is approximately true in ice, then the activation energy is seen to be that of transferring a proton along an infinite chain of water molecules.

Considering the simplicity of the model, the predicted value of $E_A = 0.6145$ eV compares quite well with that calculated by Scheiner[17] for a pentameter (0.694 eV).

3 Discussion

It is hoped that by using known properties of the model, quantitative predictions will be possible in respect of: (1) change in conductivity with added impurities; (2) a relationship between ionization and electrochemical potentials, and (3) light absorption in the IR and UV but not the visible region.

One feature that is of particular significance for biological systems is the much greater 'hole' (i.e. proton) mobility with the increased structure of the solid phase. It is well known that in biological materials the water is more structured (ice-like).[18,19,20] This would provide a mechanism for the observed rectifying properties of membrane junctions.

Semiconduction as a feature of biological importance has been advocated by Szent-Györgyi,[21] Cope,[22] Rosenberg[23] and Pethig.[14] The significance of water—if this conjecture is correct—has been overlooked.

Footnote The concept of ice as a 'protonic' semiconductor, as opposed to the viewpoint presented above that it is an electronic semiconductor having protons as the positive charge carriers (holes), was put forward by Eigen and De Maeyer[24] in the most comprehensive survey of this subject.

The concept of liquid water as a semiconductor has been put forward independently by Grand, Bernas and Amouyal.[25]

References

1. M. G. Sceats and S. A. Rice, *J. Chem. Phys.*, **70**, 3927 (1979).
2. J. B. Verberne, H. Loman, J. M. Warman, M. P. de Haas, A. Hummel and L. Prinsen, *Nature*, **272**, 343 (1978).
3. M. Kunst and S. M. Warman, *Nature*, **288**, 467 (1980).
4. D. F. Evans, T. Tominaga, J. B. Hubbard and P. G. Wolynes, *J. Phys. Chem.*, **83**, 2669 (1979).
5. R. S. Berry, S. A. Rice and J. Ross, *Physical Chemistry*, p. 998, J. Wiley & Sons (1980).
6. P. W. Atkins, *Physical Chemistry*, O.U.P., p. 326 (1978).
7. O. Ya. Samoilov, *Structure of Aqueous Electrolyte Solutions and the Hydration of Ions*. (Trans. D. J. G. Ives) Consultants Bureau, N.Y. (1965).
8. S. S. Raju and S. V. Talekar, *Physiol. Chem. Phys.*, **10**, 375 (1978).
9. R. Gomer and G. Tryson, *J. Chem. Phys.*, **66**, 4413 (1977).
10. A. J. Bard, A. B. Bocarsley, Fu-Ren F. Fan, E. G. Walton and M. S. Wrighton, *J. Amer. Chem. Soc.*, **102**, 3671 (1980).
11a. R. Williams, *J. Appl. Phys.*, **50**(4), 2848 (1979).
11b. J. F. McCann and L. J. Handley, *Nature*, **283**, 843 (1980).

12. A. K. Pikaev, 'The solvated electron in radiation chemistry'. Israel Program for Scientific Translations (1971).
13. J. Burgess, *Metal Ions in Solution*. Ellis Horwood Ltd. p. 181 (1978) (as determined by H. F. Halliwell and S. C. Nyberg, *Trans. Faraday Soc.*, **59**, 1126 (1980)).
14. R. Pethig, *Dielectric and Electronic Properties of Biological Materials*, John Wiley & Sons (1979).
15. H. C. Duecker and W. Haller, *J. Phys. Chem.*, **66**, 225 (1962).
16. B. Knight, D. M. Goodall and R. C. Greenhow, *J. Chem. Soc. Faraday Trans.*, II **75**, 874 (1979).
17. S. Scheiner, *J. Amer. Chem. Soc.*, **103**, 315 (1981).
18. H. E. Whipple, ed: Forms of Water in Biologic Systems, *Ann. N.Y. Acad. Sci.*, **125**(2) H. P. Schwan p. 344; E. H. Grant p. 418; O. Hechter p. 625 (1965).
19. R. H. Pearson and I. Pascher, *Nature*, **281**, 499 (1979).
20. J. S. Clegg and W. Drost-Hansen, in *Physical Basis of Electromagnetic Interactions*, Biol. Sys. Proc. Workshop, p. 121. (Ed. Taylor and Cheung) (1977).
21. A. Szent-Györgyi, *Nature*, **148**, 157 (1941). For later references see 14.
22. F. W. Cope, *Ann. N.Y. Acad. Sci.*, **204**, 416 (1973).
23. B. Rosenberg and E. Postow, *Ann. N.Y. Acad. Sci.*, **204**, 161 (1973).
24. M. Eigen and L. De Maeyer, *Proc. Roy. Soc. Lond.*, **A247**, 505 (1958).
25. D. Grand, A. Bernas and E. Amouyal, *Chem. Phys.*, **44**, 73 (1979).

Kinetics of vacuum dehydration in the study of tissue water

Aurel I. Popescu, Eva Katona, Constanţa Ganea and Vasile Vasilescu
Medical Faculty, Bucharest, Romania

Summary

The dehydration kinetics of frog sciatic nerve trunks previously immersed in H_2O-Ringer and D_2O-Ringer solutions were followed up. The mathematical approach of the dehydration curves proves the existence of at least two water molecule subpopulations extractable by vacuum dehydration.

We developed a controlled vacuum dehydration technique,[1,2] which permitted us to follow up by direct weighing the time course of water mass eliminated under vacuum (0.1 Torr pressure). This technique enabled us to obtain the kinetic curves of vacuum dehydration both for normal frog sciatic nerves and for nerves previously immersed in D_2O-Ringer solution (20 hours at 4 °C). The immersion was performed in order to substitute normal water existing in the tissue with heavy water by simple diffusion.

By mathematical computation of the experimental kinetic curves, these can be split into multiexponential components as presented below

$$m(t) = m_d[1 - C_1 \exp(-\alpha_1 t) - C_2 \exp(-\alpha_2 t) - \cdots] \qquad (1)$$

where m_d is the total amount of water extractable by vacuum dehydration technique, $m(t)$ is the water amount extracted at time t, and C_i, α_i ($i = 1, 2, \ldots$) are the coefficients deduced from experimental data, by computation. The following conditions are imposed

$$m(0) = 0; \qquad m(\infty) = m_d; \qquad \sum_i C_i = 1 \qquad (2)$$

It must be emphasized that by this technique we cannot extract the whole quantity of water existing in the nerve trunk. Thus, after 4 h of vacuum dehydration the tissue contains a percentage of water extractable by heating the tissue at 105 °C. This water molecule subpopulation corresponds perhaps to so-called 'tightly bound water'.

In the case of normal sciatic nerve, the dehydration kinetic curve is described by the following expression

$$m(t) = m_d^{H_2O}[1 - 0.104 \exp(-0.968t) - 0.798 \exp(-0.046t) - \cdots] \quad (3)$$

while for the nerves previously deuterated, the corresponding curve described by the function

$$m(t) = m_d^{D_2O}[1 - 0.154 \exp(-0.706t) - 0.735 \exp(-0.033t)$$
$$- 0.092 \exp(-0.048t) - \cdots] \quad (4)$$

Taking into account the notation used in ref. 1 it is easily observed that $\alpha_1 \gg \alpha_2$ in both Equations (3) and (4), demonstrating that the water molecule subpopulation characterized by the component $C_1 \exp(-\alpha_1 t)$ is more easily extractable (this may correspond to so-called 'free water') compared with the water subpopulation characterized by $C_2 \exp(\alpha_2 t)$; this may correspond to so-called 'bound water'. The component $C_3 \exp(-\alpha_3 t)$ from Equation (4) is due, in our opinion, to the normal water not yet exchanged by diffusion after nerve immersion in D_2O-Ringer solution.

At the same time Equations (3) and (4) show

$$\alpha_1(H_2O) > \alpha_1(D_2O) \quad \text{and} \quad \alpha_2(H_2O) > \alpha_2(D_2O) \quad (5)$$

These inequalities demonstrate that heavy water (that could occupy the same 'compartments' as normal water) is more tightly bound in nerve tissue than normal water. This result may be explained on the basis of the existing difference between the hydrogen and deuterium bridge, the former being weaker than the latter by 15%, as well as to mobility differences between protons and deuterons.

Finally, it is interesting to mention the equality of the following ratios: $\alpha_1(H_2O)/\alpha_1(D_2O) = 1.37$ and $\alpha_2(H_2O)/\alpha_2(D_2O) = 1.39$.

The following conclusions are drawn:

(1) Vacuum dehydration technique revealed the existence of two water molecule subpopulations in the case of frog sciatic nerve.
(2) After 4 h of vacuum dehydration there still remains in the tissue a subpopulation of water molecules (approximately 2%) extractable only by heating the tissue at 105 °C.
(3) The three water molecule subpopulations probably correspond to the so-called 'free water', 'bound water' and 'tightly bound water', respectively.
(4) H_2O is almost completely exchanged by D_2O during nerve trunk immersion in D_2O (20 h at 4 °C).

(5) The differences in $\alpha_i(H_2O)$ and $\alpha_i(D_2O)$ ($i = 1, 2, \ldots$) are tentatively ascribed to differences in mobility and interaction properties of protons and deuterons.
(6) It is to be expected that further improvement of this technique will lead to interesting data concerning water states and properties in biological systems.

References

1. V. Vasilescu, A. I. Popescu and D. Eremia, The IInd National Symposium on Freeze-Drying, Bucharest, Romania, November 16–17 (1978).
2. A. I. Popescu, C. Ganea, D. Eremia and V. Vasilescu, The 1st International Conference of Water and Ions in Biological Systems, Bucharest, Romania, June 25–27 (1980).

The occurrence and extent of vicinal water

W. Drost-Hansen
University of Miami, USA

1 Vicinal water

The subject of possible long-range effects in aqueous interfacial systems is not one which has enjoyed overwhelming popularity in recent years. In the interest of maximum conceptual economy many efforts have been made to explain experimental data on aqueous interfacial systems within the minimum number of known theories, such as those used to describe electrical double layers and van der Waals forces, but without considering the possibility of changes in the interfacial water. Indeed, such efforts are salutory as long as one is willing to recognize and make allowance for exceptions which cannot readily be fitted into existing theories. In science it is often the examination of anomalies and exception which leads to new advances; Niels Bohr maintained that there is 'no progress without paradox'.

The possible ability of confining surfaces to influence the structure, and hence properties, of water over large distances (say > or $\gg$ 5 molecular diameters of a water molecule, d_{H_2O}) was quite readily accepted 50 years ago, and indeed it must, for instance, have been quite obvious and natural to cell physiologists. With the advent of the Debye–Hückel theory, the DLVO theory and a more fundamental understanding of van der Waals forces, the notion of long-range effects of solid surfaces on water structure became far less acceptable. Contributing to this was the lack of progress in describing the structure of water in bulk. Over the past decade the question of possible long-range effects of solid surfaces on water structure has, however, again begun to attract some attention. This development is in no small part due to advances in experimental techniques, the most dramatic of such improvements probably being the force-measuring devices of Peschel et al.[1] and of Israelachvili et al.[2] No doubt the results of these developments and their impact on our understanding of interfacial structuring will be amply covered in this conference. Hence, I wish now instead to address some other specific aspects of vicinal water.

Vicinal water is defined as interfacial water (usually near a 'solid' surface) the properties of which differ from the corresponding bulk properties due to structural differences induced by proximity to the surface.

The studies, for instance, by Peschel[3] and others appear to show the existence of water structure modifications which decay (likely exponentially) from the surface with a characteristic decay length of the order of one (or at most a few) nanometers (in other words, a decay distance of the order of 4 (to 10) water molecular diameters). In contrast to such estimates, the present author[4] believes that subtle structural effects may be observed over distance of the order of 0.01 to 0.05 μm (i.e. 30 to 200 molecular diameters). Such vicinal water appears to exist near most (or all) solid surfaces (and likely occurs as well around macromolecules in aqueous solution—for MW > 1000 to 5000 daltons) regardless of the specific chemical nature of the surface (see also Clifford[5]). It is of course agreed that 'local' water/surface interactions will exist due to, for instance, ion–dipole or dipole–dipole interactions; such interactions, however, are all relatively highly energetic (>kT) and of relatively short range. Vicinal water, on the other hand, appears to exist regardless of specific surface interactions, and to extend far beyond the range of these specific effects. It appears also that vicinal water occurs independently of the existence and effects of electrical double layers. We now review briefly a few relatively recent measurements from which one may obtain estimates for the thickness, Δr, of vicinal water.

II Experimental aspects

Ballario, et al.[6] have studied the dielectric properties of suspensions, especially of polystyrene (PS) spheres (but also of a bacterial suspension). From their measurements (at 10 GHz) they conclude that the amount of 'modified water' in the PS suspension at 40 °C, amounts to at least 10% (or perhaps as much as 20%). For a 10% suspension of particles with a diameter of 0.126 μm, this corresponds to spherical, concentric shells of 'modified water' with a thickness of

$$\Delta r = 0.017 \, \mu m$$

However, one must bear in mind that this estimate is based on the use of one particular dielectric 'mixture formula' proposed by Ballario et al. Such formulae are all approximations, at best, and certainly open to criticism. On the other hand, Henry and Berteaud[7] have undertaken a large systematic study of the dielectric properties of PS suspensions, and preliminary calculations of Δr, based on these data,[8] yield essentially the same estimates as obtained by Ballario et al., even when using a number of different empirical mixture formulae. Ballario et al. also notes in passing that Jacobson[28] concluded from a study of DNA solutions that the 'structure action' of these macromolecules may extend over distances $\Delta r \simeq 0.05$ to 0.1 μm.

Deryaguin and co-workers[9] have championed the idea of extensive 'boundary-layer' modifications for over 40 years and while some of the experimental techniques employed have been subject to criticism, the overall impression is that Deryaguin has indeed provided substantial evidence for modified layers of the order

$$\Delta r \sim 0.01 \, \mu m$$

or larger. Because of space limitations, Deryaguin's many signal contributions cannot be reviewed here.

Schufle et al.[10] have measured the thermal expansion of H_2O and D_2O in narrow capillaries. Their primary objective was to identify the temperature of maximum density, T_{md}, as influenced by proximity to a solid (in other words, as a function of capillary radius). Figure 1 shows some of their data. There is little doubt that T_{md} is strongly influenced by proximity to the capillary wall. Most surprising, however, is the apparent levelling-off (in the case of D_2O) of T_{md} for capillary radii below about 3 or 4 μm! In the case of H_2O, no such levelling-off seems to occur, but T_{md} definitely decreases with decreasing capillary radius. Note that two points (differing by only 0.4 °C) are shown for the 10 μm (diameter) capillaries; in one case the capillary was made of glass; the other of quartz. This argues strongly against the notion that the observed lowering the T_{md} merely reflects the result of 'contamination' due to dissolu-

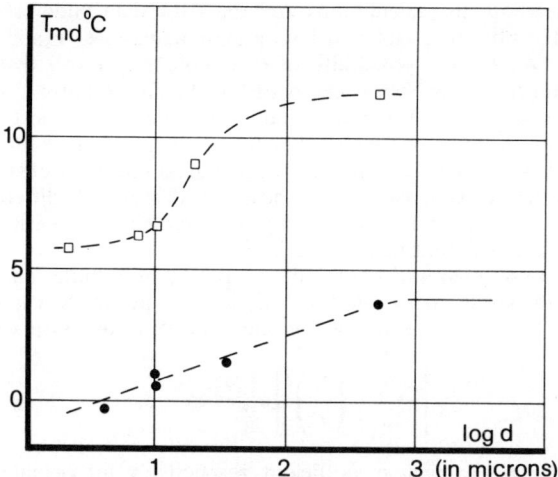

Figure 1 Temperature of maximum density (T_{md}) as a function of log (capillary diameter). Top curve (squares) for D_2O. Bottom curve (circles) for H_2O

tion of the capillaries. It is of interest also that Deryaguin et al. have reported notable lowerings of T_{md}, most recently in narrow pores ($d = 0.03$ μm) of TiO_2 and previously in silica gel. Deryaguin[11] has also argued that the effect of dissolved impurities is far too small to account for the observed decrease in T_{md}.

It is remarkable that relatively few attempts have been reported of direct measurements of the density of interfacial water. An important attempt to provide density data was made by van Gils[12] working with fibres. He investigated the density of water near the fibre surfaces after observing that in pycnometric displacement measurements, using water and heptane, the water data always resulted in larger apparent values for the fibre densities than similar measurements using heptane. For a sample of Dacron the absorption of water into the fibre can be neglected (as well as in the measurements with glass fibres and glass powders.) From Dacron a 'surface excess' of water of 0.7 to 1.1×10^{-5} g/cm² was observed. As a specific case, an excess of 1.07×10^{-5} corresponds to a net density, ρ (at 25 °C) of all the water present of 1.0030 g/cm³. (The surface area was calculated from fibre dimensions (1360 cm²/g) and this value was agreed with BET data, using xenon, of 1380 cm²/g.)

If we assume a 'concentric layer' model consisting of the fibre, a concentric layer of vicinal water (of thickness Δr and density ρ_{vw}) and bulk water (ρ_0 beyond Δr from the surface) it is obvious, from the observed surface excess, that

$$\Delta r(\rho_{vw} - \rho_0) = 1.07 \cdot 10^{-5}$$

Thus, one readily obtains values for the density of vicinal water, for various possible values of Δr.

Δr (μm)	0.01	0.1	1	10	100
ρ_{vw} (g/cm³)	11.7	2.067	1.104	1.0078	0.99815

Unless one is willing to accept unreasonably large values for the density of vicinal water, one must accept dimensions of vicinal water of the order 0.1 to 1 μm. Even if one suspects that both the calculations and the BET data underestimate the total surface area of the fibre by a factor of 10 (an extreme case) Δr is still of the order of 0.01 to 0.1 μm. As for the possibility of contamination, recall that to produce a solution, for instance, of NaCl with density of 1.100 g/cm^3 requires a concentration of 14 wt%. Thus, it seems highly unlikely that 'contamination' could give rise to such excess densities as reported by van Gils. Finally, nearly identical results were obtained by van Gils with Nylon and E-glass fibres, while glass powder yielded 3 to 16 times larger values for the excess density. (Note, however, that entirely different results have been reported by Anderson and Quinn who observed surface densities *less* than the bulk value for water adjacent to graphite surfaces.)

It is possible to use quantitatively the data reported by Schufle et al.[10] to obtain an estimate of the thickness, Δr, of the layer of vicinal water in the capillaries (used to determine T_{md}). Thus a simple 'concentric shell' model leads to the expression

$$\left[\frac{2\Delta r}{r} + \left(\frac{\Delta r}{r}\right)^2\right]\alpha_{vw} = \alpha_a - \alpha_0$$

Where α is the thermal expansion coefficient, respectively, for vicinal water (vw), the observed (apparent) value (a) and the bulk (o). The apparent (total) thermal expansion is readily calculated from Schufle's polynomial expressions (in temperature) for the relative lengths of water in the capillaries. For the 17 μm diameter quartz capillary, $\alpha_a \simeq 360 \times 10^{-6}\ °\text{C}^{-1}$ at 25 °C. From this one obtains the following set of values:

Δr (μm)	0.01	0.03	0.1	0.3	0.5	1.0
$\alpha_{vw} \times 10^6$	88435	29435	8814	2921	1745	859

The values are far higher than for bulk water ($\alpha_0 = 257 \times 10^{-6}\ °\text{C}^{-1}$).

For most normal liquids α is of the order $1000 \times 10^{-6}\ °\text{C}^{-1}$. For want of a better guide, one may suggest that vicinal water may more nearly resemble a 'normal' liquid than does bulk water, and hence choose a value for α_{vw} of the order of 1000 (to perhaps 3000) $\times 10^{-6}\ °\text{C}^{-1}$. This then suggests that $\Delta r \simeq 0.3$ to 0.5 μm. An examination of all the available data for water in quartz and glass capillaries suggest that the average Δr is 0.05–0.1 μm.

It is of interest also to note the T_{md} data yield notably larger values for the thermal expansion coefficient of the water in the pores of the TiO$_2$ than for bulk water.[11]

In Table 1 are listed some additional, fairly recent estimates of Δr. In each case specific objections may possibly be raised, regardless of the experimental procedures

Table 1

Authors	Δr (μm)	Method (or material)
Roberts and Zundel[13]	0.004	IR
Roberts and Zundel[13]	0.004	tracer diffusion
Schufle, Huang and Drost-Hansen[14]	0.02 to 0.1	surface conductance
Strenge et al.[15]	0.003	viscosity of suspensions
Horne and Young[16]	0.017	ion exclusion
Bruun, Sorensen and Drost-Hansen[17]	0.01 to 0.02	ultrasonics; PS suspensions
Peschel and Belouschek[18]	0.003 to 0.008	disjoining pressure
Metzik et al.[19]	0.1	various (see discussion below)

used or the interpretation of the results. However, it appears highly unlikely that all of the studies reported admit to complete alternate analysis in terms of a more 'classical' picture (i.e., Δr of only one (to, say, 5) molecular diameters).

The various estimates of Δr differ significantly; this, however, may not be too surprising, as the methods employed do indeed differ significantly. As an example, the value reported by Strenge et al. was obtained from a viscosity study, based on the assumption that the vicinal water had effectively infinitely high viscosity. The measurements by Peschel et al. suggest that the viscosity at, say, 0.05 μm may only be ~10 times larger than the bulk viscosity. (Note also that it is possible and indeed likely that vicinal water is shear-rate sensitive): this is suggested both in Peschel's studies as well in our own measurements of viscosity, subject to *very* low shear rates (Kerr[20]) and in some recent dilatometric studies on suspensions (Braun[21]). The 'recovery time' may be very long (of the order of hours) depending on the type of system studied, making the detection and characterization even more difficult.

Metzik et al.[19] have reported on the thermal conductivity of water between mica plates. They observed that for plate separations of about 0.1 μm, the heat conductivity is about two orders of magnitude larger than the bulk value (and larger than the thermal conductivity of ice). This is a good example of a case where it would be difficult indeed to ascribe the observed effect merely to an orientational effect of one or a few molecular layers. It is of interest also to note that the thermal conductivity decreases to 'normal' values above about 65 to 70 °C. Many anomalous aqueous properties, ascribed to vicinal water structure, do indeed disappear above this temperature range (cf. Peschel et al.).

Wiggins[22] has reported highly unusual ion partitioning effects by water in narrow pores in quartz. Similar measurements by Hurtado and Drost-Hansen[23] have confirmed these results and these more recent results agree quantitatively with those reported by Wiggins. Experimentally, however, there is one major difference: Wiggins worked with pores of about 25 Å whereas the newer results were obtained with 140 Å pores. This suggests that even in the larger pores, all the water possesses the same properties as that in the smaller pores. In that case Δr is thus likely 70 Å or larger.

III Discussion

It is perplexing and embarrassing that little can be said presently about the dependence of vicinal structuring on distance from the surface inducing the effect. Does the vicinal structuring effect occur over a finite distance (with a more or less abrupt change ('interface') beyond which is 'bulk water') or does it decrease smoothly (for instance exponentially) as one goes from the surface to the bulk region? My own intuitive feeling is that the latter situation prevails (notwithstanding that we usually, for 'arithmetic convenience', operate with a definite thickness, Δr). The problem is obviously of profound importance, and it is particularly significant in dealing with juxtaposed surfaces, such as encountered in cellular systems.

Based on our inspection of the range of values for Δr, it appears that the most likely depth of vicinal water is from 0.02 μm to 0.05 μm. However, one may not interpret this to mean that vicinal water extends this far from the solid interface as a 'homogeneous solid' structure but rather that the suggested range indicates the geometric extent over which attributes of vicinal water may be most readily detected, perhaps 'fading out' with a 'decay length' of, say, 0.01 μm.

There can be little doubt that vicinal water exists. There is, however, great uncertainty as to its extent, structure and energetics. It appears that vicinal water does not differ greatly in its energetics from that of bulk water; obviously, this circumstance makes its experimental detection and characterization difficult. Both Peschel and the present author[24] have estimated the difference in energy between bulk and vicinal water to be very small, of the order of 10 to 100 cal/mol. Extensive DSC measurements currently underway in the author's laboratory (with Mr J. Cianci) appear strongly to confirm this estimate.

Considering that a change in surface potential of 1 mV corresponds to 23 cal/mol, it may be little wonder that many electrochemical studies have failed to detect the effects of vicinal water. On the other hand Peschel[18] claims that his instrument is capable of detecting total excess energies as low as 1 cal/mol. In view of the energetics, it is hardly surprising that most theoretical studies (such as Monte Carlo or Molecular Dynamics calculations) fail to recognize vicinal water. At best, extensions of such calculations as those initiated by Barnes, Finney and coworkers[25] or by Stanley and Teixeira[26] may be sufficiently sensitive to provide a picture of vicinal water.

The extent of vicinal water, should it indeed prove to be in the range $0.02~\mu m < \Delta r < 0.05~\mu m$, is most significant from a cell-biological point of water. Clegg[27] has elegantly argued that nowhere within a cell is one likely to be more than 0.005 to 0.01 μm from a 'surface', especially if, as for instance implied by Jacobson,[28] macromolecules also possess vicinal hydration structures (a view with which the present author fully agrees, for molecules with molecular weights $>10^3$ to 5×10^3 Daltons). Thus, it would appear that all (or nearly all) cell water is vicinal water. Recall, however the uncertainties regarding Δr: do the vicinal water characteristics 'fade away' with a fixed exponential decay length or is there a certain definite thickness beyond which the water possesses normal bulk structure. Thus it is still possible that 'pools' of bulk-like water may occur in cells.

In biological systems, one obviously expects extreme complexity. The proteins are highly temperature sensitive and without a doubt lipid phase transitions also occur (with dramatic importance for the cell functioning). One must now add to this the complexity of the vicinal water structures. Hence, it is little wonder that for instance the thermal responses of organisms sometimes appear *highly* complex. In this connection, it may be of interest to quote Robert Rosen[29] '... Complexity is a property of system description rather than a property of the systems themselves. Indeed, we may say that a system *appears* complex when it is possible to generate many apparently independent descriptions of its behaviour. Each such independent description must arise out of a different process for observing the system and hence out of a distinct available mechanism that enables us to interact with the system.' Rosen also notes: 'Thus, complexity appears as a *contingent*, rather than an *intrinsic*, property and ultimately reflects interactive capabilities reflected in observation or measurement.'

Regarding thermal responses, recall the existence of thermal anomalies in aqueous interfacial properties (observed in physico-chemically well defined systems). The reality of these anomalies, usually observed, for instance near 15, 30 or 45 °C has repeatedly been demonstrated.[30] It is also certain that no such anomalies exist in bulk aqueous systems, and hence it appears inescapable that interfacial structural effects must exist to explain the thermal anomalies. One possibility is that the anomalies reflect first and/or higher-order phase transitions in the vicinal water. In that case distinct structured entities must exist in vicinal water. Furthermore, in view of the magnitude of the changes often observed,[22,23] these changes are indeed not restricted to one or a few molecular layers. It is obvious that the existence of the thermal anomalies impose severe demands on the theoretician: any ultimate theory of aqueous interfacial behaviour must be able to account for, and predict, the existence of anomalies. By the same token, any experimental testing of current or future theories must be carried out at closely spaced temperature intervals. Life wasn't meant to be easy.

The occurrence and extent of vicinal water

Acknowledgement

The author wishes to thank Dr A.-J. Berteaud for his kind hospitality during his residence (1981) at CNRS (Thiais, France) at which time these notes were prepared. Thanks are due also to Dr J. Teixeira for some helpful insight into the Stanley–Teixera percolation model of water.

References

1. J. Peschel and K. H. Adlfinger, *Z. Naturforschung*, **26a**, 707 (1971).
2. J. N. Israelachvili and G. E. Adams, *J. Chem. Soc., Faraday Trans.*, I **74**, 975 (1978); see also *Faraday Disc.*, **65**, 20 (1978).
3. J. Peschel and P. Belouschek, in *Cell-Associated Water*, eds W. Drost-Hansen and J. S. Clegg, Acad. Press, pp. 3–52 (1979).
4. W. Drost-Hansen, (a) *Phys. Chem. Liquids* **7**, 243 (1977); see also: (b) *Chemistry of the Cell Interface*, vol. 'B', ed. H. D. Brown; Acad. Press, pp. 1–84 (1971); and (c) *Ind. and Eng. Chemistry*, **61**, (November) 10 (1969).
5. J. Clifford, in *Water—A Comprehensive Treatise*, Vol. 5, ed. F. Franks, Plenum Press, pp. 75–132 (1975).
6. C. Ballario, A. Bomincontro, C. Cametti and A. DiBiasio, *J. Coll. Interface Sci.*, **78**(1), 242 (1980); see also ibid., **63**, 567 (1978) and *Lett. Nuovo Cimento*, **6**, (15), 611 (1973).
7. F. Henry and A.-J. Berteaud, *J. Microwave Power*, **15** (4), 233 (1980).
8. F. Henry, A.-J. Berteaud and W. Drost-Hansen, unpublished results, 1980–1981.
9. B. Deryaguin, *Croatia Chem. Acta*, **50**, 187 (1977); see also *J. Coll. Interface Sci.*, **49** (2), 249 (1974) and *Doklady Akad. Nauk SSSR*, **207** (3), 572 (1972).
10. J. A. Schufle and S.-Y. Huang, *Texas J. of Sci.*, XXIV (2), 197 (1972); see also *J. Geophys. Res.*, **73** (10), 3345 (1968).
11. B. V. Deryaguin, V. V. Karasev and E. N. Khromova, *J. Coll. Interface Sci.*, **78** (1), 274 (1980).
12. G. E. van Gils, *J. Coll. Interface Sci.*, **30** (2), 272 (1969).
13. N. K. Roberts and G. Zundel, *J. Phys. Chem.*, **84**, 3655 (1980); see also ibid., **85**, 2706 (1981).
14. J. A. Schufle, C. T. Huang and W. Drost-Hansen, *J. Coll. Interface Sci.*, **54**, 184 (1976).
15. K. Strenge, *Z. Phys. Chemie* (Leipzig), **259** (1), 102 (1978).
16. R. A. Horne and R. P. Young, *Electrochim. Acta*, **17**, 763 (1972).
17. S. G. Bruun, P. Graae Sorensen and W. Drost-Hansen, submitted for publication.
18. J. Peschel and P. Belouschek, in *Cell-Associated Water*, eds W. Drost-Hansen and J. S. Clegg, Acad. Press, pp. 22–24 (1979).
19. M. S. Metsik, V. D. Perevertaer, V. A. Liopo, G. T. Timoshtchenko and A. B. Kiselev, *J. Coll. Interface Sci.*, **43** (3), 662 (1973).
20. J. E. D. Kerr, Ph.D. Dissertation, Univ. of Miami, 1970; see also W. Drost-Hansen, in *L'eau et les Systèmes Biologiques*, Publ. by C.N.R.S., Paris, France, pp. 177–186 (1976).
21. C. V. Braun, Jr., M.S. Dissertation, Univ. of Miami, 1980.
22. P. M. Wiggins, *Clin. and Exp. Pharmacology and Physiology*, **2**, 171 (1975); see also: *Cell-Associated Water*, eds W. Drost-Hansen and J. S. Clegg, Acad. Press, pp. 69–114 (1979).
23. R. M. Hurtado and W. Drost-Hansen in *Cell-Associated Water*, pp. 115–123 (1979).
24. W. Drost-Hansen, *Phys. Chem. Liquids*, **7**, 295 (1977).
25. P. Barnes, J. L. Finney, J. D. Nicholas and J. E. Quinn, *Nature*, **282**, 459 (1979).
26. H. E. Stanley and J. Teixeira, *J. Chem. Phys.*, **73** (7), 3403 (1980).
27. J. S. Clegg, *Collective Phenomena*, **3**, 289 (1981).
28. B. Jacobson, *J. Amer. Chem. Soc.*, **77**, 2919 (1955).
29. R. Rosen, *Ann. N.Y. Acad. Sci.*, **316**, 178 (1979).
30. W. Drost-Hansen, see ref. (4) and *Ann. N.Y. Acad. Sci.*, **125** 471 (1965).

The non-exchangeable water fraction inside microsomes

G. Pifat
Ruder Bošković Institute, Zagreb, Yugoslavia

Summary

Presentation is made of the most salient facts regarding the encaged water in the cisternal cavities of rat liver microsomes. The semipermeability of microsomes is shown to be related to non-exchangeable water found by solvent proton magnetic relaxation measurements.

Endoplasmic reticulum of liver cells contains a complex monooxygenatic drug metabolizing enzyme system consisting of three essential components: terminal oxydase cytochrome P-450, NADPH dependent flavoprotein called NADPH cytochrome P-450 reductase and the heterogeneous phospholipid fraction.[1] This lipoprotein membranous network is transversally ruptured upon the homogenization and centrifugation of liver cells into microsomes which have the same inside-outside membrane orientation and therefore could be considered as the biochemical equivalent of the ER despite its different morphology.

Solvent proton magnetic relaxation measurements can gather information at short distances between the protons in the quasi-solid (microsomal) and liquid (water) interfaces, spreading very efficiently to the bulk of the solvent by the rapid diffusion of water molecules. If the protons can sense the macromolecular surface close by, the proton relaxation measurements can provide specific information which may not be detectable by other methods. Thus, the dynamic (and indirectly structural) information manifested by the changes in the nuclear relaxation time, T_1, could answer the question of whether the proton relaxation behaviour in the cisternal liquid of the microsomes is equal to that within the cytoplasmic liquid.

Only the most salient facts bearing on this problem are examined in this presentation.

The rationale behind the approach of Ruckpaul et al.[2] is that although the two compartments behave identically under a given set of conditions, they are less likely to do so consistently if some of the parameters conditioning their behaviour are varied. In their 1976 study of the solvent proton relaxation of microsomes,[2] more than a twofold increase was found in the total relaxation (from the initial H_2O amount in suspension) after the establishment of an isotopic (D_2O) dialysis equilibrium, with about 20% of the initial protons non-exchanged by the dialysis (Figure 1). This could be rationalized as the fraction of water very probably within the hollow interior of microsomes where water may be considerably restricted in its long-range motions, and the protons of which are non-exchangeable with bulk water. This was confirmed by the same authors[2] with the reverse experiments starting from the fully deuterated microsomes after the addition of 19% H_2O. The low relaxation rate (marked by the asterisk in Figure 1) indicates that the water restricted motionally by the macromolecular structures is encaged in the cisternal lumen prior to the D_2O dialysis, since proton communication between the cisternal and cytoplasmic compartments does not exist.

If the cisternal and cytoplasmic liquids differ in the structure and dynamics of their water, the two phases of the solvent should imply that the free induction decay is composed of two relaxation rates. Grasdalen et al.[3] in 1978 did not observe two exponential magnetic relaxation decays in their pulsed NMR measurements of deuter-

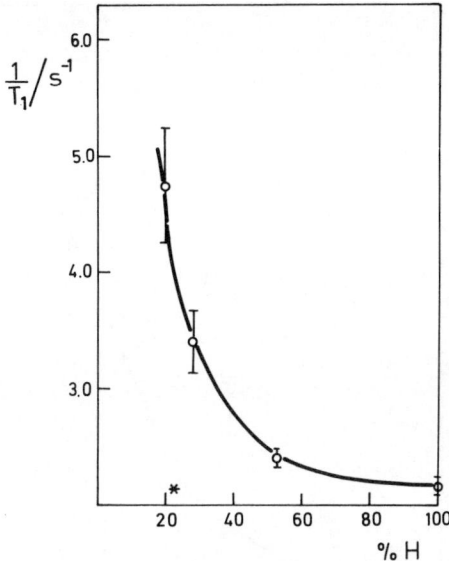

Figure 1 $1/T_1$ of microsomes depending on isotopic dilution of the solvent at room temperature; * is $1/T_1$ for deuterated microsomes with 19% H_2O added. (From reference 2)

ated microsomes since their study was performed at extreme magnetic dilution with 5% residual water. Under those conditions, the relaxation behaviour may be complicated due to the cross-relaxation between the very efficient spin-diffusion controlled relaxation of the protons from the quasi-solid membrane phase and the protons in the liquid, efficiently averaging out relaxation mechanisms throughout the whole microsomal suspension and resulting in the entire spin system relaxing as one phase. In Ruckpaul's study,[2] the addition of 19% H_2O in excess of the deuterated amount assumed to be encaged (~10%) made possible the observation of two relaxation rates from the two separate water phases.

Further evidence in favour of encaged water within the cisternal cavities is found in the results of Maričić et al.[4] with experiments in freezing microsomal water suspensions (Figure 2), where the total temperature-dependent magnetization was followed as the indicator of the percentage of 'unfrozen' protons. According to Kuntz et al.,[5] this experiment could be explained by the immobilization of the external hydration down to -7 °C, whereas the rest of the water could only be encaged within the microsomal cisternal lumen.

An interesting insight into the encaged water question is obtained through reconsideration of the studies on the permeability of microsomal membranes by Share et al. and Nilssen et al.[6,7] Using different methods but not proton magnetic relaxation measurements, the latter presented evidence along several lines which indicates that the amount of intramicrosomal water is not appreciably affected by changes in the solute concentration if solutes are uncharged molecules, e.g. sucrose or glucose, confirming a lack of osmotic response towards these solutes. With charged acetate, a marked osmotic response was found (Figure 3). Sucrose can penetrate into 77% of the intramicrosomal water compartment (which contains 44% of the total amount of microsomal

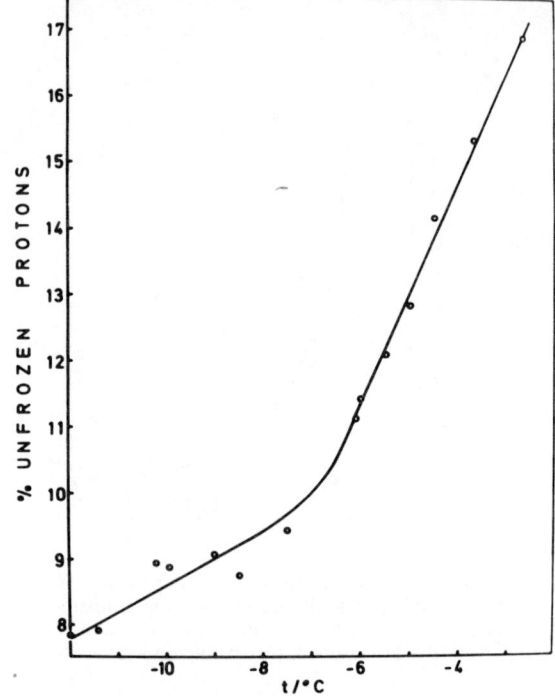

Figure 2 The temperature-dependence of the total magnetization, M_0, of microsomes. (From reference 4)

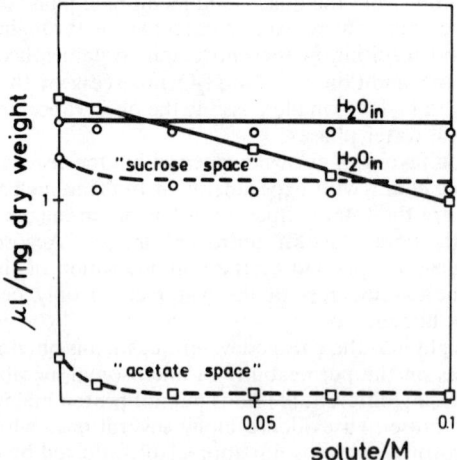

Figure 3 The effect of solute concentration on the intramicrosomal water compartment: ○ = sucrose, □ = acetate. (Dashed lines: corresponding 'solute space'.) (From reference 7)

water) leaving sucrose-inaccessible space at 23%, while acetate leaves the cisternal side of the microsomes intact. Their results can be summarized as follows: rat liver microsomes are penetrable by uncharged molecules of up to relatively high molecular weight (600 daltons) but they are impermeable to small charged molecules (90 daltons). It is interesting to mention that in 1967 Maude[8] found 16–27% of water inaccessible to sucrose in renal microsomes.

Thus Nilssen's, as Share's and Maude's results concerning permeability measurements, yield similar percentages of inaccessible (non-exchangeable) water to the proton relaxation measurements.

In summary, although water as well as sucrose can penetrate into the cisternal lumen, the fraction of intramicrosomal water is inaccessible to sugar and non-exchangeable with the bulk cytoplasmic water. This implies that this water fraction is somehow structurally 'hidden' in the interior of the microsomal vesicles. Is this functionally important?

References

1. K. Ruckpaul, *Die Pharmazie*, **33**, 310 (1978).
2. K. Ruckpaul, S. Maričić, C. R. Jänig, B. Benko, S. Vuk-Pavlović and H. Rein, *Croat. Chem. Acta*, **48**, 69 (1976).
3. H. Grasdalen, L. E. G. Eriksson, A. Ehrenberg and D. Bäckström, *Biochem. Biophys. Acta*, **541**, 521 (1978).
4. S. Maričić, B. Benko and S. Vuk-Pavlović, unpublished results.
5. I. D. Kuntz and W. Kauzman, *Adv. Protein Chem.*, **28**, 239 (1974).
6. L. Share and R. W. Hausrote, *J. Cell. Biol.*, **7**, 239 (1960).
7. R. Nilssen, E. Peterson and G. Dallner, *J. Cell. Biol.*, **56**, 762 (1973).
8. D. L. Maude, *Biochem. Biophys. Acta*, **135**, 365 (1967).

Some electrical properties of small isolated water molecule arrays

D. T. Edmonds
The Clarendon Laboratory, Oxford, UK

Summary

Some of the calculated electrical properties of small assemblies of water molecules, isolated within a protein or within a membrane, are discussed. In particular their ability to provide low energy, highly selective binding sites for ions and the consequences of ferro-electrically ordered arrays of water molecules are described.

Considerable controversy surrounds the extent to which water within living cells and even that surrounding biologically active molecules in solution differs in its properties from normal water. For a small aggregate of water molecules trapped within a protein or a membrane there can be little doubt that its properties will be markedly different if only because of the large proportion of water molecules at its surface. For example in an approximately spherical assembly of water molecules some 2.7 nm in diameter, 50% of the 320 water molecules are on the surface.

One approach to the study of water in biology is to study small isolated assemblies of water molecules that form one extreme in the spectrum of the properties of water just as bulk water forms the other extreme. Here I will concentrate on two electrical properties of such small assemblies that have received little notice to date.

The first is the extent to which very small numbers of water molecules suitably arranged can provide binding sites for small ions with energies as low as water in bulk. To exist in a low energy state a water molecule requires four hydrogen bonds (two donors and two acceptors) arranged tetrahedrally. Two structures that satisfy these requirements are the planar pentagon and the puckered hexagon. Normal ice consists of puckered hexagons and both pentagons and hexagons are found in the clathrate hydrates.[1] Calculations, including the effects of dipole–dipole and dipole–quadrupole interactions and also those of induced dipoles, reveal[2] that the centres of these water rings are very low energy sites for particular small ions.

The electrostatic self-energy of an isolated spherical ion of charge Q is given by

$$U = (1/2)QV_S$$

where V_s is the electrostatic potential at its surface. For a small ion like Na^+ the energy can be very large (12×10^{-19} J/ion or 720 kJ/mol). The energy is substantially lowered when the ion is embedded in an electrically polarizable material (high dielectric constant) such as water. The positive charge of the ion induces time averaged dipoles in the surrounding fluid pointing away from the centre ion. The negative ends of the induced dipoles point toward the central ion and reduce V_s, thus reducing U. With a Na^+ ion situated at the centre of a planar pentagon of water molecules the electrical dipoles of the water molecules tip to point away from the ion again reducing V_s. Even allowing for the hydrogen bond rupture that occurs when the water molecules rotate to reorient their dipole moments, the calculated energy of the ion and water ring is as low as that of an ion in bulk water. An interesting feature of the interstitial water ring sites is that the low energy depends on the closeness of fit of the unhydrated ion within the water ring and it is particularly low for Na^+ in the planar pentagon and K^+ in the puckered hexagon. The energy also depends on the valence state of the ion and, through the water quadrupole interaction, on the sign of the ionic charge. Such ion selectivity that is provided by static water rings is not provided by bulk water. Another interesting feature is that the ion binding sites may be as close together as 0.3 nm without raising the resting electrical dipolar energy of the water molecule assembly, thus allowing high[2] ionic mobility.

The second interesting electrical property of small water molecule assemblies is that suitably shaped assemblies, if they are shielded from high dielectric constant fluids, will order ferro-electrically and thus give rise to large electric fields. Although normal room temperature ferromagnets order through the (essentially electrostatic) exchange interaction, paramagnetic crystals will order as ferromagnets or antiferromagnets solely through the magnetic dipole interaction at sufficiently low temperatures,[3] usually of order 0.1 K. Even assemblies of nuclei order[4] through their much weaker magnetic dipole interaction at temperatures of order 10^{-6} K. The energy of interaction in a vacuum of two electric dipoles each of strength 1 Debye is 11,644 times as strong as that of two magnetic dipoles each of strength 1 Bohr magneton and separated by the same distance, so that we might expect electrical order due to dipolar interactions at temperatures of order hundreds of K. In fact few ferro-electrics due to electric dipole interaction alone are known experimentally. However, lattice sums calculated for water molecule arrays that are long in comparison with their diameter,[2,5] do show that the electrically ordered state has an energy substantially below the disordered state. The presence of surrounding material with a dielectric constant of order 5 or even 10, as may be expected within a protein or a membrane, reduces the energy advantage of the ordered state but does not remove it.

Besides the long range electric dipolar interaction, for tetrahedrally bonded water molecules, there is a short range force. As has been shown for ice,[6] in the absence of hydrogen bonding defects (i.e. two protons or zero protons in a given oxygen to oxygen bond), there is a correlation in the alignment of the electric dipole moments to second nearest neighbours. This may be thought of as a short range contribution to the Onsager[7] reaction field although Onsager only considered long range forces in his calculation. Following the arguments of Onsager this correlation cannot cause ferroelectric order but can aid its stability once established.

Ferro-electrically ordered water molecule arrays can give rise to large electric fields and could interact strongly with, for example, the known axial electric dipole moment of a protein α-helix backbone which is of order 3.5 D per residue.[8] Also the axial dipole moment of an electrically ordered cylindrical water molecule array could be forced to reverse[5] by the proximity of a charged molecule to one end, thus converting a short range action into a long range (the length of the water column) effect.

If these two calculated electrical properties of small water assemblies are confirmed by experiment it will be surprising indeed if nature has not taken advantage of them. I have previously described at some length[2,5,9] a model membrane ion channel based upon an ordered water structure which is capable of reproducing many of the measured properties of real ion channels, including the current-voltage characteristic[10] of Na^+ and K^+ channels in nerve membrane, without the need of 'gating particles'. Recently X-ray diffraction has revealed several[11,12,13] large scale water structures, in one case[13] consisting of five successive edge-connected water pentagons in a deoxydinucleoside-drug complex. It is interesting to speculate if such networks exist in real biological systems and, if so, how they could assist in charge transfer or long range signal transmission.

References

1. D. W. Davidson, in *Water: A Comprehensive Treatise*, Chap. 4, Vol. 2, Plenum Press (1974).
2. D. T. Edmonds, *Proc. R. Soc. (London)*, **B211**, 51 (1980).
3. A. H. Cooke, D. T. Edmonds, C. B. P. Finn and W. P. Wolf, *J. Phys. Soc. Japan*, **17** (B-1), 481 (1962).
4. F. Jacquinot, W. T. Wenckebach, M. Chapellier, M. Goldman and A. Abragam, *C.R. Acad. Sci.* Paris, **B278**, 93 (1974).
5. D. T. Edmonds, *Chem. Phys. Letters*, **65**, 429 (1979).
6. C. A. Coulson and D. Eisenberg, *Proc. R. Soc. (London)*, **A291**, 445 (1966).
7. L. Onsager, *J. Amer. Chem. Soc.*, **58**, 1486 (1936).
8. W. G. J. Hol, P. T. van Duijnen and H. J. C. Berendsen, *Nature (London)*, **273**, 443 (1978).
9. D. T. Edmonds, *Biochem. Soc. Symp.*, No. 46, London (1980).
10. D. T. Edmonds, *Trends in Biochem. Sci.*, April 92 (1981).
11. W. Saenger, *Nature (London)*, **279**, 343 (1979).
12. I. R. Hanson and M. R. Truter, *J. Chem. Soc. Perkin II*, 1 (1981).
13. S. Neidle, H. M. Berman and H. S. Shieh, *Nature (London)*, **288**, 129 (1980).

Molecular mechanism of the hydration force

S. Marčelja

Australian National University, Canberra, Australia

Introduction

Evidence for interactions which depend on changes in water structure near surfaces is plentiful; much of it precedes this conference by several decades. Interaction between inert solute molecules which do not like to mix with water is for historical reasons called 'hydrophobic'. Colloidal particles which failed to coagulate were drawn with schematic 'hydration spheres' by Kruyt and Bungenberg de Jong in 1929. But old research led to only a vague picture of the origin of either of the two types of interaction. Much of the recent work is also difficult to interpret. For example, NMR data frequently show line splittings or other changes in spectra, which lead to a conclusion of 'structured water'—another vague description. Computer simulations may show tremendous detail: positions of dozens of water molecules around an ion or few ions, which again may be difficult to translate to conceptual understanding of physical changes in the structure. Like in statistical mechanics, we do not want to know all coordinates, momenta and momentary values of pairwise interactions. We need to find appropriate physical quantities and calculate spatial averages and ensemble averages which will help us to understand the system.

Molecular picture

(a) *Hydrophobic interaction:* Recent simulation work has improved our knowledge of changes in water structure near small hydrophobic solutes. The intuitive picture, i.e. a dynamically distorted and smeared version of the structures seen in clathrate hydrates has been shown to be qualitatively correct. But we still do not have a reasonably simple and accurate method of calculating changes in free energy and the force associated with that structure.

The structure near macroscopic hydrophobic surfaces is not understood, the most elementary example being the free surface of water. In the macroscopic case, clathrate cages are not possible, and an increase in straining and breaking of bonds will occur. Since water molecules are not spherically symmetrical, there is surface orientation and surface potential.[1] Changes in structure induced by a macroscopic hydrophobic surface thus include a combination of several effects. Interesting old work by Fletcher[2] is now well deserving of more attention. A lot of experimental ingenuity would be needed to obtain data from which molecular parameters can be deduced. Finally, simulation with polarizable water molecules[3] will in this case be particularly interesting.

(b) *Hydration interaction:* This old problem has in the last five years received most valuable input from repulsive force measurements by Rand, Parsegian and co-workers[4,5] and by Israelachvili and Pashley.[6,7] From their results, it is seen that surfaces with electrical charges and/or dipoles interact via two mechanisms: (i) a diffuse double-layer repulsion. When surface charge regulation is included, this interaction is for monovalent electrolytes and moderate ionic concentrations well described by the classical picture and (ii) strong, short-range, repulsive force, independent of ionic concentration. This 'hydration force' follows an exponential law, with a characteristic length of 2–3 Å.

The molecular mechanism of the hydration force presents an interesting and challenging problem. The natural assumption concerning changes in the structure of water is that surface charges or dipoles induce local dielectric polarization. Due to correla-

Molecular mechanism of the hydration force

tions in the fluid, the perturbation spreads some distance away from the surface. Quite general statistical mechanics arguments[8] show that in the continuum limit* the corresponding repulsion must follow an exponential law.

More detailed information regarding the structural perturbation near a charged surface can be obtained from computer simulation and from analytical work on the ice lattice.[10,11] The coupled differential equations governing spatial dependence of the electrical field and the polarization field can be set up and solved for the ice structure. In ice, sources and sinks for the polarization field are Bjerrum L and D defects, which thus play a fully analogous role to cations and anions in a diffuse double layer. If ρ_0 is the equilibrium density of Bjerrum defects, and a the interlayer distance, the characteristic length describing the spatial variation of the polarization field in ice is given by $\xi^2 = a^2/(2\rho_0\varepsilon)$.

The physical picture which has emerged from all the mentioned work does not apply just to ice. I believe that it provides a natural framework in which we can describe a perturbation induced in aqueous solutions by the presence of a charged surface. Electrical field and polarization field associated with surface charges appear as a superposition of two solutions of the corresponding equations, relating to the two distinct physical regimes.

(i) Associated with *a net surface charge*, there is a long-range electrical field, screened by ions present in the solution. This classical electrical double layer is only weakly affected by the molecular nature of the aqueous solvent. Only in conditions where the Debye screening length λ_D is short, solvent polarization cannot follow very rapid spatial changes in the field, and the effective screening length is increased compared to the Debye length.[12] The approximate formula is

$$\lambda_1^2 \approx \lambda_D^2 + (\varepsilon - 1)\xi^2,$$

where ξ is the characteristic length associated with spatial variation of dielectric polarization and given previously for the case of ice. Experiments indicate that in water ξ is of the order of 2–3 Å.

(ii) *Surface dipoles or multipoles* lead to strong, short-ranged electrical fields confined to the neighbourhood of the charges. Those fields will lead to some average orientation of water molecules near a surface. A net *surface-induced dielectric polarization* causes a strong, repulsive force, which, however, decays rapidly with separation. If ions are present in solution, the decay is slightly faster, but the interference is minimal. The decay length is given by:

$$\lambda_2^2 \approx \xi^2[1 - (\varepsilon - 1)\xi^2/\lambda_D^2].$$

A general solution is the superposition of both short and long-range fields, which satisfies the boundary conditions. It should be stressed that the values of E and P at the boundary depend on the nature and the distribution of surface charges and dipoles. There is no reason to assume that the macroscopic relation $P = \chi E$ will hold; it has been derived for spatially uniform fields. For the long-range solution, associated with the diffuse double layer, $P_1 \approx \chi E_1/(1 - \varepsilon\xi^2/\lambda_1^2)$, where χ is the dielectric susceptibility

---

* I have often been criticized for predicting smooth monotonic behaviour without oscillations which are due to the molecular structure. We have always been aware (e.g., discussion in Ref. 9) that the continuum limit is an idealization, and that in a real fluid, interaction will show some structure. I believe that the behaviour of the envelope contains more interesting physical information than the superposed oscillations, which merely reflect the size of the molecule. In aqueous solutions, interaction between macroscopic surfaces does not show much structure, perhaps due to the open nature of the underlying continuous random network.

for spatially uniform fields. For the short-range solution $P_2 \approx -E_2/4\pi$. The limit of the classical theory of dielectrics is obtained by assuming that there is no spatial variation in the applied field. Alternatively, one may assume $\xi = 0$. In the ice picture, this means that the density of Bjerrum defects is very large. Then there is no increase in the free energy associated with spatial variation of the polarization field. The long range solution becomes the classical diffuse double layer, and the spatial extent of the short range solution shrinks to zero.

Conclusion

Recent experiments[4-7] which have provided quantitative data on the 'hydration force' have been of tremendous importance. They have enabled us to make first steps towards understanding of the molecular origin of that force. I hope that in future other clever experiments will be devised in order to characterize changes in molecular structure near surfaces. If average orientation of water dipolar moments could be measured, it could provide a direct test of the physical picture proposed in this discussion report.

References

1. U. del Pennino, A. Loria, S. Mantovani and E. Mazzega, *Nuovo Cimento*, **24B**, 108 (1974).
2. N. H. Fletcher, *Phil. Mag.*, **18**, 1287 (1968).
3. P. Barnes, J. L. Finney, J. D. Nicholas and J. E. Quinn, *Nature*, **282**, 459 (1979).
4. D. M. Le Neveu, R. P. Rand and V. A. Parsegian, *Nature*, **259**, 601 (1976).
5. A. C. Cowley, N. L. Fuller, R. P. Rand and V. A. Parsegian, *Biochemistry*, **17**, 316 (1978).
6. J. N. Israelachvili and G. E. Adams, *J. Chem. Soc. Faraday Trans.*, I **74**, 975 (1978).
7. R. M. Pashley, *J. Colloid Interface Sci.* (in press).
8. S. Marčelja and N. Radić, *Chem. Phys. Letters*, **42**, 129 (1976); S. Marčelja, *Croat. Chem. Acta*, **49**, 347 (1977).
9. S. Marčelja, D. J. Mitchell, B. W. Ninham and M. J. Sculley, *J. Chem. Soc. Faraday Trans.*, II **73**, 630 (1977).
10. D. W. R. Gruen, S. Marčelja and B. A. Pailthorpe, this proceedings and *Chem. Phys. Letters* (in press).
11. D. W. R. Gruen and S. Marčelja, to be published.
12. N. Radić and S. Marčelja, *Chem. Phys. Letters*, **55**, 377 (1978).

Water at the protein surface

Robert G. Bryant
University of Minnesota, USA

There is a wealth of thermodynamic, kinetic and chemical evidence supporting the view that water at a surface is different in several ways from water in the bulk. A difficulty in coming to an understanding of water at a surface, however, is agreeing on what constitutes fair or answerable questions about this possibly unique environment. On one hand, the surface presents structural and dynamic components that are similar to the solid. For example, X-ray structures of proteins sometimes include oxygen atom positions for water molecules at the protein surface, though these positions are consid-

Water at the protein surface

erably less certain than those of the protein atoms.[1] On the other hand, there is no compelling evidence for arrangements of solvent molecules at the surface of a protein which are immobilized in particular orientations for periods longer than the order of a microsecond. Thus, while there may be unique structure in the interfacial region, the system remains essentially fluid.

Unlike the pure solid or liquid, the interface region provides a marked anisotropy in many properties as one passes from the interior of the protein through the transition region to bulk liquid or solvent. This observation is an important beginning point for formulating an hypothesis for the behaviour of water at the surface of a protein or other biological surface. The present model is based in part on deductions from NMR relaxation data,[2] but its consequences are general. Most features of the model are not new, but it is presented so that it may stimulate fruitful discussion at this meeting, clarify my own ideas about this complex problem, and stimulate additional experimentation aimed at improving or disproving the model.

The heterogeneity of the protein surface suggests that of the several hydrogen bonds which hold the water to the protein, one will be stronger than the others. This likelihood suggests that motion of water at the surface will be rotationally anisotropic; that is, it will reorient more slowly about one axis than about others. In the simplest case the model introduces two correlation times into the water reorientation problem; one characterizing the very rapid motion about the strongest hydrogen bond, and one characterizing the slower reorientation of the fast rotation axis.[3] A schematic representation of the situation is shown in Figure 1 for two orientations of water at the surface.

Focusing on just NMR relaxation there are very important spectroscopic consequences of such an anisotropic motion of water at the surface: (1) The longitudinal NMR relaxation rate would sense only the high frequency motion in the usual temperature study because temperatures that are well above room temperature are likely to be required to sense the slower motion, particularly at the higher NMR frequencies more generally used today. (2) The very rapid reorientation about one axis will partially average several interactions that drive relaxation events, thus the apparent strength of the proton magnetic dipole–dipole interaction, for example, will be diminished more or less depending on the angle that the rapid rotation axis makes with the interproton vector.[3] That is, relaxation rates will be smaller than expected. (3) The transverse NMR relaxation rate will be drastically increased relative to the longitudinal relaxation rate by the contribution of the slow reorientation of the rapid rotation axis; however, depression of T_2 is not definitive evidence in support of such an anisotropic model because at least two other mechanisms could cause similar effects: (i) chemical exchange events that mix water protons with exchangeable protein protons, and (ii) distributions of correlation times.[4] (4) Relaxation measurements made over a wide frequency range would show a high frequency dispersion as well as a low frequency

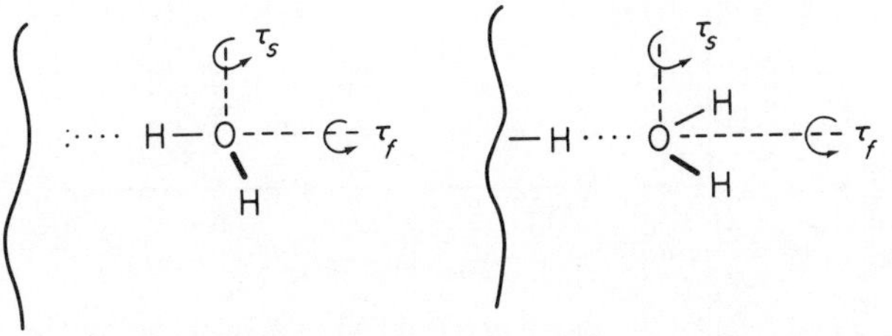

Figure 1 Anisotropic motion of water at the surface

dispersion where the inflection points should correspond to the rapid and the slow correlation times of Figure 1.

The existence of the fast motion of water at the protein surface is well supported by several types of measurement notably NMR and dielectric relaxation.[5] Characterization of the slower motions of water at the surface are considerably less definitive. There are several lines of evidence which support it, however. (1) The decrease in the water self-diffusion coefficients in protein solutions and on protein aggregates suggests a significant deviation from the liquid values.[6] (2) The coupling of the proton NMR relaxation rate of the water to the rotational motion of the protein reported accurately by NMR dispersion measurements suggests that there is a component of water motion that is at least on the order of the protein rotational correlation time which is considerably slower than the rapid rotation sensed by the higher frequency NMR relaxation measurements.[7] (3) The hydrodynamic discrepancy between the calculated size and the hydrodynamic size of protein molecules when their volumes are measured by sedimentation or light scattering, for example, suggest some slower water motion at the protein surface.[8] (4) NMR dispersion measurements carried out on solids provide at this point preliminary evidence for a slower correlation time in the problem as shown below in Figure 2.[9]

This picture of water at a protein surface is essentially a site model in which the water at a particular site is more or less free to rotate about one direction and less free

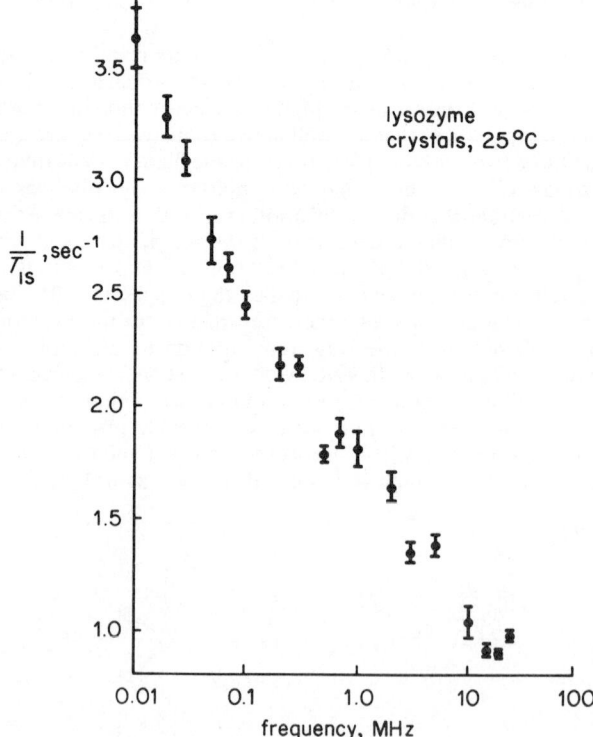

Figure 2 ^{1}H NMR relaxation rate for water in lysozyme crystals as a function of frequency at 298 K

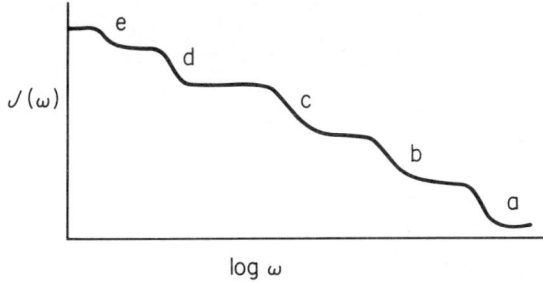

Figure 3 Proposed spectral density plot for water in water–protein systems

to rotate about the others. The absence of significant ^2H_2O quadrupole splittings in the spectrum implies, however, that the fast rotation axis must reorient in times short compared to times of order a microsecond. The fundamental heterogeneity of the protein surface implies a distribution in the parameters that characterize both the thermodynamics and dynamics of the water. There is considerable evidence for such distributions, but we may anticipate that as water is titrated into a protein system, the properties of the water already there are modified by the additional mobile dipoles so that precise or unique characterization of the distribution appropriate to water parameters is elusive. Nevertheless, the above picture of a two-correlation time model must certainly be modified somewhat to include a distribution of barriers for both the rapid and slow correlation times suggested in Figure 1. One may estimate the width of such a distribution in the high frequency case from the NMR data;[2] however, there is little direct evidence available on the nature of the distribution appropriate to the slower correlation times.

In summary, the working hypothesis for water dynamics at a protein or other surface that I propose be discussed and evaluated further is represented by Figure 1 and the spectral density plot drawn schematically in Figure 3. The inflections are tentatively identified as follows: (a) the very high frequency motion appropriate to bulk water in a protein solution; (b) the rapid rotation of water about a unique hydrogen bond direction in the surface bound state; (c) the reorientation of the rapid rotation axis, which should also approximate to the time constant for the surface diffusion; (d) the averaging of long range anisotropies imposed by the macroscopic features of samples such as collagen fibres or protein crystals; (e) the contribution from chemical exchange of protons between water and the ionizable protein groups.

References

1. K. Watenpaugh, T. Margulis, L. Sieker and L. Jensen, *J. Mol. Biol.*, **122**, 175 (1978).
2. W. M. Shirley and R. G. Bryant, *J. Amer. Chem. Soc.*, submitted.
3. D. E. Woessner, *J. Chem. Phys.*, **36**, 1 (1962).
4. H. A. Resing, *Adv. Mol. Relax. Processes*, **1**, 109 (1967).
5. R. G. Bryant and W. M. Shirley, *Biophysical Journal*, **32**, 3 (1980).
6. T. L. James and K. T. Gillen, *Biochem. Biophys. Acta*, **286**, 10 (1972).
7. S. H. Koenig, in Amer. Chem. Soc. Symposium Series: *Water in Polymers*, ed. S. P. Rowland, American Chemical Society, Washington, D.C., **127**, 157–76 (1980).
8. I. D. Kuntz, Jr. and W. Kauzmann, in *Advances in Protein Chemistry*, Eds C. B. Anfinsen, J. T. Edsall and F. M. Fichards, Academic Press, New York, **28**, 239–345 (1974).
9. R. G. Bryant and S. H. Koenig, unpublished results.

Biophysics of Water
Edited by F. Franks
© 1982 John Wiley & Sons Ltd

Double-layer, van der Waals and hydration forces between surfaces in electrolyte solutions

J. N. Israelachvili and **R. M. Pashley**

The Australian National University, Canberra, Australia

Summary

We review the experimental evidence concerning the applicability and limitations of the DLVO theory (of electric double-layer and van der Waals forces) between surfaces in aqueous solutions. It is concluded that observed deviations below ~30 Å are not due to a breakdown of DLVO forces but to the existence of additional exponentially repulsive hydration forces. Measurements of these forces between mica surfaces in various 1:1 and 2:1 electrolytes at different concentrations and pH show that only when hydrated cations bind to the negatively charged surfaces do hydration forces appear, and that their strength correlate with the known hydration of the cations. Surfaces which already contain hydrated surface groups chemically attached to them (e.g. surfactants, lipids) apparently exhibit intrinsic hydration forces. The results allow for a rationalization of many phenomena not previously understood, and their biological significance is demonstrated.

Introduction

In the following we review our current state of knowledge concerning the forces between surfaces and between charged groups in electrolyte solutions, with particular attention to the role of 'water structure' in such interactions. The experimental options for direct intermolecular force measurements are limited, and are restricted to measuring the forces between macroscopic surfaces, the results of which may be compared with theory, and then extrapolated to the microscopic world of biology: to cell surface and membrane interactions, intermicelle and protein interactions, etc.

The DLVO theory: van der Waals and electric double-layer forces

The two major forces between identical, charged (ionized) surfaces in aqueous solutions are believed to be attractive van der Waals forces and repulsive double-layer forces.[1,2] To a first approximation the attractive forces follow an inverse power law with distance, while the repulsive forces are exponential. The van der Waals forces are largely independent of the type and concentration of electrolyte, while the magnitude and decay length of the double-layer forces are sensitive to both. The DLVO theory considers the interplay of these two interactions, and has enjoyed great success in describing the stability* of many colloidal systems and is currently being gleefully rediscovered by biologists—particularly those interested in cell membrane interactions.

It is important to note that both van der Waals and double-layer force theories assume that water can be treated as a structureless medium, defined solely by its bulk dielectric permittivity (dielectric constant, refractive index, etc.).

Hydration forces

When the force-law between two surfaces or molecules cannot be described by continuum theories, the assumption that the solvent is behaving as a structureless fluid breaks down, and the effects of molecular ordering or structuring near surfaces have to be considered. In such cases we can talk of 'solvation forces', 'structural forces' or, for water, 'hydration forces'. Unfortunately experimental results purporting to show the existence of such forces have been plagued with confusion and controversy, exacerbated no doubt by the polywater caper[3] which has had the negative effect of somewhat discouraging research in this important area, but also the positive effect of bringing home the effect of impurities in yielding spurious results. But the evidence for the existence of *short-range* forces is now overwhelming, and one of the main objectives here will be to correlate them with the chemical nature of surfaces which give rise to such interactions, and then to assess their biological significance.

There are many systems where DLVO theory clearly fails, where

---

* A 'stable' dispersion of colloidal particles is one where the particles do not coagulate, i.e. the repulsive double-layer forces dominate. Instability occurs when the double-layer forces are reduced to the point where the attractive van der Waals forces now dominate, and the particles coagulate (adhere). This is usually brought about by increasing the valency or concentration of the electrolyte ions, or shifting the pH towards the isoelectric point of the surfaces.

additional short-range (<50 Å) repulsive forces are observed, and where the reasons are highly unlikely to be due to contamination. For example, certain clays,[4,5] surfactant[6] and lipid bilayers[7,8] are known to swell spontaneously in aqueous solutions; silica dispersions[9] and polystyrene lattices[10] are also stable at high ionic strengths. There is also the remarkable phenomenon that gas bubbles do not coalesce in aqueous solutions once the electrolyte concentration exceeds a certain value;[11,12] and the forces between two mercury surfaces obey DLVO theory in various electrolyte solutions, but the surfaces fail to coalesce once ionic species, e.g. I$^-$, specifically bind to the surfaces at higher concentrations.[13,14] Concerning biological membranes and lipid bilayers, plant thylakoid membranes adhere in pure water but fail to do so in the presence of 1:1 electrolytes[15] such as 10^{-3} M NaCl (more of that later). More recently Rand[7,8] and coworkers were the first to measure exponentially repulsive hydration forces between lecithin and mixed lipid bilayers (with an exponential decay length of about 3 Å) extending to about 30 Å, beyond which van der Waals and double-layer forces take over. The occurrence of short-range hydration effects between surfactant bilayers had previously been observed by Clunie and co-workers.[6]

The unexpected swelling of clays, the stability of some colloidal dispersions and the additional repulsion between air bubbles all occur or are brought about by high concentrations of electrolyte where according to the DLVO theory the surfaces should coagulate. The hydration forces observed between zwitterionic lecithin bilayers, however, occur in *pure* water. Thus electrolyte or surface charge density effects cannot be invoked in this case and while there now appears to be some consensus concerning their exponential decay and their effective range[7,8,16] (~30 Å), their origin is still not apparent. We believe that the results of a long series of experiments carried out in this laboratory over the last five years now provide a clear picture of the origin and nature of hydration forces, and rationalize many previously reported and apparently disjointed observations of such forces. These will now be described.

Measurements of van der Waals, double-layer and hydration forces between molecularly smooth surfaces

An apparatus capable of measuring the force as a function of distance (to 1 Å) between two curved mica surfaces immersed in liquid has previously been described. Experiments by Israelachvili and Adams[16] have recently been extended by Pashley.[17] These were carried out in various 1:1 and 2:1 electrolyte solutions of LiCl, NaCl, KCl, CsCl, $Ca(NO_3)_2$, $CaCl_2$, $MgCl_2$, etc., over the concentration range 10^{-6} M to 1 M, and the pH range 3–11. These results now provide an almost complete picture of the particular conditions under which the DLVO theory fully describes the interaction and those under which it does not.

Conditions where DLVO theory applies: no hydration forces

In general we find that in dilute ($\gtrsim 10^{-4}$ M) 1:1 and 2:1 electrolyte solutions the DLVO theory is obeyed right down to the *force maximum* or *energy barrier*, which determines the activation energy for coalescence (see Figure 1). Such force barriers typically occur at surface separations of 20–50 Å, below which the DLVO force becomes rapidly attractive allowing final adhesive contact in a primary minimum (at $D = 0$). These results vindicate the DLVO theory even in the short distance regime where the theory may not be expected to hold. Thus, we find that in very dilute electrolyte the double-layer force is well described by theory even at a separation of 1/50th of a Debye-length. Further, from the measured magnitude of the double-layer forces in dilute electrolyte solutions it is apparent that the surface charge density can be as low as one electronic charge per 7000 Å^2 and yet the DLVO theory—which assumes a smeared out surface charge—still appears to be valid at distances much smaller than the mean spacing between the discrete surface charge sites. Finally, the agreement implies that down to a separation of about 20 Å both the dielectric constant and refractive index of water are not significantly different (if at all) from their bulk values, since these values are used to compute the theoretical double-layer and van der Waals forces.

By comparing the measured forces with double-layer force theory it was possible to obtain the surface potential and surface charge density of the surfaces, as well as establish whether the double-layer interaction occurs at constant surface potential or surface charge or whether there is some charge regulation of the surfaces as they approach each other.[17] Such information was obtained at different electrolyte concentrations and at different pH values and allowed for a detailed analysis of the amounts of cations and protons bound to the surfaces under different solution conditions.

It was concluded that in water or dilute electrolyte solutions the

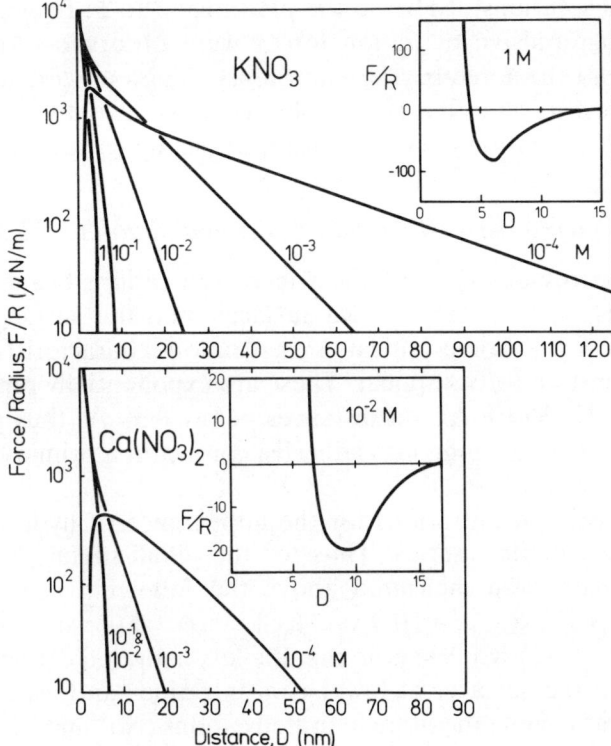

Figure 1 Measured forces F between curved mica surfaces of radius $R \sim 1$ cm in electrolyte solutions at pH ~ 6. In $\sim 10^{-4}$ M the results closely follow the theoretical DLVO force law. At higher electrolyte concentrations an additional short-range repulsion appears above a certain critical concentration for each electrolyte cation (see text). At very high concentrations this additional force is the only repulsive force between the surfaces, and together with the attractive van der Waals force gives rise to a force or energy minimum analogous to the secondary minimum in a DLVO interaction (insets). From measurements such as these the hydration force for a particular cation can be obtained by subtraction of the theoretical DLVO force

negatively charged sites on mica surfaces are covered (neutralized) mainly by protons H^+ or oxonium H_3^+O ions. It is apparent therefore that *when the surface bound counterions are protons there are no repulsive hydration forces, and in dilute solutions no deviations from DLVO theory are observed*.

To further test this conclusion, experiments were carried out in purely acid solutions of HCl in the pH range 7 to 3. In acid solutions pH = 3 no repulsive hydration forces were observed—the surfaces jumped from the force-barrier to primary minimum contact. (It is of some interest to note that air bubbles are not prevented from coalescence in HCl solution even at concentrations up to several molar.)

Conditions giving rise to hydration forces in addition to DLVO forces

As the electrolyte concentration is increased cations begin to replace the protons on the anionic mica surfaces, and the surface potential falls. However, at some critical concentration, characteristic for each cation, hydration forces appear. These are exponentially repulsive and exceed the DLVO forces at distances below ~30 Å, thus preventing the surfaces from coming into adhesive contact in a primary minimum (Figure 1).

The critical concentrations for the appearance of hydration forces follows the lyotropic series. Thus for the alkali metal chlorides hydration forces were measured above the following concentrations: 10^{-4}–10^{-3} M CsCl, ~10^{-4} M KCl, 10^{-3}–10^{-2} M NaCl and 10^{-2}–6×10^{-2} M LiCl. We note that the less hydrated cations (Cs^+ and K^+) bind to the surfaces at lower concentrations and give rise to hydration forces, while the more hydrated cations (Na^+ and Li^+) do this at higher concentrations. K^+ is somewhat exceptional: it binds at a lower concentration than 'expected' probably because of its site binding specificity for mica (K^+ is the natural ion in the mica crystal). Concerning the appearance of the hydration forces the only plausible conclusion is that *on binding to negatively charged surfaces cations are only partially dehydrated and the remaining hydration shells give rise to repulsive hydration forces*. Consistent with this conclusion are the following observations: (i) the hydration forces between surfaces fully covered with Na^+ ions are stronger than for K^+ which are in turn stronger than for Cs^+ covered surfaces. This correlation between the measured hydration forces and the known degree of hydration of the cations in solution further implies that these forces between the surfaces are actually centred around the bound cations. (ii) Above the *critical hydration force concentration* the strength of these forces for any particular cation does not further increase. A simple mass-action or site-binding model[17] shows that at these concentrations the mica surface sites are already almost fully covered with electrolyte cations. Thus the rapid saturation in the magnitude of the hydration forces correlates with the saturation of the surfaces by cations, as would be expected. (iii) At any particular electrolyte concentration where hydration forces are observed a decrease in the pH results in their disappearance. Since lowering the pH leads to proton replacement of the surface cations, and since protons were previously shown not to give rise to hydration forces, this effect is also consistent with the above conclusion.

The long range of the measured hydration forces (Figure 2(A))—well in excess of ten water diameters—is worth commenting upon. This may appear too long-range to be believable. But 'the range' of a force is not really a useful or even meaningful criterion. Since we have established that these forces are probably centred around the surface bound cations it is a simple matter to translate the measured hydration force to the corresponding energy between two cationic centres. If the force F between two curved surfaces as a function of distance D is exponential: $F/R = \text{Const.} \times e^{-D/D_0}$, where D_0 is the decay length, and if this force arises from a simple superposition of ion

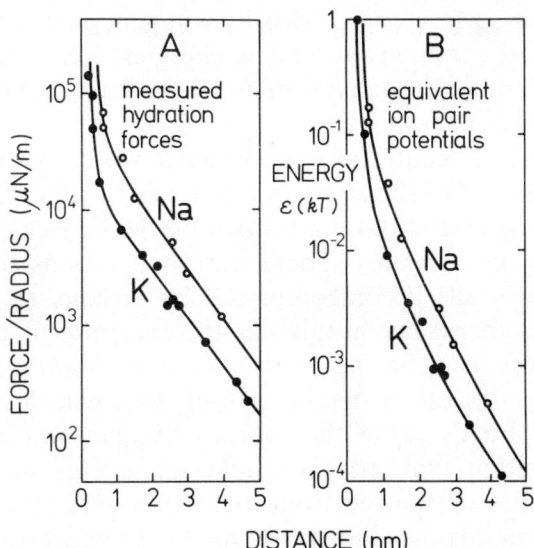

Figure 2 (A) Hydration *forces* between two mica surfaces saturated with Na^+ or K^+ ions (about one bound per ~ 50 Å^2). At distances greater than about 1 nm the forces are exponentially repulsive with a decay length of $D_0 \approx 1$ nm. (B) Corresponding hydration *energy* ε between two Na^+ or K^+ cations, in kT units

pair interactions between surface cations, then a simple summation or integration shows that the cation pair-potential $\varepsilon(D)$ is related to $F(D)$ by $\varepsilon(D) = F(D)/4\pi^2 RDD_0\sigma^2 \propto e^{-D/D_0}/D$, where σ is the surface cation density. For Na$^+$ and K$^+$ ions the hydration pair potentials deduced from our experiments are shown in Figure 2(B). We note that the pair interaction energy is *not* large—of order 1 kT at 3 Å and below 10^{-3} kT at 30 Å! Thus the measured hydration forces correspond to rather *small* interaction energies between individual ion pairs. It is, however, possible that cooperative hydration interactions occur at the surfaces; this would imply that the pair potentials of Figure 2(B) are overestimates. Either way, the measured hydration forces cannot be considered as unreasonably large at distances where they manifest themselves between surfaces.

Hydration regulation, critical hydration concentration, hydration stabilization, and hydration minimum

According to double-layer force theory when two surfaces approach each other their surface charge density will generally vary depending on the surface pK, counterion binding energies, etc. This is known as charge regulation. We find that similar effects also occur due to hydration forces.

At electrolyte concentrations well below where hydration forces arise, a mass-action analysis[17] shows that most of the cations in the diffuse double-layer and those adsorbed on the surfaces are the electrolyte cations, not protons. These adsorbed cations together with their hydration shells become replaced by protons as the surfaces approach each other, since in this way the energetically unfavourable hydration forces can be reduced (*cation hydration regulation*).* Experimentally this effect manifests itself by small deviations from DLVO forces already below the *critical hydration concentration*, and by the observation that the final adhesion energy in the primary minimum remains unchanged from that measured in purely acid solutions at the same pH—an indication that final contact occurs between protonated surfaces.

Pashley[17] has further shown that the critical hydration concentration

---

* Tentative estimates of the proton diffusion rates required for this exchange suggest that it is so rapid that true 'exchange' does not occur. Rather, the expelled hydrated cations probably leave behind a bound H$^+$ ion created by hydrolysis of their water of hydration. Such a mechanism has obvious biological implications.

occurs when the energetically favourable proton–cation exchange is now opposed by the unfavourable mixing entropy at high electrolyte cation concentrations; i.e. once $\Delta G_{ex} + \Delta G_{mix} \gtrsim kT$ it becomes unfavourable to exchange (hydration regulate); the cations now remain bound to the surfaces, the *critical hydration concentration* is reached, and hydration forces come in. Simple theoretical considerations show that the transition should be sharp, as observed, though experimentally a narrow transition concentration regime, varying by a factor of 2–3, was actually observed over which the hydration repulsion grows from zero to its final strength.

Thus the more strongly hydrated the cation, e.g. Li^+, the less ready it is to remain adsorbed and the higher is the electrolyte concentration needed for it to remain bound and hence give rise to hydration forces. In comparison, Ca^{2+} and Mg^{2+} appear to be so hydrated that they can always be finally desorbed before final contact. They therefore behave differently to monovalent cations which give rise to hydration forces right down to zero surface separation (no adhesive primary minimum). But for Ca^{2+} and Mg^{2+} solutions final adhesive contact was always observed—even well above the critical hydration concentration. However, for all the electrolytes studied the hydration force itself can stabilize the surfaces or hold them in a weak potential energy minimum (Figure 1 insets). This is of particular importance at high ionic strengths when the double-layer repulsion becomes insignificant. To distinguish such a minimum from the DLVO-type secondary minimum we may refer to it as a *hydration minimum*.

Consequences of hydration forces

The above results provide a readily understandable picture of the mechanism by which adsorbed ion hydration forces arise. For the first time a correlation has been obtained between hydration forces, cation exchange, and the hydration properties of ions in aqueous solution and hence with the lyotropic series. But the nature of the surface sites also enters into the mechanisms in determining the cation binding affinity, and in particular the competition between hydrated cations and protons for surface sites. However, the results are not consistent with the view that the mere existence of a solid surface, or a particular surface lattice configuration, or a high surface charge density, is sufficient to give hydration forces. Thus in pure water or dilute electrolyte solutions one should not expect hydration forces, unless the surfaces already contain hydrated ionic species chemically attached to them, as occurs on the surfaces of surfactant and lipid micelles and bilayers. The hydration forces observed between lecithin bilayers[7,8] are probably due to such forces, centred around the charged phosphate and choline groups on these surfaces.

Our results show that so long as there is no cation binding on mica surfaces there are no hydration forces. The unexpected stability observed for many colloidal dispersions, mentioned in the Introduction, all occur at high concentrations of hydrated cations where specific ion adsorption occurs to particle surfaces. On a speculative note, the coagulation of negatively charged particles at low pH or near the isoelectric point may turn out to be due not only to the lowering or neutralization of surface charge (DLVO theory) but also to the elimination of hydration forces as protons replace bound hydrated ions on the surfaces.

Repulsive hydration forces apparently also occur when anions bind to positively charged surfaces. We have found that the hydration forces between hexadecyltrimethylammonium bromide (CTAB) bilayers in water become more repulsive at small distances (<30 Å) when the Br^- concentration is increased.[18] Such effects are of particular importance to both inter- and intra-micelle and membrane interactions. Since such structures are not rigid, any repulsive hydration forces due to surface bound ions will also act laterally—in the interfacial plane of these structures, and thereby affect their stability and shape. For example CTA^+Br^- and Cs^+DS^- micelles are large and cylindrical while CTA^+Cl^- and Li^+DS^- are small and spherical—a result that would be expected if the larger hydration shells of bound Cl^- and Li^+ lead to a larger surface area per surfactant molecule.[19] Also related to this effect is the observation that when lecithin bilayers bind Na^+ and K^+ at high electrolyte concentrations their head-group area *increases*, while in acid HCl solutions the area *decreases*.[20]

Finally, we would like to discuss the implications of our results for the stacking and unstacking properties of plant thylakoid membranes. This membrane system has been more thoroughly studied than any other, especially as regards its inter-membrane interactions.[15] There is no doubt that DLVO forces are important in determining the stacking and unstacking behaviour of thylakoids.[21] But a full description of thylakoid stacking requires consideration of hydration forces. For example, in distilled water or in very dilute electrolyte solutions thylakoid membranes remain stacked, and only on addition of low levels of monovalent cations (e.g. 1–5 mM NaCl) do they unstack. This is entirely consistent with our observations: i.e. in dilute electrolyte solutions there are no repulsive hydration forces and surfaces can adhere; addition of ~1–10 mM NaCl displaces the bound H^+ by Na^+ and leads to 'unstacking' via the appearance of hydration repulsion. At higher electrolyte concentrations thylakoids once again restack as expected from DLVO theory, but we note that the membranes do not come into true molecular contact (primary minimum) but remain well separated by 40–60 Å of water—indicative of a hydration minimum at about the same separation as occurs between mica surfaces (Figure 1 insets). Finally, on lowering the pH the equilibrium separation between stacked thylakoid membranes is significantly *decreased*[22]—again indicative that the equilibrium separation cannot be a true primary minimum but variable, and again consistent with a reduced short-range hydration repulsion brought about by proton replacement of bound cations.

It may be too early to speculate on the full biological implications of hydration forces. The correlation between the removal of bound hydrated cations and proton release may have consequences for both proton and electron transport mechanisms; and it is not unlikely that protein reconformations may be triggered off by the 'relaxation' of these repulsive forces brought about by cation release or exchange. The whole matter is wide open, but there should be no doubt any longer that hydration forces exist, and that they are probably equal in importance to electrostatic and hydrophobic interactions.

References

1. B. V. Derjaguin and L. Landau, *Acta phys.-chim. URSS*, **14**, 633 (1941); *JETP (USSR)*, **15**, 633 (1945).
2. E. J. W. Verwey and J. Th. G. Overbeek, *Theory of the Stability of Lyophobic Colloids*, Elsevier, Amsterdam (1948).
3. F. Franks, *Polywater*, The MIT Press, Cambridge, MA, 1981.
4. H. van Olphen, *An Introduction to Clay Colloid Chemistry*, Wiley–Interscience (1st Edition 1963, 2nd Edition 1977).
5. K. Norrish, *Disc. Faraday Soc.*, No. 18, 120 (1954).
6. J. S. Clunie, J. F. Goodman and P. C. Symons, *Nature*, **216**, 1203 (1967).
7. V. A. Parsegian, N. Fuller and R. P. Rand, *Proc. Natl. Acad. Sci. USA*, **76**, 2750 (1979).
8. A. C. Cowley, N. L. Fuller, R. P. Rand and V. A. Parsegian, *Biochemistry*, **17**, 3163 (1978).
9. L. H. Allen and E. Matijević, *J. Coll. Int. Sci.*, **33**, 420 (1970).
10. T. W. Healy, A. Homola, R. O. James and R. J. Hunter, *Faraday Disc.*, No. 65, 156 (1978).

11. R. R. Lessard and S. A. Sieminski, *Ind. Eng. Chem. Fundam.*, **10**, 260 (1971).
12. J. B. Melville and E. Matijević, in *Foams* (R. J. Ackers, ed.), p. 216. Academic Press (1976).
13. S. Usui and T. Yamasaki, *J. Phys. Chem.*, **71**, 3195 (1967).
14. S. Usui and T. Yamasaki, *J. Coll. Int. Sci.*, **29**, 629 (1969).
15. J. Barber, *FEBS Letters*, **118**, 1 (1980).
16. J. N. Israelachvili and G. E. Adams, *J. Chem. Soc. Faraday I*, **74**, 975 (1978); *Faraday Disc.*, No. 65, 20 (1978).
17. R. M. Pashley, *J. Coll. Int. Sci.* (two papers, in press).
18. R. M. Pashley and J. N. Israelachvili, *Colloids and Surfaces*, **2**, 169 (1981).
19. R. S. Farinato and R. L. Rowell, in *Solution Chemistry of Surfactants* (K. L. Mittal, ed.), p. 311. Plenum, N.Y. (1979).
20. M. H. Gottleib and E. D. Eanes, *Biophys. J.*, **12**, 1533 (1972).
21. M. J. Sculley, J. T. Duniec, S. W. Thorne, W. D. Chow and N. K. Boardman, *Arch. Biochem. Biophys.*, **201**, 339, 347 (1980).
22. S. Murakami and L. Packer, *J. Cell Biol.*, **47**, 332 (1970).

Effects of macroscopic surfaces on interactions involving water

Reporter: **Paula T. Beall**

Poster discussion

Světina commented that in connection with the poster presented by Wittmann and Gros, he would like to refer to the results of his own theoretical studies of the anomalous osmotic behaviour of red blood cells (M. Brumen and S. Světina, *Proc. 1st Int. Conf. Water and Ions in Biological Systems*, Bucharest, 1980, *Stud. Biophys.* [1981]). In his model calculations, he took into consideration, beside data on the haemoglobin osmotic coefficient, also the electrostatic interactions between haemoglobin and ions of the electrolyte solution. The calculated cell volume and chloride ratio were compared with the corresponding data of Dalmark, *J. Physiol.*, **250**, 65 (1975), whereby the pH dependence of the cell water content on cell solutes was chosen as the mean criterion. It was found that with the haemoglobin osmotic coefficient alone it was not possible to explain this pH dependence. Inclusion of electrostatic interactions improved the model and quantitative agreement could be obtained only by invoking twice as strong a dependence of the haemoglobin osmotic coefficient on haemoglobin concentration than given by existing data. These theoretical guesses seemed now to be confirmed by the new data on the haemoglobin osmotic coefficient reported by Wittmann and Gros.

Gros replied that, as far as he remembered, the experiments of Dalmark were performed with red cells made cation permeable by nystatin. This should be kept in mind when comparing the results with experiments of normal cation impermeable red cells. But, as to whether Světina's calculations were in keeping with his (Gros') conclusions was uncertain, because predictions based on the osmotic coefficient measurements fail to explain the observed volume changes in the hypertonic case.

Pusch asked for information about the kind of membrane used for measuring the osmotic pressure. He also thought that a double layer membrane might cause problems by concentration polarization effects within the non-selective layer. Finally, he emphasized that one has to define the solution/membrane system before one can extract an apparent osmotic pressure. For this reason, one has to know the reflection coefficient of the membrane for the permeable species, for instance. It is then still not possible to extract individual osmotic coefficients from the measured entire osmotic pressure of a multicomponent system.

Wittmann replied that he used two-layer membranes with a thin selective layer exposed to the haemoglobin solution, and a thick porous support exposed to the reference solution. Reference solution and solvent were always identical. With the isoelectric haemoglobin solutions, the chloride concentration was found to be identical in the upper and lower compartment of the osmometer.

Franks commented that in DSC measurements one usually uses the known latent heat of fusion to calculate the amount of ice melting, or vice versa. How can one determine independently the latent heat of fusion of 'structured water' (how does it differ from ice) as well as the amount of water melted? Ter-Minassian-Saraga replied that with fully hydrated bilayers (= 50% lipid) there is structural water between the bilayers as well as some bulk water. Water external to the bilayers melts at 0 °C with water in a parallel reference cell. One is left with a small endotherm on the side of the reference peak which is used to calculate independently the amount of structural water. The structural water melts between -10 and -1 °C. The heat corresponding to this peak is measured and divided by the amount of structural water; this yields the molar entropy of the frozen structural water. Israelachvili enquired whether the experimental results on the hydration forces between lipid bilayers, using differential scanning calorimetry, can be compared with those on the same hydration forces, but measured by osmotic and other techniques. Ter-Minassian-Saraga replied that Rand's data were not all exponential. Her own experiments were carried out without any filtration pressure, under equilibrium conditions. Rand's experiments are carried out in the presence of an ultrafiltration pressure, so that one cannot expect an exponential decay for the surface forces, because the data do not correspond to the same region. Her aim was to prove that the surface force–distance law is of the form of Equation (1) in her summary, in which α is an exponent of the distance between one water molecule and the phospholipid bilayer. Equation (2) expressed the power w absorbed by the sample, which is related to the temperature by a term $(\alpha + 1)/\alpha$ on a log–log plot. Rand added that the exponential relationship between interbilayer pressure and bilayer separation applies in the region where hydration force dominates. Neutral phospholipid bilayers separate to finite limits, and therefore deviate from exponential results, because near those limits van der Waals attraction between bilayers becomes significant, and in fact equals the repulsion at the limit of separation; thus at that point $\log P = -\infty$.

Lehmann was asked whether his neutron scattering experiments showed no excluded volume for the water–papain system when ethanol was present. How did this compare to the preferential hydration of large molecules described by Timasheff. Lüdemann commented that Timasheff fitted his data in ternary systems (H_2O, protein, ethanol) by introducing an excluded volume around the protein that cannot be penetrated by ethanol molecules. Lehmann, on the other hand, did not find any significant excluded volume in his neutron scattering studies on H_2O/papain/ethanol. Could this discrepancy be resolved. Timasheff replied that the composition of the solvents was not the same, so that he had no data for comparison.

Lehmann asked whether a value could be put on the excluded water volume. Timasheff replied that excluded volumes were not meant to be boundaries or volumes, but were introduced to signify effects on the chemical potential of the cosolvent which could be translated into effects on binding. The hypothetical layer of water has no real meaning, since it must really be a continuous change out from the surface.

Several questions related to Lehmann's claim that there was no structural (conformational) change in the EtOH–water system, as compared to water. He confirmed that the structure (conformation) remains unchanged; however, the enzyme does not function. Apparently, the active site is blocked. Ter-Minassian-Saraga stated that when proteins are spread out as thin films, alcohol is added to achieve this.

Lehmann reiterated that while many proteins denature in 30% alcohol, papain is very stable and can be crystallized from 80% EtOH.

Ter-Minassian-Saraga asked McIver to develop his statement of the effects of ligands on Ca^{++} binding. McIver explained that the relationships between surface calcium and surface thermodynamics were investigated in model systems and living cells. In model systems, the surface calcium concentration is controlled by varying $[Ca^{++}]$ in the bulk phase; experimentally, a good correlation is found between interfacial free energies of lipid–water interfaces and $[Ca^{++}]$. The addition of Ca^{++} raises γ_{AC}, removal of Ca^{++} lowers γ_{AC}. Modelistic considerations relate these alterations to alterations in the biosurface–water interaction, and indicate a significant desorption of interfacial water by calcium ion, which would be expected to produce a significant entropic contribution to γ_{AC}. Preliminary measurements of the temperature dependence of γ_{AC} are consistent with this suggestion that surface entropies are elevated following calcium binding. In living cells, surface energy measurements indicate that γ_{AC} decreases under conditions of ligand binding (for example addition of the chemotactic peptide F-met-leu-phe to leukocytes), and the decrease correlates with estimates of cell surface calcium. Thus, cell adhesion and chemotaxis may actually involve reduction in surface calcium, with attendant lowering of γ_{AC} and increased rates, contrary to the popular view of 'calcium bridges'.

Bank stated that the precipitation of pyroantimonate by cation is dependent upon the ionic strength, buffer system and cation present. Not only Ca^{++}, but also Na^+, Mg^{++} and K^+ compete for the antimonate anion; therefore what was the independent evidence that the charge effect is predominantly calcium mediated? McIver replied that pyroantimonate is not specific for calcium, but two lines of evidence are consistent with the idea that ligand–biosurface interactions do involve relatively specific displacement of calcium. First, X-ray dispersive electron microprobe spectra correlate well with pyroantimonate data, and second, cell surface 'ion-pyroantimonate' complexes move from the exterior to the interior of cells following stimulation. Thus movement correlates with measurement of total cell calcium and calcium fluxes under similar conditions.

Kell asked to what extent is Ca^{++} *binding* (at the inner Helmholtz plane) distinguished from *screening* (at the outer Helmholtz plane), and are these quite distinct both energetically and mechanistically. McIver did not consider the concept very useful because he was attempting to correlate macroscopic events with physical measurements. Ter-Minassian-Saraga commented on some experiments done in the early 70's on how ion exchange in monolayers can change surface potentials. The Ca^{++} (tracer)/Na^+ ratio between the solution and a polymaleic acid-vinyl hexadecyl ether co-polymer monolayer was determined. The surface potential correlated with exchange of calcium for sodium in the inner Helmholtz layer.

Pusch enquired whether pH had been adjusted, because by changing the concentration ratio, the pH in the Helmholtz layer is also changed. He also asked whether binding or cross-binding of Ca^{++} with OH^- groups had been considered. Ter-Minassian-Saraga replied in the affirmative on both counts.

Franks commented that the ion selectivity of water channels discussed by Edmonds, originates from their dimensions. The hydration energies of K^+ and Na^+ are very different. Could the slight (?) difference in water molecule topology account for such hydration energy differences.

Edmonds thought that selectivity derives from the different sized water rings in the channels. A pentagon of five water molecules just fits Na^+, and a hexagon of six water molecules just fits K^+. These structures are optimum low energy states. In these structures the water dipoles reorient to hydrate the ion.

In answer to a question about the role of dynamics in the interpretation of his results, Edmonds said that the stability of a channel is due to the matching up of the H bonds to the protein rods. Electron microscopy shows five and six rod configurations for acetylcholine stimulated ion channels. The size of the pores is $\simeq 10$ Å, very similar to his model, and the repeat distance is 0.62–0.58 Å, compared to 0.6 for the model. He was not sure if such channels exist, but they are consistent with what hard information there is. With this model, one can explain the properties of channels without the concept of gating particles. The function of the model is to suggest experiments. There are five or six experiments suggested by this model, now it was up to the experimentalists. Maass commented on the approximate agreement between the behaviour required by the model and that of the Hodgkin–Huxley model. Could any differences be explained by Edmonds' model, not assuming a particular gating mechanism.

Edmonds did not want to assume an extra gating mechanism. He thought that the gating mechanism is built into the structure of the channel. Channels do not open or shut, they exist in configuration A or B and change between the two in response to the electric field. One should not be too impressed by the agreement with Hodgkin–Huxley, since both must satisfy the Nernst potential and are normalized to unity at zero membrane voltage. Hempling commented that the acetylcholine sensitive site which is characterized by the structure which Edmonds used for his model is different from the channel where specific gating of Na^+ occurs and which leads to an action potential. Edmonds agreed that they are distinct types of channels. He used the acetylcholine channels because the molecular structure of the squid Na^+ channel is not known. The major difference is that one is chemically gated and one electrically gated. Israelachvili wondered whether Edmonds could rationalize the unfavourable energetics of the process. He suggested a hydrophilic surface with tight water molecules and at the same time proposed to neglect water bound to the ion. Edmonds speculated that the ion leaves its hydration water behind, and is locally hydrated by water in the channel, similar to ions travelling in water filled channels in clays.

Israelachvili further enquired why the ion could not pull the whole column of water in the channel along with it. Edmonds preferred that there be no translational movement of water in this model, only rotational motion.

Israelachvili also enquired what was in the cylindrical cages of water in the channel when the ion was not there.

Edmonds replied that the cages were empty, but one could pack them with clathrate forming compounds to study their effects.

Finney suggested that such cages should dissolve inert gases.

Edmonds claimed that the chemists say that inert gases would be much more likely to dissolve in the lipid membrane.

In answer to a question by Hempling, how much energy was required to move an ion through the channel, Edmonds replied that it took ten hydrogen bond defects. He also stated that the conductivity changes as a function of temperature; at $+10$ °C the peak goes up by a factor of 1.5, the current decreases, and the rate increases.

Haglund stated that in the electron microscope one can see two morphological types of channels. Could Edmonds estimate the ratio between the two types that would be consistent with his model?

Edmonds said that they could be seen but he had never counted them. He offered to produce pictures and suggested to Haglund that she might count the channels.

In reply to Hempling, who asked whether separate channels for water movement were proposed, Edmonds replied that the one channel had got him in so much trouble, that he was going back to physics.

Clegg stated that Kell had described where he thought the protons were transferred in mitochondria. Could he tell the meeting what happens to these protons, how they are involved with ATP synthesis, and whether or not the water that is produced figures in the energetics of ATP synthesis.

Kell replied that mitochondria tend to swell when respiring. Water passes freely through their membranes. Water movements are driven by differences in concentration in different ionic compartments. As soon as protons move, it sets up a field, and the work is recovered later. Protons are not osmotically active. They are possibly retained in the Helmholtz layer of the membrane. One should distinguish between osmotic compartments and proton location.

Clegg insisted that the synthesis of water was not trivial, but Kell thought that it was, because the difference in water potential was small. Wiggins asked whether the protons participate directly in the ADP/ATP reaction or whether they induce a conformational change. Kell stated that they induce a conformational change.

Panel discussion

Israelachvili reminded Drost-Hansen that not long ago, he was proposing surface effects of micrometer distances, but now he was suggesting a less than 1 μm effect. He further commented that Peschel's force measurements are made between surfaces with surface roughness of $\simeq$ 240 Å, and yet conclusions are drawn at 'surface separations' well below that value. This could not be acceptable.

Drost-Hansen was pleased that effects at 0.01–0.05 μm were now being accepted as respectable. As to Peschel's measurements, surface roughness was estimated to be 50 Å. Lüdemann asked how it could take minutes for vicinal water structure to be re-established. Was it caused by impurities dissolving out of the surface material. Drost-Hansen stated that there were too many experimental results that ruled out impurities. With polystyrene spheres for example, volume changes are maintained for days. Derbyshire suggested that many people were unfamiliar with the measurement and utility of disjoining pressures. Could Drost-Hansen explain the technique and the measurements in greater detail. Drost-Hansen explained that the disjoining pressure is the force pushing two smooth plates apart. It is a combination of electrostatic and van der Waals forces and the structural modification due to the medium. He observed oscillations as a function of temperature. Since the electrostatic and van der Waals forces do not exhibit oscillations, these must be due to structural factors.

On a general note, Dore presented some neutron diffraction results for thin films of D_2O water on a high surface area silica (D. Steytler, J. Dore and C. J. Wright, unpublished data). The diffraction measurements were made on spherisorb which was a well-characterized pore size of 70 Å. The water was equilibrated at a partial pressure to give a coverage corresponding to about ten (or less) molecular layers and measurements were made at various temperatures. The main peak in the diffraction pattern for the D_2O was broadened, as expected for the scattering from a thin film compared to the bulk liquid. Furthermore, the peak position was found to have exactly the same temperature dependence as bulk water, indicating no structural differences between the liquid in the bulk and film phases. The results are therefore in direct conflict with proposals that the structure of water is different in the region close to the silica surface. Further experiments on thinner liquid films are to be made.

Dore then discussed what is meant by the word 'structure' in this context. The usual connotation means the spatial relationships between the quantities under investigation—in this case, the time-averaged molecular arrangement. This structure is strictly available only by direct observation through diffraction studies. The term 'structure' is often used more loosely to denote effects interpreted through some thermodynamic argument or a measurement of some dynamic quantity by spectroscopic or other means. These latter procedures may be helpful in collating a large quantity of interrelated data but it is important to recognize that the structural interpretation is based on assumptions which may later prove to be uncertain. Clearly, there is a need to combine and correlate the structural and dynamic observations but discrepancies will occasionally occur and the resolution of the differences will probably lead to a greater understanding than either can give individually.

It is therefore possible that 'bound' water may be a convenient way of visualizing certain changes in the physical properties of water near an interface, but this does not necessarily imply significant structural alteration of the molecular arrangement. The present studies are for a hydrophilic substrate and further studies for other materials would obviously be of interest.

Ter-Minassian-Saraga commented that Edmonds showed the energy profile of a negatively charged surface. The implication was that the minimum energy was achieved when a positive charge was in direct opposition to the negative charge. She believed that the minimum energy occurs when the positive charge actually slightly penetrates between two negative charges on the monolayer, Edmonds said that his model potential was for a row of point charges on a surface, not for a monolayer. Kell thought that a model for moving charge across a membrane by flipping an array of oriented dipoles would only work once. Reorientation is necessary to get back to the beginning of the cycle so the net charge displacement is zero. What are the current carriers for net charge transport. Edmonds replied that the dipole array is static. This means that it cannot affect the energy of an ion that has passed completely through it (curve $E = 0$). What the dipole distribution did was to redistribute the electrostatic potential so that the rise in potential occurs over a small distance and the potential falls across the membrane. In the model of an ion pump if the ion can be placed within the channel mouth by some chemical agency, the channel will convey the ion across the membrane, thus converting a short range action into a long range effect.

Franks commented on Bryant's presentation. Dynamic measurements can distinguish between different modes of motion associated with water near solutes or surfaces. Also, Robson showed that when water distributions and orientations are perturbed by a large solute molecule, these perturbations are attenuated by some unexpected hydrogen bond distributions in the second and third water molecule layers. Thus, the perturbations that are monitored by NMR (etc.) methods are indicative of 'hydration' but are limited to a few molecular layers. They could, moreover, be significant as regards stability of biopolymers and transport (diffusion) or in in vivo systems. Could one treat hydration on a dynamic basis. Marčelja preferred to treat it in terms of induced polarization effects.

Careri asked how T_1 relaxation times compare to dielectric relaxation measurements on the same material. Bryant replied that one should compare correlation times (τ_c) from the two techniques. The derivation of τ_c from NMR is very model dependent. Anisotropic motion predicts two correlation times. At the same temperature, τ_c from dielectric relaxation in the 0.1 nsec range compares well with τ_c for water determined by NMR. But because powerful enough magnets cannot yet be built, there is a component of τ_c that cannot yet be measured in the high frequency range. He added that there are aspects of the dielectric work which still puzzled him, but the basic features of the NMR interpretation must also be supported by the dielectric relaxation measurements. Leaving aside matters of detail, he thought generally that the NMR and the dielectric work on protein powders was more consistent now than it had been for a long time.

Hallenga replied to Franks' previous comment by agreeing that it would certainly be useful to use the term hydration, be it with more subtle distinctions in terms of dynamics. Both NMR and dielectric methods will be able to help make these distinctions: NMR measurements can now be made up to 500–600 MHz, and with special equipment down to about 50 Hz. Dielectric measurements do see more easily the high frequency processes, while NMR on the other hand is increasingly sensitive to slower processes, because the observed relaxation rate is proportional to the correlation time. The magnitude of the dielectric relaxation process will depend on the magnitude of the polarization involved which probably means fewer molecules at the lower frequencies.

Grigera commented on Bryant's mention of the temperature dependence of the dielectric experiments on lysozyme by Hoekstra. He thought it peculiar that the relaxation frequency decreases and the amplitude increases with temperature. He had obtained a similar result on collagen, *Biopolymers*, **18**, 42 (1979), and gave a different explanation, considering that the relaxation was not due to water. This explanation could fit the lysozyme data as well.

Grigera also questioned Hallenga's statement that dielectric experiments are more sensitive to shorter relaxation times than those one might expect in such complex systems. Moreover, interfacial (Maxwell–Wagner type) effects would probably interfere.

Lüdemann observed that anisotropic rotation has little relevance if bulk water is present, since water molecules can form up to four hydrogen bonds.

Bryant responded that the question was if T_s and T_f for the anisotropic motion of water on the protein surface were significant when bulk water was added to the system. As water is added, broadening of the signals causes these two maxima to disappear.

Finney referred to the ordered water in the channels proposed by Edmonds. Would one expect to be able to detect the apparently very strongly ordered water in these clathrate-type channels by relaxation measurements.

Edmonds replied that in normal cells, there are just too few of these channels to be detectable. Even in the purified protein, the bulk water of the solution would probably obscure the effect.

Derbyshire said that he did not understand Pifat's isotopic dilution studies; also he saw a similarity between the microsomal systems and the microemulsion studied by Lüdemann. Had either of them made a comparison of the results. Pifat replied that she would appreciate any help in the interpretation of the results. In answer to several questions she said that the microsomes were of 20 nm diameter, suspended in 0.1 M phosphate. Molecules of up to 600 daltons can penetrate them, but the membranes are impermeable to sucrose and acetate.

Ninham made a final comment which bore on Franks' plea to define more closely the notion of 'hydration'. From the point of view of a physicist, it seemed absurd to study systems of water alone, if one actually wanted to understand water at interfaces or in the neighbourhood of a solute molecule. There were so many competing molecular effects (polarization, charge, hydrogen bond orientation, hard sphere repulsion, surface geometry, etc.) which could give rise to ('structural, hydration, solvophobe') forces that the water problem in isolation must remain extremely difficult to unravel—especially in the absence of any theory of pure water. This was already clear from a consideration of simple questions like hydrophobic solution thermodynamics, oil–water and benzene–water interfaces (as a function of temperature), hydrophilic solutions (e.g. sucrose forms nearly ideal solutions, indicating a cancellation of hard sphere repulsive contributions to virial coefficients by attractive structural forces) and ionic solution activities.

It would be useful if people could give some thought to experiments in model liquids, less complicated than water, but which still have some of the properties characteristic of water. Examples which came to mind were propylene carbonate, a hard sphere dipolar liquid with high dielectric constant, which ought to be more easily accessible to theoretical modelling; and the remarkable fused salt ethyl ammonium nitrate, reported by D. F. Evans and collaborators (*J. Amer. Chem. Soc.*, **103**, 481 (1981)).

Discussion after Israelachvili's lecture

Frank said that in view of the fact that true biological membranes carry a charge, had he considered coating the mica plates with gold and applying an electric current.

Israelachvili replied that he had a long list of possible experiments.

Kay referred to Israelachvili's really exciting measurements of the hydration forces for the alkali metal cations. Had he made similar measurements for the tetraalkylammonium ions, and in particular the tetrabutylammonium ions? Further, had he been able to look at other solvents besides water? Israelachvili replied in the negative. In reply to a question by Beall, he said that the forces had been measured up to 50 °C, without any indication of oscillatory effects.

Middendorf asked whether photon correlation spectroscopy could be used to obtain some idea of what is happening dynamically. Israelachvili thought not, because it was hard to get very large surfaces of mica; the area of contact is $\simeq 0.1$ mm in diameter.

Franks noted that the magnitude of the forces seemed to follow the lyotropic series. Neutron diffraction data suggested that all the ions studied are hydrated identically by six water molecules per ion. Israelachvili replied that eleven different methods showed that the forces follow the lyotropic series.

Franks further noted that the only definitive method, neutron diffraction, indicated that the spatial arrangement of water molecules around Na^+ and K^+ is the same. Israelachvili countered that he measured the forces, not the geometry.

Holzwarth commented on the dependence of the surface interaction of alkali cations on their radius (or state of hydration). He measured the rate of electron transfer between anionic ligand substitution 'inert' transition metal complexes and found that at the same ionic strength, the rate of electron transfer changed by more than four orders of magnitude in the series

$$Li^+ < Na^+ < K^+ = NH_4^+ < Cs^+$$

The tetraalkylammonium salts had the effect: $N(CH_3)_4^+ \simeq K^+$, but $N(t-Bu)_4N^+ \simeq Li^+$. He wondered if one could measure what the effect of those tetraalkylammonium ions might be in respect to their surface interaction. He was especially interested in the question if there is something like a hydration sphere around such ammonium ions. Israelachvili said that he was too wise to comment; the ions must bind, but perhaps the more hydrated the less binding, and there may be a counterion effect.

Kell said that in distilled water, protons are hydrated with one or two water molecules, but he would prefer four for a minimum energy. Israelachvili accepted four H_2O molecules as probable but stated that he could not measure forces accurately over the last few angstroms, where van der Waals forces are overcome.

Section 3 Dynamics of water in cellular systems

Biophysics of Water
Edited by F. Franks
© 1982 John Wiley & Sons Ltd

Osmosis: the push and pull of life

H. G. Hempling
Medical University of South Carolina, USA

Summary

This paper discusses the osmotic forces which govern the bulk movement of water and direct the shape and form of living organisms. It emphasizes the osmotic asymmetry which emerges when a barrier permits free access to small ions and to water but is impermeable to polyvalent macromolecules. It contrasts the regulatory mechanisms resident in the membrane barrier with those present intracellularly and points out how each contributes to the regulation of cell volume. Several questions are offered for discussion: How do mammalian cells during the cell cycle alter the osmotic activity of intracellular water and small solutes without changing their ability to exchange readily with the environment? Are these changes a cause or an effect of the cell cycle? What is the relation between the composition and organization of the cell membrane and its effect on the permeability to water?

I have entitled this talk Osmosis: The Push and Pull of Life because the forces which govern the bulk movement of water direct the shape and form of living things. Life goes on in watery compartments and the shape and form which these compartments take reflect the delicate balance between forces which would expand the compartment and those which would compress it.

In the beginning, the living stuff marshalled these forces for its future evolution by separating itself from its environment by a selective phase boundary. Within the boundaries of this phase the evolving substructure of organized macromolecules formed the scaffold of the living cell and ordered its own composition to generate forces which would guarantee that the water filled out the spaces between.

What were these forces? The forces were osmotic in nature because we were concerned with the redistribution of *bulk* water. They were not diffusive because much of the filler of the cell was a continuum of water molecules rather than an emulsion of discrete molecules dispersed in non-water domains. Therefore water moved as a continuum between compartments and not as a series of random walks between non-water molecules.

What was the nature of the selectivity of the limiting boundary? Certainly it would have to be selective to water, for this was the necessary solvent for life and was to be the means for future growth. What about the dissolved gases O_2 and CO_2, the raw material and byproduct of oxidative metabolism? Most certainly. Small nutrient molecules? Of course. Charged or neutral? Ah, there was the rub, because all the ingredients for an osmotic disaster were present if the macromolecules should go negative or positive. Eons later, the great Willard Gibbs, ably documented by F. Donnan, predicted the consequences of a boundary freely permeable to ions and water but selectively impermeable to a charged macromolecule. Let me illustrate the consequences of the Gibbs–Donnan distribution by a simple example (Table 1).

Given a cell suspended in an infinite environment containing the concentrations of diffusible ions shown and a polyvalent anion with a net charge of $12(-)$, what will happen to the distribution of diffusible ions which will satisfy the requirement that each compartment be electrically neutral, and that the product of diffusible ions in one compartment be equal to the product of diffusible ions in the second compartment? Most of us are familiar with the asymmetry of ion distribution which occurs: viz., a higher concentration of the diffusible cation on the side of the impermeable anion and the reverse for the anion. What often escapes people is the osmotic disequilibrium which also ensues. For this reason, I have always preferred to speak of the

Table 1 Charge distribution between a cell and its environment. The cell contains a macromolecule with twelve negative charges: B^+ and A^- are diffusible ions

CELL			ENVIRONMENT		
mosmoles/l	meq/l		meq/l		mosmoles/l
16	B^+	16	8	B^+	8
4	A^-	4	8	A^-	8
1		12			
	$16B^+ = 4A^- + PR^{(12-)}$		$8B^+ = 8A^-$		
	$16(B^+) \times (4A^-) = 64$		$8(B^+) \times (8A^-) = 64$		
$16 + 4 + 1 = 21$					$8 + 8 = 16$

Gibbs–Donnan distribution rather than the Gibbs–Donnan equilibrium.

As long as the small ions are free to distribute themselves between the two compartments, the consequent asymmetry in osmolarity will produce a net entry of water into the cell. Unless the cell takes action, its volume will increase until cell lysis occurs. We seem to be willing to pay for the luxury of evolutionary privacy with the eternal spectre of a watery death.

It would seem necessary then to develop a force which would counter the entry of water. One way would be to limit the distensibility of the phase boundary and allow a hydrostatic pressure to build up inside the cell. Plants have solved this problem by surrounding the cells with a cell wall. Turgor pressure builds up inside the cell until it equals the difference in osmolarity between the intracellular compartment and the environment.

The other alternative, employed by many animal cells, is to limit the osmotic potential of the Gibbs–Donnan distribution. Two mechanisms have been proposed. The first is the membrane hypothesis. In this hypothesis specificity of ion movement has been imparted to the bimolecular leaflet which forms the limiting boundary of the cell. The specificity resides in intrinsic proteins embedded in the phospholipid bilayer which through binding properties and conformation in the membrane select the ions to enter or leave and at what rate. Moreover these proteins may act as energy transducers to convert the energy of metabolism into osmotic work. Selected ions may be transferred against their electrochemical gradients into or out of the cell with a consequent change in the osmotic activity of the cell solution. In effect the osmotically active ions which, unfettered, would produce osmotic death, are restrained by a continuous expenditure of metabolic energy and rendered functionally impermeable.

Implicit in this hypothesis is the view that the cell membrane separates two dilute solutions each of which is free to express the Gibbs–Donnan relationship. A small but growing number of investigators has proposed that a substantial fraction of intracellular water and solute is in a physical state different from that of the environment. Further, intracellular function may be regulated by subtle changes in the organized state of intracellular water and differential changes in the thermodynamic activity of intracellular ions. We know that the structure of water in contact with macromolecules or with surfaces is different from that in bulk water and the literature in this field is voluminous.[1,2] When we note that modern electron microscopy has given us an image of the cell replete with endoplasmic reticulum, microtubules, and microfilaments, it is a wonder at all that there is room for bulk water.

Gilbert Ling has been a leading exponent for this alternative hypothesis for almost thirty years. In his papers of 1965 and 1972,[3,4] Ling proposed that the water in the cell was oriented in multilayers polarized by alternating fixed charges on the surface of extended proteins, and that these multilayers extended over considerable distances. Further, the water was neither bound nor ice-like and no part of it was truly non-solvent. Rather, the water was capable of excluding solutes on entropic and enthalpic grounds.

More recently, Negendank[5] summarized in concise terms the major features of Ling's hypothesis which dealt with the behaviour of electrolytes inside cells. Ions are assumed to associate with fixed charges on cell macromolecules. The degree of binding and the species bound are subject to change and are influenced by (1) polarizability of the site; (2) nature and relative numbers of competing ions; (3) the number and dielectric saturation of intervening water molecules; and (4) direct and indirect electrostatic effects upon the site. Cardinal sites act as receptors capable of communication with the external environment. When these sites are filled by specific adsorbants, they can initiate a chain of induced changes in the electron distribution around each site along the extended protein and produce cooperative interactions between sites with subsequent changes in the association and dissociation of specific ligands. Signals originating from the external medium, then, may have ready access to the cell interior along chains of extended protein while signals from internal organelles have similar opportunities to act at the cell periphery.

Over the years these two hypotheses have grown apart and proponents of each have adopted an either/or position. Fortunately experience has taught us that the final solution in such cases is somewhere in between. I have little doubt today of the effectiveness of the membrane hypothesis. Its ability to distribute ions asymmetrically is responsible for the potential differences across most cells and many tissues. In excitable cells, this property coupled to mechanisms which can control the conductances of the membrane with exquisite specificity, has provided propagated electrical disturbances which form the digital code for perception, integration and execution. At a more visceral level (in a moment of weakness I was going to say, 'gut level', but I didn't have the intestinal fortitude) the asymmetric distribution of these osmotic transducers in the epithelial lining of the kidney, secretory glands and gastro-intestinal tract have been responsible for the homeostasis of the internal milieu.

Viewed from the safe distance of non-involvement, these two hypotheses offer an interesting contrast of ideas. On the one hand we have the hustle-bustle of the West with its osmotic pumps churning furiously to maintain the status quo. On the other we survey a placid Nirvana of the East where life is a spider's web of ordered structure, responding to change with gentle ripples along its charged surface.

Since the truth is somewhere in between and blessed are the peacemakers, I have suggested a compromise in the block diagram of Figure 1. In simplest terms, the membrane regulates the exchange of solutes and water between the external environment and an intracellular compartment, in which water and solutes are freely exchangeable. In addition, this intracellular compartment communicates with a compartment of osmotically excluded solute and a compartment of osmotically excluded water. These may be one and the same, but we are treating them as separate in order to identify the different exchange coefficients for water and solutes.

Since my instructions as a plenary speaker were to avoid too specialized a presentation, I will use only one example to help you to understand why I am operating with this particular model. This example will also serve to illustrate some of the phenomenological parameters which we use. In our studies we use the Boyle–van't Hoff relation as a measure of the volume of osmotically active water. When mammalian cells are placed in a medium made hyperosmotic with a functionally impermeable solute like NaCl, they shrink. A plot of the volume of the

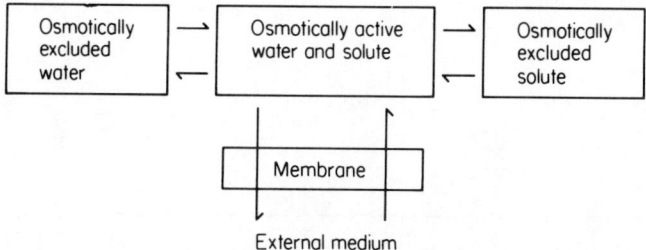

Figure 1 The role of the membrane in regulating the exchange of water and solutes between the cell and its environment

cell versus the reciprocal of the osmolarity produces a straight line whose y intercept defines the 'b value' or the volume of osmotically inactive volume.[6] The value $(1 - b)$ defines the osmotically active water. The slope of the line defines the *amount* of osmotically active solute inside the cell which is functionally impermeable. Figure 2 illustrates the use of this parameter with the human lymphocyte. The upper line is the response of normal lymphocytes. The next lower line which is almost superimposable is the response of lymphocytes which had been exposed to a hypo-osmotic medium of 200 m Osmole/l and then after a few minutes were resuspended in an isosmotic medium. They served as a control for lymphocytes which were exposed to the same hypo-osmotic medium and were maintained in this medium for 20 hours. Note that these latter cells have a volume after 20 hours which is much less than the volume predicted by the Boyle–van't Hoff relation, and that the amount of osmotically active solute inside the cell is less since the slope is less. The cognoscenti among you will

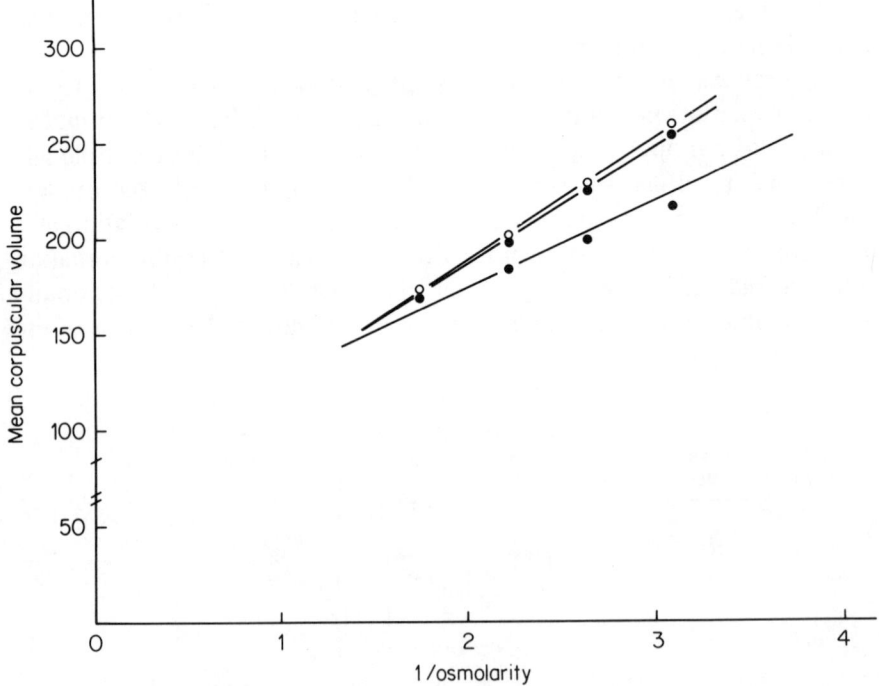

Figure 2 Boyle–van't Hoff plot for the determination of the volume of osmotically active water in human lymphocytes subjected to various treatments; for details see text

recognize the phenomenon of volume regulation by these cells, but that subject could become an entire lecture on its own. My purpose in this context is to illustrate how these simple measurements can tip you off to important conceptual problems.

We have also used Ponder's R as a measure of that volume of cell water which is osmotically active and by difference, that volume of cell water which is not active osmotically. In 1948, Ponder demonstrated that red blood cells did not obey the Boyle–van't Hoff relation. The cells shrank less in hyperosmotic solutions and swelled less in hypo-osmotic media than predicted. Therefore, the volume of osmotically active water was less than the total cell water under isotonic conditions. To relate experimental observation to osmotic theory, Ponder[7] introduced an empirical factor, R where $R =$ (cell volume $- b$)/cell water. A value for Ponder's R equal to 1 meant that all of the cell's water was osmotically active. Values less than 1 meant that a fraction of the water was osmotically active and the remainder was restricted in some fashion.

Now let me deal with a specific example from our studies on the cell cycle of the Ehrlich mouse ascites tumour cell.[8] What we found from this study was confirmation that the state of water and electrolytes differed from that in dilute solution and that these differences varied during the cell cycle. The key points were that the percentage of water in the cell remained constant, but the fraction which was osmotically active decreased as the cell progressed through the cell cycle. Further the total content of electrolyte per litre of cells did not change, but doubled when normalized to osmotically active water. We are forced to the conclusion therefore that if the cells are to be in osmotic equilibrium, both solute and solvent must be rendered osmotically inactive. Nevertheless it turns out that a representative ion like Na^+ is totally exchangeable. Do you see, therefore, without going into additional experiments and examples, why I have been thinking about compartmentalization of water and electrolytes intracellularly?

I would now like to ask some questions about the state of water in the membrane barrier of the cell. These questions have been a consequence of our studies of the membrane permeability to water in a variety of mammalian cells. Of particular interest are studies on the Ehrlich mouse ascites tumour cell during the cell cycle and also membrane differentiation of a line of rat megakaryoblasts in culture.[8,9,10]

We measure the net loss of water from cells when they are placed in hyperosmotic media. We define the permeability coefficient, Lp, as the μm^3 of water crossing 1 μm^2 of membrane surface area per minute under an osmotic gradient of 1 atmosphere. We make these measurements at different temperatures. Using Arrhenius plots and the conceptual approach of Eyring's theory of absolute reaction rates, we calculate heats and entropies of activation.

With the exception of the erythrocyte and its progenitors, all the cells we have studied have heats of activation for their membrane permeability to water which are three to four times those obtained when measurements of viscosity or self-diffusion are made at different temperatures. The question we would ask is whether this parameter is a property of the water as it traverses the membrane or whether it is a property of the membrane through which it moves. For a number of years we held the view that water was highly structured within the continuous water matrix which formed the permeability path. This view was heavily influenced by the Davson–Danielli model of the cell membrane with its lipid bilayer sparsely populated with water channels only a few angstroms wide. The high heats of activation were viewed as measures of the hydrogen bonding of water to membrane constituents.

The Singer model[11] gave us other alternatives to explain the high heats of activation for membrane permeability to water. In the Singer model, intrinsic proteins with a high degree of tertiary and quaternary structure span the membrane. Individual protein chains may form complex clusters of subunits formed both radially and laterally in the membrane. It is this ordering of protein subunits in the lipid bilayer which may offer another set of explanations for our high heats of activation.

One explanation which is advocated by Macey[12] from his studies on human erythrocytes would assign considerable structure to the water within the channels of the intrinsic proteins. This view is similar to the view we held from our Davson–Danielli days except that the aqueous pathways have moved from the lipid bilayer to the intrinsic proteins. Tacit in that argument and in ours, as well, was the belief that the channel was already there, preformed in the membrane, as it were. Lately though, we have considered that the permeability coefficient which we use is not measuring the conductance through preformed channels, but rather the probability that a channel or a continuous pathway will form. The rate-limiting step then becomes not the transit time across the membrane, but rather the transit time for subunits to form a continuous channel, either by insertion in the radial direction or association in the lateral direction. Our high heats and entropies of activation then become measures of the microviscosity of the lipid bilayer and the insertion and orientation of hydrophobic groups of intrinsic protein complexes. Therefore, another question I would pose is, What is the state of water in the membrane? Can we monitor the making and unmaking of aqueous channels?

By way of summary, and as a stimulus for discussion allow me to ask some additional questions which continue to puzzle me. What is the significance of changes in the intracellular state of water and small solutes during the cell cycle or during cellular maturation and differentiation? Do they *regulate* macromolecular reorganization or are they the *expression* of macromolecular reorganization? Are water and small solutes the passive stuff of protoplasm or do they have a dynamic life of their own? I intimated earlier that shape and form were expressions of asymmetric forces at work. Can some of these forces be osmotic as a consequence of the asymmetrical distribution and compartmentalization of solutes and water? Can this asymmetry be regulated by the charge density of non-diffusible solutes? I do not wish to diminish the importance of contractile proteins which produce the directed forces of muscle contraction or form the scaffolding of the cell. I have in mind the more pervasive, plastic forces which our scientific forebears labelled sol-gel transformations.

If the state of water changes during the cell cycle, can water regulate or is it acting as a universal solvent responding to the bidding of the charge distribution of the macromolecule? When was the last time DNA replicated in a desiccator? In summing up the distribution of forces, can we obtain long range control of genetic expression through membrane function? Since the extent of membrane differentiation and specificity resides in part in its biochemical composition, can the membrane in turn, through control of water and solute distribution, feed back on genetic expression to alter its composition? These are the kinds of questions which I as a cell physiologist plan to ask my colleagues in biophysics and physical chemistry during the meeting. I hope against hope that I receive a better answer than the one I received at a Gordon conference on water some years ago. 'Oh', he said in reply to my questions, 'don't ask me. I came here to learn about the structure of water by the way it interacts with proteins.'

References

1. W. Drost-Hansen, in H. D. Brown (ed.): *Chemistry of the Interface Part B*. Academic Press, New York (1971).

2. C. F. Hazelwood, *Ann. N.Y. Acad. Sci.*, **204**, 593 (1973).
3. G. N. Ling, *Ann. N.Y. Acad. Sci.*, **125**, 401 (1965).
4. G. N. Ling, in P. A. Horne (ed.): *Water and Aqueous Solutions*. Wiley–Interscience, New York, 663 (1972).
5. W. Negendank and C. Shaller, *J. Cell Physiol.*, **98**, 95 (1979).
6. B. Lucke and M. McCutcheon, *Physiol. Revs.*, **12**, 68 (1932).
7. E. Ponder, *Hemolysis and Related Phenomena*. Grune and Stratton, 83 (1948).
8. A. M. DuPre and H. G. Hempling, *J. Cell. Physiol.*, **97**, 381 (1978).
9. A. D. Cicoria and H. G. Hempling, *J. Cell. Physiol.*, **105**, 105 (1980).
10. A. D. Cicoria and H. G. Hempling, *J. Cell. Physiol.*, **105**, 129 (1980).
11. S. J. Singer, in L. I. Rothfield (ed.): *Structure and Function of Biological Membranes*. Academic Press, New York, 145 (1971).
12. R. J. Macey, Federation Proceedings, In Press 1981.

Protonic beta-aluminas: model systems for proton transfer in biological processes

John O. Thomas

University of Uppsala, Sweden

and

Gregory C. Farrington

University of Philadelphia, USA

Summary

The superionic proton conducting system $NH_4^+/H_3O^+/H_2O$ β''-alumina is suggested as a convenient model system for studying the Grotthus mechanism for proton transfer in biological systems.

Efficient proton translocation across or along the surface of a membrane is a *common* and particularly important phenomenon in living organisms. A typical example is the movement of protons across a cell membrane after their generation in some oxidation process. (See also Ref. 1 and references given therein.) It is interesting to note, however, that a high level of proton conductivity is extremely *rare* in crystalline solids. Studies of the mechanism(s) responsible for proton transfer in well-defined crystalline proton conductors can thus provide valuable information at the atomic level about the chemical, structural and dynamical conditions favourable to the creation of an efficient proton transfer pathway in a biological system.

We propose here that the proton conduction mechanism in one of the very best crystalline proton conductors so far studied is a useful model mechanism for biological proton transfer. The material, ammonium/hydronium β''-alumina, has a proton conductivity as high as 10^{-3} Ω^{-1} cm^{-1} at ambient temperature.[2] Its structure comprises impenetrable spinel blocks (Al atoms

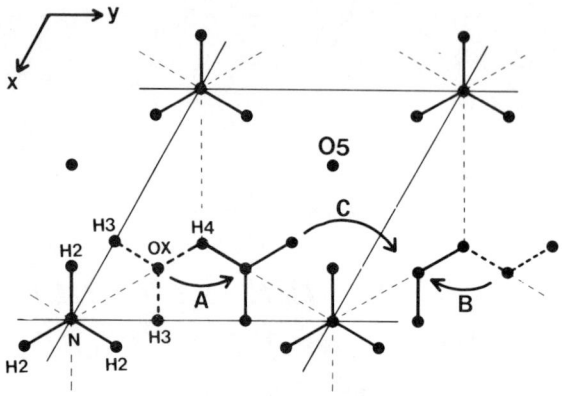

Figure 1

octahedrally and tetrahedrally coordinated to O atoms) interleaved by two-dimensional layers in which the conduction process takes place. This layer (see Figure 1) contains interlinked hexagonal pathways around the spinel block bridging oxygen atoms (O5). Equivalent sites (denoted in the figure by N and H4) in the conducting layer are statistically occupied by NH_4^+ ions (to ~80%), H_3O^+ ions (to ~10%) and H_2O molecules (to ~10%). The proton conduction mechanism deduced from an accurate single-crystal neutron diffraction study[3] involves a classical Grotthus-type mechanism, possibly enhanced by rotation of the NH_4^+ ions about an axis through N and perpendicular to the conduction plane. Components of the mechanism are: (a) rotational displacement of H_3O^+; (b) rotational displacement of H_2O; and (c) proton transfer from an H_3O^+ ion to a conveniently placed H_2O molecule. The net result is a proton transfer from left to right in the figure.

Applying this model to the structurally ill-defined ionophorous systems involved in *in vivo* biological proton transfer processes, we can suggest certain of its features as being conducive to the realization of an efficient Grotthus-type mechanism:

1. A suitably hydrophobic character around the proton transfer pathway, so hindering the formation of 'braking' or 'blocking' H-bonds.
2. An appropriate ratio of H_3O^+ ions to H_2O molecules along the pathway, so that an H_3O^+ ion has access to a nearby H_2O molecule to which it can transfer a proton.
3. An appropriate geometrical relationship between the H_3O^+ and H_2O positions, so that proton transfer is energetically feasible.
4. Rotating or vibrating groups in the vicinity of the pathway which can provide some form of dynamical enhancement to the proton transfer.

References

1. D. B. Kell, D. J. Clarke and J. G. Morris, *FEMS Microbiol. Letts.*, **11**, 1 (1981).
2. G. C. Farrington and J. L. Briant in *Fast Ionic Transport in Solids*, Eds P. Vashishta *et al.*, North-Holland, New York, p. 395 (1979).
3. J. O. Thomas and G. C. Farrington (1982). To be published.

Evidence for an increase in viscosity of water associated with ion pumping

Philippa M. Wiggins and Graham A. Bowmaker
University of Auckland, New Zealand

Summary

The electron spin resonance spectrum of the water-soluble nitroxide free radical TEMPOL has been measured in concentrated suspensions of sarcoplasmic reticulum vesicles. With addition of ATP there was an initial loss of 1–2% of the signal which returned as ATP was consumed.

The Ca^{2+}-adenosine triphosphatase (ATPase) of sarcoplasmic reticulum binds two Ca^{2+} ions and Mg^{2+} ions at specific sites on its cytoplasmic surface and only then can be phosphorylated by ATP to form a phosphoenzyme, during the lifetime of which the two Ca^{2+} ions dissociate from their binding sites and appear on the other side of the membrane. Transmembrane Ca^{2+} gradients of 10^3 can be generated and maintained by this pump. We have proposed a molecular mechanism for this and similar processes, in which the dissociation of the Ca^{2+} ions from their binding sites, the establishment of a gradient in chemical potential and the direction in which diffusion down that gradient is allowed, are all determined by an increase in the structure, hydrogen-bond energy and viscosity of interfacial water contained within oligomers of the phosphoenzymes. Previously we have shown that formation of the phosphoenzyme is accompanied by anomalous light scatter[1] that one would expect to result from fluctuations in density, by an increase in the polarization of the fluorescence of fluorescein[2] reflecting an increase in the microscopic viscosity of its environment, and increases in activity of H^+ and Na^+ and a decrease in that of K^+ consistent with changes in solvent structure.[3] In this report we describe experiments in which the effect of formation of the phosphoenzyme upon the microscopic viscosity of water was investigated using the spin probe, 4-hydroxy-2,2,6,6-tetramethylpiperidine-1-oxyl (TEMPOL).

Sarcoplasmic reticulum vesicles were prepared by standard methods from rabbit back and leg muscle, and finally suspended at a protein concentration of 100 mg cm^{-3} in KCl (100 mol m^{-3}) buffered with tris (hydroxymethyl) aminomethane(Tris) maleate (5 mol m^{-3}; pH 7). Electron spin resonance (e.s.r.) spectra were recorded at room temperature on a Varian E-4 spectrometer operating at about 9.1 GHz with a modulation frequency of 100 kHz. The resonance spectrum of TEMPOL in a concentrated (100 mg cm^{-3}) suspension of vesicles is a sharp triplet due to hyperfine coupling with one ^{14}N nucleus. The peak–peak amplitude (h) of the upfield resonance of the first derivative spectrum was assumed to be proportional to the concentration of rapidly tumbling spin probes. When a suspension containing TEMPOL was frozen at -50 °C spectral broadening reduced h almost to zero. With time h decreased slowly, its rate of decay depending upon the concentrations of protein and TEMPOL and the composition of the supporting medium. In paired experiments on one preparation of vesicles the difference between the two plots of log h against time was linear. When, however, ATP was added to one sample at zero time, the difference plot consistently showed a departure from linearity, indicating that during cycling of the ATPase some signal was lost, and that it returned as ATP was consumed; i.e. the probe was not chemically transformed during the reaction. The fraction of signal lost increased with protein concentration and was independent of TEMPOL concentration, suggesting that the loss of signal was not due to immobilization by binding of the probe to some intermediate of the ATPase reaction. The loss was greatest at the earliest time after addition of ATP, and its return followed the same time-course as ATP hydrolysis.

The findings are consistent with the proposed model of active transport. Probe molecules present in aqueous solution inside the cytoplasmic cleft between the monomeric polypeptides are immobilized when the enzyme is phosphorylated and the viscosity of the interfacial aqueous phase greatly increased. With their immobilization in random orientations there is spectral broadening and a decrease in h. The loss of signal then depends only on the fraction of total water in the system involved in the phase change and is independent of probe concentration.

An estimate of the maximal concentration of phosphoenzyme under the conditions of these experiments is approximately 4 μmol g^{-1} protein;[4] the volume occupied by membrane in 1 cm^3 of a suspension containing 100 mg protein cm^{-3} is approximately 0.18 cm^3.[5] Using these values, and assuming that the fraction of signal lost was equal to the fraction of total water that underwent a phase change with formation of the phosphoenzyme, the volume of structurally perturbed water associated with one polypeptide chain of MW 110 000 is 40.7 ± 5.24 nm^3 (mean and standard deviation of 25 determinations from nine different preparations of vesicles). The absolute value awaits a better estimate of the concentration of phosphoenzyme, but at least the order of magnitude seems plausible. It can be compared with the 200 water molecules (6 nm^3) of increased sorption by bacteriorhodopsin, the simplest proton pump of 26 000 daltons, when it is illuminated.[6]

References

1. P. M. Wiggins, *Bioelectrochem. Bioenerget.*, **6**, 123 (1979).
2. P. M. Wiggins and V. A. Knight, *Bioelectrochem. Bioenerget.*, **6**, 323 (1979).
3. P. M. Wiggins, *J. Biol. Chem.*, **255**, 11365 (1980).
4. T. Kanazawa, S. Yamada, T. Yamamoto and Y. Tonomura, *J. Biochem.*, **70**, 95 (1971).
5. D. Scales and G. Inesi, *Biophys. J.*, **16**, 135 (1976).
6. Y. A. Lazarev and E. Terpugov, *Biochim. Biophys. Acta*, **590**, 324 (1980).

NMR of water nuclei in heterogeneous systems
Relaxation theory and oxygen-17 data from aqueous solutions of proteins, polyelectrolytes and micelles

B. Halle, L. Piculell, G. Carlström, T. Andersson, H. Wennerström and B. Lindman

Chemical Centre, Lund, Sweden

Summary

A general theoretical framework for the interpretation of NMR data from water nuclei in heterogeneous systems is presented. Oxygen-17 NMR data from aqueous solutions of proteins, polyelectrolytes and micelles are used to test the theory and to give microscopic information about the state of hydration water.

The technique of nuclear magnetic resonance is well suited to provide microscopic information about the state of water in complex aqueous systems. While a vast number of ^{1}H and ^{2}H NMR studies have been reported, the third magnetic water nucleus, ^{17}O, has only recently been employed in connection with these systems. With conclusive evidence now at hand of cross-relaxation and proton (deuteron) exchange involving non-water nuclei—phenomena which complicate the interpretation of ^{1}H and ^{2}H data—and with the widespread use of FT spectrometers, ^{17}O now stands out as the most powerful nucleus for studies of water in complex systems.

It has been demonstrated repeatedly during the past two decades that NMR signals from water nuclei in macroscopically anisotropic systems exhibit line splittings, albeit an order of magnitude smaller than the rigid-lattice splitting. On account of these observations we can exclude the two extremes of water–surface interaction: the isotropic water distribution and the rigid binding. These fundamental implications have, however, been slow to penetrate into the field of macromolecular hydration. In particular, there has long been a need for a consistent theoretical framework for interpreting NMR data from water nuclei in heterogeneous systems; a theory founded on the two basic characteristics of hydration water: anisotropic orientational distribution and rapid tumbling.

Such a theory has now been presented;[1] it constitutes a slight elaboration and generalization of the relaxation theory presented by Wennerström in 1974 with special emphasis on ionic nuclei.[2] This so-called two-step model exploits the fact that the anisotropic tumbling of hydration water (correlation time τ_f), on the one hand, and the reorientation of macromolecules or molecular aggregates (correlation time τ_s), on the other, occur on widely separated time-scales. This time-scale separation leads to time-correlation functions (for the quadrupole or the dipole–dipole interaction) which decay in two steps:

$$G(t) \propto (1 + \eta^2/3 - A^2)\widetilde{G}_f(t; \tau_f) + A^2\widetilde{G}_s(t; \tau_s) \qquad (1)$$

where η is the field-gradient asymmetry parameter ($\eta = 0$ for dipolar relaxation). The reduced correlation functions $\widetilde{G}_f$ and $\widetilde{G}_s$ may, or may not, be exponential. The surface-induced bias in hydration water orientation is explicitly taken into account through the residual anisotropy

$$A = \alpha S_0 + \beta S_2 \qquad (2)$$

where the constants α and β depend on the identity of the nucleus (^{1}H, ^{2}H or ^{17}O). The order parameters S_0 and S_2 are coefficients in the expansion of the orientational distribution function for the hydration water relative to the aggregate surface.

On the basis of Equations (1) and (2), we have calculated the ratios of splittings and of slow contributions to relaxation rates from different pairs of water nuclei (^{1}H, ^{2}H or ^{17}O), normalized with respect to spin interactions. We conclude[1] that the well-known invariance of the ratio of normalized splittings is due, not to an invariance of the order parameters to the chemical nature of the surface, as often stated, but to the insensitivity of this ratio to the nature of the orientational constraint.

The longitudinal (R_1) and transverse (R_2) relaxation rates for hydration water, as predicted by the two-step model for a typical case, are shown in Figure 1 as functions of the resonance frequency ω. The fast motion contributes equally to R_1 and R_2 in the entire accessible frequency range, whereas the slow contribution falls off in the typical frequency 'window'. Note also that R_2 carries information about the slow component even at high frequencies, where R_1 is completely determined by the fast motion.

Assuming that a water molecule can be (operationally) assigned to either of two states: 'free' or 'bound', and that 'bound' water obeys the two-step model, the theory contains four parameters: τ_f, τ_s, A and P_B (the fraction

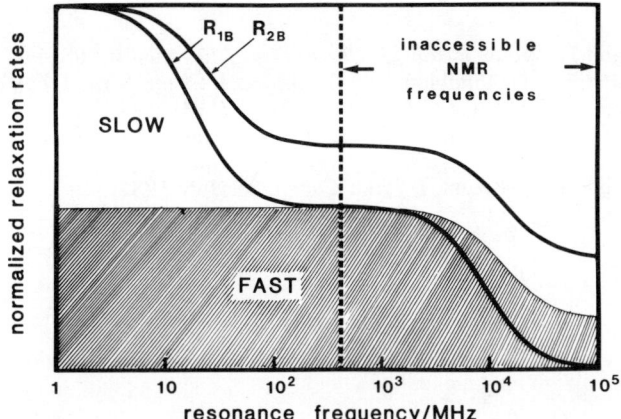

Figure 1 Relaxation rates for hydration water according to the two-step model with $\tau_f = 10$ ps, $\tau_s = 5$ ns and $A = 0.05$

'bound' water). The system can often be made macroscopically anisotropic without significantly altering the interfacial region (cf. micelle/liquid crystal or protein solution/protein crystal). It is then possible to determine all four parameters. The next step is to identify the motions represented by the two correlation times τ_f and τ_s. Possible candidates for the fast local motion include water tumbling, libration of surface residues or polymer segments, and monomer fluctuations in micelles. The slow motion usually consists of aggregate tumbling and/or water exchange between the 'free' and 'bound' states. By increasing the aggregate size until the reorientational time greatly exceeds the 'bound' water lifetime, the latter can be obtained. In certain cases, the lifetime can also be extracted from the ^{17}O scalar relaxation due to proton exchange between water molecules and acidic surface groups.[3]

We have followed these approaches in ^{17}O NMR studies of aqueous solutions of two linear polyelectrolytes,[3] seven globular proteins[4] and nine ionic surfactant micelles.[5] In all cases, the results verify the basic assumptions in the two-step model. The main conclusions from our studies are as follows.

(1) Hydration water tumbles rapidly; less than an order of magnitude slower than in the bulk, under a weak orientational constraint from the surface.
(2) We find no indications of long-range (more than ca. two water layers) hydration structures.
(3) Hydration water lifetimes are on the order of 10 ns.
(4) Charged surface groups, carboxylates in particular, and small counterions, induce larger structure and/or dynamical perturbations than uncharged or non-polar groups.
(5) In ionic surfactant micelles, less than two methylene groups are exposed to water.

References

1. B. Halle and H. Wennerström, *J. Chem. Phys.*, **75** (August 1981).
2. H. Wennerström, G. Lindblom and B. Lindman, *Chem. Scripta*, **6**, 97 (1974).
3. B. Halle and L. Piculell, *J.C.S. Faraday Trans. I*, **77**, (1981).
4. B. Halle, T. Andersson, S. Forsén and B. Lindman, *J. Am. Chem. Soc.*, **103**, 500 (1981).
5. B. Halle and G. Carlström, *J. Phys. Chem.*, **85** (July 1981).

Facilitated proton transfer in protein solutions by rotational and translational protein diffusion

G. Gros and H. Gros
Universitätsklinikum Essen, West Germany

and

D. Lavalette
Institute Curie, Orsay, France

Summary

From measurements of facilitated diffusion of CO_2 and H^+ in protein solutions, evidence is presented to show that (1) translational protein diffusion results in a highly effective facilitation of H^+ diffusion in solutions of proteins of widely differing size (mol.wt. 1.7×10^4 to 3.7×10^6), and (2) rotational protein diffusion leads to a similarly effective proton transfer but seems to do so in solutions of very high molecular weight proteins (4.5×10^5 to 3.7×10^6) only.

Two modes of molecular motion of carrier molecules can, in principle, lead to a facilitated transport of a substrate: translational and rotational diffusion. This study intends to show that both types of facilitation may be involved in proton transport in protein solutions.

We have shown earlier that facilitated CO_2 diffusion in protein solutions is a process whose limiting step is a protein-facilitated proton transport.[1,2] We have now evaluated proton transport in protein solutions from measurements of the facilitated diffusion of CO_2 across thin layers of such solutions. Measurements were performed in solutions of a variety of globular proteins using a previously published method.[3]

Demonstration of facilitated diffusion of CO_2 in protein solutions

Facilitated diffusion of CO_2 can be quantitated by comparing the CO_2 diffusion coefficient determined in a high CO_2 partial pressure range with the CO_2

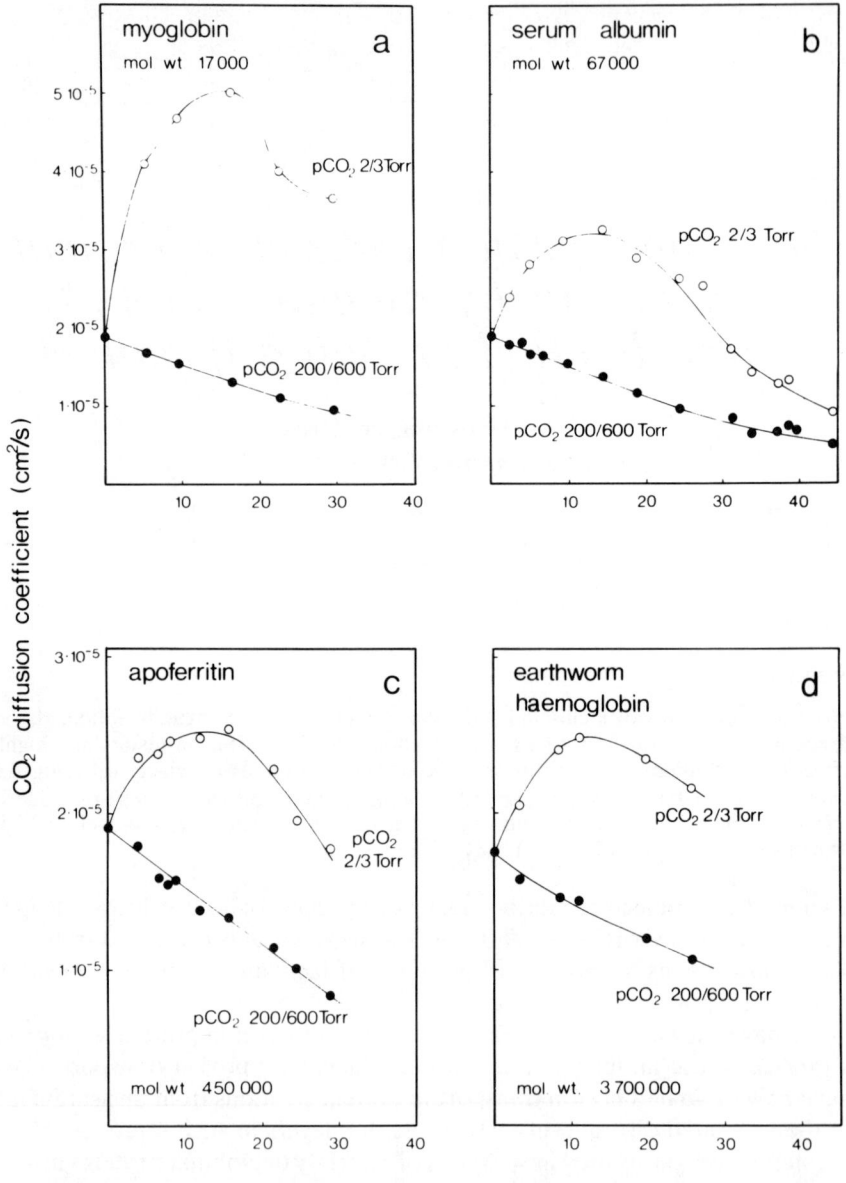

Figure 1 Facilitated CO_2 diffusion in myoglobin (a), serum albumin (b), apoferritin (c) and earthworm haemoglobin (d) solutions. The CO_2 diffusion coefficients were measured in a high pCO_2 range (●; 200 and 600 Torr at the boundaries of the diffusion layers) and in a low pCO_2 range (○; 2 and 3 Torr at the boundaries). The CO_2 diffusion coefficient is greater at low pCO_2 than at high pCO_2 indicating that a facilitation of CO_2 diffusion occurs at low pCO_2

diffusion coefficient obtained in a low pCO_2 range. When the pCO_2 range employed is high, e.g. at 200 to 600 Torr, no facilitation of CO_2 diffusion occurs under the present conditions[3] and any elevation of the CO_2 diffusion coefficient, D_{CO2}, at lower pCO_2 values is indicative of a facilitated CO_2 flux occurring in addition to the free flux of CO_2. Figure 1(a)–(d) shows that in all protein solutions investigated a facilitation of CO_2 diffusion occurs: D_{CO2} measured in a low pCO_2 range (2–3 Torr) is significantly higher than D_{CO2} measured in a pCO_2 range of 200–600 Torr. This holds for all four proteins studied, myoglobin (mol.wt. 17 000), bovine serum albumin (mol.wt. 67 000), apoferritin (mol.wt. 450 000) and earthworm haemoglobin (mol.wt. 3.7×10^6), and at all concentrations of these proteins.

Mechanism of facilitated CO_2 diffusion in protein solutions

We have previously shown that facilitated diffusion of CO_2 in protein solutions is a diffusion of HCO_3^- combined with a protein-facilitated H^+ transport (free diffusion of H^+ being negligible): thus, a facilitated CO_2 flux, $F_{CO2,fac}$, as well as the underlying proton flux, $F_{H^+,fac}$, can be expressed as follows:

$$F_{CO_2,fac} = F_{H^+,fac} = D_{post} \frac{\Delta[H^+b]}{\Delta x} \quad (1)$$

where D_{post} is the protein diffusion coefficient necessary to explain the measured fluxes, and $\Delta[H^+b]/\Delta x$ is the concentration gradient of buffered protons. Equation 1 predicts that the facilitated proton flux per concentration gradient, $F_{H^+,fac}/(\Delta[H^+b]/\Delta x)$, should be related to the protein mobility. Figure 2, in which $F_{H^+,fac}/(\Delta[H^+b]/\Delta x)$ as derived from the data of Figure 1(a)–(d) is plotted for various proteins, provides further support for the crucial role of protein diffusion, $F_{H^+,fac}/(\Delta[H^+b]/\Delta x)$, (i) at a given protein concentration decreases with increasing protein molecular weight and (ii) for a given protein decreases with increasing protein concentration. Both observations are consistent with known dependencies of protein diffusivity.[4]

Role of translational protein diffusion for facilitated proton transport

Figure 3(a)–(d) shows the protein diffusion coefficients, D_{post}, that have to be postulated to quantitatively explain the measured H^+ fluxes on the basis of Equation 1. For the four proteins studied, values of D_{post} are compared to directly measured values of the translational protein diffusion coefficient D_{trans}. Values of D_{trans} were determined as self-diffusion coefficients using ^{14}C-labelled proteins.[4] Figure 3(a) and 3(b) show that for the two smaller proteins studied, myoglobin and serum albumin, there is good agreement between D_{post} and D_{trans}, i.e. the measured facilitated proton fluxes can be quantitatively accounted for by translational protein diffusion alone. In the case of two larger proteins, apoferritin and earthworm haemoglobin, D_{post} is

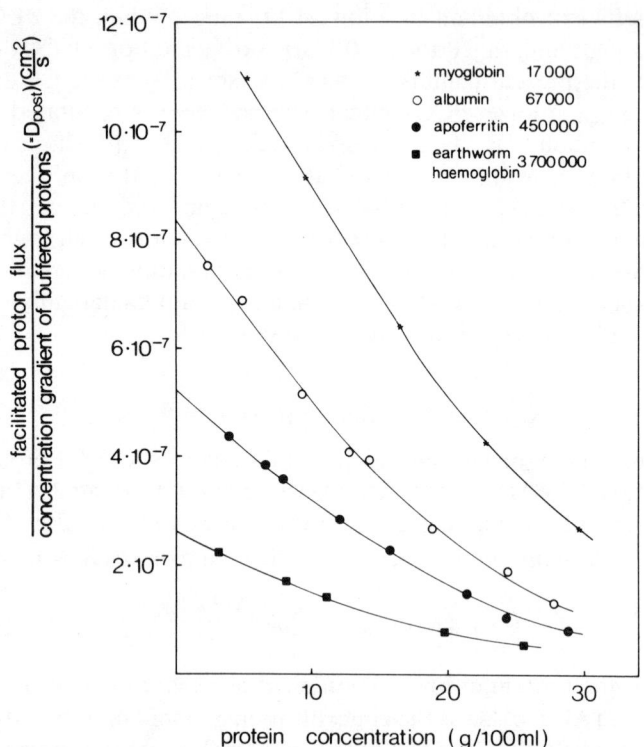

Figure 2 Facilitated proton flux per concentration gradient of buffered protons as a function of protein concentration for proteins of various molecular weights. The values shown represent protein diffusivities (D_{post}) necessary to explain the experimental facilitations seen in Figure 1. D_{post} decreases with increasing protein molecular weight and with increasing protein concentration

greater than D_{trans} at all protein concentrations studied which implies that a mechanism in addition to protein translation leads to a facilitated H$^+$ transport in the case of these proteins.

A role of rotational protein diffusion for facilitated proton transport?

Can rotational protein diffusion account for those proton fluxes occurring in addition to what is expected from translational protein diffusion? To answer this question we have (i) derived an equation describing rotation-facilitated proton diffusion in terms of the protein rotational diffusion coefficient and (ii) measured the rotational diffusion coefficient of earthworm haemoglobin.[5,6]

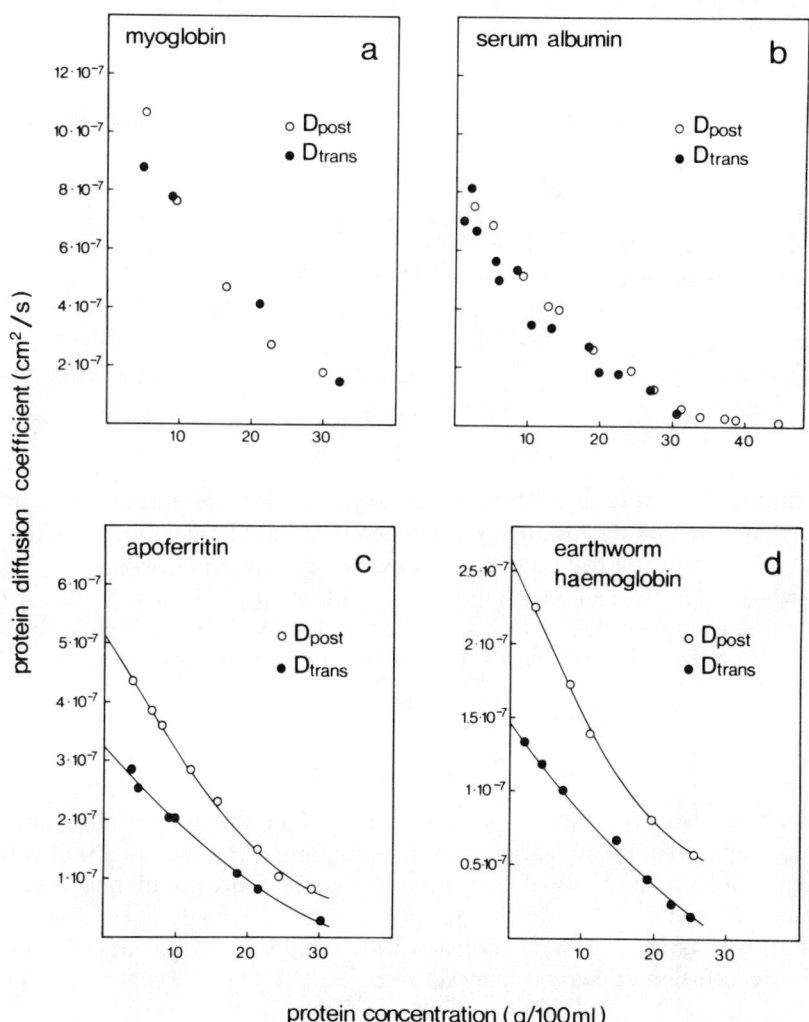

Figure 3 Postulated (○) and translational (●) protein diffusivities as a function of protein concentration for the four proteins studied. The agreement of D_{post} and D_{trans} in Figure 3(a) and (b) indicates that, in the case of myoglobin and serum albumin, translational protein diffusion can quantitatively explain the measured H^+ fluxes. Figure 3(c) and (d) show, that, for the large proteins apoferritin and earthworm haemoglobin, a mechanism in addition to protein translation leads to a facilitated proton transport

If the chemical reaction is not a rate-limiting step, the protein-facilitated proton flux by rotational diffusion is given by:

$$F_{H^+,rot} = \tfrac{2}{3} R^2 \theta \frac{\Delta[H^+b]}{\Delta x}, \quad (2)$$

where R is the molecular radius of the protein and θ is its rotational diffusion coefficient.

For *earthworm haemoglobin* at low protein concentration, $\theta_0^{25°}$ was measured to be 6.94×10^4 s^{-1} which gives a value of 0.9×10^{-7} cm^2/s for $\tfrac{2}{3}R^2\theta$, while $D_{trans,o}^{25°}$ is read from the curve of Figure 3(d) after extrapolation to zero concentration to be 1.5×10^{-7} cm^2/s. Thus, for infinite dilution,

$$D_{trans} + \tfrac{2}{3}R^2\theta = 2.4 \times 10^{-7} \text{ cm}^2/\text{s}$$

is in close agreement with the limiting value of D_{post} as obtained by extrapolation in Figure 3:

$$D_{post} = 2.6 \times 10^{-7} \text{ cm}^2/\text{s}$$

This implies that, at least at low protein concentration, the measured facilitated H$^+$ flux can be quantitatively explained in terms of a combined facilitation of H$^+$ transfer by rotational and translational protein diffusion.

For *apoferritin*, $\theta_0^{25°}$ can be estimated to be 4.8×10^5 s^{-1} from its molecular dimensions giving a value of 1.7×10^{-7} cm^2/s for $\tfrac{2}{3}R^2\theta$. $D_{trans,o}^{25°}$ is read from Figure 3(c) to be $3.3 \cdot 10^{-7}$ cm^2/s. For infinite dilution we obtain:

$$D_{trans} + \tfrac{2}{3}R^2\theta = 5.0 \times 10^{-7} \text{ cm}^2/\text{s}$$

while

$$D_{post} = 5.1 \times 10^{-7} \text{ cm}^2/\text{s}.$$

We conclude that the proton transfer observed in solutions of two large proteins, apoferritin and earthworm haemoglobin, can be quantitatively accounted for on the basis of translational together with rotational protein diffusion. In solutions of smaller proteins, such as myoglobin and serum albumin, translational protein diffusion only results in proton transfer and rotational diffusion appears to play no role.

References

1. G. Gros and W. Moll, *J. Gen. Physiol.*, **64**, 356 (1974).
2. G. Gros, W. Moll, H. Hoppe and H. Gros, *J. Gen. Physiol.*, **67**, 773 (1976).
3. G. Gros and W. Moll, *Pflügers Arch.*, **324**, 249 (1971).
4. G. Gros, *Biophys. J.*, **22**, 453 (1978).
5. D. Lavalette, D. Amand and F. Pochon, *Proc. Natl. Acad. Sci., USA*, **74**, 1407 (1977).
6. G. Gros, H. Gros, D. Lavalette, B. Amand and F. Pochon, in *Biophysics and Physiology of Carbon Dioxide*, eds C. Bauer, G. Gros and H. Bartels, Springer, Berlin–Heidelberg–New York (1980).

Proton NMR relaxation and diffusion study of water sorbed in oriented DNA and hyaluronic acid samples

G. Lahajnar and I. Zupančič
University of Ljubljana, Yugoslavia

and

A. Rupprecht
University of Stockholm, Sweden

Summary

Pulsed proton NMR relaxation and diffusion study of water sorbed in solid oriented NaDNA and hyaluronic acid samples has been performed in the range of relative humidities η between 86.6% and 48.8%. The strong angular dependence of the spin–spin relaxation time T_2 for DNA is indicative of a high dynamic preferential orientation of water molecules arising from the interaction with ordered DNA. T_2 gives evidence of structural changes in DNA induced by varying η, and—in combination with the spin–lattice relaxation (T_1) and diffusion (D) data—to specify dynamics and average distance of H_2O molecules in the hydration shell of DNA. No such conclusions can be made for hyaluronic acid where T_2 is angular independent though anisotropy of D is found.

Water plays a stabilizing role in the maintenance of native conformations of biomacromolecules. Of the various techniques used to study hydration of macromolecules, nuclear magnetic resonance (NMR) has proved to be particularly useful when the structure and dynamics of preferentially oriented interfacial water can be studied in macroscopically ordered biopolymers.

In this study structural and dynamic characteristics of water sorbed in oriented solid samples of NaDNA[1] and potassium hyaluronate[2] have been examined in the relative humidity (η) range between 86.6% and 48.8% through proton NMR relaxation and diffusion measurements. Earlier measurements on oriented NaDNA have been done down to $\eta = 34$% r.h.[3] Room temperature proton spin–lattice (T_1) and spin–spin relaxation time (T_2) measurements were done at the resonance frequency $\nu_H = 57.9$ MHz. Diffusion coefficient D was determined for a wide range of diffusion times (Δ) between 3 ms and 100 ms, using a quadrupole coil system producing gradient fields of 330 gauss/cm. The usual pulsed gradient spin–echo method[4] was used, while for long Δ Hahn's stimulated echo[5] was explored.

T_2 data for NaDNA (Figure 1) depend strongly on the angle θ between the sample orientational axis and the direction of the external magnetic field B_0. In the whole η range studied $1/T_2$ closely obeys the angular relation $1/T_2 = 1/T_{2,0} + A(3\cos^2\theta - 1)^2$, where both $T_{2,0}$ and A vary with moisture content. Such a behaviour of T_2 is interpreted in terms of fast rotational movement of H_2O molecules (correlation time $\tau_o \ll 10^{-10}$ sec) which is anisotropic because of interactions with the oriented polymer surface, so that the dipolar interaction is not completely averaged out. The angular part of the non-zero residual coupling points along the sample orientational axis as indicated by the observed angular dependence of T_2. A slower diffusional motion of H_2O molecules further influences the dipolar interaction and determines the spin–lattice relaxation time T_1. A is proportional to the square of the local order parameter of H_2O molecules and to the proton exchange time.[6] Variation of A from 0.78 ms^{-1} at 48.8% r.h. to 0.61 ms^{-1} at 75% is rather smooth

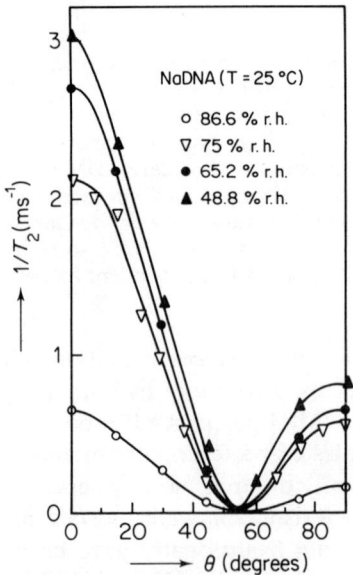

Figure 1 Angular dependence of the spin–spin relaxation rate $1/T_2$ for different humidities

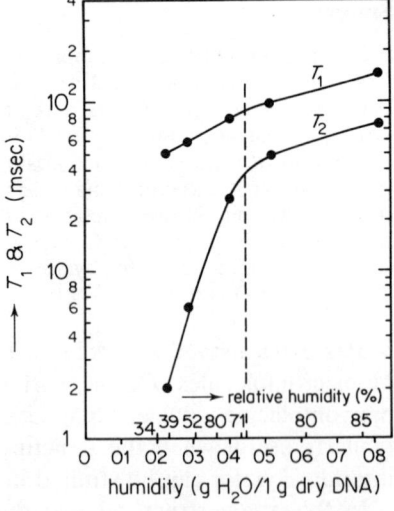

Figure 2 Dependence on the spin–lattice (T_1) and magic angle (54.7°) spin–spin (T_2) relaxation time on the water content. (Magic angle T_2 equals $T_{2,0}$)

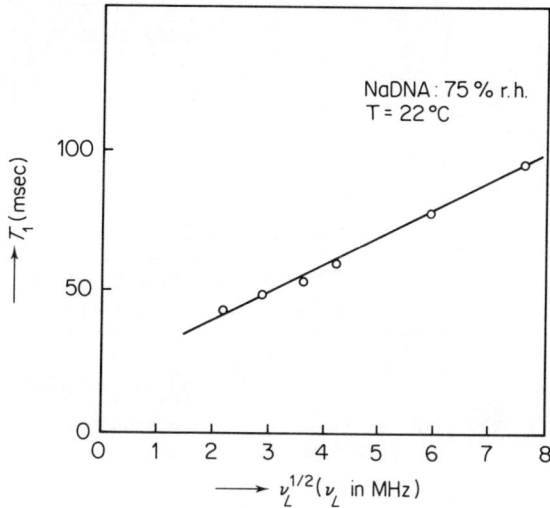

Figure 3 Dispersion of T_1 for NaDNA at 75% r.h.

and falls down to 0.17 ms^{-1} at 86.6% r.h., since hydration above ~75% r.h. proceeds with considerable swelling and water is relatively less preferentially oriented. Also a 'knee' in the plot of $T_{2,0}$ and T_1 against η (Figure 2) is observed around $\eta \approx 75\%$ r.h. This supports the finding[7] that up to 75% r.h. the solid NaDNA is in a partly disordered configuration while above this r.h. value the native clustering together of relatively non-polar aromatic bases is realized through the hydrophobic effect.[8] The disappearance of the angular dependence of T_2 below ~40% r.h.[3] confirms the observation[7] that at low η a complete loss of base stacking order takes place.

T_1 is approximately proportional to the square root of the Larmor frequency ($T_1 \propto \nu_L^{1/2}$) (Figure 3). This confirms that translational diffusion is rate determining mechanism for T_1. In terms of Krüger's theory[9] a correlation time $\tau = 10^{-9}$ s is estimated from the ratio $T_1/T_{2,0}$, which together with the experimentally determined D values allows us to calculate the closest approach distance of H$_2$O molecules as $d \approx 6$ Å.

Diffusion data (Figure 4) have been determined for a wide range of diffusion times ($\Delta = 3 - 100$ ms). Diffusion coefficient parallel ($D_\parallel$) and perpendicular ($D_\perp$) to the sample orientation shows a systematic anisotropy $(D_\parallel - D_\perp)/D$ of $10 \div 20\%$. In the limits of experimental error no evidence for restricted diffusion is found though data at shortest Δ indicate that it may exist below $\Delta = 3$ ms.

Hyaluronic acid samples behave differently. No angular dependence of T_2 is found though D is found anisotropic similarly as in DNA. From the ratio of

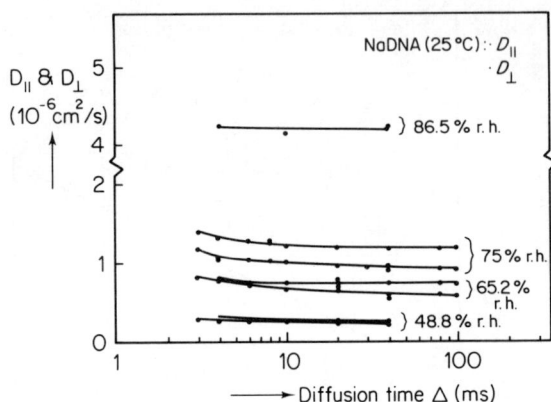

Figure 4 Diffusion coefficient for a wide range of diffusion times Δ

T_1 (T_1 = 115 ms) and T_2 (T_2 = 2.6 ms) at 86.6% r.h. a longer correlation time is estimated ($\tau \approx 3 \times 10^{-8}$ sec) indicating that isotropic relaxation time $T_{2,0}$ may dominate the observed T_2.

References

1. A. Rupprecht, *Biotechnol. Bioeng.*, **12**, 93 (1970).
2. A. Rupprecht, *Acta Chem. Scand.*, **B33**, 779 (1979).
3. G. Lahajnar, I. Zupančič, Lj. Miljković and A. Rupprecht, *Period. Biol.*, **80**, 135 (1978).
4. E. O. Stejskal and J. E. Tanner, *J. Chem. Phys.*, **42**, 288 (1965).
5. E. L. Hahn, *Phys. Rev.*, **80**, 580 (1950).
6. S. B. Ahmad, K. J. Packer and J. M. Ramsden, *Mol. Phys.*, **33**, 857 (1977).
7. M. Falk, K. A. Hartman and R. C. Lord, *J. Am. Chem. Soc.*, **85**, 391 (1963).
8. T. T. Herskovits, S. T. Singer and E. P. Geiduschek, *Arch. Biochem. Biophys.*, **94**, 99 (1961).
9. G. J. Krüger, *Z. Naturforsch.*, **24a**, 560 (1969).

Dynamics of water in the peripheral nerve

Eva Katona, Constanţa Ganea, A. I. Popescu and V. Vasilescu
Medical Faculty, Bucharest, Romania

Summary

At least three distinguishable water components are disclosed both by deuteration kinetics and by nuclear magnetic relaxation behaviour of water protons in nerve. Their dependence on tissue state and possible involvements in nerve function and anaesthesia are examined. Analysing the parameters of molecular dynamics, heterogeneity and liquid-likeness of the so-called 'bound' water fraction are pointed out.

Peripheral nerve is a highly heterogeneous system having a water content up to 76% of the total fresh weight. The water component itself also is heterogeneous. Interactions between water molecules and a large variety of macromolecular components from different regions of the nerve tissue change water properties to different extents and in a different manner.[1] These kinds of changes and their role in the structure and function of nerve are not entirely understood.[2]

Here we present some nuclear magnetic relaxation and deuteration studies concerning the dynamics of water molecules in frog peripheral nerve revealing at least three distinct water components having different motional properties. Dependence on nerve state of the tissue water distribution between these different water components and their possible involvements in molecular mechanisms of nerve anaesthesia and nerve influx condition are discussed.

The kinetics of water replacement with heavy water in the sciatic nerve of the frog under isotonic conditions, studied both gravimetrically and by infrared photometry, discloses three water compartments, one non-exchangeable and two others, slow and fast exchanging, respectively.[3,4] In a resting frog sciatic nerve the non-exchangeable water component represents 8% of the total water content of the fresh nerve, while the slow and fast exchanging water compartments are 71% and 21% respectively. In a continuously stimulated or acetylcholine treated nerve both the permeability coefficients and the amount of the fast exchanging water are increased. Exposure to glutaraldehyde increases both the permeability coefficients and the amounts of the fast exchanging and the non-exchangeable water components.

The nuclear magnetic relaxation behaviour of water protons is also dependent on the nerve state. In freshly dissected normal nerves, at temperatures above the freezing point of the bulk water, the spin–lattice relaxation behaviour, studied by the inversion recovery and/or by the saturation recovery method, is always simply exponential. At the same temperatures spin–spin relaxation decays of nerve water protons obtained by the Carr–Purcell–Meiboom–Gill technique are always multiexponential, temperature-dependent at fixed sequence pulse spacing (τ), and τ-dependent at fixed temperature.[5] Exposure to acetylcholine or glutaraldehyde results in an increase of slowly relaxing component. After-death changes in nerve seem to lead to the loss of multiexponentiality of spin–spin relaxation behaviour of water protons. In anaesthetized nerves the spin–spin relaxation process as a whole becomes slower and a marked decrease in the amount of fast relaxing component can be observed. Both spin–spin and spin–lattice relaxation processes are dependent on the degree of nerve deuteration and/or dehydration, the relaxation behaviour of water protons being quite different in deuterated and dehydrated nerves.

At 265 K the bulk of nerve water is frozen. The non-freezing water fraction at this temperature represents 21% of the total water content of the nerve and decreases linearly with temperature lowering. The spin–spin relaxation behaviour of nerve water protons becomes biexponential at these temperatures. Graphical analysis of spin–spin relaxation decays disclosed two distinct components: one of constant size and relaxation rate, and the other having a size and relaxation time decreasing with temperature lowering. Spin–lattice relaxation behaviour remains simply exponential but T_1 variation as a function of temperature shows two distinct minima at each resonance frequency. Assuming that the non-freezing water can be treated as molecules undergoing translational and rotational motions governed by a bimodal log-normal distribution of correlation times, and considering temperature-independent distribution widths and temperature-dependence of the medians of correlation time distributions to be of Eyring-type, by fitting of T_1 data parameters of molecular dynamics in the non-freezing water fraction of nerve can be obtained (Table 1).

Several main conclusions can be drawn:
1. At least three distinct water components can be disclosed in the peripheral nerve. 2. The temperature-dependent exchange processes occurring between various components are slow as compared with spin–spin relaxation rates and rapid if compared to spin–lattice relaxation rate. 3. The sizes and properties of different water components are dependent on the state of

Table 1 Parameters characterizing molecular dynamics in non-freezing water fractions of nerve

No.	Fractional population at 273 K	Median correlation time at 273 K (s)	Distribution width β	Activation enthalpy (kJ/mol)	Activation entropy (J/K)
1	0.79	1.5×10^{-10}	2.0	39.3	88
2	0.21	4×10^{-11}	0.4	113.0	364

nerve. 4. In the nerve on function both the permeability coefficients and the amount of fast exchanging water are increased. 5. Water ordering during anaesthesia is unlikely. There is a marked decrease in the amount of so-called 'bound' water of the nerve. 6. The non-exchangeable water from deuterated nerves seems to have quite different motional properties to that from dehydrated nerves. 7. At least two distinct populations of water molecules are found in the non-freezing water fraction of the nerve. 8. From the viewpoint of molecular mobility both components of non-freezing water fraction are more liquid-like than ice-like.

References

1. D. C. Chang and C. F. Hazlewood, *Biochim. Biophys. Acta*, **630**, 131 (1980).
2. R. Mathur-De Vré, *Progr. Biophys. molec. Biol.*, **35**, 103 (1979).
3. V. Vasilescu, D. -G. Mărgineanu and E. Katona, *Experientia*, **33**, 192 (1977).
4. E. Katona, D. -G. Mărgineanu and V. Vasilescu, *Cell Tissue Res.*, **203**, 331 (1979).
5. V. Vasilescu, E. Katona, V. Simplăceanu and D. Demco, *Experientia*, **34**, 1443 (1978).

The influence of the dynamic properties of water on protein fluctuations

Roger B. Gregory and Andreas Rosenberg
University of Minnesota, USA

Summary

A study of the viscosity and temperature dependence of the rates of hydrogen isotope exchange in lysozyme has demonstrated a strong dynamic coupling between protein conformational fluctuations and the dynamic properties of the solvent.

Introduction

There is now considerable experimental support for the dynamic view of protein structure. The existence of a broad distribution of structural fluctuations which may be correlated in time can be accounted for by the 'Mobile Defect' hypothesis,[1] which forms the basis upon which rearrangements of free volume and free energy support function in proteins. Hydrogen isotope exchange provides considerable information about the conformational dynamics of globular proteins. We have therefore employed this technique to investigate the dynamic coupling between the solvent and the protein interior.

Results

Hydrogen-tritium exchange of lysozyme was measured as a function of temperature and solvent viscosity in water–glycerol cosolvent mixtures (data of Gregory, Knox, Percy and Rosenberg in preparation, 1981). Complete outexchange curves of the number of hydrogens remaining per protein molecule at time t, $H(t)$, corrected to pH 7.5, were constructed by methods described previously.[2] The rate function $K(t) = d \ln H(t)/dt$ was obtained by numerical differentiation of the outexchange curves. The dependence of $K(t)$ on solvent viscosity, η at fixed $H(t)$ values is shown in Figure 1 for data at 25 °C. The plot of log $K(t)$ against log η for the fastest exchanging hydrogens

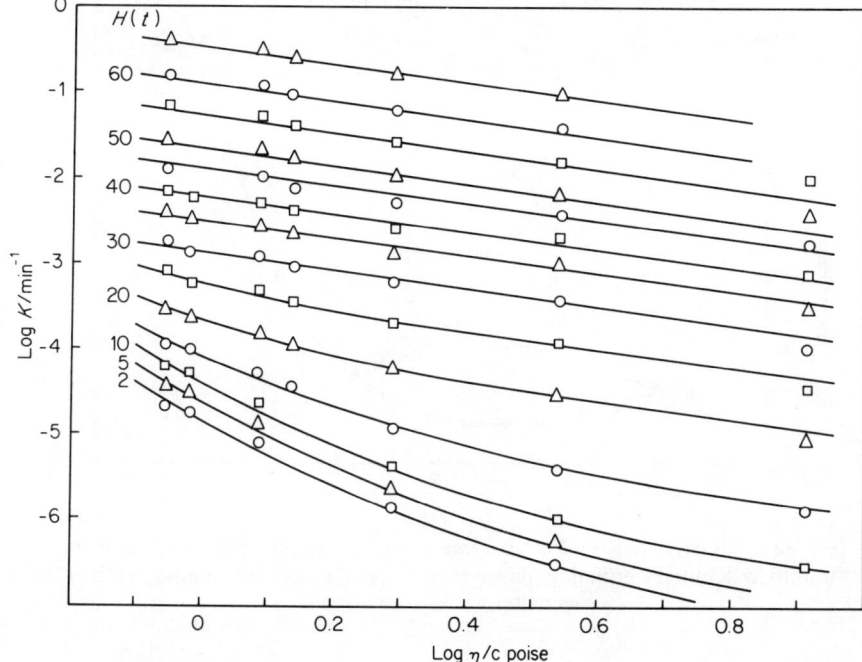

Figure 1 The rate function $K(t)$ for lysozyme at pH 7.5 and 25° plotted as a function of viscosity

that are observed $(65 \geq H(t) \geq 30)$ is linear with a slope of -1, behaviour that is commonly associated with diffusion processes. The exchange of the last 25 hydrogens shows a viscosity dependence that becomes increasingly non-linear.

Analysis of $K(t)$ as a function of both T and η employed a modified Kramers equation;[3,4] $K = A\eta^{-k} \exp -\Delta Q/RT$, which, with k equal to one, describes the rate of transfer, K, of Brownian particles over a potential energy barrier of height ΔQ in a medium of viscosity η. Plots of Δ and k against $H(t)$ are shown in Figure 2. The fastest hydrogens exchanged with k values in the range 1.5 to 1.2 and were associated with barrier heights of between 5 and 15 kcal mol^{-1}. The slowest hydrogens, thought to exchange by a thermal unfolding mechanism,[2] exchanged with a ΔQ of 30 kcal mol^{-1} and a k value that approaches 4.

Discussion

The viscosity dependence of the exchange of the fastest hydrogens is similar to that predicted by the Smoluchowski diffusion equation: $K = 4\pi rD$.

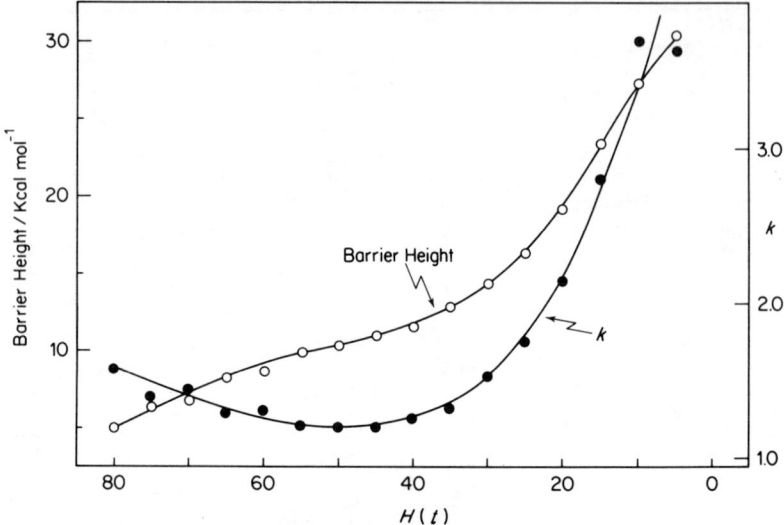

Figure 2 Barrier heights for lysozyme exchange and the parameter K from modified Kramers equation plotted as a function of the number of hydrogens remaining unchanged

However, it is apparent that the reaction is *not* diffusion limited in the solvent, for, the activation energy for such a process would be 4–5 kcal mol^{-1}, characteristic of the temperature dependence of the viscosity of water–glycerol cosolvent mixtures and the barrier height obtained with the Kramers equation would be zero, in contrast to the range of 5–15 kcal mol^{-1} observed here. In addition, the rates of hydrogen exchange observed for lysozyme in the present experiments are all less than 10^6 M^{-1} sec^{-1}, rates that are too slow to be consistent with OH$^-$ ion diffusion in bulk solvent at the viscosities employed here. Instead, the results support the view that exchange of the fastest hydrogens proceeds by a solvent penetration pathway in which the reaction is rate limited by catalyst diffusion to and from the exchange sites *within the protein*. This process is perhaps more appropriately termed percolation since it is the fluctuations in the network of protein secondary structural interactions which provide the mobile regions of free volume for catalyst penetration.

More importantly, in the present context, the results demonstrate that momentum transfer from the solvent to the protein interior is very efficient, such that the dynamic properties of the protein are well coupled to those of the solvent.

The deviations from a Kramers viscosity dependence ($k = 1$) are not well understood, particularly for the slowest hydrogens when k approaches a value of 4, but may result from the correlated conformational fluctuations of many barriers that are necessary for catalyst penetration and protein unfolding (the

Kramers equation strictly applies only to a single, static barrier). It is possible that much of the effectiveness of cosolvents such as glycerol, ethylene glycol and sucrose in stabilizing proteins derives from their increased viscosities which attenuate protein conformational fluctuations and hence reduce the probability of excess solvation of buried peptide groups that destabilize the native state. Finally, it is apparent that solvent viscosity, through its coupling to conformational fluctuations which support protein function, may be an important factor in determining enzyme activities in biological systems.

References

1. R. Lumry and A. Rosenberg, *Colloques internationaux du CNRS*, **246**, 53 (1975).
2. D. G. Knox and A. Rosenberg, *Biopolymers*, **19**, 1049 (1980).
3. H. A. Kramers, *Physica*, **7**, 284–304 (1940).
4. D. Beece, L. Eisenstein, H. Frauenfelder, D. Good, M. D. Marden, L. Reinisch, A. H. Reynolds, L. B. Sorensen and K. T. Yue, *Biochem.*, **19**, 5147 (1980).

Tritiated water distribution in the glycerol-extracted muscle during contraction, relaxation and rigor. Relevance for ionic changes in muscle activity

C. T. Dragomir, Mihaela Perianu, Angela Petre, Simona Botea, Daria Călin, Anca Barbier and Rodica Chirvasie

Victor Babeş Institute, Romania

Summary

Glycerol extracted striated muscle is able to accumulate tritiated water when the latter is introduced into the incubation medium. We have demonstrated that the tritiated water uptake by the biological structure can be used for indicating the degree of hydration of the macromolecule, and that differences in tritiated water uptake are largely correlated with modifications in the ionic behaviour of muscle.

Investigations carried out by us have demonstrated that the state of water in the contractile system of striated muscle fibres is a phenomenon basically correlated with the contractile process and development of the active force of contraction. The state of water was investigated by measuring T_2O distribution between muscle water and medium, by scintillation spectrometry in liquid phase. The tritium bond is stronger than the hydrogen bond;[1] consequently, tritiated water tends to accumulate in an aqueous phase in which hydrogen bonds are formed in higher number as compared with another aqueous phase, according to the relation:

$$R = [T_2O]i/[T_2O]o = \exp\{-\Delta[H\sim]io \cdot \Delta G_{TH}/RT\}$$

where $\Delta[H\sim]$ = excess hydrogen bonds in phase i as compared with phase o, as molar fraction (with respect to the total possible hydrogen bonds), and ΔG_{TH} the difference between the binding energy of tritium and of hydrogen.

Therefore, the percent variation of excess $\Delta[\text{H}{\sim}]io$, on transition of phase i from state 1 to state 2 may be deduced as being:

$$\Delta[\text{H}{\sim}]io\ 1, 2 = (\ln R_2 - \ln R_1) \cdot 100/\ln R_1$$

The experiments were carried out on rabbit psoas muscle glycerinated by the conventional procedures. Earlier findings[2] showed adsorption of deuterium oxide on the glycerinated muscle. The new experiments indicated excess accumulation of tritiated water in muscle water. This accumulation exceeds $R = 3$ and is strongly dependent on muscle pH in rigor (Figure 1). R tends towards value 1 at the isoelectric point of the myofibril contractile proteins, proving the reliability of the studies on the distribution of tritiated water as indicator of macromolecular hydration. Similar dependence has been observed in the case of the relaxed muscle (Figure 2). Transition from con-

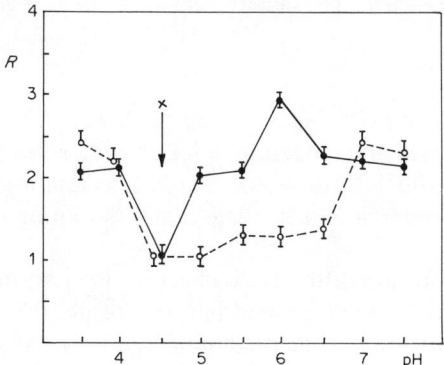

Figure 1 Abscissa—pH; ordinate—$R = [\text{T}_2\text{O}]i/[\text{T}_2\text{O}]o$; ●——● rigour without MgCl$_2$; ○——○ 4 mM MgCl$_2$ in incubation media

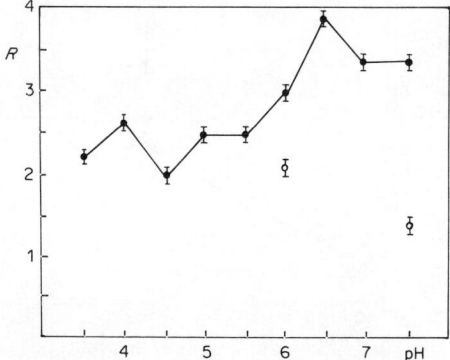

Figure 2 See Figure 1; ●——● glycerinated muscle in relaxation; ○ contraction

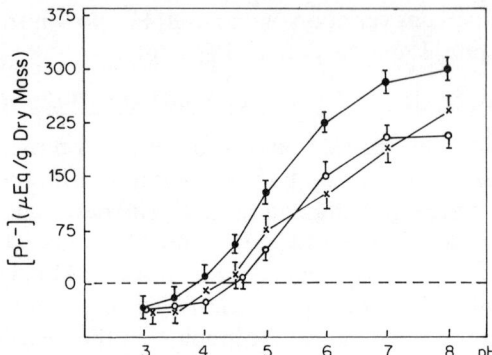

Figure 3 Charge concentration on myofilaments [Pr$^-$] as a function of pH in contraction (●——●), relaxation (○——○) and rigor (×——×)

traction to relaxation at pH 6.0 and 7.5 sharply lowers R values (Figure 2). At pH 6.0 contraction is characterized by a fall in the excess hydrogen bonds in muscle water (Δ[H~]io 1, 2) of -36%; at pH 7.5 variation is of -80%. Thus, contraction implies reduction of the degree of association of water molecules in the muscle.

When the concentration of the fixed charges [Pr$^-$] on the myofilaments of the glycerinated muscle is determined in terms of pH (Figure 3), or in terms of the saline concentration of the medium (Figure 4), their level shows a net increase in contraction as compared to relaxation or rigor. This phenomenon lends strong support to the swelling theories of contraction.[3-5] Variations in

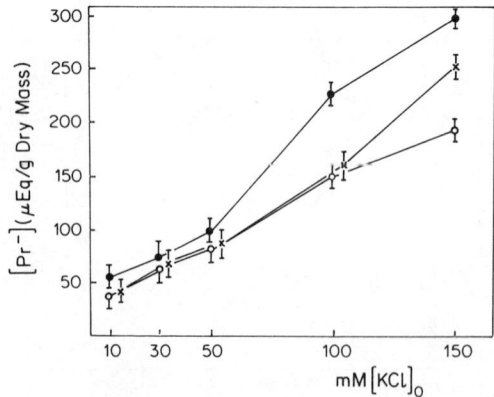

Figure 4 [Pr$^-$] as depending on saline concentration. For symbols see Figure 3

the state of water explain the ionic changes that appear during contraction. In the simplest form ionic behaviour of the contractile system of the fibres is described by the following set of equations (belonging to the Gouy–Chapman and Stern theories and to the theory of water adsorption on the charged surfaces):[6]

$$[Pr^-] = \frac{D}{4\pi F}\sqrt{\frac{4C_{el}RT}{D}}(e^{\psi_0 F/2RT} - e^{-\psi_0 F/2RT})$$

$$\psi'_0 = \psi_0 + Pr^- F \cdot \frac{1}{C_{dip.}} = Pr^- \cdot F\left(\frac{1}{C_{charge}} + \frac{1}{C_{dip.}}\right)$$

$$Pr^- = \frac{Pr^t}{1 + [H^+]\left[1 - \frac{W_{CH}}{RT}\right]\left[1 - \frac{\psi'_0 F}{RT}\right]}$$

$$\frac{1}{C_{dip.}} = \frac{16\pi^2\mu^2 N_T}{D^2 KT} \cdot \frac{1 - (N/N_T)^2}{1 + \frac{u \cdot i}{KT}[1 - (N/N_T)^2]}$$

where C_{charge} is the electric capacity of the diffuse layer, $C_{dip.}$ is the capacity of the adsorbed dipoles, N_T is the total number of adsorbed water dipoles, and N is the number of adsorbed dipoles oriented towards the surface. If N_T tends towards zero [Pr$^-$] then ψ_0 will tend towards maximum values. Calculations show that the [Pr$^-$] and ψ_0 variations found are sufficient to explain contraction according to the swelling model.[5]

References

1. G. S. Kell, in 'Water', ed. F. Franks, Vol. 1, pp. 363–412. Plenum Press, New York (1972).
2. C. T. Dragomir, I. Mărgineanu, D. Ungureanu, G. Filipescu, A. Barbier and D. Alexianu, *Physiol. Chem. Phys.*, **12**, 69 (1980).
3. C. T. Dragomir, *J. Theor. Biol.*, **27**, 343 (1970).
4. G. F. Elliott, E. M. Rome and M. Spencer, *Nature (Lond.)*, **226**, 417 (1970).
5. C. T. Dragomir, A. Barbier and D. Ungureanu, *J. Theor. Biol.*, **61**, 221 (1976).
6. I. Rădoi, M. Nemeş and C. Radovan, 'Electrochimie', Facla-Timişoara (1974).

O-17 and proton spin–lattice relaxation time studies in supercooled H_2O and D_2O enriched with O-17

E. W. Lang and H.-D. Lüdemann
Universität Regensburg, W. Germany

Summary

From O-17-T_1 studies in D_2O and H_2O in supercooled water emulsion the dynamic isotope effect is derived. It is shown that the isotope effect increases significantly in the supercooled range.

It is common practice, to use a combination of deuterium T_1 in D_2O solution and proton T_1 in H_2O solution to separate the different contributions to the proton relaxation in aqueous solutions of biopolymers. However, the presence of hydrophobic solutes in the aqueous phase influences the mobility of the water molecules in the immediate vicinity of the solute, and one must expect that these effects are quantitatively different when D_2O and H_2O are compared.

In order to study these effects, we have investigated the O-17-T_1 in light and heavy water in a wide range of temperatures and have included pressure as an additional parameter.

The complete O-17 data are in print.[1] Figure 1 compiles the ratio of the O-17-T_1 for a series of pressures.

This ratio increases significantly with falling temperature. Comparison of the $^{17}_{8}O$-T_1 and the $^{2}_{1}H$-T_1 in D_2O[3] shows an identical pressure and temperature dependence for both T_1. Furthermore, identical correlation times τ_θ are obtained, when the quadrupole coupling constants of ice I_h are inserted in the relaxation equations. This shows that the rotational diffusion of the single water molecule is isotropic.

Studying the $^{1}_{1}H$-T_1 in H_2O enriched with O-17 permits the analysis of the complete proton relaxation rate in the temperature and pressure range, where

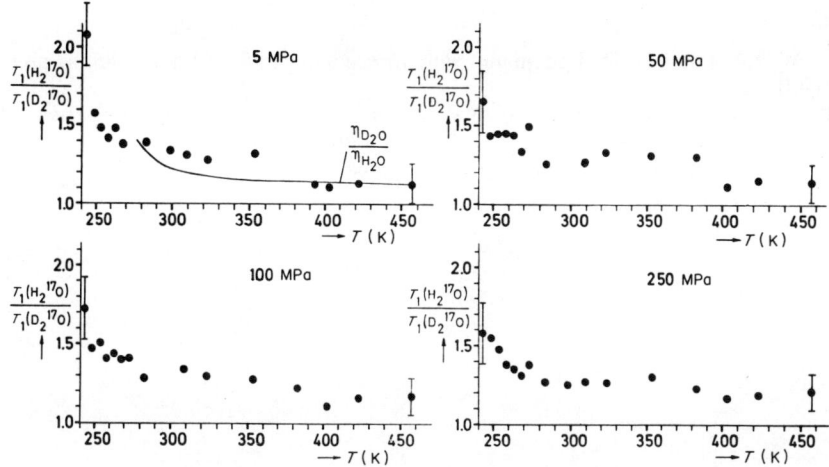

Figure 1 Ratio of the $^{17}_{8}\text{O-}T_1$ obtained in H_2O and D_2O as function of temperature for the pressures indicated in the diagrams. Solid line in the 5 MPa-diagram: Ratio of the viscosities at 0.1 MPa[2]

the O-17–T_1 becomes too short to be measurable. The interaction between O-17 and the protons is practically an additional *intra*molecular relaxation path:

$$\frac{1}{T_1} = K \sum <r^6_{X-H}> f(\tau_\theta)$$

$$H_2{}^{16}O: \quad \left(\frac{1}{T_1}\right)_{{}^1H} = \left(\frac{1}{T_1}\right)^{\text{intra}}_{HH} + \left(\frac{1}{T_1}\right)^{\text{inter}}_{HH}$$

$$H_2{}^{17}O: \quad \left(\frac{1}{T_1}\right)_{{}^1H} = \left(\frac{1}{T_1}\right)^{\text{intra}}_{HH} + \left(\frac{X}{T_1}\right)^{\text{intra}}_{{}^{17}O-H} + \left(\frac{1}{T_1}\right)^{\text{inter}}_{HH}$$

X is the mole fraction of $^{17}_{8}O$-isotope.

Analysis of the data shows that in the supercooled liquid the ^1_1H-relaxation is almost completely described by the intramolecular contribution, and this result leads to the conclusion that in the supercooled liquid the next neighbour geometry of a given water molecule is essentially tetrahedral.

The data presented in Figure 1 show that the dynamic isotope effect between light and heavy water at $T < 300$ K cannot be scaled by a constant factor.

For the analysis of ^1_1H-T_1 obtained in the aqueous solution of biopolymers it is thus preferable to include into the study $^{17}_{8}O$-T_1 data obtained in light water.

References

1. E. W. Lang and H.-D. Lüdemann, *Ber. Bunsenges. f. Phys. Chem.*, **85**, in press (1981).
2. I. B. Rabinowich, *Influence of Isotopy on the Physicochemical Properties of Liquids*, Consultants Bureau, N.Y. (Plenum Publishing Corp.) 211–212 (1970).
3. E. W. Lang and H.-D. Lüdemann, *Ber. Bunsenges. f. Phys. Chem.*, **84**, 462 (1980).

Dynamics of water in cellular systems

W. Derbyshire
University of Nottingham, UK

Introduction

There is a general question that should be borne in mind. It is 'Does incorporation into a cellular system modify the structure, and implicitly the dynamics of water, in any manner other than that expected by the presence of semipermeable membranes? One's first attempt at an 'answer' would be that it all depends upon the distance and time scales of the structure and dynamics under consideration. Clearly the situation would be different on distance scales much less than and much greater than cellular dimensions, and on time scales much less and much greater than a water molecule requires to diffuse through a mean cellular dimension. However, irrespective of the time and distance scale of the measurement, if water structures and dynamics can be determined they can then be compared in different cells, and correlated with any physiological and biochemical changes to determine if water is influential, or if it is merely a passive medium in which the more active biomolecules play out their roles. There is of course a small practical problem concerned with the availability of suitable techniques. As this meeting is specifically concerned with water we should address ourselves to the problem of its observation. Ideally we would like to have a technique, or better still techniques, capable of discriminating in favour of water and remaining insensitive to other molecules and ions present. A second consideration is that the technique should be capable of examining materials as presented, and should not require special sample preparation, e.g. clear solutions, thin films, etc., that would modify the very properties that we wish to record. These twin restrictions ensure that the list of techniques is not a long one. The selectivity requirement excludes bulk mechanical and thermodynamic measurements. However, radioactive tracer studies could be undertaken, as could X-ray and particle, e.g. neutron scattering. Dielectric relaxation appears possible, but because of cell filling problems, somewhat troublesome. On turning to spectroscopy the conventional forms appear to be difficult, although the reflectance and photoacoustic modes could be utilized. Thus nuclear magnetic resonance appears to be outstanding. The prime reason is that the instruments can be operated to detect specific nuclei, ^{1}H, ^{2}H and ^{17}O, and whilst other molecular constituents contain these nuclei and thus will be detected, they can often be distinguished on the basis of their different chemical shifts and/or different mobilities and resultant different relaxation properties. However, all is not as good as it seems as the NMR parameters derived are quantities like chemical shifts, spin–spin interactions, quadrupole coupling constants, relaxation rates, etc., and a theory is required to relate these measurements to terms of immediate relevance, degree of H bonding, the distribution of bond angles, and the mean rates of rotation and translation. Whilst theories are available, their applications to complex heterogeneous systems are full of traps for the unwary and inexperienced operator, and indeed for the seasoned practitioner.

In summary, the range of available techniques is dangerously small, and must result in qualifications being applied to any deductions made from them. Recourse has still to be made to model systems, where a wider range of techniques can be employed, and secondly to the less selective techniques when information on the state of the water can be obtained by choice of appropriate systems. In the time remaining I would like to examine the applications of NMR, past, present and potential.

Nuclear magnetic resonance of cellular systems

On examining the various NMR parameters in turn, the chemical shift of water in cellular systems is similar to that of bulk water; the diffusion rate is reduced by a factor of two, whereas the two common relaxation rates are enhanced by considerable factors and would therefore appear to be more immediately interesting and useful. The two relaxation rates are the spin–lattice, $1/T_1$, which is a measure of the rate at which the nuclear spins or magnetizations reattain an equilibrium with the lattice after a disturbance; and secondly the spin–spin relaxation, $1/T_2$, which is a measure of the rate at which they attain a mutual equilibrium. As NMR utilizes a relatively low frequency where the probability of a spontaneous transition is negligibly small, NMR transitions and therefore equilibrium have to be induced. In the absence of an external irradiation of appropriate frequency this irradiation has to be produced from within the sample itself. The spin–lattice relaxation rate depends upon the product of a function of a 'local' field produced within the sample and the components of motion at the resonance frequency, whereas the spin–spin relaxation rate has an additional contribution from low frequency motions. There are several mechanisms for the production of this local field, e.g. the presence nearby of other magnetic nuclei, and the anisotropy of any local susceptibility or chemical shift, etc. For nuclei with spin greater than $\frac{1}{2}$, the dominant field term is normally the electric field gradient experienced by the nucleus due to the local charge distribution.

The observation of relaxation rates enhanced relative to bulk water values indicates the occurrence of a greater proportion of low frequency motions. This and the absence of NMR signals with normal bulk water relaxation have been interpreted by Ling, Cope and Damadian[1] as evidence that all cellular water is restricted in some manner and taken as evidence that it has a structure different to that of bulk water. However, this is a minority view. Difficulties of explaining greatly enhanced relaxation rates together with an only slightly reduced diffusion, the observation of similar effects in non-cellular systems, and problems associated with the detailed interpretation of the concentration, temperature and frequency dependencies of the T_1 and T_2 measurements have led to the development of a more popular model. This is based upon measurements of the radial distribution function which indicate that 'order' persists for 1 nm, 3 or 4 molecular dimensions, and a deduction that a water molecule will be sensitive to the presence of other structures within this distance. The crudest model that we can adopt is one where a small fraction of the water in a cellular system is considered to be 'bound' and the remainder to be 'free'. It is envisaged that when bound the water molecules have different molecular properties. A relevant example is that the presence of a rigid surface or a relatively slow moving macromolecule would be expected to have an inhibitory effect on the motions of adjacent water molecules. The reorientation rates are typically reduced from 10^{12} to 10^9 s^{-1}, thereby causing an increase in their intrinsic relaxation rates from the order of 1 to 10^3 s^{-1}. However, at temperatures above the bulk freezing point exchange between the bound and free 'phases' is, although slow on a time scale of 10^{-9} to 10^{-12} s, rapid on one between 10^{-3} and 1 s, and average relaxation rates are observed. For bound water populations of more than 0.1% the amount and type of bound water dominates the observed relaxation behaviour. There is some dispute as to the detailed explanation of the well reported increase in ^{1}H spin–lattice relaxation time in tumourous tissue material,[2] as to whether an increase in the water content is sufficient to account for the increase or whether it is only a major factor. The observation of non-exponential relaxation in cellular systems, and the dependence of the relaxation upon various physiological processes, e.g. rigor in muscle cells[3,4] and the cell cycle in the HELA cell[5] have led to proposals that the different relaxation rate components correspond to water in different regions where the proportions of bound and free water and/or the intrinsic relaxation rates of the bound water are different. The changes observed would correspond to changes in the bound water relaxation and in turn its host matrix, or to long term movement of the water from one region to another. There was some speculation on the identities of these regions, intra-cellular extra-cellular regions associated with the sarcoplasmic reticulum, etc., being suggested. However, the observation of similar non-exponential relaxation in membrane free samples, e.g. in aqueous preparations of soya proteins and in gluten doughs, suggest that a spatial composition heterogeneity may provide an alternative mechanism.

On attempting to apply an increased degree of sophistication we are immediately confronted with the problem that there is one measurable parameter: the observed relaxation rate, and two unknowns: the amount of bound water and its intrinsic relaxation rate, and if these quantities are to be determined separately supplementary evidence must be sought. This can be from ad- or absorption isotherms with the bound water being equivalent to three or so BET monolayers, or it can be identified with the water of crystallization. More universally it may be assumed that the bound water has a modified structure that is generally not compatible with that of bulk ice, and that it consequently remains unfrozen at the bulk freezing point. On freezing, the rate of reorientation of the water molecules is reduced by a factor of 10^6, the spin–spin relaxation rate T_2 is correspondingly reduced from seconds to microseconds, and on this reduced time scale the exchange of water molecules between bound water and bulk ice is slow, and the two phases are separately observable. In general the separate estimates of the bound water content agree to within 10 to 20%. Utilizing these estimates of the bound water together with its directly measured relaxation rates, estimates can be made of the relaxation rates expected above the freezing point when the exchange with the bulk water phase again becomes rapid. These estimates are consistent with observations, indicating that there is no abrupt change in the amount or mobility of the bound water on passing through the freezing point. Additional confirmation is supplied by the observation that the relaxation of a sample containing only bound water, recorded below the bulk freezing point, is similar to that of one containing excess water, indicating that the mobility of the bound water is independent of the presence or absence of a bulk ice phase.

The dependences of bound water relaxation upon frequency and temperature are themselves complex and require a distribution of correlation frequencies for adequate characterization of the molecular motions responsible, implying the existence of a range of binding sites. However, the observation of an exponential spin–spin relaxation is consistent with the occurrence of a rapid exchange between them, even though exchange with a bulk phase, when present, may be slow. In order to simultaneously fit the spin–lattice and spin–spin relaxation data, the distribution of correlation frequencies often requires an enhanced low frequency contribution. This can be interpreted in terms of the presence of a species of water that is even more inhibited in its motion, and might thus be termed 'very tightly bound'. Alternatively, an anisotropic motion or a preferential alignment may be imposed by the presence of an extensive surface or fibre axis. A resulting motion would generally produce a non-zero average magnetic dipolar interaction between neighbouring nuclei, or a non-zero average electric field gradient. In favourable cases usually where the planar surface or fibre is sufficiently extensive these interactions are observable directly.[6] In other cases movement between differently oriented planes and fibres yields an averaged interaction but still results in additional low frequency components of motion.

Additional evidence that the bound water phase is complex is produced by examining the relaxation at sub-bound water levels. In general the relaxation rates are further enhanced, consistent with the preferential removal of the more mobile less tightly bound components. Often re-addition of water appears not to modify the intrinsic relaxation rates of the bound water already present, and indeed in some cases, hydrated films of polyalanine and polyglycine, the data can be plotted to seemingly indicate the presence of various sublayers.[7] In others, additional water acts as a plasticiser rendering water already present more mobile.[8]

Interpretations of the measurements are complicated by two NMR artefacts, which could if used correctly yield potentially useful information. As temperature and the molecular mobilities are reduced the rate of exchange between the different bound species is also decreased, and a proportion of the bound water can attain a slow exchange condition and no longer contribute to the bound water signal.[9] The symptoms of this are that the bound water signal shows a progressive reduction in amplitude with decreasing temperature. Of course, the reduction may really represent a progressive immobilization of water molecules to a state motionally equivalent in NMR terms to that of ice. The second effect occurs because magnetic energy can be redistributed within a nuclear spin system by a series of mutual spin flips involving no net exchange of energy with the lattice. It is a process by which the nuclear spins can attain an internal equilibrium. If this mechanism is effective all the nuclei within the spin-exchange pool then attain an equilibrium with the lattice at a common rate after a short initial spin exchange period. For spin exchange to be effective, nuclei must be adjacent as the spin exchange rate is a product of a function involving their mutual dipolar interaction and the low frequency components of motion, but it is only effective when their spectra overlap and mutual spin flips can occur without a net gain or loss of energy. It therefore only applies to nuclei of the same species and has a characteristic relaxation time $T_{ex} \approx T_2$. The process will be effective in situations where T_1 exceeds T_2. It has been demonstrated that these conditions apply to the bound water macromolecular protons system and consequently the ^{1}H spin–lattice relaxation rate of the signal attributed to bound water is also influenced by the polymer protons.[10]

There is one further point, it has been assumed that relaxation behaviour can be used to distinguish between the macromolecules and water. We have already noted that the macromolecular nuclei can, by means of the spin-exchange process influence the spin–lattice relaxation of the water. This observation prompts the more general question of whether the signal attributed to water corresponds to all the water, and as a corollary, is it solely due to water. The answer to both of these questions is 'probably no'. In hydrated cellulose a component of the water ≈ 0.05 g H_2O/g cellulose forms part of a rigid cellulose network, and is not detected as a water signal.[11] With hydrated nylon, water in excess of a certain critical level acts as a plasticiser rendering previously immobile water NMR visible.[12] At the higher temperatures proton as opposed to spin exchange occurs between water and macromolecular OH and NH protons, and the latter then contribute directly to the water signal.[8,13] In addition if the macromolecule, or its side chains become sufficiently mobile they will also contribute, but in this case recourse can usually be had to the chemical shifts for their resolution.

Conclusions

NMR is a powerful technique, or rather family of techniques, because many experiments can be undertaken. It is influenced by, but in turn can provide information on, many interactions. The new generation of spectrometers currently coming on line enable the investigator, by the use of tailored pulse sequences, to discriminate between the different interactions, and these sequences should, with careful and sympathetic handling, prove to be very powerful in their elucidation. I would make two heartfelt pleas, please continue to give encouragement to, and show patience with the NMR spectroscopist, and secondly could the other techniques be developed and used in parallel with NMR on the same systems to give complementary information? The NMR spectroscopist should in turn also make complementary measurements on the other components, the macromolecules, ions, metabolites, phospholipids, etc.

On the measurements themselves, clearly there is something, no matter how nebulous the definition, which might be termed 'bound' water and has modified molecular dynamical properties. As similar effects are observed with inert substrates there would seem to be nothing specifically biological or biophysical about it. It should be noted also that whilst the conformations of the macromolecules appear to be independent of water content, once basic hydration requirements have been satisfied the bulk mechanical properties are influenced by the amount of excess bulk water, and that whilst NMR relaxation is not very dependent upon the larger scale organization this appears to be influential in determining the mechanical properties.

References

1. C. F. Hazlewood, ed. *Ann. N.Y. Acad. Sci.*, **204** (1973).
2. R. Damadian, *Science*, **171**, 1151 (1971).
3. R. T. Pearson, I. D. Duff, W. Derbyshire and J. M. V. Blanshard, *Biochim. Biophys. Acta*, **362**, 188 (1974).
4. D. C. Chang, C. F. Hazlewood and D. E. Woessner, *Biochim. Biophys. Acta*, **437**, 253 (1976).
5. P. T. Beall, C. F. Hazlewood and P. N. Rao, *Science*, **192**, 904 (1976).
6. H. J. C. Berendsen, *J. Chem. Phys.*, **36**, 3297 (1962).
7. S. C. Capelin, Ph.D. Thesis, University of Nottingham (1977).
8. S. Ablett, P. J. Lillford, S. M. A. Baghdadi and W. Derbyshire, *J. Coll. and Inter. Sci.*, **67**, 355 (1975).
9. H. A. Resing, *J. Chem. Phys.*, **43**, 669 (1965).
10. H. T. Edzes and E. T. Samulski, *Nature*, **265**, 521 (1977).
11. E. Forslind, *NMR Basic Principles and Progress*, **4**, 145 (1971).
12. H. G. Olf and A. Peterlin, *J. Poly. Sci.*, **9**, 2033 (1971).
13. D. R. Woodhouse, W. Derbyshire and P. J. Lillford, *J. Mag. Res.*, **19**, 267 (1975).

Hydrogen exchange kinetics as a tool in the study of macromolecule water interactions

Andreas Rosenberg
University of Minnesota, USA

Summary

Studies of hydrogen exchange kinetics have led to models depicting the dynamics of the native structure of a protein molecule. Recent advances in the mathematical description of the complex rate process, and studies of viscosity effects on the reaction, have led us to postulate that the fluctuations of the native structure are coupled to the Brownian motion of water molecules.

The rate of the isotope exchange reaction $RCONHR' + TOH \rightleftharpoons RCONTR' + HOH$ in proteins and polypeptides, specifically the exchange of peptide hydrogens, is strongly influenced by the conformation of the biopolymer. The rate constant of the reaction, well characterized in reactions involving random coil polypeptides and peptides, is attenuated if the polypeptide chain shows secondary and tertiary structure. The kinetics of such an exchange process can be followed by radioactive tracers and by spectroscopic and NMR methods.[1] If the conditions of the experiment are chosen carefully, the exchange from a polypeptide or protein can be represented by a sum of many parallel first order reactions. We can write $H(t) = \sum_{i=1}^{n} A_i e^{-k_i t}$ where $H(t)$ represents the number of hydrogens remaining unexchanged at time t, k_i the rate constant for the ith site and A_i the number of sites with rate constant k_i. Each single rate constant can be written as $b_i k_i$ where k' represents the rate constant for the site in a random coil state and b_i is the contribution by the conformation. It represents, in free energy terms, the barrier which must be overcome in order to make contact between the peptide bond and the catalyst. A similar conformational contribution to rates is detected in studies of fluorescence quenching. The advantage of the exchange method lies in the fact that it expresses the sum of properties for all sites, describing the behaviour of the whole molecule and not a specific residue. Our method enables us to judge the extent to which the molecule is influenced by a specific change in conditions, whereas the localization of the specific group responsible for a single rate constant is difficult. The mathematical difficulties lie in the handling of assemblies of rate constants. Instead of studying single rate constants, sometimes possible in NMR studies, we have to develop distribution functions for the large number of rate constants observed as well as functions describing the distribution of activation energy barriers involved in exchange. The experimental data stretch over a very long time period, the rate constants for a protein typically spanning 7 to 8 orders of magnitude. Figure 1 shows the calculated exchange curves for a number of distributions. From this data base we can

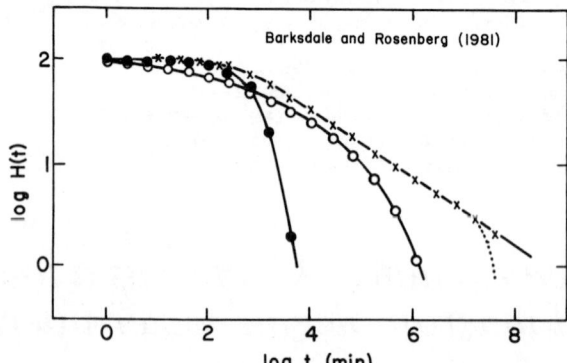

Figure 1 The exchange curves that are observed for 100 sites if: all sites have the same rate constant $k = 0.001$ min^{-1} (—●—); rate constants are distributed log normally with an average k of 0.001 min^{-1} (—○—); constants occupy a power law type of distribution with the most probably $k = 0.001$ min^{-1} (—×—)

Hydrogen exchange kinetics

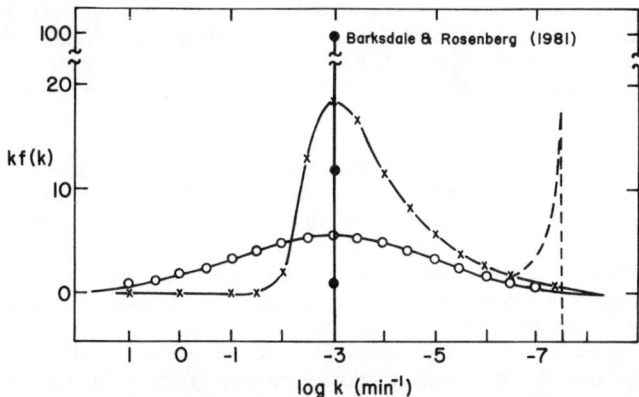

Figure 2   The corresponding distribution functions for the exchange curves in Figure 1 obtained by closed form Laplace inversion

construct a distribution function, $kf(k)$, expressing the probability of finding a rate constant with a particular value of k. Such distribution functions for data in Figure 1 are shown in Figure 2. They can be obtained, either by analytical or numerical Laplace inversion.[2] For the power law the broad peak that is seen characterizes exchange from the native state while the singularity to the right represents exchange proceeding through cooperative thermal unfolding of the molecule. We can go further and by numerical differentiation of the data in Figure 1 and similar curves obtained under different conditions, arrive at a rate function describing the apparent first order rate of exchange as a function of $H(t)$. As the next step we can study the influence of temperature, pressure or viscosity on such functions. Such an example is presented in the communication by Gregory and Rosenberg in this volume. Although the results demonstrate the dynamic nature of protein structures and that all peptide hydrogens will over a period of time exchange with those of the solvent, a physical model for such a process has been more difficult to construct. Molecular dynamics calculations currently available, although showing surprisingly large movements, limit themselves to a very short time interval and do not take into account the movements of the bulk solvent molecules. Available packing density calculations, although showing the possibility for large fluctuations, do not address the question of the role solvent molecules play in this process. The experimentally based models advocated by hydrogen exchange practitioners, are at best, qualitative. The early Carlsberg model attributed the attenuation of rates to an equilibrium between solvent accessible and inaccessible states for each of the exchange sites. However, this model gave no easily interpretable information about the nature of such states. The more recent studies follow, basically, two different lines of reasoning. The first considers the fluctuations between accessible and inaccessible states to be similar to thermal unfolding only differing in the size of the unfolding unit. Such a model predicts that exchange only occurs from the accessible state in bulk solvent. Modification of this picture relates exchange to rare 'global fluctuations' of structure not identical to unfolding but correlated to that process in the sense that a less stable structure has a larger probability for global fluctuations to take place. The second school of thought considers exchange to occur by catalyst penetration to and from the exchange sites within the native structure. A mechanism for such a model of exchange is provided by the 'mobile defect' hypothesis[4] which asserts that proteins in their states of minimum free energy contain mobile regions of poor hydrogen bonding which may be redistributed to provide the necessary pathways for catalyst penetration to the buried peptide sites. Both models visualize domains that can remain quite immobile. The motion is supposed to take place predominantly at the domain interfaces as suggested by Kuntz.[3] These models differ in essence only in the extent to which the accessible state retains structural restrictions and to which extent it becomes hydrated. Although these models all assume the contact with or penetration by catalyst to be the essential feature of the exchange process, the linkage between the activation barriers for exchange and the dynamics of solvent water has remained elusive. Recent experiments presented at the poster session of this conference,[5] however, shed new light on the problem. It can be shown that the rate of exchange from proteins is inversely proportional to the viscosity of the bulk solvent over a wide range of viscosities including that of pure water. The same type of kinetic behaviour has been observed for ligand diffusion within the protein matrix.[6]

Interpreting the results in the framework of Kramers concept of reaction rates, we can postulate that the Brownian motions of water governs the movements of the protein structure. If these findings are confirmed and observed in proteins in general, it should have interesting consequences for the description of processes where structural movement of the macromolecules is assumed to play a role.

Acknowledgement

This investigation was supported by NSF Grant No. PCM-8003744.

References

1. A. Barksdale and A. Rosenberg in *Methods of Biochemical Analysis*. ed. D. Glick. In press (1981).
2. D. Knox and A. Rosenberg, *Biopolymers*, **19**, 1049 (1980).
3. I. Kuntz, *J. Am. Chem. Soc.*, **94**, 8568 (1972).
4. R. Lumry and A. Rosenberg, *Colloq. Int. C.N.R.S.*, **246**, 53 (1975).
5. R. Gregory and A. Rosenberg, this volume.
6. D. Beece, L. Eisenstein, H. Frauenfelder, D. Good, M. C. Marden, L. Reinisch, H. M. Reynolds, L. B. Sorensen and K. T. Yue, *Biochemistry*, **19**, 5147 (1980).

Determination of water relation parameters of individual higher plant cells

A. Deri Tomos
University College of North Wales

and

U. Zimmermann
Kernforschungsanlage Jülich, West Germany

Summary

The macroscopic behaviour of water in and around the individual plant cell appears to be largely governed by a few 'water relations parameters' such as cell turgor, cell wall elasticity and membrane hydraulic conductivity. An instrument for measuring these parameters directly is described and some examples of its potential in describing whole-plant processes are given.

Much effort has been applied in recent years to elucidate the behaviour of water in plants, especially with regard to pathways of flow, osmotic relations and growth regulation.[1] The pathways of flow are governed by the resistances both of the extracellular (apoplasmic) space and of the cell membranes. The properties of the cells with regard to water are governed by a number of physical parameters such as the membrane hydraulic conductivity (Lp^*), the reflection coefficients of the individual cells to the solutes present (σ) and the elasticity of the cell wall (represented by its volumetric elastic modulus ε). The turgor pressures (P) are largely determined by the water potential gradient across the plasmalemma. ε is defined empirically as:

$$\varepsilon = \frac{dP}{dV} V \simeq \frac{\Delta P}{\Delta V} V \qquad (1)$$

Lp and σ are defined according to non-equilibrium thermodynamics[2,3] as:

$$J_v = Lp(\Delta P - \sigma \Delta \pi) \qquad (2)$$

An instrument for measuring these parameters in individual cells has been developed in the laboratory of Zimmermann and Steudle. It consists of an oil-filled glass microcapillary which may be inserted into a cell and through which the cell's hydrostatic pressure can be simultaneously recorded and manipulated. This allows direct measurement of P, ε and the half-time of pressure relaxation due to water flow following an induced volume change ($T_{1/2}$). Lp is related to ε, $T_{1/2}$ and the cell dimensions according to an expression derived from Equation (2):[2]

$$T_{1/2} = \frac{\ln 2 \cdot V}{A \cdot Lp \cdot (\varepsilon + \pi_i)} \qquad (3)$$

This Lp generally represents the conductivity of the whole pathway from vacuole to extracellular space, since (with the exception of certain experiments on *Acetabularia*) the tip can only be inserted directly into the vacuole. Pressure can be measured with an accuracy of $\pm 3 \times 10^{-3}$ MPa (3×10^{-2} bar) and the volume changes to ± 0.5 pl. (This latter accuracy is increased by measuring several $\Delta P/\Delta V$ values and determining ε graphically.) The early version of the probe was suitable only for studying the giant cells of certain algae, which can have volumes in excess of 200 μl. This allowed the properties of the apparatus to be assessed and the response of cells to puncture to be observed.

With the exception of the large epidermal bladder cells of *Mesembryanthemum crystallinum* (300–1200 nl), work on higher plants began with the development of a miniaturized version of the apparatus.[4] Results are now available for a rapidly growing number of cell types, including various cells of *Capsicum annuum*,[4] *Tradescantia virginiana*,[5,6] *Kalanchoë daigremontiana*,[7] *Chenopodium rubrum*,[8] *Pisum sativum*[9] and *Suaeda maritima* (Tomos and Wyn Jones, p. 327). Cells with volumes down to 30 pl have been studied using probe tips of about 1 μl in diameter.

To date the major drawback of the system is that the volume and surface areas of the cells have to be determined visually with the microscope, hence the cells must

---

* Abbreviations: Lp, membrane hydraulic conductivity; σ, reflection coefficient; ε, volumetric elastic modulus; P, turgor pressure; V, cell volume, J_v, volume flow (in practice this is equal to the water flow); $T_{1/2}$, half time of water exchange into or out of a cell following an induced change in cell turgor; A, cell surface area; π, osmotic potential; π_i, intracellular osmotic potential.

generally be on the surface of the issue. In practice it is also difficult to determine V and A of irregularly shaped cells with accuracy. These difficulties are being relieved by modifications of apparatus and technique to allow measurement of unseen cells. These are based on an electrical determination of surface area, in which the cell is treated as a capacitor, is charged and the kinetics of discharge followed. Knowledge of the specific capacitance of biological membranes (c 1 $\mu F/cm^2$) allows accurate estimation of cell surface area.[10] Knowing the area, the cell volume may be determined by a technique involving a short 'pressure clamp' experiment.[11] These developments have necessitated development of a single probe housing both a micro-electrode and pressure sensing facility.

A previous modification of the probe allowed pressure relaxation experiments to be performed automatically.[4] For the measurements of rapid relaxation times (< some 5 sec), however, the apparatus has to be operated manually, since the automatic response time is relatively long.

During measurements of *Chenopodium rubrum* cells[8] the water-relation parameters of cells in a tissue (leaf parenchyma) were compared with those of isolated cells derived from the same tissue. The similarity of the results obtained for each (Table 1) indicate that the mathematical analysis, developed for isolated cells in a well stirred medium, is valid for cells embedded in a tissue. Further experiments involved embedding these tissue culture cells in a gel matrix, thus imposing an enormous 'unstirred layer' around the cells. The lack of effect of this on the water relations (Table 1) indicates that unstirred layers are not a significant source of error in the analysis.

The ε values determined for higher plant cells vary considerably from tissue to tissue (Table 1). For the fruit cells of *Capsicum*, the tissue culture cells of *Chenopodium* and the epidermal cells of *Suaeda* a clear pressure dependence of ε has been observed (as is seen for the giant celled algae). A dependence of ε on volume, also observed for the giant celled algae, has only been observed for the fruit cells of *Capsicum* and the bladder cells of *Mesembryanthemum*. The values of Lp determined for the higher plant cells, although at the higher end of the range, are not dissimilar to those reported for giant algal and other cells using a variety of measuring methods.[2]

The pressure probe can also be used for determining the reflection coefficient of solutes, although to date this has only been applied to those of giant-celled algae.[2]

Using epidermal cells of *Tradescantia virginiana* an apparent activation energy for water exchange across the cell membranes has been determined.[6] The mean value of 106.9 (±55) kJ/mol, although a little high, is not in disagreement with figures quoted in this volume for other systems and is probably still consistent with simple diffusion.

The investigation of turgor mediated responses, such as the effect of pressure on the potassium fluxes of *Valonia utricularis*[1] has not yet been extended to higher plant cells.

Such measurements describe the behaviour of individual cells. The same parameters, however, must influence whole tissue or plant behaviour in predictable ways. Three examples will illustrate this approach, each involving a different water-relation parameter.

1 Drought tolerance and succulence in *Kalanchoë daigremontiana*

Equation (3) allows interpretation of the water flow across the cell membranes in terms of an electrical circuit, in which the quotient $1/Lp \cdot A$ is analogous to the resistance term and $V/(\varepsilon + \pi_i)$ to the capacitance. This latter term describes the water storage capacity of the cell. Steudle *et al.*[7] have quantified this for the leaves of *Kalanchoë daigremontiana*. They show that the 'morphological succulence' (i.e., cell size) is not the real factor involved in water storage of a tissue. The appropriate measure is the 'physiological succulence' which is as dependent on the value of ε as it is on the cell volume. A dependence of ε on turgor may also play an important role in such 'dynamic' cases.

Table 1 Water relations parameters P, $T_{1/2}$, ε and L_P of higher plant cells measured with the pressure probe

Species	Cell type	Cell vol. V (nl)	Turgor pressure P (MPa)	Half-time of water exchange $T_{1/2}$ (s)	Elastic modulus ε (MPa)	Hydraulic conductivity L_P (m/s · MPa)	Remarks and references
Mesembryanthemum crystallinum	Bladder cell	300–1200	0.3–0.5 (0.05–0.25 at high salinity)	200–2000	0.5 ($P \to 0$) 5–11 ($P = 0.3$–0.4)	$2 \cdot 10^{-7}$	ε increases with cell size (see 1)
Capsicum annuum	Fruit tissue	2–15	0.2–0.3	150–250	0.2–0.5 ($P \simeq 0.05$) 0.5–2.5 ($P \simeq 0.35$)	0.4–$0.6 \cdot 10^{-7}$	$\varepsilon = f(P), \varepsilon = f(V)$ (4)
Tradescantia virginiana	Epidermal cell	0.24–5.64	0.09–0.96	1–35	4–36	0.2–$11 \cdot 10^{-7}$	(6)
	Epidermal cell	0.24–4.16	0.18–0.66	3.8–98.4	3.9–23.9	0.14–$5.45 \cdot 10^{-7}$	
	Subsidiary cell	0.03–0.62	0.13–0.44	2.9–34.0	3.2–20.1	0.22–$3.54 \cdot 10^{-7}$	(5)
	Mesophyll cell	0.04–0.08	0.20–0.35	55–95	0.64–1.4	0.36–$0.59 \cdot 10^{-7}$	
Chenopodium rubrum	Parenchyma	0.05–1.07	0.17–0.41	11.5–35.4	1.2–3.7	0.68–$1.97 \cdot 10^{-7}$	
	Cell suspension	0.03–0.95	0.21–0.52	13.5–27.1	1.1–4.8	0.48–$1.87 \cdot 10^{-7}$	(8) $\varepsilon = f(P)$
	Embedded cells	0.12–0.31	0.27–0.35	11.9–18.0	2.1–3.2	1.0–$1.40 \cdot 10^{-7}$	
Kalanchoë daigremontiana	Mesophyll cell	0.42*	0.08–0.20	2.6–8.8	1.3–12.7	2.0–$8.8 \cdot 10^{-7}$	(7)
Suaeda maritima	Epidermal cell	0.04–2.12	0.03–0.49	2.5–22.3	1.4–20.4	0.3–$4.3 \cdot 10^{-7}$	$\varepsilon = f(P)$ (Tomos and Wyn Jones, p. 327)

* Mean value of volume.

2 Water flow through leaves of *Tradescantia virginiana*

Studies of the leaf cells of *Tradescantia virginiana* have thrown some light on the movement of water in leaves. The values of $T_{1/2}$ for the epidermal cells are rather short (in the order of a few seconds). Therefore a dynamic change in the water potential at a point in the epidermis (e.g., due to stomatal movement) would propagate rapidly from cell to cell, as described quantitatively by Philip's theory.[6,7] As a result it is unlikely that significant water potential gradients can be set up in the epidermis. This has a bearing on the control of stomatal movement.

It may also be surmised that over short distances (such as those between xylem and stomata in *Tradescantia* leaves) a cell-to-cell pathway may compete with the apoplasmic pathway for the transpiration flow.[6] (This pathway need not involve the plasmodesmata.)

These features are at present being further investigated by the insertion of two pressure probes into the same tissue.

Finally, some comparison can be made of the two contending pathways of water flow in the transpiring *Tradescantia* leaf, i.e. the epidermis or the mesophyll.[6]

3 Turgor in *Suaeda maritima* cells

Turgor regulation is of the utmost importance to almost every living plant. The problems faced by plants growing under salt stress (halophytes) are of particular interest. The contribution of the pressure probe to our understanding of osmoregulation in halophytes is described elsewhere in this volume (Tomos and Wyn Jones, p. 327).

In addition, measurement of the turgor of tissue cells before and after washing, or vacuum infiltration, with a solution of known osmotic potential provides indirect information concerning the distribution of solutes in a tissue. Experiments with beetroot tissue (Leigh and Tomos, unpublished) have provided data that agree with independent measurements of intercellular solute distribution.

These three examples illustrate the flexible role of the probe as a tool for the study of the water relations of the entire plant. More extensive use of the probe will soon allow such extrapolations of single cell measurements to be tested against 'wholeplant' measurements.

Finally, two other techniques have been developed that further facilitate the use of the probe. One, referred to above, involves embedding cells in a rigid gel matrix (Ca-alginate), allowing the insertion of the probe into plant protoplasts and into isolated vacuoles. With the support of the gel, pressure pulses can be applied, allowing measurement of Lp values. Secondly, a technique has been developed[12] by which small wall-less cells, or organelles, can be fused in an electric field by taking advantage of the phenomena of dielectrophoresis to position the cells and field-induced membrane breakdown to allow fusion. The potential of this technique extends far beyond this present application, but it will allow the formation of cells, organelles, etc., large enough for the insertion of the pressure probe. Cells can be fused in controlled numbers allowing, for example, for pairs of cells or for giants (such as erythrocytes 1 mm in diameter!)[13] Followed by embedding these cells in a gel, this technique will allow hitherto unaccessible plant cells to be available for study, e.g. fused stomatal guard cell protoplasts.

References

1. U. Zimmermann and E. Steudle, *Plant Membrane Transport: Current Conceptual Issues.*, eds. R. M. Spanswick, W. J. Lucas and J. Dainty, Elsevier/North Holland, 113–127 (1980).
2. U. Zimmermann and E. Steudle, *Adv. Bot. Res.*, **6**, 45 (1978).

3. A. Katchalsky and P. F. Curran, *Non-equilibrium Thermodynamics in Biophysics*. Harvard University Press, Cambridge, Mass (1965).
4. D. Hüsken, E. Steudle and U. Zimmermann, *Plant Physiol.*, **61**, 158 (1978).
5. U. Zimmermann, D. Hüsken and E. -D. Schulze, *Planta*, **149**, 445 (1980).
6. A. D. Tomos, E. Steudle, U. Zimmermann and E. -D. Schulze, *Plant Physiol.* (in press).
7. E. Steudle, J. A. C. Smith and U. Lüttge, *Plant Physiol.* **66**, 1155 (1980).
8. K. -H. Büchner, U. Zimmermann and F. -W. Bentrup, *Planta*, **151**, 95 (1981).
9. D. Cosgrove and E. Steudle, *Planta* (in press).
10. U. Zimmermann, R. Benz and H. Koch, *Planta* (in press).
11. S. Wendler and U. Zimmermann, *Plant Physiol.* (in press).
12. U. Zimmermann and P. Scheurich, *Planta*, **151**, 26 (1981).
13. U. Zimmermann, P. Scheurich, G. Pilwat and R. Benz, *Angew. Chemie*, **20**, 325 (1981).

The contribution of dielectric relaxation and nuclear magnetic relaxation measurements to our understanding of the dynamics of hydration in solutions of biomolecules and in cellular systems

K. Hallenga
Free University, Brussels, Belgium

Summary

In order to deal with the dynamics of water in cellular systems we ought to understand the phenomena that occur in solution as well as what happens on hydrated protein surfaces in the solid phase. I will therefore try to connect the results that have been obtained in the liquid and the solid phase from NMR and dielectric relaxation data.

First something about the dynamics of water in solutions containing mainly hydrophobic groups. It has become possible to measure the decrease of the dielectric relaxation frequency of bulk water in solutions containing higher alcohols and carboxylic acids. Taking a monolayer of water molecules around an alkylgroup as the only directly influenced solvent, the molecular reorientation time τ_M in this layer turns out to be increased by a factor 2–3. This means actually at 25 °C a change from 7 to 15–20 psec. More interesting is the correlation between the relative increase in τ_M, or rather the relative change in the dielectric relaxation frequency ω expressed as $\omega = \omega_o (1 + d.\text{conc.})$— and the entropy of transfer for the hydrophobic solute from its own liquid phase into an aqueous solution.[1] This is shown in Figure 1 where d in percent is plotted versus the entropy of transfer ΔS. No immobilized water relative to the solute exists in solutions of hydrophobic solutes. From a simple hindered rotator model it follows that the measured increase in relaxation times can account for part of the ΔS value. Since cold neutron scattering data on solutions of t.butanol[2] have indicated that the translational motions of the solvent are also slowed down, it appears certain now that the negative entropy of transfer for hydrophobic substances from apolar surroundings into water should be interpreted as changes in the dynamics of the solvent, water.

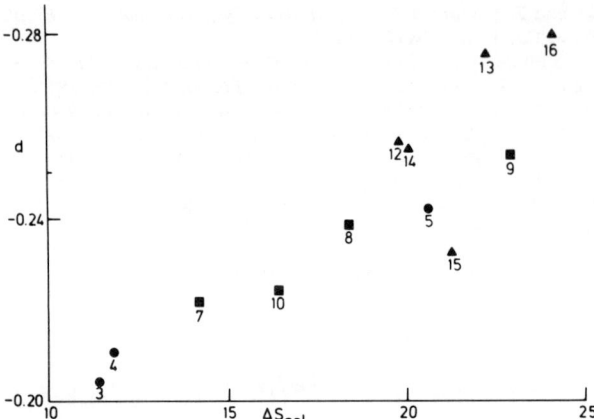

Figure 1 Relative shift per molar solute in water dielectric relaxation frequency for a series of solutions containing propanols, butanols, pentanols and hexanols plotted versus the corresponding entropy of transfer for the alcohols from their own liquid to aqueous solution. (After Reference 1)

What can dielectric measurements do for us below the GHz range? In solutions the rotational diffusive motion of proteins has been found[3,4] which gives τ_M values for the protein, depending on its size, between 10 nsec and 10 μ sec. Another small dispersion in the 1 nsec range has been reported,[5,6] but it is not at all certain that this dispersion is due to water reorientations.

What may we expect to see in cellular systems using dielectrics? Large dispersions, certainly, but not with a molecular basis. Let us just recall the observation made by Cole and Cole that the dielectric relaxation process:

$$\varepsilon^* = \varepsilon_\infty + (\varepsilon_0 - \varepsilon_\infty)/(1 + i\omega\tau)$$

can be represented by a very simple electronic circuit: a resistor in parallel with a series circuit of another resistor and a capacitor. It is immediately clear from this that a heterogeneous system like a cell suspension which has at least two regions with different ratios of dielectric constant over conductivity will show a dispersion which has nothing to do with a molecular reorientation process.

What is known about the dynamics of water molecules which make hydrogen bonds to proteins? They are usually called the specifically bound waters. In the solid state (hydrated collagen fibres) a residence time of approximately 10^{-7} sec has emerged from extensive NMR studies.[7] This number has also come out of a NMR study by Bryant on lysozyme powders.[8] Dielectric measurements on hydrated collagen in the GHz range have shown that the hydration water which is *not* specifically bound, has reorientation times in the range of 100 psec. When we bring our proteins in solution the residence and reorientation times mentioned for solid materials will certainly not become longer, but rather somewhat shorter. We may expect residence times as short as 10^{-8} sec or even less.

If we were to measure with NMR the water correlation times by spin–lattice relaxation over a very large frequency range, what do we expect to see? An enhanced relaxation rate due to the 100 psec reorientation time of the non-specifically bound waters but certainly not what has experimentally been found (see Figure 2). With rather special

Dynamics of hydration

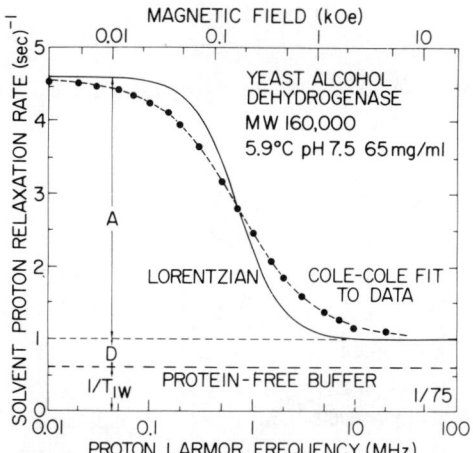

Figure 2 Dispersion of $1/T_1$, the magnetic relaxation rate of solvent water protons for a 65 mg/ml solution of alcohol dehydrogenase from yeast, 160,000 daltons 5.9 °C. (After Reference 9)

equipment it is possible to measure from 5 kHz to 50 MHz the spin–lattice time T_1, of water in protein solutions and in solid proteins as well.[9] Recently with improved low field performance a relaxation process in pure H_2O has been found as a dispersion in $1/T_1$. The effect is caused by the ^1H–^{17}O interactions, modulated by the exchange time τ_e of a proton in a water molecule (at 25 °C τ_e is 3×10^{-4} sec). The effect of a protein (here yeast alcohol dehydrogenase) on the solvent relaxation rate is twofold: a low frequency dispersion (amplitude A) with an inflection frequency ν_I characterized by the rotational diffusion of the protein, and a high frequency term with amplitude D. The dispersion is broader than a Lorentzian and can be represented by the heuristic Cole–Cole equation: dashed line through the points in Figure 2.[9] The dependence of the inflection frequency on protein molecular weight is shown in Figure 3 where dispersion curves for a variety of proteins at the same protein concentration (in mg/ml) are given. Before going into details concerning the mechanism of the observed phenomena two conclusions should be drawn from these observations for relaxation measurements in cellular systems.

(a) Whenever an organization of cellular proteins into larger assemblies takes place, this will cause enhancement of spin–lattice relaxation rates at frequencies in the range of the low frequency dispersion.

(b) Since the enhancement is proportional to protein concentration the influence of cell water content on relaxation rates should be visible at *all* frequencies.

It has been demonstrated experimentally that the inflection frequency ν_I of the dispersion curves, or rather $1/\nu_I$, correlates with protein molecular weight over almost three decades as can be seen in Figure 4. Although results for deuterium and ^{17}O are not as abundant as the proton data, they are qualitatively the same. This is shown in Figure 5 for ^1H and ^2H where the rates have been normalized with respect to the respective pure solvent rates. The amplitude A of the low frequency dispersion is about half as large for deuterons as it is for protons. It was suggested several years ago[10] that cross-relaxation between solvent protons and protein protons plays a role in the solvent–proton relaxation rates. This effect has been substantiated since[11,12] and

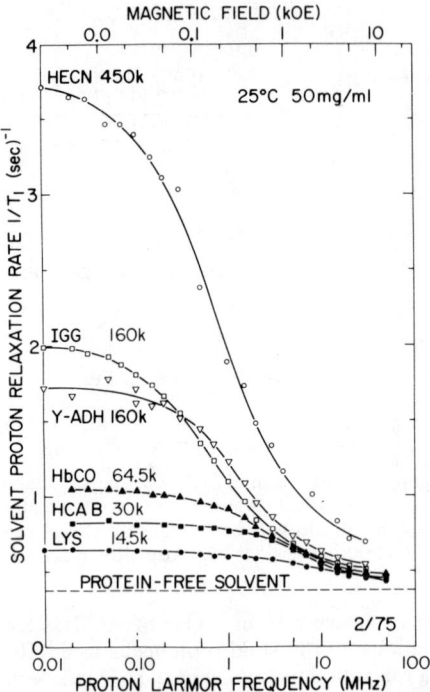

Figure 3 Dispersion of $1/T_1$ for 50 mg/ml solutions of proteins with a range of molecular weights at 25 °C. Abbreviations are: HECN, haemocyanin from Helix pomatia; IGG, non-specific human γ-immunoglobulin; Y-ADH, alcohol dehydrogenase from yeast; HbCO, human adult carbon monoxyhaemoglobin; HCA B, human erythrocyte carbonic anhydrase B; and LYS hen egg white lysozyme. The numbers next to the abbreviations give the molecular weights in units of thousands of daltons. (After Reference 9)

it has important implications for relaxation studies on protons using isotopic dilutions. There is no time to go into any detail at this point, however.

In order to understand the origin of the high frequency D term one can use the results from NMR on hydrated collagen[7] and the dielectric data obtained in protein solutions.[5,6] The specifically bound water molecules which may have residence times on the protein shorter than 10^{-8} sec will probably contribute to the D term. It has been stated[13] that there is a dispersion around 200–300 MHz which could be caused by the specifically bound waters, but the evidence can not be considered to be conclusive. The non-specifically bound waters will disperse at much higher frequencies far beyond the upper frequency limits of modern NMR equipment.

Some hypotheses exist for the origin of the low frequency dispersion.[9,14] There is a so-called hydrodynamic model implying essentially that the protein molecules 'stir up' the solution such that the water picks up some of the low frequency motion of the

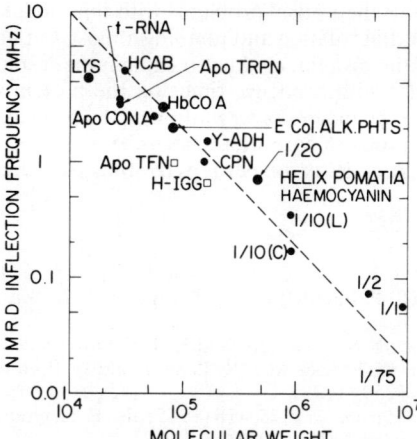

Figure 4 Variation of the inflection frequency v_I as a function of molecular weight for the relaxation dispersion of solvent protons for solutions of macromolecules at 25 °C. Abbreviations are as in Figure 3 with additional: CON A, demetallized concanavalin A; TRPN, demetallized porcine trypsin; tRNA, non-specific yeast transfer ribonucleic acid; TFN, demetallized human transferrin, CPN, human ceruloplasmin; HC 1/20, 1/10 (L), 1/10 (C), 1/2, 1/1 various states of association of elix pomatia haemocyanin. (After Reference 9)

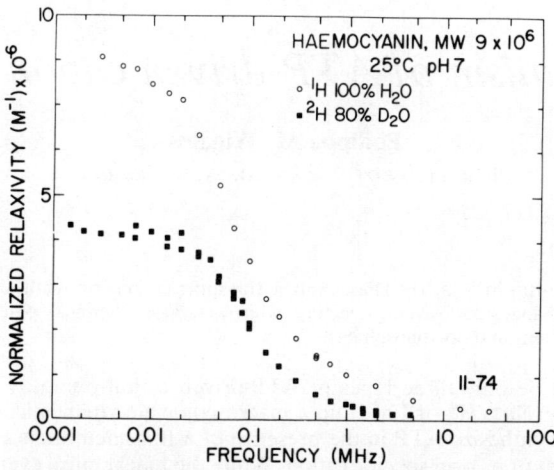

Figure 5 Protein contribution to the nuclear relaxation rates, $1/T_1$ of solvent (○) ^{1}H and (■) ^{2}H in aqueous solutions of haemocyanin (containing 11.5 and 30.6 mg protein per ml respectively) at 25 °C, as a function of the Larmor frequency of the respective nuclei. (After Reference 9)

protein. There are serious theoretical problems with this model, however. Specifically bound waters that by partial rotation and jumping almost, but not completely, average out the slow motion of the protein, could also explain the results. It is very difficult to see how water molecules with residence times on the protein surface of 10^{-8} sec or smaller would still sense the much slower motion of the protein, however.[15] It will still be clear that there is a problem here which needs to be solved by more experimental evidence as well as by more discussion perhaps by some participants of this conference.

References

1. K. Hallenga, J. R. Grigera and J. C. Berendsen, *J. Phys. Chem.*, **84**, 2381 (1980).
2. F. Franks, J. Ravenhill, P. Egelstaff and D. I. Page, *Proc. R. Soc. London Ser A*, **319**, 189 (1970).
3. E. H. Grant, G. P. South, S. Takashima and H. Ichimura, *Biochem. J.*, **122**, 691 (1971).
4. M. Y. Rosseneu-Motreff, F. Soeteweg, R. Lamote and H. Peeters, *Biopolymers*, **10**, 1039 (1971), and *ibid*, **12**, 1259 (1973).
5. E. H. Grant, *Ann. N.Y. Acad. Sci.*, **125**, 418 (1965) also E. H. Grant and G. P. South, *Advan. Mol. Relaxation Processes*, **3**, 355 (1972).
6. H. P. Schwan, *Ann. N.Y. Acad. Sci.*, **125**, 344 (1965).
7. J. R. Grigera and H. J. C. Berendsen, *Biopolymers*, **18**, 47 (1979) and references cited therein.
8. R. G. Bryant, This conference.
9. K. Hallenga and S. H. Koenig, *Biochemistry*, **15**, 4255 (1976).
10. R. Kimmich and F. Noack, *Z. Naturforsch.*, **A25**, 1680 (1970), and in *Ber. Bunsenges. Phys. Chem.*, **75**, 269 (1971).
11. H. T. Edzes and E. T. Samulski, *Nature London*, **265**, 521 (1977).
12. S. H. Koenig, R. G. Bryant, K. Hallenga and G. S. Jacob, *Biochemistry*, **17**, 4348 (1978).
13. R. K. Gupta and A. S. Mildvan, *J. Biol. Chem.*, **250**, 246 (1975).
14. R. H. Walmsley and M. Shporer, *J. Chem. Phys.*, **68**, 2584 (1978).
15. S. H. Koenig in ACS Symposium Series n° 127: *Water in Polymers.*, Ed. S. P. Rowland, American Chemical Society (1980).

A mechanism of ATP-driven cation pumps

Philippa M. Wiggins
University of Auckland, New Zealand

Summary

A possible mechanism by which ATPases might transport cations or synthesize ATP invokes surface-induced changes in solvent structure which increase chemical potentials of highly hydrated small cations and polyphosphates.

There appear to be only three types of ATP-driven cation pumps. Each transports one small cation (Na^+, H^+ or Ca^{2+}) up a macroscopic electrochemical potential gradient; each can synthesize ATP in the presence of a transmembrane electrochemical potential gradient of its own specific cation. While the biochemical events accompanying transport or synthesis are well understood, the physical mechanisms by which reaction of the enzyme with ATP or with a cation gradient can lead to transport or synthesis are not. Figure 1 illustrates the model that we have been developing over the

A mechanism of ATP-driven cation pumps

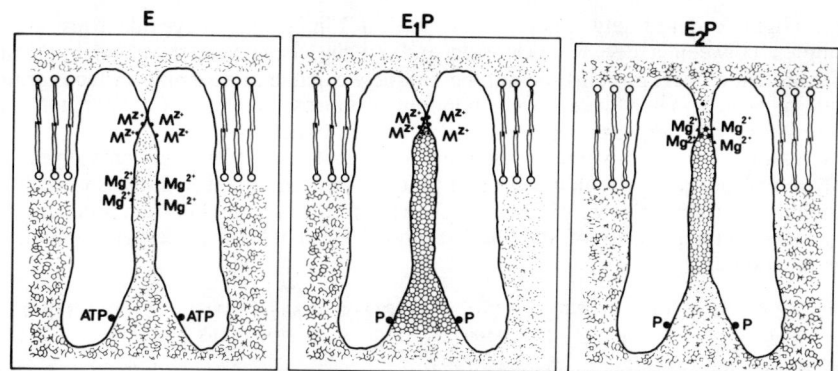

Figure 1 The three principal conformations of an ATP-driven cation pump during a transport cycle. For further details see text. M^{z+} can be Na^+ or Ca^{2+} or H^+

last few years. Each polypeptide chain spans the membrane, and has binding sites for its specific cation (M^{z+}), hydrated Mg^{2+} ions and ATP as shown. The source of energy for cation transport or for ATP synthesis lies in increases in chemical potential with increasing degree of hydration of small cations and polyphosphate anions in the highly structured interfacial aqueous phase of the two phosphorylated intermediates. The phase change starts at the phosphorylation site and moves up the cleft; Mg^{2+} dissociates and remains in the normal aqueous phase until it is overtaken at the apex, when it displaces the less highly hydrated M^{z+} from the binding sites and E_1P relaxes to E_2P, the equilibrium conformation of the phosphoenzyme when Mg^{2+} occupies its specific cation binding sites. E_2P, with its open channel selectively permeable to M^{z+}, and its high local concentration of M^{z+} with high activity coefficient, is the actively transporting conformation; its short lifetime is terminated by hydrolysis of its phosphate, when it relaxes back to E with closed channel and a normal interfacial aqueous phase.

When the concentration of M^{z+} is high enough to saturate the high affinity binding sites, each ATPase hydrolyses ATP and transports M^{z+}. Under physiological conditions this represents the normal running of the Na^+ and Ca^{2+} pumps. When local concentrations of M^{z+} are very low, those sites are occupied by Mg^{2+} ions, and E_2P can be formed by interaction with inorganic phosphate (P_i). Then, if its transmembrane electrochemical potential gradient is steep enough, M^{z+} diffuses through its open perm-selective channel, displaces Mg^{2+} from E_2P which then relaxes to E_1P, the predominant conformation with M^{z+} bound. If ADP is present, ATP is synthesized, because the reaction takes place inside the highly structured phase. The dephosphoenzyme then relaxes to E, which binds Mg^{2+} and can be rephosphorylated by P_i. Physiologically this is the normal mode of operation of the ATPase-synthetase of mitochondria. Electron transfer generates and maintains a high pH inside the mitochondria, and an accessible pool of protons, distributed probably in networks traversing the external surface of the membrane, can diffuse through E_2P, convert it to E_1P and synthesize ATP.

Evidence upon which the model is based

1. A change in solvent structure does change activities of solutes. For example, the individual free energies of transfer of ions from D_2O to H_2O are specific for each ion and increase with free energy of hydration.[1]

2. Highly ordered networks of water molecules in crystals of cyclodextrins[2] and a complex between a deoxydinucleoside and a drug[3] have been revealed by X-ray analysis. Moreover, proteins seem to be uniquely capable of assuming surface configurations which match water–water-bonding distances, and both C=O and N—H groups confer strong directionality upon hydrogen bonds.[4]

3. George and co-workers[5] pointed out that the solvation enthalpies of polyphosphates are extremely high and that the free energy of hydrolysis of ATP is probably determined by the difference in solvation free energies between products and reactants. In the presence of Mg^{2+} and at physiological pH the species participating in the reaction are:

$$MgATP^{2-} + H_2O \rightleftharpoons ADP^{3-}/ADPH^{2-} + Mg^{2+}/H^+ + H_2PO_4^-/HPO_4^{2-}$$
$$600 \qquad\qquad\qquad 1500 \quad\; 600 \qquad\quad 1998 \;\; 1168 \qquad 318 \quad\; 1251$$

The figures beneath each reactant or product are estimates of the enthalpies of hydration in kJ mol^{-1}.[1,5] Clearly the products as written are more highly hydrated than the reactants, so that a change in solvent structure which increases activity most for the most highly hydrated species will displace the equilibrium to the left with some synthesis of ATP.

4. The $(Na^+ + K^+)$-ATPase and the Ca^{2+}-ATPase are remarkably similar in structure and in reaction sequence, both of which are consistent with the representation of Figure 1. While less detailed information is available about the proton ATPase all three require Mg^{2+} for transport and phosphorylation, and many workers have suggested that all ATP-driven ion pumps use essentially the same mechanism.[6]

Properties of the cleft water

In order for this mechanism to work efficiently the water must have quite specific properties, and this is the aspect of the model that I would like to be discussed.

(i) The maximal macroscopic gradient up which each ATPase transports its specific cation can be estimated from equations of the kind:

$$\Delta G_{transfer} = -RT \ln c_i/c_e - zEF$$

where c_i and c_e are the intracellular and extracellular concentrations of the cation, z its charge, and E the transmembrane potential difference of the steady state. $\Delta G_{transfer}$ ranges from approximately 11–26 kJ mol^{-1}, with the highest value for Ca^{2+}. If the cations have a primary hydration number of 6–8, the change in chemical potential per mol of water is 2–3 kJ mol^{-1}. Similarly, the free energy of hydrolysis of ATP under physiological conditions is approximately 55 kJ mol^{-1}, a small fraction of the free energies of hydration of reactants and products.

(ii) Displaced cations M^{z+} must not be permitted to diffuse back down the cleft during the lifetime of E_2P. The water must therefore be viscous so that diffusion by random walk is slow. A computer simulation (Lewis and Wiggins, unpublished data) showed that efficiency of pumping required a long diffusion pathway, short lifetime of E_2P and high viscosity. Tunnelling of protons helps prevent back diffusion by generating a diffusion potential.

(iii) The cross-sectional area of the cleft must be small so that no water molecule is more than a few diameters from a structure-promoting surface.

(iv) Efficient operation of the $(Na^+ + K^+)$-ATPase seems to require that the chemical potential of K^+ decreases in the highly ordered phase. The properties of the water must then be such that lightly hydrated solutes (large univalent cations and anions and small non-electrolytes) decrease in chemical potential when the phase change occurs.

Can water with these properties exist, even transiently, at room temperature and up to 37 °C?

Experimental methods

Experimental design is dominated by the difficulty of detecting a signal from a microscopic abnormal phase when it is swamped by the signal from the bulk aqueous phase. We have used the techniques of light scatter, polarization of fluorescence and electron spin resonance of different water-soluble probes, and measurements with ion-specific electrodes. Suggestions of other techniques would be most welcome.

References

1. H. L. Friedman and C. V. Krishnan, in *Water: A Comprehensive Treatise*, ed. F. Franks, Plenum Press, N.Y. vol. 3, 1–118 (1973).
2. W. Saenger, *Nature*, **279**, 343 (1979).
3. S. Neidle, H. M. Berman and H. S. Shieh, *Nature*, **288**, 129 (1980).
4. J. L. Finney, in *Water: A Comprehensive Treatise*, ed. F. Franks, Plenum Press, N.Y. vol. 6, 47–122 (1979).
5. P. George, R. J. Witonsky, M. Trachtman, C. Wu, W. Dorwart, L. Richman, W. Richman, F. Shurayh and B. Lentz, *Biochim. Biophys. Acta*, **223**, 1 (1970).
6. E. Racker, in *Electron transfer chains and oxidative phosphorylation*, eds. E. Quagliariello, S. Papa, F. Palmieri, E. C. Slater and N. Siliprandi. North-Holland Publishing Company, Amsterdam. 401–406 (1975).

Water permeation through lipid bilayer membranes

D. A. Haydon
University of Cambridge, UK

Summary

Lipid bilayer membranes are appreciably permeable to water. Typical values for the permeability and activation energy for permeation are given and the mechanism by which water crosses the membranes is discussed. The water permeability of a polypeptide channel (gramicidin A) which forms readily in lipid membranes is also described.

The rôle played by lipid bilayer membranes in the water permeability of biological cell and organelle membranes is not yet clear. However, from the fact that the water permeability (unlike the ion permeability) of lipid bilayers is of similar magnitude to that of many types of biological membrane, it must be assumed for the present that the lipid contributes significantly to the overall permeability. This being so, the detailed mechanism of the water permeability of bilayers is clearly of some interest.

Because at ambient temperatures membrane lipids are mostly in the liquid crystalline rather than in the gel state, attention will be confined to bilayers in the former condition. The water permeabilities and the activation energies for permeation for egg phosphatidylcholine vesicles and black films at 25 °C, fall into the ranges 24–49 μm s^{-1} and 35–45 kJ mol^{-1} respectively.[1] These data were obtained from osmotically driven water fluxes but, in similar systems, it has been shown that isotopic exchange and osmotic experiments yield essentially the same permeabilities.[1] It may be noted that the bilayer is orders of magnitude less permeable to non-electrolytes such as urea and glycerol than it is to water.

The mechanisms of water permeation fall broadly into two classes, those which involve aggregation of the water within the bilayer so as to form either substantial intrusions or continuous channels, and those which operate if the water is molecularly dispersed, as in a dilute solution. There is a considerable amount of evidence against the presence of water channels or substantial aggregates. Thus, (i) the permeability coefficients measured by osmotic and isotopic exchange techniques are the same, indicating that interaction between water molecules crossing the bilayer is absent or very weak; (ii) the specific conductance of the membrane material, calculated from the conductance per unit area of the bilayer, is effectively that of alkanes saturated with water and not obviously consistent with the presence of water channels; (iii) the activation energy for transfer across the bilayer is about twice that for the self-diffusion of water and (iv) there is no unequivocal spectroscopic evidence for water within the chain region of the bilayer.

In the alternative, molecular solubility and diffusion mechanism, there are two obvious possibilities for the rate limiting process—diffusion through the chains or a barrier in the surface of the bilayer. Direct evidence which distinguishes between these possibilities is scarce. In monoglyceride black films it has been found that changes in the chain structure under conditions where the polar group layers are largely unaffected result in changes in the water permeability,[2] but the effects could conceivably have arisen from a high sensitivity of the water permeability to the area per molecule. Indirect evidence is available in that, if it is assumed that the diffusion and solubility in the chain region is limiting and that equilibrium exists across the bilayer surfaces, the permeability may be estimated theoretically. It is known that the partial molar volume of $-CH_2-$ in the phospholipid bilayer is very similar to the value in liquid hydrocarbons[3] and the segmental order, although significantly higher than in bulk liquid alkanes, is nevertheless low.[4] A not unreasonable though crude model for the hydrocarbon region of a bilayer is therefore a layer of liquid n-hexadecane of appropriate thickness (say, $ca.$ 30 Å). Both the solubility of water and its diffusion coefficient in n-hexadecane are known and the permeability of such a layer may thus be calculated. The permeability and activation energy for such a system are found to be 58–99 μm s^{-1} and 47–56 kJ mol^{-1} respectively at 25 °C.[1] The agreement with the observed values, given earlier, is not perfect but is remarkably close. It may be concluded that there is support for the idea that the solubility and diffusion of water in the chain region of the bilayer is rate determining, although there still remain some doubts on this question.

The water permeability of lipid bilayers can be increased by certain polypeptides, and polyenes such as nystatin and amphotericin.[1] In several cases it is clear that the added molecules form pores through the lipid of the bilayer. By far the best characterized of these pores is that of the 15-amino acid polypeptide gramicidin A, which folds into a left-handed helix and dimerizes end to end in the bilayer to form a channel approximately 28 Å in length and of internal diameter 4 Å.[5] Alkali metal ions and particularly hydrogen ions (but not anions) pass readily through the pore, apparently in a partially hydrated state. Recently, water permeability measurements have been carried out both by osmotic or net flow and by isotopic exchange diffusion methods.[6] The osmotic method yields a water permeability for a single channel of 9.58×10^{-15} cm^3 s^{-1}. In contrast to the results for the lipid bilayer, the isotopic exchange method gives a significantly lower result such that the ratio of the osmotic to the exchange permeabilities is about five. If it is assumed on the basis of the relative diameters of the water molecule ($ca.$ 3 Å) and the polypeptide channel ($ca.$ 4 Å) that molecules may not pass each other in the channel (i.e. they move in single file) it may be inferred from single-file kinetic equations that there are about five molecules present in the channel. A similar number has been deduced from electrokinetic experiments.[7]

There is considerable evidence for the importance of proteins in the water permeability of biological membranes particularly those, such as epithelia, in which specific control mechanisms operate. While there is no reason to think that the gramicidin channel resembles in detail the protein pathways of the biological membranes, it is of interest that the epithelial channels activated by anti-diuretic hormone are, like gramicidin, impermeable to urea.

References

1. R. Fettiplace and D. A. Haydon, *Physiological Rev.*, **60**, 510 (1980).
2. R. Fettiplace, *Biochim. Biophys. Acta*, **513**, 1 (1978).
3. J. F. Nagle and D. A. Wilkinson, *Biophys. J.*, **23**, 159 (1978).
4. J. Seelig and A. Seelig, *Q. Rev. Biophys.*, **13**, 19 (1980).
5. D. A. Haydon and S. B. Hladky, *Q. Rev. Biophys.*, **5**, 187 (1972).
6. P. A. Rosenberg and A. Finkelstein, *J. Gen. Physiol.*, **72**, 341 (1978).
7. P. A. Rosenberg and A. Finkelstein, *J. Gen. Physiol.*, **72**, 327 (1978).

The dynamics of water in cellular systems

Reporter: Walter Drost-Hansen

In response to Hempling's lecture, Bank enquired about microtubules. Hempling responded that such might assist in organizing water in the cells. The microfilaments and microtubules might provide a means of rapid passage of information into the cell (interior) via cooperativity.

Marsden called attention to the fact that in measuring Ponder's R-value one changes the cell, hence the R-value has been influenced by the process of its measurement. Hempling agreed, noting that this does not invalidate the usefulness of the R-value, as defined operatively. He also noted that rat red cells may be made to shrink profoundly, but when subsequently placed in distilled water do not haemolyse.

Zimmermann pointed out that Hempling's volume data were suspect. At least in older models of Coulter Counters the field strength in the orifice is about 15 kV/cm, but the 'breakdown' voltage for most cells is of the order of 2 kV/cm. Thus, as the field lines now penetrate the cells, the apparent volume observed is too low.

Hempling replied that he was perfectly well aware of the difficulties and pitfalls noted by Zimmermann. He stressed that all measuring methods were calibrated against more direct volume measuring techniques, such as direct packing-volume determinations, correcting for external space. Identical results were obtained by the various methods. Zimmermann noted that one cannot correct such data by using data from another, also incorrect method.

Hempling, later in the session, elaborated on his calibration methods. These included direct microscopic measurements with an ocular micrometer, a laborious method, usually averaging over 100 individual sets of observations. Light densitometer methods were also used together with direct packed cell volume determinations. Hempling also suggested that perhaps his measurements were not made above the breakdown potential in his particular Coulter Counter, and that, anyhow, reproducible results were obtained.

Zimmermann next pointed out that he expected membrane folding to occur because of local, internal concentration gradients. Thus the Boyle/van't Hoff law cannot apply. Hempling noted that he routinely obtains correlation coefficients between 0.997 and unity, lending considerable confidence to the data.

Knight enquired if Hempling had used the Argon laser technique for measurements of the hydrodynamic radii of the particles, noting that such technique could (a) resolve the problem of 'true' determinations of particle (cell) radii, and (b) allow the size, and osmotic measurements to be carried out simultaneously.

Hempling responded that this technique was not used in his Laboratory, and he did not feel a laser nephelometer would add anything significant.

Steponkus asked Zimmermann to elaborate on membrane folding. In response, Zimmermann stated that he had seen folding in electron micrographs and also hints of small folding at the molecular level. He concluded on this basis that thermodynamic equations become useless because of local concentration differences. Steponkus commented that one does not observe folding with protoplasts.

Kell noted that as osmolarity is increased, work is done on the membrane so that other factors, in addition to the Boyle/van't Hoff relationship are involved.

Pusch noted also the need to take into account mechanical effects.

Finally, Marsden observed that Ponder never obtained values of $R = 1.000$ and Hempling pointed out that $R = 1.000$ is the exception rather then the rule, although he has obtained such results for megakaryocites.

Discussion of posters

Robson enquired of Halle as to the consistency of NMR data. Halle, in response, noted that NMR data can, in principle, yield the two second-rank order parameters σ_0 and σ_2. These are, however, merely two coefficients in the (possibly slowly converging) expansion of the orientational distribution function, $P(\Omega)$. It may be possible to rule out some extreme models of 'bound' water orientation, but it is in general not possible to make detailed statements about $P(\Omega)$ on the basis of σ_0 and σ_2.

Finney addressed Halle regarding his hydration water lifetimes of 10^{-8} sec. Finney noted that the extensive work by the IBM group seems to exclude the possibility of characterizing such a quantity. Halle responded by observing that previous inconsistencies in ^{1}H and ^{2}H NMR results are due to contributions from cross-relaxation and non-water [i.e. protein] protons/deuterons. In the ^{17}O studies two approaches have been used to determine the lifetime, τ_l of 'bound' water (a) increasing aggregate size and thus aggregate tumbling correlations τ_r leads to identity between observed slow correlation times, τ_s, and lifetime, since

$$\frac{1}{\tau_s} = \frac{1}{\tau_r} + \frac{1}{\tau_l}$$

(b) ^{17}O scalar relaxation enhancement due to water-proton/surface-proton exchange being rate-limited by *water* exchange between 'bound' and 'free' water. Both of these methods give lifetimes of the order of 10 nsec. The very long correlation times (of the order 10^{-6} sec) observed for large proteins by Koenig *et al.* are probably due to protons/deuterons residing on protein surface residues—not due to water proton/ deuterons. These correlation times are thus not related to *water* dynamics. (*Editor's note:* A more detailed exposition of Halle's interpretations of his data is given at the end of the final discussion report.)

Holzwarth asked Halle if he was familiar with a new model of a typical micelle, proposed by Fromherz. This postulates structures ('random sticks') which may offer advantages in explaining, for instance, fast exchange between monomers in solution

The dynamics of water in cellular systems

and the aggregates. Halle replied that he did not accept the Fromherz model as realistic, and went on to note that he was not aware of any unambiguous experimental data which would require extensive water penetration into the micelle. Model-building, of course, could not prove any particular structure—although it may conceivably rule out some possibilities. Halle went on to observe that he could not determine the position along the hydrocarbon chain of the exposed methylene groups. However, recent NMR studies by Ulmius and Lindman, using selectively fluorinated amphiphiles—show that it is mainly the CH_2-groups proximal to the head group that are exposed, as expected from the classical Hartley model of micelles.

Kay commented regarding the possible penetration of water into a micelle (in connection with the Fromherz model). He also asked if such micelles should not show a phase-transition in view of the fact that the hydrocarbon chains are all in the *trans*-configuration. At some temperatures the hydrocarbon chains must be expected to take on some *gauche* configuration.

The consensus of the Conference was that the conventional micelle model was adequate to account for most experimental findings and was to be preferred over the Fromherz model.

Timasheff commented that thirty years ago, Kirkwood developed a theory of charge fluctuations on protein molecules (Kirkwood and Schumaker, *PNAS*, 1951). This theory was fully verified by light scattering experiments. The postulate of charge fluctuations which actually originated with Linderstrøm–Lang was shown to be capable of leading to a number of phenomena, including the generation of large dipole moments on proteins, the pH dependence of the activity of proteolytic enzymes and the rapid generation of charge clusters at specific sites on proteins involving the rapid redistribution of protons. Since then, this concept had been elaborated by others. Timasheff specifically wondered if Gros had considered the possible contribution of charge fluctuations to the facilitation of proton transfer which had been measured.

Pusch also addressed Gros, asking if the sorption isotherm of CO_2 was taken into account in his measurements. He furthermore wondered how the diffusion coefficient of the H^+ ion was extracted from the measured transport of CO_2 across the membrane.

In reply to Timasheff, Gros stated that with smaller protein molecules, the measured proton fluxes are well correlated with the translational diffusion coefficients of the protein. Increasing diffusivity (by choosing smaller proteins) leads to measured proton flux; upon decreasing proton diffusivity (e.g. by adding agar-agar, by using larger proteins or higher protein concentrations) the proton fluxes decrease. In all cases of smaller proteins and buffers, quantitative agreement between the measured H^+ fluxes and the fluxes expected from translational protein diffusivities were found. So, there is much evidence that these proton fluxes are based on protein diffusion rather than on H^+ movements within the hydration shell of the protein.

In answer to Pusch, he stated that CO_2 transport rates across thin layers of protein solutions were measured. Knowing thickness and area of the layer and the CO_2 partial pressure difference across the layer, it is possible to calculate the CO_2 diffusion constant $k[cm^2/min/atm]$, and, using independently determined CO_2 solubilities of these solutions [ml/ml/atm], the CO_2 diffusion coefficients $D[cm^2/S]$ is obtained.

It has previously been shown that facilitated CO_2 fluxes are based on bicarbonate and proton fluxes of equal size. They have to be equal (1) for reasons of electroneutrality, and (2) because a continuous production of H^+ and HCO_3^- at the high pCO_2 side and the opposite process at the low pCO_2 side under steady state conditions require that equal amounts of H^+ and HCO_3^- are transported continuously from the sites of production to the sites of consumption. This implies that the facilitated CO_2 flux can be equated to the underlying proton flux.

In connection with the interchange between Gros and Timasheff, Kell observed that the Kirkwood–Schumaker theory does not concern H^+ transport *along* the protein surface (i.e. inside the double layer), but rapid exchange of H^+, from different protein groups, with the bulk, leading to a fluctuating dipole and a dielectric dispersion mechanism different from Debye rotation. The theories of Schwarz and of Schneider *do* have surface H^+ conduction between different protein groups *directly*, and one should distinguish these, since they are quite different, both kinetically and mechanistically, from the Kirkwood–Schumaker theory.

Careri commented briefly on the Kirkwood–Schumaker theory involving dipole fluctuations. Such are difficult to measure directly; in fact, they are rather ill-defined and remain vague conceptually. However, the instantaneous dipole fluctuations no doubt lead to strong effects.

Careri questioned Rosenberg if he would generalize his observed dependence of the hydrogen–deuterium exchange on the viscosity of the solvent, in terms of the fluctuation–disruption theorem well known in statistical mechanics.

In response, Rosenberg noted that Careri's suggestion of generalization is a valid one. However, he was looking at the problem strictly from the experimental point of view. The Kramer equation becomes valid if the viscosity exceeds a defined critical value. At lower viscosities the transition state theory is a good way of describing reactions. However, that does not mean that Brownian motion does not exist. Thus, although Brownian motion in bulk solutions is a general phenomenon, it becomes rate determining in Kramer's sense only in a limited viscosity range.

In connection with Rosenberg's presentation, Rialdi wondered if he had tried to modify the solvent viscosity by using glycerol as the other molecule with OH^- groups. Rosenberg stated that he intended to do so but the problem lies in experimental difficulties: H_i^+ and OH^- distributions may not be allowed to vary. Work is under way using sucrose, but not enough is known about the solvent effects on the various pK values.

The discussion now turned to the presentation by Pressey. Bank was distressed by the juxtaposition of layers of semiconductors (wondering humorously if we had here a potential new source of electrical power). Pressey pointed out that there is a continuum from electrons, protons, ions to ionizable particles. He did not feel he was able to give a more definite answer. Kell suggested it might be helpful to note that when one discusses 'semiconduction' one means that the electrical conductivity of the material in question is intermediate between that of metals and insulators. The conductivity also follows a particular activation law. Many biological materials appear to fulfil these requirements and one may then speak of them in terms of a band-gap model.

At this point Careri warned that one cannot transfer information directly from *bulk* semiconduction to a *localized* spot in a lattice. At this point someone also paraphrased Careri's comment, by pointing out that the utility of thinking of a given system as an electrical semiconductor depends on the energy width of the conduction bands. This in turn depends on the degree of overlap of the electronic wave functions. In water or ice it appears that the energy bands will be so narrow as to permit very little electron conductivity.

In response to these statements, Pressey noted whether a material is an insulator, amorphous semiconductor, or semiconductor is determined by the short-range interactions.

In ice the dielectric constant is about 4, rising to about 80 for water. In salt solution is it much higher. The work required to ionize a proton is inversely proportional to the dielectric constant and going from water to 'structured' water there is a considerable change in dielectric constant which will determine whether ions are formed.

Edmonds thought that the latter points were irrelevant. The width of the bands are related to the overlap of the orbitals but one was dealing here with bands so narrow that the concept of semiconductor was not useful in the present case.

Pressey made the point that the detailed mechanism of the conduction is not known. This prompted Derbyshire to ask if the sign of the carriers in aqueous protein solutions was known from Hall Effect measurements. Pressey did not know off-hand but suspected that the information was available. Kell informed the meeting that the sign (+ or −) depended on the particular protein. He also pointed out that Pethig reports the effect can be quite large.

Maass asked Thomas what one can expect to find inside a channel of the type described by him. Thomas elaborated on the system which is extremely well defined (and an excellent proton conductor). The processes involved are very complex and difficult to describe. In this connection Thomas wondered how biophysics can ever hope to cope with the horrendous complexity of a living system when the extremely simple system that formed the basis of his studies required such complex description.

Panel discussion

Beall stressed the model dependent aspects of NMR interpretation. She particularly observed that whatever model is used it must explain several criteria: (1) it must explain both T_1 and T_2 behaviour which are not similar, (2) it must explain frequency and temperature dependence, (3) it must explain the apparent reduction of the translational diffusion of water which is dominated by the bulk water, not by some small amount of 'boundary water', (4) it must reconcile H, D and ^{17}O NMR data, and (5) it must be consistent with evidence from other techniques which suggest a continuum of changes away from a surface.

Those who do not accept the concept of a small amount of 'boundary' water, the rest being bulk, do not have to support totally the polarized multilayer hypothesis either. NMR will not be able to tell us a lot about water in heterogeneous systems; however, it is a beautiful technique with which non-destructively to monitor living cells for changes of state.

In reply, Derbyshire noted that it is not obvious how to apply NMR (especially to heterogeneous systems) and he enquired if Beall could elaborate on Hazlewood's stand regarding NMR interpretation.

Beall replied that she felt that the Houston group will go along with a distribution of correlation times for water, although it will not be the one shown by Derbyshire of a Gaussian distribution between 10^{-11} sec for free water and 10^{-6} sec for ice. This conference had already been discussing correlation times of 10^{-7} sec for very immobile water and even 10^{-9} sec for water on the surface of dry DNA and hyaluronic acid. Therefore the limits move in from each side. This forces more of the water in the system to have altered correlation times to satisfy NMR data than in the simple boundary-free type model. More a continuum of effects is implied.

Marsden commented that in Wiggins' description it is suggested that, as the cleft opens, the cation cannot move back in because of the structure of the water in the cleft and also possibly because of proton tunnelling. However, it seems that other cations already in the cleft but not located at the sites will be able to leak out. This means that if one attempts to measure the cation leakage, for instance, from red cells by cooling, so as to inactivate the pump, the leak may be reduced and thus underestimated.

Wiggins emphatically agreed with this observation. She also pointed to the Na, K-ATPase versatility, all depending on the driving force. All the processes are ouabain inhibited. As long as the channel is open, ions can move either way. Wiggins also agreed that Ca^{++} will move out.

Kell asked Wiggins to comment on the experiment of Knowles and Racker in which these authors added Ca^{2+} to the sarcoplasmic reticulum ATPase in homogeneous solution (*not* in a membrane) and observed the production of ATP.

Wiggins noted that Knowles and Racker had indeed solubilized the enzyme. Specifically, they phosphorylated the solubilized sarcoplasmic reticulum vesicles with Mg^{2+} and inorganic phosphate to produce E_2P. They then added a high concentration of Ca^{2+} to the solution. In terms of this model Ca^{2+} cannot diffuse to its binding sites from the cytoplasmic side because of the high viscosity of the water. But it can diffuse through its permoselective channel of E_2P and displace Mg^{2+} from the binding sites. E_2P relaxes to E_1P, and if ADP is added ATP is synthesized.

Careri next addressed Rosenberg, admiring his experiments, but rejecting the proposed explanation in terms of 'mobile defects', because to concentrate disorder in one spot costs more than to distribute it over a larger region. This always holds in physics. Now the fluctuations that give rise to point defects are of higher energy and therefore more unlikely that those distributed over large fractions of the macromolecule, like the domains. In other words, domain fluctuations are more likely than local defects and are equally effective towards D_2O motions inside the macromolecules.

Rosenberg replied first that his primary interest was that of an experimentalist. He also observed that Careri could be correct that defects may primarily occur between domains (this point has been discussed by I. D. Kuntz). However, Rosenberg felt that there is no direct experimental evidence for this.

Grigera commented on the current interest in the dielectric properties of electrolyte solutions. Preliminary experiments in his laboratory suggest a value of about 500 (!) for 0.1 molar NaCl solution—obviously in a range of concentration of interest to cell-physiology. He also showed graphs of $\Delta\varepsilon/_{conc}$ versus concentration. These curves begin with rapidly increasing curve segments at low concentration (nearly linear increase) to level off at higher concentrations.

In a response to a statement by McIver, Wiggins proposed to borrow an idea from Blumenfeld, namely that the enzyme active site comes to a fast equilibrium with the solution at the protein/solution interface but that the rest of the protein relaxes slowly. She also noted that the 'phase change' in the water likely starts at certain (surface) sites.

Edmonds asked Haydon if it is known how many water molecules are in contact with the small cations when they pass through a gramicidin channel. One water fore and one aft would not seem sufficient to lower the electrostatic self-energy of the ion (to 'hydrate' it).

In reply, Haydon noted that it is known from X-ray diffraction studies that the ions are indeed in the channels. It is also clear from kinetic studies that in these narrow 'pores' (equivalent diameter ~4 Å) the number n_1 of water molecules corresponds to $n = 1, 2, 3 \ldots$. Neither the ions nor the water molecules can pass each other ('overtake one another'). $Na-H_2O$ may exist together but not other ions. NMR studies on this topic are under way.

Edmonds pointed to the difficulty in accounting for the energy of hydration if each ion (Na) only has one H_2O molecule 'fore and aft'. To this Haydon noted that the ion transport may be associated with a deformation of the ring.

Ratkovič asked if Tomos and Zimmermann had estimated the hydraulic conductivity or diffusional permeability with the pressure probe method. Specifically, is the plant cell membrane permeability high or low. He also expressed concern about the effect of the position of the probe within a cell.

Tomos replied that a value of $L_p \sim 2 \times 10^{-6}$ was obtained and this appears to be the same, regardless of the type of plant cells used. A 'blown-up' cell relaxes in seconds. The opening of a single stomata will affect a whole leaf.

Section 4 Physiological water stress

Biophysics of Water
Edited by F. Franks
© 1982 John Wiley & Sons Ltd

Physiological water stress

Felix Franks
University of Cambridge, UK

Summary

Any change in the physical or chemical conditions required for the optimum function of living organisms introduces a stress which the organism must either resist or adapt to. Stresses can be of several types, but the majority of them are basically water stresses, that is, they result from changes in the intermolecular nature of water and/or solute hydration induced by changes in temperature, pressure, or solute concentration. The most widespread stress condition is that produced by low temperatures. The mechanisms that have evolved to counter water stress utilize a wide variety of physical and chemical principles, such as inhibition of ice nucleation (undercooling), efficient ice nucleation, the synthesis of freezing point depressants, or substances known to perturb the diffusional motions of water (water binding) and the redistribution of cell water so that freezing occurs in those parts of the tissue where it does not cause injury.

The preceding review lectures have demonstrated how water acts at a molecular level in maintaining native macromolecular structures, how conventional continuum approaches to describe interactions in aqueous media fail at short range (<5 nm) and how a cell has to maintain itelf in osmotic equilibrium vis-à-vis its external environment. Indeed, Dr Hempling used the term 'osmotic death' in connection with the absolute requirement for osmoregulation. We have also discussed how the diffusive motions of water are perturbed in restricted spaces. A common conclusion of many of these investigations is that the proper functioning of a living organism is sensitively attuned to the intermolecular nature of the aqueous substrate, and this, in turn, is very sensitive to changes in pressure, temperature and solute perturbations of various types. A physiological stress can be defined as an external factor acting on a cell or an organism in such a way that it interferes with its normal functioning. Different types of stress have been

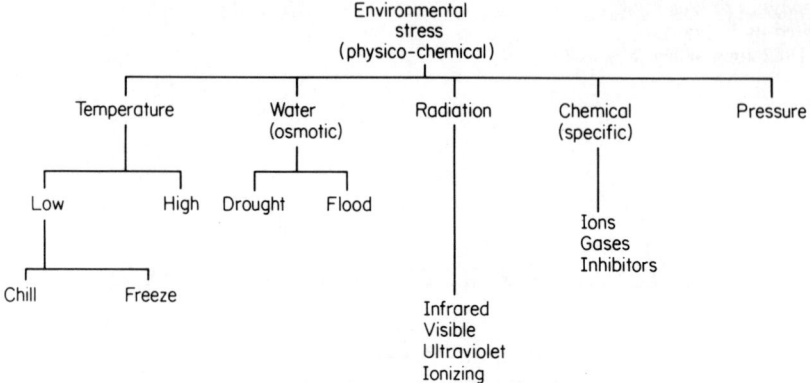

Figure 1 Different types of physico-chemical parameters which can lead to physiological stress conditions. Adapted from reference 1

described;[1] they are summarized in Figure 1. Such a classification is somewhat arbitrary, because several of the stress conditions are inter-related and can, in the final analysis, be reduced to a water stress. For instance, drought, salt and freezing stresses give rise to some identical symptoms, because they all have an osmotic component.

In order to counter a stress an organism has to make available extra energy resources, and this prevents it from functioning optimally. Two resistance mechanisms can be defined: stress avoidance and stress tolerance. The former is the biological analogue of elasticity, where the organism will attempt to resist the imposed stress. For instance, under conditions of high salt concentrations the organism dissipates energy in trying to avoid injury by excluding salt and operating at its normal internal salt level. Tolerance can be compared to plastic strain, where the body responds to the applied stress by deformation (compliance). A salt tolerant organism will therefore counter the stress by functioning at higher than optimal salt concentrations. Similarly, freeze avoidance implies that the organism will survive low temperatures by undercooling, whereas a freeze tolerant organism can survive the freezing of some of its tissue water.

Let us first of all consider stress conditions brought about by changes in the chemical composition of the aqueous substrate. At the lowest level of resolution most solutes can be regarded as physiological perturbants because, at the very least, they generate an osmotic gradient across the plasma membrane, causing the cell to lose water. The only exceptions are those substances which are able to penetrate the membrane (e.g., dimethyl sulphoxide). At a higher level of resolution it is possible to distinguish between more specific effects, produced by different classes of solutes: ionic, hydrophobic or polar. Even within each class of solutes it is possible to identify a range of different effects, as manifested, for instance, by the lyotropic series of ions. Some of these effects have been characterized by physico-chemical measurements on model systems, such as dilute aqueous solutions of proteins; results of such studies have been reported at this Conference.

Water structure perturbations which in physical terms appear minor, even trivial, may have considerable chemical consequences and can produce profound, even lethal, physiological disturbances. An example of such physiological amplication of seemingly minor physical effects is provided by the substitution of D_2O for H_2O. In a sense, this example is artificial, because D_2O does not occur in appreciable concentrations in the biosphere and therefore can hardly be considered as a cause of physiological water stress. However, its physical, chemical and biological properties are well documented and it is, after all, the molecular species that most closely resembles water, with which it forms almost ideal mixtures.

In terms of physics the differences between the two species are accounted for by the difference in their zero-point energies. It can then be shown that the vapour pressure ratio $P_{H_2O}/P_{D_2O} = 1.05$. This is indeed found to be the case, but only at temperatures approaching the critical point. Within the normal liquid range the vapour pressure ratio is 0.87.[2] The reason lies in the relatively strong intermolecular interactions which are reflected in the vibrational (hydrogen bonding) spectral modes. The relevant vibrational frequencies of D_2O are lower than those of H_2O because of the large difference in the moments of inertia. Hence, on this basis, H_2O should be more volatile than D_2O, as is indeed the case at moderate temperatures. Chemists recognize the existence of problems that have their origin in this subtle balance between intra- and intermolecular effects. For instance, the difference in the melting points of the two isotopic species is only 4 °C, but the difference in the temperatures of maximum density is 7 °C. There are also other important isotopic differences. For instance, H_2O is more dissociated than D_2O. The well studied kinetic isotope effects still pose many problems that are only partly explicable in terms of zero-point energies. Of possible relevance to life processes is the large (30%) difference in the self-diffusion coefficients which still awaits an adequate explanation. Of possible pertinence to problems of protein sol-

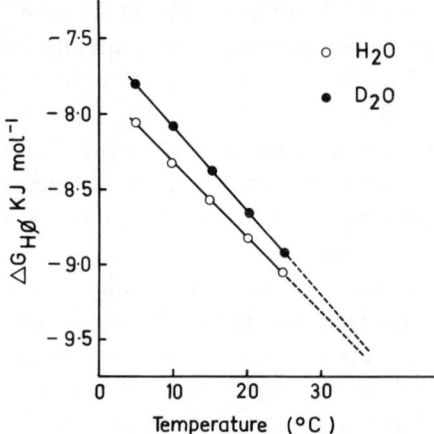

Figure 2 The Gibbs free energy of the hydrophobic interaction between two methane molecules in water, as a function of temperature. Adapted from reference 3

vation and stability are the results of Ben-Naim, shown in Figure 2, according to which the hydrophobic interaction between two methane molecules is stronger in H_2O than in D_2O, although this difference appears to decrease with rising temperature.[3]

At the physiological level D_2O produces a severe stress which in all higher forms of life becomes lethal as the D_2O substitution exceeds 40%. Only some primitive unicellular organisms are able to adapt to the gradual replacement of H_2O by D_2O. Studies of the effects of D_2O on isolated biochemical functions in excitable cells indicate up to 40% reductions in cellular ATP production, the gradual loss of electric excitability and changes in membrane enzyme activity.[4] The effect of a 50% D_2O substitution on plant (*Lemna minor*) metabolism is equally drastic: a complete inhibition of protein synthesis for 4 h, and an eventual reduction of 20% in the soluble protein content. At the same time there is a 100% enhancement in protein degradation.[5] With *Nicotiana tabacum* a 60% D_2O substitution has been found to be lethal. Lower degrees of substitution lead to reductions in the plant size and rate of flowering, and also to a loss of the ability of the plant to use selectively ^{12}C rather than ^{13}C in its metabolism.[6] Results such as these have led various investigators to conclude that D_2O is a non-specific chaotropic agent;[5] but this is hardly consistent with some estimaters of native state stabilities performed on dilute solutions of globular proteins.[7]

The role of water in physiological stress conditions can be discussed from different points of view. At constant pressure and temperature, stress is brought about by solutes. The observed symptoms can arise from general osmotic, specific or non-equilibrium effects. It is common, especially in microbiology, to relate the limits of biological viability of a given organism to the water activity a_w which is itself a measure of the osmotic pressure.[8] This seems to be a fairly crude approximation, because of the mounting evidence that the range of a_w within which an organism can function depends on the actual solute used to adjust a_w. It therefore becomes necessary to consider specific effects. Such effects seem to be particularly important for resistance towards partial or almost complete dehydration, where specific carbohydrates promote the rehydratability of the organism, while other, chemically very similar carbohydrates do not exhibit the same protective ability.[9] In the light of the profoundly toxic effects of D_2O it would in any case be quite surprising if viability and injury were to be functions simply of a_w, irrespective of the nature of the solute.

So-called bound water, already discussed at some length during this conference, also seems to play an important part in resistance to solute stress. It is a non-equilibrium phenomenon, in the sense that water binding by solutes is the manifestation of a very high free energy of activation to diffusion and *not* an equilibrium binding process. Being dominated by kinetics, the phenomenon is subject to large hysteresis effects, as demonstrated, for instance, by sorption isotherms at low water contents.[10] In such cases a description in terms of a_w is not only meaningless but misleading, although the stress which the cell actually experiences has the appearance of a purely colligative effect.

Turning now to water stress resulting from extremes in temperature, a distinction must be made between the effects of temperature *per se* and those due specifically to freezing. Where freezing or evaporation do not occur, the stress can be related to changes in the properties of water. Such changes with temperature are well documented,[11] and Figure 3 shows the dependence on temperature of selected physical properties of water, normalized to 25 °C. Although these temperature effects vary in magnitude, there is a common trend: the temperature dependences of all properties become more pronounced with decreasing temperature. In the region of undercooled water some of the properties (e.g., specific heat and compressibility) appear to diverge at a temperature close to −45 °C,[12] although the experimental limit of undercooling *in vitro* is −39 °C, at which temperature ice is nucleated

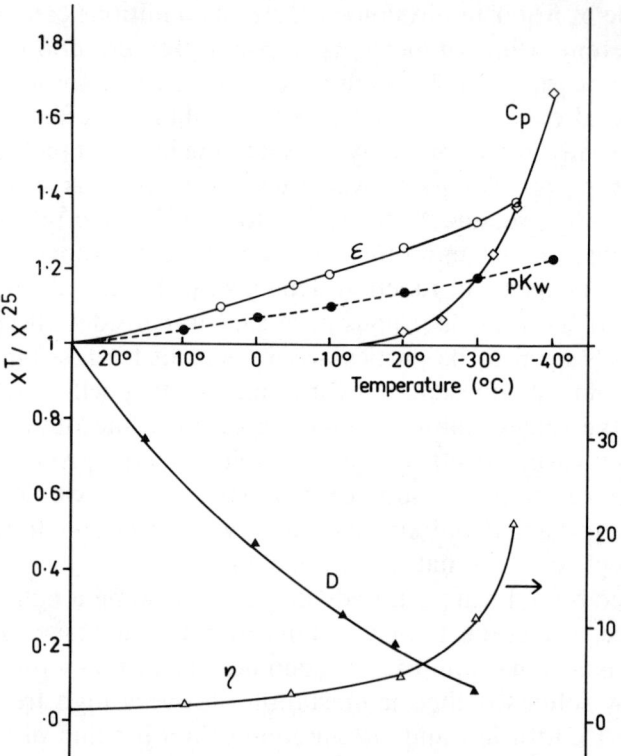

Figure 3 Temperature dependence of some physical properties of undercooled water (X^T) compared to the property at 25 °C (X^{25}): pK_w, dielectric constant (ε), isobaric specific heat (C_p) and self-diffusion coefficient (D)—left ordinate; viscosity (η)—right ordinate

spontaneously. Under *in vivo* conditions, undercooling to lower temperatures (as low as -70 °C) has been observed in organisms that exhibit freeze avoidance. Of particular relevance to biochemical processes must be the effect of temperature on K_W: between $+25°$ and -35 °C K_W decreases by three orders of magnitude, a change which is likely to have a profound effect on the delicately balanced tertiary and quaternary structures of biopolymers and supramolecular assemblies. The implications of such a change in K_W are not always fully appreciated:[13] at -35 °C $-\log a_{H^+} = 8.5$ and this constitutes neutrality. In low temperature biochemical studies it would be incorrect to buffer back to a nominal pH 7 in order to simulate conditions as they exist at physiological temperatures.[14] This caveat is particularly important where mixed aqueous solvent media are employed (e.g., in low temperature cell preservation and cryoenzymology), because acid/base dissociation equilibria in such media and at low temperatures are extremely complex.

The increase in the dielectric permittivity (ε) of water at low temperatures must also affect biological systems, via changes in the electrostatic contributions to protein stability. Thus, the value of the constant A in the simple Debye–Hückel limiting law which is given by constant $\times (\varepsilon T)^{-3/2}$ decreases by 6% over the temperature range $+20°$ to $-20\,°C$.[15] Such a reduction in ion–ion interactions on the periphery of a globular protein could well help to destabilize the native conformation.

Perhaps of greatest impact is the effect of temperature on the hydrophobic interaction. Although in the absence of credible potential energy functions it is not yet possible to calculate such an effect from first principles, experimental data on the temperature dependences of thermodynamic properties of a range of hydrophobic solutes indicate the weakening of the interaction at low temperatures (see, for instance, Figure 2). This is also demonstrated by the low temperature induced depolymerization of multi-subunit structures, such as tubulin, tobacco mosaic virus and enzymes,[16] where it is believed that the aggregation is mainly controlled by hydrophobic interactions.

The resultant of the various temperature effects on protein stability is illustrated by the $\Delta G°(N \rightarrow D)$ profile shown in Figure 4. Here $\Delta G°(N \rightarrow D)$ is defined as the standard free energy difference between the native (N) and some biologically inactive denatured (D) state. Because of the large heat capacity contributions, $\Delta G°(N \rightarrow D)(T)$ usually exhibits appreciable curvature, to the extent that the N-state exists only within a limited temperature range (ΔT).[17] $\Delta G°(T)$ seems to approximate to a symmetrical parabola about T^*, the temperature of maximum stability. The position of this parabola with respect to the T-axis, its depth and its curvature determine the stability range of the N-state. Displacements in T^* and/or ΔT values from those characteristic for mesophilic organisms are observed for thermophilic and psychrophilic mutants. For instance, mammalian cytochrome c-552 has a $T^* = 12\,°C$, whereas the protein from a thermophilic bacterium has $T^* = 27\,°C$, a remarkable shift in the stability of the protein.[18] Also its $\Delta G°(N \rightarrow D)$ at 25 °C is larger than that observed for the mammalian protein.

The effects here described need not necessarily cause observable

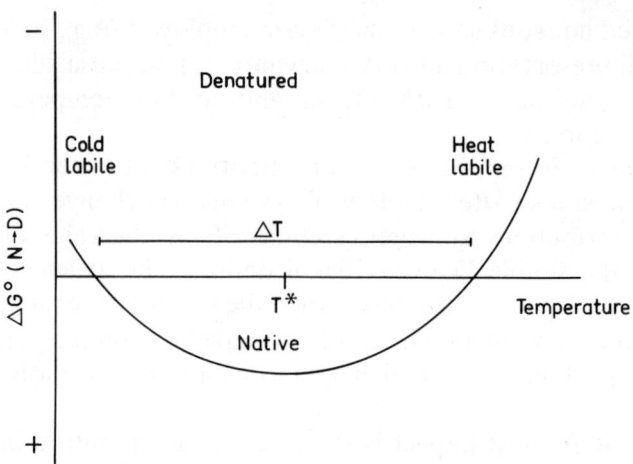

Figure 4 Standard free energy–temperature profile of globular proteins; ΔT is the temperature region of stability and T^* is the temperature of maximum stability

stress symptoms or injury, because protein dissociation can be fully reversible, as it is with many viruses. In a higher organism, on the other hand, the low temperature inactivation of selected enzymes can produce damage that is partly or wholly irreversible. An example is the cold induced sweetening of potatoes after storage at $\leqslant 10\ °C$. This results from the dissociation and partial inactivation of phosphofructokinase tetramer and leads to the accumulation of hexose phosphates which are subsequently converted to sucrose.[19] Even apart from inactivation through subunit dissociation, it is likely that temperature changes will produce stress symptoms in systems that depend on delicately coupled reactions for their optimal functioning. If the energies of activation of the various component reactions differ significantly, then a change in temperature will cause differential changes in the various rate constants. The inevitable result is that certain intermediate products will accumulate, whereas others are used up faster than they are produced. The overall result of a temperature change is therefore difficult to estimate. For instance, the overall rate of cell wall degradation by lysozyme is reduced by factor 200 for a temperature change from $40°$ to $-20\ °C$.[13] Temperature also affects the diffusive properties of water to a marked extent. The temperature dependence in the subzero range exhibits large deviations from typical Arrhenius behaviour, as shown in Figure 3. For a temperature drop from $25°$ to

−35 °C the viscosity increases by two orders of magnitude. In one sense, therefore, a decrease in temperature is equivalent to the substitution of H_2O by D_2O; they both increase the viscosity of the aqueous substrate. However, such an analogy is probably too simplistic.

In examining the results of low temperature stress, the possibility of processes other than those immediately associated with the solvent medium must also be considered, although their full discussion lies beyond the scope of this lecture. Much has been written about thermotropic phase transitions in membranes and their relevance to problems posed by chill and freeze injury in plants. It is argued, for instance, that such transitions can be the direct cause of enzyme inhibition and inactivation. The evidence for such effects is usually derived from observed discontinuities in Arrhenius plots of enzyme activity.[20] Despite obvious attractions of this hypothesis, its intrinsic validity is meeting increasing criticism.[21] Following on from the membrane transition hypothesis of injury, the process of cold hardening has been associated with observed seasonal changes in membrane lipid composition. However, plants respond very quickly to hardening and de-hardening conditions, whereas the synthesis and metabolism of lipids do not exhibit the same rapid response to external factors but take place gradually during the hardening season.[22]

When exposure to low temperature results in freezing, this will produce its own type of stress which is of a very different nature from that described above. It resembles solute stress because (1) the process of freezing removes water from the system and thereby increases the concentrations of all cellular solutes, and (2) freezing in tissue is invariably initiated in the extracellular spaces, so that an osmotic gradient is established across the cell membrane, leading to partial cell dehydration.

It is probably a coincidence that the essential substance of life, water, has its freezing point in the middle of the temperature range which we associate with life processes on this planet. This makes freezing the most important physiological stress condition in the natural environment, much more widespread than soil salinity or drought. The rate and degree to which a cell can respond to extracellular freezing depend on the temperature, the supersaturation of the cellular solutes and the water permeability of the plasma membrane. The relationships between these variables have been established by Mazur.[23] They provide the main basis for successful laboratory cryopreservation. The rate of change of temperature is not so important under field conditions because climatic changes are always slow compared to water diffusion rates through membranes.

Freezing, i.e. the growth of ice crystals, must be preceded by nucleation. A nucleus is a cluster, produced by random density fluctuations, in which the spacings and orientations of the water molecules are such that other water molecules 'recognize' the cluster as ice-like and condense on its surface. The other requirement for nucleation is that the cluster has a lifetime sufficiently long for such diffusion and condensation to take place. Whereas nuclei can arise spontaneously within the body of a liquid, their rate of formation is vastly enhanced by particulate matter capable of acting as catalyst. The freezing in tissues is invariably initiated by this type of mechanism,[24] although it is not at all certain what are the properties that make a given structure a good ice nucleator. Size and interfacial free energy (with respect to ice) are believed to play an important part.[25] Some structures, e.g. certain bacteria, provide high concentrations of nuclei at fairly high subzero temperatures; the nucleating potential of *Pseudomonas syringae* is shown in Figure 5.[26]

It is not understood why, in living tissues, freezing is always initiated in the extracellular spaces and why most cells can apparently tolerate a degree of undercooling, in the neighbourhood of 15 °C, before intracellular ice nucleation occurs. This means that the plasma membrane provides an effective barrier to ice nucleation and propagation.

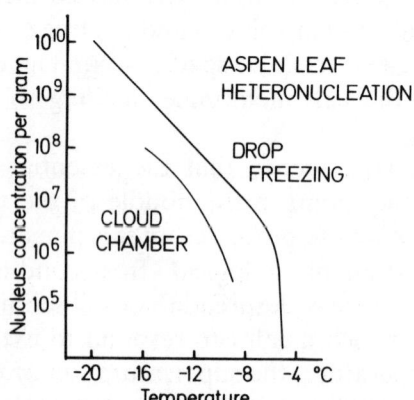

Figure 5 Concentration of active ice nuclei as function of temperature for *Pseudomonas syringae* isolated from aspen leaves. Data from reference 26

Despite some earlier suggestions that cells freeze by a homogeneous nucleation mechanism,[27] our experiments on isolated plant cells, cooled under conditions of maximal undercooling, indicate that cell freezing is nucleated by particulate matter, although at substantially lower temperatures (in the range of −23° to −33 °C) than had been inferred from experiments based on less direct methods.

From the foregoing discussion it is clear that freezing stress contains an osmotic element; the similarities between the effects of freezing and osmotic shock have been described by Farrant,[28] who, nevertheless also points out certain differences. For instance, a sublethal osmotic shock can sensitize cells, rendering them less resistant to a future freezing stress. There are also subtle, but important differences between stress symptoms produced by equiosmolal NaCl and sucrose,[8] indicating that the stresses cannot be of a purely osmotic nature.

Until recently it was a generally held belief that intracellular freezing is invariably lethal, so that freeze resistance mechanisms must rely on an inhibition of the complete osmotic dehydration of the cells, without allowing the intracellular water to freeze. Although some recent studies on the cryopreservation of mammalian embryos have cast doubt on this dogma of equating intracellular ice with death,[29] such experiments are of only limited relevance to the topic of natural water stress, because they are performed under highly artificial conditions on tissues that do not possess the natural property of cold acclimation or osmoregulation.

For the sake of completeness pressure is included among the various forms of water stress, although living organisms are not normally subjected to fluctuations in pressure. Jaenicke has rightly pointed out that much of aquatic life takes place at an average pressure of 38 MPa which makes the question of pressure effects on life processes one of profound interest and importance. Comparative studies on enzymes derived from barotolerant and barophobic species of microorganisms show significant differences.[17] The combined effects of pressure and temperature on the physical properties of water, and therefore also on the native state stabilities of proteins, are complex in the extreme.[30] Despite the fact that many species have always existed in high pressure environments, it is not at all certain that barophilic mutants have evolved. The possibility therefore exists that pressure is always a stress condition.

It serves little purpose to discuss the many symptoms associated with water stress, because the catalogue is a long one.[1] Rates of many reactions, both enzymic and non-enzymic, are markedly affected by substrate concentration, pH, salts and, of course, temperature. The possibility of changes in the membrane permeability and transport behaviour have already been referred to. It is probably more instructive to consider the processes associated with acclimation to a gradually developing stress (the coming of winter or the dry season), or response to a rapidly applied stress (salt shock). Comparative studies on mesophilic, thermophilic and psychrophilic mutants (or isolated systems derived from such mutants) may also help to promote a better insight into various mechanisms of resistance. On the other hand it must be borne in mind that psychrophily and thermophily do not correspond to stress conditions, because the organism is fully adapted to its 'unnatural' environment.

At the present time it is still hard to distinguish between cause and effect. For instance, the development of freezing resistance in plants is associated with many chemical changes,[1] including (a) accumulation of unsaturated lipids and exchange of phospholipids by glycolipids,[22] (b) accumulation of water soluble solutes (e.g. sugars), (c) accumulation of membrane proteins, (d) decrease in the hydrophobicity of soluble proteins, (e) reduction in the levels of growth substances. However, none of these changes can yet be related unambiguously to seasonal cold resistance, be it through freeze tolerance or undercooling.

The picture looks somewhat clearer where response to a suddenly applied stress is involved, as shown by Gould later in this volume. The phenomenon known as osmoregulation involves the rapid synthesis (and/or accumulation) within the cell of high concentrations of certain molecules which do not give rise to enzyme inactivation or other toxic symptoms.[8] These substances have been named 'compatible solutes', although the suitability of this epithet is open to question. Even the description of the process as osmoregulation may disguise its real nature: the substances involved, e.g. proline and the betaines, are known to affect water so as to render it 'unfreezable'. The same substances are also implicated in producing cold and salt tolerance in plants.[31] As has already been pointed out several times during this Conference, this effect cannot be of an osmotic origin, but must be of a kinetic nature, *preventing* the establishment of osmotic equilibrium by a large kinetic barrier. The practical consequence is the prevention of cell dehydration by the externally applied stress. In this connection the observations of Williams that cells will shrink osmotically only to a certain minimum volume are also of relevance.[32] The mystery which

Physiological water stress

still surrounds the phenomenon of osmoregulation is emphasized by the discussions during this Conference.

Finally, let me summarize the various methods employed by living organisms to counter the severe physiological water stress conditions in their natural environments. As already pointed out, freezing is by far the most widespread of these. Among cold acclimated woody plants three types of resistance are encountered;[33] they are shown schematically in Figure 6. The most complete protection is absolute freeze tolerance, as exhibited by dogwood stem tissue which freezes with very little undercooling and will then withstand exposure to very low (liquid nitrogen) temperature. The second type of behaviour is commonly found with buds of fruit trees. Here the tissue water again freezes at high subzero temperatures, but another, minor freezing exotherm in the neighbourhood of -35 °C is observed and cooling to even lower temperatures is invariably lethal. Freeze tolerance is therefore limited to just above the temperature of this secondary freezing event. The third type of resistance is known as deep undercooling (freeze avoidance), where the water in the hardened tissue undercools to some low temperature; in the case of fully acclimated hickory this is below -40 °C. The freezing of the tissue water at this temperature is then lethal. The means by which ice nucleation is inhibited are unknown; it appears that deep undercooling can involve temperatures

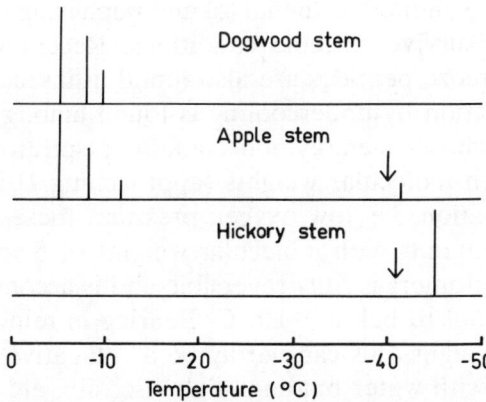

Figure 6 Different types of responses of hardy plants when exposed to subzero temperatures. Vertical lines correspond to observed freezing exotherms and arrows denote the limit of recovery. Adapted from reference 33

well below the generally accepted homogeneous nucleation temperature of liquid water ($-39\,°C$).

A completely different type of resistance has recently been reported for *Lobelia teleki* which grows in a high altitude environment where the temperature cycles between $+10°$ during day and $-10\,°C$ during night.[34] The inflorescence contains a very effective ice nucleating substance, probably of carbohydrate origin, which causes freezing when the temperature drops during the night. In the morning the ice melts and the plant can once again function under normal growth conditions.

While freeze tolerance is common among hardy plants, it is very rare among animals, most of which survive by freeze avoidance. This can take a variety of forms. The most publicized protection method is that found in Polar fish species, the so-called antifreeze proteins and glycoproteins.[35,36] These chemically simple antifreeze polymers enable the blood to undercool to just below the temperature of the ocean, but their detailed mode of operation is as yet obscure, despite considerable speculation. One common feature of all the known antifreeze peptides is their high alanine content, but whether this is a functional requirement is not certain.

A rather more direct method of protection is commonly found among insects, namely the accumulation of glycerol and/or other polyols in the haemolymph.[37] In some cases the storage carbohydrates are almost completely converted to glycerol during acclimation, thus promoting undercooling to temperatures below that of the environment. Protection is limited to the larval and pupal stages, adult insects being unable to survive extreme conditions. Recent work has suggested that antifreeze peptides are also found in insects. Yet another method of protection by undercooling is found among molluscs, e.g. *Helix pomatia*, whose haemolymph contains respiratory proteins of exceptionally high molecular weights (approaching 10^7). Under conditions of hibernation, i.e. low oxygen pressure, these haemocyanins dissociate into subunits with molecular weights of 5×10^5; such dissociation into protomers is fully reversible and is accompanied by the ability to undercool to below $-10\,°C$. Bearing in mind the still very high molecular weight, this can hardly be a colligative effect but has been associated with water binding, high viscosity, etc.[38] Such effects can be simulated with synthetic polymers in aqueous solution.

Although freeze dehydration is uncommon among animals, desiccation due to evaporation is not, and protection against this type of stress is achieved through the synthesis of high concentrations of specific carbohydrates which are apparently able to replace water in maintaining native structures of the functional macromolecular assemblies, thus preventing irreversible denaturation.[39] This phenomenon is discussed by Crowe et al. in this volume. While in their desiccated state, such organisms are in the state of suspended animation, but they begin to function normally upon rehydration to surprisingly low levels, e.g. 0.6 g water/g.

In summary, the responses of living organisms to water stress involve a wide range of physical and chemical principles, including osmotic regulation, specific hydration phenomena, promotion or inhibition of nucleation and/or ice growth, unfreezable (bound) water and, possibly, the redistribution of water within the organism to render it freeze tolerant. In some cases resistance is acquired over an extended period, but this can often be speeded up by the imposition of suitable laboratory conditions.[40] In other cases the response to a water stress can be almost instantaneous. In very few cases are the details of the hardening and dehardening processes understood beyond the most elementary level. It is to be hoped that a judicious combination of the principles of physics, chemistry and physiology may eventually lead to a better insight into the fascinating subject of water stress resistance.

I wish to thank the Leverhulme Trust, the Royal Society and the Agricultural Research Council for supporting our research in low temperature biology.

References

1. J. Levitt, *Responses of Plants to Environmental Stresses*, Academic Press, New York (2nd edition), 1980.
2. H. S. Frank, in *Water, A Comprehensive Treatise*, F. Franks, ed. Plenum Press, Vol. 1, 1971.
3. A. Ben-Naim, J. Wilf and M. Yaacobi, *J. Phys. Chem.*, **77**, 95 (1973).
4. V. Vasilescu and E Katona, in *Frontiers of Bioorganic Chemistry and Molecular Biology*, S. N. Ananchenko, ed. Pergamon Press, Oxford, 1980, p. 445.
5. R. J. Cooke, S. Grego, J. Oliver and D. D. Davies, *Planta*, **146**, 229 (1979).
6. R. A. Uphans, M. I. Blake and J. J. Katz, *Can. J. Bot.*, **53**, 2128 (1975).
7. F. Franks, unpublished results.
8. G. W. Gould and J. C. Measures, *Phil. Trans. Roy. Soc.*, **B278**, 151 (1977).
9. J. H. Crowe and J. S. Clegg, eds. *Anhydrobiosis*, Dowden, Hutchinson and Ross, Stroudsburg, PA, 1973.
10. R. J. Williams and H. J. Hope, *Cryobiology*, **18**, 133 (1981).
11. F. Franks, in *Biological Membranes at Low Temperatures*, G. J. Morris and A. Clarke, eds., Academic Press, London, 1981.
12. C. A. Angell, J. C. Shuppert and J. C. Tucker, *J. Phys. Chem.*, **77**, 3092 (1973).
13. P. Douzou, *Cryobiochemistry*, Academic Press, London, 1977.

14. M. J. Taylor, *Cryo-Letters*, **2**, 231 (1981).
15. E. C. W. Clarke and D. N. Glew, *J. Chem. Soc. Faraday Trans.*, I **76**, 1911 (1980).
16. M. A. Lauffer, in *Physical Aspects of Protein Interactions*, N. Catsimpoolas, ed. Elsevier, New York, 1978, p. 115.
17. R. Jaenicke, *Ann. Rev. Biophys. Bioeng.*, **10**, 1 (1981).
18. H. Nojima, K. Hon-Nami, T. Oshima and H. Noda, *J. Mol. Biol.*, **122**, 33 (1978).
19. W. Dixon, F. Franks and T. apRees, *Phytochem*, **20**, 969 (1981).
20. J. M. Lyons and J. K. Raison, *Comp. Biochem. Physiol.*, **37**, 405 (1970).
21. A. C. McMurdo and J. M. Wilson, *Cryo-Lett.*, **1**, 231 (1980).
22. C. Critchley, Ph.D. Thesis, Düsseldorf University, 1976.
23. P. Mazur, *Science*, **168**, 939 (1970).
24. S. F. Mathias, P. Galfré and F. Franks, *Cryobiology*, **18**, 616 (1981).
25. N. H. Fletcher, *The Chemical Physics of Ice*, CUP, 1970.
26. G. Vali, M. Christensen, R. W. Fresh *et al.*, *J. Atmos. Sci.*, **33**, 1565 (1976).
27. D. H. Rasmussen, M. N. Macaulay and A. P. MacKenzie, *Cryobiology*, **12**, 328 (1975).
28. J. Farrant, *Phil. Trans. Roy. Soc.*, **B278**, 191 (1977).
29. W. F. Rall, D. S. Reid and J. Farrant, *Nature*, **286**, 511 (1980).
30. A. Zipp and W. Kauzmann, *Biochem*, **12**, 4217 (1973).
31. A. Pollard and R. G. Wyn-Jones, *Planta*, **144**, 291 (1979).
32. R. J. Williams and T. Takahashi, *Cryobiology*, **15**, 688 (1978).
33. M. J. Burke, L. V. Gusta, H. A. Quamme *et al.*, *Ann. Rev. Plant Physiol.*, **27**, 507 (1976).
34. J. O. Krog, K. E. Zachariassen, B. Larsen and O. Smidsrød, *Nature*, **282**, 300 (1979).
35. Y. Yeh and R. E. Feeney, *Acc. Chem. Res.*, **11**, 129 (1978).
36. A. L. DeVries and Y. Lin, *Biochim. Biophys. Acta.*, **495**, 388 (1977).
37. W. Block and S. R. Young, *Cryo-Lett.*, **1**, 85 (1979).
38. P. Douzou and C. Balny, *Compt. rend.*, **279**, 851 (1974).
39. J. H. Crowe and L. M. Crowe, *Cryobiology*, **18**, 613 (1981).
40. L. A. Withers and P. J. King, *Plant Physiol.*, **64**, 675 (1979).

Hydration dependent phase changes in a biological membrane

John H. Crowe, Lois M. Crowe and David W. Deamer
University of California, USA

Summary

In the region of 20% H_2O content lipids in sarcoplasmic reticulum were shown to undergo a phase change to hexagonal phase. Upon rehydration the morphology and activity of the membranes were disrupted. Thermal analysis during drying also suggested a phase change at *ca*. 20% water content.

Hydration-dependent phase changes in phospholipid bilayers are well-known, due primarily to the X-ray diffraction work of Luzzati, Reiss-Husson and their colleagues[1,2] and to the electron microscopy of Stoeckhenius,[3] Deamer *et al.*[4] and others. Probably the best understood phase change in phospholipids is the lamellar to hexagonal II change that occurs in some, but not all, phospholipids at near 0.25 g H_2O/g lipid (g/g). The hexagonal II phase consists of tubes of lipid, with the polar ends oriented into a hydrated core (Figure 1). In

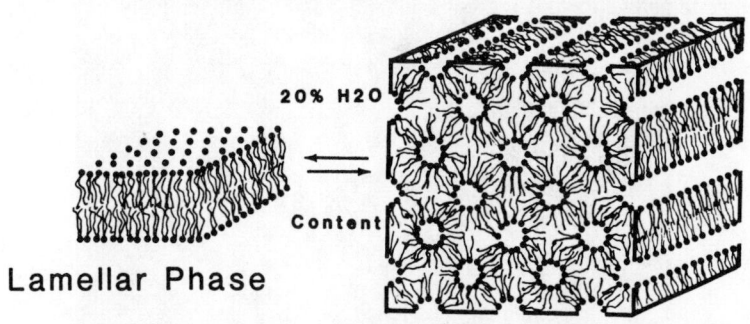

Figure 1

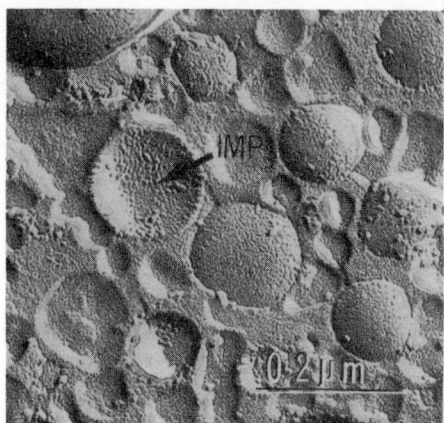

Figure 2

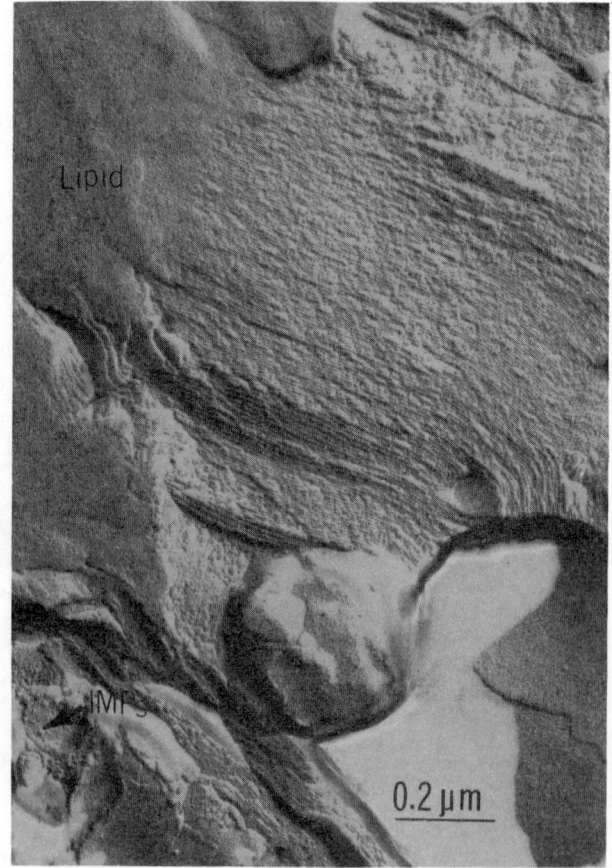

Figure 3

recent years, Simon[5] has hypothesized that if such a phase change were to occur in biological membranes, important consequences would result for cells that normally survive dehydration, such as those found in seeds, cysts of certain crustaceans, and some species of nematodes.[6] However, there is little evidence for the existence of hydration-dependent phase changes in natural biological membranes. We provide such evidence in this paper.

We have studied the consequences of dehydration on isolated vesicles of sarcoplasmic reticulum (SR). In the presence of ATP these vesicles accumulate Ca from the surrounding medium and possess a characteristic morphology, thus providing physiological and morphological assays for the effects of dehydration. In freeze fracture, the freshly prepared vesicles were seen to possess intramembrane particles (IMPs; known to represent the Ca-ATPase) found primarily on the P face (Figure 2). When the vesicles were dehydrated and freeze-fractured at known water contents, the following was observed. At

Figure 4

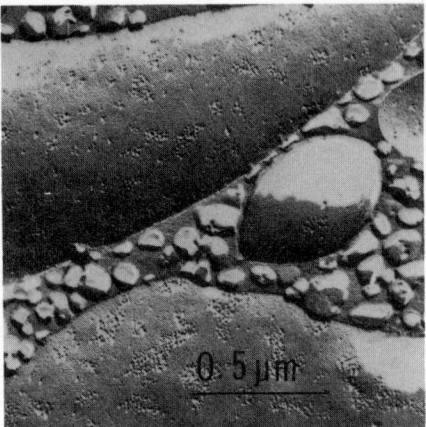

Figure 5

about 0.3 g/g lipid domains devoid of IMPs were observed, with an apparent phase separation of the IMPs (Figure 3). At lower water contents, lipid domains appear to orient into tubes of lipid, which we interpret as hexagonal phase (Figure 4(a), longitudinal fracture; Figure 4(b), cross fracture). Other phases exist as well; particularly prominent are lipid crystals and a phase similar to cubic phase. When vesicles that had been dehydrated were rehydrated, large vesicles were obtained, with IMPs distributed approximately equally on the P and E faces (Figure 5). Such vesicles showed low Ca-transport, high ATPase activity and poor coupling between Ca-transport and ATP utilization.

Further evidence for the phase change in the region of 0.25 g/g was obtained from thermal analysis. Figure 6 shows a continuous recording of water content and temperature of SR. Under dehydrating conditions, the

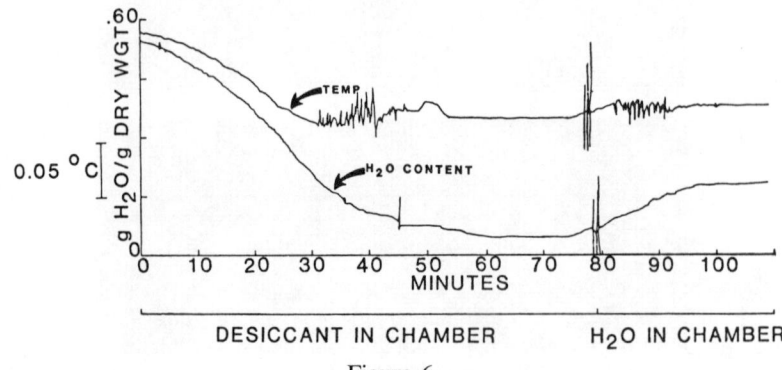

Figure 6

sample cooled due to evaporative water loss, and near 0.25 g/g a series of exothermic events was recorded. When the same sample was rehydrated from the vapour phase, it warmed and a series of endothermic events was recorded in the region of 0.25 g/g.

We conclude that dehydration of natural biological membranes can lead to phase separations of IMPs and lipids and phase changes in the lipids, with detrimental consequences for biological activity in the rehydrated membranes. We are actively studying the mechanisms by which cells that normally survive dehydration escape such consequences. (Supported by grants PCM-80-04720 from the National Science Foundation, U.S. and RA/41 from the National Sea Grant.)

References

1. U. Luzzati and A. Tardieu, *Ann. Rev. Phys. Chem.*, **25**, 79 (1974).
2. P. Saludjian and F. Reiss-Husson, *Proc. Nat. Acad. Sci. USA.*, **77**, 6991 (1980).
3. W. Stoeckhenius, *J. Cell Biol.*, **12**, 221 (1962).
4. D. W. Deamer, R. Leonard, A. Tardieu and D. Branton, *Biochim. Biophys. Acta* **219**, 47 (1970).
5. E. W. Simon, in *Dry Biological Systems*, eds J. H. Crowe and J. S. Clegg, Academic Press. New York (1978).
6. J. H. Crowe and J. S. Clegg (eds.). *Anhydrobiosis*, Dowden, Hutchison, and Ross. Stroudsburg, Pa. (1973).

Membrane water and its role in a thermodynamic model of membrane damage

J. J. McGrath
Michigan State University, USA

Summary

A working model is presented describing thermodynamic and kinetic aspects of membrane changes induced by freezing. In this model water is the dominant component of the membrane system on a molar basis and changes in state of the membrane are mediated by changes in state of the water.

Freezing a biological cell imposes two major physiological stresses on the cell: temperature reduction and exposure to hypertonic solution. It is known that either the thermal perturbation or the chemical perturbation applied independently may induce cell damage. During freezing when thermal and chemical changes are occurring simultaneously there appears to be a complex coupling of these two factors which may lead to damage. Furthermore, the rates of freezing and thawing are known to affect the observed recovery of cells, indicating the importance of rate information for understanding freezing injury. Finally, a number of investigators suggest that cell membranes are the site of injury in many cases and that the damage mechanism involves the loss of membrane material from the membrane during freezing/thawing.

As a means of understanding more about such freezing injury a working model has been developed which defines the membrane as a thermodynamic system. Simple reaction kinetics concepts are introduced in order to account for the known dependence of freezing injury on rates of perturbation induced by freezing.

Thermodynamic description of the membrane

The membrane system is described in terms of Gibbs–Duhem equation which places constraints on possible changes in intensive property variations:

$$0 = -S\,dT + V\,dP - \Sigma n_j\,d\bar{\mu}_j - A\,d\gamma \tag{1}$$

where

$$\mu_j = \mu_j^*(T) + \bar{V}_j P + RT\,\log_e a_j + ZF\psi \tag{2}$$

The importance of this relationship is that it explicitly states and links various forms of energy terms which can alter the chemical energy of one or more 'labile' membrane components. The relationship indicates that such energy changes which might lead to a driving potential for membrane alteration may arise from thermal, chemical, mechanical and electrical changes.

It is obvious, for example, that alteration of the chemical potential of the water associated with the membrane system would alter the chemical potential of other membrane components in a case where $(dT = dP = d\gamma = 0)$. Thus changes in extra-membraneous water which equilibrate with membrane water would mediate membrane alterations.

The Gibbs–Duhem relation has been useful in assessing qualitative trends, order of magnitude analyses and understanding events involving simultaneous changes such as freezing where thermal and chemical effects (and probably others) occur.

Formation of a simple kinetic model

A membrane alteration is assumed to occur by an unspecified unimolecular, rate-limiting reaction which transforms a 'labile' reactant molecule through an activated state to a product molecule. As an example, membrane 'blebbing' may be the macroscopic manifestation of the unimolecular damage reaction. Forward and reverse reaction rate expressions are developed:

$$K_f = \frac{KT}{h} \exp\left[\frac{-\Delta\mu_f^{\neq}}{KT}\right] \tag{3}$$

$$K_r = \frac{KT}{h} \exp\left[\frac{-\Delta\mu_r^{\neq}}{KT}\right] \tag{4}$$

The net rate of change of membrane molecules per unit area can be expressed as:

$$\frac{d\Gamma}{dt} = K_r\Gamma - K_f\Gamma \tag{5}$$

where the activation energies $\Delta\mu^{\neq}$ would be altered by solution perturbations in the general case.

Comparison of theory and experiment

Haemolysis kinetics experiments were performed and activation thermodynamic parameters were derived based upon the initial rate of haemolysis. The activation free energy ($\Delta\mu_f^{\neq}$) for the initial haemolytic reaction was a function of the perturbation of water activity away from the isotonic value which could be fit in the following form:

$$\Delta\mu_f^{\neq} = \Delta\mu_f^{\neq\circ} + \beta RT \log_e(a\omega/a\omega^\circ) \qquad (6)$$

where $r^2 = 0.997$ and the activation free energy barrier in the isotonic state, $\Delta\mu_f^{\neq\circ}$, was 21.1 Kcal/mol. The form of Equation (6) would be expected from the Gibbs–Duhem equation based upon simplifying assumptions.

A computer model for the release of membrane material leading to haemolysis has been developed synthesizing Equations (3)–(6). Two major qualitative trends were obtained from the computer simulations of the loss of membrane material which agree with experimental haemolysis kinetic data: (a) the greater the degree of perturbation in water activity the greater the extent of reaction (haemolysis or predicted loss of membrane material); (b) the characteristic time for loss of material is found to be comparable to that observed for isothermal haemolysis kinetics.

The model also predicts that initial hydration of the membrane material and that cellular shrinkage morphology also effects the exchange of membrane material.

While it is clear that many assumptions have been incorporated in the model presented, it is felt that the thermodynamic and kinetic aspects incorporated into the model provide a working basis for further progress in understanding a complex damage reaction. It is clear that membrane water plays an important role in the reaction in the sense that typical membrane systems may require a large mole fraction of water in order to exist as a bilayer and in the sense that rapid water exchange may mediate the injury process.

Physical and temporal factors involved in the death of embryos that contain ice

W. F. Rall and **C. Polge**
A.R.C. Institute of Animal Physiology, Cambridge, UK

and

D. S. Reid
University of California, USA

Summary

Successful cryopreservation is thought to depend primarily on the fate of intracellular water during cooling and warming. We have examined the responses of mammalian embryos to the formation of intracellular ice by crystallization of vitreous water during slow warming. The use of low temperature light microscopy and parallel experiments of the survival of the embryos has permitted the correlation of observed changes and their consequences during cooling and warming.

The responses of living cells to subzero temperatures and the solidification of water are of practical concern and theoretical interest. Studies of the processes which lead to the long-term preservation of living cells at low temperatures often provide information on the role of water in the maintenance of normal biological structure and function.[1,2] Successful cryopreservation is thought to depend primarily on the fate of intracellular water during cooling and warming. In addition, metazoan cells often require the presence of a cryoprotective additive such as glycerol or dimethyl sulphoxide (DMSO) to survive the deleterious effects of freezing and thawing. Such additives are thought to prevent injury by their colligative action in decreasing the rise in electrolyte concentration,[3] and/or by increasing the probability of attaining partial vitrification of the cell suspension.[4]

Recently we have examined the responses of mammalian embryos to the formation of intracellular ice caused by the crystallization of vitreous cytoplasm during slow warming.[5] Eight-cell mouse embryos in the presence of 1.5 M DMSO were cooled slowly (0.5 °C/min) to temperatures between −35 and −45 °C and then rapidly (~500 °C/min) by transfer into liquid nitrogen. The survival of embyros on thawing was found to depend on the rate of warming: none of the embryos survived warming at rates below 15 °C/min but high survival (~80%) was observed under rapid warming (~500 °C/min).[6,5] Parallel low-temperature light microscopy of embryos cooled and warmed under these conditions indicated that embryos 'flashed' or darkened during slow warming but did not during either rapid cooling or rapid warming.[5,7] On the basis of these observations, we concluded that extracellular crystallization and partial cellular dehydration during slow cooling was interrupted by the apparent vitrification of the remaining liquid solution during rapid cooling. If the rate of warming was too low, however, the metastable vitreous cytoplasm would 'devitrify' or crystallize during warming.

We now report that differential scanning calorimetry (DSC) of model DMSO–NaCl–H$_2$O solutions indicates that the extracellular solution (and presumably the cytoplasm) is indeed capable of vitrifying during rapid cooling from ~ −40 °C and ice will form during slow warming. First, we modelled one effect of slow cooling on the extracellular solution by preparing a series of DMSO–NaCl solutions with decreasing water content but with the same weight ratio of DMSO to NaCl ($R = 14.9$) as found in 1.5 M DMSO in isotonic saline.[8,9] Then we measured the melting points, glass forming abilities, glass transformation temperatures, and devitrification (crystallization) temperatures of these solutions during rapid cooling (~300 °C/min) and slow warming (5 or 10 °C/min). The DSC results indicate that when the water content is reduced to ~53.5 wt %, one obtains a solution with a melting endotherm of −40 °C. This solution will readily vitrify when cooled at ~300 °C/min and exhibits a glass transition at ~ −130 °C and a devitrification (crystallization) exotherm at ~ −85 °C during slow warming. No additional thermal events were observed during slow warming. When these results are combined with the survival measurements and parallel cryomicroscope observations reported previously, they indicate that: (1) the 'flashing' or darkening of embryos during slow warming shows a direct correlation with crystallization of model vitreous solutions. (2) The formation of intracellular ice is not invariably lethal but the survival depends on a subsequent series of changes that are temperature and time dependent. (3) The amount of cellular dehydration before rapid cooling plays a critical role in determining whether vitrification can occur.

References

1. P. Mazur, *Science*, **168**, 939 (1970).
2. J. Farrant, *Phil. Trans. R. Soc. London*, **B278**, 191 (1977).

3. J. E. Lovelock, *Biochim. Biophys. Acta*, **11**, 28 (1953).
4. B. J. Luyet, in *Cryobiology*, ed. H. T. Meryman. Academic Press, New York, pp. 115–138 (1966).
5. W. F. Rall, D. S. Reid and J. Farrant, *Nature*, **286**, 511 (1980).
6. D. G. Whittingham, M. Wood, J. Farrant, H. Leeg and J. A. Halsey, *J. Reprod. Fert.*, **56**, 11 (1979).
7. W. F. Rall, in *Frozen Storage of Laboratory Animal Embryos*, ed. G. H. Zeilmaker. Gustav Fischer Verlag, in press (1981).
8. F. H. Cocks and W. E. Brower, *Cryobiology*, **11**, 340 (1974).
9. A. P. MacKenzie, *Phil. Trans. R. Soc. London*, **B278**, 167 (1977).

Fish glycopeptide and peptide antifreezes: their interaction with ice and water

A. L. DeVries
University of Illinois, USA

Summary

Glycopeptide and peptide antifreeze agents are present in the body fluids of polar fishes and allow them to avoid freezing in ice-laden seawater. These antifreezes lower the freezing point 200 times more than predicted by colligative relations, but have little effect on the melting point of ice. They bind to ice and appear to inhibit growth by raising the curvature of growth steps on the ice crystal surface.

During most of the year the polar oceans are at -1.9 °C, the freezing point of seawater. This temperature is well below -0.8 °C, the freezing temperature of a typical marine teleost. Fishes living in freezing seawater cannot survive this 1.1 degree of supercooling because ice is always present which quickly leads to seeding, ice growth and death.

In the past several years the body fluids of polar fishes living in such waters have been shown to contain either glycopeptides or peptides which lower their freezing points to -2 °C, a temperature below the freezing point of seawater. These glycopeptides and peptides are present in the body fluids at concentrations of 4% (W/V) and account for approximately 1 °C of the body freezing-point depression.[1]

The glycopeptides present in the antarctic fishes consist of a repeating tripeptide, Ala-Ala-Thr-, with the disaccharide galactose-N-acetylgalactosamine attached to each threonyl residue and are found in eight discrete molecular weights ranging from 2600 to 23 500 daltons. Carbohydrate-free peptides are present in several species of arctic fishes which include the winter flounder and arctic sculpin. These peptides occur in three sizes with molecular weights of 3200, 5000 and 8000 daltons and all three are nearly identical in composition. Like the glycopeptides, two-thirds of the peptides consist of alanine residues while most of the remaining residues are threonine, serine, aspartate and glutamate, which are polar.[2]

These molecules make a negligible contribution to the osmotic pressure of the fishes' body fluids and thus cause a depression of the 'freezing point' by some mechanism other than a colligative process. This view is supported by the fact that these compounds lower the temperature at which ice growth occurs but not the temperature at which it melts. A 2% aqueous solution of the glycopeptides or peptides will not freeze in the presence of a seed crystal until the temperature is lowered to -1.2 °C, but the ice that forms will not melt until the temperature is raised to -0.02 °C (Figure 1) a melting temperature determined by colligative effects. Thus, these colloidal solutes can be characterized as having 'antifreeze' properties where it is stressed that the freezing process and not the melting process is affected in a non-colligative manner.

At one time it was speculated that this unusual antifreeze activity resulted from the 'structuring' of water around the polar side-chains of the antifreezes. Nuclear magnetic resonance studies and isopiestic determinations of water binding indicate that the amount of water that is bound is not significantly greater than that bound by other molecules which lack antifreeze properties and are of similar size and composition.[3,4]

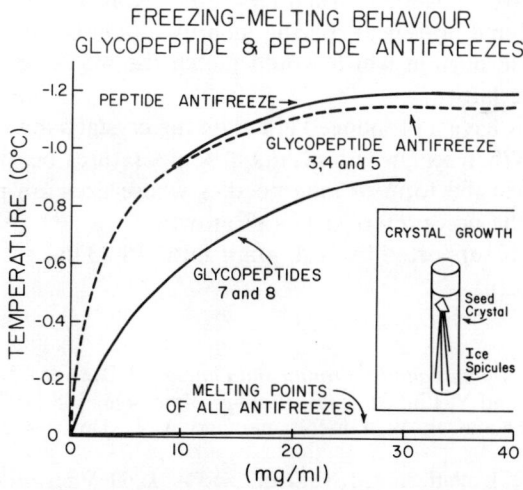

Figure 1 Freezing and melting points of aqueous solutions of glycopeptide and peptide antifreezes as a function of concentration. Inset shows the spicular type crystal growth which occurs in the presence of the antifreezes

The freezing and melting behaviour of aqueous solutions of the antifreeze glycopeptides and peptides have been studied in detail.[5,6]

The antifreezes appear to produce the non-colligative depression of the freezing point by an adsorption–inhibition mechanism. One of the important features of this model is the recognition of the ice by the antifreezes, and their binding to it, which results in inhibition of crystal growth. It appears that the adsorbed antifreezes act as a barrier to the advancing front of water molecules which are joining the ice lattice at the step during crystal growth. Inhibition of growth apparently results from the fact that the advancing ice front can neither 'overgrow' the adsorbed antifreezes nor pass around them. The adsorbed antifreezes appear to prevent propagation of the step because they force the ice to grow between them in the form of many highly curved fronts. The highly curved fronts have higher surface energies than straight fronts. In order for the highly curved fronts to grow energy must be removed from the system. Thus crystal growth is stopped until energy is removed from the system by lowering the temperature, i.e., by depressing the freezing point.

Both the glycopeptide and peptide antifreezes have been shown to bind to ice. The peptide antifreezes are helical molecules in which the polar clusters of amino acids project from the same side of the coil. In these polar clusters the residues threonine and aspartic acid are separated by 4.5 Å, a repeat distance which also separates adjacent oxygens to the ice lattice parallel to the a-axis. The peptide probably binds to the ice through hydrogen bonding between these residues and the oxygens in the ice lattice. Although the glycopeptides have expanded structures[7,8] the secondary structure has not been established and no repeat spacing identified in either the carbohydrate moiety or peptide portion which would match the 4.5 Å or 7.36 Å repeat spacing in the ice lattice.

The antifreezes have a pronouced effect on the crystal habit of ice grown in their presence. When ice growth occurs at temperatures below the freezing point, growth is in the form of long needles whose axes are parallel to the c-axis, which is the non-preferred axis of growth.

This research is supported by NSF grant DPP 78-23462.

References

1. A. L. DeVries, *Animals and Environmental Fitness*, ed. R. Gilles, 583–607 (1980).
2. A. L. DeVries and Y. Lin, *Biochim. Biophys. Acta*, **495**, 388 (1977).
3. A. E. V. Haschemeyer, W. Guschlbauer and A. L. DeVries, *Nature*, **269**, 87 (1977).
4. J. G. Dumen, J. L. Patterson, J. J. Kozak and A. L. DeVries, *Biochim. Biophys. Acta*, **626**, 332 (1980).
5. A. L. DeVries, *Science*, **172**, 1152 (1971).
6. J. A. Raymond and A. L. DeVries, *Proc. Natl. Acad. Sci.*, **74**, 2589 (1977).
7. F. Franks and E. R. Morris, *Biochim. Biophys. Acta*, **540**, 346 (1978).
8. E. Berman, A. Allerhand and A. L. DeVries, *J. Biol. Chem.*, **255**, 4407 (1980).

Evidence for a protein stabilizing mechanism in plant cells under water stress

B. Schobert
University of California, USA

Summary

Investigations with model systems showed that proline and betaine (trimethylglycine) were able to antagonize different modes of protein denaturation induced by chaotropic salts. The mode of action of the denaturants and the mechanism of protein stabilization are discussed.

During water stress (drought and salinity), cells of unicellular algae and higher plants accumulate various low molecular weight organic compounds, such as proline, trimethylglycine (betaine) or several polyols. It was the aim of these investigations to gain more insight into the injurious processes during the onset of water stress, and to elucidate the function of the accumulated organic substances.

Investigations with pure enzymes as model systems showed that proline and trimethylglycine were able to diminish protein denaturation induced by urea, guanidinium hydrochloride, sodium dodecylsulphate, KSCN or $NaClO_3$.[1] The stabilizing ability was not restricted to these compounds, but was also true for many other substances. It has been demonstrated in detail elsewhere[2] that the protective ability was related to the molecular structure of these compounds: the presence of several methyl-groups promoted enzyme stabilization, whereas completely polar substances were always ineffective. Furthermore, the protective ability was dependent on the concentration of these cosolutes present.

The mode of action of the denaturants, as well as the mechanism of protein stabilization, is still not completely understood. Two different interpretations may be used to describe the phenomenon of protein destabilization.

(1) The treatment used by several authors is based on binding equilibria. It is assumed that a complex exists between the denaturant and the protein, but there are a greater number of binding sites in the denatured state. Due to the preferential binding of the denaturant to the unfolded protein molecule, the equilibrium between the native and the denatured state is shifted towards the disordered conformation of the protein.

Although there is evidence for direct interaction between denaturants and proteins, the binding sites and the nature of binding are still beyond a satisfactory explanation. From the present results it is questionable whether binding of the denaturants is a prerequisite for protein unfolding.

(2) The second approach in explaining the denaturing mechanism is to invoke changes in water structure. A change in the water–polymer interactions, transmitted by alterations of the water structure has been proposed for urea.[3] It is assumed that the denaturant displaces the equilibrium between different water species to short range structures and the extended organization of pure water is greatly destroyed. Similarly, the solubilization of apolar groups by other chaotropic solutes (e.g., SCN^-, ClO_3^-) is interpreted as being related to a disordered water structure, associated with positive entropies.[4]

The second hypothesis provides a better basis for the mechanistic explanation of the present investigations. The entropy of water is of primary importance in maintaining the native state of many proteins. Since hydrophobic residues induce an increase in water organization in their vicinity, they cause the entropy of water to decrease.[5] Due to this positive energy contribution, the value of $\Delta G_{solution}$ of the protein is less negative or even positive. Since the conformation, adopted by a protein molecule, represents the free-energy minimum of the whole system, the contact between water and apolar groups is largely avoided by withdrawing many of the hydrophobic groups from the protein surface and by burying them in the interior of the molecules.

The transition from the native to the denatured state of a protein must involve a negative free energy change in order to be spontaneous. This condition is initiated by the presence of other solutes, causing a loss of structured water. In these solutions, the exposure of non-polar groups is connected with a lower positive energy contribution and therefore, the solvation of hydrophobic groups is energetically possible. The driving force for protein denaturation is an entropy gain, due to the relaxed, unfolded conformation of the protein molecule itself. From this consideration it is proposed that the effect of both the different denaturants and the stabilizing cosolutes is transmitted by entropy changes in water. All the chaotropic solutes are thus proposed to decrease the structural organization of water, whereas the stabilizing compounds act in an opposite way and increase the proportion of ordered water molecules, thus stabilizing the native conformation by an entropy-driven process. Therefore, the only real denaturing or stabilizing agent is water itself.

What is the possible denaturant in cells? Model investigations with solutions of bovine serum albumin (1–40%, w/v) and egg white (1–10%, w/v) demonstrated a denaturing activity for these proteins as a function of their concentration.[6] This result was also achieved with a solution of 5% (w/v) poly-L-arginine, whereas other poly-amino-acids were less effective. It indicates that the denaturing effectivity is due to the nature of the polar groups on the surface of the proteins. In the presence of stabilizing cosolutes, such as proline, betaine or tetra methyl ammonium chloride this denaturing effectivity was greatly diminished. These proteins are therefore classified as water structure breakers and it is proposed that their destabilizing mechanism is consistent with the mode of action of other chaotropic solutes. Preliminary experiments showed that this activity was also true for bulk proteins from several plant species. Therefore, proteins are supposed to be the 'biological denaturants', their destabilizing activity increasing with their concentration. During the accumulation of proline or betaine it is the disordered water structure, created by proteins, that is compensated for.

Spin label studies with the diatom *Phaeodactylum tricornutum* revealed that during the onset of high osmotic strain approximately 50–60% of the aqueous space was removed from the cytoplasm of the cells,[7] indicating that the protein concentration is more than doubled. Since the protein concentration is already high in the cytoplasm during the non-stress state, such concentration changes could contribute to changes in water structure. In respose to the accumulation of proline the water content of the cells recovered up to 80% only. Calculations of the correlation times of the spin label showed that the recovery in microviscosity of the aqueous phase was considerably less than that observed in the cell volume. This result indicates that the adapted cells differed from the non-stress cells. Therefore, volume regulation of the cells does not seem to be the primary aim of this regulatory mechanism, rather a regulation in the state of the aqueous phase.

References

1. B. Schobert and R. Hartlieb, *Arch. Biochem. Biophys.* (submitted).
2. B. Schobert and H. P. Jennisen, *Cryobiology* (submitted).
3. H. S. Frank and F. Franks, *J. Chem. Phys.*, **48**, 4746 (1968).
4. Y. Hatefi and W. G. Hanstein, *Proc. Natl. Acad. Sci. USA*, **62**, 1125 (1969).
5. H. S. Frank and M. W. Evans, *J. Chem. Phys.*, **13**, 507 (1945).
6. B. Schobert and R. Hartlieb, *Arch. Biochem. Biophys.* (submitted).
7. B. Schobert and D. Marsh, *Biochim. Biophys. Acta* (submitted).

Biological systems with low water content: NMR approach to the state of water in plant seed

S. Ratković and M. Denić
Maize Research Institute, Beograd, Yugoslavia

and

G. Lahajnar and I. Zupančič
Institut 'Josef Stefan', Ljubljana, Yugoslavia

Summary

The proton T_1, T_2 and diffusion constant (D) were studied in endosperm of maize seed and the results support the multifractional behaviour of water in these systems. A possible correlation between the state of water in seed (particularly in embryo) and seed viability was suggested.

There have been some studies on the state of water in different classes of seed by using proton spin–spin (T_2) measurements.[1] In this report we present measurements of spin-relaxation times (T_1, T_2) and diffusion constant (D) on the endosperm and embryo of maize kernal separated from each other. The main constituent of endosperm is starch (60–80%), then proteins (<10%) and variable amount of water. The embryo contains mostly lipids, proteins and water.

For water in endosperm two T_1 components were found at proton resonance frequencies of 16 and 32 MHz, respectively. T_1 was measured as a function of hydration between 0.025 and 0.7 g H_2O/g d.m. and a minimum in T_1 was obtained at around 0.25 g H_2O/g d.m. for both genotypes studied (W 64 A+, W 64 AO_2). Such dependence is also found in pure starch/water systems. At hydration levels below 0.05 g H_2O/g d.m. a single T_1 was observed (Figure 1).

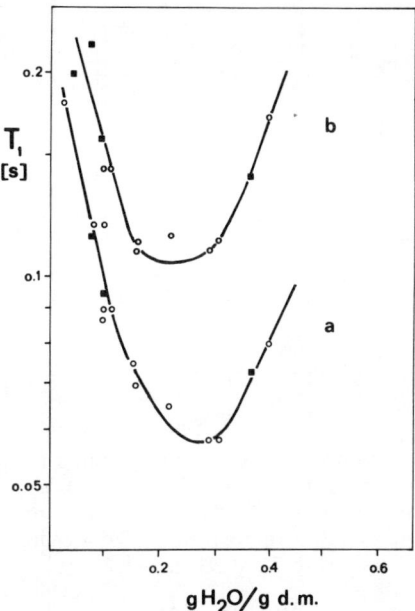

Figure 1 Proton spin-lattice relaxation time (T_1) versus water content for *endosperm* of two maize genotypes: ○ W 64 A+; ■ W 64 AO$_2$

For seed with water content below this limit two well separated components of proton FID signal from endosperm were obtained at resonance frequency $v_H = 57.9$ MHz (Bruker pulsed spectrometer, B-KR 322s). A 'solid' component with $T_{2a} \approx 10$ μs (Gaussian form), which is the same for both types of endosperm, arises mostly from macromolecular protons (starch, proteins) and from H$_2$O protons in intimate contact with these molecules. The 'semi-solid' component (Lorentzian form) is characterized with $T_{2b} \approx 0.4$ ms (8–9% water) and probably represents water molecules immobilized by starch in the endosperm matrix. The T_{2b} is in positive correlation with water content and it seems that it shows up some species specificity. Above 0.1 g H$_2$O/g d.m. a third 'liquid' component arises with $T_2 \geq 5$ ms.

In endosperm with lower water content another 'liquid' component is found at higher amplifications with $T_2 = 8$ ms (W 64 A+) and $T_2 = 11.5$ ms (W 64 AO$_2$), similar to T_{2c} component of water. The signal of this component makes <0.5% of the total proton signal (solid + adsorbed water). To identify this fraction the diffusion constant (D) was measured at different temperatures using the PGSE method. The small value of $D \approx 10^{-7}$ cm^2 s^{-1} and relatively high activation energy $E_a = 19.3$ kJ suggest that this component arises from traces of lipids distributed within the endosperm tissue.

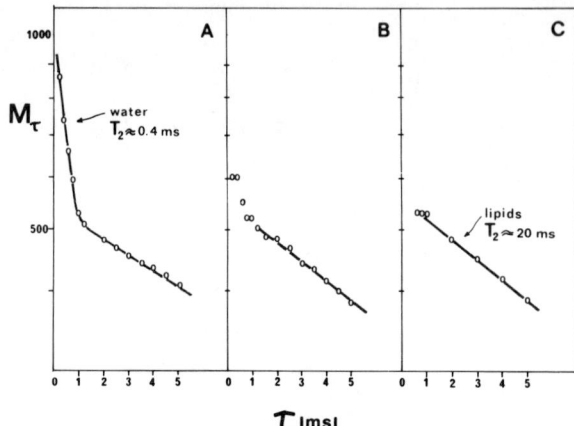

Figure 2 Proton spin echo signal versus τ for *embryo* of the maize genotype W 64 A+. A. Embryo with H_2O content ~8%; B. Partially dried embryo; C. Drying at elevated temperature (the signal of lipids with $T_2 \approx 20$ ms is left)

As far as the embryo is concerned the proton signal of H_2O was discriminated from the signal of lipids by successive drying or by exchange with D_2O. In relatively dry seed (water content 5–10%) a component with $T_2 \approx 0.4$ ms, similar to the 'semi-liquid' component in endosperm, is probably a result of partial immobilization by proteins (Figure 2).

Seed viability is in close correlation with water content of the seed but the mechanism of the action is not known.[2] Our efforts are concentrated to identification of the fraction of water in the embryo, using NMR, which is 'responsible' for seed viability. This is done by combining the NMR measurements and the germination tests. Possible candidates for preserving seed alive are 'solid' and 'semi-liquid' fractions of water.

References

1. S. I. Aksenov, N. A. Askochenskaya and N. S. Petinov, *Fiz. Rast.*, **16**, 58 (1969).
2. E. H. Roberts, *Viability of Seeds*, Chapman and Hall, London (1972).

The effects of growth under water stress on the structure, metabolism and cryopreservation of cultured sycamore cells

Hugh W. Pritchard, Brian W. W. Grout and **Keith C. Short**
North East London Polytechnic, UK

and

David S. Reid
University of California, USA

Summary

The transfer of liquid-grown sycamore cells to medium with 6% w/v mannitol added decreases both cell division and biomass production. Vacuolar volume and cell wall thickness are reduced in the smaller cells of the population and their walls contract in hypertonic cryoprotectant. The respiration rate of such cells is increased and their water content apparently reduced. A high proportion of these modified cells are able to withstand cooling into liquid nitrogen using the appropriate protocol.

Pregrowth and survival after freezing

A number of plant cell cultures show enhanced survival after cryopreservation when pregrown in the presence of solutes such as mannitol and proline.[1] These solutes may have their effects directly within the cell interior or externally by the imposition of a degree of osmotic stress.

Withers and King[2] have reported enhanced survival of *Acer pseudoplatanus* (sycamore) cells after freezing and thawing by pregrowth for 7 days in culture medium with 6% w/v mannitol as an additive. The following freezing protocol was employed: (i) cryoprotectant of 0.5 M DMSO + 0.5 M glycerol + 1 M proline, (ii) cooling at 1 °C/min to −35 °C, (iii) holding time of 30 min at

−35 °C, (iv) plunge into LN$_2$ from holding temperature, (v) thaw by plunging into water at 40 °C.

In this investigation we have begun to study the effects of the mannitol pregrowth in this system with respect to alteration of cellular structure and function.

The effects of mannitol pregrowth

The addition of 6% w/v mannitol to the basic sycamore cell growth medium increases the osmolality from 121 ± 11 to 511 ± 17 milliosmols kg^{-1}. This will pose a degree of osmotic stress on the cell if the mannitol does not cross the plasmalemma and reach an equilibrium. Whilst this assumption is generally accepted for higher plants there is some evidence of mannitol penetration into algal cells[3] with alterations in metabolism resulting from raised internal and not external osmotic pressures. Experiments to determine the extent, if any, of mannitol uptake in the system described below are in hand.

Pregrowth with the mannitol additive for 7 days depresses both cell division and total biomass production by c. 35% (Table 1). This reduced growth rate may cause changes in cellular composition and metabolism resulting in increased freeze tolerance as has been previously described for a number of organisms.[4]

The cell size distribution within the population is not significantly altered by pregrowth but certain morphological differences can be seen. Thin-sectioning shows that the outer cell walls of smaller pregrown cells (<30 μm diam.) are significantly thinner than their control counterparts (Table 1). More detailed examination of these sections at high magnification and freeze-fracture experiments showed no other changes in cell wall architecture. Other properties of the cell walls are altered however, for when placed in the

Table 1 The effects of mannitol pregrowth (7 days) on cultured sycamore cells

Parameter	Control	Mannitol pregrown
[a] Osmolality of medium (milliosmols/kg)	121 ± 11	511 ± 17
Cell number ($\times 10^5$ per ml)	5.04	3.33
Dry weight (mg/ml)	3.35	1.95
[b] Respiration (μlO$_2$/mg/h)	11.07	14.18
[a] 50% plasmolysis point (milliosmols/kg)	621	836
[c] Cell wall thickness (μm)	0.41	0.30
[c] Vacuolar volume (% of whole cell)	34	14

[a] freezing point osmometer; [b] Gilson respirometer; [c] electron microscopy.

hypertonic cryoprotectant solution (1820 ± 104 milliosmols kg^{-1}) prior to freezing the entire cell shrinks and not just the protoplast as in control cells. This shrinkage significantly alters the cell size distribution during the incubation prior to freezing, bringing 78.7% of the pregrown cells into the 15–25 μm diam. size class compared with 55% of control cells. Smaller cells have been shown to be more amenable to freezing[1] and it is possible that a reduced volume : surface area ratio aids water movement during protective dehydration and subsequent rehydration. This 'osmotic' behaviour of the cell wall may also regulate water movement in and out of the cell in some way, particularly with respect to the solution between the protoplast and cell wall and the external medium.

Further ultrastructural studies showed a marked reduction in vacuolar volume (60% redn. of total vol.) as a result of pregrowth. This increased cytoplasm : vacuole ratio increases freeze-tolerance,[1] perhaps by decreasing damaging stresses during plasmolysis and deplasmolysis and facilitating loss of water outside the plasmalemma.

The osmotic behaviour of pregrown cells (15–25 μm diam.) is also altered, with the 50% plasmolysis point being reached at a much higher osmolality than for control cells (Table 1). For any hypertonic external solution mannitol-grown cells will therefore need to shrink less than control cells during plasmolysis. This may reduce the extent of shrinkage-related injuries. Further, the increase in external osmolality needed to produce 50% plasmolysis is reduced in pregrown cells indicating a reduced cytoplasmic water content, with its obvious benefits for freeze tolerance. The altered cell wall properties may also affect the point at which plasmolysis is seen for as the wall shrinks together with the protoplast plasmolysis may be less evident. This would result in the differences shown by the data being understated.

Examination of rates of oxygen uptake show a 28% increase during mannitol pregrowth (Table 1). This may result from active solute uptake or increased rates of synthesis of compounds including cytoplasmic solutes. Increased respiratory rates in plant tissues in response to osmotic stress have been reported although the mechanisms involved are not clear. An increase in respiration has also been associated with cold hardening.[5]

The freeze/thaw response

Using a programmable cryomicroscope it can be seen that both pregrown and control cells are plasmolysed by the cryoprotectant and shrink a little further in immediate response to the passage of the ice-front. There is no further reduction in protoplast volume during the holding period and if protective dehydration does occur during this period it does so without further shrinkage.

The phenomenon of 'flashing' was only seen in unprotected cells of both pregrown and control populations. This may be as a result of the high water content of these cells whereas the protected cells are plasmolysed and at a much reduced water content.

After thawing the benefits of pregrowth are clear, for surviving cells (estimated by a positive fluorescein diacetate reaction) are found only in these cultures and not in controls. The surviving cells are predominantly (82%) in the 15–25 μm diam. class. Cultures that give positive FDA reactions postthaw will regrow to produce cell colonies when plated on to semi-solid medium, although there is a further reduction in viable cell number at this stage. This loss is at present variable and unpredictable in our laboratory and is the subject of further study.

The value of pregrowth

The smaller cells (15–25 μm diam.) of the mannitol pregrown population survive the freeze/thaw procedure whereas their counterparts from the control populations do not. Cell size *per se* is not of principal importance in survival therefore, and perhaps more important are: (i) cytoplasm:vacuole volume ratio; (ii) quantity and localization of cellular water; (iii) accumulation of cytoplasmic solutes; (iv) osmotic behaviour of the cells, especially with regard to protoplast shrinkage.

Mannitol pregrowth appears to alter these aspects of cell structure and function favourably with respect to freeze. tolerance and may have other beneficial metabolic effects as yet undetected. Current experiments are looking for alterations in membrane composition and soluble lipids and proteins as a result of pregrowth.

Similar data to those briefly described here are being collected using sorbitol as an additive and experiments are under way to test the hypothesis that the observed modifications are solely the result of osmotic stress. If the hypothesis is proven this would imply that the sycamore cell line is in some way 'hardenable' and considerable value would be gained from further work with a non-responsive cell line.

Acknowedgement

HWP wishes to acknowledge support from an SRC studentship.

References

1. L. A. Withers, in: *Tissue Culture Storage for Genetic Conservation*, IBPGR Technical Report, Rome, p. 91 (1980).
2. L. A. Withers and P. King, *Cryoletters*, **1**, 213 (1980).
3. R. L. Heath, *Plant Physiol.*, **59**, 911 (1977).
4. G. J. Morris, in: *Low Temperature Preservation in Medicine and Biology*, Pitman Medical, 253–283 (1980).
5. S. Hatano, in: *Plant Cold Hardiness and Freezing Stress*, Academic Press, pp. 175–196 (1978).

Freeze-induced dehydration: effects on the plasma membrane of isolated plant protoplasts

P. L. Steponkus, M. F. Dowgert, R. Y. Evans and W. J. Gordon-Kamm
Cornell University, USA

Summary

Freeze–thaw injury to isolated protoplasts (*Secale cereale* L. cv. Puma) is ascribed to two dehydration-induced lesions in the plasma membrane. In non-acclimated protoplasts (LT_{50} = −1 to −2 °C), sufficiently large surface areal contractions (>1000 μm^2) are irreversible and the protoplasts lyse during expansion upon thawing. In contrast, in acclimated protoplasts (LT_{50} = −25 to −28 °C), large surface areal contractions (<3000 μm^2) are reversible but injury results from the loss of osmotic responsiveness following dehydration at high solute concentrations. The molecular basis for these two lesions is discussed.

Introduction

Although there is a consensus that the plasma membrane is the primary site of freezing injury, the molecular aspects of injury are rarely considered. We have elected to study the cryobehaviour of the plasma membrane *in situ* using enzymatically isolated protoplasts of leaves of *Secale cereale* L. cv. Puma. Isolated protoplasts behave as ideal osmometers over a wide range of osmolalities.[1,2] As they remain spherical, the extent of dehydration can be quantified by direct cryomicroscopic observations.[3] During a freeze–thaw cycle, a protoplast contracts with the minimum volume a function of the lowest temperature attained and subsequently expands upon thawing to an extent determined by the osmolality of the suspending medium.

Dehydration results in several cellular consequences—most notably surface areal contraction and solute concentration. We propose that (1) both stresses are potentially lethal—depending on the freeze–thaw protocol (minimum temperature attained and composition of the suspending medium) and the hardiness of the tissue from which the protoplasts were isolated; (2) there is a unique membrane lesion resulting from each stress, i.e. expansion-induced lysis during warming or total loss of osmotic responsiveness following cooling; and (3) cold acclimation is a complex of cellular alterations which collectively contribute to the increase in freezing tolerance.

Expansion-induced lysis

Although osmometric behaviour is best described as a function of volume, lysis resulting from volumetric changes is a function of the surface area of the plasma membrane.[1] Protoplasts do not, however, possess a fixed maximum surface area at which lysis occurs. Instead, the expansion potential is characterized by an absolute Tolerable Surface Area Increment (TSAI).[1,2,3] In a population of protoplasts, the absolute magnitude of change in the mean surface area of the population which results in lysis of 50% of the population ($TSAI_{50}$) is constant and independent of the extent of contraction. For non-acclimated Puma rye protoplasts, the $TSAI_{50}$ is 1000 μm^2. This value is exceeded if protoplasts are frozen to -1 to -2 °C (the LT_{50}) and subsequently thawed. This lesion quantitatively accounts for the incidence of injury incurred by non-acclimated protoplasts. In acclimated protoplasts, the $TSAI_{50}$ increases to 3000 μm^2. This value exceeds the extent of contraction which would be incurred if the protoplasts were completely dehydrated and then returned to isotonic conditions.

Recently, we have reported that the stress–strain relation (SSR) of isolated protoplasts depends strongly on the time scale of deformation.[4,5] Over periods of up to a few seconds, the plasma membrane behaves elastically. The area elastic modulus (k_A) is similar (~ 150 mN $\cdot$ m^{-1}) for both acclimated and non-acclimated protoplasts.[6] As the critical lysing tension (γ_c) is also similar for both (3 to 4 mN $\cdot$ m^{-1}), elastic surface areal expansion is limited to 2%. Over longer periods (minutes), area increases with time under large tension and decreases under sufficiently small tension, suggesting that material is incorporated into or deleted from the plane of the membrane and a surface energy law applies. The fact that protoplasts remain spherical after large surface areal deformations suggests that the membrane is under tension at all areas. Resting tensions (γ_r) of 110 $\mu N \cdot m^{-1}$ and 204 $\mu N \cdot m^{-1}$ have been measured in protoplasts isolated from non-acclimated and acclimated tissues, respectively.[6]

We propose that upon exposure to hypertonic conditions, volumetric contraction results in the rapid relaxation of γ_r and membrane material is subducted from the membrane into a reservoir. Electron micrographs document that extensive vesiculation is observed following contraction and that the plasma membrane remains smooth without folding or pleating.[7] Upon return to isotonic conditions, the increase in tension alters the reservoir/membrane equilibrium and induces reincorporation of membrane material. In nonacclimated protoplasts the excursion is not totally reversible, however, because not all of the subducted material is reincorporated into the membrane.[7]

Contraction-induced loss of osmotic responsiveness

When non-acclimated protoplasts are frozen below -5 °C (lower than the LT_{50}) and acclimated protoplasts to -25 to -28 °C (the LT_{50}), injury is manifested as a total loss of osmotic responsiveness and they remain contracted during warming. Therefore the influence of hypertonic exposures without subsequent expansion was investigated.[8] The incidence of injury in either an ionic ($CaCl_2$ + NaCl) or non-ionic (sorbitol) osmoticum was determined in the contracted state using fluorescein diacetate. While the molecular nature of this form of injury has not been investigated, inactivation or loss of specific membrane components conferring semipermeable characteristics is assumed.

In non-acclimated protoplasts, the extent of injury was similar at equiosmolal concentrations of either $CaCl_2$ + NaCl or sorbitol. In both osmotica, injury was both time and concentration dependent with no specific injurious concentration apparent. In acclimated protoplasts, a similar extent of injury was observed in $CaCl_2$ + NaCl—albeit at higher (2×) concentrations. In contrast, the extent of injury was markedly reduced in acclimated protoplasts exposed to all hypertonic sorbitol treatments.

When suspended in $CaCl_2$ + NaCl, the extent of injury in non-acclimated and acclimated protoplasts is similar if compared at similar extents of cellular dehydration, i.e. equivolumes. As an increase in the internal solute concentration (osmotic adjustment) is observed following cold acclimation,[3] the difference in the extent of injury between non-acclimated and acclimated protoplasts at equiosmolalities is ascribed to differences in the extent of dehydration incurred. In contrast, when suspended in sorbitol, the extent of injury is significantly less in acclimated protoplasts even when compared at equivolumes. Hence, cold acclimation results in an increased tolerance to cellular dehydration in addition to mitigation of the extent of dehydration due to osmotic adjustment.

References

1. P. L. Steponkus and S. C. Wiest, in *Plant Cold Hardiness and Freezing Stress*, eds. P. H. Li and A. Sakai, Academic Press, New York, pp. 75–91 (1978).
2. S. C. Wiest and P. L. Steponkus, *Plant Physiol.*, **62**, 699 (1978).
3. P. L. Steponkus and S. C. Wiest, in *Low Temperature Stress in Crop Plants: The Role of the Membrane*, eds. J. M. Lyons, D. G. Graham and J. K. Raison, Academic Press, New York, pp. 231–254 (1979).

4. J. Wolfe and P. L. Steponkus, *Biochim. Biophys. Acta*, **643**, 663 (1981).
5. P. L. Steponkus, J. Wolfe and M. F. Dowgert, in *Effects of Low Temperatures on Biological Membranes*, p. 307, eds. G. J. Morris and A. Clarke, Academic Press (1981).
6. M. F. Dowgert and P. L. Steponkus, *Plant Physiol.*, **67** (Suppl), 64 (1981).
7. W. J. Gordon-Kamm and P. L. Steponkus, *Plant Physiol.*, **67** (Suppl), 122 (1981).
8. R. Y. Evans and P. L. Steponkus, *Plant Physiol.*, **67** (Suppl), 122 (1981).

NMR relaxation times of water protons in cultured cells under freezing and osmotic stress conditions

Paula T. Beall
Baylor College of Medicine, Texas, USA

Summary

The behaviour of water in cells under temperature and osmotic stress can be monitored by nuclear magnetic resonance (NMR) relaxation times for water protons. The motional freedom of water molecules in cells under these conditions is a complex function of the ratio of water to dry solids, the organization of the macromolecular cell structure, and the response of macromolecular conformation to these stresses.

Populations of cultured cells have some advantages over animal tissues in the study of the behaviour of water molecules in biological systems. Increased sample homogeneity, a single cell type, lack of blood and lymph and a constant and measurable extracellular volume are only a few of these. In these experiments, populations of highly characterized mammalian cells were grown as monolayers under tissue culture conditions (L-15 medium for SW 613, human colon cancer, MEM for Hela, and CHO—Chinese hamster ovary cells at 37 °C in equilibrium with air or air and 5% CO_2) for the study of two important questions on the behaviour of water molecules inside cells under stress conditions. The spin–lattice relaxation time (T_1) and the spin–spin relaxation time (T_2) of water protons were measured by 90°-τ-180° pulse sequence and a Carr–Purcell–Meiboom–Gill spin echo sequence respectively on a Bruker SXP pulsed nuclear magnetic resonance (NMR) spectrometer at 30 MHz. Water contents of cell pellets were determined by desiccation and weighing.

In human cancer of the breast cell line SW 613, the bulk of water in the cell pellet freezes at -13 °C when the cells are cooled slowly (1 °C/10 min). Signal intensity for protons drops to $\simeq 15\%$ of the original value and these

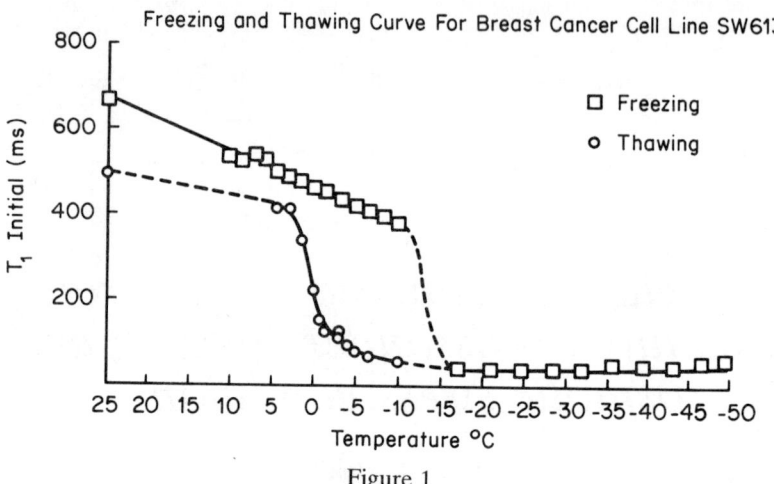

Figure 1

protons remain unfrozen to $-52\ °C$. T_1 values decrease linearly from 668 msec at $25\ °C$ to 380 msec at $-10\ °C$ (Figure 1) and then drop abruptly to 48 msec at $-13\ °C$. T_2 values decrease linearly from 102 to 93 msec over the $25-(-10)\ °C$ range and then drop to 1.3 msec and less for the non-frozen water in these cells (Figure 2). A value of $\simeq 15\%$ non-frozen water in these

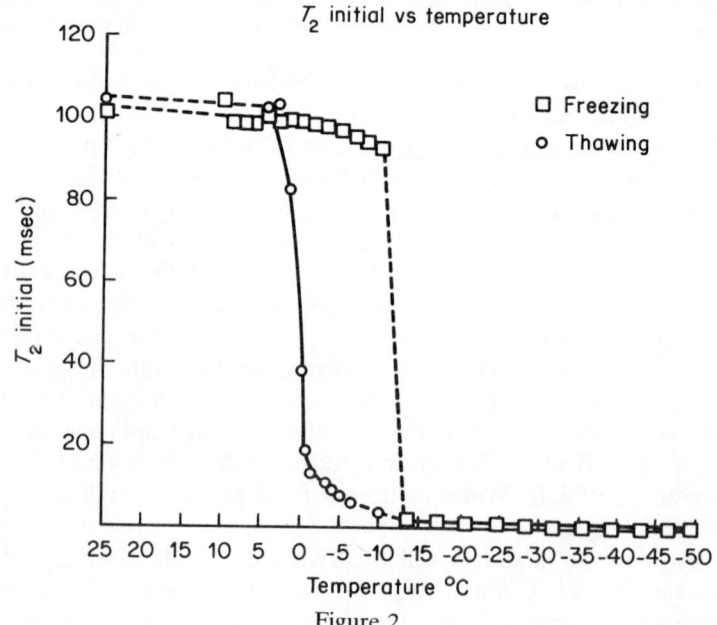

Figure 2

pure cells is consistent with findings for mouse[1,2] and porcine[3] muscle and rat kidney tissues.[4] A distinct hysteresis is apparent in both T_1 and T_2 patterns upon slow rewarming of the cell pellet (Figure 1 and 2). The majority of water in the cells (without cryoprotectant) did not thaw until 0–5 °C. Similar hysteresis seen in rat kidney tissue[4] and porcine muscle[3] has been interpreted to be due to ice crystal formation during the first freezing rupturing cell membranes and changing the properties of macromolecular structures in the system which affect water in their vicinity. The failure of both parameters to return to their original values upon thawing also indicates considerable disruption of the organized cell structure by freezing. NMR relaxation times may be used to evaluate the effects of freezing damage on cells, including those of frozen foods.[5]

Cultured cells are good experimental systems to study the effects of osmotic stress since they can be suspended in solutions of varying osmotic strengths, allowed to equilibrate, and then collected for NMR measurements. Human cervical carcinoma cells (Hela) and Chinese hamster ovary cells (CHO) were suspended in sodium chloride solutions ranging from 0.03 M to 0.5 M for 30 min at 37 °C. Figure 3 displays the relationship between $1/T_1$ of the water protons in these cells and the ratio of dry solids to water. Within the narrow physiological range in which cells can survive the shrinking and swelling procedure, $1/T_1$ correlates well with water content. However, outside this range macromolecular structural changes begin to occcur that will prevent recovery of the cell to a viable state. Hypertonicity results in crenated membranes, cytoplasmic precipitates and condensed chromatin. Hypotonicity causes swollen and broken cells, cytoplasmic vacuoles, and disorganized

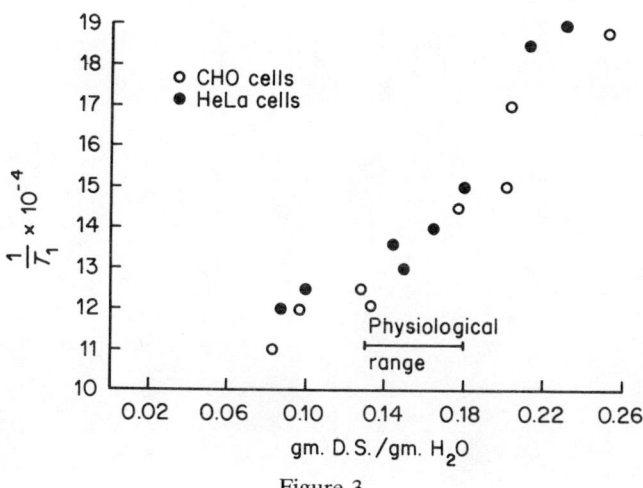

Figure 3

chromatin. T_1 values for Hela and CHO cells in our experiments and for V79-S171 mammalian cells in the experiments of Raaphorst *et al.*,[6] reflected not only water content but also macromolecular rearrangements and conformational changes. At molarities above 1.0 M, water content and cell volume are decreased[6] however T_1 increases because macromolecular condensation releases water from hydration shells. The response of cells to osmotic stress is not linear, but rather a complex function of the water holding capacity and conformational state of their macromolecular constituents. Cells which are resistant to such stresses may have more stable macromolecular organization.

Acknowledgements

This work supported in part by the Office of Naval Research contract N00014-81-K-0167 and the National Institutes of Health grant CA-21624. The assistance of Jim Fogal on the freezing experiments is gratefully acknowledged.

References

1. B. M. Fung, *Bioch. Biophys. Acta*, **362**, 209 (1974).
2. S. N. Rustgi, H. Peemoeller, R. T. Thompson, D. W. Kydon and M. M. Pintar, *Biophys. J.*, **22**, 439 (1978).
3. W. Derbyshire and J. L. Parsons, *J. Mag. Res.*, **6**, 344 (1972).
4. V. V. Morariu, I. C. Kiricuta and C. F. Hazlewood, *Physiol. Chem. Phys.*, **10**, 517 (1978).
5. J. A. Troller and J. H. B. Christian, Eds., *Water Activity and Food*, Academic Press, New York (1978).
6. G. P. Raaphorst, P. Law and J. Kruuv, *Physiol. Chem. Phys.*, **10**, 177 (1978).

Water relations in the epidermal cells of the halophyte Suaeda maritima

A. Deri Tomos and R. Gareth Wyn Jones
University College of North Wales

Summary

Certain factors that influence the behaviour of water at a cellular level in plants can be measured by continuous measurement and manipulation of individual cell turgor. An attempt to determine whether halophytes possess unusual properties is described. No fundamental differences were found.

The transport of water at a cellular level is important in controlling many whole-plant processes, including transpiration, gas exchange across stomata and osmotic adaptation. With reference to this last feature, it is of particular interest to study halophytic plants, such as *Suaeda maritima* which face special problems with regard to water flow through their tissues and to osmotically driven growth. However, these plants grow successfully in environments of moderate salinity (salt marshes). Such growth is associated with considerable morphological changes, as leaves and stems become succulent due to a general enlargement of the cells.[1] Since succulence is generally associated with plants growing under conditions of water stress, a study of the water relations of *Suaeda* may also provide information about this little understood phenomenon.

The micro pressure-probe of Zimmermann and Steudle[2,3] which provides a direct method of measuring certain water-relations parameters (turgor, P; cell wall elastic modulus, ε; and cell membrane hydraulic conductivity, Lp) has been applied to the individual cells of the *S. maritima* leaf (see also Tomos and Zimmermann, pp. 256–261). Preliminary results obtained with epidermal cells of *S. maritima* plants grown hydroponically under conditions of varying (NaCl) salinity are described here.

1 Cell turgor pressure

(a) Within experimental error, epidermal cells from varying sites of the same leaf have the same turgor (Table 1). This suggests that the distribution of osmotic solutes is uniform throughout the epidermis. In this experiment, turgor ranged from 60 to 380 kPa for the different leaves measured. (The full range of turgor pressures recorded can be deduced from Figure 1.)

(b) This uniformity of turgor appears to extend to different leaves within the same plant (Table 1). There is some indication, however, that younger leaves have slightly higher turgor than older ones. This may indicate a process that allows higher turgor to develop in those cells that are undergoing expansion (i.e. developing succulence).

(c) There appears to be no correlation between cell turgor and the water potential of expressed leaf sap, or of the hydroponic culture solution, despite a large range observed for each parameter. The range of turgor is similar to

Table 1 Measurements of the osmotic pressure of the hydroponic culture solution and of the expressed leaf sap in comparison to the turgor pressure of epidermal cells of *Suaeda maritima*. The table also notes the relative ages of the leaves from the same plant (O.P., osmotic pressure measured in a vapour point osmometer)

Plant	Culture solution O.P. (MPa)	Leaf no.	Leaf sap O.P. (MPa)	Cell no.	Cell turgor (MPa)	Relative leaf age
A.	0.02	1	1.52	1	0.13	
				2	0.16	
				3	0.16	
B.	0.69	1	2.40	1	0.35	Younger
				2	0.35	
				3	0.38	
		2	2.42	1	0.33	Older
				2	0.35	
				3	0.34	
C.	0.80	1	1.85	1	0.06	Younger
				2	0.06	
D.	0.80	1	3.64	1	0.11	Younger
				2	0.12	
		2	3.76	1	0.07	Older
				2	0.12	
				3	0.05	
E.	2.01	1	2.94	1	0.28	
F.	2.03	1	2.55	1	0.12	Younger
				2	0.14	
		2	2.55	1	0.09	Older
				2	0.11	
				3	0.09	

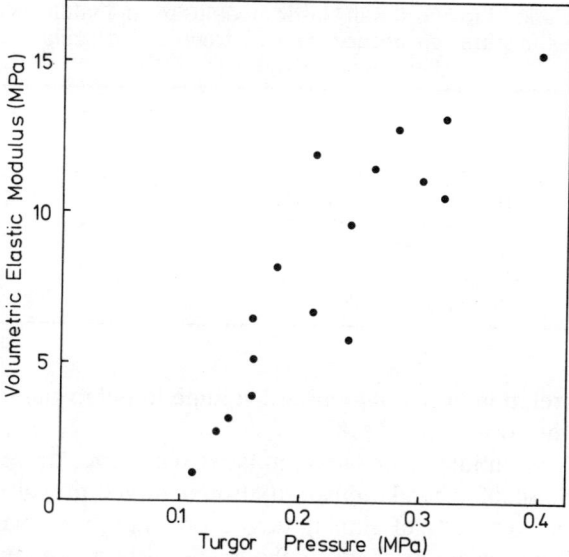

Figure 1   The pressure dependence of cell wall elastic modulus at 0 mM NaCl

that previously described for non-halophytes grown under uniform conditions and having only a small range of leaf-sap water potential.[4,5,6] It is therefore evident that the plant maintains its turgor within a certain limit. No measurement of root or shoot water potential was made, but it appears likely that a large water potential gradient exists from the culture solution to the leaf (up to 3 MPa; Table 1); this gradient is not reflected in cell turgor. The water potential of the leaf cell walls and intercellular spaces must, therefore, be rather low (i.e. rather similar to that of the cells). This suggests that this extracellular space may play an important role in osmoregulation, and that this could be the basis for the apparent increased turgor of young leaves. Certainly no information of the turgor can be obtained by measurement of expressed sap alone.

2   Cell wall elastic modulus (ε)

(a) There is a strong relationship between ε and cell turgor. This relation, which can be shown clearly for the giant cells of certain algae[2] has proved difficult to demonstrate in higher plants. The shape of the epidermal cells of S. maritima, however, allow clear demonstration of this relationship. The same relationship occurs for plants grown both in the absence of NaCl (Figure 1) and in its presence (data not presented).

Table 2 The relationship of cell wall elastic modulus (ε) and salt induced succulence. Due to the strong pressure dependence of ε, data from cells of similar turgor were used (between 0.25 and 0.35 MPa)

Culture solution salt conc. (mM NaCl)	Range of cell volumes (pl)	No. of plants used	No. of cells used	Elastic modulus (±S.D) (MPa)
0	110–143	4	5	11.8 ± 1.1
100	337–682	2	6	11.1 ± 2.8
150	67–873	2	5	10.9 ± 2.1

(b) The correlation between ε and cell volume found in giant celled algae,[2] however, was not observed.

(c) There is no influence of salt-stimulated succulence on cell wall elastic modulus. Because of the relationship between turgor pressure and ε, data were collected from cells of similar turgor pressure from plants grown in different salt concentrations. Table 2 shows that within experimental error ε was unchanged by salt concentration despite a large variation of cell volumes. (The increase in cell volume of salt-treated plants reflects the development of succulence of the tissue—but only qualitatively—too few cells are included to provide quantitative data.)

3 Cell membrane hydraulic conductivity (Lp)

(a) From the limited data obtained, there appears to be no change in the Lp of the cell membranes accompanying the change in morphology (Table 3). The Lp values of 0.3 to 4.3 × 10^{-7} m.s^{-1} MPa^{-1} obtained were similar to those measured for non-halophytic plants[4,5,6] and of a comparable scatter.

Table 3 The relationship of cell membrane hydraulic conductivity (Lp) and salt-induced succulence

Culture solution salt conc. (mM NaCl)	Cell no.	No. of relaxation experiments	Cell turgor (MPa)	Relaxation half-times (±S.D) (sec)	Hydraulic conductivity (±S.D) (m.sec^{-1} MPa^{-1})
0	1	3	0.12	3.1 ± 0.3	1.9 ± 0.4 (×10^{-7})
	2	4	0.18	22.3 ± 2.2	0.3 ± 0.03 (×10^{-7})
100	1	8	0.48	2.5 ± 0.4	1.9 ± 0.5 (×10^{-7})
150	1	1	0.10	6.0	4.3 (×10^{-7})
	2	8	0.11	13.0 ± 3.0	1.9 ± 0.5 (×10^{-7})
	3	6	0.15	9.1 ± 2.9	2.0 ± 0.4 (×10^{-7})

References

1. A. R. Yeo and T. J. Flowers, *J. Exp. Bot.*, **31**, 1171 (1980).
2. U. Zimmermann and E. Steudle, *Adv. Bot. Res.*, **6**, 45 (1978).
3. D. Husken, E. Steudle and U. Zimmermann, *Plant Physiol.*, **61**, 158 (1978).
4. E. Steudle, J. A. C. Smith and U. Luttge, *Plant Physiol.*, **66**, 1155 (1980).
5. K.-H Buchner, U. Zimmermann and F. W. Bentrup, *Planta.*, **151**, 95 (1981).
6. A. D. Tomos, E. Steudle, U. Zimmermann and E.-D. Schulze, *Plant Physiol.*, in press (1981).

Water relations and resistance mechanisms in bacteria

G. W. Gould
Unilever Research Laboratory, Bedford, UK

Summary

Although structurally simple, some vegetative bacteria avoid water loss in environments of widely varying water activities by the intracellular accumulation of specific amino acids at concentrations sufficient to balance the osmolality of the external medium. If this osmoregulation mechanism is overcome, and water loss occurs, then metabolism is arrested and under certain conditions cell resistance, e.g. to heat, increases, sometimes many hundred-fold. Such cells become superficially spore-like, and it now seems likely that in the endospore forms of bacteria, such water loss from the central compartment of the cell, and then maintenance of a low water level whatever the environmental a_w, is a major factor in their dormancy and enormous resistance to heat.

Bacteria are prokaryotes and are therefore morphologically simple, uncompartmented, normally unicellular, and therefore always in intimate contact and tending to osmotic equilibrium with their environment. However, in order to metabolize and multiply, the vegetative forms of bacteria must maintain a high intracellular water content whatever the environmental osmolality, and osmoregulatory mechanisms have therefore evolved that very effectively ensure this.

The major mechanism involves the cell synthesizing or accumulating from the environment, free amino acids to an intracellular concentration sufficient to balance the external osmotic pressure, thus avoiding water loss.

In non-halophilic bacteria, the most common osmoregulatory amino acids are glutamic acid, γ-amino butyric acid and proline, the latter being used by the most osmotolerant organisms,[1] and rising to well over molar in the cytoplasm of such bacteria growing in media of sufficiently low a_w. Adaptation to low a_w can occur remarkably quickly, for example, in response to transfer to medium containing 1 M salt, the proline concentration within cells of *Bacillus subtilis* rose more than 100-fold, and growth then recommenced, all within about 50 minutes.[2]

Enzymes within the cell continue to operate in the presence of high levels of the amino acids, whereas the extracellular solute would often inhibit them, hence such intracellular osmoregulatory substances have been termed 'compatible solutes'.[3]

Exactly what triggers the osmoregulatory response is still not known. The response is certainly to some parameter related to water loss, or potential water loss from the cell, rather than to the environmental a_w or osmolality *per se*. This is clear because externally added solutes that do *not* readily penetrate the cell membrane (e.g. sodium chloride, sucrose) and which therefore tend to remove water from the cell osmotically, elicit the response, whereas solutes that readily penetrate the membrane, and therefore remove water less effectively (e.g. glycerol), do not.

If bacteria are osmotically dehydrated beyond the level that can be combatted by the cell's osmoregulatory system, then metabolism and growth are, of course, inhibited. In a sense the cells become dormant. Interestingly, they may also become very resistant to heat. For example, the heat resistance of cells of some *Salmonella* species was increased by about 700-fold by suspension in non-permeant solutes that withdrew water and 'plasmolysed' the cells.[4]

Bacteria with depleted intracellular pools of low molecular weight solutes were made more resistant to heat by suspension in non-permeant solutes, than were bacteria with enriched pools, suggesting again that removal of water from the cytoplasm was more important in imposing heat resistance than the lowering of a_w per se.[5]

The large increases in heat resistance that can be brought about by osmotic dehydration of vegetative bacteria has led to attempts being made to establish links with the enormous heat resistance that is typical of bacterial endospores. These cells remain resistant and extremely dormant, even in pure water, and maintain their resistance unchanged for many years.

That a low water content in the central core of the spore contributes to resistance is indicated, but not proven, by a number of observations. For example, when spores germinate their heat resistance falls, commonly more than 10^4-fold within a minute or two. However, if the just germinated spores are quickly suspended in solutions of non-penetrating solutes, their heat resistance can be completely reimposed.[6] The longer the time lag between the initiation of germination and the resuspension in non-permeant solute, the less is the consequent rise in heat resistance, probably reflecting the rising level of low molecular weight pool components in the germinated cells.

It used to be thought that calcium dipicolinate (pyridine-2,6-dicarboxylate), which is present at levels as high as 10% of dry weight, and is situated in the central core of the spore, was directly involved in the heat resistance mechanism of these cells. However, the isolation of dipicolinate—negative, low calcium, yet fully heat resistant mutant spores[7] has made this idea untenable.

Rather, more recent evidence has implicated the cortex of the spore, which is the region surrounding the central core, in somehow controlling resistance. For instance, hydrolysis of cortex which is composed of loosely cross-linked, electronegative peptidoglycan polymer, by lysozyme, reduces spore heat resistance: mutant spores with defective cortexes are heat sensitive.[8]

If the cortex does protect the underlying core components from denaturation by heat, then it is 'acting at a distance' from those normally heat sensitive components of the spore. Recent interest has therefore centred around the possible mechanisms by which this may occur.

Current hypotheses include the possibility of a cortex that squeezes water out of the core either by contraction[9] or by expansion.[10] Partial dehydration may result from anisotropic expansion[11] brought about by partial hydrolysis of the peptidoglycan or by cation exchange, or from radial growth of the cortex during spore formation and consequent generation of pressure on the core and dehydration through 'reverse osmosis'.[12] Alternatively, the core may be kept low in water simply by being in osmotic equilibrium with the surrounding cortex, which contains the electronegative peptidoglycan and, presumably, counterions;[13] however dielectric measurements indicate the presence of 'mobile ions' in the cortex of some, but not all, types of spores.[14]

The variety of mechanisms suggested highlights the considerable fundamental interest and practical importance of spore resistance. It also highlights the major current problem, which is the lack of sound information concerning the actual state of macromolecules, ions and water in the various compartments within a heat resistant spore in water.

References

1. J. C. Measures, *Nature Lond.*, **257**, 398 (1975).
2. G. W. Gould and J. C. Measures, *Phil. Trans. Roy. Soc. B.*, **278**, 151 (1977).
3. A. D. Brown and J. R. Simpson, *J. Gen. Microbiol.*, **72**, 589 (1972).
4. J. E. L. Corry, *J. Appl. Bact.*, **37**, 31 (1974).
5. G. W. Gould and G. J. Dring, *Spore Research 1976*, Ed. A. N. Barker et al. 421–430. Academic Press (1977).
6. G. J. Dring and G. W. Gould, *Biochem. Biophys. Res. Commun.*, **66**, 202 (1975).
7. R. S. Hanson, M. V. Curry, J. V. Garner and H. O. Halvorson, *Can. J. Microbiol.*, **18**, 1139 (1972).
8. Y. Imae and J. L. Strominger, *J. Bact.*, **126**, 907 (1976).
9. J. C. Lewis, N. S. Snell and H. K. Burr, *Science. N.Y.* **132**, 544 (1960).
10. G. Alderton and N. S. Snell, *Biochem. Biophys. Res. Commun.*, **10**, 139 (1963).
11. A. D. Worth, *Adv. Microbial Physiol.*, **15**, 1 (1977).
12. J. E. Algie, *Current Microbiol.*, **3**, 287 (1980).
13. G. W. Gould and G. J. Dring, *Nature Lond.*, **258**, 402 (1975).
14. E. L. Carstensen, R. E. Marquis, S. Z. Child and G. R. Bender, *J. Bact.*, **140**, 917 (1979).

Towards a physical chemical characterization of compatible solutes

R. Gareth Wyn Jones and Anne Pollard
University College of North Wales

Summary

While concentrated solutions of glycinebetaine and other compatible solutes do not inhibit a variety of enzymic activities and in certain cases may partially protect the enzymes from NaCl and KCl inhibition, they do not bind to the proteins. It seems probable that these solutes are excluded from the hydration sphere of protein. The close correlation between the behaviour of stabilizing (see Timasheff et al. in this volume) and compatible solutes is noted.

With the exception of the Halobacteriaceae, the accumulation of organic relatively non-toxic, solutes is a nearly ubiquitous response of cells to hyperosmotic stress. Following Borowitzka and Brown, these are usually termed compatible solutes. They are primarily accumulated as osmotica in the cytoplasmic compartments of cells and contribute to the regulation of cell volume and/or turgor pressure (see Tomos and Zimmermann, in pp. 256–261).

In relation to this workshop the major question posed by this phenomenon is whether the physico-chemical properties of compatible solutes tell us anything about the 'state' of cellular (cytoplasmic) water and its relationship to the structural stability and functional integrity of cellular constituents. Although many putative compatible solutes have been described, they can be grouped (albeit crudely) into two main groups; polyhydric alcohols and their derivatives, and small zwitterions typified by proline and glycinebetaine (N,N',N''-trimethylglycine). Several of this latter group are methylated quaternary ammonium or tertiary sulphonium compounds. While this paper will concentrate on these dipolar ions, it must be recognized that under extreme hyperosmotic conditions glycerol is the solute utilized.

Enzyme interactions with glycinebetaine and related compounds

Unlike NaCl and KCl, glycinebetaine and proline, at concentrations of 500mM, do not inhibit a range of enzymes *in vitro*.[1] In some cases, but not all, glycinebetaine also ameliorates the inhibitory effects of the inorganic salts. Using barley malic dehydrogenase (decarboxylating) as a model enzyme, this protective action was found apparently not to depend on glycinebetaine binding to the enzyme[2] but to be mediated through the solvent water. The protective effect was modulated by altering the degree of methylation of the charged nitrogen (Figure 1). On a molar basis the protective action of proline and glycerol in this system closely resembled that of dimethylglycine in Figure 1. An identical rank order of protection was reported by Shkedy-Vinkler and Avi-Dor[3] studying a moderately halotolerant bacterium.

In view of Schobert's hypothesis of protein stabilization by solute binding, glycinebetaine–protein interactions were further tested by two techniques. Binding of solute to purified bovine serum albumin (BSA) and pig heart glutamine-oxaloacetate transaminase (an enzyme partly protected against NaCl inhibition by glycinebetaine) was assessed by equilibrium gel filtration.[4] Typical results are shown in Figure 2. No evidence of binding was obtained. A second technique was developed, utilizing the colligative nature of freezing point depression (ΔT). It was reasoned that 'binding' of solute to protein should be manifested by a less than additive ΔT of mixtures of BSA (2, 7 and 20% w/v) and glycinebetaine and proline (100–900 mmol kg^{-1}) compared with individual solutions. Representative data, shown in Figure 3, demonstrated that

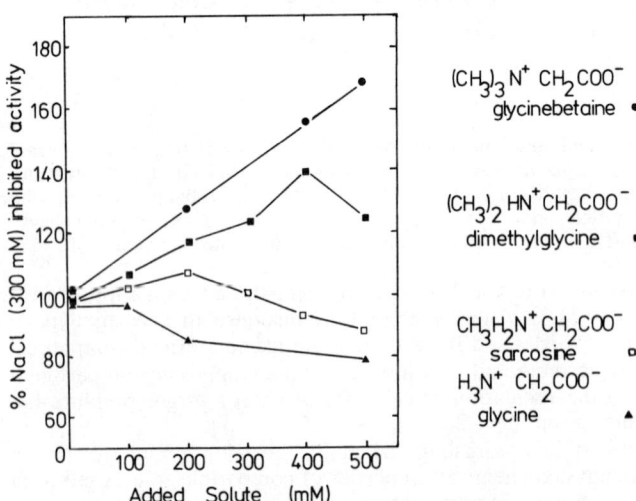

Figure 1 Comparative effects of progressively methylated derivatives of glycine on the inhibition of barley leaf malate dehydrogenase (decarboxylating) by 300 mM NaCl[1]

Towards a physical chemical characterization of compatible solutes

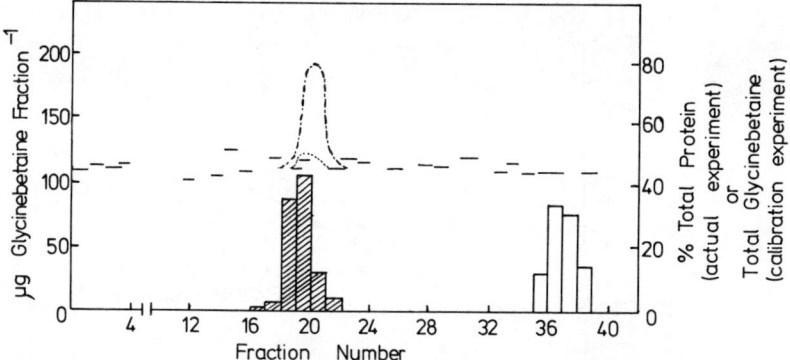

Figure 2 The equilibrium of filtration profile from a Sephadex G 25 column, equilibrated with 1 mM glycinebetaine, during elution of 1 mg BSA in 1 mM glycinebetaine. BSA elution peak ▨, glycinebetaine elution peak (□) when solute (0.1 mmol) run independently. The lines above protein peak represent the hypothetical glycinebetaine concentrations that would result from the binding of 1 mol (····) and 10 mols (·—·—·—·—·) of glycinebetaine per mol of BSA. Actual glycinebetaine values from column eluate shown as (–)[4]

the experimentally determined ΔT of mixtures *exceeded* the additive values of the components. This is interpreted as indicating a partial exclusion of the solute from the hydration sphere (domain) of the protein in sharp contrast to the binding hypothesis, but in agreement with early data.[5]

Some solution properties of these solutes

The data generated further interest in the solution chemistry of these and related solutes. Both glycinebetaine and proline are extremely water soluble (respectively 157 g/100 ml H_2O 19 °C, 162 g/100 ml H_2O 25 °C; cf. glycine 25 g/100 ml H_2O 25 °C).[6] Early studies on the solution properties of a wide variety of amino acids are summarized by Edsall.[7] Unlike glycine, its betaine and proline have activity and osmotic coefficients markedly exceeding unity of concentrations below 1 molal. Both are dipolar with no net charge at physiological pHs and have dielectric increments in water at 25° in the range 18–26. The difference between the calculated and observed apparent molal volumes, termed 'electrostriction', was smaller with glycinebetaine than glycine or proline; this difference being attributed to a smaller interaction of the former with solvent water. More recently the entropies and heat capacities of transfer of mono-, di-, and trimethylglycine in relation to water–solute interactions were studied.[8] Despite being highly polar, the betaine, unlike unsubstituted amino acids, had a negative heat capacity of transfer resembling apolar molecules. The authors suggest that the solute might have strong water 'structure-building' properties but in a subsequent paper,[9] a study of the temperature dependence of the viscosity B coefficient failed to confirm this. These data showed glycine to be strongly solvated and a water 'structure-breaker' but that these effects diminished with progressive methylation. Glycinebetaine interaction with the solvent was small with little indication of 'structure-making'. The compound was unusual in having an apparent molal volume which decreased with increasing concentration at low temperature. Kozak *et al.*[10] used early activity coefficient data to examine solute–solute and solute–solvent interactions

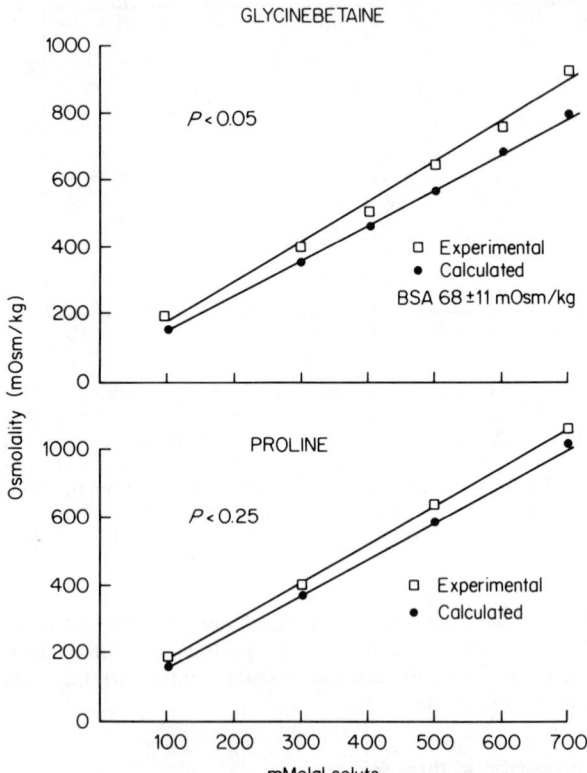

Figure 3 The relationship of the osmolalities of solutions of glycine–betaine and proline (100–700 mmol kg^{-1} in bovine serum albumin (20% w/v) (experimental values, □) with the calculated osmolalities from the summation of values from separate solutions of the equivalent molality (calculated values, ●) values determined by freezing point depression (ΔT) in an Advanced Instruments Osmometer calibrated against standard NaCl solutions and using the relationship, ΔT for osmolal solution equals -1.858 °C

for a range of biologically important solutes; some evidence for glycinebetaine–solvent interactions was deduced.

Concluding discussion

These data lead to the speculation that the various glycinebetaine–water interactions—hydrophilic, hydrophobic, cationic and anionic—are so balanced that the net effect on the thermodynamic state of the water is small but with some enhancement of 'structure'. Perhaps it should be considered a 'benign' solute. Thus it may behave in a similar way but for different physical reasons, to the polyols, whose nearest neighbour oxygen–oxygen distances correspond to those of oxygen in water.[11] However, the adsorption isotherm of glycinebetaine (Eden and Pethig, unpublished data) indicate a strong and markedly hysteretic binding of 1 to 3 mols of H_2O per mol of solute. But it must be assured that in solution this hydration does not grossly perturbate the surrounding water.

In this volume Timasheff et al., pp. 48–50, discuss the role of solvation in the stabilization and destabilization of protein structure, concluding that stabilizing compounds are excluded from the domain of proteins allowing their preferential hydration. Our evidence on glycinebetaine concurs. Further, the close identity of the stabilizing (salting-out) compounds of Timasheff and the compatible solutes found in biological systems suggests that there is a general correspondence.

Additionally, consideration of the molecular architecture of glycinebetaine (essentially tetramethyl ammonium cation and carboxylate) in relation to the position of those moieties in the lyotropic series[12] suggests that it should salt-out (stabilize) proteins. Indeed this solute (and to lesser extent proline) effectively salt-out lactoglobulin near its isoelectric point (Wyn Jones and Owen unpublished data).

In addition to providing some physico-chemical basis for 'compatibility', these concepts imply that these solutes not only act as colligative osmotic solutes in the bulk water of the cytoplasm (cf. Clegg, pp. 365–385) but may also contribute to macromolecular stability; the maintenance of metabolic integrity being important in addition to any specific requirement for volume and/or pressure regulation. Further, these small and readily modified molecules could be utilized as probes for studies on protein stability and hydration. Finally it must be noted that the maintenance of membrane semi-permeability is as biologically important as protein stability, although not discussed,[13] and that any specifically biochemical constraints on solute levels must be superimposed on this broad physico-chemical picture.

References

1. A. Pollard and R. G. Wyn Jones, *Planta*, **144**, 291 (1979).
2. B. Schobert, *J. Theor. Biol.*, **68**, 17 (1977).
3. C. Shkedy-Vinkler and Y. Avi-Dor, *Biochem. J.*, **150**, 219 (1975).
4. J. P. Hummel and W. J. Dreyer, *Biochim. Biophys. Acta*, **63**, 530 (1962).
5. M. London, J. Fuld, E. Crane and J. J. Marymont, *Arch. Biochem. Biophys.*, **122**, 439 (1967).
6. R. M. C. Dawson, D. C. Elliott, W. H. Elliott and K. M. Jones, Data for Biochemical Research. 2nd Edn. (1969).
7. J. T. Edsall, in *The Chemistry of Amino Acids and Proteins*, ed. C. L. A. Schmidt 2nd edition. C. C. Thomas, Springfield, (1944).
8. M. Kennerley and H. J. V. Tyrrell, *J. Chem. Soc.*, (A) 607 (1968).
9. H. J. V. Tyrrell and M. Kennerley, *J. Chem. Soc.*, (A) 2724 (1968).
10. J. J. Kozak, W. S. Knight and Walter Kauzmann, *J. Chem. Phys.*, **48**, 675 (1968).
11. D. T. Warner, *Nature*, **196**, 1055 (1962).
12. P. H. Von Hippel and T. Schleich, in *Structure and Stability of Biological Macromolecules*, eds. S. N. Timasheff and G. D., Fasman, Dekker, pp. 417–574 (1969).
13. R. G. Wyn Jones and A. Pollard, in *Encyclopedia of Plant Physiology*, N.S. Vol. 12 Plant Nutrition, eds. A. Lauchli and R. Bieleski, (1982).

The relation between ionic selectivity and enhanced interactions of water molecules in Halobacterium marismortui

Ben-Zion Ginzburg and Margaret Ginzburg
The Hebrew University of Jerusalem, Israel

Summary

H. marismortui, a unique form of life, has a high power of selective discrimination between K^+ and Na^+. It is suggested that enhanced interactions of water molecules are involved in the molecular basis of the selectivity. Evidence for the existence of such enhancement comes from NMR and DSC measurements.

Halobacterium marismortui, a species of halophilic bacteria isolated from the Dead Sea, seems to be a unique form of life as compared either to mesophilic forms or to other halophilic organisms. *H. marismortui* possesses very high powers of selective discrimination between K and Na. The selectivity $(K_{in}/Na_{in})/(K_{out}/Na_{out})$ can exceed 20,000. This high selectivity is maintained even when there is no measurable output of metabolic energy, under conditions when there is fast communication between the inside and outside phases. It is suggested that the retention of the K is a property of the bulk of the cytoplasm rather than of the membrane. K does not appear to be bound by any special compound such as a macrocyclic antibiotic, since the dry-weight content of the bacteria is insufficient to accommodate the amount of material that would be needed to bind all the K present. Nor can there be direct binding by the cell proteins, since the ratio of K to amino-acid residues ranges around 1.2 ions per amino acid residue. It is therefore suggested that *water* might be involved in the molecular basis of the selectivity for K in these organisms. On theoretical grounds, it has been postulated that if a macromolecular surface has an ordering effect on the water in its neighbourhood, such 'structured' water might prefer K to Na ions because of the better fit of the former within the water lattice.

I wish to demonstrate the chief pieces of evidence in favour of the interaction of water molecules in *Halobacterium marismortui*. The subject has been reviewed quite recently.[1]

Figure 1 shows the response of the cell ions to a drastic reduction in the rate of metabolism (to less than 3% of the control) which was brought about by subjecting cells to low temperature. The K concentration did not change significantly during a 24-h period, even though the K gradient across the cell membrane is enormous. On the other hand, the cells lost about the same amounts of Na and Cl against the concentration gradient. Thus, high ionic concentration gradients were maintained even when the output of metabolic energy was very low.

Table 1 shows the results of experiments in which cells of *H. halobium* and *H. marismortui* were deprived of organic nutrients. Logarithmic-phase cells were suspended in solutions composed only of inorganic salts. The cell suspension was kept vigorously aerated and the pH maintained at 7.0. After 4 h of resuspension, net protein changes stopped altogether; oxygen uptake stopped, there was no further change in pH of the medium. These observations were taken to signify that endogenous metabolism had fallen to a very low rate. We see from the table that the cells of *H. halobium* lost 2/3 of their potassium, and the Na concentration increased almost to the

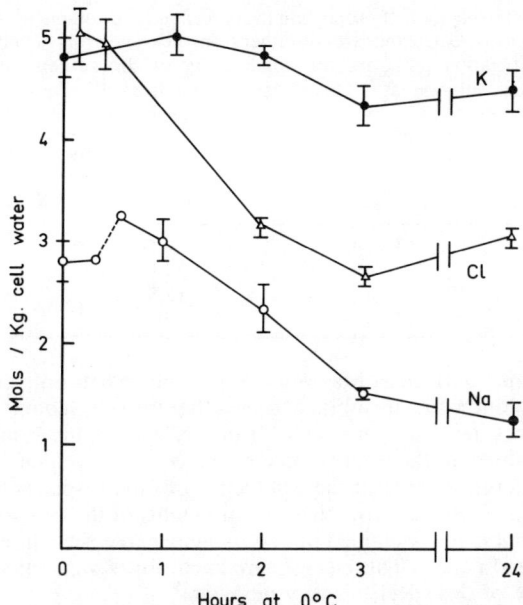

Figure 1 Effect of incubation at 0 °C on cell ion concentrations of *Halobacterium sp*. The cultures were aerated for the first 3 h. For composition of medium, *see* ref. [8]. pH of incubation medium maintained at 7.0. Mean of seven experiments. ● K; ○ Na; △ Cl (reproduced from *J. Membrane Biology*, **5**, 1971, by permission of Springer-Verlag, Heidelberg)

level of the outside solution. Thus, cells of *H. halobium* grown in dim light require an organic substrate to energize the metabolism needed to maintain their ionic gradients. This is of course typical of all other cells.

Cells of *H. marismortui* behaved quite differently. The K concentration fell only slightly, and the gradients of Na and Cl increased even though oxygen uptake and glycolysis were reduced to 1% or less of their usual values. These starved cells can be kept for 3 weeks without important changes in their ionic composition.

Secondly, cells of the two species differ in their passive permeability properties. By

Table 1 Effect of starvation on cell ion concentrations of *Halobacterium halobium* and *H. marismortui*

		Cell ion concentrations, Molal	
Species	Culture	K^+	Na^+
H. halobium	logarithmic	4.5	0.85
	starved (24 h)	1.4	3.3
H. marismortui	logarithmic	3.7	2.0
	starved (24 h)	3.0	1.1

Table 2 Determination of proportion (as percentage) of volume of suspension occupied by cells. Calculations made either from measurements of pellet volume after centrifugation, or from the conductivity of the suspension and the corresponding solution at 20 KHz (reproduced from *Biophysical Structure Mechanism*, **4**, 1978, by permission of Springer-Verlag, Heidelberg)

		Cell volume fraction %	
Species	Solution	Conductivity	Centrifugation
Yeast	40 mM	24.0	25.0
	4 M	37.9	40.9
H. halobium	4 M	12.5	13.0
H. marismortui	4 M	9.3	22.4

using an equation first derived by Maxwell, it is possible to determine whether cells are enclosed by a non-conducting membrane, or whether the cells seem to be 'transparent' to electrical currents, i.e. very permeable. If the cell membrane is impermeable, and therefore non-conducting, the total volume of the cells in a suspension can be calculated from the difference between the conductivity of the suspension and that of the suspending medium. Table 2 shows that measurements of the cell volume fraction of yeast and *H. halobium* cells obtained by conductivity agree with direct measurements made on centrifuged pellets. This lack of agreement for *H. marismortui* suggests that the cell membrane of this species is very permeable.

This conclusion is consistent with the permeability to organic materials shown in Table 3. It can be seen that *H. halobium* was not permeable to the organic molecules listed there. On the other hand, equilibration of the same compounds across the *H. marismortui* membrane took less than 100 sec. However, the compounds equilibrated with only about 40% of the cell-water. As there are no inner membranes within the bacterial cells, it has been suggested that the remaining 60% is not available to organic molecules. In other words, there must be more than one phase of water within the cell. Further evidence in favour of more than one phase has come from NMR measurements.[2] The visible intensity of water in the pellets of *H. marismortui* accounted for 101 ± 7% of the total water present. When the cells were cooled gradually down from 40 °C, the intensity of the signal did not change until −18 °C was reached. In the vicinity of −20° (the temperature at which the culture medium freezes) some freezing occurred, and only 40% of the initial signal could be observed. Since extracellular water accounts for 28% of the total water, it is concluded that, at −20°, all the extracellular water freezes together with 45% of the cellular water. Thus, the NMR data indicate that there are two or possibly three water environments.

The ratio of unfrozen water to protein is 7–10 mols H_2O per 100 g protein, or 3–4

Table 3 Determination of intercellular space of centrifuged pellets of *Halobacterium*, as determined by several carbohydrates. The bacteria were centrifuged at 12,000 g for 20 min. Intercellular water expressed as percent of total pellet water

		% intercellular water	
Compound	Molecular weight	H. halobium	H. marismortui
Blue Dextran	2,000,000	26.5	28.0
Inulin	7000	30.3	36–62
Sucrose	342	28.3	36–45
Fructose	180	27.5	38–66

Table 4 Molar heat of dehydration ($\Delta \bar{H}$) as measured by Differential Scanning Calorimetry in pellets of various cells (from ref. 3)

Cells	kJ mol^{-1} H$_2$O	
	Pellets	Supernatant
Human red blood	40.6	~41.0
H. halobium	46.2	~44.5
H. marismortui	50.4	~44.5

times more than has been found for several well defined proteins. If it is ruled out that exchange between the water environments is across a very tight membrane, it must be concluded that 55% of the cell-water has an average translational diffusion coefficient of 10^{-8} cm^2 sec^{-1} (3 orders of magnitude lower than that of aqueous solution). From the NMR of deuterated water, it can be concluded that the rotational motions of cellular water involve processes of reorientation with rates slower than 10^8 sec^{-1} (as compared with 10^{11} sec^{-1} for the rotational diffusion rate of pure water at 20°).

From differential scanning calorimetry it has been shown that the excess molar heat of dehydration $\Delta(\Delta\bar{H})$, in kJ mol^{-1} H$_2$O is -0.4, 1.7 and 6.0 for pellets of erythrocytes, H. halobium cells and H. marismortui cells respectively. $\Delta(\Delta\bar{H})$ is distributed over all the pellet water, which is partly intra-, partly extracellular. For the two bacterial species, about 30–50% of total pellet water is in free solution, i.e. there are no interactions with macromolecules, and thus the excess molar heat is nil. The rest of the cell water must have a $\Delta(\Delta\bar{H})$ of at least twice that indicated in the table, i.e. 3.4 and 12.0 kJ mol^{-1} H$_2$O. In H. marismortui there are 9.6 mols H$_2$O per 100 g protein. This is 3–4 times more than is usual with proteins. About 20% seems to be primary hydration water, i.e. H$_2$O molecules interacting with protein, while the rest shows enhanced interactions between the water molecules themselves.

References

1. M. Ginzburg, in *Energetics and Structure of Halophilic Microorganisms*, Ed. S. R. Caplan and M. Ginzburg, Elsevier, North-Holland (1978).
2. H. T. Edzes, Ph.D. thesis, University of Gronigen (1976).
3. B. Z. Ginzburg, *Thermochimica Acta*, in press.

Freezing injury and cold acclimation in plants

John V. Carter
University of Minnesota, USA

Summary

Intracellular and extracellular freezing of water in plant tissue can both result in injury. The nature of these injuries, as well as cold acclimation, the process by which overwintering plants avoid them, are briefly discussed. Solved and unsolved problems within these research areas are pointed out and suggestions about methods and areas in which future research might be fruitful are made.

Freezing injury

Plants can be damaged in several ways when ice forms within them. Intracellular freezing, invariably lethal to those plant cells in which it occurs in nature,[1] is fairly uncommon, no doubt occurring only after tissue water has undercooled to at least -5 °C or more if the freezing rate is fast.[2-5] More common is what has been termed secondary freezing injury.[6] In its most common form, ice nucleation occurs slightly below 0 °C, on the tissue surface, caused by a heterogeneous nucleator or by ice from another source such as airborne microcrystals, and propagates in intercellular spaces. Intracellular water permeates the plasma membrane and crystallizes on the developing ice front, the driving force being the difference in vapour pressure of the ice and the intracellular water which is still liquid. It is this combination of freeze-induced dehydration and accompanying low temperature which produces the injury referred to in this article as freeze-dehydration injury.

Cold acclimation

Physiological and biochemical changes which are triggered by environmental cues can transform certain plants into a state in which they can survive temperatures significantly below 0 °C. These changes are referred to as cold acclimation, which as would be expected of a trait crucial to the survival of a species, is complex. Because of its complexity there are several levels on which cold acclimation can be studied. One oft-used approach is to probe the mechanism of freezing injury, reasoning that coming to an understanding of freezing injury will simultaneously lead to an uncovering of the most critical aspect(s) of cold acclimation. Another path which has been followed is the measurement under acclimating conditions of changes in cellular concentrations of compounds suspected to be involved in cold acclimation. A third body of knowledge has built up around the nature of the environmental changes which are both necessary and sufficient to cause cold acclimation.

Solved and unsolved problems

The very large collection of correlative data, evident from a perusal of Levitt's book,[6] represents many solved problems and yet is itself a manifestation of a larger unsolved problem. Changes in sugars,[7] starch,[8] hormones,[9] lipid unsaturation,[10] cell wall thickness,[11] membrane fluidity,[12] ascorbic acid,[13] phospholipids,[14] total RNA[15] and rRNA[16] have been correlated with cold acclimation, to name a few. From this incomplete list it is evident that much has been learned about changes which take place during cold acclimation. However, this type of information makes it appear that we know more than we do, because of at least two factors. First, determination of changes in a given component or property averaged over an entire tisssue masks potentially important changes that it could have in certain cell types and, even more importantly, in different locations within a single cell.

Second, we don't know whether many of these changes are essential for cold hardiness or whether they are responses to environmental changes making it possible for better growth under new conditions. If we are to understand the mechanism(s) of cold acclimation, control experiments should be carried out to test the essentiality to cold acclimation of any correlation which is discovered. One approach to this question has been to expose related plant varieties, differing in cold acclimating ability, to the same

Freezing injury and cold acclimation in plants

acclimating conditions and examine in each the correlation in question. If it exists in the least acclimatable as well as in the most acclimatable variety, it has been argued that this is sufficient to show that it is not related to hardiness. An alternative and perhaps equally reasonable conclusion would be that the correlation is related to cold acclimation but that something else must also occur which does not occur in the least acclimatable variety. Another approach which has been used is to produce the change of interest by a method not involving environmental alterations to see if a change in cold hardiness of the plant also occurs. Great specificity is an obvious prerequisite of any such method, or conclusions drawn from the results cannot be unambiguous.

To conclude this section, in my view some of the chief unsolved problems are: (1) Which of the many correlations that have been found are essential to cold acclimation? (2) Is there an order in which the changes essential to cold acclimation must occur and if so what is it? At least, what happens first? (3) What is the critical factor in freeze–dehydration injury? (4) Does the same factor remain the most critical throughout the annual life cycle of an overwintering plant? (5) How important is avoidance of tissue-water undercooling? (6) By what means does the water which undergoes deep undercooling (down to $-45\ °C$) remain liquid while in close proximity to extracellular ice? (7) Do phase transitions occur in any cell membranes of overwintering plants at temperatures close to their killing temperature?

Suggestions for future research

Significant progress in plant cold hardiness research can be made by developing an understanding of freezing injury, particularly freeze–dehydration injury. Death due to freeze–dehydration results over a narrow temperature range, which is to say that, at any stage of development, plants have well-defined killing points. For example, fully acclimated *Solanum commersonii* can withstand freezing at $-2\ °C$ and subsequent slow cooling to $-12\ °C$, but dies at $-13\ °C$.[17] Thus, seeking the source of freeze-dehydration injury requires consideration of processes which exhibit relatively high cooperativity.[3] Since death due to freeze-dehydration injury is not caused by the initial freezing of tissue water, that very cooperative process can be eliminated. Other cooperative processes which should be considered are: (1) low temperature denaturation of proteins; (2) aggregation of highly concentrated proteins; (3) membrane lipid phase transitions; (4) mechanical rupture of plasma membranes due to adhesion to developing ice crystals.

First let us consider membrane phase transitions. Both decreasing temperature and decreasing water content can affect the intermolecular ordering of membrane lipids dispersed in water. Since permeability is much lower through gel phase lipid bilayers than through liquid-crystalline or mixed gel-liquid-crystalline phase bilayers it has long been felt that this phase transition in a plasma membrane would be potentially harmful to a plant cell undergoing freeze-dehydration since it would slow the efflux of water from the cell making intracellular freezing more likely. The entire liquid-crystalline-to-gel phase transition in a biomembrane typically takes place over a $10°$ to $20\ °C$ range because of the diversity of fatty acids and head groups present, and thus is not very cooperative. However, the final stages of the transition, in which conversion to gel phase is completed, can occur in a small temperature range and there is reason to believe that it is this portion of the phase transition which is potentially damaging.[18] Research is needed in this area because there is as yet no unambiguous demonstration that gel-to-liquid-crystalline phase transitions occur in membranes of cold hardy plant cells.

When cell water content is reduced below a certain value, a bilayer to hexagonal phase transition occurs, in which the phospholipids are distributed in long, discontinuous cylinders.[19] Such a transition could produce the electrolyte leakage which is associated with freeze-dehydration injury as well as with imbibition of highly desiccated plant material.

While these phase transitions are reversible, death is not. Thus they themselves could not individually or collectively be the primary cause of death by freeze–dehydration; if they cause other changes which are irreversible they could still be labelled as prime suspects, however. Intracellular freezing of water trapped in a cell whose plasma membrane lipid has totally gone to gel phase is an attractive hypothesis, but it must be pointed out that many plants have killing points at temperatures low enough so that all but a small fraction of freezable water has already frozen extracellularly. Release of toxic materials such as proteases which would result from the loss of compartmentalization attending a bilayer–hexagonal phase transition could result in lethal injury.

Next, let us focus on items (1) and (2) from the above list of cooperative processes. Protein denaturation, both high- and low-temperature induced, is a cooperative process which at low concentrations is reversible. At higher concentrations aggregation, also apparently cooperative, accompanies denaturation, rendering it irreversible. These related processes are central to Levitt's hypothesis, also called the SH hypothesis, advanced as an explanation of freeze–dehydration injury almost 20 years ago.[20,6]

The SH hypothesis has proved difficult to verify. Using purified ribulose-1,5-bisphosphate carboxylase (RuBPCase) it has been shown that denaturation-aggregation does occur both in response to freeze–thaw treatment[21] and to dehydration at room temperature,[22] and that aggregation occurs through disulphide bond formation. However, it has not been shown *in vivo*. Nevertheless, the hypothesis is attractive because it accommodates much of what is known about freeze-dehydration injury; more research is warranted to determine whether it is valid.

An avenue of plant cold hardiness research that to my knowledge has not been explored is the effect of freeze-dehydration on the integrity of the cytoskeleton. Many researchers have verified that microtubules, microfilaments, and the microtrabecular lattice are depolymerized by exposure of cells to low temperature. Ordinarily this is reversible. However, if this depolymerization takes place at the same time that dehydration is occurring, as it would during freeze-induced dehydration, the monomer proteins can aggregate both homogeneously and with other denatured cytoplasmic proteins, and thus be rendered incapable of participation in reassembly upon warming. The resultant destruction of the cytoskeleton would certainly constitute serious injury. One indication that this scenario may have some validity is that cessation of cytoplasmic streaming is a good indicator of lethal freeze-dehydration injury, and cytoplasmic streaming is known to involve at least a part of the cytoskeleton. Also, suggestive evidence exists that microtubule depolymerization may be associated with chilling injury.[23] Plant cold hardiness scientists have been warned to concentrate on membranes, especially the plasma membrane; indeed, the benefits of research on cytoplasmic components and their relationship to cold acclimation and/or freezing injury have been called into question.[24] Without negating the importance of membranes in both cold acclimation and freezing injury, it should be noted that the division between membrane and cytoplasm is not sharp. The proteinaceous cytoskeleton connects the plasma membrane with the various organellar membranes; it also compartmentalizes the cytoplasm. An hypothesis has been advanced that the cytoskeleton provides a matrix for cytoplasmic enzymes and substrates allowing the reaction sequences of which they are a part to be spatially linked,[25,26] so that the cytoplasm may be as ordered as are membranes. Because of connections between plasma membrane and cytoskeleton, any technique which purports to measure a property of the plasma membrane in an intact cell actually does not make a clear distinction between membranous and cytoplasmic properties. Learning whether cytoskeletal disassembly is associated with freeze-dehydration injury and whether cold acclimation retards or prevents it could constitute a significant advance in plant cold hardiness research.

References

1. D. Siminovitch and G. W. Scarth, *Can. J. Res.*, **C16**, 467 (1938).
2. C. R. Olien, *Barley: Patterns of Response to Freezing Stress*. A.R.S. U.S.D.A. Tech. Bull. No. 1558, pp 1–8 (1977).
3. M. J. Burke and C. Stushnoff, in *Stress Physiology in Crop Plants*, eds H. Mussell and R. C. Staples, Wiley-Interscience, New York, pp. 197–225 (1979).
4. M. J. Burke, L. V. Gusta, H. A. Quamme, C. J. Weiser and P. H. Li, *Ann. Rev. Plant Physiol.*, **27**, 507 (1976).
5. M. F. George and M. J. Burke, *Curr. Adv. Plant Sci.*, **8**, 349 (1976).
6. J. Levitt, *Responses of Plants to Environmental Stresses*, 2nd ed., Vol. I, Academic Press, New York, Ch. 6 (1980).
7. K. A. Santarius and H. Milde, *Planta*, **136**, 163 (1977).
8. J. Levitt, *ibid*, pp. 207–208.
9. M. Waldman, A. Rikin, A. Dorvat, and A. E. Richmond, *J. Exp. Bot.*, **26**, 853 (1975).
10. E. D. Gerloff, T. Richardson and M. A. Stahmann, *Plant Physiol.*, **41**, 1280 (1966).
11. N. P. A. Huner, J. P. Palta, P. H. Li and J. V. Carter, *Bot. Gaz.*, in press.
12. L. Vigh, L. I. Horvathm, D. Dudits and T. Farkas, *FEBS Letters*, **107**, 291 (1979).
13. I. D. Shmatok, *Fiziol. Rast.*, **5**, 341 (1958).
14. J. Levitt, *ibid*, pp. 193–196.
15. D. Siminovitch, B. Rheaume and R. Sachar, in *Molecular Mechanisms of Temperature Adaptation*, ed. C. L. Prosser, Pub. No. 84. Amer. Assoc. Adv. Sci. Washington, D.C. (1967).
16. M. DeVay and E. Paldi, *Plant Sci. Lett.*, **8**, 191 (1977).
17. H. H. Chen and P. H. Li, *Plant Physiol.*, **66**, 414 (1980).
18. J. V. Carter, *Cryo-Letters*, **1**, 408 (1980).
19. M. A. Toivio-Kinnucan and C. Stushnoff, *Cryobiol.*, **18**, 72 (1981).
20. J. Levitt, *H. Theoret. Biol.*, **3**, 355 (1962).
21. N. P. A. Huner and F. D. H. MacDowall, *Can. J. Biochem.*, **57**, 155 (1979).
22. N. P. A. Huner and J. V. Carter, *Can. J. Biochem*, in press.
23. A. Rikin, D. Atsmon and C. Gitler, *Plant & Cell Physiol.*, **21**, 829 (1980).
24. P. Steponkus, in *Stress Physiology in Crop Plants*, eds. H. Mussell and R. C. Staples, Wiley, New York, pp. 143–158 (1979).
25. J. J. Wolosewick and K. R. Porter, *J. Cell. Biol.*, **82**, 114 (1979).
26. B. E. Batten, H. J. Aalberg and E. Anderson, *Cell*, **21**, 885 (1980).

Membrane damage following freeze-induced dehydration

G. J. Morris
Culture Centre of Algae and Protozoa, Cambridge, UK

Summary

A model of membrane damage at low rates of cooling is discussed. During osmotic shrinkage there is evidence that an increase in membrane surface pressure occurs; the responses of the cellular membrane to this applied stress during freezing and thawing are discussed.

Introduction

During freezing cells are exposed to an osmotic stress, liquid water is removed from solution as ice and the residual aqueous solution becomes increasingly concentrated, upon thawing the reverse process occurs and the cell is diluted from a hypertonic to isotonic environment. Whilst there are many parallels between physiological water stress and freezing injury two important differences exist. First, during freezing the imposed stress is not simply osmotic, other variables including membrane phase separations, pH and gas solubility are changing simultaneously. Secondly, following the hypertonic exposure there is a subsequent dilution during thawing.

It is generally accepted that an early event of damage during freeze-induced dehydration is at the level of the cellular membrane. A current hypothesis of damage is presented schematically in Figure 1.[1-3] Exposure to hypertonic solutions induces osmotic shrinkage and assuming that the cell remains spherical during shrinkage an increase in the interfacial membrane pressure occurs. At a maximum packing density within the membrane any further increase in applied pressure may be accommodated by the loss of membrane components. If such loss does not exceed a critical value, then the cell is osmotically active during thawing. However, because of the loss of effective surface area it cannot return to its isotonic volume, which is determined by the intracellular solute concentration, and lysis may occur. At lower subzero temperatures a loss of membrane selective permeability may occur as the result of either the release of an excess amount of membrane or a second independent mechanism of injury such as membrane fusion, a mesomorphic lipid phase change or protein denaturation and such cells will not be osmotically responsive during thawing. This argument does not only apply to the plasmalemma, similar stresses must occur in the organelles of shrunken eukaryotic cells, which may be important for vacuoles and result in the release of lytic enzymes.

The above sequence is derived largely from theoretical considerations, whilst some experimental data can be interpreted as part of this sequence, the whole chain of events has not been demonstrated during freezing and thawing. This article will review some of the evidence which supports this hypothesis and will discuss future experimentation.

Increase in intramembrane pressure during dehydration

Using the technique of micropipette aspiration the resting tension of the plasma membrane of isolated plant protoplasts has been measured. For small amounts of osmotic shrinkage over short periods of time (seconds) the amount of material in the plane of the membrane is conserved and deformations follow an elastic relationship. Under more extensive conditions of dehydration the interfacial membrane tension remains constant possibly indicating the release of membrane material.[4]

In liposomes containing the probe 1,6-diphenyl 1,3,5-hexatriene (DPH) a direct relationship exists between the fluorescence anisotropy and surface pressure within the bilayer.[5] Osmotic shrinkage of liposomes containing DPH induces a decrease in fluorescence anisotropy (Figure 2) which is consistent with either an isothermal decrease in fluidity or an increase in lateral pressure. A minimum value is observed following shrinkage in 1.0 M NaCl, this change occurs within 15 sec of exposure and remains constant for 15 min. The phenomenon is reversible, liposomes shrunken in 1.0 M NaCl and then diluted exhibit a decrease in lateral pressure. Similar results have been reported for the hypotonic swelling of liposomes.[6] At higher concentrations of NaCl where direct membrane damage occurs there is a relaxation in lateral pressure. Extension of this technique to cell suspensions will determine the stresses imposed on the membrane during isothermal dehydration.

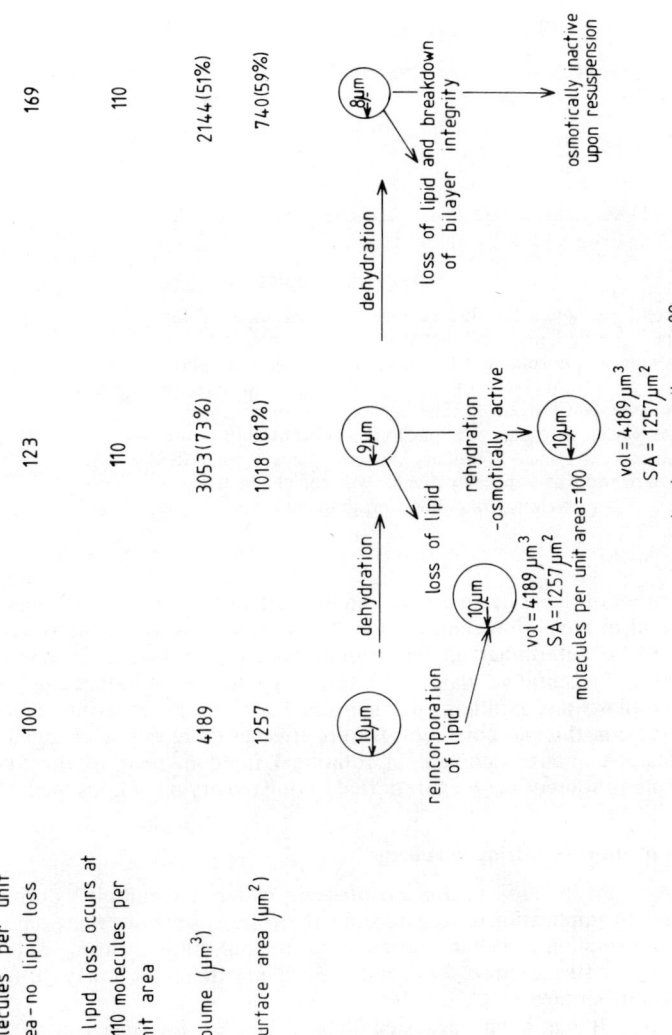

Figure 1 Schematic representation of cellular damage at low rates of cooling. The following assumptions are made: a spherical cell of diameter 20 μm with one limiting membrane which is composed entirely of phospholipid. During shrinkage and expansion the cell remains spherical and there is no physical limitation to shrinkage or any alteration in the intracellular solute concentration. The number of molecules per unit area of membrane is arbitrarily taken to be 100 in the isotonic condition, the maximum packing density is 110 molecules per unit area

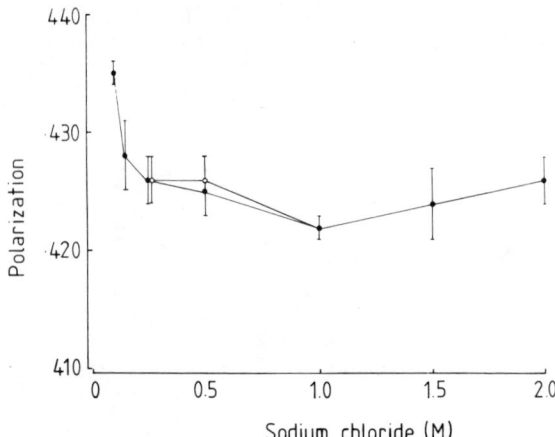

Fgiure 2 Steady-state fluorescence depolarization of the probe 1,6-diphenyl-1,3,5-hexatriene in liposomes of dipalmitoyl phosphatidylcholine:cholesterol:dicetyl phosphate at a mol ratio of 7:2:1, following exposure to hypertonic NaCl at 20 °C. The liposomes were prepared in 0.1 M NaCl. A range of liposome concentrations was examined at each sodium chloride level and the depolarization at zero absorbance was calculated using a maximum likelihood programme

Unfortunately, neither of the above methods can be used during freezing and thawing. It is thus essential to develop techniques which allow changes in the interfacial membrane tension to be determined in the frozen state; electron spin resonance (ESR) provides useful, if qualitative, data. ESR studies of the freeze-induced dehydration of plant protoplasts and multilamellar liposomes indicate an ordering of the phospholipid polar regions, this was not a temperature effect as there was no change in undercooled samples.[7] A similar decrease in rotational freedom near to the hydrophilic regions of phospholipids has been reported during the drying of liposomes.[8,9]

The response of the membrane during shrinkage

Assuming that there is an increase in applied pressure within a membrane during osmotic shrinkage and by implication during freezing, there are at least five reactions:
  1. Non-spherical contraction. A cell may attain osmotic equilibrium by losing water with a negligible change in surface area, for example a cell may flatten or it may shrink with projections from its surface.
  2. Protein 'bobbing'. It has been suggested that surface area changes may be accommodated by the movement of conical shaped membrane proteins into or away from the plane of the membrane.[10]
  3. Loss of bilayer structure. Significant changes in bilayer thickness, consistent with an elastic response do not occur. However, the demonstration of membrane lipid polymorphism[11] provides a mechanism for the conversion of some lipid to inverted micelles within a bilayer matrix. Such a transition would allow large changes in effective surface area.

4. Phase transitions from the liquid crystalline to gel state. In monolayer studies an increase in lateral pressure induces a condensation of the liquid phase to gel.[12]

5. Loss of membrane material. This does not invoke a novel or pathological mechanism, a dynamic equilibrium exists between cellular membranes and their environment, the stresses associated with freezing and thawing may alter the position of this equilibrium.[1] The solubility of phospholipids in aqueous solutions is low, in the order of 10^{-10} M,[13] and it is unlikely that at low temperatures a significant amount of lipid is released rapidly in a molecular form. Alternatively, larger units of membrane may be lost, the nature of which is dependent on the physical state of the membrane.

At temperatures above a lipid phase separation an evagination of membrane has been observed into hypertonic solutions.[3,4,14] At an intermediate stage these evaginations are attached to the cell membrane and are thus equivalent to reaction 1 above. However, as a more extreme reaction, they then may detach, it is not known what determines the release into the intra-or extracellular compartment. At temperatures below a lipid lateral phase separation, in which state gel and liquid-crystalline phases coexist, a preferential loss of gel material has been demonstrated from erythrocytes following hypertonic exposure at low temperature[15] or freezing.[16] Molecular packing faults occur at the gel to liquid-crystalline boundary.[17] Any increase in lateral pressure would then result in a subduction of gel material, which would then form vesicles when warmed above their phase transition temperature.

The response of the membrane during rehydration

During rehydration the intramembrane surface pressure will decrease (Figure 2). Assuming that membrane selective permeability is retained then reactions 1–4 are potentially reversible. In cells in which membrane material is released, lysis will occur before the cell retains its original volume;[2] however, in some cell-types a reincorporation of lipid may occur[3,4] and this may be an important strategy of freeze-tolerance. The specific mechanism is not understood, a lipid-transfer protein has been implicated[4] but for this to be effective during thawing it will have to have a high activity at subzero temperatures.

Conclusions

The hypothesis of damage discussed provides a description of freezing injury at the membrane level. If not correct in all details, or of universal application, it is, however, a scheme which is open to experimentation and will enable more sophisticated models to be developed.

References

1. J. J. McGrath, in *Effects of Low Temperatures on Biological Membranes* Eds. G. J. Morris and A. Clarke, Academic Press (1981).
2. P. L. Steponkus and S. C. Wiest, in *Low Temperature Stress in Crop Plants: the role of the membrane* Eds. J. M. Lyons, D. Graham and J. K. Raison, pp. 231–254, Academic Press (1979).
3. R. J. Williams and H. J. Hope, *Cryobiology*, **18**, 133 (1981).
4. P. L. Steponkus, J. Wolfe and M. F. Dowgert, in *Effects of Low Temperatures on Biological Membranes* Eds. G. J. Morris and A. Clarke, Academic Press (1981).
5. A. J. C. Fulford and W. E. Peel, *Biochim. Biophys. Acta*, **598**, 237 (1980).
6. A. Borochov and H. Borochov, *Biochim. Biophys. Acta*, **550**, 546 (1979).
7. J. Singh and R. W. Miller, *Plant Physiol.*, **66**, 349 (1980).

8. O. H. Griffith, P. J. Dehlinger and S. P. Van, *J. Membr. Biol.*, **15**, 159 (1974).
9. P. Jost, L. J. Libertini, V. C. Herbert and O. H. Griffith, *J. Mol. Biol.*, **57**, 77 (1971).
10. W. Niedermeyer, G. R. Parish and H. Moor, *Cytobiologie*, **13**, 364 (1976).
11. P. R. Cullis and B. de Kruijff, *Biochim. Biophys. Acta*, **559**, 399 (1979).
12. M. N. Jones, *Biological Interfaces*, Elsevier, Amsterdam. (1975).
13. C. Tanford, *The Hydrophobic Effect: Formation of micelles and biological membranes.* 2nd Edition, Wiley–Interscience, New York (1980).
14. J. P. Reeves and R. M. Dowben, *J. Cell. Physiol.*, **73** (1969).
15. T. Araki, *FEBS Letters*, **97**, 237 (1979).
16. S. Fujikawa, in *Effects of Low Temperatures on Biological Membranes.* Eds. G. J. Morris and A. Clarke, Academic Press (1981).
17. S. Marcelja and J. Wolfe, *Biochim. Biophys. Acta*, **557**, 24 (1979).

Physiological water stress: cellular components under extremes of physical conditions

Rainer Jaenicke
Universität Regensburg, West Germany

Summary

Among the cellular components most exposed to extreme environments, proteins and membrane constituents require maximum adaptation. Chemical mechanisms to cope with low water activity (halophily) and high temperature (thermophily) have been recently elucidated. Barophily is a more complex phenomenon requiring stabilization of assembly structures.

Living systems are sensitive to their environment in that they are only able to maintain metabolic activity and viability within certain limits of temperature, pressure, water activity, pH, nutrient concentration, etc. The respective limits of viability in natural habitats are: $-1 < T < 100\ °C$, $1 < p < 1200$ bar, ≤ 5.5 M salt (NaCl, KCl), $0 < \text{pH} < 12$, ≥ 0.2 g H_2O/g biomass (hydration).

A great variety of procaryotic and eucaryotic organisms has been observed that are capable of growth and multiplication under the given extremes of environmental conditions. Obviously there is no variable that has not been specifically selected for by certain organisms such that they require the extreme condition for their survival ('obligate' thermophiles, psychrophiles, halophiles, acidophiles, etc.). Ecological specialization as the consequence of selective pressure causes the most extreme environments to be characterized by minimum species diversity to the extreme that pure cultures with only a single species may be observed.[1,2]

In analysing mechanisms of resistance or adaptation, three points need consideration: (1) Environmental factors may be grouped into two categories depending on whether the intracellular conditions correspond to the extracellular ones or not (e.g. extremes of pH or salt[1-3]). (ii) Environmental factors may affect an organism directly and/or indirectly, through effects on other factors (e.g., T- or p-effects on the solubility of gases or the ionization of (poly-)electrolytes). (iii) Environmental extremes often refer to a whole set of conditions superimposed in an ill-defined way (e.g. deep sea as 'high pressure habitat'); as a consequence, conclusions from certain 'indicator molecules', like enzymes may be doubtful.

Physiological water stress

Specific environmental factors are not necessarily reflected by adaptive changes of the structure of intracellular cytoplasmic 'marker enzymes'; on the other hand, membranes and peripheral protein components exposed to the outside world are expected to be optimum marker systems for all environmental factors. However, so far it has not been possible to purify and crystallize such systems; therefore soluble enzymes have been generally applied to investigate the molecular basis of adaptation.

As indicated, adaptation is expected to be characterized by the anomalous stability of cell constituents relevant for viability. Progress in elucidating adaptation mechanisms at the enzyme level has been recently achieved with respect to temperature adaptation (thermophily) and adaptation to low water activity (halophily); concerning acidophilic, alkalinophilic, and barophilic organisms, studies at the molecular level are still in a preliminary state.[4]

I. Extremes of temperature

Evolutionary adaptation to extremes of temperature is connected with the structural and functional integrity of cell constituents, as well as their kinetic interplay in the metabolic network.

1. Increased thermostability (thermotolerance and thermophily) is commonly reflected by a flattening of the temperature profile of the free energy of denaturation causing a shift of the temperature maximum of conformational stability towards high temperatures ($T \leq 100\ °C$ at normal atmospheric pressure). In addition, the temperature profile of catalytic activity of thermophilic enzymes turns out to be shifted in thermophiles, eventually giving rise to 'cold inactivation' in a temperature range where the mesophilic counterparts still show enzyme activity.

Regarding their metabolism and their existence as aerobes, anaerobes, autotrophs, or heterotrophs, thermophiles do not differ significantly from their mesophilic counterparts. In general it is the intrinsic thermostability of cell components rather than enhanced turnover or specific stabilizing factors which is responsible for the increase in optimum temperature. Thermostability refers to a large number (if not all) of the proteins in a given thermophilic organism. The increase in the free energy of stabilization that is necessary to confer thermophilic characteristics ($\Delta G \sim 20\ kJ/mol$) represents only a relatively small increment in the total interaction energy of the molecule. Interaction energies of the given magnitude can arise in different ways from a limited number of aminoacid replacements providing supplemental non-covalent interactions without drastic perturbations in the overall backbone structure. The expected stabilizing effect of increased hydrophobic interactions cannot be convincingly demonstrated if statistical analysis involves aminoacid analyses of a great number of functionally unrelated enzymes from thermophilic and mesophilic organisms. Comparing the primary sequences and their respective three-dimensional structures of closely related enzymes (e.g., ferredoxins, haemoglobins, lactic dehydrogenases, etc.), thermostability is found to be enhanced by (i) the additive effect of small improvements at many locations in the three-dimensional structure, (ii) an increased number of ion-pairs, (iii) a significant preference for ala, thr, arg, instead of gly, ser, lys, and (iv) increased hydrophobicity whenever the aminoacid exchange is primarily internal and vice versa.

2. With respect to the *catalytic properties* of thermophilic enzymes at high temperature, the temperature dependence of the formation of the Michaelis complex has been shown to be important. Due to enthalpy–entropy compensation the free energy of enzyme ligand interaction is found to be only slightly temperature dependent. A comparison of homologous enzymes from species adapted to a wide range of temperatures reveal that ligand binding affinities and specific catalytic activity are conserved, so that cold- and warm-adapted organisms show similar metabolic rates at the respective temperatures of their natural habitats.

3. In contrast to the general requirement of thermostability for the majority of cell constituents of a thermophilic organism, *temperature sensitivity* only requires a small number of mutations. Apart from the effects on microorganisms, physiological phenomena in higher organisms such as cold inactivation, sweetening, growth limits, hypothermia, hibernation, etc. have been interpreted in terms of temperature sensitivity. Again hydrophobic interactions are assumed to be of importance, in addition to the ionization of groups involved in intermolecular ion pairs, and effects on the dielectric constant of the aqueous solvent which is significantly increased at low temperature. All three mechanisms are expected to affect the state of association and conformation of proteins, and thereby to modulate metabolic regulation.

4. Regarding evolutionary adaptation to $T < 10\ °C$, available knowledge on cellular structures, enzyme patterns, and regulatory properties of the respective *psychrophiles* is almost non-existent. The low maximum temperature of growth observed for these organisms is considered to be caused by the thermolability of certain essential constituents of the cell. Examples have been reported where a clear correlation of temperature sensitivity of specific enzymes and maximum temperature of growth may be assumed. However, as yet no attempts have been made to analyze the specific structural features of these enzymes.

II. Low water activity

Systematic studies on hydration-dependent metabolic transitions and the state of water during 'cryptobiosis', i.e. under conditions of excessive dehydration prove 0.3 g/g to be the minimum water content required for metabolism and enzymatic activity. Since small shifts in water activity can result in large physiological changes, the majority of organisms have evolved mechanisms for keeping constant the composition of their intracellular fluids. In this connection, organisms exposed to high salt or solute concentrations had to adapt their whole intracellular inventory to the respective solute, or to some low molecular weight metabolite (aminoacids, carbohydrate derivatives, polyhydric alcohols, etc.) with equal osmolarity. In the latter case, it is only the cell membrane or cell wall that has to be adapted to the extreme environment (e.g. by forming ether type isoprenoid lipids replacing the fatty acid esters in the normal cellular membrane). Enzymes from halotolerant or halophilic bacteria require high concentrations of specific cations and anions. The respective concentrations (~ 5.3 M KCl) mainly affect the aqueous solvent, favouring hydrophobic interactions, and (to a lesser extent) screening off electrostatic interactions. The significance of both effects is clearly indicated by the decrease of the average hydrophobicity per residue, and the large excess of acidic aminoacids, comparing halophiles and non-halophiles. Because of the complications connected with the purification of halophilic enzymes, quantitative enzymological information with respect to the primary sequence and three-dimensional structure is scarce. The following features of halophilic enzymes may be generalized: (i) the basic metabolic patterns and the corresponding enzymes in halophiles and non-halophiles are identical; (ii) halophily of an organism corresponds to a salt requirement of its ribosomal, cytoplasmic, and membrane proteins; (iii) high salt concentrations affect the enzyme-substrate affinity, while V_{max} is affected to a lesser degree; (iv) halophilic enzymes show a significant deficiency of non-polar aminoacids, and a large excess of acidic ones (corresponding chemical modification generates halophilic properties of cell constituents); (v) ATP dependent cation pumps (Na^+/K^+ ATPases) may take part in the regulation of the intracellular salt concentration, at the level of osmoregulation as well as specific ion regulation.[4]

III. Extremes of pH

The central role of water in all cellular processes implies that the hydrogen ion is one of the most important factors defining the boundaries of growth and reproduction of organisms. Despite that, there is life in the whole range of pH (pH 0–12).[1] 'Acidophiles' and 'alkalinophiles' requiring extreme pH values are rare. Their adaptation mechanism is unknown. In many cases, acidophily is connected with thermostability ('acidothermophiles').[1–3]

A remarkable feature of acidophiles and alkalinophiles is the fact that the intracellular pH is found to be close to neutrality, suggesting a huge transmembrane pH gradient the nature of which is unknown; apparently the intactness of the cell-wall is of crucial importance. As in the case of halophiles, the stability of those parts of the cell envelope accessible to the attack of the environment is achieved by anomalous non-polar lipids and highly stable extracellular or membrane proteins. Adequate analysis of the respective structures is lacking so that at the enzyme level no specific requirements for acidophily can be given so far. Due to the normal intracellular pH, the intracellular enzyme pattern does not show peculiarities regarding structure, function and regulation.

IV. High pressure

Hydrostatic pressure in the biosphere ranges from 0.1–120 MPa (1–1200 bar). Seventy per cent of the earth's surface is covered by the oceans, 86% of which exceed a depth of 2000 m; the average pressure on the ocean floor is ~380 bar. Since adaptation to extreme depths in general implies adaptation to low temperature, low nutrient concentration, low oxygen content, and complete darkness, the analysis of 'barophily' (if it exists) refers to a complex situation.

Due to the subtle balance of weak intermolecular interactions stabilizing the native structure of proteins, structural alterations induced by high pressure may cause inhibition as well as acceleration of enzyme reactions. Both effects cooperate *in vivo* to cause a variable degree of 'metabolic dislocation', which is known to affect the growth and reproduction of non-adapted organisms.

Model studies using cell constituents of normal, non-'barophilic' organisms prove high pressure to shift thermodynamic equilibria, and to alter the rate of chemical reactions, depending on the magnitude and sign of the reaction volume, and the volume of activation. Targets in the given context are (i) protonation–deprotonation, (ii) hydrophobic solvation, and (iii) dissociation–association, especially regarding protein assembly and protein denaturation.[4] Since nucleic acids have been shown to be stable within the given pressure range, high pressure adaptation is expected to involve mainly proteins, especially enzymes. Dissociation of ribosomes[5,6] and (oligomeric) enzymes[7–9] seems to be the key of barosensitivity, i.e. stabilization of the quaternary structure is expected to be the basic mechanism of pressure adaptation. Structural studies involving assembly systems (e.g., oligomeric enzymes) from organisms living at different depth are still lacking; so far the existence of obligate barophilic organisms has not been proven in an unequivocal way.

Investigating the effects of pressure on barosensitive oligomeric enzymes proves denaturation to be accompanied by deactivation and dissociation. Both processes run parallel in a strictly reversible way. In the range of transition oligomer $\rightleftharpoons$ monomer, deactivation is found to be a slow first-order reaction, while reconstitution follows a consecutive folding-association mechanism.

The importance of hydrophobic interactions in the pressure dependent assembly–disassembly processes is demonstrated by water release effects, observed, e.g. in the temperature and pressure dependent 'polymerization' of the coat protein of tobacco mosaic virus. The respective thermodynamic quantities, as well as the corresponding data for a number of oligomeric enzymes corroborate the hypothesis that hydration effects govern the pressure dependent denaturation.

The *biological* significance of the previously mentioned stress conditions is obvious, considering the ecological, physiological, evolutionary, and taxonomic implications.[2] From the *chemical* point of view, variation of temperature, pressure, and pH is relevant for the elucidation of reaction mechanisms, or groups involved in enzyme catalysis (cf. cryo-enzymology, interpretation of ΔV and $\Delta V^{\ddagger}$, titration of active sites, etc.). Finally, microorganisms, or enzymes adapted to extremes of physical conditions may clearly gain *technological* importance (enzyme technology), with special emphasis on highly specific redox and group transfer reactions.

Experimental developments in the three fields at the cellular and molecular level aim at two different goals. On one hand, whole cells or organisms are studied in order to determine how life processes are affected in the natural habitat; on the other hand, purified cellular components (e.g., individual enzymes) are used to describe the thermodynamics and kinetics of specific biochemical reactions. Deductions from the latter approach in connection with evolutionary and ecological aspects of physiological stress have to be made with care, because *in vitro* data may not be directly applicable to the intracellular processes. *In vivo*, the abundance, activity and stability of an enzyme depends on coupled reactions, coenzymes, feedback mechanisms and protein turnover, which may not be adequately simulated *in vitro*. Therefore, in the future the current approach involving the purification and characterization of selected constituents from thermophiles, halophiles, etc. will be increasingly replaced by structural and functional studies on systems with increasing complexity.

References

1. T. D. Brock, *Thermophilic Microorganisms and Life at High Temperature*. New York/Heidelberg/Berlin. 465 pp. (1978).
2. D. J. Kushner, (Ed.) *Microbial Life in Extreme Environments*. London/New York/San Francisco. 465 pp. (1978).
3. M. Shilo, (Ed.) *Strategies of Microbial Life in Extreme Environments*. Wienheim/New York. 514 pp. (1979).
4. R. Jaenicke, *Ann. Rev. Biophys. Bioeng.*, **10**, in press (1981).
5. E. Schulz, H.-D. Lüdemann and R. Jaenicke, *FEBS Letters*, **64**, 40 (1976).
6. E. Schulz, R. Jaenicke and W. Knoche, *Biophys. Chem.*, **4**, 253 (1976).
7. B. C. Schade, R. Rudolph, H.-D. Lüdemann and R. Jaenicke, *Biochemistry*, **19**, 1121 (1980).
8. B. C. Schade, H.-D. Lüdemann, and R. Jaenicke, *Biophys. Chem.*, **11**, 257 (1980).
9. K. Müller, H.-D. Lüdemann and R. Jaenicke, *Biochemistry and Biophys. Chem.* in press (1981).

Physiological water stress

Reporter: Helen leB. Skaer

On the general topic of undercooled water, Dore reported on recently performed neutron diffraction measurements on D_2O down to $-16\ °C$. Such studies show that the structure of water changes significantly with temperature and that this is probably due to changes in the orientational correlation between adjacent molecules. A typical diffraction pattern for D_2O (Figure 1) has a main diffraction peak followed by an oscillatory function. The position of the diffraction peak is very sensitive to the temperature of the sample, as shown in Figure 2. It shows a smooth behaviour as the

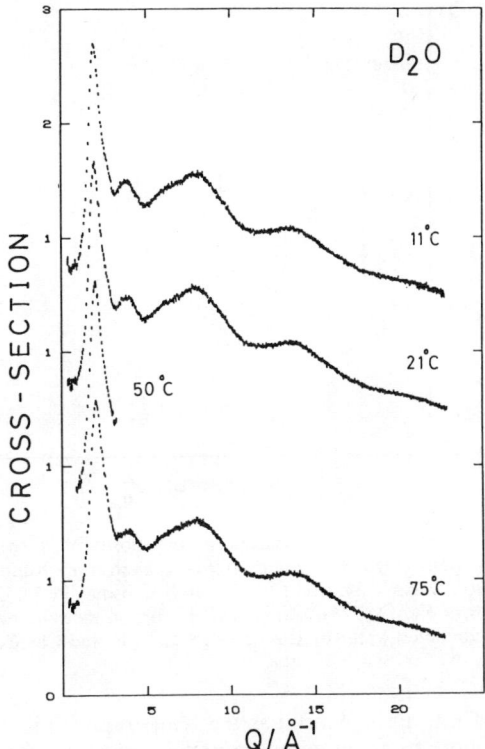

Figure 1 Typical neutron diffraction measurements for liquid D_2O at various temperatures (Gibson and Dore, unpublished data); detailed comparison of the curves reveals significant variation which can be correlated with orientational changes due to hydrogen-bonding effects

temperature is reduced and there are no dramatic effects as the liquid becomes undercooled (m.p. for D_2O is 4 °C). The $g(r)$ plot at room temperature has a broad peak at ~1.7 Å^{-1} which is the residual contribution of a hydrogen-bond as seen in the crystalline solids. The 'so-called' hydrogen-bond in the liquid does not correspond to a specified distance and is spread over a range of values due to variations in the relative positions of adjacent molecules. It is interesting to compare this behaviour with that of a completely hydrogen-bonded random structure. Amorphous ice prepared by vapour-deposition has recently been shown (M. Chowdhury, J. Dore and J. Wenzel, unpublished data) to be such a structure and is compared with the results for liquid water in Figure 3. The peak position in the neutron diffraction pattern has shifted down to 1.7 Å^{-1} and it is tempting to suggest that the extrapolation of the graph in Figure 2 would give this value, at a temperature of −45 °C which is the 'critical temperature' predicted from the anomalous physical properties of undercooled water. However, there are arguments against this, as there is apparently no evidence to support a continuity of state between amorphous ice and undercooled water; the situation therefore remains somewhat paradoxical. The experiments do show that

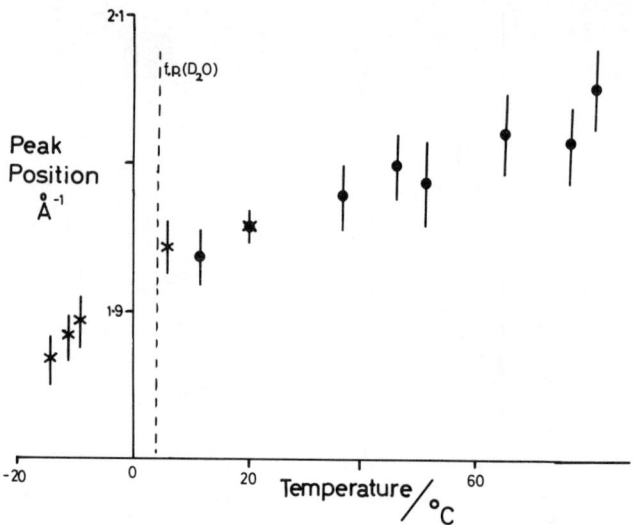

Figure 2 The systematic variation in the position of the main diffraction peak (Figure 1); circles are data taken from Walford and Dore, *Mol. Phys.*, **34**, 21 (1977), and Gibson, Ph.D. Thesis, University of Kent (1978), and crosses are recent measurements on supercooled water by Bosio, Texeira, Dore and Chieux

hydrogen-bonding effects are enhanced as the temperature is lowered and that this behaviour becomes more pronounced in the initial part of the undercooled region.

The discussion then turned to a general consideration of cryoprotection, prompted by Derbyshire who asked how and why different cryoprotectants (e.g., Me_2SO, glycoproteins) operate by different mechanisms. While polar fish glycoproteins allow freezing *avoidance* (the fish die if they freeze), some insects can *tolerate* freezing and thawing as a result of the presence of glycerol in their body fluids. Similarly, glycerol or Me_2SO can be used to confer freeze tolerance on isolated animal cells (de Vries). Me_2SO appears to act by raising the volume of osmotically inactive water in cells beyond that expected simply by the addition of solute. This is not as a result of osmotic imbalance, as Me_2SO permeates cells very readily (Hempling). The influence on cell survival of intracellular (permeant) and extracellular (impermeant) cryoprotective agents are distinct and highly dependent on cooling rate. For example, with rat granulocytes, the optimal cooling rate with Me_2SO is *ca.* 0.3 K min^{-1}, viability decreasing with increasing rate. However, with the addition of hydroxyethyl starch (HES, an extracellular additive), the cooling rate optimum is *ca.* 12 K min^{-1}, with a sharp drop off in viability for both higher and lower cooling rates. The two agents act synergistically at cooling rates of 12 K min^{-1} but HES is deleterious to survival at cooling rates of 1 K min^{-1} (Bank).

The discussion then shifted to the mechanism of action of 'compatible solutes' such as betaine and proline. Wyn-Jones pointed out that these substances protect some enzymes against inhibition by high salt concentration and also against denaturing agents such as urea. He suggested that, since some compounds which appear to accumulate in cells as 'osmoregulators' are present in a high enough concentration to contribute to the osmotic potential, there might be a correlation between their colliga-

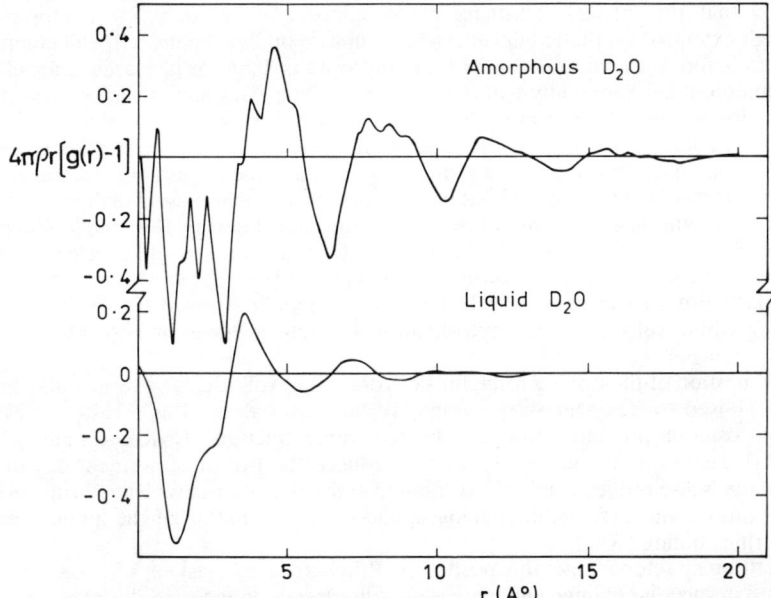

Figure 3 A comparison of the composite pair correlation function for neutron scattering by liquid water and amorphous ice. The a-D_2O data (Chowdhury and Dore) are in good agreement with the continuous random network (CRN) model of Boutron and Alben (*J. Chem. Phys.*, **187**, 428 (1975)) based on a continuous hydrogen-bonded structure. Changes in the structure of liquid water are consistent with an increased correlation of molecular orientation through hydrogen-bonding, as the temperature is reduced

tive activity and their ability to act as protectants. Timasheff, however, suggested that these molecules are excluded from the hydration sphere of proteins. This is true also for ions that are 'hydrated' such as $SO_4^=$, which are excluded from the proximity of macromolecules. This process is called salting-out. The type of ionic hydration seems to be incompatible with the macromolecular hydration. The same appears to be true for 'compatible solutes'. The problem is posed by the lyotropic series which has not yet been solved, e.g. $SO_4^=$ and ClO_4^- have similar geometry, yet one is salting-out and the other salting-in, a process that cannot be explained at all in terms of electrostatics (Franks). Schobert, however, pointed out that proteins cannot be salted-out in solutions of high protein concentration. She further emphasized that the mechanism of accumulation of 'compatible' solutes is variable; proline is accumulated after rapid osmotic shock, whereas betaine is more important under long term water stress conditions. Thus it is not known at present which structures are protected, nor why they should have to be protected.

The problem associated with accumulation of high urea concentrations as the osmoregulating compound, for example in cartilaginous fish, was raised (Hempling). Pain pointed out that a number of globular proteins are stable in high concentrations of urea.

Franks raised the problem of osmotic shrinkage in terms of the plasma membrane, by asking about the degree of lateral compression that a membrane can tolerate. It appears that the intrinsic elasticity of membranes allows only 2% compression, although extended synthetic bilayers (which rupture on 2% expansion), will compress 20–30% before they rupture. Similarly, in protoplasts, large surface area changes can be accommodated apparently without folds or ruffling. This may be accomplished by protein loss. If membranes are labelled with conA-fluorescein, the fluorescence is internalized during shrinkage and it remains internalized during re-expansion (Steponkus, Robson). Yeast vacuoles during shrinking accommodate lateral pressure increases by movements of proteins in and out of the plane of the membrane. Further, there is a release of membrane proteins following freezing and thawing (Morris). Steponkus queried the interpretation of protein movements in membranes and emphasized that the loss of membrane material during shrinkage had been demonstrated not only in protoplasts but also in yeast and HeLa cells. Dragomir stressed the importance of studying whole cells, since the cytoskeleton is likely to have an important role in volume changes.

The question of the driving force for dehydration of cells during extracellular freezing was raised by Ter-Minassian-Saraga. Water leaves the cell as a result of raised external osmotic pressure, produced by the transformation of solvent water to ice (Franks). However, as the temperature is reduced the hydraulic permeability of the membrane is also reduced and this, combined with calculations involving diffusion rate considerations and permeability changes, allows the estimation of the amount water lost during cooling (Rall).

MacRobbie, referring to the poster by Pritchard et al., asked why the relative decrease in vacuolar volume and increase in cytoplasmic volume, exhibited by cultured sycamore cells grown under conditions of water stress, should enhance survival. The importance of an unaltered cell volume and water content but a change in the vacuolar volume may relate to the redistribution of water from the vacuole to the cytoplasm in response to an increased solute concentration in the latter. This redistribution may aid the osmotic withdrawal of water in the presence of extracellular ice. The increase in cytoplasmic solute concentration is to some extent unexplained, i.e. it is not clear whether mannitol permeates the cell and accumulates in the cytoplasm, or whether the cells are capable of synthesizing a non-toxic intracellular solute which would osmotically balance the increased osmolality of the 'pregrowth' medium. Experiments to elucidate the importance of both of these alternatives are in hand (Pritchard).

There followed some discussion concerning the difficulty of defining vacuolar volume when it is known that vacuoles will readily fuse and subdivide (Steponkus, MacRobbie). Bank pointed out that freeze fracture evidence indicates that yeast vacuoles are more prone to crystallization during freezing and also to subsequent recrystallization than is the cytoplasm. Thus, the vacuole would tend to sequester water from the remaining unfrozen cytoplasm and might thereby render the cell more resistant to freezing damage.

Wyn Jones, referring to the work of Krog et al. (1979) on the freezing tolerance of a plant which promotes premature freezing by a biosynthetic nucleating agent, asked in which compartment of the plant this ice seeding occurs. It appears that there is no special compartment, both the inflorescence and the vital tissues of the plant are protected against a decrease in temperature by the heat of fusion of water. The temperature of the plant is kept close to 0 °C, with only a small amount of ice forming. The nucleating agent is believed to be a carbohydrate. If the fluids are extracted and the extract is added to saline, 1 mg of which will normally undercool to -1.5 °C, the mixture will not undercool at all. Thus, there must be an active ingredient that promotes nucleation (Franks) and it should be emphasized that these plants are exploiting the promotion rather than the avoidance of nucleation (MacRobbie).

Physiological water stress

The discussion then moved on to the consideration of the freeze protection of polar fish. Franks posed a problem for de Vries: if one invokes the Kelvin effect, i.e. that crystals of small radius of curvature are unstable and will not grow, this must represent a precarious state of affairs over the long term, since any ice formed, however slowly, cannot melt. Would ice not accumulate slowly and the fish eventually freeze? Ice crystals are never found in polar fish even though many of them live permanently at -2 °C. However, if any ice did form, there is no evidence for a thermal cycle which might result in melting. One is forced to conclude that the antifreeze acts at the level of an 'ice-embryo'—a critical cluster which, with time, would grow to a crystal. Perhaps in the presence of the anti-freeze agent these clusters disappear with time but it is hard to prove or disprove this idea (de Vries). Polar fish make use of a device demonstrated in mammalian hibernators—the selective uncoupling of oxidative phosphorylation. The following possibility could be tested—that phagocytes ingest the 'ice embryos' (which are marked for ingestion by the antifreeze complex) and then uncouple their mitochondria in order to generate enough heat to melt the ice (Clegg). Alternatively, increased muscular activity might raise the body temperature (Marsden). However, the body temperature remains very close to that of the surrounding water. Even if the fish struggles a lot, the body temperature rises only by 0.8 °C. The large surface area of the gills, necessary for oxygen uptake, in any case prevents the conservation of metabolic heat (De Vries). The fish freeze at -2.2 °C and can exist in a slush of freezing sea water (~ -1.6 °C). Wiggins pointed out that the turnover rate of the protein or glycoprotein antifreeze should be taken into account in making any kinetic analysis. Finally it was generally agreed that two new compounds termed 'meltase' and 'ice nuclease' should be identified and extracted, preferably by adsorbing them on to mica plates! (Israelachvili).

Hefford suggested that a single macromolecule could act either as a nucleating agent or an antifreeze agent depending on its concentration. At low concentration it might act as a crystal nucleation site and at higher concentration as a crystal poison.

Hallenga raised the problem of undercooling in cells and suggested an approach based on the use of non-equilibrium thermodynamics. It seems that there must be an increase in the kinetic barrier towards ice crystal formation on the scale of molecular clusters. This barrier can never be high enough to prevent the formation of small clusters but perhaps the proteins in the cell have an influence on the size requirements of these clusters before they can start to grow into macroscopic ice crystals. This theory was considered unlikely by Franks who felt that once ΔG of cluster growth becomes negative, crystallization is too fast to interrupt, except by kinetically efficient means, such as the adsorption of anti-freeze molecules at the surface of the growing cluster.

Section 5   Matters arising

Biophysics of Water
Edited by F. Franks
© 1982 John Wiley & Sons Ltd

Alternative views on the role of water in cell function

James S. Clegg
University of Miami, USA

Summary

Current thought about cellular function is heavily influenced by the view that almost all of the water in cells exhibits properties that are the same as those of water in bulk aqueous solutions. This paper briefly summarizes some alternative descriptions of cell water and considers their consequences to various cellular activities.

Introduction

Most of the functions carried out by living cells require the participation of water and it has generally been taken as a matter of course that intracellular water is chemically and physically equivalent to the water in bulk aqueous solutions. That simplifying assumption has been used with apparent success in the description of a wide variety of cellular activities, ranging from solute transport and the regulation of intermediary metabolism, to assembly-disassembly of cellular components. Such success notwithstanding, this paper will show that there is good reason to question that assumption and will indicate that the functions of water in cells are far more pervasive than this traditional view has allowed.

Space limitations prevent anything approaching a review or detailed analysis of the available data, so I must be brief and selective in my choice of examples; only the most recent work of authors will be cited. Finally, I will utilize diagrams for the sake of brevity. However, this simplicity of description can be deceptive if taken literally so the reader is warned that, like all cartoons, they must not be confused with real life.

The traditional view

This conception (Figure 1) considers that well in excess of 90% of total cellular water exhibits properties that are the same as those of the water in bulk aqueous solutions which will be referred to by the initials 'Bw', and conveniently illustrated by blank space in this and subsequent diagrams. Such water is located in the 'aqueous compartments' of cells: cytosol, nucleoplasm, and cytoplasmic organelle interiors (Figure 1). The remainder of the water is found immediately adjacent to surfaces, be these free ions, metabolites, macromolecules or ultrastructurally demonstable cell components. It is generally agreed that this water, within 3 to 6 Å from surfaces, exhibits properties that distinctly differ from those of Bw. This fraction of cell water will be indicated in diagrams by stippling and referred to as 'Hw', since it can be considered as the water of primary hydration. Some would call this 'bound water', a term I will avoid. Thus, the traditional view can be summed up: $\geqslant 90\%$ Bw, $\leqslant 10\%$ Hw. Several important consequences of this view to cellular functions can be recognized:

1. The Bw is taken to be a single aqueous phase even though it may be partitioned by membranes into several compartments in eucaryotic cells. Further, the solvent properties of Bw are taken to be the same for all solutes in all intracellular compartments, and equivalent in that respect to the surrounding aqueous environment. The consequences of this are important: first, total cell concentrations are usually taken as reliable indicators of chemical activity since the activity coefficients are considered to be the same as those of an equivalent salt solution, as well as the extracellular phase; second, results from *in vitro* studies can evidently be extrapolated to the intracellular environment without significant trepidation, at least with respect to solvent considerations. That point is of some importance with regard to studies of enzyme reactions in dilute solutions, and the physiological significance of such results.

2. In the absence of binding, this description requires that unequal concentrations of solutes across the cell membrane, and across intracellular membrane-bounded compartments, are maintained by membrane processes which selectively transport the relevant solute between two ordinary aqueous phases using ATP or equivalent free energy sources.

3. In effect, the traditional view considers the functions of cell water to be a solvent, a substrate and product of various enzymes, and an

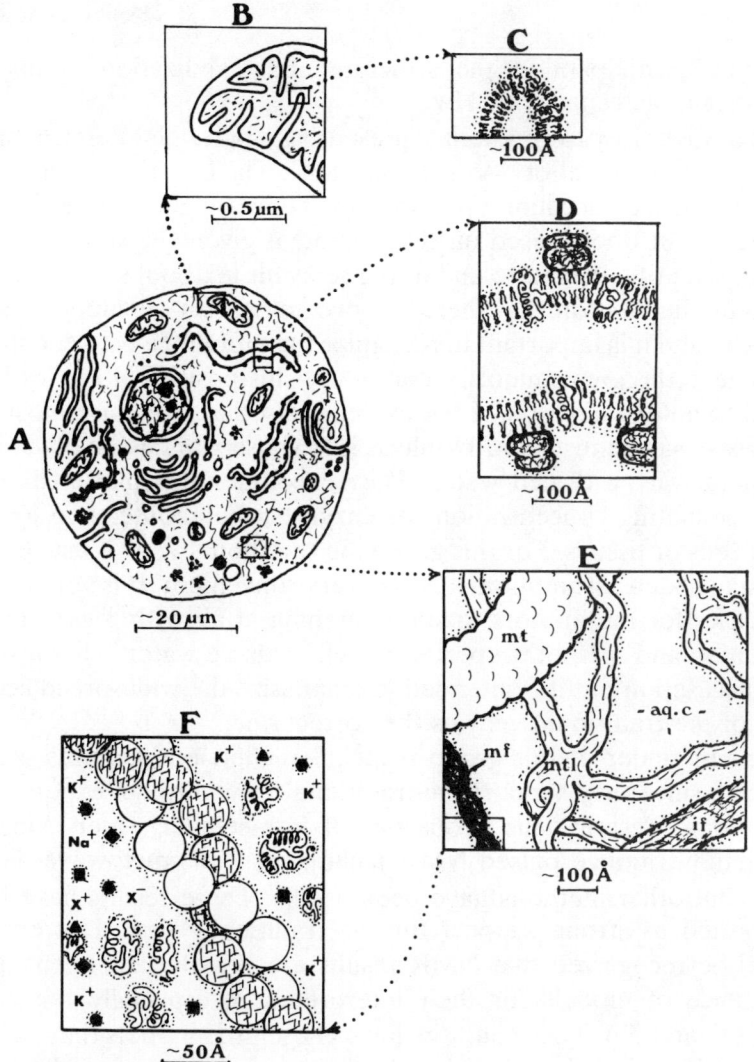

Figure 1 Cell structure and the traditional view of cell water. Part A is a diagrammatic representation of a eucaryotic cell. The inserts B and C illustrate mitochondria, and D represents the endoplasmic reticulum with attached ribosomes. Insert E represents the cytoskeletal elements (mt = microtubule, mf = microfilament, if = intermediate filament), and the microtrabecular lattice (mtl). The intervening volume is the aqueous cytoplasm (aq.c) which is shown in more detail in insert F along with part of a microfilament. X^+ and X^- in insert F represent free cations and anions other than Na^+ and K^+, and metabolites are depicted by the darkened symbols. In all diagrams stippling represents primary hydration water (Hw); the remainder of the water is considered equivalent to pure water (Bw) according to this view, and is represented by empty space

important participant in the structure and stabilization of macromolecules in its capacity as Hw.

It is always risky to generalize, presenting a particular description as an accurate portrayal of a 'consensus view'. The question is, does this represent such an account, upon which to compare alternative views? I believe that it does, based on the treatment given the subject in the current scientific literature and in the relevant textbooks. However, it is also my impression that there are two categories of 'supporters' of this view, and it is important to recognize the difference between them.

I believe the great majority that adopt this position do so without regard to an examination of the evidence. In this group are most cell biologists, biochemists and biophysicists whose work is involved in a peripheral way with cell water. They encounter this matter directly when estimating concentrations of enzymes, metabolites and ions in whole cells or tissues. For this group the traditional view is usually not just an unstated assumption, it is also very convenient. It is very rare in such cases for the authors to state anything at all with regard to the disposition and solvent properties of cell or tissue water. That is not a petty accusation but it is intended to emphasize the widespread acceptance of the traditional view as the correct one.

The remainder of this group is much smaller, but requires special attention since they support the traditional view through experiments designed to describe the properties of intracellular water. Most of these studies utilize pulsed NMR techniques[1-5] or microwave dielectrics[6,7] but other methods have been used.[8,9] These results have been interpreted as strong support for the traditional view. However, it should be recognized that NMR results are heavily dependent upon the choice of models for their interpretation, especially relaxation times (T_1 and T_2). These authors have chosen the models they believe to be most appropriate, but that does not necessarily mean they have chosen the correct ones, any more than have those who choose to interpret very similar NMR data in an entirely different way, namely that none of the water in cells behaves like BW.[10-13] It appears to me that more work will be required to produce compelling evidence either way from the use of NMR, and this research is in progress.[12]

Fewer studies have been carried out on the microwave dielectric properties of intracellular water, almost all of the published work originating from Schwan, Foster and their colleagues.[6,7] I believe two interpretive problems apply to this work. One is that the frequency range examined has not exceeded about 10 GHz at physiological temperatures, well below the characteristic relaxation frequency of bulk water. Thus, considerable extrapolations to high frequency are employed and the assumption is generally made that intracellular water exhibits simple Debye relaxation. The second problem concerns the use of 'mixture equations' that are unlikely to apply to complex cellular systems. Because these equations are used to estimate the fraction of cell water that has dielectric properties identical to those of bulk water, the conclusions would appear to be less than compelling.

Finally, a significant amount of evidence for the traditional view comes from studies on mammalian red blood cells.[8,14] These are such unusual cells that I think it is fair to question the generality of the conclusions.

In summing up this very brief account of evidence in support of the traditional view it can be said that a considerable amount of data from NMR and dielectric analysis can be interpreted as consistent with that description of the physical properties of intracellular water, and that a limited amount of evidence from other kinds of studies also supports that view. In the following sections of this paper I will summarize some of the alternatives that have been advanced.

The association–induction hypothesis

The most specific extant alternative view of cell water is this hypothesis, first formulated by Gilbert Ling about 30 years ago. Since that time he and his associates have carried out a vigorous research programme to test and modify the hypothesis, the published work being so voluminous that even a listing of the papers would be prohibitive. Access to this literature can be obtained through the most recent publications.[15-17] The major features of this hypothesis, which contain certain aspects in common with the early views of Troshin[18] and Ernst[19] are as follows (Figure 2(A)).

1. Virtually all of the water in cells is considered to exist as polarized multilayers arising from fixed charges on extended protein surfaces, these water layers being generated over considerable distances from the surface relative to a monolayer of water.

2. The water multilayers exclude ions and other solutes to varying degree, and the contribution of membrane processes such as active transport are considered to be negligible in the regulation of solute distributions.

3. Ions are also associated with fixed charges on cellular macro-

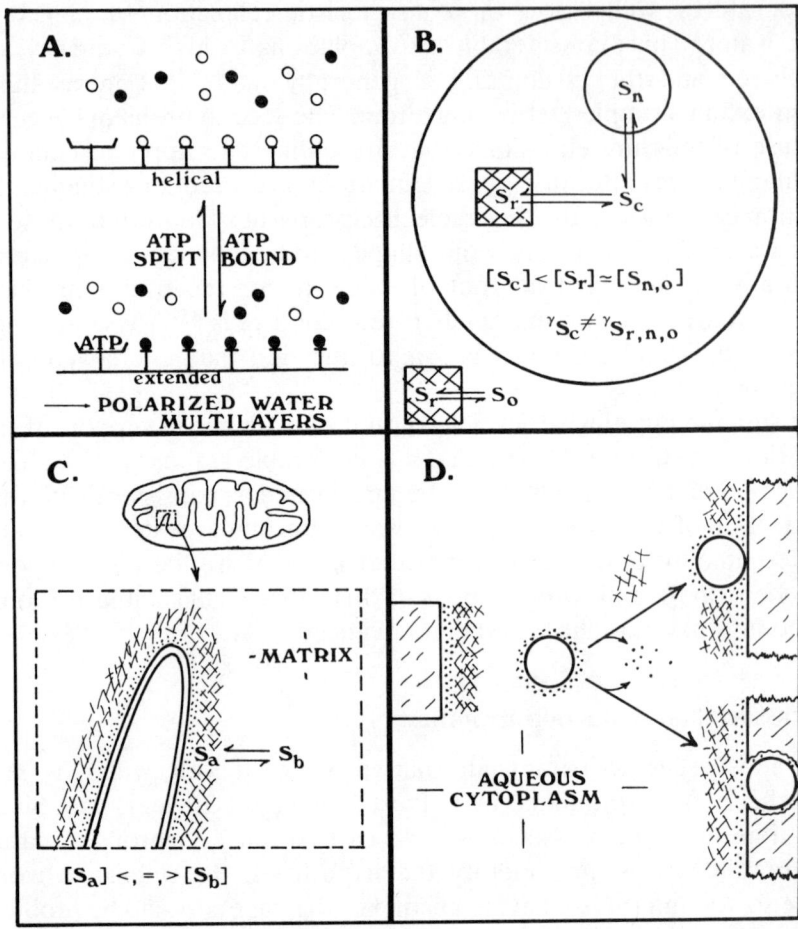

Figure 2 Some features of alternative views on cell water. In part A the horizontal lines represent protein chains (helical or extended) containing binding sites for ions (empty and filled circles). A cardinal site is shown to the left of each chain. Part B illustrates the reference phase technique and some of the observed results. The cross-hatched squares represent a dilute gelatin reference phase containing a given solute (S). Subscripts are n = nucleus, r = reference phase, c = cytoplasm, 0 = cell interior, and γ is the activity coefficient. Part C shows a proposed description of the water in the matrix of mitochondria. 'S' represents a solute partitioned between two aqueous phases: a = 'abnormal' (cross-hatching) and b = 'normal' (empty space). Part D describes proposed interactions between enzymes and other macromolecules (spheres) in the aqueous cytoplasm with the surfaces of cytoplasmic structures (rectangles, see Figure 1(D) and (E)). Cross-hatched regions represent vicinal water. Stippling in parts C and D represents the water of primary hydration. See text for the authors whose work is summarized in this figure, and for further details

molecules, notable proteins, the degree of binding for a given ion being influenced by a number of factors.

4. Cardinal sites exist on these particular proteins which, when filled with specific adsorbents such as ATP, initiate cooperative interactions within the protein–ion–water system (Figure 2(A). Such things as hormones and regulatory cyclic nucleotides are included in the list of cardinal adsorbents.

5. ATP binding at the cardinal site leads to cooperative alterations and the selective accumulation of K^+ over Na^+, and generates the polarized multilayers of water; ATP splitting and the removal of ADP results in a movement of the system to a lower energy state in which the ion selectivity is lost as is the polarization of water. Figure 2A summarizes a few of these features in the case where the concentrations of free ions do not change.

This is a mere skeletal outline of the hypothesis which includes far more specific detail than I have been able to consider here. In its complete form it provides an alternative explanation for a wide variety of cellular functions ranging from the characteristic ion-selectivity of cells to the generation of action potentials in excitable cells and mechanisms of hormone action. Because the A-I hypothesis differs so dramatically from the traditional view, in essentially all regards, its consequences to cell function are profound, to say the least.

This hypothesis has been strongly supported, most notably by the extensive work of Hazlewood, Chang and their associates[10–13] and Negendank.[17,20] Further support comes from the work of Minkoff and Damadian,[21] Cope[22] and Edelmann.[23,24] Most of this evidence has been obtained from pulsed NMR studies (subject to the same interpretive difficulties as described earlier), sorption isotherms, freezing experiments, ion flux measurements, solute distribution studies *in vivo* and *in vitro*, X-ray microanalysis, and calculations on the energetic requirements for active transport.

Nevertheless, the scientific community as a whole has been reluctant to accept the A-I hypothesis. Presumably, this reluctance stems from less than compelling evidence for the actual existence of polarized multilayers of water in cells and for the extended proteins that generate them and selectively bind ions.

While one might disagree with details of Ling's hypothesis it is not so easy to dismiss the objections he has raised against several key studies whose results are considered to be firm evidence for the validity of the traditional view. His recent review with Negendank[17] clearly shows that serious experimental problems and interpretive weaknesses do exist in a number of these studies.

Whether or not Ling is correct will eventually be decided by customary scientific practice. Certainly, his work and writings have generated a great deal of research. If he is correct, cell biology will undergo a revolution.

A number of alternative views on intracellular water have been proposed more recently. I can say at the outset that they have received no wider acceptance than has the A-I hypothesis.

The reference phase technique

The work of Horowitz, Paine and colleagues[25] provides direct experimental evidence that the traditional view of cellular water requires modification. They have developed an elegant method for examining the solvent properties of intracellular water *in situ* called the reference phase technique.[26,27] Because this technique is new and a powerful one, I will consider some details (Figure 2(B)). A microdrop of gelatin sol (the reference phase) containing an appropriate radioactive solute is injected into the cytoplasm of amphibian oocytes and made to gel by temperature reduction within the physiological range. After diffusion equilibrium is achieved the cells are placed at $-160°$ to $-190°$, and the reference phase, nucleus, and selected areas of cytoplasm are microdissected at $-45\ °C$, and then analysed for solute and water contents. The properties of the solute and water in the reference phase are apparently very similar to those of the surrounding Ringer's salt solution.[26,27] Therefore, it can be predicted that if the traditional view is correct, then cytoplasmic concentrations must equal reference phase concentrations for the solute when diffusion equilibrium has been achieved. However, that is not the result they observed for several ions and a number of non-metabolizable compounds. In fact, none of the solutes follow this prediction. Thus, they have shown that cytoplasm exhibits solvent properties that differ distinctly from those of the bulk liquid.

One example must suffice to illustrate the magnitude of this difference. Use of labelled sucrose in the reference phase shows that cytoplasmic water excludes this solute. In fact, the results can be interpreted on the basis that only one-third of the total cytoplasmic water behaves as the 'normal' solvent (Bw), the remainder being completely nonsolvent. However, it is my impression that these investigators do not exclude the possibility that all of the cytoplasmic water exhibits altered solvent properties. In contrast to the cytoplasm of these oocytes the nuclear water appears to have solvent properties more similar to Bw.[25,28] It is possible that this result could be related to developmental stage since Palmer and Civan[29] have shown using ion-sensitive microelectrodes that both nucleus and cytoplasm of differentiated epithelial cells contains Na^+ and K^+ activities that are comparable but both differing from those of ordinary saline.

This is a very inadequate and brief summary of the findings of this research group and a reading of the original work is recommended. It must suffice here to emphasize a few of their general conclusions: the aqueous interior of cells is not a single homogeneous phase, so that total cell concentrations of solutes do not adequately represent solute concentration distributions within different parts of cells; cytoplasmic concentrations can *not* be considered equal to chemical activities because of the occurrence of intracellular binding and the markedly altered solvent properties of the cytoplasm (Figure 2(B)).

It is difficult to find fault with this work. One possible problem concerns the achievement of diffusion equilibrium since their intepretation rests upon that. The authors assure us this is the case. They also mention that cytoplasmic membrane bounded vesicles could contribute to solute exclusion. Although such involvement has not been completely ruled out, they believe the weight of available evidence does not suggest that it contributes appreciably to their results.[30]

These studies have important consequences to cell function, the most obvious being solute transport. Since it is the electrochemical activity gradient across any cellular membrane that determines the direction and driving force for transport, current estimates of the energy requirements for, and even the direction of transport are likely to be less than accurate approximations in many cases. Because Na^+ and K^+ concentrations in the nucleus differ appreciably from those of the cytoplasm, and since these distributions are determined by differences in binding and/or solvent properties in these two compartments and *not* by active transport,[25] the possibility arises that changes in binding and/or solvent properties of the cytoplasm could be intimately involved with the regulation of these cations in the nucleus. That is not trivial since Na^+ and K^+ have been implicated in processes involved with gene expression.[25] Another consequence to cell function concerns the effects of the hormone insulin on amino acid and sugar-analog transport, and their intracellular distributions.[30] This work indicates that insulin acts at the level of cytoplasmic solute exclusion as well as at the cell membrane. An interesting explanation of 'counterflow' transport is also presented in that study. Finally, they have observed that these cells maintain certain solutes and ions against electrochemical gradients between cytoplasm and the cell exterior. Therefore, it was concluded that active transport functions are performed by the cell membrane in this system.

It is obvious that one must be careful about generalizing from the results of experiments carried out on giant amphibian oocytes, and studies of this sort on other cell types are needed. Horowitz, Paine *et al.* are fully aware of this qualification; nevertheless, they make a good case for similar solvent behaviour in several other cell types.[26,27,30] The reference phase technique is a powerful experimental tool, one of its most notable virtues being that interpretation of results does not depend on model building. Unfortunately, the current technique is applicable only to large cells.

The two-phase model

Garlid[14,31] has emphasized that both the traditional view and the A-I hypothesis bear in common the description of cell water as a single aqueous phase. Using rat liver mitochondria as a model of the aqueous compartments of cells, he has measured equilibrium distributions of polar, non-metabolized small solutes across the inner mitochondrial membrane at 0 °C. The results lead him to conclude that water in the mitochondrial matrix (inner compartment) exists as two contiguous but immiscible aqueous phases which can selectively exclude, concentrate, or not discriminate between various solutes, relative to Bw (Figure 2(C)). One of these phases is considered to exhibit the solvent properties of Bw, whereas the other phase he calls 'abnormal' because of its altered solvent properties. The abnormal phase constitutes about 30% of the matrix water and is postulated to be located next to the matrix side of the inner mitochondrial membrane in a layer about 25 Å thick (Figure 2(C)), equivalent to about 7 molecular layers of water.

An interesting feature of Garlid's model is that it allows for the partitioning of metabolites and even macromolecules between these two phases. Because of the thinness of the abnormal phase adjacent to the membrane this would reduce diffusion to essentially two dimensions which, if true, has some very interesting metabolic implications.[32-34]

Garlid also concluded that a substantial bulk aqueous phase exists within the matrix and that active transport by the inner membrane is required to account for solute movements and distribution. Thus, like that of Horowitz, Paine et al., this model does not require a rejection of widely held views on active transport.

It is reasonable to question whether or not results from studies carried out on mitochondria from an endotherm performed at 0 °C can be safely generalized to the entire cell. Another relevant point concerns the extraordinary concentrations of organic compounds in the mitochondrial matrix, the protein alone amounting to over 50 wt.%; indeed, the matrix has even been modeled as a protein crystal by Srere who has carried out some very interesting calculations, including the water volume and content of the matrix.[35,36] How these considerations relate to Garlid's model is not clear to me since Srere's calculations indicate that virtually all of the matrix water is consumed by the equivalent of one or two monolayers of water around each protein. Consequently, one wonders how a substantial bulk aqueous phase can also be present. Further study is needed.

While on the subject of mitochondria and their low water content it should be recognized that the synthesis of ATP might be strongly influenced by matrix water concentration. For instance, it has long been known that when mitochondria are respiring and phosphorylating ADP, the matrix volume contracts to about one-half that of non-respiring mitochondria, thereby reducing the water concentration even more drastically.[37] This could be quite significant since H_2O figures prominently in the equation: $ADP + Pi \rightarrow ATP + H_2O$. The articles by Kell and by Wiggins in the present volume should be consulted for additional consequences of water structure to phosphorylation mechanisms. Ling and Negendank's critical review of such matter in isolated vesicles is also important in this regard.[17]

A compromise hypothesis

Hempling and co-workers[38] have advanced an hypothesis that incorporates certain aspects of traditional views with those of Ling's hypothesis. Since Hempling has contributed to this volume my treatment will be very brief. Using evidence from solute distribution, osmotically induced volume changes, and cell cycle studies on three different cell types they conclude that the cell membrane does indeed regulate the exchange of water and solutes between extracellular and intracellular phases. However, this exchangeable intracellular phase communicates with osmotically excluded water and solute compartment(s). The size of the excluded compartment is appreciable, and varies with the cell cycle in an interesting way. This hypothesis bears at least some resemblance to the previously discussed findings of Horowitz and Paine, and has even more in common with the model proposed by Garlid. Interestingly, none of these three cite the others in their most recent papers.[14,30,38]

The water powered pump

In a very interesting series of studies Wiggins[39-41] has obtained evidence that the activity of membrane-bound ATPases might involve changes in the microscopic viscosity of a significant fraction of the surrounding water, thereby changing its affinity for all solutes. Using sarcoplasmic reticulum vesicles *in vitro* she has recently shown that the driving force for active transport might be developed by a change in the structure of an appreciable amount of water near and within a cleft of the Ca^{++}-ATPase. Wiggins has also contributed to the present volume and that paper and those cited above should be consulted for details.

The vicinal water network model

When cells are disrupted a large fraction of their enzyme complement is released into the suspending medium. It has long been assumed that these enzymes also exist free in solution within the aqueous intracellular compartments, operating by random collision, simple mass-action principles. However, there is reason to believe that these enzymes are somehow weakly associated with the internal architecture of cells[33,34] and I have proposed that water interactions might be involved with these associations.[32,42] The general idea (Figure 2(D)) is that intracellular surfaces, notably the cytoskeletal elements (see Figures 1(E) and (F)) perturb water in their vicinity over distances of the order of 30–50Å, generating an aqueous phase whose structure and properties differ from Hw as well as from the water that is more distant (but not necessarily Bw).

It was proposed that the 'soluble' enzymes might preferentially associate with this vicinal phase (and/or the surface) due to an increase in the system's entropy that would accompany the release of the 'more structured' water (Hw) at the enzyme surface into the surrounding 'less structured' cytoplasmic water. Changes in the amount of 'vicinal water' might also be involved. The enzymes making up a given pathway are believed to self-associate in the vicinal phase. As a result, metabolic activity in the aqueous cellular compartments is considered to occur in a highly organized two-dimensional phase, rather than in the randomness of a three-dimensional solution, which the traditional view assumes.

The experimental evidence in support of this view is indirect, and obtained largely from the study of water and metabolism in a somewhat unusual system, the cells of *Artemia* cysts. However, it is also consistent with a large body of observations made on a variety of other cell types, and can be experimentally tested.

An important feature of this model, and essentially all of the views summarized in this paper, concerns the influence of intracellular surfaces upon the properties of intracellular water, the topic of the next section.

Intracellular surfaces

Figure 1 illustrates a few of the major formed structures found in eucaryotic cells. The total suface area presented to the water in cells is enormous, and the aqueous compartments are very crowded indeed. It is worth attempting to estimate this area since we know that water adjacent to surfaces differs from the bulk liquid. Rat liver cells are reasonably well known in this regard, and estimates of their total *membrane* surface suggest a figure of roughly 100,000 μm^2 per cell; a monolayer of 'close-packed' water on this surface would require only about 1% of the total cell water.[32,43] Since it is evident that membrane integrity requires more than a single water layer we can suppose that the membranes alone will consume between 5–10% of the total water. However, it should be realized that the surface area of the nuclear matrix and especially the various cytoskeletal elements (microtubules, microfilaments and intermediate filaments) is even larger. In addition, an extensively branched and interconnected cytoplasmic network known as the 'microtrabecular lattice' (MTL) has recently been described by Porter, Wolosewick and co-workers.[44–46] Visual inspection of these various elements certainly shows that their collective surface area greatly exceeds that of the membranes, at least by a factor of 5. Therefore, if we use 500,000 μm^2 as a minimum estimate of the cytoskeleton and MTL surface area per cell, then 5% of the total water will be required just for monolayer coverage. We might suppose then that just the membranes, cytoskeleton and MTL will require of the order of 15% of the total water to achieve primary hydration. If we allow all these elements to perturb five layers of water the figure increases to about 30% of the total.

One must be impressed by the close packed nature of all these structures and the relatively small volume between them which, of course, is the location of the aqueous cytoplasm (Figures 1(E) and (F)). One wonders how any of the cytoplasmic water can find itself sufficiently distant from these and other surfaces to allow for the existence of an ordinary bulk water phase. Although subject to large error I find these estimates to be instructive in at least one respect: if surfaces do indeed perturb water and alter its properties over distances of hundreds of Ångstroms as Drost-Hansen[47,48] has argued, then with confidence we can conclude that *all* of the water in the cytoplasm must differ to some extent from Bw. For these reasons it is of utmost importance to understand the properties of interfacial water, and particularly the distances involved.

I believe it is also worth considering the possible functions that water might play in the assembly and disassembly of the cytoskeleton and MTL. These structures are formed from protein subunits which undergo reversible polymerization and it is evident that those processes involve the participation of water. Assembly–disassembly studies on these structures are usually carried out *in vitro*, and it is significant that organic 'compatible' solvents such as glycerol are frequently used in the reaction mixtures. For instance, Lee and Timasheff[49] have shown that the *in vitro* polymerization of tubulin into microtubules is entropy driven and that glycerol enhances this assembly by nonspecific protein–solvent thermodynamic interactions. It seems likely that all such assembly–disassembly processes will be influenced by the physical properties of water in their microenvironment, but it is very risky to assume that those properties will be the same as those of Bw.

A few words are also in order on the relationship between cell water and cytoskeletal elements during cell transformations. Viral and malignant transformations are often accompanied by significant changes in the cytoskeleton, most notably in the actin-containing components.[50-52] Correlated with these changes are increases in the total cell water content, and NMR studies indicate that the water in such cells behaves more like the bulk liquid than the corresponding non-transformed cell type.[10, 11, 53] Several of the 'alternative views' summarized in this paper would assign an important and perhaps even a casual role to water during cell transformation. The traditional view provides no basis at all for water involvement and, as a result, such possibilities have rarely been considered.

Water and enzyme activity

I have already mentioned that the organization of metabolism in the aqueous compartments might directly involve the participation of water. It is agreed that water plays an important role in enzyme catalysis as a 'stabilizing' solvent and, in many cases as a substrate, but it might be far more important than that[33,34] A recent series of provocative papers by Low, Somero and their associates[54] very strongly suggests, if not proves, that changes in protein solvation during enzyme catalysis contribute significantly to the thermodynamic activation parameters. These hydration effects are believed to arise from altered exposure to water of side chains and peptide linkages distant from the active site during catalytic conformational changes in the enzyme. It appears that major contributions to rate enhancement arise from differences in the entropy of water immediately adjacent to such groups relative to that of the surrounding more distant aqueous phase. In the case of *in vitro* studies this would be the bulk water of the incubation medium. But that might not be the case for such an enzyme operating within the aqueous intracellular components where, as this paper has indicated, the properties of at least a large fraction of the water differ from the bulk fluid; thus, these enzymes might not be functioning in Bw. Similar sorts of hydration contributions to such things as antibody–antigen, and ligand–receptor interactions are also possible.

Concluding remarks

I have summarized a few examples of research that strongly suggest the traditional view of cellular water is less than an acceptable description. Space limitations have not allowed coverage of all the relevant evidence and I apologize to those whose work has not been included. My choices have been influenced by research that indicates alternative roles for water in cell function, in addition to the study of its physical properties. I believe the evidence is sufficient to suggest that this long held conception of the aqueous compartments of cells should be abandoned if we are ever to understand the structure and properties of water in cells; to continue with its unqualified acceptance will also inhibit study of the diverse and potentially vital role that water plays in cell functions, several of which have been considered here.

At the same time I have recognized that a significant amount of evidence has been produced in support of the traditional view, notably from the use of NMR and dielectrics. In view of that it is fair to ask why I should choose my conclusion over theirs. One reason is that certain experiments, like those using the reference phase technique for example, provide much more direct and reliable information about the nature of cell water, and with far fewer assumptions, than the heavily model-dependent NMR, and the dielectric studies. I believe the evidence is compelling that the solvent properties of a very large fraction of cytoplasmic water differ distinctly from those of the bulk liquid.[14,17,25-28,30] One can therefore ask whether it is better to choose a model that requires over 95% of the cell's water to exhibit rotational and translational behaviour identical to that of pure water in order to interpret NMR results, when these data can equally well be explained by other models that seem more consistent with evidence from other techniques. I am also influenced by the enormous surface area present in cells and its effects on the properties of the surrounding water. Finally, I admit to the bias that comes from a classical training in biology: it is hard to accept the assumption that several billions of years of evolution would have produced aqueous intracellular compartments that exhibit no more organization than the chaos of a solution.

If the traditional view is to be discarded, then we should try to decide between the various alternatives that have been advanced. I believe that decision cannot be made at present. While there is reason to believe that at least a third of the water in cells differs from both 'bulk' and 'hydration' water in some of its properties, that is not necessarily the upper limit. This proportionality will be heavily influenced by the particular methodology employed,[55] a point of which I am aware but have been guilty of glossing over in this paper. There is evidence to suggest that some of the water in cells exhibits properties that are very similar to those of Bw; nevertheless, the possibility remains that none of it behaves that way, particularly in the case of cytoplasmic water.

Different cell types vary in total water content, and it can be expected that differences will also exist in the properties and disposition of their water, and in the functions it performs. We can also expect that cell transformations, normal and pathological, will result in comparable variation. Recent advances in intracellular ultrastructure clearly demonstrate that an extraordinary degree of structural integration exists in the cytoplasm which, only a decade or two ago was believed to be a relatively homogeneous aqueous compartment; the nucleus also exhibits considerable ultrastructural complexity. This macromolecular architecture is vital to normal cellular function. It seems reasonable to speculate that the versatile properties of water would allow for the development of a comparable degree of structural organization of this dominant component of cells, linking it inextricably to virtually all of their functions.

Acknowledgements

Travel funds and research support were provided by a grant from the U.S. National Science Foundation (PCM 79 25609). I am very grateful to Drs S. Horowitz and P. Paine for providing preprints of their work. The skilled assistance of Lynda Weller in the preparation of the manuscript is appreciated.

References

1. E. E. Burnell, M. E. Clark, J. A. M. Hinke, and N. R. Chapman, *Biophys. J.*, **33**, 1 (1981).
2. E. D. Finch, in *The Aqueous Cytoplasm* (ed. A. D. Keith), pp. 61–90. Marcel Dekker, Inc., New York (1979).
3. B. M. Fung and T. W. McGaughy, *Biophys. J.*, **28**, 293 (1979).
4. K. R. Brownstein and C. E. Tarr, *Phys. Rev.*, A, **19**, 2446 (1979).
5. G. P. Raaphorst and J. Kruuv, in *The Aqueous Cytoplasm* (ed. A. D. Keith), pp. 91–136. Marcell Dekker, Inc., New York (1979).
6. K. R. Foster, J. L. Shepps, and H. P. Schwan, *Biophys. J.*, **29**, 271 (1980).
7. J. L. Schepps and K. R. Foster, *Phys. Med. Biol.*, **6**, 1149 (1980).
8. D. A. T. Dick, in *Membranes and Ion Transport* (ed. E. E. Bittar), Vol. 3, pp. 211–227. Wiley–Interscience, London (1971).
9. A. D. Brown and J. M. Sturtevant, *J. Membrane Biol.*, **54**, 21 (1980).
10. C. F. Hazlewood, in: *Cell-Associated Water* (eds. W. Drost-Hansen and J. S. Clegg), pp. 165–260, Academic Press, New York (1979).
11. P. T. Beall, in: *Nuclear-Cytoplasmic Interactions in the Cell Cycle* (ed. G. L. Whitson), pp. 223–247. Academic Press, New York (1980).
12. P. K. Seitz, D. C. Chang, C. F. Hazlewood, H. E. Rorschach and J. S. Clegg, *Arch. Biochem. Biophys.*, **210**, 517 (1981).
13. G. C. Cleveland, D. C. Chang, C. F. Hazlewood and H. E. Rorschach, *Biophys. J.*, **16**, 1043 (1976).
14. K. D. Garlid, in *Cell-Associated Water* (eds. W. Drost-Hansen and J. S. Clegg), pp. 293–362. Academic Press, New York (1979).

15. G. N. Ling, in *The Aqueous Cytoplasm* (ed. A. D. Keith), pp. 23–60. Marcel Dekker, Inc., New York (1979).
16. G. N. Ling, C. L. Walton and M. M. Ochsenfeld, *J. Cell. Physiol.*, **106**, 385 (1981).
17. G. N. Ling and W. Negendank, *Persp. Biol. Med.*, **24**, 215 (1980).
18. I. A. Gamaley, A. B. Kaulin and A. S. Troshin, *Cytology* (in Russian), **19**, 1309 (1977).
19. E. Ernst, *Acta Biochim. Biophys. Acad. Sci. Hungary*, **11**, 143 (1976).
20. W. Negendank, *J. Cell. Physiol.*, **104**, 443 (1980).
21. L. Minkoff and R. Damadian, *Biophys. J.*, **13**, 167 (1973).
22. F. W. Cope, *Physiol. Chem. Phys.*, **8**, 569 (1976).
23. L. Edelmann, *Microsc. Acta*, **2** (suppl.), 166 (1978).
24. L. Edelmann, *Physiol. Chem. Phys.*, **9**, 313 (1977).
25. P. L. Paine and S. B. Horowitz, in *Cell Biology* (eds. L. Goldstein and D. Prescott), Vol. 4, pp. 299–338. Academic Press, New York (1980).
26. S. B. Horowitz, P. L. Paine, L. Tluczek and J. K. Reynhout, *Biophys. J.*, **25**, 33 (1979).
27. S. B. Horowitz and P. L. Paine, *Biophys. J.*, **25**, 45 (1979).
28. P. L. Paine, T. W. Pearson, L. J. M. Tluczek and S. B. Horowitz, *Nature, Lond.*, **291**, 558 (1981).
29. L. G. Palmer and M. M. Civan, *J. Membr. Biol.*, **33**, 41 (1977).
30. S. B. Horowitz and T. W. Pearson, *Mol. Cell. Biol*, **1**, 769 (1981).
31. K. D. Garlid, in *L'eau et les Systemes Biologiques* (eds. A. Alfsen and A. J. Berteaud), pp. 317–321. Colloq. Intern. CNRS No. 246, Paris (1976).
32. J. S. Clegg, in *Cell-Associated Water* (eds. W. Drost-Hansen and J. S. Clegg), pp. 117–155. Academic Press, New York (1979).
33. J. S. Clegg, *Collective Phenom.*, **3**, 289 (1981).
34. J. S. Clegg, *J. Exp. Zool.*, **215**, 303 (1981).
35. P. A. Srere, *Trends Biochem. Sci.*, **5**, 120 (1980).
36. P. A. Srere, *Trends Biochem. Sci.*, **6**, 4 (1981).
37. C. R. Hackenbrock, *Proc. Natl. Acad. Sci. U.S.A.*, **61**, 508 (1968).
38. H. G. Hempling, A. D. Cicoria, A. M. Dupre and S. Thompson, *J. Exp. Zool.*, **215**, 259 (1981).
39. P. W. Wiggins, in *Cell-Associated Water* (eds. W. Drost-Hansen and J. S. Clegg), pp. 60–114. Academic Press, New York (1979).
40. P. W. Wiggins and V. A. Knight, *Bioelectrochem. Bioenerget.*, **6**, 323 (1979).
41. P. W. Wiggins, *J. Biol. Chem.*, **255**, 11365 (1980).
42. J. S. Clegg, in Cold Spring Harbor Symposium (eds. J. D. Watson and G. Albrecht-Buehler), Vol. 46, Cold Spring Harbor, New York, in press (1982).
43. J. S. Clegg and W. Dorst-Hansen, in *The Physical Basis of Electromagnetic Interactions with Biological Systems* (eds. L. S. Taylor and A. Y. Cheung), pp. 121–131. HEW Publ. (FDA) 78-8055, Washington, D.C. (1978).
44. J. J. Wolosewick and K. R. Porter, *J. Cell Biol.*, **82**, 114 (1979).
45. K. R. Porter and K. Anderson, in Cold Spring Harbor Symposium (eds. J. D. Watson and G. Albrecht-Buehler), Vol. 46, Cold Spring Harbor, New York, in press (1982).
46. M. Schliwa and J. van Blerkom, in Cold Spring Harbor Symposium (eds. J. D. Watson and G. Albrecht-Buehler), Vol. 46, Cold Spring Harbor, New York, in press (1982).
47. W. Drost-Hansen, in *Chemistry of the Cell Interface. B*, (ed. H. D. Brown), pp. 1–184. Academic Press, New York (1971).

48. W. Drost-Hansen, in *Physics and Chemistry of Liquids*, Vol. 7, pp. 243–348. Gordon and Breach Science Publishers, Ltd., Holland (1978).
49. J. C. Lee and S. N. Timasheff, *Biochemistry*, **16**, 1754 (1977).
50. J. L. Pastan and M. Willingham, *Nature, Lond.*, **274**, 645 (1978).
51. T. T. Puck, *Proc. Natl. Acad. Sci. U.S.A.*, **74**, 4491 (1977).
52. S. L. Wolin and R. S. Kucherlapati, *J. Cell Biol.*, **82**, 76 (1979).
53. G. N. Ling and M. Tucker, *J. Natl. Cancer Inst.*, **64**, 1199 (1980).
54. G. S. Greaney and S. N. Somero, *Biochemistry*, **18**, 5322 (1979).
55. M. Pezolet, M. Pigeon-Gosselin, R. Savoie and J-P Caille, *Biochim. Biophys. AScta*, **544**, 394 (1978).

Discussion following Clegg's lecture

Reporter: **Helen leB. Skaer**

Elmgren commented that several techniques (NMR, ultracentrifugation, ESR) suggest that the translational diffusion rate of solvent decreases with increasing concentration of macromolecules. This is usually explained by some 'obstruction effect'. However, the picture that the obstruction is a geometric one cannot be true. The measurement does not follow one particular solvent molecule and its movement in the solution, but takes in the motion of billions of molecules. As the mean free path of the solvent molecules is several orders of magnitude less than the average distance between the macromolecules (as long as their volume fraction is ≤0.3), their presence cannot influence the measured mobility. Otherwise, the measurements would be dependent on the particular geometry of the measuring cell.

There are several ways to show that obstruction effects are negligible. One is that the diffusion between parallel plates can sterically be hindered in only one dimension. Nevertheless, the diffusion is not reduced to 2/3 of the bulk value, but to much lower values. Another way to show that obstruction is not important is that *rotational* diffusion is affected at least as much as *translational* diffusion. (They are affected equally if the observed particles are approximately isotropic.) Geometrical obstruction is thus negligible, and the law of energy equipartition is valid in the solutions.

The change in diffusion with the concentration of the macromolecules can be transformed to changes in diffusion resulting from the proximity of the surface of the macromolecules (*Polymer Letters* **18**, 339 (1980)). The solvent mobility profiles around macromolecules can give rise to the observed results.

Wyn Jones commented that many biochemists are happy to accept the idea of some form of intracellular supramolecular architectures. There followed some discussion concerning the mobility of water and ions in such a supramolecular complex. It was agreed that the methods used at present to study the binding and dynamics of ions, particularly K^+, give only indirect measures, so that the interpretation of the behaviour of intracellular K^+ is controversial (Kay, Clegg).

Summarizing discussion

Reporters: **Helen leB. Skaer** and **Felix Franks**

The discussion was opened by the chairman (Kay) with some timely philosophy concerning the difficulty of measuring interactions both within and outside the cell. Franks took this up by asking specifically what information was required and how it could be obtained in order to draw conclusions about interactions involving 'compatible solutes.' Ninham suggested that most of the data *are* already available in measurements of activity coefficients, osmotic coefficients and so on. These data have not been properly analysed. One must convert from the experimental Lewis–Randall (constant pressure) ensemble to the constant density ensemble appropriate to statistical mechanics. The virial coefficient then measures the interacting forces between two solutes, and one can get a good idea of how much the solvent structure is perturbed by a given solute. There would probably be a good deal of progress if people took the trouble to learn some statistical mechanics and physical chemistry.

Wyn Jones pointed out that molecules like betaine can be considered as molecules of minimum interaction and thus a better term for them might be 'benign solutes'. Slade felt that, regarding the exclusion of sucrose and proline from the protein surface (negative binding), each experiment should be analysed separately when considering protein stability. Low sucrose concentrations can increase the equilibrium constant for subunit dissociation of dehydrogenases and lower the enzyme activity at a given substrate concentration (cooperative enzyme). High sucrose concentrations (*ca.* 1 M) decrease the K_{diss} (enhancement of the associated state) and result in maximum activity for the same given substrate concentration. Clearly at 1 M sucrose there is no way of distinguishing complex formation between enzyme and sucrose from simple coexistence in the same test tube, since $K_{diss} \sim 1$ M for the sugar/protein interaction implies an interaction free energy of zero. Nevertheless, it seems that sucrose concentrations below any appreciable K_{diss} for interaction with protein have a different effect from much higher sucrose concentrations. It is necessary to specify the protein concentration with respect to K_{diss} protein–protein and the small molecule concentration with respect to a possible K_{diss} protein–ligand.

Yet another discussion on 'bound' water developed, following a request that we should agree on the extent of 'bound' water, at least within the confines of a single experimental system (Bank). Careri pointed out the problems of sampling: if the system is uniform, an average can be produced and bound water can be defined as water with energy $>kT$. However, in a non-uniform system (such as a biological system), averaging is not possible. The real task is then to classify the types of water molecules.

Bryant pointed out a practical problem with experimental measures of the amount

Summarizing discussion

of water which is bound to a protein and not included in the criterion suggested by Careri. NMR is well able to measure the amount of unfrozen water next to a protein or other macromolecule system, when a solution is frozen. However, the reference state for this measurement is ice; i.e. the water that fails to freeze is the water which has a lower free energy by remaining next to the protein unfrozen and the measurement yields a value of 0.34 g H_2O/g lysozyme. When other reference states are used, the result is different. For example, Rupley and Careri used heat capacity data from lysozyme powders to detect at what hydration ratio various physical properties became constant and found >0.4 g H_2O/g lysozyme. There are thus good measures of the amount of associated water, but they do depend on what reference state is implied by the measurement.

Further difficulties are encountered when comparisons are made between different properties. Derbyshire illustrated this with an example. His interest is in understanding mechanical and thermodynamic properties in terms of molecular interactions. Because of its ease of use NMR is a favourite technique, water proton T_1 and T_2 have been measured in sols and gels of soya protein in different states. No difference can be detected in the ^1H relaxation between a gel and a sol, even though the mechanical effects are grossly different. This reflects the feature that NMR relaxation is sensitive to 'short' range interactions, whereas the mechanical properties are dependent upon 'large scale' organization.

Israelachvili suggested that we should draw on the analogous situation occurring at a surface in an electrolyte solution, in looking for operational definitions for bound water, structured water, solvation layers and so on. In an electrolyte solution it is usually clear which ions are bound and which are in the diffuse double-layer. Similarly water at surfaces can be envisaged as 'bound' out to one or two molecular distances, and then 'diffusely structured' or 'solvated' beyond that, out to many molecular diameters, depending on the surface or binding site. The figure of one to two layers for water of restricted mobility was generally agreed (Beveridge, Robson) but Franks pointed out that at low water concentrations (for example in partly frozen systems) kinetic effects make an analysis difficult, because the system is metastable.

In this connection Bryant suggested that care must be taken in using strictly dynamical criteria in discussing hydration effects. One might argue, for instance, that the water next to a large alkali metal ion moves as fast as water would in the bulk and by that dynamical criterion, the ion is not significantly hydrated. But if the same charged ion is plunged into water from the gas phase, there are very large thermodynamic effects and the energies associated with the solvation process cannot be dismissed. The problem is only apparently different for say Mg^{2+} ion which is certainly hydrated with six long-lived water molecules in its first condensation sphere. It is a grave error to use the dynamical observation to conclude that only six water molecules are involved in solvation of Mg^{2+} ion and then ascribe all of the ΔH of hydration for example to those six water molecules. While the protein case is obviously more heterogeneous, the same care must be taken not to mix dynamic and thermodynamic reasoning.

On the question of semantics, Robson felt that the term 'solvation' water was preferable to 'bound' water, since not all the molecules near a solute are necessarily happy there. The energy of the solute–solvent interaction could be less favourable at some surfaces than the solvent–solvent interaction, but it would be more favourable than a vacuum near the surfaces! Certainly water may be actually bound, but solute–solvent and solvent–solvent hydrogen bonds may be of comparable stability. Moreover, water near a non-polar group *dislikes* to be there in the special sense that non-polar groups are brought together by the hydrophobic effect. Yet for an isolated non-polar group, some water still has to *be* there.

Levine was concerned whether the terms used to describe intermediate types of water which are neither bound nor bulk, such as 'capillary', 'vicinal', 'loosely bound' and 'diffusely hydrating' are in fact synonymous. Further, he asked for a maximum capillary diameter which might contain only bound and 'capillary' water, but no bulk water. Ter-Minassian-Saraga gave a rough estimate of 6 nm diameter. However, Bryant pointed out that in protein crystals such as lysozyme there is a significant fraction of the total water content that freezes and which leads to fracture of the crystal. That water is also very liquid, as measured by NMR relaxation times. The sizes of the spaces in which this apparently normal water resides must be of the order of the sizes of protein molecules or smaller. 1.5 nm pores for lysozyme perhaps. This suggests that the size of a confining volume which will make water very abnormal must be below this volume.

The discussion then moved on to consider certain aspects of NMR. Israelachvili asked if there was any correlation between the lifetime of a bound molecule on a surface, as measured by NMR relaxation, and its binding energy. Derbyshire thought that in principle this is true. However, Bryant pointed out the fundamental difference between dynamics and thermodynamics, i.e. the difference between the enthalpy change or free energy change for the process and the activation enthalpy or activation energy for the same process. What NMR relaxation will give is the activation barrier and the rate constant and these are not necessarily in some simple proportion to the thermodynamic driving force for the process. On the other hand, since the lifetime of a bound molecule is reflected in the dissociation rate constant, if one knows in addition the rate constant of association, then the ratio of these two kinetic constants gives the equilibrium constant and from that value ΔG can be calculated (Maass). Halle pointed out the value of analysing water and ion mobility in terms of NMR, while Beall warned against assuming that water that is simply trapped inside a large molecule is necessarily bound.

The discussion then shifted to the nature of the cytoskeletal structures in the cytoplasm. Kay asked why it is that one cannot see the cytoskeletal components in the cell, and Clegg explained that they can only be visualized at present by cytological methods such as fixation, specific staining (such as tannic acid), freeze-etching and immunofluorescence, and referred those interested to a recent Cold Spring Harbor symposium on the cytoskeleton and microtrabercular systems. Steponkus pointed out that cells with lysed membranes remain structurally remarkably intact, as if the cytoplasm was held together in some way. In addition, in certain cells the organelles show remarkably little movement around the cell, indicating perhaps some restriction imposed by cytoskeletal structures. Careri further suggested that actin components in the cytoskeleton might act as 'water carriers' within the cell.

There followed an interaction (physical/biological) that could be said to underline the differing viewpoints. Concern was expressed that, whereas work with metal surfaces always involved great precautions to purify the surface, in biological systems the surface properties of proteins are studied in the presence of numerous contaminants and it is entirely possible that one is actually studying interactions of water with these impurities rather than with the protein surface (Kay). The response to this was that impurities *are* biology and one should not need to worry whether the interaction under study is with impurities or with the macromolecular surface.

NMR relaxation of water in heterogeneous systems—consensus views?

R. G. Bryant and **B. Halle**

Since there had been considerable discussion about the usefulness of NMR methods in studies of water dynamics in heterogeneous systems and about the interpretation of experimental data in terms of parameters that describe hydration phenomena, those participants with experience of such techniques were asked to go into conclave and produce a consensus view. The following statement is the result of their deliberations, prepared by their convenor, Robert G. Bryant—Editor.

With the general spirit of reviewing the situation on the state of 'bound water' on proteins as perceived by the NMR spectroscopist and with the particular intention of attempting a partial answer to Finney's apparently simple question on the lifetime of a water molecule at a protein surface, we here assemble several aspects of the NMR results presented and/or referred to at this meeting. The intent is to indicate areas of consensus and, more importantly, major outstanding problems. In this effort let us sweep aside many interesting points of detail, while still attempting to present the major features of a consensus achieved by us last night, no doubt by the dubious strategy of adding alcohol to the problem.

We must remember that the actual measurements are the rate constants for the recovery of magnetization to equilibrium values following a perturbation. The decay times themselves, T_1 or T_2 for example, are long, ranging from seconds to tens of microseconds. To deduce the rates of the faster motions of the system, we must depend on models for the nuclear relaxation itself that couple the slow time constants, among the longest lifetimes in spectroscopy, to motions in the system at and above the spectrometer frequency. For simple isotropic liquids and for crystalline solids these models or equations are very well documented and tested. In pure water, for example, the proton relaxation rate is given by

$$1/T_1 = Q/r^6 \left(\frac{\tau_c}{1 + \omega^2 \tau_c^2} + \frac{4\tau_c}{1 + \omega^2 \tau_c^2} \right) \tag{1}$$

where r is the interproton distance and τ_c is the correlation time for reorientation of this vector, ω the resonance frequency and Q a constant. The correlation time at 25 °C is about 8 psec but the T_1 about 3.6 sec.

It is important to recognize that not all of the systems discussed are directly comparable, because the basic dynamical input is different. In particular, the work discussed on adsorbed water (Bryant's poster on lysozyme powder, Ratkovič's results on seeds) represented a dynamically simpler system to characterize than a protein or other macromolecule dissolved in water, because in the case of a solid the macromolecule is not free to rotate and in the dryer systems there is no bulk water, and hence, no chemical exchange between the free and bound states to be concerned with. Thus, in these systems the major task is to characterize the motion at the surface. While this effort is complete with its own difficulties, the major features of the problem appear to be well in hand. That is, the motion of the water at the surface is anisotropic, leading directly to the involvement of two correlation times in the problem; in addition, each of these appears very likely to have a significant distribution of values; or equivalently the dynamical events that lead to the water reorientations about different directions have a distribution of activation energies. The uncertainties in these conclusions or what disagreements exist are basically about how anisotropic the water motion is and precisely how wide the correlation time distributions might be. Of two proposed correlation time distributions, we know a great deal more about the higher frequency process. A surprising feature seems to be that the correlation times for the rapid water motions, even in fairly dry protein systems, are in the 0.1–10 nsec range, depending of course on temperature and water content.

In the case of aqueous solutions the situation is much more complicated because now the macromolecule surface is free to rotate with correlation times of the order of 10^{-7} sec or shorter, depending on size. Water at the protein surface is now free to exchange with the pool of bulk water present. Hallenga summarized many of the critical facts that must be accounted for in any comprehensive explanation of the relaxation of water nuclei induced by dissolved macromolecules. Focusing just on proteins, the NMR dispersion curves illustrate the problems. The NMR relaxation is dramatically affected by the macromolecule at low frequencies, but the effect falls off markedly with resonance frequency as shown schematically in Figure 1. There are two major points to explain: (1) the frequency of the dispersion curve inflection and (2) the amplitude. The data shown by Hallenga, collected in Seymour Koenig's laboratory, indicate that the frequency of the inflection points reports the rotational correlation time of the protein molecule over a very wide range of protein molecular weights. This point is critical. The magnitude of the change in NMR relaxation rate on passing through the dispersion curve and the coupling of the water relaxation rate to the rotational motion of the protein require a dynamical model; there have been several. The following list is not intended to be exhaustive.

An early idea was that water was tightly bound to sites on the protein and exchanged between these bound sites, where it could not move except with the rotational correlation time of the protein, and the bulk water pool. If several hundred molecules of water were so bound to the protein, the effects of the NMR relaxation would have to

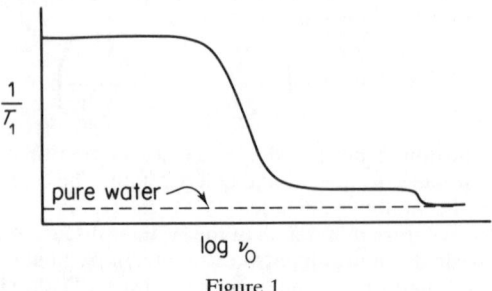

Figure 1

NMR relaxation of water in heterogeneous systems

be about 100 times larger than observed. The model therefore had to be modified to include only a few such irrotationally bound water molecules at the surface. As Finney indicated, Koenig and coworkers pointed out that the model gets into grave difficulty when proton, deuteron and oxygen-17 data are considered at the same time. Briefly, the water in the bound state must stay there long enough to sense the rotational correlation time of the protein, $ca.$ 10^{-8} sec, but short enough so that all the water nuclei sample the bound environment in a time short compared with the relaxation time measured. The relaxation times and hence the constraints are different for the different nuclei; and what happened was that there was no one set of lifetimes that could be consistent with all three nuclei at the same time. In addition the model does not provide for a high frequency dispersion process which is implied by the NMR dispersion and the work on solids. Therefore, the model was eliminated. In its place Koenig has suggested a weak dynamical coupling between the rotational motion of the protein molecule and the water molecule which follows in a rather involved manner from the basic conservation of angular momentum in such a system. Those who have studied this effect in terms of hydrodynamic theory have not been able to find a coupling that is sufficiently large to account for the observed NMR measurements. Therefore, while this possibility has certainly not been eliminated, its likelihood seems somewhat diminished, at least in the form most of us understand.

Halle has suggested that chemical exchange of protons and deuterons between water and ionizable groups on the protein may account for the observations on these nuclei. Koenig and coworkers considered this possibility some time ago. Such an exchange may happen in the time of the T_1 measurement, but that in itself is not sufficient, since the proton exchange must be sufficiently fast in the remainder of the water to average the effect over all water molecules. This seems unlikely, but this point, too, is still open.

An alternative or even parallel pathway for the coupling of the slow rotation of the protein to the water molecule NMR relaxation is some protein induced anisotropy in the water motion. There are several versions of such a coupling model, one was presented by Halle in his poster, and it is not clear at this time what the precise features of the dynamical model are, except that the water molecule motion next to a protein must have two correlation times, a slow one and a fast one. In any such model, regardless of the details, the slow correlation time is the time constant for the averaging of the residual anisotropy in the water molecule motion. Several different types of motion could do that: (1) rotation of the protein, (2) exchange of the water out of the bound environment, (3) diffusion of the water along the surface of the protein. Thus, the measured correlation time becomes a mix of contributions:

$$\frac{1}{\tau_{slow}} = \frac{1}{\tau_{rotation \; (protein)}} + \frac{1}{\tau_{exch}} + \frac{1}{\tau_{surface \; diffusion}} + \cdots \qquad (2)$$

We know rotational correlation times for the protein are of the order of 10^{-7} to 10^{-8} sec, depending on size and temperature. The exchange lifetimes are usually thought to be fast too, of the order of 10^{-7} sec, or faster. The measurements on lysozyme suggest an estimate of the surface diffusion time even on dry lysozyme (20 g/100 g) will be of the order of 10^{-7} sec; adding more water should speed it up. Setting aside the difficulty of defining bound water for such models, now it should be clear why we cannot come to a simple answer to Finney's question of how long the water resides at the surface. The measurements need not provide such a number directly, but rather a mix of times as suggested in Equation (2), and a great deal would depend upon which interaction was dominant.

[Even with the free flow of alcohol during the deliberations of the NMR spectroscopists, unanimity could not be obtained. Halle therefore prepared a 'minority report' which differs in some respects from the consensus report. It is printed below and I apologize to the reader, if after the above clear exposition, he will now be thrown back into confusion. On the other hand, I hope that these two very concise discussions of the same set of problems will demonstrate the state-of-the-art reached in the translation of spectroscopic parameters into molecular processes.—Editor.]

The theory of spin relaxation in general, and its application to heterogeneous systems in particular, tends to be shrouded in a rather heavy formalism. In the following, I try to emphasize the basic physics of the problem, which, I believe, can be appreciated also by those who are less than fluent in the NMR jargon. For details see B. Halle and H. Wennerström, *J. Chem. Phys.*, **75**, (1981).

The task is to identify the indisputable experimental facts about water in heterogeneous systems and to use them as a basis for the construction of a physical model. This model should be simple, i.e. contain as few adjustable parameters as possible, and general, i.e. it should be applicable to relaxation in isotropic as well as anisotropic systems, to line splittings, and to all three magnetic water nuclei (^1H, ^2H and ^{17}O).

Consider first an aqueous region adjacent to an immobile, although not necessarily rigid surface. Typical examples include phospholipid bilayers, surfactant liquid-crystalline mesophases, clays and protein crystals. Such systems have been studied extensively—using all three water nuclei—during the past few decades and two important conclusions have been drawn

(1) The NMR absorption lines exhibit splittings, indicating a preferential water orientation relative to the surface, and
(2) The splittings are much smaller than expected for rigid water binding to the surface, i.e. the orientational bias is small.

This is qualitatively what one would predict on the basis of our present knowledge of the water–water and water–surface interactions.

But how much water is perturbed? (Perturbed in the sense that it gives rise to an NMR behaviour which is measurably different from that of bulk water. This is what NMR practitioners actually mean by the elusive concept of 'bound' water.) By varying the water content in several kinds of systems it has been shown, primarily by Woessner, that significant perturbations occur only in the first two water layers.

This picture is by no means inconsistent with the existence of repulsive hydration forces operative over distances of 10 or more water molecular diameters. This is because NMR experiments monitor the average behaviour of individual water molecules, whereas the hydration force is a collective effect from a vast number of water molecules, most of which are only exceedingly weakly perturbed ('bulk' water to the NMR spectroscopist).

Let us now focus our attention on a different kind of system, e.g. a dilute aqueous solution of a globular protein. The most important experimental observation in these isotropic systems is the frequency dependence of the relaxation rates. (The inequality of longitudinal and transverse relaxation rates may be viewed as a frequency dependence.) This indicates that the relaxation is induced by molecular motions on two time-scales: typically, the slow one is in the nsec range, while the fast one is in the psec range. The main source of controversy in the water NMR literature of recent years concerns the nature of these motions and the mechanism whereby they induce spin relaxation.

There can be little doubt that the local environment of a water molecule close to the protein surface is very similar to that in the previously discussed anisotropic systems. Thus, the water molecules in the first few layers around the protein molecule experience a slight preferential orientation with respect to the protein surface and the fast motion can be identified with local water tumbling and side-chain libration.

In order to understand the origin of the low-frequency dispersion, we must recall some basic concepts from the theory of spin relaxation. Relaxation is induced by time-dependent interactions and proceeds at a rate which is essentially proportional to the characteristic time of the fluctuations in the interaction. This so-called correlation time is a measure of the time that a water molecule 'remembers' its orientation relative to the external magnetic field. The fast local water tumbling will cause a water molecule to lose most of its orientational 'memory' very quickly. But because of the slight average orientational bias (quantified by the so-called residual anisotropy involving certain order parameters), the water molecules near the protein surface will also have a 'long-term memory', the loss of which is characterized by a long correlation time τ_s.

The fast motion can thus be viewed as fluctuations in the orientation of a water molecule relative to the protein surface, and the slow motion as fluctuations in the orientation of the local constraint axis or director relative to the external field. This step-wise loss of orientational memory or correlation, characterized by a fast and a slow correlation time and by the residual anisotropy, constitutes the essence of our so-called two-step model for spin relaxation in heterogeneous sytems.

Finally, to return to the question about 'bound' water lifetimes, which was raised earlier by Finney, if we continue to discuss the dilute protein solution there are at least two types of motion that could wash out the long-term memory. The most obvious one is protein reorientation (correlation time τ_r), which modulates the orientation of the local director with respect to the external field. However, the same result can be accomplished also by translational diffusion of water molecules from one protein molecule to another one. It is the correlation time for this latter process ('chemical exchange' in the NMR jargon) that we refer to as the 'bound' water lifetime. If both of these processes are operative, the slow correlation time becomes

$$\frac{1}{\tau_s} = \frac{1}{\tau_r} + \frac{1}{\tau_l} \tag{3}$$

If the protein is sufficiently large, it will tumble so slowly that a 'bound' water molecule will diffuse away before the protein has time to reorient appreciably. Then $\tau_r \gg \tau_l$ and, according to Equation (3), the measured slow correlation time equals the lifetime. This way of deducing the lifetime may be viewed as a kind of self-diffusion measurement where a water molecule is labelled by the orientation of its local constraint axis.

In this connection it may be worthwhile to point out an obvious, but sometimes forgotten point of distinction between the diffusion of water molecules and ions in heterogeneous systems. When an ion undergoes a diffusive step in an external field there is, in general, a change in the energy. Water molecules, however, are usually displaced by other water molecules; hence there is no change in energy (even in an inhomogeneous field)—only a kinetic barrier. Consequently, water molecules associated to a protein surface are not trapped in a potential well as are the counter-ions. However, in the case of strongly hydrated counter-ions, e.g. Li^+ or Mg^{2+}, the counter-ion hydration sheath may be sufficiently long-lived for these water molecules to be effectively trapped with the ions. In such cases it may be pertinent to add a third term, corresponding to surface diffusion, to Equation (3). This may also be the case in systems with very low water contents, as discussed by Bryant.

Subject index

Action potential, 150, 371
Activation energy, 157, 240, 286, 301, 388
Active site, 58, 61, 196
Active transport, 138, 219, 267, 373, 375, 376
Amorphous ice, 154, 155, 357
Anisotropy, 179, 200, 201, 222, 233, 391
Anti-diuretic hormone, 271
Antifreeze proteins, 292, 306–308, 360
 non-colligative action of, 308
Antigenicity, 67

Bacterial spore, 334
Binding site, 174, 188, 267, 276
 primary, 41
Bjerrum defects, 177, 178
Bound water, 28, 46, 98, 136, 161, 199, 222, 237, 250–253, 262, 264, 266, 272, 307, 386, 389–393
 life time of, 272, 387, 388, 393
Boyle–van't Hoff relation, 209, 210, 272

Cell fusion, 67, 260
Charge transfer, 148, 149
 gating, 149
Chemical exchange, 179, 181, 251, 272, 391
Chill injury, 287, 346
Clathrate, 6, 148, 174, 176
Cold acclimation, 291, 320, 321, 344–345
Cold inactivation, 354
Compatible solute, 290, 333, 335–359, 358
Computer simulation
 molecular dynamics, 6, 79, 168
 Monte Carlo, 6, 21, 32, 35, 52, 62, 63, 65, 79, 168
Concentration polarization, 195
Conductance, 154–158, 198, 215, 216, 270
Contact angle, 152, 153
Continuum theories, 112
Contractile system, 242–245
Correlation function, 17

Correlation time, 125, 179, 180, 181, 200, 222, 232, 233, 311
 distribution, 126, 275, 390
Critical spreading, 152
Cryopreservation, 287, 289, 303, 315–318, 358
Cytoplasmic streaming, 346
Cytoskeleton, 346, 376, 377, 378, 388

Debye screening length, 117, 177, 186
Decay length, 163, 185, 189
Dehydration, 160–162, 297–299, 304, 317, 320, 343, 345, 354
 isothermal, 348
Density, 48, 166
 maximum, 164, 281
 of interfacial water, 164
Dialysis equilibrium, 170
Diamagnetic susceptibility, 36, 60
Dielectric permittivity, 174, 186, 201, 274, 285
Dielectric relaxation, 41, 73, 180, 200, 261–266, 369
Dielectrophoresis, 260
Differential refractometry, 48
Differential scanning calorimetry, 127–133, 304
Diffusion, 67, 230, 232, 233, 250, 270, 273, 288, 343, 385, 391
 jump, 18
 of proteins, 225, 227, 228, 262
 passive, 4
Dipole moment, 21, 34, 148, 175, 273
 induced, 35
Disjoining pressure, 199
Dispersion forces, 110
Distribution coefficient, 23
Donnan
 distribution, 206, 207
 exclusion, 27, 122

Subject index

Double layer forces, 106, 109, 176, 177, 184, 186

Elastic modulus, 329, 330, 360
Electron correlation, 89
Electron spin resonance, 218–220, 269, 350
  spin probe, 218, 311
Electron transfer, 202
Electrostatic forces, 116–118, 174
Endoplasmic reticulum, 170–173
Entropy, 5, 7
  conformational, 11
  of sorption, 28
  of transfer, 261
Enzyme inactivation, 286, 290
Enzyme-substrate binding, 73, 99
Equation of state, 99
Erythrocyte, 195
Excluded volume, 97, 196

Flexibility, 11, 58, 98
Fluctuation, 59, 61, 99, 144, 147, 218, 238, 255, 273, 274, 276, 288, 393
Fluorescence polarization, 218, 269
Freeze avoidance, 280, 284, 291, 292
Freeze dehydration, 292
Freeze injury, 287, 300, 303, 319, 343–347
  secondary, 344
Freeze tolerance, 280, 290, 292, 316, 317, 318, 358
Freezing point depression, 308, 338

Gel, 12, 13, 14, 24, 372
  viscoelastic, 12
Gibbs–Duhem equation, 301, 302
Glass transition, 304

Haemolysis, 302
Hall effect, 275
Halophile, 340–343, 354
Halophyte, 260
Hamaker constant, 109, 110, 112
Heat capacity, 5, 36, 38, 98
Heat of dehydration, 343
Heat of sorption, 28
Helmholtz plane, 116, 138, 197, 199
Hydration, 17, 58, 190, 222, 243, 276, 366
  in low moisture systems, 312–314
  isotope effect, 46
  preferential, 49, 66, 70, 71, 339
Hydration forces, 114–116, 118, 141, 142, 176, 184, 185, 187, 188–193, 196, 202
  range, 185, 189
Hydration shell, 42, 45, 63, 97, 108, 202, 326, 337, 359
Hydrogen bond, 5, 6, 11, 13, 32, 55, 63, 75, 244
  bifurcated, 63, 89, 99, 100
  cooperativity, 13, 32, 33, 80, 81, 94, 100, 144–147, 190, 262, 357
  defects, 175, 198
  distribution, 200
  energy, 55, 387
  internal, 55
  orientation, 201
  rearrangement, 114
  tritiated, 242
Hydrophobic effect, 4, 21, 23, 55, 64, 71, 110, 176, 223, 246, 282, 285, 353, 354, 355
  free energy, 57
Hydrophobicity, 49

Intracellular ice, 304, 346
Intramembrane particles, 297, 298
Ion binding, 191, 197, 208, 371, 373, 385
Ion channel, 148–150, 174, 197, 200, 201, 213, 267
Ion distribution, 207, 208, 209, 213, 340
Ion exchange, 197
Ion hydration, 191, 387, 393
Ion selectivity, 167, 174, 197, 206, 249
Ionization potential, 157
Isotope exchange, 161, 235, 238–241, 254–256, 269, 270, 274, 281–282, 314

Kramers equation, 240, 241, 274

Lattice defect, 156
Lennard–Jones atom, 75, 112
Lifshitz theory, 107, 109, 110
Light scattering, 180, 269
Lipid bilayer, 69, 127–133, 140–142, 185, 192, 195, 269–271, 295, 392
  compressibility, 142
  phase transition, 297, 298, 351
  pressure, 196
  vesicle, 297
Lymphocyte, 210
Lyotropic series (or Hofmeister series), 67, 188, 191, 202, 281, 339, 359

Maximum density effect, 164, 281
Membrane asymmetry, 28, 206
Membrane folding, 271–272
Membrane hydration, 302
Membrane permeability, 27, 171, 211, 212, 269, 276, 287, 290, 341, 342, 345
  coefficient of, 211, 212, 236, 330
  energy of activation, 212, 269
  hydraulic, 257, 360
  selective, 11, 206, 213, 339, 348
Membrane phase transition, 287, 345 (see Lipid transition)
Membrane potential, 137, 149, 198, 268, 373

Subject index

Micelle, 223, 273
Microviscosity, 213, 218, 311, 376
Mobile defects, 238, 255

NMR
  carbon-13, 66
  cross-relaxation, 160, 263
  dispersion, 263, 264
  hysteresis, 325
  line intensity, 98
  line splitting, 41, 126, 181
  oxygen-17, 221–223, 246–247
  phosphorus-31, 69
  proton relaxation, 42, 170, 231–234, 247
  tritium, 45, 46
Nernst potential, 198
Neutron scattering, 101, 196, 199, 202, 216, 261
  quasi-elastic, 16, 17
  small angle, 134–136
Non-exchangeable water, 171, 173, 235, 236
Non-solvent water, 372
Nucleation
  biosynthetic, 360
  heterogeneous, 100, 360
  homogeneous, 283, 284
  in tissue, 288
  inhibition, 291

Order parameter, 74, 222, 232, 272
Osmoregulation, 279, 289, 290, 333, 334, 358
  in halophytes, 260, 327
Osmotic coefficient, 121, 195
Osmotic dehydration, 280, 290, 316, 335, 348, 359, 360

pH gradient, 355
Pair potential, 32, 79, 101, 190
  effective, 34
  on-additivity, 32, 33, 80, 81, 90
Partial molar volume, 337
Passive diffusion, 4
Photosynthesis, 3, 17
Polarizability, 81, 92, 94, 101, 208
Polarization, 114, 116, 200
  surface-induced, 116, 177
Polarized multilayers, 208, 369–372
Ponder's R value, 211, 271
Potential energy surface, 51, 82, 85–89
Preferential interaction parameter, 48, 70
Pressure clamp, 258
Protein aggregation, 345
Protein dissociation, 286, 292, 346, 348, 386
Protein folding, 57
  domain, 59, 256
Protein stability, 7, 71, 282, 285, 336, 339

Protein unfolding, 65, 70, 240, 254, 255, 309, 311
  free energy, 353
  kinetics, 254
Proton pump, 137–139
Proton transfer, 139, 157, 215, 216, 221, 232, 274
  by Grotthus mechanism, 216
  by tunnelling, 268, 275
  facilitated, 225–230
Protoplast, 319–321, 350
Proximity criterion, 52
Pseudomonas syringae, 288

Radial distribution function, 83, 84, 87, 100, 357
Radius of gyration, 136
Reaction field, 62
Reflection coefficient, 195, 257
Refractive index, 186
Rehydratability, 283, 351
Retardation, 110

Salting-out, 9, 339, 359
Second virial coefficient, 82, 87
Secondary structure, 10
Self-diffusion, 180, 281
Semiconduction, 154–158, 274
Smoluchowski equation, 239
Solvation site, 51
Sorption, 39, 138, 308
Sorption hysteresis, 39
Sorption isotherm, 27, 28, 38, 39, 41, 71, 251, 273, 283, 338
  BET, 165, 251
  monolayer, coverage, 38, 60, 378
Specific heat (*see* Heat capacity)
Spin diffusion, 171, 252
Spin–lattice relaxation, 45, 46, 125, 179, 180, 222, 231–234, 247, 250–253, 312–314, 323–326, 387, 389–393
Spin–spin relaxation, 46, 125, 179, 180, 222, 231–234, 247, 250–253, 312–314, 323–326, 387, 389–393
Stern layer, 116
Structure wave, 144–147
Structured water, 127, 128, 131, 196, 307
Supermolecule approximation, 63
Surface forces, 106
Surface free energy, 151–153, 288
Surface potential, 168, 176, 186, 188, 197

Thermal conductivity, 167
Thermal expansion, 164, 166
Thermophile, 353
Turgor pressure, 207, 257, 258, 260, 328, 330

Undercooled water, 246–247, 283, 284, 356–358
  in living organisms (deep undercooling), 291, 345, 360
Unfreezable water, 11, 45, 128, 171, 236, 290, 324, 342, 387

Van der Waals interactions, 4, 75, 106, 114, 184
Vicinal water, 138, 163–169, 199, 376–377, 388
  decay length, 163
  range, 168
Viscosity, 167, 238, 239, 256, 274, 287
  B-coefficient, 337

Water activity, 60, 283, 302, 333, 334

Water bridge, 59
Water dimer, 79, 82, 85
Water distribution, 4
Water exchange, 208, 235, 236
  temperature dependence of, 236
Water potential, 260, 328, 329
Water stress, 279–293, 309, 326, 327
Water structure, 5, 76–94, 142, 249, 310
  and phosphorylation, 372
  tetrahedrality, 78, 79
Water transport, 327

X-ray diffraction, 15, 140

Young's equation, 151

Zero point energy, 281
Zeta potential, 116

Compound index

ATPase, 218, 219
Ammonium sulphate, 70
Amphotericin, 270
Apoferritin, 227, 230

Bacteriorhodopsin, 220
Betaine, 290, 309, 336, 337, 338
Bovine serum albumin (BSA), 227, 336

Cellulose acetate, 27
1-Chlorobutane, 24
2-Chloroethanol, 50
Cholestrol, 141, 142
Chymotrypsin, 6
Collagen, 41
Cyclodextrin, 268
Cycloheptatriene, 25, 26
Cyclohexane, 24
Cyclopentane, 24
Cytochrome c-552, 285

DNA, 4, 41, 164, 231, 233, 274
Dextran, 152, 153
Dimethyl sulphoxide (DMSO), 134, 136, 303, 304, 315, 358

Ethanol, 134, 136

Glutamic acid, 333
Glycerol, 48, 70, 71, 72, 269, 292, 303, 315
Glycoprotein, 11, 12, 152
Glyoxal, 52, 53
Gramicidin A, 270, 276
Guanidinium chloride, 7, 10, 11, 49, 65, 97

Haemoglobin, 42, 97, 98, 121–123, 196, 227, 228, 230
Hexadecyltrimethylammonium bromide (CTAB), 192

Hyaluronic acid, 231, 233, 274
Hydroxyethyl starch, 358

Insulin, 6, 374
Isopropyl salicylate, 152

Lysozyme, 36, 38, 58, 60, 61, 63, 99, 200, 201, 238, 240, 386, 387

Malic dehydrogenase, 336
Mannitol, 318
Methoxyethanol, 50
2-Methyl-2,4-pentanediol (MPD), 48, 49, 70, 100
Myoglobin, 10, 41, 227

Nystatin, 270

Popain, 134
Penicillinase, 7, 10
Peptidoglycan, 22
Phosphatidylcholine, 69, 127, 141, 142
Phosphatidylethanolamine, 69, 141, 142
Phosphatidylinositol, 132, 141, 142
Phosphatidylserine, 141, 142
Phosphofructokinase, 286
Phycocyanin, 17
Poly-L-arginine, 311
Polyethylene glycol, 66–69, 100, 152
Polystyrene, 164
Potassium thiocyanate, 309, 310
Proline, 290, 309, 311, 315, 333, 336, 359
Propylene carbonate, 201

Ribulose biphosphate carboxylase, 346

Serine, 34
Silica, 199
Sodium dodecyl sulphate, 67

Sodium phosphate, 70
Sorbitol, 321
Sucrose, 48, 49, 70, 71, 171, 173, 201, 334, 372

Tobacco mosaic virus, 6, 285

Urea, 7, 8, 9, 10, 50, 65, 97, 269, 309, 358

Valinomycin, 4
Vitamin B12 coenzyme, 34, 35

Yeast alcohol dehydrogenase, 263